# ESSENTIALS OF
# ECONOMICS

## Eighth Edition

## N. GREGORY MANKIW

**HARVARD UNIVERSITY**

# ESSENTIALS OF
# ECONOMICS

## Eighth Edition

## N. GREGORY MANKIW

**HARVARD UNIVERSITY**

CENGAGE
Learning

Australia • Brazil • Mexico • Singapore • United Kingdom • United States

**Essentials of Economics, 8e**
N. Gregory Mankiw

Vice President, General Manager, Social Science
    & Qualitative Business: Erin Joyner

Product Director: Jason Fremder

Senior Product Manager: Michael Parthenakis

Developmental Editor: Jane Tufts

Senior Digital Content Designer: Kasie Jean

Senior Content Developer: Anita Verma

Content Development Manager: Clara
    Goosman

Product Assistant: Emily Lehmann

Executive Marketing Manager: John Carey

Senior Content Project Manager:
    Colleen A. Farmer

Senior Digital Production Project Manager:
    Derek Drifmeyer

Manufacturing Planner: Kevin Kluck

Marketing Coordinator: Casey Binder

Senior Learning Design Author: Eugenia Belova

Learning Design Author: Brian A. Rodriguez

Production Service: Lumina Datamatics Inc.,

Intellectual Property
    Analyst: Jennifer Bowes
    Project Manager: Sarah Shainwald

Senior Art Director: Michelle Kunkler

Internal and Cover Designer: Harasymczuk
    Design

Cover Image: Library of Congress Prints and
    Photographs Division Washington, DC
    20540 USA [LC-USZC4-4637];
    © AIMSTOCK/Getty Images; © Buena Vista
    Images/Getty Images

Chapter Opener Photo: © samsonovs/Getty
    Images

Custom Internal Illustrations: Bruce Morser

Unless otherwise noted, all items © Cengage Learning.

Library of Congress Control Number: 2016947885

ISBN 13: 978-1-337-09199-2

ISBN 10: 1-337-09199-5

**Cengage Learning**
20 Channel Center Street
Boston, MA 02210
USA

Cengage Learning is a leading provider of customized learning solutions with employees residing in nearly 40 different countries and sales in more than 125 countries around the world. Find your local representative at **www.cengage.com.**

Cengage Learning products are represented in Canada by Nelson Education, Ltd.

To learn more about Cengage Learning Solutions, visit **www.cengage.com**

Purchase any of our products at your local college store or at our preferred online store **www.cengagebrain.com**

Printed in the United States of America
Print Number: 02    Print Year: 2017

*To Catherine, Nicholas, and Peter,*
*my other contributions to the next generation*

# About the Author

Jordi Cabré

N. Gregory Mankiw is the Robert M. Beren Professor of Economics at Harvard University. As a student, he studied economics at Princeton University and MIT. As a teacher, he has taught macroeconomics, microeconomics, statistics, and principles of economics. He even spent one summer long ago as a sailing instructor on Long Beach Island.

Professor Mankiw is a prolific writer and a regular participant in academic and policy debates. His work has been published in scholarly journals, such as the *American Economic Review, Journal of Political Economy*, and *Quarterly Journal of Economics*, and in more popular forums, such as the *New York Times* and *The Wall Street Journal*. He is also author of the best-selling intermediate-level textbook *Macroeconomics* (Worth Publishers). In addition to his teaching, research, and writing, Professor Mankiw has been a research associate of the National Bureau of Economic Research, an adviser to the Congressional Budget Office and the Federal Reserve Banks of Boston and New York, and a member of the ETS test development committee for the Advanced Placement exam in economics. From 2003 to 2005, he served as chairman of the President's Council of Economic Advisers.

Professor Mankiw lives in Wellesley, Massachusetts, with his wife, Deborah, three children, Catherine, Nicholas, and Peter, and their border terrier, Tobin.

# Brief Contents

# Preface: To the Student

"Economics is a study of mankind in the ordinary business of life." So wrote Alfred Marshall, the great 19th-century economist, in his textbook, *Principles of Economics*. We have learned much about the economy since Marshall's time, but this definition of economics is as true today as it was in 1890, when the first edition of his text was published.

Why should you, as a student in the 21st century, embark on the study of economics? There are three reasons.

The first reason to study economics is that it will help you understand the world in which you live. There are many questions about the economy that might spark your curiosity. Why are apartments so hard to find in New York City? Why do airlines charge less for a round-trip ticket if the traveler stays over a Saturday night? Why is Robert Downey, Jr., paid so much to star in movies? Why are living standards so meager in many African countries? Why do some countries have high rates of inflation while others have stable prices? Why are jobs easy to find in some years and hard to find in others? These are just a few of the questions that a course in economics will help you answer.

The second reason to study economics is that it will make you a more astute participant in the economy. As you go about your life, you make many economic decisions. While you are a student, you decide how many years to stay in school. Once you take a job, you decide how much of your income to spend, how much to save, and how to invest your savings. Someday you may find yourself running a small business or a large corporation, and you will decide what prices to charge for your products. The insights developed in the coming chapters will give you a new perspective on how best to make these decisions. Studying economics will not by itself make you rich, but it will give you some tools that may help in that endeavor.

The third reason to study economics is that it will give you a better understanding of both the potential and the limits of economic policy. Economic questions are always on the minds of policymakers in mayors' offices, governors' mansions, and the White House. What are the burdens associated with alternative forms of taxation? What are the effects of free trade with other countries? What is the best way to protect the environment? How does a government budget deficit affect the economy? As a voter, you help choose the policies that guide the allocation of society's resources. An understanding of economics will help you carry out that responsibility. And who knows: Perhaps someday you will end up as one of those policymakers yourself.

Thus, the principles of economics can be applied in many of life's situations. Whether the future finds you following the news, running a business, or sitting in the Oval Office, you will be glad that you studied economics.

N. Gregory Mankiw
December 2016

# Video Application

**V**ideo application features the book's author introducing chapter content. Author Greg Mankiw introduces the important themes in every chapter by delivering a highly relevant deposition on the real-world context to the economic principles that will be appearing in the upcoming chapter. These videos are intended to motivate students to better understand how economics relates to their day-to-day lives and in the world around them.

# ConceptClip Videos

**C**onceptClip videos help students master economics terms. These high-energy videos, embedded throughout the interactive book, address the known student challenge of understanding economics terminology when initially introduced to the subject matter. Developed by Professor Mike Brandl of The Ohio State University, these concept-based animations provide students with memorable context to the key terminology required for your introductory economics course.

> *"I have always wanted supplemental material such as this to help me understand certain concepts in economics."*

Equilibrium

QTY (SUPPLIED) = QTY (DEMANDED)

# Graph Builder

**G**raph Builder allows students to move step-by-step through complex graphical figures. Designed specifically for introductory economics students, Graph Builder interactive exercises help students first understand complex graphs by deconstructing a graph into finite steps that build upon one another, then practice graphing by drawing out a similar scenario from scratch. This drawing method supports the kinesthetic learning approach valued by instructors, like you— all within the context of the interactive book!

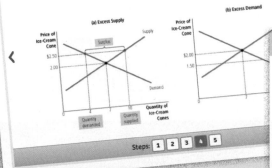

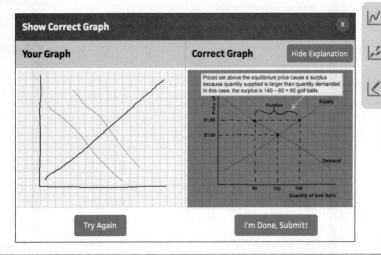

# Adaptive Test Prep Prepares Your Students for High-Stakes Testing

**A**re your students constantly asking you for more practice questions as exam time comes closer? Do your students complain because the test bank-type questions in the exam do not have the same look and feel as their homework assignments?

Adaptive Test Prep is a powerful tool that uses 4,000 new test bank-like questions to give students almost unlimited practice for each chapter and section. They can take as many tests as they like that are immediately graded for them. Students see how they did and the program gives them immediate remediation in the form of very robust feedback, a link right back into the text where the question topic resides, and for about 2,000 questions, they get a brief Quick Coach video with an instructor walking them through the exact question they missed!

Students can generate reports that show them which chapters and sections they need the most help on so they can tailor future practice tests just on the areas they are struggling with.

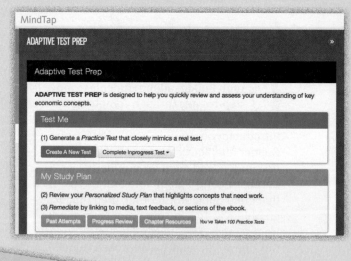

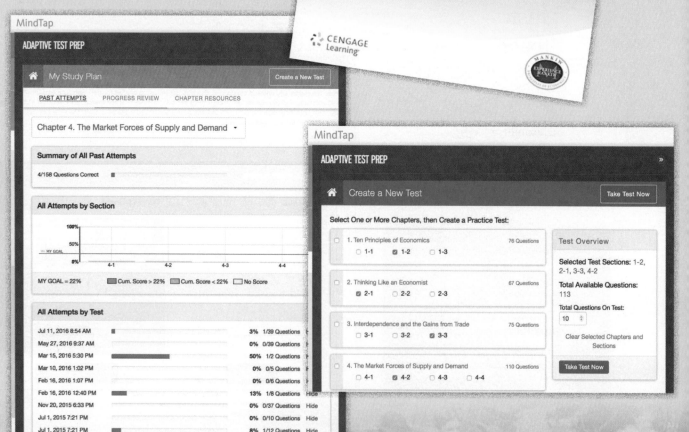

# Nobody Does Ancillaries Like We Do!

**Y**ou want your teaching tools worthy of the excellence that you bring to your class and no text has the quality and breadth of ancillaries that Mankiw, 8e has. No publisher spends the time and resources on the ancillary tools that we do!

We have a top team of veteran instructors, many of whom have been in the group since the first edition. Under the leadership and guidance of Dr. David Hakes at the University of Northern Iowa, this all-star group is relentless in making sure that the suite of ancillary materials are unmatched in the market in both quantity and quality. No other text comes close!

**Test Bank** Cengage Learning Testing (powered by Cognero®) is a powerful online cloud-based test bank system that allows you to quickly find, review, edit, and create new test question content in an instant. Tests are easy to create then export to your Learning Management System or as a document such as an Adobe .pdf or Microsoft .doc.

Our Cengage Learning testing product for Mankiw, 8e has been substantively updated by a team of award winning teaching economists. Each question in the bank was carefully reviewed and edited to align to changes made in this edition, and new questions were added. With close to 17,000 questions in the bank, our eighth edition remains the most robust and error-free test bank in the economics market!

As well, we have made it easier for you to (a) navigate and find questions when sorting/filtering based on topic, learning objective, level difficulty, question type, and so forth, and (b) find questions when moving between the print test bank and the digital versions of the test bank!

## The Art of Instruction — Premium Teaching Tools for Classroom Presentations

Available on the Instructor Companion site, the selection of PowerPoint ancillaries accompanying Mankiw, 8e not only offer you the choice and flexibility you've become accustomed to but also offer improved features to bring economics concepts to life.

**Premium PowerPoint and Lecture Notes** This popular series of chapter-by-chapter presentations comprise many innovative teaching tools, including animated graphs, additional examples not covered in the book, and FRED data, all designed to enhance your lectures and increase student involvement in class.

**Traditional Lecture PowerPoint** This comprehensive series of lecture presentations are designed to save you valuable time as you prepare for class. This supplement covers all essential topics, graphs, tables, and FRED data just as they would appear in the text.

**Polling PowerPoints Powered by TurningPoint Cloud** This pre-built series of PowerPoints offers polling questions for in-class student engagement.

**Exhibit PowerPoint** This set of presentation slides includes all of the exhibits, tables, and graphs from the text.

# Acknowledgments

I n writing this book, I benefited from the input of many talented people. Indeed, the list of people who have contributed to this project is so long, and their contributions so valuable, that it seems an injustice that only a single name appears on the cover.

Let me begin with my colleagues in the economics profession. The many editions of this text and its supplemental materials have benefited enormously from their input. In reviews and surveys, they have offered suggestions, identified challenges, and shared ideas from their own classroom experience. I am indebted to them for the perspectives they have brought to the text. Unfortunately, the list has become too long to thank those who contributed to previous editions, even though students reading the current edition are still benefiting from their insights.

Most important in this process has been David Hakes (University of Northern Iowa). David, a dedicated teacher, has served as a reliable sounding board for ideas and is a hardworking partner with me in putting together the superb package of supplements. In addition, a special thanks to Ron Cronovich, an insightful instructor and trusted advisor, for his many years of consultation.

A special thanks to the team of teaching economists who worked on the test bank and ancillaries for this edition, many of whom have been working on the Mankiw ancillaries from the beginning. To Ken McCormick for vetting the entire test bank (with 17,000 questions) for correctness, and to Ken Brown, Sarah Cosgrove, Harold Elder, Michael Enz, Lisa Jepsen, Bryce Kanago, Daniel Marburger, Amanda Nguyen, Alicia Rosburg, Forrest Spence, and Kelvin Wong for authoring new questions and updating existing ones.

The following reviewers of the seventh edition provided suggestions for refining the content, organization, and approach in the eighth.

Mark Abajian, *San Diego Mesa College*

Rahi Abouk, *University of Wisconsin Milwaukee*

Mathew Abraham, *Indiana University – Purdue University Indianapolis*

Nathanael Adams, *Cardinal Stritch University*

Seemi Ahmad, *Dutchess Community College*

May Akabogu-Collins, *Mira Costa College–Oceanside*

Ercument Aksoy, *Los Angeles Valley College*

Basil Al-Hashimi, *Mesa Community College*

Rashid Al-Hmoud, *Texas Tech University*

William Aldridge, *University of Alabama–Tuscaloosa*

Donald L. Alexander, *Western Michigan University*

Hassan Aly, *Ohio State University*

Michelle Amaral, *University of the Pacific*

Shahina Amin, *University of Northern Iowa*

Catalina Amuedo-Dorantes, *San Diego State University*

Vivette Ancona, *Hunter College–CUNY*

Aba Anil, *University of Utah*

Diane Anstine, *North Central College*

Carolyn Arcand, *University of Massachusetts Boston*

Becca Arnold, *San Diego Community College*

Ali Ataiifar, *Delaware County Community College*

Shannon Aucoin, *University of Louisiana Lafayette*

Lisa Augustyniak, *Lake Michigan College*

Wesley Austin, *University of Louisiana Lafayette*

Dennis Avola, *Framingham State University*

Regena M. Aye, *Allen Community College*

Sang Hoo Bae, *Clark University*

Karen Baehler, *Hutchinson Community College*

Sahar Bahmani, *University of Wisconsin-Parkside*

Mohsen Bahmani-Oskooee, *University of Wisconsin Milwaukee*

xvii

Richard Baker, *Copiah-Lincoln Community College*
Stephen Baker, *Capital University*
Tannista Banerjee, *Auburn University*
Bob Barnes, *DePaul University*
Hamid Bastin, *Shippensburg University*
James Bathgate, *Western Nevada College*
Leon Battista, *Albertus Magnus College*
Gerald Baumgardner, *Susquehanna University*
Christoph Bauner, *University of Massachusetts–Amherst*
Elizabeth Bayley, *University of Delaware*
Ergin Bayrak, *University of Southern California*
Nihal Bayraktar, *Pennsylvania State University*
Mike Belleman, *St. Clair County Community College*
Audrey Benavidez, *Del Mar College*
Cynthia Benelli, *University of California Santa Barbara*
Charles Bennett, *Gannon University*
Bettina Berch, *Borough of Manhattan Community College*
Stacey Bertke, *Owensboro Community & Technical College*
Tibor Besedes, *Georgia Institute of Technology*
Abhijeet Bhattacharya, *Illinois Valley Community College*
Ronald Bishop, *Lake Michigan College*
Thomas Bishop, *California State Channel Islands*
Nicole Bissessar, *Kent State University-Ashtabula*
Janet Blackburn, *San Jacinto South College*
Jeanne Boeh, *Augsburg College*
Natalia Boliari, *Manhattan College*
Antonio Bos, *Tusculum College*
Jennifer Bossard, *Doane College*
James Boudreau, *University of Texas–Pan American*
Mike Bowyer, *Montgomery Community College*
William Brennan, *Minnesota State University–Mankato*
Genevieve Briand, *Washington State University*
Scott Broadbent, *Western Kentucky University*
Greg Brock, *Georgia Southern University*
Ivy Broder, *American University*
Todd Broker, *Murray State University*

Stacey Brook, *University of Iowa*
Keith Brouhle, *Grinnell College*
Byron Brown, *Michigan State University*
Crystal Brown, *Anderson University*
Kris Bruckerhoff, *University of Minnesota-Crookston*
Christopher Brunt, *Lake Superior State University*
Laura Bucila, *Texas Christian University*
Donna Bueckman, *University of Tennessee–Knoxville*
Don Bumpass, *Sam Houston State University*
Joe Bunting, *St. Andrews University*
Benjamin Burden, *Temple College*
Mariya Burdina, *University of Central Oklahoma*
Rob Burrus, *University of North Carolina–Wilmington*
James Butkiewicz, *University of Delaware*
William Byrd, *Troy University*
Anna Cai, *University of Alabama–Tuscaloosa*
Samantha Cakir, *Macalester College*
Michael Carew, *Baruch College*
William Carner, *Westminster College*
Craig Carpenter, *Albion College*
John Carter, *California State University-Stanislaus*
Ginette Carvalho, *Fordham University*
Onur Celik, *Quinnipiac University*
Avik Chakrabarti, *University of Wisconsin–Milwaukee*
Kalyan Chakraborty, *Emporia State University*
Suparna Chakraborty, *Baruch College–CUNY*
Dustin Chambers, *Salisbury University*
Silvana Chambers, *Salisbury University*
Krishnamurti Chandrasekar, *New York Institute of Technology*
Yong Chao, *University of Louisville*
David Chaplin, *Northwest Nazarene University*
Xudong Chen, *Baldwin-Wallace College*
Yi-An Chen, *University of Washington, Seattle*
Kirill Chernomaz, *San Francisco State University*
Ron Cheung, *Oberlin College*
Hui-Chu Chiang, *University of Central Oklahoma*
Mainul Chowdhury, *Northern Illinois University*

Dmitriy Chulkov, *Indiana University Kokomo*
Lawrence Cima, *John Carroll University*
Cindy Clement, *University of Maryland*
Matthew Clements, *St. Edward's University*
Sondra Collins, *University of Southern Mississippi*
Tina Collins, *San Joaquin Valley College*
Scott Comparato, *Southern Illinois University*
Kathleen Conway, *Carnegie Mellon University*
Stephen Cotten, *University of Houston Clear Lake*
Jim Cox, *Georgia Perimeter College*
Michael Craig, *University of Tennessee–Knoxville*
Matt Critcher, *University of Arkansas Community College at Batesville*
George Crowley, *Troy University, Troy*
David Cullipher, *Arkansas State University-Mountain Home*
Dusan Curcic, *University of Virginia*
Norman Cure, *Macomb Community College*
Maria DaCosta, *University of Wisconsin–EauClaire*
Bruce Dalgaard, *St. Olaf College*
Anusua Datta, *Philadelphia University*
Earl Davis, *Nicholls State University*
Amanda Dawsey, *University of Montana*
Prabal De, *City College of New York*
Rooj Debasis, *Kishwaukee College*
Dennis Debrecht, *Carroll University*
William DeFrance, *University of Michigan-Flint*
Theresa J. Devine, *Brown University*
Paramita Dhar, *Central Connecticut State University*
Ahrash Dianat, *George Mason University*
Stephanie Dieringer, *University of South Florida St. Petersburg*
Du Ding, *Northern Arizona University*
Liang Ding, *Macalester College*
Parks Dodd, *Georgia Institute of Technology*
Veronika Dolar, *Long Island University*
Zachary Donohew, *University of Central Arkansas*
Kirk Doran, *University of Notre Dame*
Craig Dorsey, *College of DuPage*

Caf Dowlah, *Queensborough Community College–CUNY*

Tanya Downing, *Cuesta College*

Michael J. Driscoll, *Adelphi University*

Ding Du, *Northern Arizona University*

Kevin Dunagan, *Oakton community college*

Nazif Durmaz, *University of Houston–Victoria*

Tomas Dvorak, *Union College*

Eva Dziadula, *Lake Forest College*

Dirk Early, *Southwestern University*

Ann Eike, *University of Kentucky*

Harold Elder, *University of Alabama–Tuscaloosa*

Lynne Elkes, *Loyola University Maryland*

Diantha Ellis, *Abraham Baldwin College*

Noha Emara, *Columbia University*

Michael Enz, *Framingham State University*

David Epstein, *The College of New Jersey*

Lee Erickson, *Taylor University*

Sarah Estelle, *Hope College*

Pat Euzent, *University of Central Florida–Orlando*

Timothy Ewest, *Wartburg College*

Yang Fan, *University of Washington*

Amir Farmanesh, *University of Maryland*

MohammadMahdi Farsiabi, *Wayne State University*

Julie Finnegan, *Mendocino College*

Ryan Finseth, *University of Montana*

Donna Fisher, *Georgia Southern University*

Nikki Follis, *Chadron State College*

Joseph Franklin, *Newberry College*

Matthew Freeman, *Mississippi State University*

Gary Frey, *City College of New York*

Ted Fu, *Shenandoah University*

Winnie Fung, *Wheaton College*

Marc Fusaro, *Arkansas Tech University*

Todd Gabe, *University of Maine*

Mary Gade, *Oklahoma State University*

Jonathan Gafford, *Columbia State Community College*

Iris Geisler, *Austin Community College*

Jacob Gelber, *University of Alabama at Birmingham*

Robert Gentenaar, *Pima Downtown Community College*

Soma Ghosh, *Albright College*

Edgar Ghossoub, *University of Texas at San Antonio*

Alex Gialanella, *Manhattanville College*

Bill Gibson, *University of Vermont*

Kenneth Gillingham, *Yale University*

Gregory Gilpin, *Montana State University*

Robert Godby, *University of Wyoming*

Jayendra Gokhale, *Oregon State University*

Joel Goldhar, *IIT/Stuart School of Business*

Michael Goode, *Central Piedmont Community College*

Michael J Gootzeit, *University of Memphis*

Jackson Grant, *US Air Force Academy*

Jeremy Groves, *Northern Illinois University*

Ilhami Gunduz, *Brooklyn College–CUNY*

Roberts Halsey, *Indiana University*

Michele Hampton, *Cuyahoga Community College Eastern*

James Hartley, *Mount Holyoke College*

Mike Haupert, *University of Wisconsin LaCrosse*

David Hedrick, *Central Washington University*

Evert Van Der Heide, *Calvin College*

Sara Helms, *Samford University*

Jessica Hennessey, *Furman University*

Thomas Henry, *Mississippi State University*

Alexander Hill, *University of Colorado-Boulder*

Bob Holland, *Purdue University*

Paul Holmes, *Ashland University*

Kim Hoolda, *Fordham University*

Aaron Hoshide, *University of Maine*

Michael Hoyte, *York College*

Glenn Hsu, *University of Central Oklahoma*

Kuang-Chung Hsu, *University of Central Oklahoma*

Jim Hubert, *Seattle Central Community College*

George Hughes, *University of Hartford*

Andrew Hussey, *University of Memphis*

Christopher Hyer, *University of New Mexico*

Kent Hymel, *California State University–Northridge*

Miren Ivankovic, *Anderson University*

Eric Jacobson, *University of Delaware*

Bolormaa Jamiyansuren, *Augsburg College*

Justin Jarvis, *Orange Coast College*

Andres Jauregui, *Columbus State University*

Ricot Jean, *Valencia College*

Michal Jerzmanowski, *Clemson University*

Bonnie Johnson, *California Lutheran University*

Bruce Johnson, *Centre College*

Paul Johnson, *University of Alaska Anchorage*

Philipp Jonas, *KV Community College*

Adam Jones, *University of North Carolina–Wilmington*

Jason Jones, *Furman University*

Roger Jordan, *Baker College*

James Jozefowicz, *Indiana University of Pennsylvania*

Sujana Kabiraj, *Louisiana State University*

Simran Kahai, *John Carroll University*

Leo Kahane, *Providence College*

Venoo Kakar, *San Francisco State University*

David Kalist, *Shippensburg University*

Lillian Kamal, *University of Hartford*

Willie Kamara, *North Lake College*

Robert Kane, *State University of New York-Fredonia*

David Karemera, *St. Cloud State University*

Logan Kelly, *University of Wisconsin*

Craig Kerr, *California State Polytechnic University-Pomona*

Wahhab Khandker, *University of Wisconsin–LaCrosse*

Jongsung Kim, *Bryant University*

Kihwan Kim, *Rutgers*

Elsy Kizhakethalackal, *Bowling Green State University*

Todd Knoop, *Cornell College*

Fred Kolb, *University of Wisconsin–EauClaire*

Oleg Korenok, *Virginia Commonwealth University*

Janet Koscianski, *Shippensburg University*

Kafui Kouakou, *York College*

Mikhail Kouliavtsev, *Stephen F. Austin State University*

Maria Kula, *Roger Williams University*

Nakul Kumar, *Bloomsburg University*

Ben Kyer, *Francis Marion University*

Yuexing Lan, *Auburn Montgomery*

Daniel Lawson, *Oakland Community College*

Elena Lazzari, *Marygrove College*

Quan Le, *Seattle University*

Chun Lee, *Loyola Marymount University*

Daniel Lee, *Shippensburg University*

Jihoon Lee, *Northeastern University*

Jim Lee, *Texas A&M–Corpus Christi*

Junghoon Lee, *Emory University*

Ryan Lee, *Indiana University*

Sang Lee, *Southeastern Louisiana University*

James Leggette, *Belhaven University*

Bozena Leven, *The College of New Jersey*

Qing Li, *College of the Mainland*

Zhen Li, *Albion College*

Carlos Liard-Muriente, *Central Connecticut State University*

Larry Lichtenstein, *Canisius College*

Jenny Liu, *Portland State University*

Jialu Liu, *Allegheny College*

Sam Liu, *West Valley College*

Xuepeng Liu, *Kennesaw State University*

Jie Ma, *Indiana University*

Michael Machiorlatti, *Oklahoma City Community College*

Bruce Madariaga, *Montgomery College and Northwestern University*

Brinda Mahalingam, *University of Alabama-Huntsville*

C. Lucy Malakar, *Lorain County Community College*

Paula Manns, *Atlantic Cape Community College*

Gabriel Manrique, *Winona State University*

Dan Marburger, *Arizona State University*

Hardik Marfatia, *Northeastern Illinois University*

Christina Marsh, *Wake Forest University*

William McAndrew, *Gannon University*

Katherine McClain, *University of Georgia*

Michael McIlhon, *Century College*

Steven McMullen, *Hope College*

Jennifer McNiece, *Howard Payne University*

Robert Menafee, *Sinclair Community College*

Fabio Mendez, *Loyola University Maryland*

Charles Meyrick, *Housatonic Community College*

Heather Micelli, *Mira Costa College*

Laura Middlesworth, *University of Wisconsin–Eau Claire*

Meghan Mihal, *St. Thomas Aquinas College*

Eric Miller, *Oakton Community College*

Phillip Mixon, *Troy University–Troy*

Evan Moore, *Auburn University–Montgomery*

Francis Mummery, *California State University–Fullerton*

John Mundy, *St. Johns River State University*

Charles Murray, *The College of Saint Rose*

James Murray, *University of Wisconsin–LaCrosse*

Christopher Mushrush, *Illinois State University*

John Nader, *Davenport University*

Max Grunbaum Nagiel, *Daytona State College*

Mihai Nica, *University of Central Oklahoma*

Scott Niederjohn, *Lakeland College*

Mark Nixon, *Fordham University*

George Norman, *Tufts University*

David O'Hara, *Metropolitan State University*

Brian O'Roark, *Robert Morris University*

Yanira Ogrodnik, *Post University*

Wafa Orman, *University of Alabama in Huntsville*

Glenda Orosco, *Oklahoma State University Institute of Technology*

Orgul Ozturk, *University of South Carolina*

Jennifer Pakula, *Saddleback College*

Maria Papapavlou, *San Jacinto Central College*

Nitin Paranjpe, *Wayne State University*

Irene Parietti, *Felician College*

Jooyoun Park, *Kent State University*

Dodd Parks, *Georgia Institute of Technology*

Jason Patalinghug, *University of New Haven*

Michael Patton, *St. Louis Community College–Wildwood*

Wesley Pech, *Wofford College*

Josh Phillips, *Iowa Central Community College*

Germain Pichop, *Oklahoma City Community College*

Lodovico Pizzati, *University of Southern California*

Florenz Plassmann, *Binghamton University*

Lana Podolak, *Community College of Beaver County*

Gyan Pradhan, *Eastern Kentucky University*

Curtis Price, *University of Southern Indiana*

Silvia Prina, *Case Western Reserve University*

Thomas Prusa, *Rutgers University*

Conrad Puozaa, *University of Mississippi*

John Stuart Rabon, *Missouri State University*

Mark Reavis, *Arkansas Tech University*

Robert Rebelein, *Vassar College*

Agne Reizgeviciute, *California State University-Chico*

Matt Rendleman, *Southern Illinois University*

Judith Ricks, *Onondaga Community College*

Chaurey Ritam, *Binghamton University*

Jared Roberts, *North Carolina State University*

Josh Robinson, *University of Alabama-Birmingham*

Kristen Roche, *Mount Mary College*

Antonio Rodriguez, *Texas A&M International University*

Debasis Rooj, *Kishwaukee College*

Larry Ross, *University of Alaska*

Subhasree Basu Roy, *Missouri State University*

Jeff Rubin, *Rutgers University–New Brunswick*

Jason C. Rudbeck, *University of Georgia*

Jeff Ruggiero, *University of Dayton*

Robert Rycroft, *University of Mary Washington*

Allen Sanderson, *University of Chicago*

Malkiat Sandhu, *San Jose City College*

Lisle Sanna, *Ursinus College*

Nese Sara, *University of Cincinnati*

Naveen Sarna, *Northern Virginia Community College–Alexandria*

Eric Sartell, *Whitworth University*

Martin Schonger, *Princeton University*

Andy Schuchart, *Iowa Central Community College*

Michael Schultz, *Menlo College*

Jessica Schuring, *Central College*

Danielle Schwarzmann, *Towson University*

Gerald Scott, *Florida Atlantic University*

Elan Segarra, *San Francisco State University*

Bhaswati Sengupta, *Iona College*

Reshmi Sengupta, *Northern Illinois University*

Dan Settlage, *University of Arkansas-Fort Smith*

David Shankle, *Blue Mountain College*

Alex Shiu, *McLennan Community College*

Robert Shoffner, *Central Piedmont Community College*

Mark Showalter, *Brigham Young University*

Sanchit Shrivastava, *University of Utah*

Johnny Shull, *Wake Tech Community College*

Suann Shumaker, *Las Positas College*

Nicholas Shunda, *University of Redlands*

Milan Sigetich, *Southern Oregon University*

Jonathan Silberman, *Oakland University*

Joe Silverman, *Mira Costa College–Oceanside*

Silva Simone, *Murray State University*

Harmeet Singh, *Texas A&M University–Kingsville*

Catherine Skura, *Sandhills Community College*

Gary Smith, *Canisius College*

Richard Smith, *University of South Florida–St. Petersburg*

Joe Sobieralski, *Southwestern Illinois College–Belleville*

Mario Solis-Garcia, *Macalester College*

Arjun Sondhi, *Wayne State University*

Soren Soumbatiants, *Franklin University*

Matt Souza, *Indiana University – Purdue University Columbus*

Nekeisha Spencer, *Binghamton University*

Dean Stansel, *Florida Gulf Coast University*

Sylwia Starnawska, *D'Youville College*

Keva Steadman, *Augustana College*

Rebecca Stein, *University of Pennsylvania*

Dale Steinreich, *Drury University*

Paul Stock, *University of Mary Hardin-Baylor*

Michael Stroup, *Stephen F. Austin State University*

Edward Stuart, *Northeastern Illinois University*

Yang Su, *University of Washington*

Yu-hsuan Su, *University of Washington*

Samanta Subarna, *The College of New Jersey*

Abdul Sukar, *Cameron University*

Burak Sungu, *Miami University*

John Susenburger, *Utica College*

James Swofford, *University of South Alabama*

Vera Tabakova, *East Carolina University*

Ariuna Taivan, *University of Minnesota-Duluth*

Eftila Tanellari, *Radford University*

Eric Taylor, *Central Piedmont Community College*

Erdal Tekin, *Georgia State University*

Noreen Templin, *Butler Community College*

Thomas Tenerelli, *Central Washington University*

Anna Terzyan, *California State University-Los Angeles*

Petros Tesfazion, *Ithaca College*

Charles Thompson, *Brunswick Community College*

Flint Thompson, *Chippewa Valley Technical College*

Deborah Thorsen, *Palm Beach State College–Central*

James Tierney, *University of California Irvine*

Julie Trivitt, *Arkansas Tech University*

Arja Turunen-Red, *University of New Orleans*

Mark Tuttle, *Sam Houston State University*

Jennifer VanGilder, *Ursinus College*

Ross vanWassenhove, *University of Houston*

Ben Vaughan, *Trinity University*

Roumen Vesselinov, *Queens College, City University of New York*

Rubina Vohra, *St. Peter's College*

Will Walsh, *Samford University*

Chih-Wei Wang, *Pacific Lutheran University*

Jingjing Wang, *University of New Mexico*

Chad Wassell, *Central Washington University*

Christine Wathen, *Middlesex Community College*

J. Douglas Wellington, *Husson University*

Adam Werner, *California Polytechnic State University*

Sarah West, *Macalester College*

Elizabeth Wheaton, *Southern Methodist University*

Oxana Wieland, *University of Minnesota, Crookston*

Christopher Wimer, *Bowling Green State University–Firelands College*

Do Youn Won, *University of Utah*

Kelvin Wong, *University of Minnesota*

Ken Woodward, *Saddleback College*

Irena Xhurxhi, *York College*

Xu Xu, *Mississippi state university*

Ying Yang, *University of Rhode Island*

Young-Ro Yoon, *Wayne State University*

Eric Zemjic, *Kent State University*

Yongchen Zhao, *Towson University*

Zhen Zhu, *University of Central Oklahoma*

Kent Zirlott, *University of Alabama–Tuscaloosa*

Joseph Zwiller, *Lake Michigan College*

The team of editors who worked on this book improved it tremendously. Jane Tufts, developmental editor, provided truly spectacular editing—as she always does. Michael Parthenakis, senior product manager, did a splendid job of overseeing the many people involved in such a large project. Anita Verma, senior content developer, was crucial in assembling an extensive and thoughtful group of reviewers to give me feedback on the previous edition, while putting together an excellent team to revise the supplements. Colleen Farmer, senior content project manager, had the patience and dedication necessary to turn my manuscript into this book. Kasie Jean, digital content designer and a trained economist, designed and implemented all of the valuable student resources in MindTap. Michelle Kunkler, senior art director, gave this book its clean, friendly look. Bruce Morser, the illustrator, helped make the book more visually appealing and the economics in it less abstract. Pamela Rockwell, copyeditor, refined my prose, and Lumina Datamatic's indexer, prepared a careful and thorough index. John Carey, executive marketing manager, worked long hours getting the word out to potential users of this book. The rest of the Cengage team has, as always, been consistently professional, enthusiastic, and dedicated.

I am grateful also to Denis Fedin and Nina Vendhan, two star Harvard undergraduates, who helped me refine the manuscript and check the page proofs for this edition.

As always, I must thank my "in-house" editor Deborah Mankiw. As the first reader of most things I write, she continued to offer just the right mix of criticism and encouragement.

Finally, I would like to mention my three children Catherine, Nicholas, and Peter. Their contribution to this book was putting up with a father spending too many hours in his study. The four of us have much in common—not least of which is our love of ice cream (which becomes apparent in Chapter 4).

N. Gregory Mankiw
December 2016

# Contents

# PART II How Markets Work 63

## CHAPTER 4

### The Market Forces of Supply and Demand 65

## CHAPTER 5

### Elasticity and Its Application 89

## CHAPTER 6

### Supply, Demand, and Government Policies 111

# PART III Markets and Welfare  131

## CHAPTER 7

### Consumers, Producers, and the Efficiency of Markets  133

## CHAPTER 8

### Application: The Costs of Taxation  153

## CHAPTER 9

### Application: International Trade  167

# PART IV The Economics of the Public Sector 187

## CHAPTER 10

### Externalities 189

## CHAPTER 11

### Public Goods and Common Resources 211

# PART V Firm Behavior and the Organization of Industry 227

# PART VI The Data of Macroeconomics 301

# PART VII The Real Economy in the Long Run 343

# PART VIII Money and Prices in the Long Run 431

# PART IX Short-Run Economic Fluctuations 481

# PART I
# Introduction

# Ten Principles of Economics

The word *economy* comes from the Greek word *oikonomos*, which means "one who manages a household." At first, this origin might seem peculiar. But in fact, households and economies have much in common.

A household faces many decisions. It must decide which household members do which tasks and what each member receives in return: Who cooks dinner? Who does the laundry? Who gets the extra dessert at dinner? Who gets to drive the car? In short, a household must allocate its scarce resources (time, dessert, car mileage) among its various members, taking into account each member's abilities, efforts, and desires.

Like a household, a society faces many decisions. It must find some way to decide what jobs will be done and who will do them. It needs some people to grow food, other people to make clothing, and still others to design computer software. Once society has allocated people (as well as land, buildings, and machines) to various jobs, it must also allocate the goods and services they produce. It must decide who will eat caviar and who will eat potatoes. It must decide who will drive a Tesla and who will take the bus.

The management of society's resources is important because resources are scarce. **Scarcity** means that society has limited resources and therefore cannot produce all the goods and services people wish to have. Just as each member of a household cannot get everything she wants, each individual in a society cannot attain the highest standard of living to which she might aspire.

**Economics** is the study of how society manages its scarce resources. In most societies, resources are allocated not by an all-powerful dictator but through the combined choices of millions of households and firms. Economists, therefore, study how people make decisions: how much they work, what they buy, how much they save, and how they invest their savings. Economists also study how people interact with one another. For instance, they examine how the multitude of buyers and sellers of a good together determine the price at which the good is sold and the quantity that is sold. Finally, economists analyze the forces and trends that affect the economy as a whole, including the growth in average income, the fraction of the population that cannot find work, and the rate at which prices are rising.

The study of economics has many facets, but it is unified by several central ideas. In this chapter, we look at *Ten Principles of Economics*. Don't worry if you don't understand them all at first or if you aren't completely convinced. We explore these ideas more fully in later chapters. The ten principles are introduced here to give you an overview of what economics is all about. Consider this chapter a "preview of coming attractions."

**scarcity**
the limited nature of society's resources

**economics**
the study of how society manages its scarce resources

# 1-1  How People Make Decisions

There is no mystery to what an economy is. Whether we are talking about the economy of Los Angeles, the United States, or the whole world, an economy is just a group of people dealing with one another as they go about their lives. Because the behavior of an economy reflects the behavior of the individuals who make up the economy, we begin our study of economics with four principles about individual decision making.

## 1-1a  Principle 1: People Face Trade-offs

You may have heard the old saying, "There ain't no such thing as a free lunch." Grammar aside, there is much truth to this adage. To get something that we like, we usually have to give up something else that we also like. Making decisions requires trading off one goal against another.

Consider a student who must decide how to allocate her most valuable resource—her time. She can spend all of her time studying economics, spend all of it studying psychology, or divide it between the two fields. For every hour she studies one subject, she gives up an hour she could have used studying the other. And for every hour she spends studying, she gives up an hour she could have spent napping, bike riding, watching TV, or working at her part-time job for some extra spending money.

Consider parents deciding how to spend their family income. They can buy food, clothing, or a family vacation. Or they can save some of the family income for retirement or the children's college education. When they choose to spend an extra dollar on one of these goods, they have one less dollar to spend on some other good.

When people are grouped into societies, they face different kinds of trade-offs. One classic trade-off is between "guns and butter." The more a society spends on national defense (guns) to protect its shores from foreign aggressors, the less it can spend on consumer goods (butter) to raise the standard of living at home. Also important in modern society is the trade-off between a clean environment and a high level of income. Laws that require firms to reduce pollution raise the cost of producing goods and services. Because of these higher costs, the firms end up earning smaller profits, paying lower wages, charging higher prices, or some combination of these three. Thus, while pollution regulations yield the benefit of a cleaner environment and the improved health that comes with it, they come at the cost of reducing the incomes of the regulated firms' owners, workers, and customers.

Another trade-off society faces is between efficiency and equality. **Efficiency** means that society is getting the maximum benefits from its scarce resources. **Equality** means that those benefits are distributed uniformly among society's members. In other words, efficiency refers to the size of the economic pie, and equality refers to how the pie is divided into individual slices.

When government policies are designed, these two goals often conflict. Consider, for instance, policies aimed at equalizing the distribution of economic well-being. Some of these policies, such as the welfare system or unemployment insurance, try to help the members of society who are most in need. Others, such as the individual income tax, ask the financially successful to contribute more than others to support the government. Though they achieve greater equality, these policies reduce efficiency. When the government redistributes income from the rich to the poor, it reduces the reward for working hard; as a result, people work less and produce fewer goods and services. In other words, when the government tries to cut the economic pie into more equal slices, the pie gets smaller.

Recognizing that people face trade-offs does not by itself tell us what decisions they will or should make. A student should not abandon the study of psychology just because doing so would increase the time available for the study of economics. Society should not stop protecting the environment just because environmental regulations reduce our material standard of living. The poor should not be ignored just because helping them distorts work incentives. Nonetheless, people are likely to make good decisions only if they understand the options that are available to them. Our study of economics, therefore, starts by acknowledging life's trade-offs.

**efficiency**
the property of society getting the most it can from its scarce resources

**equality**
the property of distributing economic prosperity uniformly among the members of society

### 1-1b Principle 2: The Cost of Something Is What You Give Up to Get It

Because people face trade-offs, making decisions requires comparing the costs and benefits of alternative courses of action. In many cases, however, the cost of an action is not as obvious as it might first appear.

Consider the decision to go to college. The main benefits are intellectual enrichment and a lifetime of better job opportunities. But what are the costs? To answer this question, you might be tempted to add up the money you spend on tuition, books, room, and board. Yet this total does not truly represent what you give up to spend a year in college.

There are two problems with this calculation. First, it includes some things that are not really costs of going to college. Even if you quit school, you need a place to sleep and food to eat. Room and board are costs of going to college only to the extent that they are more expensive at college than elsewhere. Second, this calculation ignores the largest cost of going to college—your time. When you spend a year listening to lectures, reading textbooks, and writing papers, you cannot spend that time working at a job. For most students, the earnings they give up to attend school are the single largest cost of their education.

The **opportunity cost** of an item is what you give up to get that item. When making any decision, decision makers should be aware of the opportunity costs that accompany each possible action. In fact, they usually are. College athletes who can earn millions if they drop out of school and play professional sports are well aware that their opportunity cost of attending college is very high. It is not surprising that they often decide that the benefit of a college education is not worth the cost.

**opportunity cost**
whatever must be given up to obtain some item

### 1-1c  Principle 3: Rational People Think at the Margin

Economists normally assume that people are rational. **Rational people** systematically and purposefully do the best they can to achieve their objectives, given the available opportunities. As you study economics, you will encounter firms that decide how many workers to hire and how much of their product to manufacture and sell to maximize profits. You will also encounter individuals who decide how much time to spend working and what goods and services to buy with the resulting income to achieve the highest possible level of satisfaction.

Rational people know that decisions in life are rarely black and white but usually involve shades of gray. At dinnertime, the question you face is not "Should I fast or eat like a pig?" More likely, you will be asking yourself "Should I take that extra spoonful of mashed potatoes?" When exams roll around, your decision is not between blowing them off and studying 24 hours a day but whether to spend an extra hour reviewing your notes instead of watching TV. Economists use the term **marginal change** to describe a small incremental adjustment to an existing plan of action. Keep in mind that *margin* means "edge," so marginal changes are adjustments around the edges of what you are doing. Rational people often make decisions by comparing *marginal benefits* and *marginal costs*.

**rational people**
people who systematically and purposefully do the best they can to achieve their objectives

**marginal change**
a small incremental adjustment to a plan of action

For example, suppose you are considering calling a friend on your cell phone. You decide that talking with her for 10 minutes would give you a benefit that you value at about $7. Your cell phone service costs you $40 per month plus $0.50 per minute for whatever calls you make. You usually talk for 100 minutes a month, so your total monthly bill is $90 ($0.50 per minute times 100 minutes, plus the $40 fixed fee). Under these circumstances, should you make the call? You might be tempted to reason as follows: "Because I pay $90 for 100 minutes of calling each month, the average minute on the phone costs me $0.90. So a 10-minute call costs $9. Because that $9 cost is greater than the $7 benefit, I am going to skip the call." That conclusion is wrong, however. Although the *average* cost of a 10-minute call is $9, the *marginal* cost—the amount your bill increases if you make the extra call—is only $5. You will make the right decision only by comparing the marginal benefit and the marginal cost. Because the marginal benefit of $7 is greater than the marginal cost of $5, you should make the call. This is a principle that people innately understand: Cell phone users with unlimited minutes (that is, minutes that are free at the margin) are often prone to making long and frivolous calls.

Thinking at the margin works for business decisions as well. Consider an airline deciding how much to charge passengers who fly standby. Suppose that flying a 200-seat plane across the United States costs the airline $100,000. In this case, the average cost of each seat is $100,000/200, which is $500. One might be tempted to conclude that the airline should never sell a ticket for less than $500. But a rational airline can increase its profits by thinking at the margin. Imagine that a plane is about to take off with 10 empty seats and a standby passenger waiting at the gate is willing to pay $300 for a seat. Should the airline sell the ticket? Of course it should. If the plane has empty seats, the cost of adding one more passenger is tiny. The *average* cost of flying a passenger is $500, but the *marginal* cost is merely the cost of the can of soda that the extra passenger will consume. As long as the standby passenger pays more than the marginal cost, selling the ticket is profitable.

Marginal decision making can help explain some otherwise puzzling economic phenomena. Here is a classic question: Why is water so cheap, while diamonds are so expensive? Humans need water to survive, while diamonds are unnecessary. Yet people are willing to pay much more for a diamond than for a cup of water. The reason is that a person's willingness to pay for a good is based on the marginal benefit that an extra unit of the good would yield. The marginal benefit, in turn, depends on how many units a person already has. Water is essential, but the marginal benefit of an extra cup is small because water is plentiful. By contrast, no one needs diamonds to survive, but because diamonds are so rare, people consider the marginal benefit of an extra diamond to be large.

A rational decision maker takes an action if and only if the marginal benefit of the action exceeds the marginal cost. This principle explains why people use their cell phones as much as they do, why airlines are willing to sell tickets below average cost, and why people are willing to pay more for diamonds than for water. It can take some time to get used to the logic of marginal thinking, but the study of economics will give you ample opportunity to practice.

*"Is the marginal benefit of this call greater than the marginal cost?"*

### 1-1d  Principle 4: People Respond to Incentives

An **incentive** is something (such as the prospect of a punishment or reward) that induces a person to act. Because rational people make decisions by comparing costs and benefits, they respond to incentives. You will see that incentives play a central role in the study of economics. One economist went so far as to suggest that the entire field could be summarized as simply "People respond to incentives. The rest is commentary."

**incentive**
something that induces a person to act

Incentives are key to analyzing how markets work. For example, when the price of an apple rises, people decide to eat fewer apples. At the same time, apple orchards decide to hire more workers and harvest more apples. In other words, a higher price in a market provides an incentive for buyers to consume less and an incentive for sellers to produce more. As we will see, the influence of prices on the behavior of consumers and producers is crucial to how a market economy allocates scarce resources.

Public policymakers should never forget about incentives: Many policies change the costs or benefits that people face and, as a result, alter their behavior. A tax on gasoline, for instance, encourages people to drive smaller, more fuel-efficient cars. That is one reason people drive smaller cars in Europe, where gasoline taxes are high, than in the United States, where gasoline taxes are low. A higher gasoline tax also encourages people to carpool, take public transportation, and live closer to where they work. If the tax were larger, more people would be driving hybrid cars, and if it were large enough, they would switch to electric cars.

When policymakers fail to consider how their policies affect incentives, they often end up facing unintended consequences. For example, consider public policy regarding auto safety. Today, all cars have seat belts, but this was not true

60 years ago. In 1965, Ralph Nader's book *Unsafe at Any Speed* generated much public concern over auto safety. Congress responded with laws requiring seat belts as standard equipment on new cars.

How does a seat belt law affect auto safety? The direct effect is obvious: When a person wears a seat belt, the probability of surviving an auto accident rises. But that's not the end of the story because the law also affects behavior by altering incentives. The relevant behavior here is the speed and care with which drivers operate their cars. Driving slowly and carefully is costly because it uses the driver's time and energy. When deciding how safely to drive, rational people compare, perhaps unconsciously, the marginal benefit from safer driving to the marginal cost. As a result, they drive more slowly and carefully when the benefit of increased safety is high. For example, when road conditions are icy, people drive more attentively and at lower speeds than they do when road conditions are clear.

Consider how a seat belt law alters a driver's cost–benefit calculation. Seat belts make accidents less costly because they reduce the likelihood of injury or death. In other words, seat belts reduce the benefits of slow and careful driving. People respond to seat belts as they would to an improvement in road conditions—by driving faster and less carefully. The result of a seat belt law, therefore, is a larger number of accidents. The decline in safe driving has a clear, adverse impact on pedestrians, who are more likely to find themselves in an accident but (unlike the drivers) don't have the benefit of added protection.

At first, this discussion of incentives and seat belts might seem like idle speculation. Yet in a classic 1975 study, economist Sam Peltzman argued that auto-safety laws have had many of these effects. According to Peltzman's evidence, these laws give rise to fewer deaths per accident but also to more accidents. He concluded that the net result is little change in the number of driver deaths and an increase in the number of pedestrian deaths.

Peltzman's analysis of auto safety is an offbeat and controversial example of the general principle that people respond to incentives. When analyzing any policy, we must consider not only the direct effects but also the less obvious indirect effects that work through incentives. If the policy changes incentives, it will cause people to alter their behavior.

**QuickQuiz**  *Describe an important trade-off you recently faced. • Give an example of some action that has both a monetary and nonmonetary opportunity cost. • Describe an incentive your parents offered to you in an effort to influence your behavior.*

# 1-2 How People Interact

The first four principles discussed how individuals make decisions. As we go about our lives, many of our decisions affect not only ourselves but other people as well. The next three principles concern how people interact with one another.

### 1-2a Principle 5: Trade Can Make Everyone Better Off

You may have heard on the news that the Chinese are our competitors in the world economy. In some ways, this is true because American and Chinese firms produce many of the same goods. Companies in the United States and China compete for the same customers in the markets for clothing, toys, solar panels, automobile tires, and many other items.

Yet it is easy to be misled when thinking about competition among countries. Trade between the United States and China is not like a sports contest in which one side wins and the other side loses. In fact, the opposite is true: Trade between two countries can make each country better off.

To see why, consider how trade affects your family. When a member of your family looks for a job, she competes against members of other families who are looking for jobs. Families also compete against one another when they go shopping because each family wants to buy the best goods at the lowest prices. In a sense, each family in an economy competes with all other families.

Despite this competition, your family would not be better off isolating itself from all other families. If it did, your family would need to grow its own food, make its own clothes, and build its own home. Clearly, your family gains much from its ability to trade with others. Trade allows each person to specialize in the activities she does best, whether it is farming, sewing, or home building. By trading with others, people can buy a greater variety of goods and services at lower cost.

Like families, countries also benefit from the ability to trade with one another. Trade allows countries to specialize in what they do best and to enjoy a greater variety of goods and services. The Chinese, as well as the French, Egyptians, and Brazilians, are as much our partners in the world economy as they are our competitors.

*"For $5 a week you can watch baseball without being nagged to cut the grass!"*

## 1-2b Principle 6: Markets Are Usually a Good Way to Organize Economic Activity

The collapse of communism in the Soviet Union and Eastern Europe in the late 1980s and early 1990s was one of the last century's most transformative events. Communist countries operated on the premise that government officials were in the best position to allocate the economy's scarce resources. These central planners decided what goods and services were produced, how much was produced, and who produced and consumed these goods and services. The theory behind central planning was that only the government could organize economic activity in a way that promoted economic well-being for the country as a whole.

Most countries that once had centrally planned economies have abandoned the system and are instead developing market economies. In a **market economy**, the decisions of a central planner are replaced by the decisions of millions of firms and households. Firms decide whom to hire and what to make. Households decide which firms to work for and what to buy with their incomes. These firms and households interact in the marketplace, where prices and self-interest guide their decisions.

**market economy**
an economy that allocates resources through the decentralized decisions of many firms and households as they interact in markets for goods and services

At first glance, the success of market economies is puzzling. In a market economy, no one is looking out for the economic well-being of society as a whole. Free markets contain many buyers and sellers of numerous goods and services, and all of them are interested primarily in their own well-being. Yet despite decentralized decision making and self-interested decision makers, market economies have proven remarkably successful in organizing economic activity to promote overall economic well-being.

In his 1776 book *An Inquiry into the Nature and Causes of the Wealth of Nations*, economist Adam Smith made the most famous observation in all of economics: Households and firms interacting in markets act as if they are guided by an "invisible hand" that leads them to desirable market outcomes. One of our goals in this book is to understand how this invisible hand works its magic.

As you study economics, you will learn that prices are the instrument with which the invisible hand directs economic activity. In any market, buyers look at the price when determining how much to demand, and sellers look at the price when deciding how much to supply. As a result of the decisions that buyers and sellers make, market prices reflect both the value of a good to society and the cost to society of making the good. Smith's great insight was that prices adjust to guide these individual buyers and sellers to reach outcomes that, in many cases, maximize the well-being of society as a whole.

Smith's insight has an important corollary: When a government prevents prices from adjusting naturally to supply and demand, it impedes the invisible hand's ability to coordinate the decisions of the households and firms that make up an economy. This corollary explains why taxes adversely affect the allocation of resources: They distort prices and thus the decisions of households and firms. It also explains the great harm caused by policies that directly control prices, such as rent control. And it explains the failure of communism. In communist countries, prices were not determined in the marketplace but were dictated by central planners. These planners lacked the necessary information about consumers' tastes and producers' costs, which in a market economy is reflected in prices. Central planners failed because they tried to run the economy with one hand tied behind their backs—the invisible hand of the marketplace.

---

### FYI

## Adam Smith and the Invisible Hand

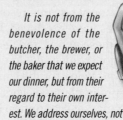

It may be only a coincidence that Adam Smith's great book *The Wealth of Nations* was published in 1776, the exact year in which American revolutionaries signed the Declaration of Independence. But the two documents share a point of view that was prevalent at the time: Individuals are usually best left to their own devices, without the heavy hand of government guiding their actions. This political philosophy provides the intellectual basis for the market economy and for free society more generally.

Why do decentralized market economies work so well? Is it because people can be counted on to treat one another with love and kindness? Not at all. Here is Adam Smith's description of how people interact in a market economy:

Adam Smith

*Man has almost constant occasion for the help of his brethren, and it is in vain for him to expect it from their benevolence only. He will be more likely to prevail if he can interest their self-love in his favour, and show them that it is for their own advantage to do for him what he requires of them. . . . Give me that which I want, and you shall have this which you want, is the meaning of every such offer; and it is in this manner that we obtain from one another the far greater part of those good offices which we stand in need of.*

*It is not from the benevolence of the butcher, the brewer, or the baker that we expect our dinner, but from their regard to their own interest. We address ourselves, not to their humanity but to their self-love, and never talk to them of our own necessities but of their advantages. Nobody but a beggar chooses to depend chiefly upon the benevolence of his fellow-citizens. . . .*

*Every individual . . . neither intends to promote the public interest, nor knows how much he is promoting it. . . . He intends only his own gain, and he is in this, as in many other cases, led by an invisible hand to promote an end which was no part of his intention. Nor is it always the worse for the society that it was no part of it. By pursuing his own interest he frequently promotes that of the society more effectually than when he really intends to promote it.*

Smith is saying that participants in the economy are motivated by self-interest and that the "invisible hand" of the marketplace guides this self-interest into promoting general economic well-being.

Many of Smith's insights remain at the center of modern economics. Our analysis in the coming chapters will allow us to express Smith's conclusions more precisely and to analyze more fully the strengths and weaknesses of the market's invisible hand. ■

BETTMANN/CORBIS

**CASE STUDY**

**ADAM SMITH WOULD HAVE LOVED UBER**
You have probably never lived in a centrally planned economy, but if you have ever tried to hail a cab in a major city, you have likely experienced a highly regulated market. In many cities, the local government imposes strict controls in the market for taxis. The rules usually go well beyond regulation of insurance and safety. For example, the government may limit entry into the market by approving only a certain number of taxi medallions or permits. It may determine the prices that taxis are allowed to charge. The government uses its police powers—that is, the threat of fines or jail time—to keep unauthorized drivers off the streets and to prevent all drivers from charging unauthorized prices.

Recently, however, this highly controlled market has been invaded by a disruptive force: Uber. Launched in 2009, this company provides an app for smartphones that connects passengers and drivers. Because Uber cars do not roam the streets looking for taxi-hailing pedestrians, they are technically not taxis and so are not subject to the same regulations. But they offer much the same service. Indeed, rides from Uber cars are often more convenient. On a cold and rainy day, who wants to stand on the side of the road waiting for an empty cab to drive by? It is more pleasant to remain inside, use your smartphone to arrange for a ride, and stay warm and dry until the car arrives.

Uber cars often charge less than taxis, but not always. Uber allows drivers to raise their prices significantly when there is a surge in demand, such as during a sudden rainstorm or late on New Year's Eve, when numerous tipsy partiers are looking for a safe way to get home. By contrast, regulated taxis are typically prevented from surge pricing.

Not everyone is fond of Uber. Drivers of traditional taxis complain that this new competition eats into their source of income. This is hardly a surprise: Suppliers of goods and services usually dislike new competitors. But vigorous competition among producers makes a market work well for consumers.

That is why economists love Uber. A 2014 survey of several dozen prominent economists asked whether car services such as Uber increased consumer well-being. Yes, said every single economist. The economists were also asked whether surge pricing increased consumer well-being. Yes, said 85 percent of them. Surge pricing makes consumers pay more at times, but because Uber drivers respond to incentives, it also increases the quantity of car services supplied when they are most needed. Surge pricing also helps allocate the services to those consumers who value them most highly and reduces the costs of searching and waiting for a car.

If Adam Smith were alive today, he would surely have the Uber app on his phone. ●

*Technology can improve this market.*

## 1-2c Principle 7: Governments Can Sometimes Improve Market Outcomes

If the invisible hand of the market is so great, why do we need government? One purpose of studying economics is to refine your view about the proper role and scope of government policy.

One reason we need government is that the invisible hand can work its magic only if the government enforces the rules and maintains the institutions that are key to a market economy. Most important, market economies need institutions to enforce **property rights** so individuals can own and control scarce resources.

**property rights**
the ability of an individual to own and exercise control over scarce resources

A farmer won't grow food if she expects her crop to be stolen; a restaurant won't serve meals unless it is assured that customers will pay before they leave; and a film company won't produce movies if too many potential customers avoid paying by making illegal copies. We all rely on government-provided police and courts to enforce our rights over the things we produce—and the invisible hand counts on our ability to enforce those rights.

Another reason we need government is that, although the invisible hand is powerful, it is not omnipotent. There are two broad rationales for a government to intervene in the economy and change the allocation of resources that people would choose on their own: to promote efficiency or to promote equality. That is, most policies aim either to enlarge the economic pie or to change how the pie is divided.

Consider first the goal of efficiency. Although the invisible hand usually leads markets to allocate resources to maximize the size of the economic pie, this is not always the case. Economists use the term **market failure** to refer to a situation in which the market on its own fails to produce an efficient allocation of resources. As we will see, one possible cause of market failure is an **externality,** which is the impact of one person's actions on the well-being of a bystander. The classic example of an externality is pollution. When the production of a good pollutes the air and creates health problems for those who live near the factories, the market left to its own devices may fail to take this cost into account. Another possible cause of market failure is **market power,** which refers to the ability of a single person or firm (or a small group) to unduly influence market prices. For example, if everyone in town needs water but there is only one well, the owner of the well is not subject to the rigorous competition with which the invisible hand normally keeps self-interest in check; she may take advantage of this opportunity by restricting the output of water so she can charge a higher price. In the presence of externalities or market power, well-designed public policy can enhance economic efficiency.

Now consider the goal of equality. Even when the invisible hand yields efficient outcomes, it can nonetheless leave sizable disparities in economic well-being. A market economy rewards people according to their ability to produce things that other people are willing to pay for. The world's best basketball player earns more than the world's best chess player simply because people are willing to pay more to watch basketball than chess. The invisible hand does not ensure that everyone has sufficient food, decent clothing, and adequate healthcare. This inequality may, depending on one's political philosophy, call for government intervention. In practice, many public policies, such as the income tax and the welfare system, aim to achieve a more equal distribution of economic well-being.

To say that the government *can* improve on market outcomes does not mean that it always *will*. Public policy is made not by angels but by a political process that is far from perfect. Sometimes policies are designed simply to reward the politically powerful. Sometimes they are made by well-intentioned leaders who are not fully informed. As you study economics, you will become a better judge of when a government policy is justifiable because it promotes efficiency or equality and when it is not.

**market failure**
a situation in which a market left on its own fails to allocate resources efficiently

**externality**
the impact of one person's actions on the well-being of a bystander

**market power**
the ability of a single economic actor (or small group of actors) to have a substantial influence on market prices

QuickQuiz   *Why is a country better off not isolating itself from all other countries?*
*• Why do we have markets, and according to economists, what roles should government play in them?*

# 1-3 How the Economy as a Whole Works

We started by discussing how individuals make decisions and then looked at how people interact with one another. All these decisions and interactions together make up "the economy." The last three principles concern the workings of the economy as a whole.

## 1-3a Principle 8: A Country's Standard of Living Depends on Its Ability to Produce Goods and Services

The differences in living standards around the world are staggering. In 2014, the average American had an income of about $55,000. In the same year, the average Mexican earned about $17,000, the average Chinese about $13,000, and the average Nigerian only $6,000. Not surprisingly, this large variation in average income is reflected in various measures of quality of life. Citizens of high-income countries have more TV sets, more cars, better nutrition, better healthcare, and a longer life expectancy than citizens of low-income countries.

Changes in living standards over time are also large. In the United States, incomes have historically grown about 2 percent per year (after adjusting for changes in the cost of living). At this rate, average income doubles every 35 years. Over the past century, average U.S. income has risen about eightfold.

What explains these large differences in living standards among countries and over time? The answer is surprisingly simple. Almost all variation in living standards is attributable to differences in countries' **productivity**—that is, the amount of goods and services produced by each unit of labor input. In nations where workers can produce a large quantity of goods and services per hour, most people enjoy a high standard of living; in nations where workers are less productive, most people endure a more meager existence. Similarly, the growth rate of a nation's productivity determines the growth rate of its average income.

The fundamental relationship between productivity and living standards is simple, but its implications are far-reaching. If productivity is the primary determinant of living standards, other explanations must be of secondary importance. For example, it might be tempting to credit labor unions or minimum-wage laws for the rise in living standards of American workers over the past century. Yet the real hero of American workers is their rising productivity. As another example, some commentators have claimed that increased competition from Japan and other countries explained the slow growth in U.S. incomes during the 1970s and 1980s. Yet the real villain was not competition from abroad but flagging productivity growth in the United States.

The relationship between productivity and living standards also has profound implications for public policy. When thinking about how any policy will affect living standards, the key question is how it will affect our ability to produce goods and services. To boost living standards, policymakers need to raise productivity by ensuring that workers are well educated, have the tools they need to produce goods and services, and have access to the best available technology.

**productivity**
the quantity of goods and services produced from each unit of labor input

## 1-3b Principle 9: Prices Rise When the Government Prints Too Much Money

In January 1921, a daily newspaper in Germany cost 0.30 marks. Less than two years later, in November 1922, the same newspaper cost 70,000,000 marks. All other prices in the economy rose by similar amounts. This episode is one of history's most spectacular examples of **inflation,** an increase in the overall level of prices in the economy.

**inflation**
an increase in the overall level of prices in the economy

*"Well it may have been 68 cents when you got in line, but it's 74 cents now!"*

Although the United States has never experienced inflation even close to that of Germany in the 1920s, inflation has at times been an economic problem. During the 1970s, for instance, when the overall level of prices more than doubled, President Gerald Ford called inflation "public enemy number one." By contrast, inflation in the first decade of the 21st century ran about 2½ percent per year; at this rate, it would take almost 30 years for prices to double. Because high inflation imposes various costs on society, keeping inflation at a low level is a goal of economic policymakers around the world.

What causes inflation? In almost all cases of large or persistent inflation, the culprit is growth in the quantity of money. When a government creates large quantities of the nation's money, the value of the money falls. In Germany in the early 1920s, when prices were on average tripling every month, the quantity of money was also tripling every month. Although less dramatic, the economic history of the United States points to a similar conclusion: The high inflation of the 1970s was associated with rapid growth in the quantity of money, and the return of low inflation in the 1980s was associated with slower growth in the quantity of money.

### 1-3c  Principle 10: Society Faces a Short-Run Trade-off between Inflation and Unemployment

Although a higher level of prices is, in the long run, the primary effect of increasing the quantity of money, the short-run story is more complex and controversial. Most economists describe the short-run effects of monetary injections as follows:

- Increasing the amount of money in the economy stimulates the overall level of spending and thus the demand for goods and services.
- Higher demand may over time cause firms to raise their prices, but in the meantime, it also encourages them to hire more workers and produce a larger quantity of goods and services.
- More hiring means lower unemployment.

This line of reasoning leads to one final economy-wide trade-off: a short-run trade-off between inflation and unemployment.

Although some economists still question these ideas, most accept that society faces a short-run trade-off between inflation and unemployment. This simply means that, over a period of a year or two, many economic policies push inflation and unemployment in opposite directions. Policymakers face this trade-off regardless of whether inflation and unemployment both start out at high levels (as they did in the early 1980s), at low levels (as they did in the late 1990s), or someplace in between. This short-run trade-off plays a key role in the analysis of the **business cycle**—the irregular and largely unpredictable fluctuations in economic activity, as measured by the production of goods and services or the number of people employed.

Policymakers can exploit the short-run trade-off between inflation and unemployment using various policy instruments. By changing the amount that the government spends, the amount it taxes, and the amount of money it prints, policymakers can influence the overall demand for goods and services. Changes in demand in turn influence the combination of inflation and unemployment that the economy experiences in the short run. Because these instruments of economic policy are potentially so powerful, how policymakers should use them to control the economy, if at all, is a subject of continuing debate.

This debate heated up in the early years of Barack Obama's presidency. In 2008 and 2009, the U.S. economy, as well as many other economies around the world, experienced a deep economic downturn. Problems in the financial system, caused by bad

**business cycle**
fluctuations in economic activity, such as employment and production

bets on the housing market, spilled over into the rest of the economy, causing incomes to fall and unemployment to soar. Policymakers responded in various ways to increase the overall demand for goods and services. President Obama's first major initiative was a stimulus package of reduced taxes and increased government spending. At the same time, the nation's central bank, the Federal Reserve, increased the supply of money. The goal of these policies was to reduce unemployment. Some feared, however, that these policies might over time lead to an excessive level of inflation.

**QuickQuiz** *List and briefly explain the three principles that describe how the economy as a whole works.*

# 1-4 Conclusion

You now have a taste of what economics is all about. In the coming chapters, we develop many specific insights about people, markets, and economies. Mastering these insights will take some effort, but it is not an overwhelming task. The field of economics is based on a few big ideas that can be applied in many different situations.

Throughout this book, we will refer back to the *Ten Principles of Economics* highlighted in this chapter and summarized in Table 1. Keep these building blocks in mind: Even the most sophisticated economic analysis is founded on the ten principles introduced here.

**TABLE 1**

**Ten Principles of Economics**

**How People Make Decisions**
1: People Face Trade-offs
2: The Cost of Something Is What You Give Up to Get It
3: Rational People Think at the Margin
4: People Respond to Incentives

**How People Interact**
5: Trade Can Make Everyone Better Off
6: Markets Are Usually a Good Way to Organize Economic Activity
7: Governments Can Sometimes Improve Market Outcomes

**How the Economy as a Whole Works**
8: A Country's Standard of Living Depends on Its Ability to Produce Goods and Services
9: Prices Rise When the Government Prints Too Much Money
10: Society Faces a Short-Run Trade-off between Inflation and Unemployment

## CHAPTER QuickQuiz

1. Economics is best defined as the study of
   a. how society manages its scarce resources.
   b. how to run a business most profitably.
   c. how to predict inflation, unemployment, and stock prices.
   d. how the government can stop the harm from unchecked self-interest.

2. Your opportunity cost of going to a movie is
   a. the price of the ticket.
   b. the price of the ticket plus the cost of any soda and popcorn you buy at the theater.
   c. the total cash expenditure needed to go to the movie plus the value of your time.
   d. zero, as long as you enjoy the movie and consider it a worthwhile use of time and money.

3. A marginal change is one that
   a. is not important for public policy.
   b. incrementally alters an existing plan.
   c. makes an outcome inefficient.
   d. does not influence incentives.

4. Adam Smith's "invisible hand" refers to
   a. the subtle and often hidden methods that businesses use to profit at consumers' expense.
   b. the ability of free markets to reach desirable outcomes, despite the self-interest of market participants.
   c. the ability of government regulation to benefit consumers, even if the consumers are unaware of the regulations.
   d. the way in which producers or consumers in unregulated markets impose costs on innocent bystanders.

5. Governments may intervene in a market economy in order to
   a. protect property rights.
   b. correct a market failure due to externalities.
   c. achieve a more equal distribution of income.
   d. All of the above.

6. If a nation has high and persistent inflation, the most likely explanation is
   a. the central bank creating excessive amounts of money.
   b. unions bargaining for excessively high wages.
   c. the government imposing excessive levels of taxation.
   d. firms using their monopoly power to enforce excessive price hikes.

## SUMMARY

- The fundamental lessons about individual decision making are that people face trade-offs among alternative goals, that the cost of any action is measured in terms of forgone opportunities, that rational people make decisions by comparing marginal costs and marginal benefits, and that people change their behavior in response to the incentives they face.
- The fundamental lessons about interactions among people are that trade and interdependence can be mutually beneficial, that markets are usually a good

way of coordinating economic activity among people, and that the government can potentially improve market outcomes by remedying a market failure or by promoting greater economic equality.
- The fundamental lessons about the economy as a whole are that productivity is the ultimate source of living standards, that growth in the quantity of money is the ultimate source of inflation, and that society faces a short-run trade-off between inflation and unemployment.

## KEY CONCEPTS

scarcity, p. 4
economics, p. 4
efficiency, p. 5
equality, p. 5
opportunity cost, p. 6
rational people, p. 6

marginal change, p. 6
incentive, p. 7
market economy, p. 9
property rights, p. 11
market failure, p. 12
externality, p. 12

market power, p. 12
productivity, p. 13
inflation, p. 13
business cycle, p. 14

## QUESTIONS FOR REVIEW

1. Give three examples of important trade-offs that you face in your life.

2. What items would you include to figure out the opportunity cost of a vacation to Disney World?

3. Water is necessary for life. Is the marginal benefit of a glass of water large or small?

4. Why should policymakers think about incentives?

5. Why isn't trade among countries like a game with some winners and some losers?

6. What does the "invisible hand" of the marketplace do?

7. What are the two main causes of market failure? Give an example of each.

8. Why is productivity important?

9. What is inflation and what causes it?

10. How are inflation and unemployment related in the short run?

## PROBLEMS AND APPLICATIONS

1. Describe some of the trade-offs faced by each of the following:
   a. a family deciding whether to buy a new car
   b. a member of Congress deciding how much to spend on national parks
   c. a company president deciding whether to open a new factory
   d. a professor deciding how much to prepare for class
   e. a recent college graduate deciding whether to go to graduate school

2. You are trying to decide whether to take a vacation. Most of the costs of the vacation (airfare, hotel, and forgone wages) are measured in dollars, but the benefits of the vacation are psychological. How can you compare the benefits to the costs?

3. You were planning to spend Saturday working at your part-time job, but a friend asks you to go skiing. What is the true cost of going skiing? Now suppose you had been planning to spend the day studying at the library. What is the cost of going skiing in this case? Explain.

4. You win $100 in a basketball pool. You have a choice between spending the money now and putting it away for a year in a bank account that pays 5 percent interest. What is the opportunity cost of spending the $100 now?

5. The company that you manage has invested $5 million in developing a new product, but the development is not quite finished. At a recent meeting, your salespeople report that the introduction of competing products has reduced the expected sales of your new product to $3 million. If it would cost $1 million to finish development and make the product, should you go ahead and do so? What is the most that you should pay to complete development?

6. A 1996 bill reforming the federal government's antipoverty programs limited many welfare recipients to only two years of benefits.
   a. How does this change affect the incentives for working?
   b. How might this change represent a trade-off between equality and efficiency?

7. Explain whether each of the following government activities is motivated by a concern about equality or a concern about efficiency. In the case of efficiency, discuss the type of market failure involved.
   a. regulating cable TV prices
   b. providing some poor people with vouchers that can be used to buy food
   c. prohibiting smoking in public places
   d. breaking up Standard Oil (which once owned 90 percent of all oil refineries) into several smaller companies
   e. imposing higher personal income tax rates on people with higher incomes
   f. instituting laws against driving while intoxicated

8. Discuss each of the following statements from the standpoints of equality and efficiency.
   a. "Everyone in society should be guaranteed the best healthcare possible."
   b. "When workers are laid off, they should be able to collect unemployment benefits until they find a new job."

9. In what ways is your standard of living different from that of your parents or grandparents when they were your age? Why have these changes occurred?

10. Suppose Americans decide to save more of their incomes. If banks lend this extra saving to businesses, which use the funds to build new factories, how might this lead to faster growth in productivity? Who do you suppose benefits from the higher productivity? Is society getting a free lunch?

11. During the Revolutionary War, the American colonies could not raise enough tax revenue to fully fund the war effort. To make up the difference, the colonies decided to print more money. Printing money to cover expenditures is sometimes referred to as an "inflation tax." Who do you think is being "taxed" when more money is printed? Why?

To find additional study resources, visit cengagebrain.com, and search for "Mankiw."

# Thinking Like an Economist

**E**very field of study has its own language and its own way of thinking. Mathematicians talk about axioms, integrals, and vector spaces. Psychologists talk about ego, id, and cognitive dissonance. Lawyers talk about venue, torts, and promissory estoppel.

Economics is no different. Supply, demand, elasticity, comparative advantage, consumer surplus, deadweight loss—these terms are part of the economist's language. In the coming chapters, you will encounter many new terms and some familiar words that economists use in specialized ways. At first, this new language may seem needlessly arcane. But as you will see, its value lies in its ability to provide you with a new and useful way of thinking about the world in which you live.

The purpose of this book is to help you learn the economist's way of thinking. Just as you cannot become a mathematician, psychologist, or lawyer overnight, learning to think like an economist will take some time. Yet with a combination of theory, case studies, and examples of economics in the news, this book will give you ample opportunity to develop and practice this skill.

Before delving into the substance and details of economics, it is helpful to have an overview of how economists approach the world. This chapter discusses the field's methodology. What is distinctive about how economists confront a question? What does it mean to think like an economist?

# 2-1  The Economist as Scientist

Economists try to address their subject with a scientist's objectivity. They approach the study of the economy in much the same way a physicist approaches the study of matter and a biologist approaches the study of life: They devise theories, collect data, and then analyze these data in an attempt to verify or refute their theories.

To beginners, the claim that economics is a science can seem odd. After all, economists do not work with test tubes or telescopes. The essence of science, however, is the *scientific method*—the dispassionate development and testing of theories about how the world works. This method of inquiry is as applicable to studying a nation's economy as it is to studying the earth's gravity or a species' evolution. As Albert Einstein once put it, "The whole of science is nothing more than the refinement of everyday thinking."

Although Einstein's comment is as true for social sciences such as economics as it is for natural sciences such as physics, most people are not accustomed to looking at society through a scientific lens. Let's discuss some of the ways economists apply the logic of science to examine how an economy works.

*"I'm a social scientist, Michael. That means I can't explain electricity or anything like that, but if you ever want to know about people, I'm your man."*

## 2-1a  The Scientific Method: Observation, Theory, and More Observation

Isaac Newton, the famous 17th-century scientist and mathematician, allegedly became intrigued one day when he saw an apple fall from a tree. This observation motivated Newton to develop a theory of gravity that applies not only to an apple falling to the earth but to any two objects in the universe. Subsequent testing of Newton's theory has shown that it works well in many circumstances (albeit not in all circumstances, as Einstein would later show). Because Newton's theory has been so successful at explaining observation, it is still taught in undergraduate physics courses around the world.

This interplay between theory and observation also occurs in economics. An economist might live in a country experiencing rapidly increasing prices and be moved by this observation to develop a theory of inflation. The theory might assert that high inflation arises when the government prints too much money. To test this theory, the economist could collect and analyze data on prices and money from many different countries. If growth in the quantity of money were completely unrelated to the rate of price increase, the economist would start to doubt the validity of this theory of inflation. If money growth and inflation were strongly correlated in international data, as in fact they are, the economist would become more confident in the theory.

Although economists use theory and observation like other scientists, they face an obstacle that makes their task especially challenging: In economics, conducting experiments is often impractical. Physicists studying gravity can drop many objects in their laboratories to generate data to test their theories. By contrast, economists studying inflation are not allowed to manipulate a nation's monetary policy simply to generate useful data. Economists, like astronomers and evolutionary biologists, usually have to make do with whatever data the world happens to give them.

To find a substitute for laboratory experiments, economists pay close attention to the natural experiments offered by history. When a war in the Middle East interrupts the supply of crude oil, for instance, oil prices skyrocket around the world. For consumers of oil and oil products, such an event depresses living standards. For economic policymakers, it poses a difficult choice about how best to respond. But for economic scientists, the event provides an opportunity to study the effects of a key natural resource on the world's economies. Throughout this book, therefore, we consider many historical episodes. These episodes are valuable to study because they give us insight into the economy of the past and, more important, because they allow us to illustrate and evaluate economic theories of the present.

## 2-1b The Role of Assumptions

If you ask a physicist how long it would take a marble to fall from the top of a ten-story building, he will likely answer the question by assuming that the marble falls in a vacuum. Of course, this assumption is false. In fact, the building is surrounded by air, which exerts friction on the falling marble and slows it down. Yet the physicist will point out that the friction on the marble is so small that its effect is negligible. Assuming the marble falls in a vacuum simplifies the problem without substantially affecting the answer.

Economists make assumptions for the same reason: Assumptions can simplify the complex world and make it easier to understand. To study the effects of international trade, for example, we might assume that the world consists of only two countries and that each country produces only two goods. In reality, there are numerous countries, each of which produces thousands of different types of goods. But by considering a world with only two countries and two goods, we can focus our thinking on the essence of the problem. Once we understand international trade in this simplified imaginary world, we are in a better position to understand international trade in the more complex world in which we live.

The art in scientific thinking—whether in physics, biology, or economics—is deciding which assumptions to make. Suppose, for instance, that instead of dropping a marble from the top of the building, we were dropping a beach ball of the same weight. Our physicist would realize that the assumption of no friction is less accurate in this case: Friction exerts a greater force on the beach ball because it is much larger than a marble. The assumption that gravity works in a vacuum is reasonable when studying a falling marble but not when studying a falling beach ball.

Similarly, economists use different assumptions to answer different questions. Suppose that we want to study what happens to the economy when the government changes the number of dollars in circulation. An important piece of this analysis, it turns out, is how prices respond. Many prices in the economy change infrequently: The newsstand prices of magazines, for instance, change only once every few years. Knowing this fact may lead us to make different assumptions when studying the effects of the policy change over different time horizons. For studying the short-run effects of the policy, we may assume that prices do not change much. We may even make the extreme and artificial assumption that all prices are completely fixed. For studying the long-run effects of the policy, however, we may assume that all prices are completely flexible. Just as a physicist uses different assumptions when studying falling marbles and falling beach balls, economists use different assumptions when studying the short-run and long-run effects of a change in the quantity of money.

### 2-1c  Economic Models

High school biology teachers teach basic anatomy with plastic replicas of the human body. These models have all the major organs—the heart, the liver, the kidneys, and so on—which allow teachers to show their students very simply how the important parts of the body fit together. Because these plastic models are stylized and omit many details, no one would mistake one of them for a real person. Despite this lack of realism—indeed, because of this lack of realism— studying these models is useful for learning how the human body works.

Economists also use models to learn about the world, but unlike plastic manikins, their models mostly consist of diagrams and equations. Like a biology teacher's plastic model, economic models omit many details to allow us to see what is truly important. Just as the biology teacher's model does not include all the body's muscles and capillaries, an economist's model does not include every feature of the economy.

As we use models to examine various economic issues throughout this book, you will see that all the models are built with assumptions. Just as a physicist begins the analysis of a falling marble by assuming away the existence of friction, economists assume away many details of the economy that are irrelevant to the question at hand. All models—in physics, biology, and economics—simplify reality to improve our understanding of it.

### 2-1d  Our First Model: The Circular-Flow Diagram

The economy consists of millions of people engaged in many activities—buying, selling, working, hiring, manufacturing, and so on. To understand how the economy works, we must find some way to simplify our thinking about all these activities. In other words, we need a model that explains, in general terms, how the economy is organized and how participants in the economy interact with one another.

**circular-flow diagram**
a visual model of the economy that shows how dollars flow through markets among households and firms

Figure 1 presents a visual model of the economy called a **circular-flow diagram.** In this model, the economy is simplified to include only two types of decision makers—firms and households. Firms produce goods and services using inputs, such as labor, land, and capital (buildings and machines). These inputs are called the *factors of production*. Households own the factors of production and consume all the goods and services that the firms produce.

Households and firms interact in two types of markets. In the *markets for goods and services*, households are buyers, and firms are sellers. In particular, households buy the output of goods and services that firms produce. In the *markets for the factors of production*, households are sellers, and firms are buyers. In these markets, households provide the inputs that firms use to produce goods and services. The circular-flow diagram offers a simple way of organizing the economic transactions that occur between households and firms in the economy.

The two loops of the circular-flow diagram are distinct but related. The inner loop represents the flows of inputs and outputs. The households sell the use of their labor, land, and capital to the firms in the markets for the factors of production. The firms then use these factors to produce goods and services, which in turn are sold to households in the markets for goods and services. The outer

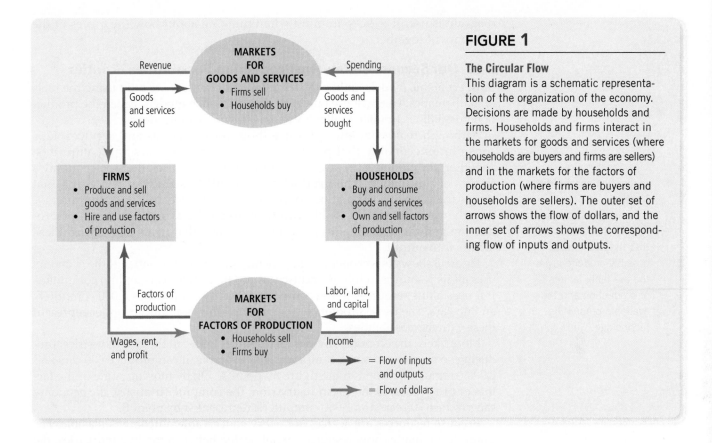

**FIGURE 1**

**The Circular Flow**
This diagram is a schematic representation of the organization of the economy. Decisions are made by households and firms. Households and firms interact in the markets for goods and services (where households are buyers and firms are sellers) and in the markets for the factors of production (where firms are buyers and households are sellers). The outer set of arrows shows the flow of dollars, and the inner set of arrows shows the corresponding flow of inputs and outputs.

loop of the diagram represents the corresponding flow of dollars. The households spend money to buy goods and services from the firms. The firms use some of the revenue from these sales to pay for the factors of production, such as the wages of their workers. What's left is the profit of the firm owners, who are themselves members of households.

Let's take a tour of the circular flow by following a dollar bill as it makes its way from person to person through the economy. Imagine that the dollar begins at a household—say, in your wallet. If you want to buy a cup of coffee, you take the dollar (along with a few of its brothers and sisters) to one of the economy's markets for goods and services, such as your local Starbucks coffee shop. There, you spend it on your favorite drink. When the dollar moves into the Starbucks cash register, it becomes revenue for the firm. The dollar doesn't stay at Starbucks for long, however, because the firm uses it to buy inputs in the markets for the factors of production. Starbucks might use the dollar to pay rent to its landlord for the space it occupies or to pay the wages of its workers. In either case, the dollar enters the income of some household and, once again, is back in someone's wallet. At that point, the story of the economy's circular flow starts once again.

The circular-flow diagram in Figure 1 is a very simple model of the economy. A more complex and realistic circular-flow model would include, for instance, the roles of government and international trade. (A portion of that dollar you gave to Starbucks might be used to pay taxes or to buy coffee beans from a farmer in Brazil.) Yet these details are not crucial for a basic understanding of how the economy is organized. Because of its simplicity, this circular-flow diagram is useful to keep in mind when thinking about how the pieces of the economy fit together.

### 2-1e  Our Second Model: The Production Possibilities Frontier

Most economic models, unlike the circular-flow diagram, are built using the tools of mathematics. Here we use one of the simplest such models, called the production possibilities frontier, to illustrate some basic economic ideas.

Although real economies produce thousands of goods and services, let's consider an economy that produces only two goods—cars and computers. Together, the car industry and the computer industry use all of the economy's factors of production. The **production possibilities frontier** is a graph that shows the various combinations of output—in this case, cars and computers—that the economy can possibly produce given the available factors of production and the available production technology that firms use to turn these factors into output.

Figure 2 shows this economy's production possibilities frontier. If the economy uses all its resources in the car industry, it produces 1,000 cars and no computers. If it uses all its resources in the computer industry, it produces 3,000 computers and no cars. The two endpoints of the production possibilities frontier represent these extreme possibilities.

More likely, the economy divides its resources between the two industries, producing some cars and some computers. For example, it can produce 600 cars and 2,200 computers, shown in the figure by point A. Or, by moving some of the factors of production to the car industry from the computer industry, the economy can produce 700 cars and 2,000 computers, represented by point B.

Because resources are scarce, not every conceivable outcome is feasible. For example, no matter how resources are allocated between the two industries, the economy cannot produce the amount of cars and computers represented by point C. Given the technology available for manufacturing cars and computers, the economy does not have enough of the factors of production to support that level of output. With the resources it has, the economy can produce at any point on or

**production possibilities frontier**
a graph that shows the combinations of output that the economy can possibly produce given the available factors of production and the available production technology

---

## FIGURE 2

**The Production Possibilities Frontier**
The production possibilities frontier shows the combinations of output—in this case, cars and computers—that the economy can possibly produce. The economy can produce any combination on or inside the frontier. Points outside the frontier are not feasible given the economy's resources. The slope of the production possibilities frontier measures the opportunity cost of a car in terms of computers. This opportunity cost varies, depending on how much of the two goods the economy is producing.

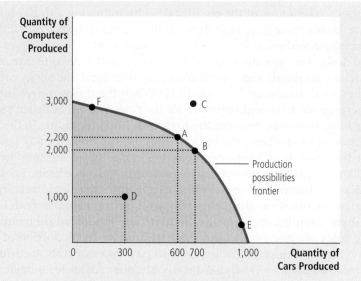

inside the production possibilities frontier, but it cannot produce at points outside the frontier.

An outcome is said to be *efficient* if the economy is getting all it can from the scarce resources it has available. Points on (rather than inside) the production possibilities frontier represent efficient levels of production. When the economy is producing at such a point, say point A, there is no way to produce more of one good without producing less of the other. Point D represents an *inefficient* outcome. For some reason, perhaps widespread unemployment, the economy is producing less than it could from the resources it has available: It is producing only 300 cars and 1,000 computers. If the source of the inefficiency is eliminated, the economy can increase its production of both goods. For example, if the economy moves from point D to point A, its production of cars increases from 300 to 600, and its production of computers increases from 1,000 to 2,200.

One of the *Ten Principles of Economics* discussed in Chapter 1 is that people face trade-offs. The production possibilities frontier shows one trade-off that society faces. Once we have reached an efficient point on the frontier, the only way of producing more of one good is to produce less of the other. When the economy moves from point A to point B, for instance, society produces 100 more cars at the expense of producing 200 fewer computers.

This trade-off helps us understand another of the *Ten Principles of Economics:* The cost of something is what you give up to get it. This is called the *opportunity cost*. The production possibilities frontier shows the opportunity cost of one good as measured in terms of the other good. When society moves from point A to point B, it gives up 200 computers to get 100 additional cars. That is, at point A, the opportunity cost of 100 cars is 200 computers. Put another way, the opportunity cost of each car is two computers. Notice that the opportunity cost of a car equals the slope of the production possibilities frontier. (If you don't recall what slope is, you can refresh your memory with the graphing appendix to this chapter.)

The opportunity cost of a car in terms of the number of computers is not constant in this economy but depends on how many cars and computers the economy is producing. This is reflected in the shape of the production possibilities frontier. Because the production possibilities frontier in Figure 2 is bowed outward, the opportunity cost of a car is highest when the economy is producing many cars and few computers, such as at point E, where the frontier is steep. When the economy is producing few cars and many computers, such as at point F, the frontier is flatter, and the opportunity cost of a car is lower.

Economists believe that production possibilities frontiers often have this bowed shape. When the economy is using most of its resources to make computers, the resources best suited to car production, such as skilled autoworkers, are being used in the computer industry. Because these workers probably aren't very good at making computers, increasing car production by one unit will cause only a slight reduction in the number of computers produced. Thus, at point F, the opportunity cost of a car in terms of computers is small, and the frontier is relatively flat. By contrast, when the economy is using most of its resources to make cars, such as at point E, the resources best suited to making cars are already at work in the car industry. Producing an additional car means moving some of the best computer technicians out of the computer industry and turning them into autoworkers. As a result, producing an additional car requires a substantial loss of computer output. The opportunity cost of a car is high, and the frontier is steep.

The production possibilities frontier shows the trade-off between the outputs of different goods at a given time, but the trade-off can change over time. For

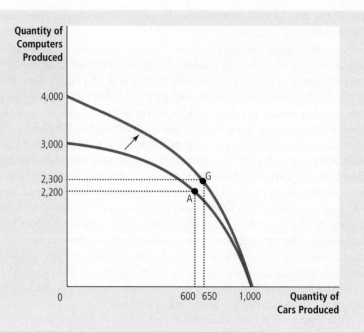

## FIGURE 3

**A Shift in the Production Possibilities Frontier**
A technological advance in the computer industry enables the economy to produce more computers for any given number of cars. As a result, the production possibilities frontier shifts outward. If the economy moves from point A to point G, then the production of both cars and computers increases.

example, suppose a technological advance in the computer industry raises the number of computers that a worker can produce per week. This advance expands society's set of opportunities. For any given number of cars, the economy can now make more computers. If the economy does not produce any computers, it can still produce 1,000 cars, so one endpoint of the frontier stays the same. But if the economy devotes some of its resources to the computer industry, it will produce more computers from those resources. As a result, the production possibilities frontier shifts outward, as in Figure 3.

This figure illustrates what happens when an economy grows. Society can move production from a point on the old frontier to a point on the new frontier. Which point it chooses depends on its preferences for the two goods. In this example, society moves from point A to point G, enjoying more computers (2,300 instead of 2,200) and more cars (650 instead of 600).

The production possibilities frontier simplifies a complex economy to highlight some basic but powerful ideas: scarcity, efficiency, trade-offs, opportunity cost, and economic growth. As you study economics, these ideas will recur in various forms. The production possibilities frontier offers one simple way of thinking about them.

### 2-1f Microeconomics and Macroeconomics

Many subjects are studied on various levels. Consider biology, for example. Molecular biologists study the chemical compounds that make up living things. Cellular biologists study cells, which are made up of many chemical compounds and, at the same time, are themselves the building blocks of living organisms. Evolutionary biologists study the many varieties of animals and plants and how species change gradually over the centuries.

Economics is also studied on various levels. We can study the decisions of individual households and firms. Or we can study the interaction of households and firms in markets for specific goods and services. Or we can study the operation of the economy as a whole, which is the sum of the activities of all these decision makers in all these markets.

The field of economics is traditionally divided into two broad subfields. **Microeconomics** is the study of how households and firms make decisions and how they interact in specific markets. **Macroeconomics** is the study of economy-wide phenomena. A microeconomist might study the effects of rent control on housing in New York City, the impact of foreign competition on the U.S. auto industry, or the effects of compulsory school attendance on workers' earnings. A macroeconomist might study the effects of borrowing by the federal government, the changes over time in the economy's rate of unemployment, or alternative policies to promote growth in national living standards.

Microeconomics and macroeconomics are closely intertwined. Because changes in the overall economy arise from the decisions of millions of individuals, it is impossible to understand macroeconomic developments without considering the associated microeconomic decisions. For example, a macroeconomist might study the effect of a federal income tax cut on the overall production of goods and services. But to analyze this issue, he must consider how the tax cut affects households' decisions about how much to spend on goods and services.

Despite the inherent link between microeconomics and macroeconomics, the two fields are distinct. Because they address different questions, each field has its own set of models, which are often taught in separate courses.

**microeconomics**
the study of how households and firms make decisions and how they interact in markets

**macroeconomics**
the study of economy-wide phenomena, including inflation, unemployment, and economic growth

**Quick Quiz** *In what sense is economics like a science? • Draw a production possibilities frontier for a society that produces food and clothing. Show an efficient point, an inefficient point, and an infeasible point. Show the effects of a drought. • Define* microeconomics *and* macroeconomics.

# 2-2 The Economist as Policy Adviser

Often, economists are asked to explain the causes of economic events. Why, for example, is unemployment higher for teenagers than for older workers? Sometimes, economists are asked to recommend policies to improve economic outcomes. What, for instance, should the government do to improve the economic well-being of teenagers? When economists are trying to explain the world, they are scientists. When they are trying to help improve it, they are policy advisers.

## 2-2a Positive versus Normative Analysis

To help clarify the two roles that economists play, let's examine the use of language. Because scientists and policy advisers have different goals, they use language in different ways.

For example, suppose that two people are discussing minimum-wage laws. Here are two statements you might hear:

> PORTIA:  Minimum-wage laws cause unemployment.
> NOAH:  The government should raise the minimum wage.

Ignoring for now whether you agree with these statements, notice that Portia and Noah differ in what they are trying to do. Portia is speaking like a scientist: She is making a claim about how the world works. Noah is speaking like a policy adviser: He is making a claim about how he would like to change the world.

In general, statements about the world come in two types. One type, such as Portia's, is positive. **Positive statements** are descriptive. They make a claim about how the world *is*. A second type of statement, such as Noah's, is normative. **Normative statements** are prescriptive. They make a claim about how the world *ought to be*.

**positive statements**
claims that attempt to describe the world as it is

**normative statements**
claims that attempt to prescribe how the world should be

A key difference between positive and normative statements is how we judge their validity. We can, in principle, confirm or refute positive statements by examining evidence. An economist might evaluate Portia's statement by analyzing data on changes in minimum wages and changes in unemployment over time. By contrast, evaluating normative statements involves values as well as facts. Noah's statement cannot be judged using data alone. Deciding what is good or bad policy is not just a matter of science. It also involves our views on ethics, religion, and political philosophy.

Positive and normative statements are fundamentally different, but within a person's set of beliefs, they are often intertwined. In particular, positive views about how the world works affect normative views about what policies are desirable. Portia's claim that the minimum wage causes unemployment, if true, might lead her to reject Noah's conclusion that the government should raise the minimum wage. Yet normative conclusions cannot come from positive analysis alone; they involve value judgments as well.

As you study economics, keep in mind the distinction between positive and normative statements because it will help you stay focused on the task at hand. Much of economics is positive: It just tries to explain how the economy works. Yet those who use economics often have normative goals: They want to learn how to improve the economy. When you hear economists making normative statements, you know they are speaking not as scientists but as policy advisers.

### 2-2b  Economists in Washington

President Harry Truman once said that he wanted to find a one-armed economist. When he asked his economists for advice, they always answered, "On the one hand, . . . . On the other hand, . . . ."

Truman was right in realizing that economists' advice is not always straightforward. This tendency is rooted in one of the *Ten Principles of Economics*: People face trade-offs. Economists are aware that trade-offs are involved in most policy decisions. A policy might increase efficiency at the cost of equality. It might help future generations but hurt current generations. An economist who says that all policy decisions are easy or clear-cut is an economist not to be trusted.

Truman was not the only president who relied on the advice of economists. Since 1946, the president of the United States has received guidance from the Council of Economic Advisers, which consists of three members and a staff of a few dozen economists. The council, whose offices are just a few steps from the White House, has no duty other than to advise the president and to write the annual *Economic Report of the President*, which discusses recent developments in the economy and presents the council's analysis of current policy issues.

The president also receives input from economists in many administrative departments. Economists at the Office of Management and Budget help formulate spending plans and regulatory policies. Economists at the Department of the Treasury help design tax policy. Economists at the Department of Labor analyze data on workers and those looking for work to help formulate labor-market policies. Economists at the Department of Justice help enforce the nation's antitrust laws.

*"Let's switch. I'll make the policy, you implement it, and he'll explain it. "*

Economists are also found outside the administrative branch of government. To obtain independent evaluations of policy proposals, Congress relies on the advice of the Congressional Budget Office, which is staffed by economists. The Federal Reserve, the institution that sets the nation's monetary policy, employs hundreds of economists to analyze economic developments in the United States and throughout the world.

The influence of economists on policy goes beyond their role as advisers: Their research and writings often affect policy indirectly. Economist John Maynard Keynes offered this observation:

> The ideas of economists and political philosophers, both when they are right and when they are wrong, are more powerful than is commonly understood. Indeed, the world is ruled by little else. Practical men, who believe themselves to be quite exempt from intellectual influences, are usually the slaves of some defunct economist. Madmen in authority, who hear voices in the air, are distilling their frenzy from some academic scribbler of a few years back.

These words were written in 1935, but they remain true today. Indeed, the "academic scribbler" now influencing public policy is often Keynes himself.

## 2-2c  Why Economists' Advice Is Not Always Followed

Any economist who advises presidents or other elected leaders knows that his recommendations are not always heeded. Frustrating as this can be, it is easy to understand. The process by which economic policy is actually made differs in many ways from the idealized policy process assumed in economics textbooks.

Throughout this text, whenever we discuss economic policy, we often focus on one question: What is the best policy for the government to pursue? We act as if policy were set by a benevolent king. Once the king figures out the right policy, he has no trouble putting his ideas into action.

In the real world, figuring out the right policy is only part of a leader's job, sometimes the easiest part. After a president hears from his economic advisers about what policy is best from their perspective, he turns to other advisers for related input. His communications advisers will tell him how best to explain the proposed policy to the public, and they will try to anticipate any misunderstandings that might make the challenge more difficult. His press advisers will tell him how the news media will report on his proposal and what opinions will likely be expressed on the nation's editorial pages. His legislative affairs advisers will tell him how Congress will view the proposal, what amendments members of Congress will suggest, and the likelihood that Congress will pass some version of the president's proposal into law. His political advisers will tell him which groups will organize to support or oppose the proposed policy, how this proposal will affect his standing among different groups in the electorate, and whether it will change support for any of the president's other policy initiatives. After hearing and weighing all this advice, the president then decides how to proceed.

Making economic policy in a representative democracy is a messy affair—and there are often good reasons why presidents (and other politicians) do not advance the policies that economists advocate. Economists offer crucial input to the policy process, but their advice is only one ingredient of a complex recipe.

Quick**Quiz**  *Give an example of a positive statement and an example of a normative statement that somehow relates to your daily life.  •  Name three parts of government that regularly rely on advice from economists.*

# 2-3  Why Economists Disagree

"If all economists were laid end to end, they would not reach a conclusion." This quip from George Bernard Shaw is revealing. Economists as a group are often criticized for giving conflicting advice to policymakers. President Ronald Reagan once joked that if the game Trivial Pursuit were designed for economists, it would have 100 questions and 3,000 answers.

Why do economists so often appear to give conflicting advice to policymakers? There are two basic reasons:

- Economists may disagree about the validity of alternative positive theories of how the world works.
- Economists may have different values and therefore different normative views about what government policy should aim to accomplish.

Let's discuss each of these reasons.

### 2-3a  Differences in Scientific Judgments

Several centuries ago, astronomers debated whether the earth or the sun was at the center of the solar system. More recently, climatologists have debated whether the earth is experiencing global warming and, if so, why. Science is an ongoing search to understand the world around us. It is not surprising that as the search continues, scientists sometimes disagree about the direction in which truth lies.

Economists often disagree for the same reason. Economics is a young science, and there is still much to be learned. Economists sometimes disagree because they have different hunches about the validity of alternative theories or about the size of important parameters that measure how economic variables are related.

For example, economists disagree about whether the government should tax a household's income or its consumption (spending). Advocates of a switch from the current income tax to a consumption tax believe that the change would encourage households to save more because income that is saved would not be taxed. Higher saving, in turn, would free resources for capital accumulation, leading to more rapid growth in productivity and living standards. Advocates of the current income tax system believe that household saving would not respond much to a change in the tax laws. These two groups of economists hold different normative views about the tax system because they have different positive views about saving's responsiveness to tax incentives.

### 2-3b  Differences in Values

Suppose that Peter and Paula both take the same amount of water from the town well. To pay for maintaining the well, the town taxes its residents. Peter has income of $150,000 and is taxed $15,000, or 10 percent of his income. Paula has income of $30,000 and is taxed $6,000, or 20 percent of her income.

Is this policy fair? If not, who pays too much and who pays too little? Does it matter whether Paula's low income is due to a medical disability or to her decision to pursue an acting career? Does it matter whether Peter's high income is due to a large inheritance or to his willingness to work long hours at a dreary job?

These are difficult questions about which people are likely to disagree. If the town hired two experts to study how it should tax its residents to pay for the well, we would not be surprised if they offered conflicting advice.

This simple example shows why economists sometimes disagree about public policy. As we know from our discussion of normative and positive analysis, policies cannot be judged on scientific grounds alone. Sometimes, economists give conflicting advice because they have different values. Perfecting the science of economics will not tell us whether Peter or Paula pays too much.

## 2-3c Perception versus Reality

Because of differences in scientific judgments and differences in values, some disagreement among economists is inevitable. Yet one should not overstate the amount of disagreement. Economists agree with one another to a much greater extent than is sometimes understood.

Table 1 contains twenty propositions about economic policy. In surveys of professional economists, these propositions were endorsed by an overwhelming

**TABLE 1**

Propositions about Which Most Economists Agree

*Proposition (and percentage of economists who agree)*

1. A ceiling on rents reduces the quantity and quality of housing available. (93%)
2. Tariffs and import quotas usually reduce general economic welfare. (93%)
3. Flexible and floating exchange rates offer an effective international monetary arrangement. (90%)
4. Fiscal policy (for example, tax cut and/or government expenditure increase) has a significant stimulative impact on a less than fully employed economy. (90%)
5. The United States should not restrict employers from outsourcing work to foreign countries. (90%)
6. Economic growth in developed countries like the United States leads to greater levels of well-being. (88%)
7. The United States should eliminate agricultural subsidies. (85%)
8. An appropriately designed fiscal policy can increase the long-run rate of capital formation. (85%)
9. Local and state governments should eliminate subsidies to professional sports franchises. (85%)
10. If the federal budget is to be balanced, it should be done over the business cycle rather than yearly. (85%)
11. The gap between Social Security funds and expenditures will become unsustainably large within the next 50 years if current policies remain unchanged. (85%)
12. Cash payments increase the welfare of recipients to a greater degree than do transfers-in-kind of equal cash value. (84%)
13. A large federal budget deficit has an adverse effect on the economy. (83%)
14. The redistribution of income in the United States is a legitimate role for the government. (83%)
15. Inflation is caused primarily by too much growth in the money supply. (83%)
16. The United States should not ban genetically modified crops. (82%)
17. A minimum wage increases unemployment among young and unskilled workers. (79%)
18. The government should restructure the welfare system along the lines of a "negative income tax." (79%)
19. Effluent taxes and marketable pollution permits represent a better approach to pollution control than the imposition of pollution ceilings. (78%)
20. Government subsidies on ethanol in the United States should be reduced or eliminated. (78%)

**Source:** Richard M. Alston, J. R. Kearl, and Michael B. Vaughn, "Is There Consensus among Economists in the 1990s?" *American Economic Review* (May 1992): 203–209; Dan Fuller and Doris Geide-Stevenson, "Consensus among Economists Revisited," *Journal of Economics Education* (Fall 2003): 369–387; Robert Whaples, "Do Economists Agree on Anything? Yes!" *Economists' Voice* (November 2006): 1–6; Robert Whaples, "The Policy Views of American Economic Association Members: The Results of a New Survey," *Econ Journal Watch* (September 2009): 337–348.

Source: IGM Economic Experts Panel, April 16, 2012.

**ASK THE EXPERTS**

**Ticket Resale**

"Laws that limit the resale of tickets for entertainment and sports events make potential audience members for those events worse off on average."

**What do economists say?**

8% disagree ——→   ←—— 12% uncertain

80% agree

majority of respondents. Most of these propositions would fail to command a similar consensus among the public.

The first proposition in the table is about rent control, a policy that sets a legal maximum on the amount landlords can charge for their apartments. Almost all economists believe that rent control adversely affects the availability and quality of housing and is a costly way of helping the neediest members of society. Nonetheless, many city governments ignore the advice of economists and place ceilings on the rents that landlords may charge their tenants.

The second proposition in the table concerns tariffs and import quotas, two policies that restrict trade among nations. For reasons we discuss more fully later in this text, almost all economists oppose such barriers to free trade. Nonetheless, over the years, presidents and Congress have chosen to restrict the import of certain goods.

Why do policies such as rent control and trade barriers persist if the experts are united in their opposition? It may be that the realities of the political process stand as immovable obstacles. But it also may be that economists have not yet convinced enough of the public that these policies are undesirable. One purpose of this book is to help you understand the economist's view on these and other subjects and, perhaps, to persuade you that it is the right one.

As you read the book, you will occasionally see small boxes called "Ask the Experts." These are based on the IGM Economics Experts Panel, an ongoing survey of several dozen of the world's most prominent economists. Every few weeks, these experts are offered a proposition and then asked whether they agree with it, disagree with it, or are uncertain. The results in these boxes will give you a sense of when economists are united, when they are divided, and when they just don't know what to think.

You can see an example here regarding the resale of tickets to entertainment and sporting events. Lawmakers sometimes try to prohibit reselling tickets, or "scalping" as it is sometimes called. The survey results show that many economists side with the scalpers rather than the lawmakers.

 *Why might economic advisers to the president disagree about a question of policy?*

## 2-4 Let's Get Going

The first two chapters of this book have introduced you to the ideas and methods of economics. We are now ready to get to work. In the next chapter, we start learning in more detail the principles of economic behavior and economic policy.

As you proceed through this book, you will be asked to draw on many of your intellectual skills. You might find it helpful to keep in mind some advice from the great economist John Maynard Keynes:

The study of economics does not seem to require any specialized gifts of an unusually high order. Is it not . . . a very easy subject compared with the higher branches of philosophy or pure science? An easy subject, at which very few

## Why You Should Study Economics

*In this excerpt from a commencement address, the former president of the Federal Reserve Bank of Dallas makes the case for studying economics.*

### The Dismal Science? Hardly!

**By Robert D. McTeer, Jr.**

My take on training in economics is that it becomes increasingly valuable as you move up the career ladder. I can't imagine a better major for corporate CEOs, congressmen, or American presidents. You've learned a systematic, disciplined way of thinking that will serve you well. By contrast, the economically challenged must be perplexed about how it is that economies work better the fewer people they have in charge. Who does the planning? Who makes decisions? Who decides what to produce?

For my money, Adam Smith's invisible hand is the most important thing you've learned by studying economics. You understand how we can each work for our own self-interest and still produce a desirable social outcome. You know how uncoordinated activity gets coordinated by the market to enhance the wealth of nations. You understand the magic of markets and the dangers of tampering with them too much. You know better what you first learned in kindergarten: that you shouldn't kill or cripple the goose that lays the golden eggs. . . .

Economics training will help you understand fallacies and unintended consequences. In fact, I am inclined to define economics as the study of how to anticipate unintended consequences. . . .

Little in the literature seems more relevant to contemporary economic debates than what usually is called the broken window fallacy. Whenever a government program is justified not on its merits but by the jobs it will create, remember the broken window: Some teenagers, being the little beasts that they are, toss a brick through a bakery window. A crowd gathers and laments, "What a shame." But before you know it, someone suggests a silver lining to the situation: Now the baker will have to spend money to have the window repaired. This will add to the income of the repairman, who will spend his additional income, which will add to another seller's income, and so on. You know the drill. The chain of spending will multiply and generate higher income and employment. If the broken window is large enough, it might produce an economic boom! . . .

Most voters fall for the broken window fallacy, but not economics majors. They will say, "Hey, wait a minute!" If the baker hadn't spent his money on window repair, he would have spent it on the new suit he was saving to buy. Then the tailor would have the new income to spend, and so on. The broken window didn't create net new spending; it just diverted spending from somewhere else. The broken window does not create new activity, just different activity. People see the activity that takes place. They don't see the activity that *would* have taken place.

The broken window fallacy is perpetuated in many forms. Whenever job creation or retention is the primary objective I call it the job-counting fallacy. Economics majors understand the non-intuitive reality that real progress comes from job destruction. It once took 90 percent of our population to grow our food. Now it takes 3 percent. Pardon me, Willie, but are we worse off because of the job losses in agriculture? The would-have-been farmers are now college professors and computer gurus. . . .

So instead of counting jobs, we should make every job count. We will occasionally hit a soft spot when we have a mismatch of supply and demand in the labor market. But that is temporary. Don't become a Luddite and destroy the machinery, or become a protectionist and try to grow bananas in New York City. ■

**Source:** *The Wall Street Journal*, June 4, 2003.

excel! The paradox finds its explanation, perhaps, in that the master-economist must possess a rare *combination* of gifts. He must be mathematician, historian, statesman, philosopher—in some degree. He must understand symbols and speak in words. He must contemplate the particular in terms of the general, and touch abstract and concrete in the same flight of thought. He must study the present in the light of the past for the purposes of the future. No part of man's nature or his institutions must lie entirely outside his regard. He must be purposeful and disinterested in a simultaneous mood; as aloof and incorruptible as an artist, yet sometimes as near the earth as a politician.

This is a tall order. But with practice, you will become more and more accustomed to thinking like an economist.

## Chapter QuickQuiz

1. An economic model is
   a. a mechanical machine that replicates the functioning of the economy.
   b. a fully detailed, realistic description of the economy.
   c. a simplified representation of some aspect of the economy.
   d. a computer program that predicts the future of the economy.

2. The circular-flow diagram illustrates that, in markets for the factors of production,
   a. households are sellers, and firms are buyers.
   b. households are buyers, and firms are sellers.
   c. households and firms are both buyers.
   d. households and firms are both sellers.

3. A point inside the production possibilities frontier is
   a. efficient but not feasible.
   b. feasible but not efficient.
   c. both efficient and feasible.
   d. neither efficient nor feasible.

4. An economy produces hot dogs and hamburgers. If a discovery of the remarkable health benefits of hot dogs were to change consumers' preferences, it would
   a. expand the production possibilities frontier.
   b. contract the production possibilities frontier.
   c. move the economy along the production possibilities frontier.
   d. move the economy inside the production possibilities frontier.

5. All of the following topics fall within the study of microeconomics EXCEPT
   a. the impact of cigarette taxes on the smoking behavior of teenagers.
   b. the role of Microsoft's market power in the pricing of software.
   c. the effectiveness of antipoverty programs in reducing homelessness.
   d. the influence of the government budget deficit on economic growth.

6. Which of the following is a positive, rather than a normative, statement?
   a. Law X will reduce national income.
   b. Law X is a good piece of legislation.
   c. Congress ought to pass law X.
   d. The president should veto law X.

## SUMMARY

- Economists try to address their subject with a scientist's objectivity. Like all scientists, they make appropriate assumptions and build simplified models to understand the world around them. Two simple economic models are the circular-flow diagram and the production possibilities frontier.
- The field of economics is divided into two subfields: microeconomics and macroeconomics. Microeconomists study decision making by households and firms and the interactions among households and firms in the marketplace. Macroeconomists study the forces and trends that affect the economy as a whole.

- A positive statement is an assertion about how the world *is*. A normative statement is an assertion about how the world *ought to be*. When economists make normative statements, they are acting more as policy advisers than as scientists.
- Economists who advise policymakers sometimes offer conflicting advice either because of differences in scientific judgments or because of differences in values. At other times, economists are united in the advice they offer, but policymakers may choose to ignore the advice because of the many forces and constraints imposed by the political process.

## KEY CONCEPTS

circular-flow diagram, p. 22          microeconomics, p. 27          positive statements, p. 28
production possibilities frontier, p. 24   macroeconomics, p. 27          normative statements, p. 28

## QUESTIONS FOR REVIEW

1. In what ways is economics a science?

2. Why do economists make assumptions?

3. Should an economic model describe reality exactly?

4. Name a way that your family interacts in the factor market and a way that it interacts in the product market.

5. Name one economic interaction that isn't covered by the simplified circular-flow diagram.

6. Draw and explain a production possibilities frontier for an economy that produces milk and cookies. What happens to this frontier if a disease kills half of the economy's cows?

7. Use a production possibilities frontier to describe the idea of "efficiency."

8. What are the two subfields into which economics is divided? Explain what each subfield studies.

9. What is the difference between a positive and a normative statement? Give an example of each.

10. Why do economists sometimes offer conflicting advice to policymakers?

## PROBLEMS AND APPLICATIONS

1. Draw a circular-flow diagram. Identify the parts of the model that correspond to the flow of goods and services and the flow of dollars for each of the following activities.
   a. Selena pays a storekeeper $1 for a quart of milk.
   b. Stuart earns $8 per hour working at a fast-food restaurant.
   c. Shanna spends $40 to get a haircut.
   d. Salma earns $20,000 from her 10 percent ownership of Acme Industrial.

2. Imagine a society that produces military goods and consumer goods, which we'll call "guns" and "butter."
   a. Draw a production possibilities frontier for guns and butter. Using the concept of opportunity cost, explain why it most likely has a bowed-out shape.
   b. Show a point that is impossible for the economy to achieve. Show a point that is feasible but inefficient.
   c. Imagine that the society has two political parties, called the Hawks (who want a strong military) and the Doves (who want a smaller military). Show a point on your production possibilities frontier that the Hawks might choose and a point that the Doves might choose.
   d. Imagine that an aggressive neighboring country reduces the size of its military. As a result, both the Hawks and the Doves reduce their desired production of guns by the same amount. Which party would get the bigger "peace dividend," measured by the increase in butter production? Explain.

3. The first principle of economics discussed in Chapter 1 is that people face trade-offs. Use a production possibilities frontier to illustrate society's trade-off between two "goods"—a clean environment and the quantity of industrial output. What do you suppose determines the shape and position of the frontier? Show what happens to the frontier if engineers develop a new way of producing electricity that emits fewer pollutants.

4. An economy consists of three workers: Larry, Moe, and Curly. Each works 10 hours a day and can produce two services: mowing lawns and washing cars. In an hour, Larry can either mow one lawn or wash one car; Moe can either mow one lawn or wash two cars; and Curly can either mow two lawns or wash one car.
   a. Calculate how much of each service is produced under the following circumstances, which we label A, B, C, and D:
      - All three spend all their time mowing lawns. (A)
      - All three spend all their time washing cars. (B)
      - All three spend half their time on each activity. (C)
      - Larry spends half his time on each activity, while Moe only washes cars and Curly only mows lawns. (D)
   b. Graph the production possibilities frontier for this economy. Using your answers to part a, identify points A, B, C, and D on your graph.
   c. Explain why the production possibilities frontier has the shape it does.
   d. Are any of the allocations calculated in part a inefficient? Explain.

5. Classify the following topics as relating to microeconomics or macroeconomics.
   a. a family's decision about how much income to save
   b. the effect of government regulations on auto emissions
   c. the impact of higher national saving on economic growth
   d. a firm's decision about how many workers to hire
   e. the relationship between the inflation rate and changes in the quantity of money

6. Classify each of the following statements as positive or normative. Explain.
   a. Society faces a short-run trade-off between inflation and unemployment.
   b. A reduction in the rate of money growth will reduce the rate of inflation.
   c. The Federal Reserve should reduce the rate of money growth.
   d. Society ought to require welfare recipients to look for jobs.
   e. Lower tax rates encourage more work and more saving.

To find additional study resources, visit cengagebrain.com, and search for "Mankiw."

# Appendix

## Graphing: A Brief Review

Many of the concepts that economists study can be expressed with numbers—the price of bananas, the quantity of bananas sold, the cost of growing bananas, and so on. Often, these economic variables are related to one another: When the price of bananas rises, people buy fewer bananas. One way of expressing the relationships among variables is with graphs.

Graphs serve two purposes. First, when developing economic theories, graphs offer a visual way to express ideas that might be less clear if described with equations or words. Second, when analyzing economic data, graphs provide a powerful way of finding and interpreting patterns. Whether we are working with theory or with data, graphs provide a lens through which a recognizable forest emerges from a multitude of trees.

Numerical information can be expressed graphically in many ways, just as there are many ways to express a thought in words. A good writer chooses words that will make an argument clear, a description pleasing, or a scene dramatic. An effective economist chooses the type of graph that best suits the purpose at hand.

In this appendix, we discuss how economists use graphs to study the mathematical relationships among variables. We also discuss some of the pitfalls that can arise in the use of graphical methods.

### Graphs of a Single Variable

Three common graphs are shown in Figure A-1. The *pie chart* in panel (a) shows how total income in the United States is divided among the sources of income, including compensation of employees, corporate profits, and so on. A slice of the pie represents each source's share of the total. The *bar graph* in panel (b) compares income in four countries. The height of each bar represents the average income in each country. The *time-series graph* in panel (c) traces the rising productivity in the U.S. business sector over time. The height of the line shows output per hour in each year. You have probably seen similar graphs in newspapers and magazines.

### Graphs of Two Variables: The Coordinate System

The three graphs in Figure A-1 are useful in showing how a variable changes over time or across individuals, but they are limited in how much they can tell us. These graphs display information only about a single variable. Economists are often concerned with the relationships between variables. Thus, they need to display two variables on a single graph. The *coordinate system* makes this possible.

Suppose you want to examine the relationship between study time and grade point average. For each student in your class, you could record a pair of numbers: hours per week spent studying and grade point average. These numbers could then be placed in parentheses as an *ordered pair* and appear as a single point on the graph. Albert E., for instance, is represented by the ordered pair (25 hours/week, 3.5 GPA),

## FIGURE A-1

### Types of Graphs

The pie chart in panel (a) shows how U.S. national income is derived from various sources. The bar graph in panel (b) compares the average income in four countries. The time-series graph in panel (c) shows the productivity of labor in U.S. businesses over time.

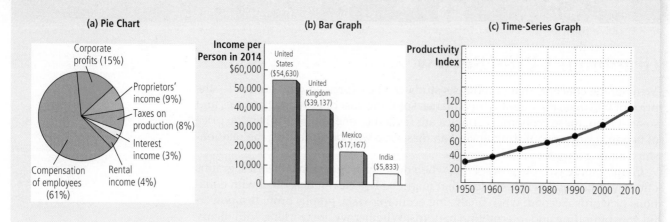

while his "what-me-worry?" classmate Alfred E. is represented by the ordered pair (5 hours/week, 2.0 GPA).

We can graph these ordered pairs on a two-dimensional grid. The first number in each ordered pair, called the *x-coordinate*, tells us the horizontal location of the point. The second number, called the *y-coordinate*, tells us the vertical location of the point. The point with both an *x*-coordinate and a *y*-coordinate of zero is known as the *origin*. The two coordinates in the ordered pair tell us where the point is located in relation to the origin: *x* units to the right of the origin and *y* units above it.

Figure A-2 graphs grade point average against study time for Albert E., Alfred E., and their classmates. This type of graph is called a *scatter plot* because it plots

## FIGURE A-2

### Using the Coordinate System

Grade point average is measured on the vertical axis and study time on the horizontal axis. Albert E., Alfred E., and their classmates are represented by various points. We can see from the graph that students who study more tend to get higher grades.

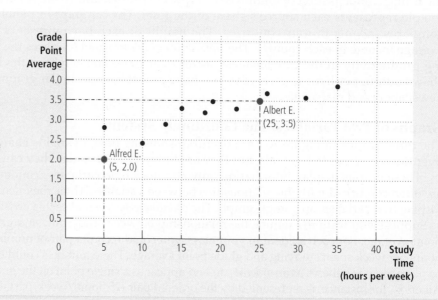

scattered points. Looking at this graph, we immediately notice that points farther to the right (indicating more study time) also tend to be higher (indicating a better grade point average). Because study time and grade point average typically move in the same direction, we say that these two variables have a *positive correlation*. By contrast, if we were to graph party time and grades, we would likely find that higher party time is associated with lower grades. Because these variables typically move in opposite directions, we say that they have a *negative correlation*. In either case, the coordinate system makes the correlation between two variables easy to see.

## Curves in the Coordinate System

Students who study more do tend to get higher grades, but other factors also influence a student's grades. Previous preparation is an important factor, for instance, as are talent, attention from teachers, even eating a good breakfast. A scatter plot like Figure A-2 does not attempt to isolate the effect that studying has on grades from the effects of other variables. Often, however, economists prefer looking at how one variable affects another, holding everything else constant.

To see how this is done, let's consider one of the most important graphs in economics: the *demand curve*. The demand curve traces out the effect of a good's price on the quantity of the good consumers want to buy. Before showing a demand curve, however, consider Table A-1, which shows how the number of novels that Emma buys depends on her income and on the price of novels. When novels are cheap, Emma buys them in large quantities. As they become more expensive, she instead borrows books from the library or chooses to go to the movies rather than read. Similarly, at any given price, Emma buys more novels when she has a higher income. That is, when her income increases, she spends part of the additional income on novels and part on other goods.

We now have three variables—the price of novels, income, and the number of novels purchased—which is more than we can represent in two dimensions. To put the information from Table A-1 in graphical form, we need to hold one of the three variables constant and trace out the relationship between the other two. Because the demand curve represents the relationship between price and quantity demanded, we hold Emma's income constant and show how the number of novels she buys varies with the price of novels.

## TABLE A-1

**Novels Purchased by Emma**
This table shows the number of novels Emma buys at various incomes and prices. For any given level of income, the data on price and quantity demanded can be graphed to produce Emma's demand curve for novels, as shown in Figures A-3 and A-4.

| Price | For $30,000 Income: | For $40,000 Income: | For $50,000 Income: |
|---|---|---|---|
| $10 | 2 novels | 5 novels | 8 novels |
| 9 | 6 | 9 | 12 |
| 8 | 10 | 13 | 16 |
| 7 | 14 | 17 | 20 |
| 6 | 18 | 21 | 24 |
| 5 | 22 | 25 | 28 |
| | Demand curve, $D_3$ | Demand curve, $D_1$ | Demand curve, $D_2$ |

## FIGURE A-3

**Demand Curve**

The line $D_1$ shows how Emma's purchases of novels depend on the price of novels when her income is held constant. Because the price and the quantity demanded are negatively related, the demand curve slopes downward.

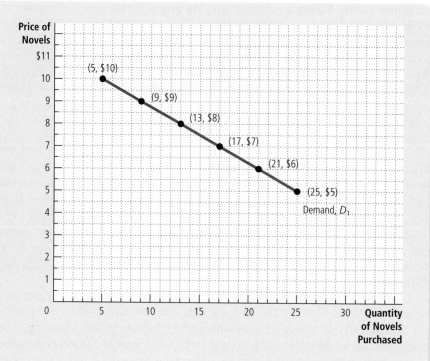

Suppose that Emma's income is $40,000 per year. If we place the number of novels Emma purchases on the *x*-axis and the price of novels on the *y*-axis, we can graphically represent the middle column of Table A-1. When the points that represent these entries from the table—(5 novels, $10), (9 novels, $9), and so on—are connected, they form a line. This line, pictured in Figure A-3, is known as Emma's demand curve for novels; it tells us how many novels Emma purchases at any given price, holding income constant. The demand curve is downward-sloping, indicating that a higher price reduces the quantity of novels demanded. Because the quantity of novels demanded and the price move in opposite directions, we say that the two variables are *negatively related*. (Conversely, when two variables move in the same direction, the curve relating them is upward-sloping, and we say that the variables are *positively related*.)

Now suppose that Emma's income rises to $50,000 per year. At any given price, Emma will purchase more novels than she did at her previous level of income. Just as earlier we drew Emma's demand curve for novels using the entries from the middle column of Table A-1, we now draw a new demand curve using the entries from the right column of the table. This new demand curve (curve $D_2$) is pictured alongside the old one (curve $D_1$) in Figure A-4; the new curve is a similar line drawn farther to the right. We therefore say that Emma's demand curve for novels *shifts* to the right when her income increases. Likewise, if Emma's income were to fall to $30,000 per year, she would buy fewer novels at any given price and her demand curve would shift to the left (to curve $D_3$).

In economics, it is important to distinguish between *movements along a curve* and *shifts of a curve*. As we can see from Figure A-3, if Emma earns $40,000 per year and novels cost $8 apiece, she will purchase 13 novels per year. If the price of

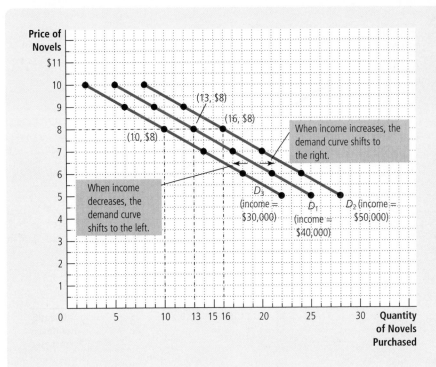

### FIGURE A-4

**Shifting Demand Curves**

The location of Emma's demand curve for novels depends on how much income she earns. The more she earns, the more novels she will purchase at any given price, and the farther to the right her demand curve will lie. Curve $D_1$ represents Emma's original demand curve when her income is $40,000 per year. If her income rises to $50,000 per year, her demand curve shifts to $D_2$. If her income falls to $30,000 per year, her demand curve shifts to $D_3$.

novels falls to $7, Emma will increase her purchases of novels to 17 per year. The demand curve, however, stays fixed in the same place. Emma still buys the same number of novels *at each price*, but as the price falls, she moves along her demand curve from left to right. By contrast, if the price of novels remains fixed at $8 but her income rises to $50,000, Emma increases her purchases of novels from 13 to 16 per year. Because Emma buys more novels *at each price*, her demand curve shifts out, as shown in Figure A-4.

There is a simple way to tell when it is necessary to shift a curve: *When a relevant variable that is not named on either axis changes, the curve shifts.* Income is on neither the *x*-axis nor the *y*-axis of the graph, so when Emma's income changes, her demand curve must shift. The same is true for any change that affects Emma's purchasing habits, with the sole exception of a change in the price of novels. If, for instance, the public library closes and Emma must buy all the books she wants to read, she will demand more novels at each price, and her demand curve will shift to the right. Or if the price of movies falls and Emma spends more time at the movies and less time reading, she will demand fewer novels at each price, and her demand curve will shift to the left. By contrast, when a variable on an axis of the graph changes, the curve does not shift. We read the change as a movement along the curve.

## Slope

One question we might want to ask about Emma is how much her purchasing habits respond to price. Look at the demand curve pictured in Figure A-5. If this curve is very steep, Emma purchases nearly the same number of novels regardless

## FIGURE A-5

**Calculating the Slope of a Line**

To calculate the slope of the demand curve, we can look at the changes in the *x*- and *y*-coordinates as we move from the point (21 novels, $6) to the point (13 novels, $8). The slope of the line is the ratio of the change in the *y*-coordinate (−2) to the change in the *x*-coordinate (+8), which equals −¼.

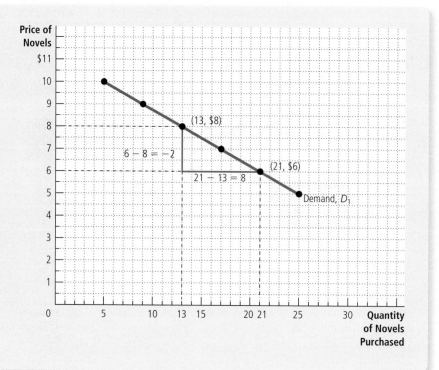

of whether they are cheap or expensive. If this curve is much flatter, the number of novels Emma purchases is more sensitive to changes in the price. To answer questions about how much one variable responds to changes in another variable, we can use the concept of *slope*.

The slope of a line is the ratio of the vertical distance covered to the horizontal distance covered as we move along the line. This definition is usually written out in mathematical symbols as follows:

$$\text{slope} = \frac{\Delta y}{\Delta x},$$

where the Greek letter Δ (delta) stands for the change in a variable. In other words, the slope of a line is equal to the "rise" (change in *y*) divided by the "run" (change in *x*). The slope will be a small positive number for a fairly flat upward-sloping line, a large positive number for a steep upward-sloping line, and a negative number for a downward-sloping line. A horizontal line has a slope of zero because in this case the *y*-variable never changes; a vertical line is said to have an infinite slope because the *y*-variable can take any value without the *x*-variable changing at all.

What is the slope of Emma's demand curve for novels? First of all, because the curve slopes down, we know the slope will be negative. To calculate a numerical value for the slope, we must choose two points on the line. With Emma's income at $40,000, she will purchase 21 novels at a price of $6 or 13 novels at a price of $8. When we apply the slope formula, we are concerned with the change between these two points. In other words, we are concerned with the difference between them, which lets us know that we will have to subtract one set of values from the other, as follows:

$$\text{slope} = \frac{\Delta y}{\Delta x} = \frac{\text{first } y\text{-coordinate} - \text{second } y\text{-coordinate}}{\text{first } x\text{-coordinate} - \text{second } x\text{-coordinate}} = \frac{6 - 8}{21 - 13} = \frac{-2}{8} = \frac{-1}{4}$$

Figure A-5 shows graphically how this calculation works. Try computing the slope of Emma's demand curve using two different points. You should get exactly the same result, −¼. One of the properties of a straight line is that it has the same slope everywhere. This is not true of other types of curves, which are steeper in some places than in others.

The slope of Emma's demand curve tells us something about how responsive her purchases are to changes in the price. A small slope (a number close to zero) means that Emma's demand curve is relatively flat; in this case, she adjusts the number of novels she buys substantially in response to a price change. A larger slope (a number farther from zero) means that Emma's demand curve is relatively steep; in this case, she adjusts the number of novels she buys only slightly in response to a price change.

## Cause and Effect

Economists often use graphs to advance an argument about how the economy works. In other words, they use graphs to argue about how one set of events *causes* another set of events. With a graph like the demand curve, there is no doubt about cause and effect. Because we are varying price and holding all other variables constant, we know that changes in the price of novels cause changes in the quantity Emma demands. Remember, however, that our demand curve came from a hypothetical example. When graphing data from the real world, it is often more difficult to establish how one variable affects another.

The first problem is that it is difficult to hold everything else constant when studying the relationship between two variables. If we are not able to hold other variables constant, we might decide that one variable on our graph is causing changes in the other variable when those changes are actually being caused by a third *omitted variable* not pictured on the graph. Even if we have identified the correct two variables to look at, we might run into a second problem—*reverse causality*. In other words, we might decide that A causes B when in fact B causes A. The omitted-variable and reverse-causality traps require us to proceed with caution when using graphs to draw conclusions about causes and effects.

**Omitted Variables**   To see how omitting a variable can lead to a deceptive graph, let's consider an example. Imagine that the government, spurred by public

## FIGURE A-6

**Graph with an Omitted Variable**

The upward-sloping curve shows that members of households with more cigarette lighters are more likely to develop cancer. Yet we should not conclude that ownership of lighters causes cancer because the graph does not take into account the number of cigarettes smoked.

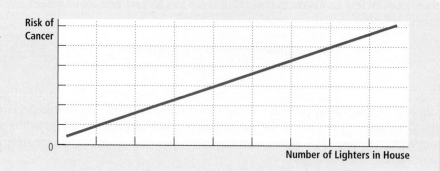

concern about the large number of deaths from cancer, commissions an exhaustive study from Big Brother Statistical Services, Inc. Big Brother examines many of the items found in people's homes to see which of them are associated with the risk of cancer. Big Brother reports a strong relationship between two variables: the number of cigarette lighters that a household owns and the probability that someone in the household will develop cancer. Figure A-6 shows this relationship.

What should we make of this result? Big Brother advises a quick policy response. It recommends that the government discourage the ownership of cigarette lighters by taxing their sale. It also recommends that the government require warning labels: "Big Brother has determined that this lighter is dangerous to your health."

In judging the validity of Big Brother's analysis, one question is key: Has Big Brother held constant every relevant variable except the one under consideration? If the answer is no, the results are suspect. An easy explanation for Figure A-6 is that people who own more cigarette lighters are more likely to smoke cigarettes and that cigarettes, not lighters, cause cancer. If Figure A-6 does not hold constant the amount of smoking, it does not tell us the true effect of owning a cigarette lighter.

This story illustrates an important principle: When you see a graph used to support an argument about cause and effect, it is important to ask whether the movements of an omitted variable could explain the results you see.

**Reverse Causality**   Economists can also make mistakes about causality by misreading its direction. To see how this is possible, suppose the Association of American Anarchists commissions a study of crime in America and arrives at Figure A-7, which plots the number of violent crimes per thousand people in major cities against the number of police officers per thousand people. The anarchists note the curve's upward slope and argue that because police increase rather than decrease the amount of urban violence, law enforcement should be abolished.

If we could run a controlled experiment, we would avoid the danger of reverse causality. To run an experiment, we would randomly assign different numbers of police to different cities and then examine the correlation between police and crime. Figure A-7, however, is not based on such an experiment. We simply

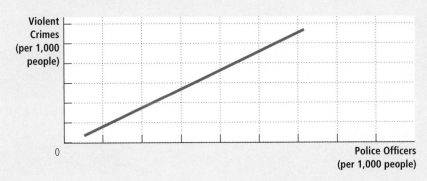

FIGURE **A-7**

**Graph Suggesting Reverse Causality**

The upward-sloping curve shows that cities with a higher concentration of police are more dangerous. Yet the graph does not tell us whether police cause crime or crime-plagued cities hire more police.

observe that more dangerous cities have more police officers. The explanation for this may be that more dangerous cities hire more police. In other words, rather than police causing crime, crime may cause police. Nothing in the graph itself allows us to establish the direction of causality.

It might seem that an easy way to determine the direction of causality is to examine which variable moves first. If we see crime increase and then the police force expand, we reach one conclusion. If we see the police force expand and then crime increase, we reach the other. This approach, however, is also flawed: Often, people change their behavior not in response to a change in their present conditions but in response to a change in their *expectations* of future conditions. A city that expects a major crime wave in the future, for instance, might hire more police now. This problem is even easier to see in the case of babies and minivans. Couples often buy a minivan in anticipation of the birth of a child. The minivan comes before the baby, but we wouldn't want to conclude that the sale of minivans causes the population to grow!

There is no complete set of rules that says when it is appropriate to draw causal conclusions from graphs. Yet just keeping in mind that cigarette lighters don't cause cancer (omitted variable) and that minivans don't cause larger families (reverse causality) will keep you from falling for many faulty economic arguments.

# Interdependence and the Gains from Trade

Consider your typical day. You wake up in the morning and pour yourself juice from oranges grown in Florida and coffee from beans grown in Brazil. Over breakfast, you read a newspaper written in New York on a tablet made in China. You get dressed in clothes made of cotton grown in Georgia and sewn in factories in Thailand. You drive to class in a car made of parts manufactured in more than a dozen countries around the world. Then you open up your economics textbook written by an author living in Massachusetts, published by a company located in Ohio, and printed on paper made from trees grown in Oregon.

Every day, you rely on many people, most of whom you have never met, to provide you with the goods and services that you enjoy. Such interdependence is possible because people trade with one another. Those people providing you with goods and services are not acting out of generosity. Nor is some government agency directing them to satisfy your desires. Instead, people provide you and other consumers with the goods and services they produce because they get something in return.

In subsequent chapters, we examine how an economy coordinates the activities of millions of people with varying tastes and abilities. As a starting point for this analysis, in this chapter we consider the reasons for economic interdependence. One of the *Ten Principles of Economics* highlighted in Chapter 1 is that trade can make everyone better off. We now examine this principle more closely. What exactly do people gain when they trade with one another? Why do people choose to become interdependent?

The answers to these questions are key to understanding the modern global economy. Most countries today import from abroad many of the goods and services they consume, and they export to foreign customers many of the goods and services they produce. The analysis in this chapter explains interdependence not only among individuals but also among nations. As we will see, the gains from trade are much the same whether you are buying a haircut from your local barber or a T-shirt made by a worker on the other side of the globe.

# 3-1  A Parable for the Modern Economy

To understand why people choose to depend on others for goods and services and how this choice improves their lives, let's examine a simple economy. Imagine that there are only two goods in the world: meat and potatoes. And there are only two people in the world: a cattle rancher named Ruby and a potato farmer named Frank. Both Ruby and Frank would like to eat a diet of both meat and potatoes.

The gains from trade are most obvious if Ruby can produce only meat and Frank can produce only potatoes. In one scenario, Frank and Ruby could choose to have nothing to do with each other. But after several months of eating beef roasted, boiled, broiled, and grilled, Ruby might decide that self-sufficiency is not all it's cracked up to be. Frank, who has been eating potatoes mashed, fried, baked, and scalloped, would likely agree. It is easy to see that trade would allow both of them to enjoy greater variety: Each could then have a steak with a baked potato or a burger with fries.

Although this scene illustrates most simply how everyone can benefit from trade, the gains would be similar if Frank and Ruby were each capable of producing the other good, but only at great cost. Suppose, for example, that Ruby is able to grow potatoes but her land is not very well suited for it. Similarly, suppose that Frank is able to raise cattle and produce meat but is not very good at it. In this case, Frank and Ruby can each benefit by specializing in what he or she does best and then trading with the other person.

The gains from trade are less obvious, however, when one person is better at producing *every* good. For example, suppose that Ruby is better at raising cattle *and* better at growing potatoes than Frank. In this case, should Ruby choose to remain self-sufficient? Or is there still reason for her to trade with Frank? To answer this question, we need to look more closely at the factors that affect such a decision.

### 3-1a Production Possibilities

Suppose that Frank and Ruby each work 8 hours per day and can devote this time to growing potatoes, raising cattle, or a combination of the two. The table in Figure 1 shows the amount of time each person requires to produce 1 ounce of each good. Frank can produce an ounce of potatoes in 15 minutes and an ounce of meat in 60 minutes. Ruby, who is more productive in both activities, can produce an ounce of potatoes in 10 minutes and an ounce of meat in 20 minutes. The last two columns in the table show the amounts of meat or potatoes Frank and Ruby can produce if they devote all 8 hours to producing only that good.

Panel (b) of Figure 1 illustrates the amounts of meat and potatoes that Frank can produce. If Frank devotes all 8 hours of his time to potatoes, he produces 32 ounces of potatoes (measured on the horizontal axis) and no meat. If he devotes all of his time to meat, he produces 8 ounces of meat (measured on the vertical axis) and no potatoes. If Frank divides his time equally between the two activities, spending 4 hours on each, he produces 16 ounces of potatoes and 4 ounces of meat. The figure shows these three possible outcomes and all others in between.

This graph is Frank's production possibilities frontier. As we discussed in Chapter 2, a production possibilities frontier shows the various mixes of output

Panel (a) shows the production opportunities available to Frank the farmer and Ruby the rancher. Panel (b) shows the combinations of meat and potatoes that Frank can produce. Panel (c) shows the combinations of meat and potatoes that Ruby can produce. Both production possibilities frontiers are derived assuming that Frank and Ruby each work 8 hours per day. If there is no trade, each person's production possibilities frontier is also his or her consumption possibilities frontier.

**FIGURE 1**

**The Production Possibilities Frontier**

**(a) Production Opportunities**

|  | Minutes Needed to Make 1 Ounce of: | | Amount Produced in 8 Hours | |
|---|---|---|---|---|
|  | **Meat** | **Potatoes** | **Meat** | **Potatoes** |
| **Frank the farmer** | 60 min/oz | 15 min/oz | 8 oz | 32 oz |
| **Ruby the rancher** | 20 min/oz | 10 min/oz | 24 oz | 48 oz |

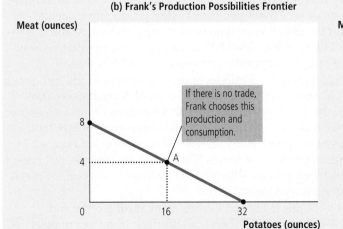

**(b) Frank's Production Possibilities Frontier**

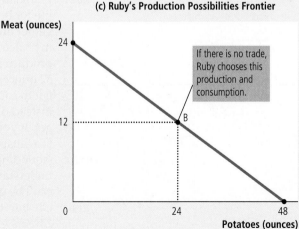

**(c) Ruby's Production Possibilities Frontier**

that an economy can produce. It illustrates one of the *Ten Principles of Economics* in Chapter 1: People face trade-offs. Here Frank faces a trade-off between producing meat and producing potatoes.

You may recall that the production possibilities frontier in Chapter 2 was drawn bowed out. In that case, the rate at which society could trade one good for the other depended on the amounts that were being produced. Here, however, Frank's technology for producing meat and potatoes (as summarized in Figure 1) allows him to switch between the two goods at a constant rate. Whenever Frank spends 1 hour less producing meat and 1 hour more producing potatoes, he reduces his output of meat by 1 ounce and raises his output of potatoes by 4 ounces—and this is true regardless of how much he is already producing. As a result, the production possibilities frontier is a straight line.

Panel (c) of Figure 1 shows the production possibilities frontier for Ruby. If Ruby devotes all 8 hours of her time to potatoes, she produces 48 ounces of potatoes and no meat. If she devotes all of her time to meat, she produces 24 ounces of meat and no potatoes. If Ruby divides her time equally, spending 4 hours on each activity, she produces 24 ounces of potatoes and 12 ounces of meat. Once again, the production possibilities frontier shows all the possible outcomes.

If Frank and Ruby choose to be self-sufficient rather than trade with each other, then each consumes exactly what he or she produces. In this case, the production possibilities frontier is also the consumption possibilities frontier. That is, without trade, Figure 1 shows the possible combinations of meat and potatoes that Frank and Ruby can each produce and then consume.

These production possibilities frontiers are useful in showing the trade-offs that Frank and Ruby face, but they do not tell us what Frank and Ruby will actually choose to do. To determine their choices, we need to know the tastes of Frank and Ruby. Let's suppose they choose the combinations identified by points A and B in Figure 1. Based on his production opportunities and food preferences, Frank decides to produce and consume 16 ounces of potatoes and 4 ounces of meat, while Ruby decides to produce and consume 24 ounces of potatoes and 12 ounces of meat.

### 3-1b  Specialization and Trade

After several years of eating combination B, Ruby gets an idea and goes to talk to Frank:

> RUBY: Frank, my friend, have I got a deal for you! I know how to improve life for both of us. I think you should stop producing meat altogether and devote all your time to growing potatoes. According to my calculations, if you work 8 hours a day growing potatoes, you'll produce 32 ounces of potatoes. If you give me 15 of those 32 ounces, I'll give you 5 ounces of meat in return. In the end, you'll get to eat 17 ounces of potatoes and 5 ounces of meat every day, instead of the 16 ounces of potatoes and 4 ounces of meat you now get. If you go along with my plan, you'll have more of *both* foods. [To illustrate her point, Ruby shows Frank panel (a) of Figure 2.]
>
> FRANK: (sounding skeptical) That seems like a good deal for me. But I don't understand why you are offering it. If the deal is so good for me, it can't be good for you too.
>
> RUBY: Oh, but it is! Suppose I spend 6 hours a day raising cattle and 2 hours growing potatoes. Then I can produce 18 ounces of meat and 12 ounces of potatoes. After I give you 5 ounces of my meat in exchange for 15 ounces of your potatoes, I'll end up with 13 ounces

The proposed trade between Frank the farmer and Ruby the rancher offers each of them a combination of meat and potatoes that would be impossible in the absence of trade. In panel (a), Frank gets to consume at point A* rather than point A. In panel (b), Ruby gets to consume at point B* rather than point B. Trade allows each to consume more meat and more potatoes.

## FIGURE 2

**How Trade Expands the Set of Consumption Opportunities**

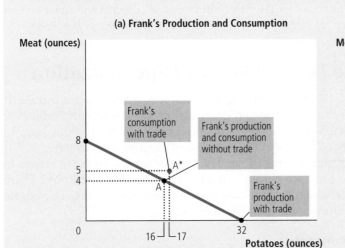

### (a) Frank's Production and Consumption

Frank's consumption with trade

Frank's production and consumption without trade

Frank's production with trade

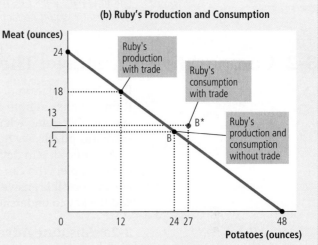

### (b) Ruby's Production and Consumption

Ruby's production with trade

Ruby's consumption with trade

Ruby's production and consumption without trade

### (c) The Gains from Trade: A Summary

|  | Frank | | Ruby | |
|---|---|---|---|---|
|  | Meat | Potatoes | Meat | Potatoes |
| **Without Trade:** | | | | |
| Production and Consumption | 4 oz | 16 oz | 12 oz | 24 oz |
| **With Trade:** | | | | |
| Production | 0 oz | 32 oz | 18 oz | 12 oz |
| Trade | Gets 5 oz | Gives 15 oz | Gives 5 oz | Gets 15 oz |
| Consumption | 5 oz | 17 oz | 13 oz | 27 oz |
| **GAINS FROM TRADE:** | | | | |
| Increase in Consumption | +1 oz | +1 oz | +1 oz | +3 oz |

of meat and 27 ounces of potatoes, instead of the 12 ounces of meat and 24 ounces of potatoes that I now get. So I will also consume more of both foods than I do now. [She points out panel (b) of Figure 2.]

FRANK: I don't know. . . . This sounds too good to be true.

RUBY: It's really not as complicated as it first seems. Here—I've summarized my proposal for you in a simple table. [Ruby shows Frank a copy of the table at the bottom of Figure 2.]

FRANK: (after pausing to study the table) These calculations seem correct, but I am puzzled. How can this deal make us both better off?

RUBY: We can both benefit because trade allows each of us to specialize in doing what we do best. You will spend more time growing potatoes and less time raising cattle. I will spend more time raising cattle and less time growing potatoes. As a result of specialization and trade, each of us can consume more meat and more potatoes without working any more hours.

> **QuickQuiz** *Draw an example of a production possibilities frontier for Robinson Crusoe, a shipwrecked sailor who spends his time gathering coconuts and catching fish. Does this frontier limit Crusoe's consumption of coconuts and fish if he lives by himself? Would he face the same limits if he could trade with natives on the island?*

# 3-2 Comparative Advantage: The Driving Force of Specialization

Ruby's explanation of the gains from trade, though correct, poses a puzzle: If Ruby is better at both raising cattle and growing potatoes, how can Frank ever specialize in doing what he does best? Frank doesn't seem to do anything best. To solve this puzzle, we need to look at the principle of *comparative advantage*.

As a first step in developing this principle, consider the following question: In our example, who can produce potatoes at a lower cost—Frank or Ruby? There are two possible answers, and in these two answers lie the solution to our puzzle and the key to understanding the gains from trade.

### 3-2a  Absolute Advantage

**absolute advantage**
the ability to produce a good using fewer inputs than another producer

One way to answer the question about the cost of producing potatoes is to compare the inputs required by the two producers. Economists use the term **absolute advantage** when comparing the productivity of one person, firm, or nation to that of another. The producer that requires a smaller quantity of inputs to produce a good is said to have an absolute advantage in producing that good.

In our example, time is the only input, so we can determine absolute advantage by looking at how much time each type of production takes. Ruby has an absolute advantage in producing both meat and potatoes because she requires less time than Frank to produce a unit of either good. Ruby needs to input only 20 minutes to produce an ounce of meat, whereas Frank needs 60 minutes. Similarly, Ruby needs only 10 minutes to produce an ounce of potatoes, whereas Frank needs 15 minutes. Thus, if we measure cost in terms of the quantity of inputs, Ruby has the lower cost of producing potatoes.

### 3-2b  Opportunity Cost and Comparative Advantage

**opportunity cost**
whatever must be given up to obtain some item

There is another way to look at the cost of producing potatoes. Rather than comparing inputs required, we can compare opportunity costs. Recall from Chapter 1 that the **opportunity cost** of some item is what we give up to get that item. In our example, we assumed that Frank and Ruby each spend 8 hours a day working. Time spent producing potatoes, therefore, takes away from time available for producing meat. When reallocating time between the two goods, Ruby and Frank give up units of one good to produce units of the other, thereby moving along the production possibilities frontier. The opportunity cost measures the trade-off between the two goods that each producer faces.

Let's first consider Ruby's opportunity cost. According to the table in panel (a) of Figure 1, producing 1 ounce of potatoes takes 10 minutes of work. When Ruby spends those 10 minutes producing potatoes, she spends 10 fewer minutes producing meat. Because Ruby needs 20 minutes to produce 1 ounce of meat, 10 minutes of work would yield ½ ounce of meat. Hence, Ruby's opportunity cost of producing 1 ounce of potatoes is ½ ounce of meat.

| | Opportunity Cost of: | | TABLE 1 |
| --- | --- | --- | --- |
| | **1 oz of Meat** | **1 oz of Potatoes** | The Opportunity Cost of Meat and Potatoes |
| **Frank the farmer** | 4 oz potatoes | ¼ oz meat | |
| **Ruby the rancher** | 2 oz potatoes | ½ oz meat | |

Now consider Frank's opportunity cost. Producing 1 ounce of potatoes takes him 15 minutes. Because he needs 60 minutes to produce 1 ounce of meat, 15 minutes of work would yield ¼ ounce of meat. Hence, Frank's opportunity cost of 1 ounce of potatoes is ¼ ounce of meat.

Table 1 shows the opportunity costs of meat and potatoes for the two producers. Notice that the opportunity cost of meat is the inverse of the opportunity cost of potatoes. Because 1 ounce of potatoes costs Ruby ½ ounce of meat, 1 ounce of meat costs Ruby 2 ounces of potatoes. Similarly, because 1 ounce of potatoes costs Frank ¼ ounce of meat, 1 ounce of meat costs Frank 4 ounces of potatoes.

Economists use the term **comparative advantage** when describing the opportunity costs faced by two producers. The producer who gives up less of other goods to produce Good X has the smaller opportunity cost of producing Good X and is said to have a comparative advantage in producing it. In our example, Frank has a lower opportunity cost of producing potatoes than Ruby: An ounce of potatoes costs Frank only ¼ ounce of meat, but it costs Ruby ½ ounce of meat. Conversely, Ruby has a lower opportunity cost of producing meat than Frank: An ounce of meat costs Ruby 2 ounces of potatoes, but it costs Frank 4 ounces of potatoes. Thus, Frank has a comparative advantage in growing potatoes, and Ruby has a comparative advantage in producing meat.

Although it is possible for one person to have an absolute advantage in both goods (as Ruby does in our example), it is impossible for one person to have a comparative advantage in both goods. Because the opportunity cost of one good is the inverse of the opportunity cost of the other, if a person's opportunity cost of one good is relatively high, the opportunity cost of the other good must be relatively low. Comparative advantage reflects the relative opportunity cost. Unless two people have the same opportunity cost, one person will have a comparative advantage in one good, and the other person will have a comparative advantage in the other good.

**comparative advantage**
the ability to produce a good at a lower opportunity cost than another producer

### 3-2c Comparative Advantage and Trade

The gains from specialization and trade are based not on absolute advantage but on comparative advantage. When each person specializes in producing the good for which he or she has a comparative advantage, total production in the economy rises. This increase in the size of the economic pie can be used to make everyone better off.

In our example, Frank spends more time growing potatoes, and Ruby spends more time producing meat. As a result, the total production of potatoes rises from 40 to 44 ounces, and the total production of meat rises from 16 to 18 ounces. Frank and Ruby share the benefits of this increased production.

We can also view the gains from trade in terms of the price that each party pays the other. Because Frank and Ruby have different opportunity costs, they can both get a bargain. That is, each of them benefits from trade by obtaining a good at a price that is lower than his or her opportunity cost of that good.

Consider the proposed deal from Frank's viewpoint. Frank receives 5 ounces of meat in exchange for 15 ounces of potatoes. In other words, Frank buys each ounce of meat for a price of 3 ounces of potatoes. This price of meat is lower than his opportunity cost for an ounce of meat, which is 4 ounces of potatoes. Thus, Frank benefits from the deal because he gets to buy meat at a good price.

Now consider the deal from Ruby's viewpoint. Ruby buys 15 ounces of potatoes at a cost of 5 ounces of meat. That is, the price for an ounce of potatoes is ⅓ ounce of meat. This price of potatoes is lower than her opportunity cost of an ounce of potatoes, which is ½ ounce of meat. Ruby benefits because she gets to buy potatoes at a good price.

The story of Ruby the rancher and Frank the farmer has a simple moral, which should now be clear: *Trade can benefit everyone in society because it allows people to specialize in activities in which they have a comparative advantage.*

### 3-2d  The Price of the Trade

The principle of comparative advantage establishes that there are gains from specialization and trade, but it raises a couple of related questions: What determines the price at which trade takes place? How are the gains from trade shared between the trading parties? The precise answers to these questions are beyond the scope of this chapter, but we can state one general rule: *For both parties to gain from trade, the price at which they trade must lie between the two opportunity costs.*

In our example, Frank and Ruby agreed to trade at a rate of 3 ounces of potatoes for each ounce of meat. This price is between Ruby's opportunity cost (2 ounces of potatoes per ounce of meat) and Frank's opportunity cost (4 ounces of potatoes per ounce of meat). The price need not be exactly in the middle for both parties to gain, but it must be somewhere between 2 and 4.

To see why the price has to be in this range, consider what would happen if it were not. If the price of meat were below 2 ounces of potatoes, both Frank and Ruby would want to buy meat, because the price would be below each of their opportunity costs. Similarly, if the price of meat were above 4 ounces of potatoes, both would want to sell meat, because the price would be above their opportunity costs. But there are only two members of this economy. They cannot both be buyers of meat, nor can they both be sellers. Someone has to take the other side of the deal.

A mutually advantageous trade can be struck at a price between 2 and 4. In this price range, Ruby wants to sell meat to buy potatoes, and Frank wants to sell potatoes to buy meat. Each party can buy a good at a price that is lower than his or her opportunity cost. In the end, each person specializes in the good for which he or she has a comparative advantage and, as a result, is better off.

**QuickQuiz**   *Robinson Crusoe can gather 10 coconuts or catch 1 fish per hour. His friend Friday can gather 30 coconuts or catch 2 fish per hour. What is Crusoe's opportunity cost of catching 1 fish? What is Friday's? Who has an absolute advantage in catching fish? Who has a comparative advantage in catching fish?*

## The Legacy of Adam Smith and David Ricardo

Economists have long understood the gains from trade. Here is how the great economist Adam Smith put the argument:

*It is a maxim of every prudent master of a family, never to attempt to make at home what it will cost him more to make than to buy. The tailor does not attempt to make his own shoes, but buys them of the shoemaker. The shoemaker does not attempt to make his own clothes but employs a tailor. The farmer attempts to make neither the one nor the other, but employs those different artificers. All of them find it for their interest to employ their whole industry in a way in which they have some advantage over their neighbors, and to purchase with a part of its produce, or what is the same thing, with the price of part of it, whatever else they have occasion for.*

This quotation is from Smith's 1776 book *An Inquiry into the Nature and Causes of the Wealth of Nations*, which was a landmark in the analysis of trade and economic interdependence.

Smith's book inspired David Ricardo, a millionaire stockbroker, to become an economist. In his 1817 book

David Ricardo

BETTMANN/CORBIS

*Principles of Political Economy and Taxation*, Ricardo developed the principle of comparative advantage as we know it today. He considered an example with two goods (wine and cloth) and two countries (England and Portugal). He showed that both countries can gain by opening up trade and specializing based on comparative advantage.

Ricardo's theory is the starting point of modern international economics, but his defense of free trade was not a mere academic exercise. Ricardo put his beliefs to work as a member of the British Parliament, where he opposed the Corn Laws, which restricted the import of grain.

The conclusions of Adam Smith and David Ricardo on the gains from trade have held up well over time. Although economists often disagree on questions of policy, they are united in their support of free trade. Moreover, the central argument for free trade has not changed much in the past two centuries. Even though the field of economics has broadened its scope and refined its theories since the time of Smith and Ricardo, economists' opposition to trade restrictions is still based largely on the principle of comparative advantage. ■

# 3-3 Applications of Comparative Advantage

The principle of comparative advantage explains interdependence and the gains from trade. Because interdependence is so prevalent in the modern world, the principle of comparative advantage has many applications. Here are two examples, one fanciful and one of great practical importance.

### 3-3a Should Serena Williams Mow Her Own Lawn?

When Serena Williams plays at the Wimbledon tennis tournament, she spends a lot of time running around on grass. One of the most talented tennis players of all time, she can hit a ball with a speed and accuracy that most casual athletes can only dream of. Most likely, she is talented at other physical activities as well. For example, let's imagine that Serena can mow her lawn faster than anyone else. But just because she *can* mow her lawn fast, does this mean she *should*?

To answer this question, we can use the concepts of opportunity cost and comparative advantage. Let's say that Serena can mow her lawn in 2 hours. In that same 2 hours, she could film a television commercial and earn $30,000. By contrast, Forrest Gump, the boy next door, can mow Serena's lawn in 4 hours. In that same 4 hours, Forrest could work at McDonald's and earn $50.

ALLSTAR PICTURE LIBRARY / ALAMY

*"They did a nice job with this grass."*

## IN THE NEWS

# Economics within a Marriage

*An economist argues that you shouldn't always unload the dishwasher just because you're better at it than your partner.*

### You're Dividing the Chores Wrong

**By Emily Oster**

No one likes doing chores. In happiness surveys, housework is ranked down there with commuting as activities that people enjoy the least. Maybe that's why figuring out who does which chores usually prompts, at best, tense discussion in a household and, at worst, outright fighting.

If everyone is good at something different, assigning chores is easy. If your partner is great at grocery shopping and you are great at the laundry, you're set. But this isn't always—or even usually—the case. Often one person is better at everything. (And let's be honest, often that person is the woman.) Better at the laundry, the grocery shopping, the cleaning, the cooking. But does that mean she should have to do everything?

Before my daughter was born, I both cooked and did the dishes. It wasn't a big deal, it didn't take too much time, and honestly I was a lot better at both than my husband. His cooking repertoire extended only to eggs and chili, and when I left him in charge of the dishwasher, I'd often find he had run it "full" with one pot and eight forks.

After we had a kid, we had more to do and less time to do it in. It seemed like it was time for some reassignments. But, of course, I was still better at doing both things. Did that mean I should do them both?

I could have appealed to the principle of fairness: We should each do half. I could have appealed to feminism—surveys show that women more often than not get the short end of the chore stick. In time-use data, women do about 44 minutes more housework than men (2 hours and 11 minutes versus 1 hour and 27 minutes). Men outwork women only in the areas of "lawn" and "exterior maintenance." I could have suggested he do more chores to rectify this imbalance, to show our daughter, in the *Free To Be You and Me* style, that Mom and Dad are equal and that housework is fun if we do it together! I could have simply smashed around the pans in the dishwasher while sighing loudly in the hopes he would notice and offer to do it himself.

But luckily for me and my husband, I'm an economist, so I have more effective tools than passive aggression. And some basic economic principles provided the answer. We needed to divide the chores because it is simply not *efficient* for the best cook and dishwasher to do all the cooking and dishwashing. The economic principle at play here is increasing marginal cost. Basically, people get worse when they are tired. When I teach my students at the University of Chicago this principle, I explain it in the context of managing their employees. Imagine you have a good employee and a not-so-good one. Should you make the good employee do literally everything?

Usually, the answer is no. Why not? It's likely that the not-so-good employee is better at 9 a.m. after a full night of sleep than the good employee is at 2 a.m. after a 17-hour workday. So you want to give at least a few tasks to your worse guy. The same principle applies in your household. Yes, you (or your spouse) might be better at everything. But anyone doing the laundry at 4 a.m. is likely to put the red towels in with the white T-shirts. Some task splitting is a good idea. How much depends on how fast people's skills decay.

In this example, Serena has an absolute advantage in mowing lawns because she can do the work with a lower input of time. Yet because Serena's opportunity cost of mowing the lawn is $30,000 and Forrest's opportunity cost is only $50, Forrest has a comparative advantage in mowing lawns.

The gains from trade in this example are tremendous. Rather than mowing her own lawn, Serena should make the commercial and hire Forrest to mow the lawn. As long as Serena pays Forrest more than $50 and less than $30,000, both of them are better off.

### 3-3b Should the United States Trade with Other Countries?

Just as individuals can benefit from specialization and trade with one another, so can populations of people in different countries. Many of the goods that

To "optimize" your family efficiency (every economist's ultimate goal—and yours, too), you want to equalize effectiveness on the final task each person is doing. Your partner does the dishes, mows the lawn, and makes the grocery list. You do the cooking, laundry, shopping, cleaning, and paying the bills. This may seem imbalanced, but when you look at it, you see that by the time your partner gets to the grocery-list task, he is wearing thin and starting to nod off. It's all he can do to figure out how much milk you need. In fact, he is just about as good at that as you are when you get around to paying the bills, even though that's your fifth task.

If you then made your partner also do the cleaning—so it was an even four and four—the house would be a disaster, since he is already exhausted by his third chore while you are still doing fine. This system may well end up meaning one person does more, but it is unlikely to result in one person doing everything.

Once you've decided you need to divide up the chores in this way, how should you decide who does what? One option would be randomly assigning tasks; another would be having each person do some of everything. One spousal-advice website I read suggested you should divide tasks based on which ones you like the best. None of these are quite right.

(In the last case, how would anyone ever end up with the job of cleaning the bathroom?)

To decide who does what, we need more economics. Specifically, the principle of comparative advantage. Economists usually talk about this in the context of trade. Imagine Finland is better than Sweden at making both reindeer hats and snowshoes. But they are much, much better at the hats and only a little better at the snowshoes. The overall world production is maximized when Finland makes hats and Sweden makes snowshoes.

We say that Finland has an *absolute advantage* in both things but a *comparative advantage* only in hats. This principle is part

ROBERT NEUBECKER

of the reason economists value free trade, but that's for another column (and probably another author). But it's also a guideline for how to trade tasks in your house. You want to assign each person the tasks on which he or she has a comparative advantage. It doesn't matter that you have an absolute advantage in everything. If you are much, much better at the laundry and only a little better at cleaning the toilet, you should do the laundry and have your spouse get out the scrub brush. Just explain that it's efficient!

In our case, it was easy. Other than using the grill—which I freely admit is the husband domain—I'm much, much better at cooking. And I was only moderately better at the dishes. So he got the job of cleaning up after meals, even though his dishwasher loading habits had already come under scrutiny. The good news is another economic principle I hadn't even counted on was soon in play: *learning by doing.* As people do a task, they improve at it. Eighteen months into this new arrangement the dishwasher is almost a work of art: neat rows of dishes and everything carefully screened for "top-rack only" status. I, meanwhile, am forbidden from getting near the dishwasher. Apparently, there is a risk that I'll "ruin it." ∎

*Ms Oster is a professor of economics at Brown University.*

**Source:** Slate, November 21, 2012.

---

Americans enjoy are produced abroad, and many of the goods produced in the United States are sold abroad. Goods produced abroad and sold domestically are called **imports.** Goods produced domestically and sold abroad are called **exports.**

To see how countries can benefit from trade, suppose there are two countries, the United States and Japan, and two goods, food and cars. Imagine that the two countries produce cars equally well: An American worker and a Japanese worker can each produce one car per month. By contrast, because the United States has more and better land, it is better at producing food: A U.S. worker can produce 2 tons of food per month, whereas a Japanese worker can produce only 1 ton of food per month.

**imports**
goods produced abroad and sold domestically

**exports**
goods produced domestically and sold abroad

## ASK THE EXPERTS

### Trade between China and the United States

"Trade with China makes most Americans better off because, among other advantages, they can buy goods that are made or assembled more cheaply in China."

**What do economists say?**

0% disagree                    0% uncertain

100% agree

"Some Americans who work in the production of competing goods, such as clothing and furniture, are made worse off by trade with China."

**What do economists say?**

0% disagree                    4% uncertain

96% agree

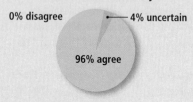

Source: IGM Economic Experts Panel, June 19, 2012.

The principle of comparative advantage states that each good should be produced by the country that has the smaller opportunity cost of producing that good. Because the opportunity cost of a car is 2 tons of food in the United States but only 1 ton of food in Japan, Japan has a comparative advantage in producing cars. Japan should produce more cars than it wants for its own use and export some of them to the United States. Similarly, because the opportunity cost of a ton of food is 1 car in Japan but only 1/2 car in the United States, the United States has a comparative advantage in producing food. The United States should produce more food than it wants to consume and export some to Japan. Through specialization and trade, both countries can have more food and more cars.

In reality, of course, the issues involved in trade among nations are more complex than this example suggests. Most important among these issues is that each country has many citizens with different interests. International trade can make some individuals worse off, even as it makes the country as a whole better off. When the United States exports food and imports cars, the impact on an American farmer is not the same as the impact on an American autoworker. Yet, contrary to the opinions sometimes voiced by politicians and pundits, international trade is not like war, in which some countries win and others lose. Trade allows all countries to achieve greater prosperity.

**QuickQuiz**   *Suppose that a skilled brain surgeon also happens to be the world's fastest typist. Should she do her own typing or hire a secretary? Explain.*

## 3-4  Conclusion

You should now understand more fully the benefits of living in an interdependent economy. When Americans buy tube socks from China, when residents of Maine drink orange juice from Florida, and when a homeowner hires the kid next door to mow her lawn, the same economic forces are at work. The principle of comparative advantage shows that trade can make everyone better off.

Having seen why interdependence is desirable, you might naturally ask how it is possible. How do free societies coordinate the diverse activities of all the people involved in their economies? What ensures that goods and services will get from those who should be producing them to those who should be consuming them? In a world with only two people, such as Ruby the rancher and Frank the farmer, the answer is simple: These two people can bargain and allocate resources between themselves. In the real world with billions of people, the answer is less obvious. We take up this issue in the next chapter, where we see that free societies allocate resources through the market forces of supply and demand.

## CHAPTER QuickQuiz

1. In an hour, Mateo can wash 2 cars or mow 1 lawn, and Tyler can wash 3 cars or mow 1 lawn. Who has the absolute advantage in car washing, and who has the absolute advantage in lawn mowing?
   a. Mateo in washing, Tyler in mowing.
   b. Tyler in washing, Mateo in mowing.
   c. Mateo in washing, neither in mowing.
   d. Tyler in washing, neither in mowing.

2. Once again, in an hour, Mateo can wash 2 cars or mow 1 lawn, and Tyler can wash 3 cars or mow 1 lawn. Who has the comparative advantage in car washing, and who has the comparative advantage in lawn mowing?
   a. Mateo in washing, Tyler in mowing.
   b. Tyler in washing, Mateo in mowing.
   c. Mateo in washing, neither in mowing.
   d. Tyler in washing, neither in mowing.

3. When two individuals produce efficiently and then make a mutually beneficial trade based on comparative advantage,
   a. they both obtain consumption outside their production possibilities frontier.
   b. they both obtain consumption inside their production possibilities frontier.
   c. one individual consumes inside her production possibilities frontier, while the other consumes outside hers.
   d. each individual consumes a point on her own production possibilities frontier.

4. Which goods will a nation typically import?
   a. those goods in which the nation has an absolute advantage
   b. those goods in which the nation has a comparative advantage
   c. those goods in which other nations have an absolute advantage
   d. those goods in which other nations have a comparative advantage

5. Suppose that in the United States, producing an aircraft takes 10,000 hours of labor and producing a shirt takes 2 hours of labor. In China, producing an aircraft takes 40,000 hours of labor and producing a shirt takes 4 hours of labor. What will these nations trade?
   a. China will export aircraft, and the United States will export shirts.
   b. China will export shirts, and the United States will export aircraft.
   c. Both nations will export shirts.
   d. There are no gains from trade in this situation.

6. Kayla can cook dinner in 30 minutes and wash the laundry in 20 minutes. Her roommate takes half as long to do each task. How should the roommates allocate the work?
   a. Kayla should do more of the cooking based on her comparative advantage.
   b. Kayla should do more of the washing based on her comparative advantage.
   c. Kayla should do more of the washing based on her absolute advantage.
   d. There are no gains from trade in this situation.

## SUMMARY

- Each person consumes goods and services produced by many other people both in the United States and around the world. Interdependence and trade are desirable because they allow everyone to enjoy a greater quantity and variety of goods and services.
- There are two ways to compare the ability of two people to produce a good. The person who can produce the good with the smaller quantity of inputs is said to have an *absolute advantage* in producing the good. The person who has the smaller opportunity cost of producing the good is said to have a *comparative advantage*. The gains from trade are based on comparative advantage, not absolute advantage.
- Trade makes everyone better off because it allows people to specialize in those activities in which they have a comparative advantage.
- The principle of comparative advantage applies to countries as well as to people. Economists use the principle of comparative advantage to advocate free trade among countries.

## KEY CONCEPTS

absolute advantage, p. 52
opportunity cost, p. 52

comparative advantage, p. 53
imports, p. 57

exports, p. 57

## QUESTIONS FOR REVIEW

1. Under what conditions is the production possibilities frontier linear rather than bowed out?

2. Explain how absolute advantage and comparative advantage differ.

3. Give an example in which one person has an absolute advantage in doing something but another person has a comparative advantage.

4. Is absolute advantage or comparative advantage more important for trade? Explain your reasoning using the example in your answer to question 3.

5. If two parties trade based on comparative advantage and both gain, in what range must the price of the trade lie?

6. Why do economists oppose policies that restrict trade among nations?

## PROBLEMS AND APPLICATIONS

1. Maria can read 20 pages of economics in an hour. She can also read 50 pages of sociology in an hour. She spends 5 hours per day studying.
   a. Draw Maria's production possibilities frontier for reading economics and sociology.
   b. What is Maria's opportunity cost of reading 100 pages of sociology?

2. American and Japanese workers can each produce 4 cars a year. An American worker can produce 10 tons of grain a year, whereas a Japanese worker can produce 5 tons of grain a year. To keep things simple, assume that each country has 100 million workers.
   a. For this situation, construct a table analogous to the table in Figure 1.
   b. Graph the production possibilities frontiers for the American and Japanese economies.
   c. For the United States, what is the opportunity cost of a car? Of grain? For Japan, what is the opportunity cost of a car? Of grain? Put this information in a table analogous to Table 1.
   d. Which country has an absolute advantage in producing cars? In producing grain?
   e. Which country has a comparative advantage in producing cars? In producing grain?
   f. Without trade, half of each country's workers produce cars and half produce grain. What quantities of cars and grain does each country produce?
   g. Starting from a position without trade, give an example in which trade makes each country better off.

3. Pat and Kris are roommates. They spend most of their time studying (of course), but they leave some time for their favorite activities: making pizza and brewing root beer. Pat takes 4 hours to brew a gallon of root beer and 2 hours to make a pizza. Kris takes 6 hours to brew a gallon of root beer and 4 hours to make a pizza.
   a. What is each roommate's opportunity cost of making a pizza? Who has the absolute advantage in making pizza? Who has the comparative advantage in making pizza?
   b. If Pat and Kris trade foods with each other, who will trade away pizza in exchange for root beer?
   c. The price of pizza can be expressed in terms of gallons of root beer. What is the highest price at which pizza can be traded that would make both roommates better off? What is the lowest price? Explain.

4. Suppose that there are 10 million workers in Canada and that each of these workers can produce either 2 cars or 30 bushels of wheat in a year.
   a. What is the opportunity cost of producing a car in Canada? What is the opportunity cost of producing a bushel of wheat in Canada? Explain the relationship between the opportunity costs of the two goods.
   b. Draw Canada's production possibilities frontier. If Canada chooses to consume 10 million cars, how much wheat can it consume without trade? Label this point on the production possibilities frontier.
   c. Now suppose that the United States offers to buy 10 million cars from Canada in exchange for 20 bushels of wheat per car. If Canada continues to consume 10 million cars, how much wheat does this deal allow Canada to consume? Label this point on your diagram. Should Canada accept the deal?

5. England and Scotland both produce scones and sweaters. Suppose that an English worker can produce 50 scones per hour or 1 sweater per hour.

Suppose that a Scottish worker can produce 40 scones per hour or 2 sweaters per hour.

a. Which country has the absolute advantage in the production of each good? Which country has the comparative advantage?

b. If England and Scotland decide to trade, which commodity will Scotland export to England? Explain.

c. If a Scottish worker could produce only 1 sweater per hour, would Scotland still gain from trade? Would England still gain from trade? Explain.

6. The following table describes the production possibilities of two cities in the country of Baseballia:

| | Pairs of Red Socks per Worker per Hour | Pairs of White Socks per Worker per Hour |
| --- | --- | --- |
| Boston | 3 | 3 |
| Chicago | 2 | 1 |

a. Without trade, what is the price of white socks (in terms of red socks) in Boston? What is the price in Chicago?

b. Which city has an absolute advantage in the production of each color sock? Which city has a comparative advantage in the production of each color sock?

c. If the cities trade with each other, which color sock will each export?

d. What is the range of prices at which trade can occur?

7. A German worker takes 400 hours to produce a car and 2 hours to produce a case of wine. A French worker takes 600 hours to produce a car and $X$ hours to produce a case of wine.

a. For what values of $X$ will gains from trade be possible? Explain.

b. For what values of $X$ will Germany export cars and import wine? Explain.

8. Suppose that in a year an American worker can produce 100 shirts or 20 computers and a Chinese worker can produce 100 shirts or 10 computers.

a. For each country, graph the production possibilities frontier. Suppose that without trade the workers in each country spend half their time producing each good. Identify this point in your graphs.

b. If these countries were open to trade, which country would export shirts? Give a specific numerical example and show it on your graphs. Which country would benefit from trade? Explain.

c. Explain at what price of computers (in terms of shirts) the two countries might trade.

d. Suppose that China catches up with American productivity so that a Chinese worker can produce 100 shirts or 20 computers. What pattern of trade would you predict now? How does this advance in Chinese productivity affect the economic well-being of the two countries' citizens?

9. Are the following statements true or false? Explain in each case.

a. "Two countries can achieve gains from trade even if one of the countries has an absolute advantage in the production of all goods."

b. "Certain talented people have a comparative advantage in everything they do."

c. "If a certain trade is good for one person, it can't be good for the other one."

d. "If a certain trade is good for one person, it is always good for the other one."

e. "If trade is good for a country, it must be good for everyone in the country."

To find additional study resources, visit cengagebrain.com, and search for "Mankiw."

# PART II
# How Markets Work

# The Market Forces of Supply and Demand

**W**hen a cold snap hits Florida, the price of orange juice rises in supermarkets throughout the country. When the weather turns warm in New England every summer, the price of hotel rooms in the Caribbean plummets. When a war breaks out in the Middle East, the price of gasoline in the United States rises and the price of a used Cadillac falls. What do these events have in common? They all show the workings of supply and demand.

*Supply* and *demand* are the two words economists use most often—and for good reason. Supply and demand are the forces that make market economies work. They determine the quantity of each good produced and the price at which it

is sold. If you want to know how any event or policy will affect the economy, you must think first about how it will affect supply and demand.

This chapter introduces the theory of supply and demand. It considers how buyers and sellers behave and how they interact with one another. It shows how supply and demand determine prices in a market economy and how prices, in turn, allocate the economy's scarce resources.

# 4-1 Markets and Competition

The terms *supply* and *demand* refer to the behavior of people as they interact with one another in competitive markets. Before discussing how buyers and sellers behave, let's first consider more fully what we mean by the terms *market* and *competition*.

### 4-1a What Is a Market?

**market**
a group of buyers and sellers of a particular good or service

A **market** is a group of buyers and sellers of a particular good or service. The buyers as a group determine the demand for the product, and the sellers as a group determine the supply of the product.

Markets take many forms. Some markets are highly organized, such as the markets for many agricultural commodities. In these markets, buyers and sellers meet at a specific time and place where an auctioneer helps set prices and arrange sales.

More often, markets are less organized. For example, consider the market for ice cream in a particular town. Buyers of ice cream do not meet together at any one time. The sellers of ice cream are in different locations and offer somewhat different products. There is no auctioneer calling out the price of ice cream. Each seller posts a price for an ice-cream cone, and each buyer decides how much ice cream to buy at each store. Nonetheless, these consumers and producers of ice cream are closely connected. The ice-cream buyers are choosing from the various ice-cream sellers to satisfy their cravings, and the ice-cream sellers are all trying to appeal to the same ice-cream buyers to make their businesses successful. Even though it is not as organized, the group of ice-cream buyers and ice-cream sellers forms a market.

### 4-1b What Is Competition?

The market for ice cream, like most markets in the economy, is highly competitive. Each buyer knows that there are several sellers from which to choose, and each seller is aware that his product is similar to that offered by other sellers. As a result, the price and quantity of ice cream sold are not determined by any single buyer or seller. Rather, price and quantity are determined by all buyers and sellers as they interact in the marketplace.

**competitive market**
a market in which there are many buyers and many sellers so that each has a negligible impact on the market price

Economists use the term **competitive market** to describe a market in which there are so many buyers and so many sellers that each has a negligible impact on the market price. Each seller of ice cream has limited control over the price because other sellers are offering similar products. A seller has little reason to charge less than the going price, and if he charges more, buyers will make their purchases elsewhere. Similarly, no single buyer of ice cream can influence the price of ice cream because each buyer purchases only a small amount.

In this chapter, we assume that markets are *perfectly competitive*. To reach this highest form of competition, a market must have two characteristics: (1) The goods offered for sale are all exactly the same, and (2) the buyers and sellers are so numerous that no single buyer or seller has any influence over the market price.

Because buyers and sellers in perfectly competitive markets must accept the price the market determines, they are said to be *price takers*. At the market price, buyers can buy all they want, and sellers can sell all they want.

There are some markets in which the assumption of perfect competition applies perfectly. In the wheat market, for example, there are thousands of farmers who sell wheat and millions of consumers who use wheat and wheat products. Because no single buyer or seller can influence the price of wheat, each takes the market price as given.

Not all goods and services, however, are sold in perfectly competitive markets. Some markets have only one seller, and this seller sets the price. Such a seller is called a *monopoly*. Your local cable television company, for instance, may be a monopoly. Residents of your town probably have only one company from which to buy cable service. Other markets fall between the extremes of perfect competition and monopoly.

Despite the diversity of market types we find in the world, assuming perfect competition is a useful simplification and, therefore, a natural place to start. Perfectly competitive markets are the easiest to analyze because everyone participating in the market takes the price as given by market conditions. Moreover, because some degree of competition is present in most markets, many of the lessons that we learn by studying supply and demand under perfect competition apply in more complicated markets as well.

 *What is a market? • What are the characteristics of a perfectly competitive market?*

# 4-2 Demand

We begin our study of markets by examining the behavior of buyers. To focus our thinking, let's keep in mind a particular good—ice cream.

## 4-2a The Demand Curve: The Relationship between Price and Quantity Demanded

The **quantity demanded** of any good is the amount of the good that buyers are willing and able to purchase. As we will see, many things determine the quantity demanded of any good, but in our analysis of how markets work, one determinant plays a central role: the price of the good. If the price of ice cream rose to $20 per scoop, you would buy less ice cream. You might buy frozen yogurt instead. If the price of ice cream fell to $0.20 per scoop, you would buy more. This relationship between price and quantity demanded is true for most goods in the economy and, in fact, is so pervasive that economists call it the **law of demand**: Other things being equal, when the price of a good rises, the quantity demanded of the good falls, and when the price falls, the quantity demanded rises.

The table in Figure 1 shows how many ice-cream cones Catherine buys each month at different prices. If ice cream is free, Catherine eats 12 cones per month. At $0.50 per cone, Catherine buys 10 cones each month. As the price rises further, she buys fewer and fewer cones. When the price reaches $3.00, Catherine doesn't buy any cones at all. This table is a **demand schedule**, a table that shows the relationship between the price of a good and the quantity demanded, holding constant everything else that influences how much of the good consumers want to buy.

The graph in Figure 1 uses the numbers from the table to illustrate the law of demand. By convention, the price of ice cream is on the vertical axis, and the

**quantity demanded**
the amount of a good that buyers are willing and able to purchase

**law of demand**
the claim that, other things being equal, the quantity demanded of a good falls when the price of the good rises

**demand schedule**
a table that shows the relationship between the price of a good and the quantity demanded

## FIGURE 1

**Catherine's Demand Schedule and Demand Curve**

The demand schedule is a table that shows the quantity demanded at each price. The demand curve, which graphs the demand schedule, illustrates how the quantity demanded of the good changes as its price varies. Because a lower price increases the quantity demanded, the demand curve slopes downward.

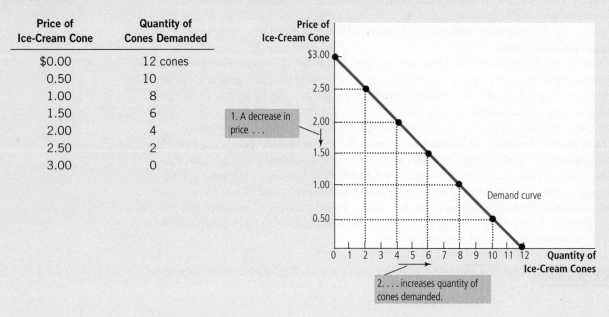

| Price of Ice-Cream Cone | Quantity of Cones Demanded |
| --- | --- |
| $0.00 | 12 cones |
| 0.50 | 10 |
| 1.00 | 8 |
| 1.50 | 6 |
| 2.00 | 4 |
| 2.50 | 2 |
| 3.00 | 0 |

**demand curve**

a graph of the relationship between the price of a good and the quantity demanded

quantity of ice cream demanded is on the horizontal axis. The line relating price and quantity demanded is called the **demand curve**. The demand curve slopes downward because, other things being equal, a lower price means a greater quantity demanded.

### 4-2b  Market Demand versus Individual Demand

The demand curve in Figure 1 shows an individual's demand for a product. To analyze how markets work, we need to determine the *market demand*, the sum of all the individual demands for a particular good or service.

The table in Figure 2 shows the demand schedules for ice cream of the two individuals in this market—Catherine and Nicholas. At any price, Catherine's demand schedule tells us how much ice cream she buys, and Nicholas's demand schedule tells us how much ice cream he buys. The market demand at each price is the sum of the two individual demands.

The graph in Figure 2 shows the demand curves that correspond to these demand schedules. Notice that we sum the individual demand curves *horizontally* to obtain the market demand curve. That is, to find the total quantity demanded at any price, we add the individual quantities, which are found on the horizontal axis of the individual demand curves. Because we are interested in analyzing how markets function, we work most often with the market demand curve. The market demand curve shows how the total quantity demanded of a good varies as the price of the good varies, while all other factors that affect how much consumers want to buy are held constant.

The quantity demanded in a market is the sum of the quantities demanded by all the buyers at each price. Thus, the market demand curve is found by adding horizontally the individual demand curves. At a price of $2.00, Catherine demands 4 ice-cream cones and Nicholas demands 3 ice-cream cones. The quantity demanded in the market at this price is 7 cones.

## FIGURE 2

**Market Demand as the Sum of Individual Demands**

| Price of Ice-Cream Cone | Catherine | | Nicholas | | Market |
|---|---|---|---|---|---|
| $0.00 | 12 | + | 7 | = | 19 cones |
| 0.50 | 10 | | 6 | | 16 |
| 1.00 | 8 | | 5 | | 13 |
| 1.50 | 6 | | 4 | | 10 |
| 2.00 | 4 | | 3 | | 7 |
| 2.50 | 2 | | 2 | | 4 |
| 3.00 | 0 | | 1 | | 1 |

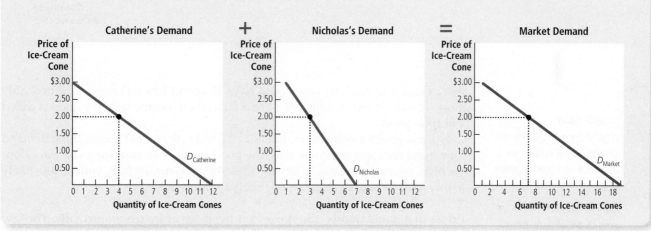

## 4-2c Shifts in the Demand Curve

Because the market demand curve holds other things constant, it need not be stable over time. If something happens to alter the quantity demanded at any given price, the demand curve shifts. For example, suppose the American Medical Association discovered that people who regularly eat ice cream live longer, healthier lives. The discovery would raise the demand for ice cream. At any given price, buyers would now want to purchase a larger quantity of ice cream, and the demand curve for ice cream would shift.

Figure 3 illustrates shifts in demand. Any change that increases the quantity demanded at every price, such as our imaginary discovery by the American Medical Association, shifts the demand curve to the right and is called an *increase in demand*. Any change that reduces the quantity demanded at every price shifts the demand curve to the left and is called a *decrease in demand*.

There are many variables that can shift the demand curve. Let's consider the most important.

**Income** What would happen to your demand for ice cream if you lost your job one summer? Most likely, it would fall. A lower income means that you have

## FIGURE 3

**Shifts in the Demand Curve**
Any change that raises the quantity that buyers wish to purchase at any given price shifts the demand curve to the right. Any change that lowers the quantity that buyers wish to purchase at any given price shifts the demand curve to the left.

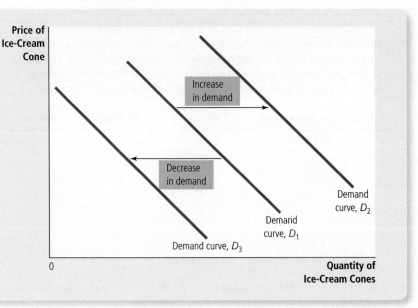

**normal good**
a good for which, other things being equal, an increase in income leads to an increase in demand

**inferior good**
a good for which, other things being equal, an increase in income leads to a decrease in demand

**substitutes**
two goods for which an increase in the price of one leads to an increase in the demand for the other

**complements**
two goods for which an increase in the price of one leads to a decrease in the demand for the other

less to spend in total, so you would have to spend less on some—and probably most—goods. If the demand for a good falls when income falls, the good is called a **normal good**.

Normal goods are the norm, but not all goods are normal goods. If the demand for a good rises when income falls, the good is called an **inferior good**. An example of an inferior good might be bus rides. As your income falls, you are less likely to buy a car or take a cab and more likely to ride a bus.

**Prices of Related Goods**   Suppose that the price of frozen yogurt falls. The law of demand says that you will buy more frozen yogurt. At the same time, you will probably buy less ice cream. Because ice cream and frozen yogurt are both cold, sweet, creamy desserts, they satisfy similar desires. When a fall in the price of one good reduces the demand for another good, the two goods are called **substitutes**. Substitutes are often pairs of goods that are used in place of each other, such as hot dogs and hamburgers, sweaters and sweatshirts, and cinema tickets and film streaming services.

Now suppose that the price of hot fudge falls. According to the law of demand, you will buy more hot fudge. Yet in this case, you will likely buy more ice cream as well because ice cream and hot fudge are often used together. When a fall in the price of one good raises the demand for another good, the two goods are called **complements**. Complements are often pairs of goods that are used together, such as gasoline and automobiles, computers and software, and peanut butter and jelly.

**Tastes**   The most obvious determinant of your demand is your tastes. If you like ice cream, you buy more of it. Economists normally do not try to explain people's tastes because tastes are based on historical and psychological forces that are beyond the realm of economics. Economists do, however, examine what happens when tastes change.

**Expectations**   Your expectations about the future may affect your demand for a good or service today. If you expect to earn a higher income next month, you may choose to save less now and spend more of your current income buying ice cream. If you expect the price of ice cream to fall tomorrow, you may be less willing to buy an ice-cream cone at today's price.

**Number of Buyers**   In addition to the preceding factors, which influence the behavior of individual buyers, market demand depends on the number of these buyers. If Peter were to join Catherine and Nicholas as another consumer of ice cream, the quantity demanded in the market would be higher at every price, and market demand would increase.

**Summary**   The demand curve shows what happens to the quantity demanded of a good when its price varies, holding constant all the other variables that influence buyers. When one of these other variables changes, the demand curve shifts. Table 1 lists the variables that influence how much of a good consumers choose to buy.

If you have trouble remembering whether you need to shift or move along the demand curve, it helps to recall a lesson from the appendix to Chapter 2. A curve shifts when there is a change in a relevant variable that is not measured on either axis. Because the price is on the vertical axis, a change in price represents a movement along the demand curve. By contrast, income, the prices of related goods, tastes, expectations, and the number of buyers are not measured on either axis, so a change in one of these variables shifts the demand curve.

| Variable | A Change in This Variable . . . |
|---|---|
| Price of the good itself | Represents a movement along the demand curve |
| Income | Shifts the demand curve |
| Prices of related goods | Shifts the demand curve |
| Tastes | Shifts the demand curve |
| Expectations | Shifts the demand curve |
| Number of buyers | Shifts the demand curve |

**TABLE 1**

**Variables That Influence Buyers**
This table lists the variables that affect how much of any good consumers choose to buy. Notice the special role that the price of the good plays: A change in the good's price represents a movement along the demand curve, whereas a change in one of the other variables shifts the demand curve.

**CASE STUDY**

**TWO WAYS TO REDUCE THE QUANTITY OF SMOKING DEMANDED**
Because smoking can lead to various illnesses, public policymakers often want to reduce the amount that people smoke. There are two ways that they can attempt to achieve this goal.

One way to reduce smoking is to shift the demand curve for cigarettes and other tobacco products. Public service announcements, mandatory health warnings on cigarette packages, and the prohibition of cigarette advertising on television are all policies aimed at reducing the quantity of cigarettes demanded at any given price. If successful, these policies shift the demand curve for cigarettes to the left, as in panel (a) of Figure 4.

Alternatively, policymakers can try to raise the price of cigarettes. If the government taxes the manufacture of cigarettes, for example, cigarette companies pass much of this tax on to consumers in the form of higher prices. A higher price encourages smokers to reduce the numbers of cigarettes they smoke. In this case, the reduced amount of smoking does not represent a shift in the demand curve.

## FIGURE 4

**Shifts in the Demand Curve versus Movements along the Demand Curve**

If warnings on cigarette packages convince smokers to smoke less, the demand curve for cigarettes shifts to the left. In panel (a), the demand curve shifts from $D_1$ to $D_2$. At a price of $4.00 per pack, the quantity demanded falls from 20 to 10 cigarettes per day, as reflected by the shift from point A to point B. By contrast, if a tax raises the price of cigarettes, the demand curve does not shift. Instead, we observe a movement to a different point on the demand curve. In panel (b), when the price rises from $4.00 to $8.00, the quantity demanded falls from 20 to 12 cigarettes per day, as reflected by the movement from point A to point C.

### (a) A Shift in the Demand Curve

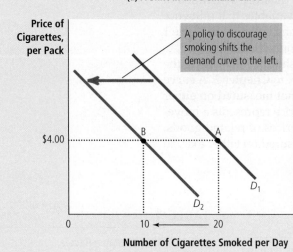

A policy to discourage smoking shifts the demand curve to the left.

### (b) A Movement along the Demand Curve

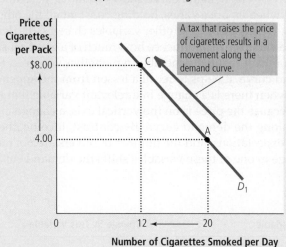

A tax that raises the price of cigarettes results in a movement along the demand curve.

*What is the best way to stop this?*

Instead, it represents a movement along the same demand curve to a point with a higher price and lower quantity, as in panel (b) of Figure 4.

How much does the amount of smoking respond to changes in the price of cigarettes? Economists have attempted to answer this question by studying what happens when the tax on cigarettes changes. They have found that a 10 percent increase in the price causes a 4 percent reduction in the quantity demanded. Teenagers are especially sensitive to the price of cigarettes: A 10 percent increase in the price causes a 12 percent drop in teenage smoking.

A related question is how the price of cigarettes affects the demand for illicit drugs, such as marijuana. Opponents of cigarette taxes often argue that tobacco and marijuana are substitutes so that high cigarette prices encourage marijuana use. By contrast, many experts on substance abuse view tobacco as a "gateway drug" leading young people to experiment with other harmful substances. Most studies of the data are consistent with this latter view: They find that lower cigarette prices are associated with greater use of marijuana. In other words, tobacco and marijuana appear to be complements rather than substitutes. ●

**Quick Quiz**   *Make up an example of a monthly demand schedule for pizza, and graph the implied demand curve. Give an example of something that would shift this demand curve, and briefly explain your reasoning. Would a change in the price of pizza shift this demand curve?*

# 4-3 Supply

We now turn to the other side of the market and examine the behavior of sellers. Once again, to focus our thinking, let's consider the market for ice cream.

## 4-3a The Supply Curve: The Relationship between Price and Quantity Supplied

The **quantity supplied** of any good or service is the amount that sellers are willing and able to sell. There are many determinants of quantity supplied, but once again, price plays a special role in our analysis. When the price of ice cream is high, selling ice cream is profitable, and so the quantity supplied is large. Sellers of ice cream work long hours, buy many ice-cream machines, and hire many workers. By contrast, when the price of ice cream is low, the business is less profitable, so sellers produce less ice cream. At a low price, some sellers may even choose to shut down, and their quantity supplied falls to zero. This relationship between price and quantity supplied is called the **law of supply**: Other things being equal, when the price of a good rises, the quantity supplied of the good also rises, and when the price falls, the quantity supplied falls as well.

The table in Figure 5 shows the quantity of ice-cream cones supplied each month by Ben, an ice-cream seller, at various prices of ice cream. At a price below $1.00, Ben does not supply any ice cream at all. As the price rises, he supplies a greater and greater quantity. This is the **supply schedule**, a table that shows the relationship between the price of a good and the quantity supplied, holding constant everything else that influences how much of the good producers want to sell.

**quantity supplied**
the amount of a good that sellers are willing and able to sell

**law of supply**
the claim that, other things being equal, the quantity supplied of a good rises when the price of the good rises

**supply schedule**
a table that shows the relationship between the price of a good and the quantity supplied

---

The supply schedule is a table that shows the quantity supplied at each price. This supply curve, which graphs the supply schedule, illustrates how the quantity supplied of the good changes as its price varies. Because a higher price increases the quantity supplied, the supply curve slopes upward.

**FIGURE 5**

**Ben's Supply Schedule and Supply Curve**

| Price of Ice-Cream Cone | Quantity of Cones Demanded |
|---|---|
| $0.00 | 0 cones |
| 0.50 | 0 |
| 1.00 | 1 |
| 1.50 | 2 |
| 2.00 | 3 |
| 2.50 | 4 |
| 3.00 | 5 |

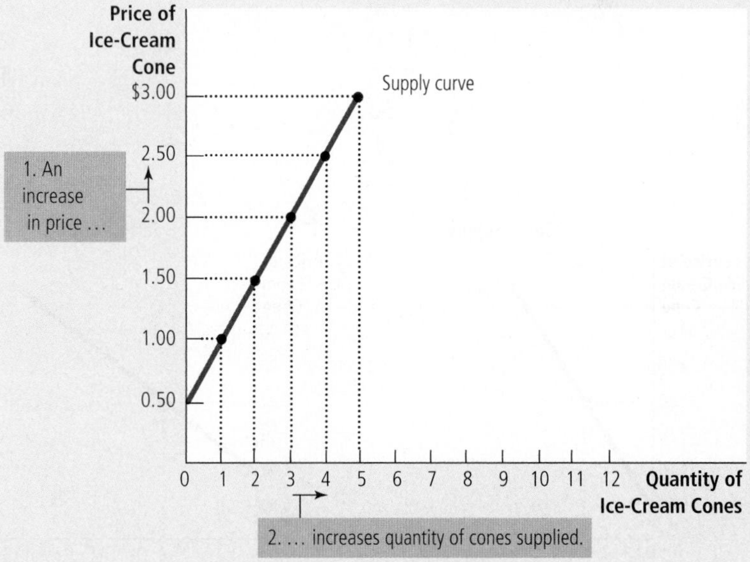

1. An increase in price …

2. … increases quantity of cones supplied.

The graph in Figure 5 uses the numbers from the table to illustrate the law of supply. The curve relating price and quantity supplied is called the **supply curve**. The supply curve slopes upward because, other things being equal, a higher price means a greater quantity supplied.

### 4-3b  Market Supply versus Individual Supply

Just as market demand is the sum of the demands of all buyers, market supply is the sum of the supplies of all sellers. The table in Figure 6 shows the supply schedules for the two ice-cream producers in the market—Ben and Jerry. At any price, Ben's supply schedule tells us the quantity of ice cream that Ben supplies, and Jerry's supply schedule tells us the quantity of ice cream that Jerry supplies. The market supply is the sum of the two individual supplies.

The graph in Figure 6 shows the supply curves that correspond to the supply schedules. As with demand curves, we sum the individual supply curves *horizontally* to obtain the market supply curve. That is, to find the total quantity supplied at any price, we add the individual quantities, which are found on the horizontal axis of the individual supply curves. The market supply curve shows how the total quantity supplied varies as the price of the good varies, holding constant all other factors that influence producers' decisions about how much to sell.

## FIGURE 6

**Market Supply as the Sum of Individual Supplies**

The quantity supplied in a market is the sum of the quantities supplied by all the sellers at each price. Thus, the market supply curve is found by adding horizontally the individual supply curves. At a price of $2.00, Ben supplies 3 ice-cream cones and Jerry supplies 4 ice-cream cones. The quantity supplied in the market at this price is 7 cones.

| Price of Ice-Cream Cone | Ben | | Jerry | | Market |
|:---:|:---:|:---:|:---:|:---:|:---:|
| $0.00 | 0 | + | 0 | = | 0 cones |
| 0.50 | 0 | | 0 | | 0 |
| 1.00 | 1 | | 0 | | 1 |
| 1.50 | 2 | | 2 | | 4 |
| 2.00 | 3 | | 4 | | 7 |
| 2.50 | 4 | | 6 | | 10 |
| 3.00 | 5 | | 8 | | 13 |

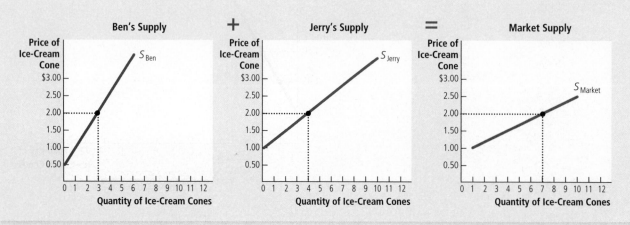

## 4-3c Shifts in the Supply Curve

Because the market supply curve is drawn holding other things constant, when one of these factors changes, the supply curve shifts. For example, suppose the price of sugar falls. Sugar is an input in the production of ice cream, so the fall in the price of sugar makes selling ice cream more profitable. This raises the supply of ice cream: At any given price, sellers are now willing to produce a larger quantity. As a result, the supply curve for ice cream shifts to the right.

Figure 7 illustrates shifts in supply. Any change that raises quantity supplied at every price, such as a fall in the price of sugar, shifts the supply curve to the right and is called an *increase in supply*. Any change that reduces the quantity supplied at every price shifts the supply curve to the left and is called a *decrease in supply*.

There are many variables that can shift the supply curve. Let's consider the most important.

**Input Prices**  To produce their output of ice cream, sellers use various inputs: cream, sugar, flavoring, ice-cream machines, the buildings in which the ice cream is made, and the labor of workers who mix the ingredients and operate the machines. When the price of one or more of these inputs rises, producing ice cream is less profitable, and firms supply less ice cream. If input prices rise substantially, a firm might shut down and supply no ice cream at all. Thus, the supply of a good is negatively related to the price of the inputs used to make the good.

**Technology**  The technology for turning inputs into ice cream is another determinant of supply. The invention of the mechanized ice-cream machine, for example, reduced the amount of labor necessary to make ice cream. By reducing firms' costs, the advance in technology raised the supply of ice cream.

**Expectations**  The amount of ice cream a firm supplies today may depend on its expectations about the future. For example, if a firm expects the price of ice cream to rise in the future, it will put some of its current production into storage and supply less to the market today.

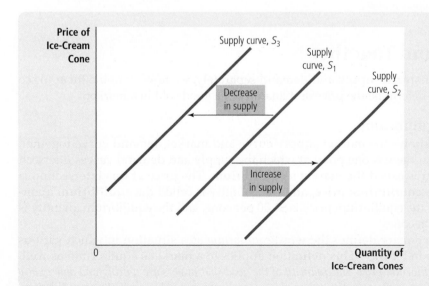

### FIGURE 7

**Shifts in the Supply Curve**
Any change that raises the quantity that sellers wish to produce at any given price shifts the supply curve to the right. Any change that lowers the quantity that sellers wish to produce at any given price shifts the supply curve to the left.

## TABLE **2**

**Variables That Influence Sellers**
This table lists the variables that affect how much of any good producers choose to sell. Notice the special role that the price of the good plays: A change in the good's price represents a movement along the supply curve, whereas a change in one of the other variables shifts the supply curve.

| Variable | A Change in This Variable . . . |
|---|---|
| Price of the good itself | Represents a movement along the supply curve |
| Input prices | Shifts the supply curve |
| Technology | Shifts the supply curve |
| Expectations | Shifts the supply curve |
| Number of sellers | Shifts the supply curve |

**Number of Sellers**   In addition to the preceding factors, which influence the behavior of individual sellers, market supply depends on the number of these sellers. If Ben or Jerry were to retire from the ice-cream business, the supply in the market would fall.

**Summary**   The supply curve shows what happens to the quantity supplied of a good when its price varies, holding constant all the other variables that influence sellers. When one of these other variables changes, the supply curve shifts. Table 2 lists the variables that influence how much of a good producers choose to sell.

Once again, to remember whether you need to shift or move along the supply curve, keep in mind that a curve shifts only when there is a change in a relevant variable that is not named on either axis. The price is on the vertical axis, so a change in price represents a movement along the supply curve. By contrast, because input prices, technology, expectations, and the number of sellers are not measured on either axis, a change in one of these variables shifts the supply curve.

QuickQuiz   *Make up an example of a monthly supply schedule for pizza, and graph the implied supply curve. Give an example of something that would shift this supply curve, and briefly explain your reasoning. Would a change in the price of pizza shift this supply curve?*

# 4-4 Supply and Demand Together

**equilibrium**
a situation in which the market price has reached the level at which quantity supplied equals quantity demanded

**equilibrium price**
the price that balances quantity supplied and quantity demanded

**equilibrium quantity**
the quantity supplied and the quantity demanded at the equilibrium price

Having analyzed supply and demand separately, we now combine them to see how they determine the price and quantity of a good sold in a market.

### 4-4a Equilibrium

Figure 8 shows the market supply curve and market demand curve together. Notice that there is one point at which the supply and demand curves intersect. This point is called the market's **equilibrium**. The price at this intersection is called the **equilibrium price**, and the quantity is called the **equilibrium quantity**. Here the equilibrium price is $2.00 per cone, and the equilibrium quantity is 7 ice-cream cones.

The dictionary defines the word *equilibrium* as a situation in which various forces are in balance. This definition applies to a market's equilibrium as well. *At the equilibrium price, the quantity of the good that buyers are willing and able to buy exactly balances the quantity that sellers are willing and able to sell.* The equilibrium price is sometimes called the *market-clearing price* because, at this price, everyone

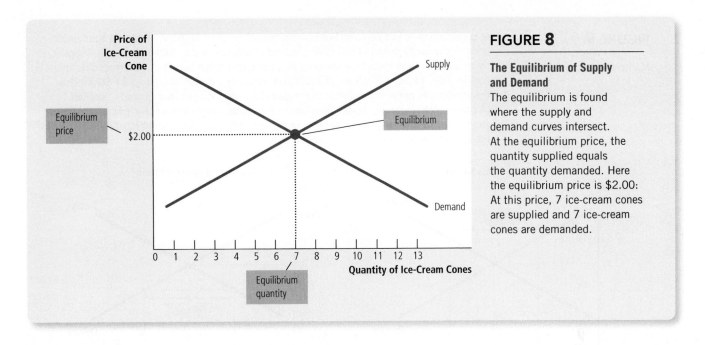

**FIGURE 8**

**The Equilibrium of Supply and Demand**
The equilibrium is found where the supply and demand curves intersect. At the equilibrium price, the quantity supplied equals the quantity demanded. Here the equilibrium price is $2.00: At this price, 7 ice-cream cones are supplied and 7 ice-cream cones are demanded.

in the market has been satisfied: Buyers have bought all they want to buy, and sellers have sold all they want to sell.

The actions of buyers and sellers naturally move markets toward the equilibrium of supply and demand. To see why, consider what happens when the market price is not equal to the equilibrium price.

Suppose first that the market price is above the equilibrium price, as in panel (a) of Figure 9. At a price of $2.50 per cone, the quantity of the good supplied (10 cones) exceeds the quantity demanded (4 cones). There is a **surplus** of the good: Suppliers are unable to sell all they want at the going price. A surplus is sometimes called a situation of *excess supply*. When there is a surplus in the ice-cream market, sellers of ice cream find their freezers increasingly full of ice cream they would like to sell but cannot. They respond to the surplus by cutting their prices. Falling prices, in turn, increase the quantity demanded and decrease the quantity supplied. These changes represent movements *along* the supply and demand curves, not shifts in the curves. Prices continue to fall until the market reaches the equilibrium.

**surplus**
a situation in which quantity supplied is greater than quantity demanded

Suppose now that the market price is below the equilibrium price, as in panel (b) of Figure 9. In this case, the price is $1.50 per cone, and the quantity of the good demanded exceeds the quantity supplied. There is a **shortage** of the good: Demanders are unable to buy all they want at the going price. A shortage is sometimes called a situation of *excess demand*. When a shortage occurs in the ice-cream market, buyers have to wait in long lines for a chance to buy one of the few cones available. With too many buyers chasing too few goods, sellers can respond to the shortage by raising their prices without losing sales. These price increases cause the quantity demanded to fall and the quantity supplied to rise. Once again, these changes represent movements *along* the supply and demand curves, and they move the market toward the equilibrium.

**shortage**
a situation in which quantity demanded is greater than quantity supplied

Thus, regardless of whether the price starts off too high or too low, the activities of the many buyers and sellers automatically push the market price toward the equilibrium price. Once the market reaches its equilibrium, all buyers and sellers

## FIGURE 9

**Markets Not in Equilibrium**

In panel (a), there is a surplus. Because the market price of $2.50 is above the equilibrium price, the quantity supplied (10 cones) exceeds the quantity demanded (4 cones). Suppliers try to increase sales by cutting the price of a cone, and this moves the price toward its equilibrium level. In panel (b), there is a shortage. Because the market price of $1.50 is below the equilibrium price, the quantity demanded (10 cones) exceeds the quantity supplied (4 cones). With too many buyers chasing too few goods, suppliers can take advantage of the shortage by raising the price. Hence, in both cases, the price adjustment moves the market toward the equilibrium of supply and demand.

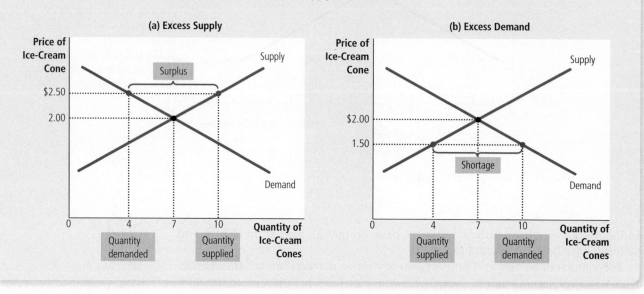

**law of supply and demand**
the claim that the price of any good adjusts to bring the quantity supplied and the quantity demanded for that good into balance

are satisfied, and there is no upward or downward pressure on the price. How quickly equilibrium is reached varies from market to market depending on how quickly prices adjust. In most free markets, surpluses and shortages are only temporary because prices eventually move toward their equilibrium levels. Indeed, this phenomenon is so pervasive that it is called the **law of supply and demand**: The price of any good adjusts to bring the quantity supplied and quantity demanded for that good into balance.

### 4-4b  Three Steps to Analyzing Changes in Equilibrium

So far, we have seen how supply and demand together determine a market's equilibrium, which in turn determines the price and quantity of the good that buyers

purchase and sellers produce. The equilibrium price and quantity depend on the position of the supply and demand curves. When some event shifts one of these curves, the equilibrium in the market changes, resulting in a new price and a new quantity exchanged between buyers and sellers.

When analyzing how some event affects the equilibrium in a market, we proceed in three steps. First, we decide whether the event shifts the supply curve, the demand curve, or, in some cases, both. Second, we decide whether the curve shifts to the right or to the left. Third, we use the supply-and-demand diagram to compare the initial equilibrium with the new one, which shows how the shift affects the equilibrium price and quantity. Table 3 summarizes these three steps. To see how this recipe is used, let's consider various events that might affect the market for ice cream.

| |
|---|
| 1. Decide whether the event shifts the supply or demand curve (or perhaps both). |
| 2. Decide in which direction the curve shifts. |
| 3. Use the supply-and-demand diagram to see how the shift changes the equilibrium price and quantity. |

**TABLE 3**

**Three Steps for Analyzing Changes in Equilibrium**

**Example: A Change in Market Equilibrium Due to a Shift in Demand**  Suppose that one summer the weather is very hot. How does this event affect the market for ice cream? To answer this question, let's follow our three steps.

1. The hot weather affects the demand curve by changing people's taste for ice cream. That is, the weather changes the amount of ice cream that people want to buy at any given price. The supply curve is unchanged because the weather does not directly affect the firms that sell ice cream.
2. Because hot weather makes people want to eat more ice cream, the demand curve shifts to the right. Figure 10 shows this increase in demand as a shift in the demand curve from $D_1$ to $D_2$. This shift indicates that the quantity of ice cream demanded is higher at every price.
3. At the old price of $2, there is now an excess demand for ice cream, and this shortage induces firms to raise the price. As Figure 10 shows, the increase in demand raises the equilibrium price from $2.00 to $2.50 and the equilibrium quantity from 7 to 10 cones. In other words, the hot weather increases both the price of ice cream and the quantity of ice cream sold.

**Shifts in Curves versus Movements along Curves**  Notice that when hot weather increases the demand for ice cream and drives up the price, the quantity of ice cream that firms supply rises, even though the supply curve remains the same. In this case, economists say there has been an increase in "quantity supplied" but no change in "supply."

*Supply* refers to the position of the supply curve, whereas the *quantity supplied* refers to the amount suppliers wish to sell. In this example, supply does not change because the weather does not alter firms' desire to sell at any given price. Instead, the hot weather alters consumers' desire to buy at any given price and thereby shifts the demand curve to the right. The increase in demand

## FIGURE 10

**How an Increase in Demand Affects the Equilibrium**
An event that raises quantity demanded at any given price shifts the demand curve to the right. The equilibrium price and the equilibrium quantity both rise. Here an abnormally hot summer causes buyers to demand more ice cream. The demand curve shifts from $D_1$ to $D_2$, which causes the equilibrium price to rise from $2.00 to $2.50 and the equilibrium quantity to rise from 7 to 10 cones.

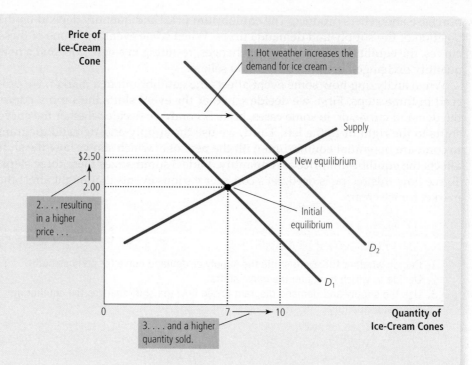

causes the equilibrium price to rise. When the price rises, the quantity supplied rises. This increase in quantity supplied is represented by the movement along the supply curve.

To summarize, a shift *in* the supply curve is called a "change in supply," and a shift *in* the demand curve is called a "change in demand." A movement *along* a fixed supply curve is called a "change in the quantity supplied," and a movement *along* a fixed demand curve is called a "change in the quantity demanded."

**Example: A Change in Market Equilibrium Due to a Shift in Supply**   Suppose that during another summer, a hurricane destroys part of the sugarcane crop and drives up the price of sugar. How does this event affect the market for ice cream? Once again, to answer this question, we follow our three steps.

1. The change in the price of sugar, an input for making ice cream, affects the supply curve. By raising the costs of production, it reduces the amount of ice cream that firms produce and sell at any given price. The demand curve does not change because the higher cost of inputs does not directly affect the amount of ice cream consumers wish to buy.
2. The supply curve shifts to the left because, at every price, the total amount that firms are willing and able to sell is reduced. Figure 11 illustrates this decrease in supply as a shift in the supply curve from $S_1$ to $S_2$.
3. At the old price of $2, there is now an excess demand for ice cream, and this shortage causes firms to raise the price. As Figure 11 shows, the shift in the supply curve raises the equilibrium price from $2.00 to $2.50 and

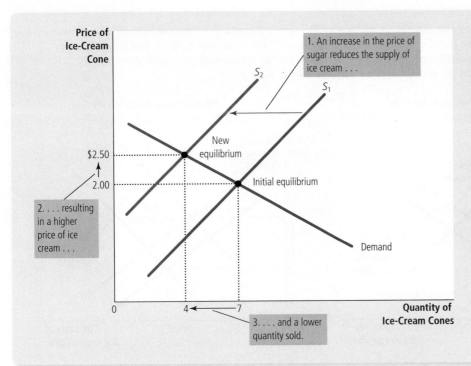

**Price of Ice-Cream Cone**

1. An increase in the price of sugar reduces the supply of ice cream . . .

$S_2$

$S_1$

New equilibrium

$2.50

2.00 ········· Initial equilibrium

2. . . . resulting in a higher price of ice cream . . .

Demand

0        4 ◄── 7

3. . . . and a lower quantity sold.

**Quantity of Ice-Cream Cones**

**FIGURE 11**

**How a Decrease in Supply Affects the Equilibrium**
An event that reduces quantity supplied at any given price shifts the supply curve to the left. The equilibrium price rises, and the equilibrium quantity falls. Here an increase in the price of sugar (an input) causes sellers to supply less ice cream. The supply curve shifts from $S_1$ to $S_2$, which causes the equilibrium price of ice cream to rise from $2.00 to $2.50 and the equilibrium quantity to fall from 7 to 4 cones.

lowers the equilibrium quantity from 7 to 4 cones. As a result of the sugar price increase, the price of ice cream rises, and the quantity of ice cream sold falls.

**Example: Shifts in Both Supply and Demand**   Now suppose that the heat wave and the hurricane occur during the same summer. To analyze this combination of events, we again follow our three steps.

1. We determine that both curves must shift. The hot weather affects the demand curve because it alters the amount of ice cream that consumers want to buy at any given price. At the same time, when the hurricane drives up sugar prices, it alters the supply curve for ice cream because it changes the amount of ice cream that firms want to sell at any given price.
2. The curves shift in the same directions as they did in our previous analysis: The demand curve shifts to the right, and the supply curve shifts to the left. Figure 12 illustrates these shifts.
3. As Figure 12 shows, two possible outcomes might result depending on the relative size of the demand and supply shifts. In both cases, the equilibrium price rises. In panel (a), where demand increases substantially while supply falls just a little, the equilibrium quantity also rises. By contrast, in panel (b), where supply falls substantially while demand rises just a little, the equilibrium quantity falls. Thus, these events certainly raise the price of ice cream, but their impact on the amount of ice cream sold is ambiguous (that is, it could go either way).

## FIGURE 12

**A Shift in Both Supply and Demand**

Here we observe a simultaneous increase in demand and decrease in supply. Two outcomes are possible. In panel (a), the equilibrium price rises from $P_1$ to $P_2$, and the equilibrium quantity rises from $Q_1$ to $Q_2$. In panel (b), the equilibrium price again rises from $P_1$ to $P_2$, but the equilibrium quantity falls from $Q_1$ to $Q_2$.

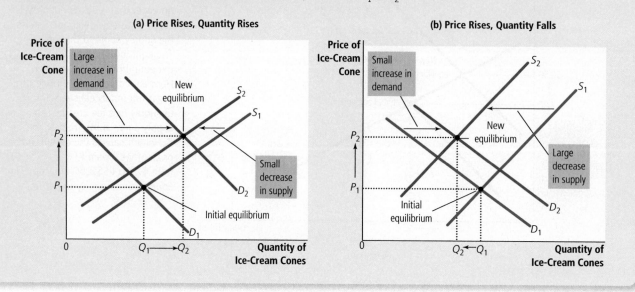

**(a) Price Rises, Quantity Rises**

**(b) Price Rises, Quantity Falls**

**Summary**   We have just seen three examples of how to use supply and demand curves to analyze a change in equilibrium. Whenever an event shifts the supply curve, the demand curve, or perhaps both curves, you can use these tools to predict how the event will alter the price and quantity sold in equilibrium. Table 4 shows the predicted outcome for any combination of shifts in the two curves. To make sure you understand how to use the tools of supply and demand, pick a few entries in this table and make sure you can explain to yourself why the table contains the prediction that it does.

## TABLE 4

**What Happens to Price and Quantity When Supply or Demand Shifts?**
As a quick quiz, make sure you can explain at least a few of the entries in this table using a supply-and-demand diagram.

|  | No Change in Supply | An Increase in Supply | A Decrease in Supply |
|---|---|---|---|
| **No Change in Demand** | P same<br>Q same | P down<br>Q up | P up<br>Q down |
| **An Increase in Demand** | P up<br>Q up | P ambiguous<br>Q up | P up<br>Q ambiguous |
| **A Decrease in Demand** | P down<br>Q down | P down<br>Q ambiguous | P ambiguous<br>Q down |

QuickQuiz | *On the appropriate diagram, show what happens to the market for pizza if the price of tomatoes rises. • On a separate diagram, show what happens to the market for pizza if the price of hamburgers falls.*

# 4-5 Conclusion: How Prices Allocate Resources

This chapter has analyzed supply and demand in a single market. Our discussion has centered on the market for ice cream, but the lessons learned here apply to most other markets as well. Whenever you go to a store to buy something, you are contributing to the demand for that item. Whenever you look for a job, you are contributing to the supply of labor services. Because supply and demand are such pervasive economic phenomena, the model of supply and demand is a powerful tool for analysis. We use this model repeatedly in the following chapters.

One of the *Ten Principles of Economics* discussed in Chapter 1 is that markets are usually a good way to organize economic activity. Although it is still too early to judge whether market outcomes are good or bad, in this chapter we have begun to see how markets work. In any economic system, scarce resources have to be allocated among competing uses. Market economies harness the forces of supply and demand to serve that end. Supply and demand together determine the prices of the economy's many different goods and services; prices in turn are the signals that guide the allocation of resources.

For example, consider the allocation of beachfront land. Because the amount of this land is limited, not everyone can enjoy the luxury of living by the beach. Who gets this resource? The answer is whoever is willing and able to pay the price. The price of beachfront land adjusts until the quantity of land demanded exactly balances the quantity supplied. Thus, in market economies, prices are the mechanism for rationing scarce resources.

Similarly, prices determine who produces each good and how much is produced. For instance, consider farming. Because we need food to survive, it is crucial that some people work on

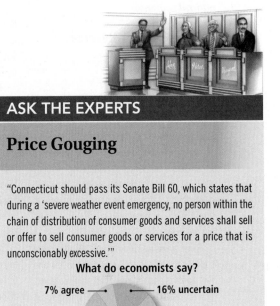

## ASK THE EXPERTS

### Price Gouging

"Connecticut should pass its Senate Bill 60, which states that during a 'severe weather event emergency, no person within the chain of distribution of consumer goods and services shall sell or offer to sell consumer goods or services for a price that is unconscionably excessive.'"

**What do economists say?**

7% agree —— • —— 16% uncertain

77% disagree

Source: IGM Economic Experts Panel, May 2, 2012.

*"Two dollars"*

*"—and seventy-five cents."*

## Price Increases after Disasters

*When a disaster such as a hurricane strikes a region, many goods experience an increase in demand or a decrease in supply, putting upward pressure on prices. Policymakers often object to these price hikes, but this opinion piece endorses the market's natural response.*

### Is Price Gouging Reverse Looting?

**By John Carney**

Four dollars for a can of coke. Five hundred dollars a night for a hotel in downtown Brooklyn. A pair of D-batteries for $6.99.

These are just a few of the examples of price hikes I or friends of mine have personally come across in the run-up and aftermath of hurricane Sandy. Price gouging, as this is often called, is a common occurrence during emergencies.

Price gouging around natural disasters is one of the things politicians on the left and right agree is a terrible, no good, very bad thing. New York Attorney General Eric Schneiderman sent out a press release warning "against price inflation of necessary goods and services during hurricane Sandy." New Jersey Governor Chris Christie issued a "forceful reminder" that price gouging "will result in significant penalties." Hotlines have been established to allow consumers to report gouging.

New Jersey's law is very specific. Price increases of more than 10 percent during a declared state of emergency are considered excessive. A New Jersey gas station paid a $50,000 fine last year for hiking gasoline prices by 16 percent during tropical storm Irene.

New York's law may be even stricter. According to AG Schneiderman's release, all price increases on "necessary goods and items" count as gouging.

"General Business Law prohibits such increase in costs of essential items like food, water, gas, generators, batteries and flashlights, and services like transportation, during natural disasters or other events that disrupt the market," the NY AG release said.

These laws are built on the quite conventional view that it is unethical for a business to take advantage of a disaster in pursuit of profits. It just seems wrong for business owners to make money on the misery of their

neighbors. Merchants earning larger profits because of a disaster seem to be rewarded for doing nothing more than raising their prices.

"It's reverse looting," a neighbor of mine in Brooklyn said about the price of batteries at a local electronic store.

Unfortunately, ethics runs into economics in a way that can make these laws positively harmful. Price gouging can occur only when there is a shortage of the goods in demand. If there were no shortage, normal market processes would prevent sudden price spikes. A deli owner charging $4 for a can of Pepsi would discover he was just driving customers to the deli a block away, which charges a buck.

But when everyone starts suddenly buying batteries or bottles of water for fear of a blackout, shortages can arise. Sometimes there simply is not enough of a particular good to satisfy a sharp spike in demand. And so the question arises: how do we decide

farms. What determines who is a farmer and who is not? In a free society, there is no government planning agency making this decision and ensuring an adequate supply of food. Instead, the allocation of workers to farms is based on the job decisions of millions of workers. This decentralized system works well because these decisions depend on prices. The prices of food and the wages of farmworkers (the price of their labor) adjust to ensure that enough people choose to be farmers.

If a person had never seen a market economy in action, the whole idea might seem preposterous. Economies are enormous groups of people engaged in a multitude of interdependent activities. What prevents decentralized decision making from degenerating into chaos? What coordinates the actions of the millions of people with their varying abilities and desires? What ensures that what needs to be done is in fact done? The answer, in a word, is *prices*. If an invisible hand guides market economies, as Adam Smith famously suggested, then the price system is the baton that the invisible hand uses to conduct the economic orchestra.

which customers get the batteries, the groceries, the gasoline?

We could hold a lottery. Perhaps people could receive a ticket at the grocery store. Winners would get to shop at the usual prices. Losers would just go hungry. Or, more likely, they would be forced to buy the food away from the lottery winners—at elevated prices no doubt, since no one would buy food just to sell it at the same price. So the gouging would just pass from merchant to lottery winning customer.

We could have some sort of rationing program. Each person could be assigned a portion of the necessary goods according to their household need. This is something the U.S. resorted to during World War II. The problem is that rationing requires an immense amount of planning—and an impossible level of knowledge. The rationing bureaucrat would have to know precisely how much of each good was available in a given area and how many people would need it. Good luck getting that in place as a hurricane bears down on your city.

We could simply sell goods on a first come, first serve basis. This is, in fact, what anti-gouging laws encourage. The result is all too familiar. People hoard goods. Store shelves are emptied. And you have to wonder,

Would you pay $4 for this?

M. UNAL OZMEN/SHUTTERSTOCK.COM

why is a first to the register race a fairer system than the alternative of market prices? Speed seems a poor proxy for justice.

Allowing prices to rise at times of extreme demand discourages overconsumption. People consider their purchases more carefully. Instead of buying a dozen batteries (or bottles of water or gallons of gas), perhaps they buy half that. The result is that goods under extreme demand are available to more

customers. The market process actually results in a more equitable distribution than the anti-gouging laws.

Once we understand this, it's easy to see that merchants aren't really profiting from disaster. They are profiting from managing their prices, which has the socially beneficial effect of broadening distribution and discouraging hoarding. In short, they are being justly rewarded for performing an important public service.

One objection is that a system of free-floating, legal gouging would allow the wealthy to buy everything and leave the poor out altogether. But this concern is overrated. For the most part, price hikes during disasters do not actually put necessary goods and services out of reach of even the poorest people. They just put the budgets of the poor under additional strain. This is a problem better resolved through transfer payments to alleviate the household budgetary effects of the prices after the fact, rather than trying to control the price in the first place….

Instead of cracking down on price gougers, we should be using our experience of shortages during this time of crisis to spark a reform of our counter-productive laws. Next time disaster strikes, we should hope for a bit more gouging and a lot fewer empty store shelves. ∎

---

## CHAPTER Quick Quiz

1. A change in which of the following will NOT shift the demand curve for hamburgers?
   a. the price of hot dogs
   b. the price of hamburgers
   c. the price of hamburger buns
   d. the income of hamburger consumers

2. An increase in _____ will cause a movement along a given demand curve, which is called a change in _____.
   a. supply, demand
   b. supply, quantity demanded
   c. demand, supply
   d. demand, quantity supplied

3. Movie tickets and film streaming services are substitutes. If the price of film streaming increases, what happens in the market for movie tickets?
   a. The supply curve shifts to the left.
   b. The supply curve shifts to the right.
   c. The demand curve shifts to the left.
   d. The demand curve shifts to the right.

4. The discovery of a large new reserve of crude oil will shift the _____ curve for gasoline, leading to a _____ equilibrium price.
   a. supply, higher
   b. supply, lower
   c. demand, higher
   d. demand, lower

5. If the economy goes into a recession and incomes fall, what happens in the markets for inferior goods?
   a. Prices and quantities both rise.
   b. Prices and quantities both fall.
   c. Prices rise and quantities fall.
   d. Prices fall and quantities rise.

6. Which of the following might lead to an increase in the equilibrium price of jelly and a decrease in the equilibrium quantity of jelly sold?
   a. an increase in the price of peanut better, a complement to jelly
   b. an increase in the price of Marshmallow Fluff, a substitute for jelly
   c. an increase in the price of grapes, an input into jelly
   d. an increase in consumers' incomes, as long as jelly is a normal good

## SUMMARY

- Economists use the model of supply and demand to analyze competitive markets. In a competitive market, there are many buyers and sellers, each of whom has little or no influence on the market price.
- The demand curve shows how the quantity of a good demanded depends on the price. According to the law of demand, as the price of a good falls, the quantity demanded rises. Therefore, the demand curve slopes downward.
- In addition to price, other determinants of how much consumers want to buy include income, the prices of substitutes and complements, tastes, expectations, and the number of buyers. If one of these factors changes, the demand curve shifts.
- The supply curve shows how the quantity of a good supplied depends on the price. According to the law of supply, as the price of a good rises, the quantity supplied rises. Therefore, the supply curve slopes upward.
- In addition to price, other determinants of how much producers want to sell include input prices, technology, expectations, and the number of sellers. If one of these factors changes, the supply curve shifts.
- The intersection of the supply and demand curves determines the market equilibrium. At the equilibrium price, the quantity demanded equals the quantity supplied.
- The behavior of buyers and sellers naturally drives markets toward their equilibrium. When the market price is above the equilibrium price, there is a surplus of the good, which causes the market price to fall. When the market price is below the equilibrium price, there is a shortage, which causes the market price to rise.
- To analyze how any event influences a market, we use the supply-and-demand diagram to examine how the event affects the equilibrium price and quantity. To do this, we follow three steps. First, we decide whether the event shifts the supply curve or the demand curve (or both). Second, we decide in which direction the curve shifts. Third, we compare the new equilibrium with the initial equilibrium.
- In market economies, prices are the signals that guide economic decisions and thereby allocate scarce resources. For every good in the economy, the price ensures that supply and demand are in balance. The equilibrium price then determines how much of the good buyers choose to consume and how much sellers choose to produce.

## KEY CONCEPTS

## QUESTIONS FOR REVIEW

1. What is a competitive market? Briefly describe a type of market that is *not* perfectly competitive.

2. What are the demand schedule and the demand curve, and how are they related? Why does the demand curve slope downward?

3. Does a change in consumers' tastes lead to a movement along the demand curve or to a shift in the demand curve? Does a change in price lead to a movement along the demand curve or to a shift in the demand curve? Explain your answers.

4. Harry's income declines, and as a result, he buys more pumpkin juice. Is pumpkin juice an inferior or a normal good? What happens to Harry's demand curve for pumpkin juice?

5. What are the supply schedule and the supply curve, and how are they related? Why does the supply curve slope upward?

6. Does a change in producers' technology lead to a movement along the supply curve or to a shift in the supply curve? Does a change in price lead to a movement along the supply curve or to a shift in the supply curve?

7. Define the equilibrium of a market. Describe the forces that move a market toward its equilibrium.

8. Beer and pizza are complements because they are often enjoyed together. When the price of beer rises, what happens to the supply, demand, quantity supplied, quantity demanded, and price in the market for pizza?

9. Describe the role of prices in market economies.

## PROBLEMS AND APPLICATIONS

1. Explain each of the following statements using supply-and-demand diagrams.
   a. "When a cold snap hits Florida, the price of orange juice rises in supermarkets throughout the country."
   b. "When the weather turns warm in New England every summer, the price of hotel rooms in Caribbean resorts plummets."
   c. "When a war breaks out in the Middle East, the price of gasoline rises and the price of a used Cadillac falls."

2. "An increase in the demand for notebooks raises the quantity of notebooks demanded but not the quantity supplied." Is this statement true or false? Explain.

3. Consider the market for minivans. For each of the events listed here, identify which of the determinants of demand or supply are affected. Also indicate whether demand or supply increases or decreases. Then draw a diagram to show the effect on the price and quantity of minivans.
   a. People decide to have more children.
   b. A strike by steelworkers raises steel prices.
   c. Engineers develop new automated machinery for the production of minivans.
   d. The price of sports utility vehicles rises.
   e. A stock market crash lowers people's wealth.

4. Consider the markets for film streaming services, TV screens, and tickets at movie theaters.
   a. For each pair, identify whether they are complements or substitutes:
      • Film streaming and TV screens
      • Film streaming and movie tickets
      • TV screens and movie tickets
   b. Suppose a technological advance reduces the cost of manufacturing TV screens. Draw a diagram to show what happens in the market for TV screens.
   c. Draw two more diagrams to show how the change in the market for TV screens affects the markets for film streaming and movie tickets.

5. Over the past 40 years, technological advances have reduced the cost of computer chips. How do you think this has affected the market for computers? For computer software? For typewriters?

6. Using supply-and-demand diagrams, show the effect of the following events on the market for sweatshirts.
   a. A hurricane in South Carolina damages the cotton crop.
   b. The price of leather jackets falls.
   c. All colleges require morning exercise in appropriate attire.
   d. New knitting machines are invented.

7. Ketchup is a complement (as well as a condiment) for hot dogs. If the price of hot dogs rises, what happens in the market for ketchup? For tomatoes? For tomato juice? For orange juice?

8. The market for pizza has the following demand and supply schedules:

| Price | Quantity Demanded | Quantity Supplied |
|---|---|---|
| $4 | 135 pizzas | 26 pizzas |
| 5 | 104 | 53 |
| 6 | 81 | 81 |
| 7 | 68 | 98 |
| 8 | 53 | 110 |
| 9 | 39 | 121 |

a. Graph the demand and supply curves. What are the equilibrium price and quantity in this market?
b. If the actual price in this market were *above* the equilibrium price, what would drive the market toward the equilibrium?
c. If the actual price in this market were *below* the equilibrium price, what would drive the market toward the equilibrium?

9. Consider the following events: Scientists reveal that eating oranges decreases the risk of diabetes, and at the same time, farmers use a new fertilizer that makes orange trees produce more oranges. Illustrate and explain what effect these changes have on the equilibrium price and quantity of oranges.

10. Because bagels and cream cheese are often eaten together, they are complements.
a. We observe that both the equilibrium price of cream cheese and the equilibrium quantity of bagels have risen. What could be responsible for this pattern—a fall in the price of flour or a fall in the price of milk? Illustrate and explain your answer.
b. Suppose instead that the equilibrium price of cream cheese has risen but the equilibrium quantity of bagels has fallen. What could be

responsible for this pattern—a rise in the price of flour or a rise in the price of milk? Illustrate and explain your answer.

11. Suppose that the price of basketball tickets at your college is determined by market forces. Currently, the demand and supply schedules are as follows:

| Price | Quantity Demanded | Quantity Supplied |
|---|---|---|
| $4 | 10,000 tickets | 8,000 tickets |
| 8 | 8,000 | 8,000 |
| 12 | 6,000 | 8,000 |
| 16 | 4,000 | 8,000 |
| 20 | 2,000 | 8,000 |

a. Draw the demand and supply curves. What is unusual about this supply curve? Why might this be true?
b. What are the equilibrium price and quantity of tickets?
c. Your college plans to increase total enrollment next year by 5,000 students. The additional students will have the following demand schedule:

| Price | Quantity Demanded |
|---|---|
| $4 | 4,000 tickets |
| 8 | 3,000 |
| 12 | 2,000 |
| 16 | 1,000 |
| 20 | 0 |

Now add the old demand schedule and the demand schedule for the new students to calculate the new demand schedule for the entire college. What will be the new equilibrium price and quantity?

To find additional study resources, visit cengagebrain.com, and search for "Mankiw."

# Elasticity and Its Application

Imagine that some event drives up the price of gasoline in the United States. It could be a war in the Middle East that disrupts the world supply of oil, a booming Chinese economy that boosts the world demand for oil, or a new tax on gasoline passed by Congress. How would U.S. consumers respond to the higher price?

It is easy to answer this question in a broad fashion: Consumers would buy less. This conclusion follows from the law of demand, which we learned in the previous chapter. But you might want a precise answer. By how much would consumption of gasoline fall? This question can be answered using a concept called *elasticity*, which we develop in this chapter.

Elasticity is a measure of how much buyers and sellers respond to changes in market conditions. When studying how some event or policy affects a market, we can discuss not only the direction of the effects but also their magnitude. Elasticity is useful in many applications, as we see toward the end of this chapter.

Before proceeding, however, you might be curious about the answer to the gasoline question. Many studies have examined consumers' response to changes in gasoline prices, and they typically find that the quantity demanded responds more in the long run than it does in the short run. A 10 percent increase in gasoline prices reduces gasoline consumption by about 2.5 percent after a year and by about 6 percent after 5 years. About half of the long-run reduction in quantity demanded arises because people drive less, and half arises because they switch to more fuel-efficient cars. Both responses are reflected in the demand curve and its elasticity.

# 5-1 The Elasticity of Demand

When we introduced demand in Chapter 4, we noted that consumers usually buy more of a good when its price is lower, when their incomes are higher, when the prices of its substitutes are higher, or when the prices of its complements are lower. Our discussion of demand was qualitative, not quantitative. That is, we discussed the direction in which quantity demanded moves but not the size of the change. To measure how much consumers respond to changes in these variables, economists use the concept of **elasticity**.

**elasticity**
a measure of the responsiveness of quantity demanded or quantity supplied to a change in one of its determinants

**price elasticity of demand**
a measure of how much the quantity demanded of a good responds to a change in the price of that good, computed as the percentage change in quantity demanded divided by the percentage change in price

## 5-1a  The Price Elasticity of Demand and Its Determinants

The law of demand states that a fall in the price of a good raises the quantity demanded. The **price elasticity of demand** measures how much the quantity demanded responds to a change in price. Demand for a good is said to be *elastic* if the quantity demanded responds substantially to changes in the price. Demand is said to be *inelastic* if the quantity demanded responds only slightly to changes in the price.

The price elasticity of demand for any good measures how willing consumers are to buy less of the good as its price rises. Because a demand curve reflects the many economic, social, and psychological forces that shape consumer preferences, there is no simple, universal rule for what determines a demand curve's elasticity. Based on experience, however, we can state some rules of thumb about what influences the price elasticity of demand.

**Availability of Close Substitutes**   Goods with close substitutes tend to have more elastic demand because it is easier for consumers to switch from that good to others. For example, butter and margarine are easily substitutable. A small increase in the price of butter, assuming the price of margarine is held fixed, causes the quantity of butter sold to fall by a large amount. By contrast, because eggs are a food without a close substitute, the demand for eggs is less elastic than the demand for butter. A small increase in the price of eggs does not cause a sizable drop in the quantity of eggs sold.

**Necessities versus Luxuries**   Necessities tend to have inelastic demands, whereas luxuries have elastic demands. When the price of a doctor's visit rises, people do not dramatically reduce the number of times they go to the doctor, although they might go somewhat less often. By contrast, when the price of sailboats rises, the quantity of sailboats demanded falls substantially. The reason is that most people view doctor visits as a necessity and sailboats as a luxury. Whether a good is a necessity or a luxury depends not on the intrinsic properties of the good but on the preferences of the buyer. For avid sailors with little concern about their health, sailboats might be a necessity with inelastic demand and doctor visits a luxury with elastic demand.

**Definition of the Market**    The elasticity of demand in any market depends on how we draw the boundaries of the market. Narrowly defined markets tend to have more elastic demand than broadly defined markets because it is easier to find close substitutes for narrowly defined goods. For example, food, a broad category, has a fairly inelastic demand because there are no good substitutes for food. Ice cream, a narrower category, has a more elastic demand because it is easy to substitute other desserts for ice cream. Vanilla ice cream, a very narrow category, has a very elastic demand because other flavors of ice cream are almost perfect substitutes for vanilla.

**Time Horizon**    Goods tend to have more elastic demand over longer time horizons. When the price of gasoline rises, the quantity of gasoline demanded falls only slightly in the first few months. Over time, however, people buy more fuel-efficient cars, switch to public transportation, and move closer to where they work. Within several years, the quantity of gasoline demanded falls more substantially.

## 5-1b Computing the Price Elasticity of Demand

Now that we have discussed the price elasticity of demand in general terms, let's be more precise about how it is measured. Economists compute the price elasticity of demand as the percentage change in the quantity demanded divided by the percentage change in the price. That is,

$$\text{price elasticity of demand} = \frac{\text{percentage change in quantity demanded}}{\text{percentage change in price}}$$

For example, suppose that a 10 percent increase in the price of an ice-cream cone causes the amount of ice cream you buy to fall by 20 percent. We calculate your elasticity of demand as

$$\text{price elasticity of demand} = \frac{20 \text{ percent}}{10 \text{ percent}} = 2$$

In this example, the elasticity is 2, reflecting that the change in the quantity demanded is proportionately twice as large as the change in the price.

Because the quantity demanded of a good is negatively related to its price, the percentage change in quantity will always have the opposite sign as the percentage change in price. In this example, the percentage change in price is a *positive* 10 percent (reflecting an increase), and the percentage change in quantity demanded is a *negative* 20 percent (reflecting a decrease). For this reason, price elasticities of demand are sometimes reported as negative numbers. In this book, we follow the common practice of dropping the minus sign and reporting all price elasticities of demand as positive numbers. (Mathematicians call this the *absolute value*.) With this convention, a larger price elasticity implies a greater responsiveness of quantity demanded to changes in price.

### 5-1c  The Midpoint Method: A Better Way to Calculate Percentage Changes and Elasticities

If you try calculating the price elasticity of demand between two points on a demand curve, you will quickly notice an annoying problem: The elasticity from point A to point B seems different from the elasticity from point B to point A. For example, consider these numbers:

|  |  |  |
|--|--|--|
| point A: | price = $4 | quantity = 120 |
| point B: | price = $6 | quantity = 80 |

Going from point A to point B, the price rises by 50 percent and the quantity falls by 33 percent, indicating that the price elasticity of demand is 33/50, or 0.66. Going from point B to point A, the price falls by 33 percent and the quantity rises by 50 percent, indicating that the price elasticity of demand is 50/33, or 1.5. This difference arises because the percentage changes are calculated from a different base.

One way to avoid this problem is to use the *midpoint method* for calculating elasticities. The standard procedure for computing a percentage change is to divide the change by the initial level. By contrast, the midpoint method computes a percentage change by dividing the change by the midpoint (or average) of the initial and final levels. For instance, $5 is the midpoint between $4 and $6. Therefore, according to the midpoint method, a change from $4 to $6 is considered a 40 percent rise because $(6 - 4) / 5 \times 100 = 40$. Similarly, a change from $6 to $4 is considered a 40 percent fall.

Because the midpoint method gives the same answer regardless of the direction of change, it is often used when calculating the price elasticity of demand between two points. In our example, the midpoint between point A and point B is:

midpoint:    price = $5    quantity = 100

According to the midpoint method, when going from point A to point B, the price rises by 40 percent and the quantity falls by 40 percent. Similarly, when going from point B to point A, the price falls by 40 percent and the quantity rises by 40 percent. In both directions, the price elasticity of demand equals 1.

The following formula expresses the midpoint method for calculating the price elasticity of demand between two points, denoted $(Q_1, P_1)$ and $(Q_2, P_2)$:

$$\text{price elasticity of demand} = \frac{(Q_2 - Q_1) / [(Q_2 + Q_1) / 2]}{(P_2 - P_1) / [(P_2 + P_1) / 2]}$$

The numerator is the percentage change in quantity computed using the midpoint method, and the denominator is the percentage change in price computed using the midpoint method. If you ever need to calculate elasticities, you should use this formula.

In this book, however, we rarely perform such calculations. For most of our purposes, what elasticity represents—the responsiveness of quantity demanded to a change in price—is more important than how it is calculated.

## 5-1d The Variety of Demand Curves

Economists classify demand curves according to their elasticity. Demand is considered *elastic* when the elasticity is greater than 1, which means the quantity moves proportionately more than the price. Demand is considered *inelastic* when the elasticity is less than 1, which means the quantity moves proportionately less than the price. If the elasticity is exactly 1, the percentage change in quantity equals the percentage change in price, and demand is said to have *unit elasticity*.

Because the price elasticity of demand measures how much quantity demanded responds to changes in the price, it is closely related to the slope of the demand curve. The following rule of thumb is a useful guide: The flatter the demand curve that passes through a given point, the greater the price elasticity of demand. The steeper the demand curve that passes through a given point, the smaller the price elasticity of demand.

Figure 1 shows five cases. In the extreme case of a zero elasticity, shown in panel (a), demand is *perfectly inelastic*, and the demand curve is vertical. In this case, regardless of the price, the quantity demanded stays the same. As the elasticity rises, the demand curve gets flatter and flatter, as shown in panels (b), (c), and (d). At the opposite extreme, shown in panel (e), demand is *perfectly elastic*. This occurs as the price elasticity of demand approaches infinity and the demand curve becomes horizontal, reflecting the fact that very small changes in the price lead to huge changes in the quantity demanded.

Finally, if you have trouble keeping straight the terms *elastic* and *inelastic*, here's a memory trick for you: *I*nelastic curves, such as in panel (a) of Figure 1, look like the letter I. This is not a deep insight, but it might help on your next exam.

---

**FYI**

## A Few Elasticities from the Real World

We have talked about what elasticity means, what determines it, and how it is calculated. Beyond these general ideas, you might ask for a specific number. How much, precisely, does the price of a particular good influence the quantity demanded?

To answer such a question, economists collect data from market outcomes and apply statistical techniques to estimate the price elasticity of demand. Here are some price elasticities of demand, obtained from various studies, for a range of goods:

| | |
|---|---|
| Eggs | 0.1 |
| Healthcare | 0.2 |
| Cigarettes | 0.4 |
| Rice | 0.5 |
| Housing | 0.7 |
| Beef | 1.6 |
| Peanut Butter | 1.7 |
| Restaurant Meals | 2.3 |
| Mountain Dew | 4.4 |

These kinds of numbers are fun to think about, and they can be useful when comparing markets.

Nonetheless, one should take these estimates with a grain of salt. One reason is that the statistical techniques used to obtain them require some assumptions about the world, and these assumptions might not be true in practice. (The details of these techniques are beyond the scope of this book, but you will encounter them if you take a course in econometrics.) Another reason is that the price elasticity of demand need not be the same at all points on a demand curve, as we will see shortly in the case of a linear demand curve. For both reasons, you should not be surprised if different studies report different price elasticities of demand for the same good. ∎

## FIGURE 1

**The Price Elasticity of Demand**

The price elasticity of demand determines whether the demand curve is steep or flat. Note that all percentage changes are calculated using the midpoint method.

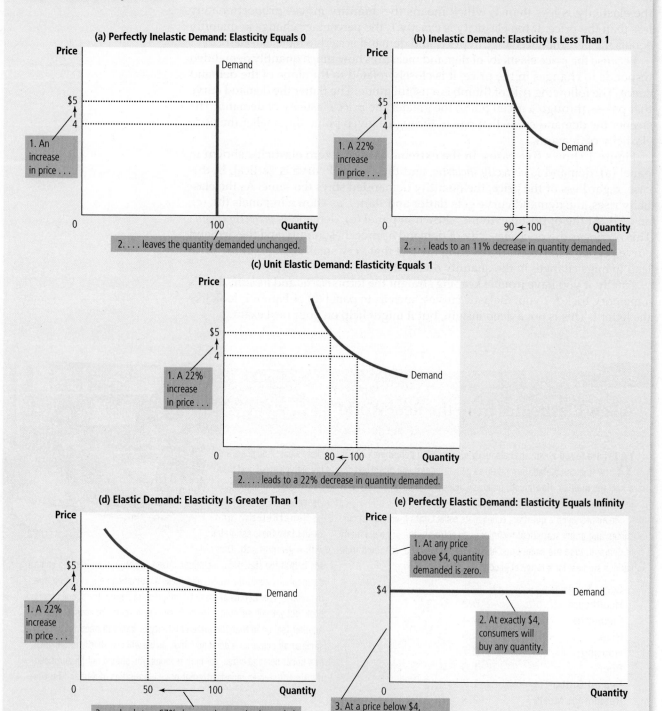

**(a) Perfectly Inelastic Demand: Elasticity Equals 0**

Price

Demand

$5
4

1. An increase in price . . .

0 ──── 100 ──── Quantity

2. . . . leaves the quantity demanded unchanged.

**(b) Inelastic Demand: Elasticity Is Less Than 1**

Price

$5
4

Demand

1. A 22% increase in price . . .

0 ──── 90 ← 100 ──── Quantity

2. . . . leads to an 11% decrease in quantity demanded.

**(c) Unit Elastic Demand: Elasticity Equals 1**

Price

$5
4

Demand

1. A 22% increase in price . . .

0 ──── 80 ← 100 ──── Quantity

2. . . . leads to a 22% decrease in quantity demanded.

**(d) Elastic Demand: Elasticity Is Greater Than 1**

Price

$5
4

Demand

1. A 22% increase in price . . .

0 ──── 50 ← ── 100 ──── Quantity

2. . . . leads to a 67% decrease in quantity demanded.

**(e) Perfectly Elastic Demand: Elasticity Equals Infinity**

Price

1. At any price above $4, quantity demanded is zero.

$4 ──────────────────── Demand

2. At exactly $4, consumers will buy any quantity.

0 ──────────── Quantity

3. At a price below $4, quantity demanded is infinite.

### 5-1e Total Revenue and the Price Elasticity of Demand

When studying changes in supply or demand in a market, one variable we often want to study is **total revenue**, the amount paid by buyers and received by sellers of a good. In any market, total revenue is $P \times Q$, the price of the good times the quantity of the good sold. We can show total revenue graphically, as in Figure 2. The height of the box under the demand curve is $P$, and the width is $Q$. The area of this box, $P \times Q$, equals the total revenue in this market. In Figure 2, where $P = \$4$ and $Q = 100$, total revenue is $\$4 \times 100$, or $\$400$.

How does total revenue change as one moves along the demand curve? The answer depends on the price elasticity of demand. If demand is inelastic, as in panel (a) of Figure 3, then an increase in the price causes an increase in total revenue. Here an increase in price from $\$4$ to $\$5$ causes the quantity demanded to fall from 100 to 90, so total revenue rises from $\$400$ to $\$450$. An increase in price raises $P \times Q$ because the fall in $Q$ is proportionately smaller than the rise in $P$. In other words, the extra revenue from selling units at a higher price (represented by area A in the figure) more than offsets the decline in revenue from selling fewer units (represented by area B).

We obtain the opposite result if demand is elastic: An increase in the price causes a decrease in total revenue. In panel (b) of Figure 3, for instance, when the price rises from $\$4$ to $\$5$, the quantity demanded falls from 100 to 70, so total revenue falls from $\$400$ to $\$350$. Because demand is elastic, the reduction in the quantity demanded is so great that it more than offsets the increase in the price. That is, an increase in price reduces $P \times Q$ because the fall in $Q$ is proportionately greater than the rise in $P$. In this case, the extra revenue from selling units at a higher price (area A) is smaller than the decline in revenue from selling fewer units (area B).

The examples in this figure illustrate some general rules:

- When demand is inelastic (a price elasticity less than 1), price and total revenue move in the same direction: If the price increases, total revenue also increases.

**total revenue**
the amount paid by buyers and received by sellers of a good, computed as the price of the good times the quantity sold

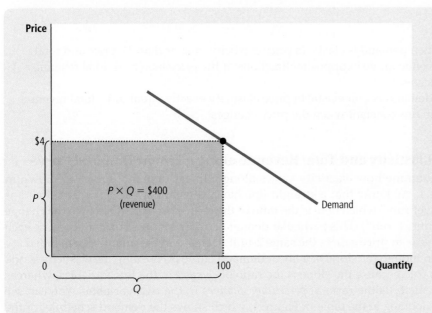

**FIGURE 2**

**Total Revenue**
The total amount paid by buyers, and received as revenue by sellers, equals the area of the box under the demand curve, $P \times Q$. Here, at a price of $\$4$, the quantity demanded is 100 and total revenue is $\$400$.

## FIGURE 3

**How Total Revenue Changes When Price Changes**

The impact of a price change on total revenue (the product of price and quantity) depends on the elasticity of demand. In panel (a), the demand curve is inelastic. In this case, an increase in the price leads to a decrease in quantity demanded that is proportionately smaller, so total revenue increases. Here an increase in the price from $4 to $5 causes the quantity demanded to fall from 100 to 90. Total revenue rises from $400 to $450. In panel (b), the demand curve is elastic. In this case, an increase in the price leads to a decrease in quantity demanded that is proportionately larger, so total revenue decreases. Here an increase in the price from $4 to $5 causes the quantity demanded to fall from 100 to 70. Total revenue falls from $400 to $350.

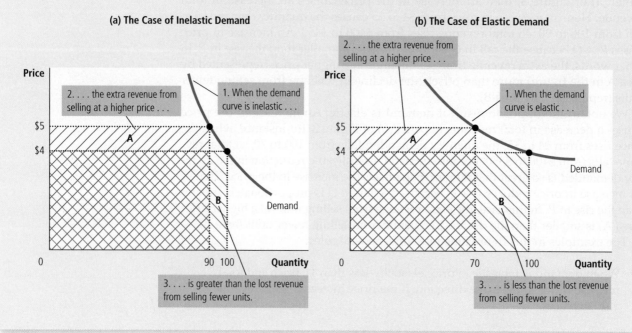

**(a) The Case of Inelastic Demand**

2. . . . the extra revenue from selling at a higher price . . .

1. When the demand curve is inelastic . . .

3. . . . is greater than the lost revenue from selling fewer units.

**(b) The Case of Elastic Demand**

2. . . . the extra revenue from selling at a higher price . . .

1. When the demand curve is elastic . . .

3. . . . is less than the lost revenue from selling fewer units.

- When demand is elastic (a price elasticity greater than 1), price and total revenue move in opposite directions: If the price increases, total revenue decreases.
- If demand is unit elastic (a price elasticity exactly equal to 1), total revenue remains constant when the price changes.

### 5-1f Elasticity and Total Revenue along a Linear Demand Curve

Let's examine how elasticity varies along a linear demand curve, as shown in Figure 4. We know that a straight line has a constant slope. Slope is defined as "rise over run," which here is the ratio of the change in price ("rise") to the change in quantity ("run"). This particular demand curve's slope is constant because each $1 increase in price causes the same 2-unit decrease in the quantity demanded.

Even though the slope of a linear demand curve is constant, the elasticity is not. This is true because the slope is the ratio of *changes* in the two variables, whereas the elasticity is the ratio of *percentage changes* in the two variables. You can see this by looking at the table in Figure 4, which shows the demand schedule for the

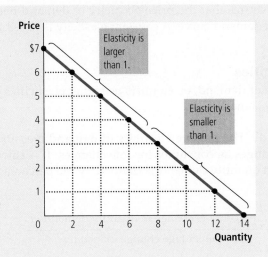

## FIGURE 4

**Elasticity along a Linear Demand Curve**
The slope of a linear demand curve is constant, but its elasticity is not. The price elasticity of demand is calculated using the demand schedule in the table and the midpoint method. At points with a low price and high quantity, the demand curve is inelastic. At points with a high price and low quantity, the demand curve is elastic.

| Price | Quantity | Total Revenue (Price × Quantity) | Percentage Change in Price | Percentage Change in Quantity | Elasticity | Description |
|-------|----------|----------------------------------|----------------------------|-------------------------------|------------|-------------|
| $7    | 0        | $0                               |                            |                               |            |             |
|       |          |                                  | 15                         | 200                           | 13.0       | Elastic     |
| 6     | 2        | 12                               |                            |                               |            |             |
|       |          |                                  | 18                         | 67                            | 3.7        | Elastic     |
| 5     | 4        | 20                               |                            |                               |            |             |
|       |          |                                  | 22                         | 40                            | 1.8        | Elastic     |
| 4     | 6        | 24                               |                            |                               |            |             |
|       |          |                                  | 29                         | 29                            | 1.0        | Unit elastic |
| 3     | 8        | 24                               |                            |                               |            |             |
|       |          |                                  | 40                         | 22                            | 0.6        | Inelastic   |
| 2     | 10       | 20                               |                            |                               |            |             |
|       |          |                                  | 67                         | 18                            | 0.3        | Inelastic   |
| 1     | 12       | 12                               |                            |                               |            |             |
|       |          |                                  | 200                        | 15                            | 0.1        | Inelastic   |
| 0     | 14       | 0                                |                            |                               |            |             |

linear demand curve in the graph. The table uses the midpoint method to calculate the price elasticity of demand. The table illustrates the following: *At points with a low price and high quantity, the demand curve is inelastic. At points with a high price and low quantity, the demand curve is elastic.*

The explanation for this fact comes from the arithmetic of percentage changes. When the price is low and consumers are buying a lot, a $1 price increase and 2-unit reduction in quantity demanded constitute a large percentage increase in the price and a small percentage decrease in quantity demanded, resulting in a small elasticity. When the price is high and consumers are not buying much, the same $1 price increase and 2-unit reduction in quantity demanded constitute a small percentage increase in the price and a large percentage decrease in quantity demanded, resulting in a large elasticity.

The table also presents total revenue at each point on the demand curve. These numbers illustrate the relationship between total revenue and elasticity. When the price is $1, for instance, demand is inelastic and a price increase to $2 raises total revenue. When the price is $5, demand is elastic and a price increase to $6 reduces total revenue. Between $3 and $4, demand is exactly unit elastic and total revenue is the same at these two prices.

The linear demand curve illustrates that the price elasticity of demand need not be the same at all points on a demand curve. A constant elasticity is possible, but it is not always the case.

## 5-1g Other Demand Elasticities

In addition to the price elasticity of demand, economists use other elasticities to describe the behavior of buyers in a market.

**income elasticity of demand**

a measure of how much the quantity demanded of a good responds to a change in consumers' income, computed as the percentage change in quantity demanded divided by the percentage change in income

**The Income Elasticity of Demand**   The **income elasticity of demand** measures how the quantity demanded changes as consumer income changes. It is calculated as the percentage change in quantity demanded divided by the percentage change in income. That is,

$$\text{income elasticity of demand} = \frac{\text{percentage change in quantity demanded}}{\text{percentage change in income}}$$

As we discussed in Chapter 4, most goods are *normal goods*: Higher income raises the quantity demanded. Because quantity demanded and income move in the same direction, normal goods have positive income elasticities. A few goods, such as bus rides, are *inferior goods*: Higher income lowers the quantity demanded. Because quantity demanded and income move in opposite directions, inferior goods have negative income elasticities.

Even among normal goods, income elasticities vary substantially in size. Necessities, such as food and clothing, tend to have small income elasticities because consumers choose to buy some of these goods even when their incomes are low. Luxuries, such as caviar and diamonds, tend to have large income elasticities because consumers feel that they can do without these goods altogether if their incomes are too low.

**cross-price elasticity of demand**

a measure of how much the quantity demanded of one good responds to a change in the price of another good, computed as the percentage change in quantity demanded of the first good divided by the percentage change in price of the second good

**The Cross-Price Elasticity of Demand**   The **cross-price elasticity of demand** measures how the quantity demanded of one good responds to a change in the price of another good. It is calculated as the percentage change in quantity demanded of good 1 divided by the percentage change in the price of good 2. That is,

$$\text{cross-price elasticity of demand} = \frac{\text{percentage change in quantity demanded of good 1}}{\text{percentage change in the price of good 2}}$$

Whether the cross-price elasticity is a positive or negative number depends on whether the two goods are substitutes or complements. As we discussed in Chapter 4, *substitutes* are goods that are typically used in place of one another, such as hamburgers and hot dogs. An increase in hot dog prices induces people to grill hamburgers instead. Because the price of hot dogs and the quantity of hamburgers demanded move in the same direction, the cross-price elasticity is positive. Conversely, *complements* are goods that are typically used together, such as computers and software. In this case, the cross-price elasticity is negative, indicating that an increase in the price of computers reduces the quantity of software demanded.

**Quick Quiz**   *Define the price elasticity of demand. • Explain the relationship between total revenue and the price elasticity of demand.*

# 5-2 The Elasticity of Supply

When we introduced supply in Chapter 4, we noted that producers of a good offer to sell more of it when the price of the good rises. To turn from qualitative to quantitative statements about quantity supplied, we once again use the concept of elasticity.

## 5-2a The Price Elasticity of Supply and Its Determinants

The law of supply states that higher prices raise the quantity supplied. The **price elasticity of supply** measures how much the quantity supplied responds to changes in the price. Supply of a good is said to be *elastic* if the quantity supplied responds substantially to changes in the price. Supply is said to be *inelastic* if the quantity supplied responds only slightly to changes in the price.

The price elasticity of supply depends on the flexibility of sellers to change the amount of the good they produce. For example, beachfront land has an inelastic supply because it is almost impossible to produce more of it. Manufactured goods, such as books, cars, and televisions, have elastic supplies because firms that produce them can run their factories longer in response to a higher price.

In most markets, a key determinant of the price elasticity of supply is the time period being considered. Supply is usually more elastic in the long run than in the short run. Over short periods of time, firms cannot easily change the size of their factories to make more or less of a good. Thus, in the short run, the quantity supplied is not very responsive to the price. Over longer periods of time, firms can build new factories or close old ones. In addition, new firms can enter a market, and old firms can exit. Thus, in the long run, the quantity supplied can respond substantially to price changes.

> **price elasticity of supply**
> a measure of how much the quantity supplied of a good responds to a change in the price of that good, computed as the percentage change in quantity supplied divided by the percentage change in price

## 5-2b Computing the Price Elasticity of Supply

Now that we have a general understanding about the price elasticity of supply, let's be more precise. Economists compute the price elasticity of supply as the percentage change in the quantity supplied divided by the percentage change in the price. That is,

$$\text{price elasticity of supply} = \frac{\text{percentage change in quantity supplied}}{\text{percentage change in price}}$$

For example, suppose that an increase in the price of milk from $2.85 to $3.15 a gallon raises the amount that dairy farmers produce from 9,000 to 11,000 gallons per month. Using the midpoint method, we calculate the percentage change in price as

$$\text{percentage change in price} = (3.15 - 2.85) \,/\, 3.00 \times 100 = 10 \text{ percent}$$

Similarly, we calculate the percentage change in quantity supplied as:

Percentage change in quantity supplied = (11,000 − 9,000) / 10,000 × 100 = 20 percent.

In this case, the price elasticity of supply is

$$\text{price elasticity of supply} = \frac{20 \text{ percent}}{10 \text{ percent}} = 2$$

In this example, the elasticity of 2 indicates that the quantity supplied changes proportionately twice as much as the price.

## 5-2c The Variety of Supply Curves

Because the price elasticity of supply measures the responsiveness of quantity supplied to changes in price, it is reflected in the appearance of the supply curve. Figure 5 (on the facing page) shows five cases. In the extreme case of zero elasticity, as shown in panel (a), supply is *perfectly inelastic* and the supply curve is vertical. In this case, the quantity supplied is the same regardless of the price. As the elasticity rises, the supply curve gets flatter, which shows that the quantity supplied responds more to changes in the price. At the opposite extreme, shown in panel (e), supply is *perfectly elastic*. This occurs as the price elasticity of supply approaches infinity and the supply curve becomes horizontal, meaning that very small changes in the price lead to very large changes in the quantity supplied.

In some markets, the elasticity of supply is not constant but varies over the supply curve. Figure 6 (presented below) shows a typical case for an industry in which firms have factories with a limited capacity for production. For low levels of quantity supplied, the elasticity of supply is high, indicating that firms respond substantially to changes in the price. In this region, firms have capacity for production that is not being used, such as plants and equipment that are idle for all or part of the day. Small increases in price make it profitable for firms to begin using this idle capacity. As the quantity supplied rises, firms begin to reach capacity. Once capacity is fully used, further increases in production require the construction of new plants. To induce firms to incur this extra expense, the price must rise substantially, so supply becomes less elastic.

Figure 6 presents a numerical example of this phenomenon. When the price rises from $3 to $4 (a 29 percent increase, according to the midpoint method), the quantity supplied rises from 100 to 200 (a 67 percent increase). Because quantity supplied changes proportionately more than the price, the supply curve has an elasticity greater than 1. By contrast, when the price rises from $12 to $15 (a 22 percent increase), the quantity supplied rises from 500 to 525 (a 5 percent increase). In this case, quantity supplied moves proportionately less than the price, so the elasticity is less than 1.

> QuickQuiz   *Define the price elasticity of supply. • Explain why the price elasticity of supply might be different in the long run than in the short run.*

---

### FIGURE 6

**How the Price Elasticity of Supply Can Vary**
Because firms often have a maximum capacity for production, the elasticity of supply may be very high at low levels of quantity supplied and very low at high levels of quantity supplied. Here an increase in price from $3 to $4 increases the quantity supplied from 100 to 200. Because the 67 percent increase in quantity supplied (computed using the midpoint method) is larger than the 29 percent increase in price, the supply curve is elastic in this range. By contrast, when the price rises from $12 to $15, the quantity supplied rises only from 500 to 525. Because the 5 percent increase in quantity supplied is smaller than the 22 percent increase in price, the supply curve is inelastic in this range.

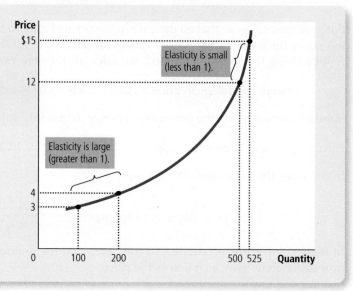

The price elasticity of supply determines whether the supply curve is steep or flat. Note that all percentage changes are calculated using the midpoint method.

**FIGURE 5**

The Price Elasticity of Supply

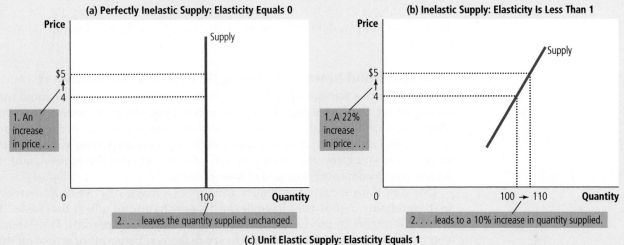

**(a) Perfectly Inelastic Supply: Elasticity Equals 0**

1. An increase in price . . .

2. . . . leaves the quantity supplied unchanged.

**(b) Inelastic Supply: Elasticity Is Less Than 1**

1. A 22% increase in price . . .

2. . . . leads to a 10% increase in quantity supplied.

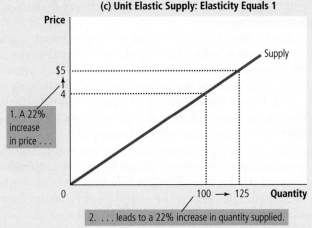

**(c) Unit Elastic Supply: Elasticity Equals 1**

1. A 22% increase in price . . .

2. . . . leads to a 22% increase in quantity supplied.

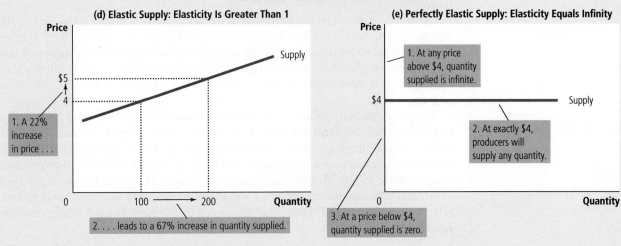

**(d) Elastic Supply: Elasticity Is Greater Than 1**

1. A 22% increase in price . . .

2. . . . leads to a 67% increase in quantity supplied.

**(e) Perfectly Elastic Supply: Elasticity Equals Infinity**

1. At any price above $4, quantity supplied is infinite.

2. At exactly $4, producers will supply any quantity.

3. At a price below $4, quantity supplied is zero.

# 5-3 Three Applications of Supply, Demand, and Elasticity

Can good news for farming be bad news for farmers? Why did OPEC, the international oil cartel, fail to keep the price of oil high? Does drug interdiction increase or decrease drug-related crime? At first, these questions might seem to have little in common. Yet all three questions are about markets, and all markets are subject to the forces of supply and demand. Here we apply the versatile tools of supply, demand, and elasticity to answer these seemingly complex questions.

### 5-3a  Can Good News for Farming Be Bad News for Farmers?

Imagine you're a Kansas wheat farmer. Because you earn all your income from selling wheat, you devote much effort to making your land as productive as possible. You monitor weather and soil conditions, check your fields for pests and disease, and study the latest advances in farm technology. You know that the more wheat you grow, the more you will have to sell after the harvest, and the higher your income and standard of living will be.

One day, Kansas State University announces a major discovery. Researchers in its agronomy department have devised a new hybrid of wheat that raises the amount farmers can produce from each acre of land by 20 percent. How should you react to this news? Does this discovery make you better off or worse off than you were before?

Recall from Chapter 4 that we answer such questions in three steps. First, we examine whether the supply or demand curve shifts. Second, we consider the direction in which the curve shifts. Third, we use the supply-and-demand diagram to see how the market equilibrium changes.

In this case, the discovery of the new hybrid affects the supply curve. Because the hybrid increases the amount of wheat that can be produced on each acre of land, farmers are now willing to supply more wheat at any given price. In other words, the supply curve shifts to the right. The demand curve remains the same because consumers' desire to buy wheat products at any given price is not affected by the introduction of a new hybrid. Figure 7 shows an example of such a change. When the supply curve shifts from $S_1$ to $S_2$, the quantity of wheat sold increases from 100 to 110 and the price of wheat falls from \$3 to \$2.

Does this discovery make farmers better off? As a first cut to answering this question, consider what happens to the total revenue received by farmers. Farmers' total revenue is $P \times Q$, the price of the wheat times the quantity sold. The discovery affects farmers in two conflicting ways. The hybrid allows farmers to produce more wheat ($Q$ rises), but now each bushel of wheat sells for less ($P$ falls).

The price elasticity of demand determines whether total revenue rises or falls. In practice, the demand for basic foodstuffs such as wheat is usually inelastic because these items are relatively inexpensive and have few good substitutes. When the demand curve is inelastic, as it is in Figure 7, a decrease in price causes total revenue to fall. You can see this in the figure: The price of wheat falls substantially, whereas the quantity of wheat sold rises only slightly. Total revenue falls from \$300 to \$220. Thus, the discovery of the new hybrid lowers the total revenue that farmers receive from the sale of their crops.

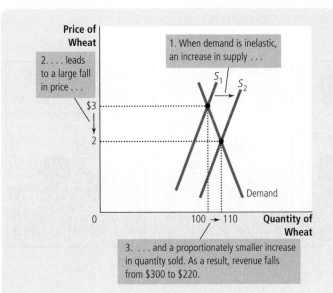

1. When demand is inelastic, an increase in supply . . .

2. . . . leads to a large fall in price . . .

$3

2

$S_1$ $S_2$

Demand

Price of Wheat

0     100 → 110     **Quantity of Wheat**

3. . . . and a proportionately smaller increase in quantity sold. As a result, revenue falls from $300 to $220.

**FIGURE 7**

**An Increase in Supply in the Market for Wheat**
When an advance in farm technology increases the supply of wheat from $S_1$ to $S_2$, the price of wheat falls. Because the demand for wheat is inelastic, the increase in the quantity sold from 100 to 110 is proportionately smaller than the decrease in the price from $3 to $2. As a result, farmers' total revenue falls from $300 ($3 × 100) to $220 ($2 × 110).

If farmers are made worse off by the discovery of this new hybrid, one might wonder why they adopt it. The answer goes to the heart of how competitive markets work. Because each farmer is only a small part of the market for wheat, she takes the price of wheat as given. For any given price of wheat, it is better to use the new hybrid to produce and sell more wheat. Yet when all farmers do this, the supply of wheat increases, the price falls, and farmers are worse off.

This example may at first seem hypothetical, but it helps to explain a major change in the U.S. economy over the past century. Two hundred years ago, most Americans lived on farms. Knowledge about farm methods was sufficiently primitive that most Americans had to be farmers to produce enough food to feed the nation's population. But over time, advances in farm technology increased the amount of food that each farmer could produce. This increase in food supply, together with the inelastic demand for food, caused farm revenues to fall, which in turn encouraged people to leave farming.

A few numbers show the magnitude of this historic change. As recently as 1950, 10 million people worked on farms in the United States, representing 17 percent of the labor force. Today, fewer than 3 million people work on farms, or 2 percent of the labor force. This change coincided with tremendous advances in farm productivity: Despite the large drop in the number of farmers, U.S. farms now produce about five times as much output as they did in 1950.

This analysis of the market for farm products also explains a seeming paradox of public policy: Certain farm programs try to help farmers by inducing them *not* to plant crops on all of their land. The purpose of these programs is to reduce the supply of farm products and thereby raise prices. With inelastic demand for their products, farmers as a group receive greater total revenue if they supply a smaller crop to the market. No single farmer would choose to leave her land fallow on her own because each takes the market price as given. But if all farmers do so together, they can all be better off.

When analyzing the effects of farm technology or farm policy, it is important to keep in mind that what is good for farmers is not necessarily good for society as a whole. Improvement in farm technology can be bad for farmers because it makes farmers increasingly unnecessary, but it is surely good for consumers who pay less for food. Similarly, a policy aimed at reducing the supply of farm products may raise the incomes of farmers, but it does so at the expense of consumers.

### 5-3b  Why Did OPEC Fail to Keep the Price of Oil High?

Many of the most disruptive events for the world's economies over the past several decades have originated in the world market for oil. In the 1970s, members of the Organization of the Petroleum Exporting Countries (OPEC) decided to raise the world price of oil to increase their incomes. These countries accomplished this goal by agreeing to jointly reduce the amount of oil they supplied. As a result, the price of oil (adjusted for overall inflation) rose more than 50 percent from 1973 to 1974. Then, a few years later, OPEC did the same thing again. From 1979 to 1981, the price of oil approximately doubled.

Yet OPEC found it difficult to maintain such a high price. From 1982 to 1985, the price of oil steadily declined about 10 percent per year. Dissatisfaction and disarray soon prevailed among the OPEC countries. In 1986, cooperation among OPEC members completely broke down, and the price of oil plunged 45 percent. In 1990, the price of oil (adjusted for overall inflation) was back to where it began in 1970, and it stayed at that low level throughout most of the 1990s. (In the first decade and a half of the 21st century, the price of oil fluctuated substantially once again, but the main driving force was not OPEC supply restrictions. Instead, booms and busts in economies around the world caused demand to fluctuate, while advances in fracking technology caused large increases in supply.)

The OPEC episodes of the 1970s and 1980s show how supply and demand can behave differently in the short run and in the long run. In the short run, both the supply and demand for oil are relatively inelastic. Supply is inelastic because the quantity of known oil reserves and the capacity for oil extraction cannot be changed quickly. Demand is inelastic because buying habits do not respond immediately to changes in price. Thus, as panel (a) of Figure 8 shows, the short-run

When the supply of oil falls, the response depends on the time horizon. In the short run, supply and demand are relatively inelastic, as in panel (a). Thus, when the supply curve shifts from $S_1$ to $S_2$, the price rises substantially. In the long run, however, supply and demand are relatively elastic, as in panel (b). In this case, the same size shift in the supply curve ($S_1$ to $S_2$) causes a smaller increase in the price.

**FIGURE 8**

A Reduction in Supply in the World Market for Oil

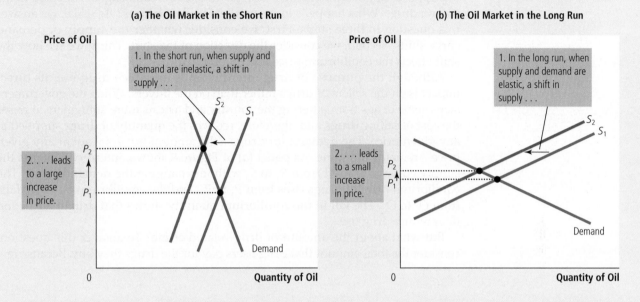

(a) The Oil Market in the Short Run

(b) The Oil Market in the Long Run

supply and demand curves are steep. When the supply of oil shifts from $S_1$ to $S_2$, the price increase from $P_1$ to $P_2$ is large.

The situation is very different in the long run. Over long periods of time, producers of oil outside OPEC respond to high prices by increasing oil exploration and by building new extraction capacity. Consumers respond with greater conservation, such as by replacing old inefficient cars with newer efficient ones. Thus, as panel (b) of Figure 8 shows, the long-run supply and demand curves are more elastic. In the long run, the shift in the supply curve from $S_1$ to $S_2$ causes a much smaller increase in the price.

This analysis shows why OPEC succeeded in maintaining a high price of oil only in the short run. When OPEC countries agreed to reduce their production of oil, they shifted the supply curve to the left. Even though each OPEC member sold less oil, the price rose by so much in the short run that OPEC incomes rose. In the long run, however, supply and demand are more elastic. As a result, the same reduction in supply, measured by the horizontal shift in the supply curve, caused a smaller increase in the price. Thus, OPEC's coordinated reduction in supply proved less profitable in the long run. The cartel learned that raising prices is easier in the short run than in the long run.

### 5-3c Does Drug Interdiction Increase or Decrease Drug-Related Crime?

A persistent problem facing our society is the use of illegal drugs, such as heroin, cocaine, ecstasy, and methamphetamine. Drug use has several adverse effects. One is that drug dependence can ruin the lives of drug users and their families.

Another is that drug addicts often turn to robbery and other violent crimes to obtain the money needed to support their habit. To discourage the use of illegal drugs, the U.S. government devotes billions of dollars each year to reducing the flow of drugs into the country. Let's use the tools of supply and demand to examine this policy of drug interdiction.

Suppose the government increases the number of federal agents devoted to the war on drugs. What happens in the market for illegal drugs? As usual, we answer this question in three steps. First, we consider whether the supply or demand curve shifts. Second, we consider the direction of the shift. Third, we see how the shift affects the equilibrium price and quantity.

Although the purpose of drug interdiction is to reduce drug use, its direct impact is on the sellers of drugs rather than on the buyers. When the government stops some drugs from entering the country and arrests more smugglers, it raises the cost of selling drugs and, therefore, reduces the quantity of drugs supplied at any given price. The demand for drugs—the amount buyers want at any given price—remains the same. As panel (a) of Figure 9 shows, interdiction shifts the supply curve to the left from $S_1$ to $S_2$ without changing the demand curve. The equilibrium price of drugs rises from $P_1$ to $P_2$, and the equilibrium quantity falls from $Q_1$ to $Q_2$. The fall in the equilibrium quantity shows that drug interdiction does reduce drug use.

But what about the amount of drug-related crime? To answer this question, consider the total amount that drug users pay for the drugs they buy. Because few

## FIGURE 9

**Policies to Reduce the Use of Illegal Drugs**

Drug interdiction reduces the supply of drugs from $S_1$ to $S_2$, as in panel (a). If the demand for drugs is inelastic, then the total amount paid by drug users rises, even as the amount of drug use falls. By contrast, drug education reduces the demand for drugs from $D_1$ to $D_2$, as in panel (b). Because both price and quantity fall, the amount paid by drug users falls.

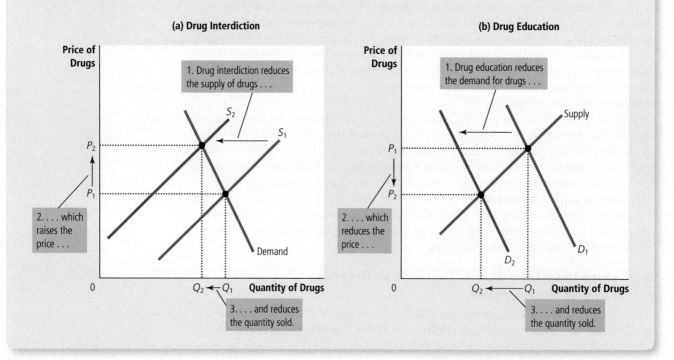

**(a) Drug Interdiction**

Price of Drugs

1. Drug interdiction reduces the supply of drugs . . .

$S_2$

$S_1$

$P_2$

$P_1$

2. . . . which raises the price . . .

Demand

0        $Q_2 \leftarrow Q_1$   **Quantity of Drugs**

3. . . . and reduces the quantity sold.

**(b) Drug Education**

Price of Drugs

1. Drug education reduces the demand for drugs . . .

Supply

$P_1$

$P_2$

2. . . . which reduces the price . . .

$D_1$

$D_2$

0        $Q_2 \leftarrow Q_1$   **Quantity of Drugs**

3. . . . and reduces the quantity sold.

drug addicts are likely to break their destructive habits in response to a higher price, it is likely that the demand for drugs is inelastic, as it is drawn in the figure. If demand is inelastic, then an increase in price raises total revenue in the drug market. That is, because drug interdiction raises the price of drugs proportionately more than it reduces drug use, it raises the total amount of money that drug users pay for drugs. Addicts who already had to steal to support their habits would have an even greater need for quick cash. Thus, drug interdiction could increase drug-related crime.

Because of this adverse effect of drug interdiction, some analysts argue for alternative approaches to the drug problem. Rather than trying to reduce the supply of drugs, policymakers might try to reduce the demand by pursuing a policy of drug education. Successful drug education has the effects shown in panel (b) of Figure 9. The demand curve shifts to the left from $D_1$ to $D_2$. As a result, the equilibrium quantity falls from $Q_1$ to $Q_2$, and the equilibrium price falls from $P_1$ to $P_2$. Total revenue, $P \times Q$, also falls. Thus, in contrast to drug interdiction, drug education can reduce both drug use and drug-related crime.

Advocates of drug interdiction might argue that the long-run effects of this policy are different from the short-run effects because the elasticity of demand depends on the time horizon. The demand for drugs is probably inelastic over short periods because higher prices do not substantially affect drug use by established addicts. But demand may be more elastic over longer periods because higher prices would discourage experimentation with drugs among the young and, over time, lead to fewer drug addicts. In this case, drug interdiction would increase drug-related crime in the short run but decrease it in the long run.

> **QuickQuiz** *How might a drought that destroys half of all farm crops be good for farmers? If such a drought is good for farmers, why don't farmers destroy their own crops in the absence of a drought?*

# 5-4 Conclusion

According to an old quip, even a parrot can become an economist simply by learning to say "supply and demand." These last two chapters should have convinced you that there is much truth to this statement. The tools of supply and demand allow you to analyze many of the most important events and policies that shape the economy. You are now well on your way to becoming an economist (or at least a well-educated parrot).

---

## CHAPTER QuickQuiz

1. A life-saving medicine without any close substitutes will tend to have
   a. a small elasticity of demand.
   b. a large elasticity of demand.
   c. a small elasticity of supply.
   d. a large elasticity of supply.

2. The price of a good rises from $8 to $12, and the quantity demanded falls from 110 to 90 units. Calculated with the midpoint method, the price elasticity of demand is
   a. 1/5.
   b. 1/2.
   c. 2.
   d. 5.

3. A linear, downward-sloping demand curve is
   a. inelastic
   b. unit elastic.
   c. elastic.
   d. inelastic at some points, and elastic at others.

4. The ability of firms to enter and exit a market over time means that, in the long run,
   a. the demand curve is more elastic.
   b. the demand curve is less elastic.
   c. the supply curve is more elastic.
   d. the supply curve is less elastic.

5. An increase in the supply of a good will decrease the total revenue producers receive if
   a. the demand curve is inelastic.
   b. the demand curve is elastic.
   c. the supply curve is inelastic.
   d. the supply curve is elastic.

6. Over time, technological advance increases consumers' incomes and reduces the price of smartphones. Each of these forces increases the amount consumers spend on smartphones if the income elasticity of demand is greater than _____ and if the price elasticity of demand is greater than _____.
   a. zero, zero
   b. zero, one
   c. one, zero
   d. one, one

## SUMMARY

- The price elasticity of demand measures how much the quantity demanded responds to changes in the price. Demand tends to be more elastic if close substitutes are available, if the good is a luxury rather than a necessity, if the market is narrowly defined, or if buyers have substantial time to react to a price change.
- The price elasticity of demand is calculated as the percentage change in quantity demanded divided by the percentage change in price. If quantity demanded moves proportionately less than the price, then the elasticity is less than 1 and demand is said to be inelastic. If quantity demanded moves proportionately more than the price, then the elasticity is greater than 1 and demand is said to be elastic.
- Total revenue, the total amount paid for a good, equals the price of the good times the quantity sold. For inelastic demand curves, total revenue moves in the same direction as the price. For elastic demand curves, total revenue moves in the opposite direction as the price.
- The income elasticity of demand measures how much the quantity demanded responds to changes

in consumers' income. The cross-price elasticity of demand measures how much the quantity demanded of one good responds to changes in the price of another good.
- The price elasticity of supply measures how much the quantity supplied responds to changes in the price. This elasticity often depends on the time horizon under consideration. In most markets, supply is more elastic in the long run than in the short run.
- The price elasticity of supply is calculated as the percentage change in quantity supplied divided by the percentage change in price. If quantity supplied moves proportionately less than the price, then the elasticity is less than 1 and supply is said to be inelastic. If quantity supplied moves proportionately more than the price, then the elasticity is greater than 1 and supply is said to be elastic.
- The tools of supply and demand can be applied in many different kinds of markets. This chapter uses them to analyze the market for wheat, the market for oil, and the market for illegal drugs.

## KEY CONCEPTS

elasticity, p. 90
price elasticity of demand, p. 90

total revenue, p. 95
income elasticity of demand, p. 98

cross-price elasticity of demand, p. 98
price elasticity of supply, p. 99

## QUESTIONS FOR REVIEW

1. Define the price elasticity of demand and the income elasticity of demand.

2. List and explain the four determinants of the price elasticity of demand discussed in the chapter.

3. If the elasticity is greater than 1, is demand elastic or inelastic? If the elasticity equals zero, is demand perfectly elastic or perfectly inelastic?

4. On a supply-and-demand diagram, show equilibrium price, equilibrium quantity, and the total revenue received by producers.

5. If demand is elastic, how will an increase in price change total revenue? Explain.

6. What do we call a good with an income elasticity less than zero?

7. How is the price elasticity of supply calculated? Explain what it measures.

8. If a fixed quantity of a good is available, and no more can be made, what is the price elasticity of supply?

9. A storm destroys half the fava bean crop. Is this event more likely to hurt fava bean farmers if the demand for fava beans is very elastic or very inelastic? Explain.

## PROBLEMS AND APPLICATIONS

1. For each of the following pairs of goods, which good would you expect to have more elastic demand and why?
   a. required textbooks or mystery novels
   b. Beethoven recordings or classical music recordings in general
   c. subway rides during the next 6 months or subway rides during the next 5 years
   d. root beer or water

2. Suppose that business travelers and vacationers have the following demand for airline tickets from New York to Boston:

| Price | Quantity Demanded (business travelers) | Quantity Demanded (vacationers) |
|---|---|---|
| $150 | 2,100 tickets | 1,000 tickets |
| 200 | 2,000 | 800 |
| 250 | 1,900 | 600 |
| 300 | 1,800 | 400 |

   a. As the price of tickets rises from $200 to $250, what is the price elasticity of demand for (i) business travelers and (ii) vacationers? (Use the midpoint method in your calculations.)
   b. Why might vacationers have a different elasticity from business travelers?

3. Suppose the price elasticity of demand for heating oil is 0.2 in the short run and 0.7 in the long run.
   a. If the price of heating oil rises from $1.80 to $2.20 per gallon, what happens to the quantity of heating oil demanded in the short run? In the long run? (Use the midpoint method in your calculations.)

   b. Why might this elasticity depend on the time horizon?

4. A price change causes the quantity demanded of a good to decrease by 30 percent, while the total revenue of that good increases by 15 percent. Is the demand curve elastic or inelastic? Explain.

5. Cups of coffee and donuts are complements. Both have inelastic demand. A hurricane destroys half the coffee bean crop. Use appropriately labeled diagrams to answer the following questions.
   a. What happens to the price of coffee beans?
   b. What happens to the price of a cup of coffee? What happens to total expenditure on cups of coffee?
   c. What happens to the price of donuts? What happens to total expenditure on donuts?

6. The price of coffee rose sharply last month, while the quantity sold remained the same. Five people suggest various explanations:

   LEONARD:  Demand increased, but supply was perfectly inelastic.
   SHELDON:  Demand increased, but it was perfectly inelastic.
   PENNY:  Demand increased, but supply decreased at the same time.
   HOWARD:  Supply decreased, but demand was unit elastic.
   RAJ:  Supply decreased, but demand was perfectly inelastic.

   Who could possibly be right? Use graphs to explain your answer.

7. Suppose that your demand schedule for pizza is as follows:

| Price | Quantity Demanded (income = $20,000) | Quantity Demanded (income = $24,000) |
|---|---|---|
| $8 | 40 pizza | 50 pizza |
| 10 | 32 | 45 |
| 12 | 24 | 30 |
| 14 | 16 | 20 |
| 16 | 8 | 12 |

a. Use the midpoint method to calculate your price elasticity of demand as the price of pizza increases from $8 to $10 if (i) your income is $20,000 and (ii) your income is $24,000.

b. Calculate your income elasticity of demand as your income increases from $20,000 to $24,000 if (i) the price is $12 and (ii) the price is $16.

8. The *New York Times* reported (Feb. 17, 1996) that subway ridership declined after a fare increase: "There were nearly four million fewer riders in December 1995, the first full month after the price of a token increased 25 cents to $1.50, than in the previous December, a 4.3 percent decline."

a. Use these data to estimate the price elasticity of demand for subway rides.

b. According to your estimate, what happens to the Transit Authority's revenue when the fare rises?

c. Why might your estimate of the elasticity be unreliable?

9. Two drivers, Walt and Jessie, each drive up to a gas station. Before looking at the price, each places an order. Walt says, "I'd like 10 gallons of gas." Jessie says, "I'd like $10 worth of gas." What is each driver's price elasticity of demand?

10. Consider public policy aimed at smoking.

a. Studies indicate that the price elasticity of demand for cigarettes is about 0.4. If a pack of cigarettes currently costs $5 and the government wants to reduce smoking by 20 percent, by how much should it increase the price?

b. If the government permanently increases the price of cigarettes, will the policy have a larger effect on smoking 1 year from now or 5 years from now?

c. Studies also find that teenagers have a higher price elasticity of demand than adults. Why might this be true?

11. You are the curator of a museum. The museum is running short of funds, so you decide to increase revenue. Should you increase or decrease the price of admission? Explain.

12. Explain why the following might be true: A drought around the world raises the total revenue that farmers receive from the sale of grain, but a drought only in Kansas reduces the total revenue that Kansas farmers receive.

To find additional study resources, visit cengagebrain.com, and search for "Mankiw."

# Supply, Demand, and Government Policies

## CHAPTER 6

E conomists have two roles. As scientists, they develop and test theories to explain the world around them. As policy advisers, they use these theories to help change the world for the better. The focus of the preceding two chapters has been scientific. We have seen how supply and demand determine the price of a good and the quantity of the good sold. We have also seen how various events shift supply and demand, thereby changing the equilibrium price and quantity. And we have developed the concept of elasticity to gauge the size of these changes.

This chapter offers our first look at policy. Here we analyze various types of government policy using only the tools of supply and demand. As you will see, the analysis yields some surprising insights. Policies often have effects that their architects did not intend or anticipate.

We begin by considering policies that directly control prices. For example, rent-control laws set a maximum rent that landlords may charge tenants. Minimum-wage laws set the lowest wage that firms may pay workers. Price controls are usually enacted when policymakers believe that the market price of a good or service is unfair to buyers or sellers. Yet, as we will see, these policies can generate inequities of their own.

After discussing price controls, we consider the impact of taxes. Policymakers use taxes to raise revenue for public purposes and to influence market outcomes. Although the prevalence of taxes in our economy is obvious, their effects are not. For example, when the government levies a tax on the amount that firms pay their workers, do the firms or the workers bear the burden of the tax? The answer is not at all clear—until we apply the powerful tools of supply and demand.

# 6-1 Controls on Prices

To see how price controls affect market outcomes, let's look once again at the market for ice cream. As we saw in Chapter 4, if ice cream is sold in a competitive market free of government regulation, the price of ice cream adjusts to balance supply and demand: At the equilibrium price, the quantity of ice cream that buyers want to buy exactly equals the quantity that sellers want to sell. To be concrete, let's suppose that the equilibrium price is $3 per cone.

Some people may not be happy with the outcome of this free-market process. The American Association of Ice-Cream Eaters complains that the $3 price is too high for everyone to enjoy a cone a day (their recommended daily allowance). Meanwhile, the National Organization of Ice-Cream Makers complains that the $3 price—the result of "cutthroat competition"—is too low and is depressing the incomes of its members. Each of these groups lobbies the government to pass laws that alter the market outcome by directly controlling the price of an ice-cream cone.

Because buyers of any good always want a lower price while sellers want a higher price, the interests of the two groups conflict. If the Ice-Cream Eaters are successful in their lobbying, the government imposes a legal maximum on the price at which ice-cream cones can be sold. Because the price is not allowed to rise above this level, the legislated maximum is called a **price ceiling**. By contrast, if the Ice-Cream Makers are successful, the government imposes a legal minimum on the price. Because the price cannot fall below this level, the legislated minimum is called a **price floor**. Let us consider the effects of these policies in turn.

**price ceiling**
a legal maximum on the price at which a good can be sold

**price floor**
a legal minimum on the price at which a good can be sold

## 6-1a How Price Ceilings Affect Market Outcomes

When the government, moved by the complaints and campaign contributions of the Ice-Cream Eaters, imposes a price ceiling in the market for ice cream, two outcomes are possible. In panel (a) of Figure 1, the government imposes a price ceiling of $4 per cone. In this case, because the price that balances supply and demand ($3) is below the ceiling, the price ceiling is *not binding*. Market forces naturally move the economy to the equilibrium, and the price ceiling has no effect on the price or the quantity sold.

In panel (a), the government imposes a price ceiling of $4. Because the price ceiling is above the equilibrium price of $3, the price ceiling has no effect, and the market can reach the equilibrium of supply and demand. In this equilibrium, quantity supplied and quantity demanded both equal 100 cones. In panel (b), the government imposes a price ceiling of $2. Because the price ceiling is below the equilibrium price of $3, the market price equals $2. At this price, 125 cones are demanded and only 75 are supplied, so there is a shortage of 50 cones.

## FIGURE 1

**A Market with a Price Ceiling**

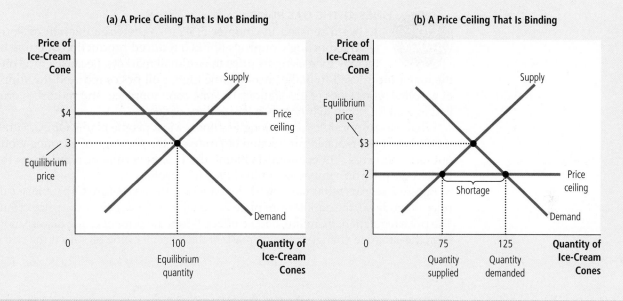

**(a) A Price Ceiling That Is Not Binding**

**(b) A Price Ceiling That Is Binding**

Panel (b) of Figure 1 shows the other, more interesting, possibility. In this case, the government imposes a price ceiling of $2 per cone. Because the equilibrium price of $3 is above the price ceiling, the ceiling is a *binding constraint* on the market. The forces of supply and demand tend to move the price toward the equilibrium price, but when the market price hits the ceiling, it cannot, by law, rise any further. Thus, the market price equals the price ceiling. At this price, the quantity of ice cream demanded (125 cones in the figure) exceeds the quantity supplied (75 cones). Because of this excess demand of 50 cones, some people who want to buy ice cream at the going price are unable to do so. In other words, there is a shortage of ice cream.

In response to this shortage, some mechanism for rationing ice cream will naturally develop. The mechanism could be long lines: Buyers who are willing to arrive early and wait in line get a cone, while those unwilling to wait do not. Alternatively, sellers could ration ice-cream cones according to their own personal biases, selling them only to friends, relatives, or members of their own racial or ethnic group. Notice that even though the price ceiling was motivated by a desire to help buyers of ice cream, not all buyers benefit from the policy. Some buyers do get to pay a lower price, although they may have to wait in line to do so, but other buyers cannot get any ice cream at all.

This example in the market for ice cream shows a general result: *When the government imposes a binding price ceiling on a competitive market, a shortage of the good arises, and sellers must ration the scarce goods among the large number of potential buyers.* The rationing mechanisms that develop under price ceilings are rarely desirable. Long lines are inefficient because they waste buyers' time. Discrimination according to seller bias is both inefficient (because the good may not go to the buyer who values it most highly) and often unfair. By contrast, the rationing mechanism in a free, competitive market is both efficient and impersonal. When the market for ice cream reaches its equilibrium, anyone who wants to pay the market price can get a cone. Free markets ration goods with prices.

### CASE STUDY

### LINES AT THE GAS PUMP

As we discussed in Chapter 5, in 1973 the Organization of Petroleum Exporting Countries (OPEC) reduced production of crude oil, thereby increasing its price in world oil markets. Because crude oil is the major input used to make gasoline, the higher oil prices reduced the supply of gasoline. Long lines at gas stations became commonplace, and motorists often had to wait for hours to buy only a few gallons of gas.

What was responsible for the long gas lines? Most people blame OPEC. Surely, if OPEC had not reduced production of crude oil, the shortage of gasoline would not have occurred. Yet economists blame the U.S. government regulations that limited the price oil companies could charge for gasoline.

Figure 2 reveals what happened. As panel (a) shows, before OPEC raised the price of crude oil, the equilibrium price of gasoline, $P_1$, was below the price ceiling. The price regulation, therefore, had no effect. When the price of crude oil rose, however, the situation changed. The increase in the price of crude oil raised the cost of

---

## FIGURE 2

**The Market for Gasoline with a Price Ceiling**

Panel (a) shows the gasoline market when the price ceiling is not binding because the equilibrium price, $P_1$, is below the ceiling. Panel (b) shows the gasoline market after an increase in the price of crude oil (an input into making gasoline) shifts the supply curve to the left from $S_1$ to $S_2$. In an unregulated market, the price would have risen from $P_1$ to $P_2$. The price ceiling, however, prevents this from happening. At the binding price ceiling, consumers are willing to buy $Q_D$, but producers of gasoline are willing to sell only $Q_S$. The difference between quantity demanded and quantity supplied, $Q_D - Q_S$, measures the gasoline shortage.

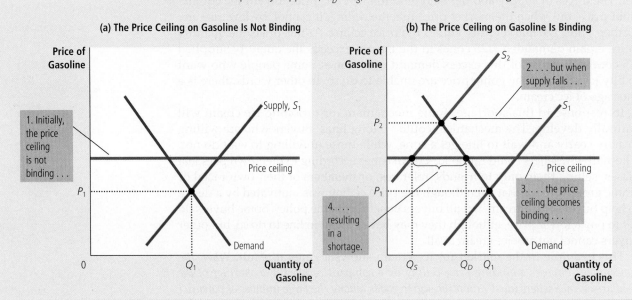

(a) The Price Ceiling on Gasoline Is Not Binding

(b) The Price Ceiling on Gasoline Is Binding

producing gasoline, and this reduced the supply of gasoline. As panel (b) shows, the supply curve shifted to the left from $S_1$ to $S_2$. In an unregulated market, this shift in supply would have raised the equilibrium price of gasoline from $P_1$ to $P_2$, and no shortage would have resulted. Instead, the price ceiling prevented the price from rising to the equilibrium level. At the price ceiling, producers were willing to sell $Q_S$, but consumers were willing to buy $Q_D$. Thus, the shift in supply caused a severe shortage at the regulated price.

Eventually, the laws regulating the price of gasoline were repealed. Lawmakers came to understand that they were partly responsible for the many hours Americans lost waiting in line to buy gasoline. Today, when the price of crude oil changes, the price of gasoline can adjust to bring supply and demand into equilibrium. ●

**CASE STUDY**

**RENT CONTROL IN THE SHORT RUN AND THE LONG RUN**

One common example of a price ceiling is rent control. In many cities, the local government places a ceiling on rents that landlords may charge their tenants. The goal of this policy is to help the poor by making housing more affordable. Economists often criticize rent control, arguing that it is a highly inefficient way to help the poor raise their standard of living. One economist called rent control "the best way to destroy a city, other than bombing."

The adverse effects of rent control are less apparent to the general population because these effects occur over many years. In the short run, landlords have a fixed number of apartments to rent, and they cannot adjust this number quickly as market conditions change. Moreover, the number of people searching for housing in a city may not be highly responsive to rents in the short run because people take time to adjust their housing arrangements. Therefore, the short-run supply and demand for housing are relatively inelastic.

Panel (a) of Figure 3 shows the short-run effects of rent control on the housing market. As with any binding price ceiling, rent control causes a shortage. But because supply and demand are inelastic in the short run, the initial shortage caused by rent control is small. The primary effect in the short run is to reduce rents.

The long-run story is very different because the buyers and sellers of rental housing respond more to market conditions as time passes. On the supply side, landlords respond to low rents by not building new apartments and by failing to maintain existing ones. On the demand side, low rents encourage people to find their own apartments (rather than living with their parents or sharing apartments with roommates) and induce more people to move into the city. Therefore, both supply and demand are more elastic in the long run.

Panel (b) of Figure 3 illustrates the housing market in the long run. When rent control depresses rents below the equilibrium level, the quantity of apartments supplied falls substantially and the quantity of apartments demanded rises substantially. The result is a large shortage of housing.

In cities with rent control, landlords use various mechanisms to ration housing. Some landlords keep long waiting lists. Others give preference to tenants without children. Still others discriminate on the basis of race. Sometimes apartments are allocated to those willing to offer under-the-table payments to building superintendents. In essence, these bribes bring the total price of an apartment closer to the equilibrium price.

To understand fully the effects of rent control, we have to remember one of the *Ten Principles of Economics* from Chapter 1: People respond to incentives. In free

## FIGURE 3

**Rent Control in the Short Run and in the Long Run**

Panel (a) shows the short-run effects of rent control: Because the supply and demand curves for apartments are relatively inelastic, the price ceiling imposed by a rent-control law causes only a small shortage of housing. Panel (b) shows the long-run effects of rent control: Because the supply and demand curves for apartments are more elastic, rent control causes a large shortage.

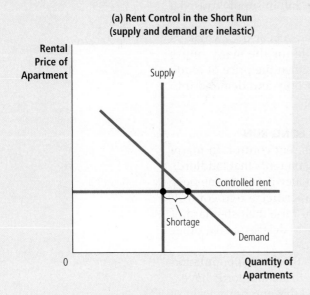

(a) Rent Control in the Short Run
(supply and demand are inelastic)

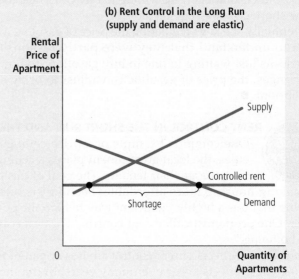

(b) Rent Control in the Long Run
(supply and demand are elastic)

markets, landlords try to keep their buildings clean and safe because desirable apartments command higher prices. By contrast, when rent control creates shortages and waiting lists, landlords lose their incentive to respond to tenants' concerns. Why should a landlord spend money to maintain and improve the property when people are waiting to move in as it is? In the end, tenants get lower rents, but they also get lower-quality housing.

Policymakers often react to the effects of rent control by imposing additional regulations. For example, various laws make racial discrimination in housing illegal and require landlords to provide minimally adequate living conditions. These laws, however, are difficult and costly to enforce. By contrast, when rent control is eliminated and a market for housing is regulated by the forces of competition, such laws are less necessary. In a free market, the price of housing adjusts to eliminate the shortages that give rise to undesirable landlord behavior. ●

### 6-1b How Price Floors Affect Market Outcomes

To examine the effects of another kind of government price control, let's return to the market for ice cream. Imagine now that the government is persuaded by the pleas of the National Organization of Ice-Cream Makers whose members feel that the $3 equilibrium price is too low. In this case, the government might institute a price floor. Price floors, like price ceilings, are an attempt by the government to maintain prices at other than

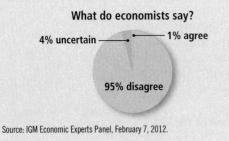

## ASK THE EXPERTS

## Rent Control

"Local ordinances that limit rent increases for some rental housing units, such as in New York and San Francisco, have had a positive impact over the past three decades on the amount and quality of broadly affordable rental housing in cities that have used them."

**What do economists say?**

4% uncertain —— 1% agree

95% disagree

Source: IGM Economic Experts Panel, February 7, 2012.

equilibrium levels. Whereas a price ceiling places a legal maximum on prices, a price floor places a legal minimum.

When the government imposes a price floor on the ice-cream market, two outcomes are possible. If the government imposes a price floor of $2 per cone when the equilibrium price is $3, we obtain the outcome in panel (a) of Figure 4. In this case, because the equilibrium price is above the floor, the price floor is not binding. Market forces naturally move the economy to the equilibrium, and the price floor has no effect.

Panel (b) of Figure 4 shows what happens when the government imposes a price floor of $4 per cone. In this case, because the equilibrium price of $3 is below the floor, the price floor is a binding constraint on the market. The forces of supply and demand tend to move the price toward the equilibrium price, but when the market price hits the floor, it can fall no further. The market price equals the price floor. At this floor, the quantity of ice cream supplied (120 cones) exceeds the quantity demanded (80 cones). Because of this excess supply of 40 cones, some people who want to sell ice cream at the going price are unable to. *Thus, a binding price floor causes a surplus.*

Just as the shortages resulting from price ceilings can lead to undesirable rationing mechanisms, so can the surpluses resulting from price floors. The sellers who appeal to the personal biases of the buyers, perhaps due to racial or familial ties, may be better able to sell their goods than those who do not. By contrast, in a free market, the price serves as the rationing mechanism, and sellers can sell all they want at the equilibrium price.

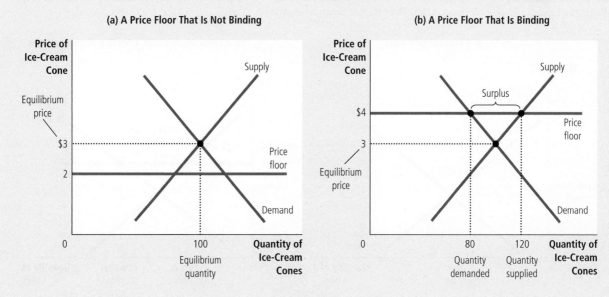

In panel (a), the government imposes a price floor of $2. Because this is below the equilibrium price of $3, the price floor has no effect. The market price adjusts to balance supply and demand. At the equilibrium, quantity supplied and quantity demanded both equal 100 cones. In panel (b), the government imposes a price floor of $4, which is above the equilibrium price of $3. Therefore, the market price equals $4. Because 120 cones are supplied at this price and only 80 are demanded, there is a surplus of 40 cones.

**FIGURE 4**

**A Market with a Price Floor**

**(a) A Price Floor That Is Not Binding**

**(b) A Price Floor That Is Binding**

### THE MINIMUM WAGE

**CASE STUDY**

An important example of a price floor is the minimum wage. Minimum-wage laws dictate the lowest price for labor that any employer may pay. The U.S. Congress first instituted a minimum wage with the Fair Labor Standards Act of 1938 to ensure workers a minimally adequate standard of living. In 2015, the minimum wage according to federal law was $7.25 per hour. (Some states mandate minimum wages above the federal level.) Many European nations have minimum-wage laws as well, sometimes significantly higher than in the United States. For example, even though the average income in France is almost 30 percent lower than it is in the United States, the French minimum wage is more than 30 percent higher.

To examine the effects of a minimum wage, we must consider the market for labor. Panel (a) of Figure 5 shows the labor market, which, like all markets, is subject to the forces of supply and demand. Workers determine the supply of labor, and firms determine the demand. If the government doesn't intervene, the wage normally adjusts to balance labor supply and labor demand.

Panel (b) of Figure 5 shows the labor market with a minimum wage. If the minimum wage is above the equilibrium level, as it is here, the quantity of labor supplied exceeds the quantity demanded. The result is unemployment. Thus, while the minimum wage raises the incomes of those workers who have jobs, it lowers the incomes of workers who cannot find jobs.

To fully understand the minimum wage, keep in mind that the economy contains not a single labor market but many labor markets for different types of workers. The impact of the minimum wage depends on the skill and experience of the worker. Highly skilled and experienced workers are not affected because their equilibrium wages are well above the minimum. For these workers, the minimum wage is not binding.

---

## FIGURE 5

**How the Minimum Wage Affects the Labor Market**

Panel (a) shows a labor market in which the wage adjusts to balance labor supply and labor demand. Panel (b) shows the impact of a binding minimum wage. Because the minimum wage is a price floor, it causes a surplus: The quantity of labor supplied exceeds the quantity demanded. The result is unemployment.

**(a) A Free Labor Market**

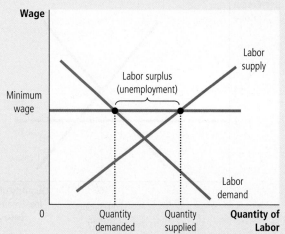

**(b) A Labor Market with a Binding Minimum Wage**

The minimum wage has its greatest impact on the market for teenage labor. The equilibrium wages of teenagers are low because teenagers are among the least skilled and least experienced members of the labor force. In addition, teenagers are often willing to accept a lower wage in exchange for on-the-job training. (Some teenagers, including many college students, are willing to work as interns for no pay at all. Because internships pay nothing, minimum-wage laws often do not apply to them. If they did, these internship opportunities might not exist.) As a result, the minimum wage is binding more often for teenagers than for other members of the labor force.

Many economists have studied how minimum-wage laws affect the teenage labor market. These researchers compare the changes in the minimum wage over time with the changes in teenage employment. Although there is some debate about how much the minimum wage affects employment, the typical study finds that a 10 percent increase in the minimum wage depresses teenage employment by 1 to 3 percent. In interpreting this estimate, note that a 10 percent increase in the minimum wage does not raise the average wage of teenagers by 10 percent. A change in the law does not directly affect those teenagers who are already paid well above the minimum, and enforcement of minimum-wage laws is not perfect. Thus, the estimated drop in employment of 1 to 3 percent is significant.

In addition to altering the quantity of labor demanded, the minimum wage alters the quantity supplied. Because the minimum wage raises the wage that teenagers can earn, it increases the number of teenagers who choose to look for jobs. Studies have found that a higher minimum wage influences which teenagers are employed. When the minimum wage rises, some teenagers who are still attending high school choose to drop out and take jobs. With more people vying for the available jobs, some of these new dropouts displace other teenagers who had already dropped out of school and now become unemployed.

The minimum wage is a frequent topic of debate. Advocates of the minimum wage view the policy as one way to raise the income of the working poor. They correctly point out that workers who earn the minimum wage can afford only a meager standard of living. In 2015, for instance, when the minimum wage was $7.25 per hour, two adults working 40 hours a week for every week of the year at minimum-wage jobs had a total annual income of only $30,160. This amount was 24 percent above the official poverty line for a family of four but was less than half of the median family income in the United States. Many advocates of the minimum wage admit that it has some adverse effects, including unemployment, but they believe that these effects are small and that, all things considered, a higher minimum wage makes the poor better off.

Opponents of the minimum wage contend that it is not the best way to combat poverty. They note that a high minimum wage causes unemployment, encourages teenagers to drop out of school, and prevents some unskilled workers from getting on-the-job training. Moreover, opponents of the minimum wage point out that it is a poorly targeted policy. Not all minimum-wage workers are heads of households trying to help their families escape poverty. In fact, less than a third of minimum-wage earners are in families with incomes below the

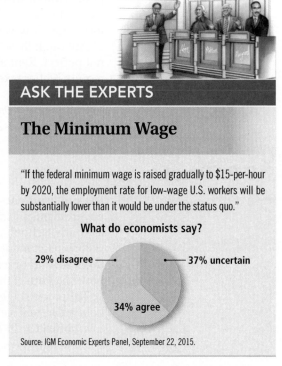

### ASK THE EXPERTS

## The Minimum Wage

"If the federal minimum wage is raised gradually to $15-per-hour by 2020, the employment rate for low-wage U.S. workers will be substantially lower than it would be under the status quo."

**What do economists say?**

29% disagree

37% uncertain

34% agree

Source: IGM Economic Experts Panel, September 22, 2015.

poverty line. Many are teenagers from middle-class homes working at part-time jobs for extra spending money. ●

### 6-1c  Evaluating Price Controls

One of the *Ten Principles of Economics* discussed in Chapter 1 is that markets are usually a good way to organize economic activity. This principle explains why economists usually oppose price ceilings and price floors. To economists, prices are not the outcome of some haphazard process. Prices, they contend, are the result of the millions of business and consumer decisions that lie behind the supply and demand curves. Prices have the crucial job of balancing supply and demand and, thereby, coordinating economic activity. When policymakers set prices by legal decree, they obscure the signals that normally guide the allocation of society's resources.

Another one of the *Ten Principles of Economics* is that governments can sometimes improve market outcomes. Indeed, policymakers are motivated to control prices because they view the market's outcome as unfair. Price controls are often aimed at helping the poor. For instance, rent-control laws try to make housing affordable for everyone, and minimum-wage laws try to help people escape poverty.

Yet price controls often hurt those they are trying to help. Rent control may keep rents low, but it also discourages landlords from maintaining their buildings and makes housing hard to find. Minimum-wage laws may raise the incomes of some workers, but they also cause other workers to become unemployed.

Helping those in need can be accomplished in ways other than controlling prices. For instance, the government can make housing more affordable by paying a fraction of the rent for poor families. Unlike rent control, such rent subsidies do not reduce the quantity of housing supplied and, therefore, do not lead to housing shortages. Similarly, wage subsidies raise the living standards of the working poor without discouraging firms from hiring them. An example of a wage subsidy is the *earned income tax credit*, a government program that supplements the incomes of low-wage workers.

Although these alternative policies are often better than price controls, they are not perfect. Rent and wage subsidies cost the government money and, therefore, require higher taxes. As we see in the next section, taxation has costs of its own.

 *Define price ceiling and price floor and give an example of each. Which leads to a shortage? Which leads to a surplus? Why?*

# 6-2  Taxes

All governments—from national governments around the world to local governments in small towns—use taxes to raise revenue for public projects, such as roads, schools, and national defense. Because taxes are such an important policy instrument and affect our lives in many ways, we return to the study of taxes several times throughout this book. In this section, we begin our study of how taxes affect the economy.

To set the stage for our analysis, imagine that a local government decides to hold an annual ice-cream celebration—with a parade, fireworks, and speeches by town officials. To raise revenue to pay for the event, the town decides to place a $0.50 tax on the sale of ice-cream cones. When the plan is announced, our two lobbying groups swing into action. The American Association of Ice-Cream Eaters claims that consumers of ice cream are having trouble making ends meet, and it argues that *sellers* of ice cream should pay the tax. The National Organization of Ice-Cream Makers claims that its members are struggling to survive in a competitive market, and it argues that *buyers* of ice cream should pay the tax. The town mayor, hoping to reach a compromise, suggests that half the tax be paid by the buyers and half be paid by the sellers.

To analyze these proposals, we need to address a simple but subtle question: When the government levies a tax on a good, who actually bears the burden of the tax? The people buying the good? The people selling the good? Or if buyers and sellers share the tax burden, what determines how the burden is divided? Can the government simply legislate the division of the burden, as the mayor is suggesting, or is the division determined by more fundamental market forces? The term **tax incidence** refers to how the burden of a tax is distributed among the various people who make up the economy. As we will see, some surprising lessons about tax incidence can be learned by applying the tools of supply and demand.

**tax incidence**
the manner in which the burden of a tax is shared among participants in a market

## 6-2a How Taxes on Sellers Affect Market Outcomes

We begin by considering a tax levied on sellers of a good. Suppose the local government passes a law requiring sellers of ice-cream cones to send $0.50 to the government for every cone they sell. How does this law affect the buyers and sellers of ice cream? To answer this question, we can follow the three steps in Chapter 4 for analyzing supply and demand: (1) We decide whether the law affects the supply curve or the demand curve. (2) We decide which way the curve shifts. (3) We examine how the shift affects the equilibrium price and quantity.

**Step One**   The immediate impact of the tax is on the sellers of ice cream. Because the tax is not levied on buyers, the quantity of ice cream demanded at any given price is the same; thus, the demand curve does not change. By contrast, the tax on sellers makes the ice-cream business less profitable at any given price, so it shifts the supply curve.

**Step Two**   Because the tax on sellers raises the cost of producing and selling ice cream, it reduces the quantity supplied at every price. The supply curve shifts to the left (or, equivalently, upward).

In addition to determining the direction in which the supply curve moves, we can also be precise about the size of the shift. For any market price of ice cream, the effective price to sellers—the amount they get to keep after paying the tax—is $0.50 lower. For example, if the market price of a cone happened to be $2.00, the effective price received by sellers would be $1.50. Whatever the market price, sellers will supply a quantity of ice cream as if the price were $0.50 lower than it is. Put differently, to induce sellers to supply any given quantity, the market price must now be $0.50 higher to compensate for the effect of the tax. Thus, as shown in Figure 6, the supply curve shifts *upward* from $S_1$ to $S_2$ by the exact size of the tax ($0.50).

**Step Three**   Having determined how the supply curve shifts, we can now compare the initial and the new equilibriums. Figure 6 shows that the equilibrium price of ice cream rises from $3.00 to $3.30, and the equilibrium quantity falls from 100 to 90 cones. Because sellers sell less and buyers buy less in the new equilibrium, the tax reduces the size of the ice-cream market.

## FIGURE 6

**A Tax on Sellers**

When a tax of $0.50 is levied on sellers, the supply curve shifts up by $0.50 from $S_1$ to $S_2$. The equilibrium quantity falls from 100 to 90 cones. The price that buyers pay rises from $3.00 to $3.30. The price that sellers receive (after paying the tax) falls from $3.00 to $2.80. Even though the tax is levied on sellers, buyers and sellers share the burden of the tax.

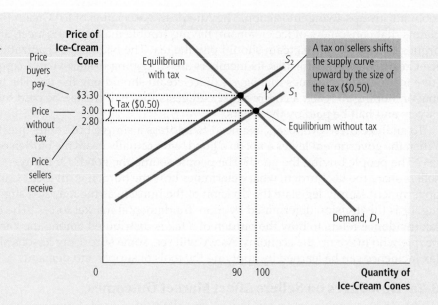

**Implications**   We can now return to the question of tax incidence: Who pays the tax? Although sellers send the entire tax to the government, buyers and sellers share the burden. Because the market price rises from $3.00 to $3.30 when the tax is introduced, buyers pay $0.30 more for each ice-cream cone than they did without the tax. Thus, the tax makes buyers worse off. Sellers get a higher price ($3.30) from buyers than they did previously, but what they get to keep after paying the tax is only $2.80 ($3.30 − $0.50 = $2.80), compared with $3.00 before the tax. Thus, the tax also makes sellers worse off.

To sum up, this analysis yields two lessons:

- Taxes discourage market activity. When a good is taxed, the quantity of the good sold is smaller in the new equilibrium.
- Buyers and sellers share the burden of taxes. In the new equilibrium, buyers pay more for the good, and sellers receive less.

### 6-2b  How Taxes on Buyers Affect Market Outcomes

Now consider a tax levied on buyers of a good. Suppose that our local government passes a law requiring buyers of ice-cream cones to send $0.50 to the government for each ice-cream cone they buy. What are the effects of this law? Again, we apply our three steps.

**Step One**   The initial impact of the tax is on the demand for ice cream. The supply curve is not affected because, for any given price of ice cream, sellers have the same incentive to provide ice cream to the market. By contrast, buyers now have to pay a tax to the government (as well as the price to the sellers) whenever they buy ice cream. Thus, the tax shifts the demand curve for ice cream.

**Step Two**   Next, we determine the direction of the shift. Because the tax on buyers makes buying ice cream less attractive, buyers demand a smaller quantity of ice cream at every price. As a result, the demand curve shifts to the left (or, equivalently, downward), as shown in Figure 7.

Once again, we can be precise about the size of the shift. Because of the $0.50 tax levied on buyers, the effective price to buyers is now $0.50 higher than the market price (whatever the market price happens to be). For example, if the market price of a cone happened to be $2.00, the effective price to buyers would be $2.50. Because buyers look at their total cost including the tax, they demand a quantity of ice cream as if the market price were $0.50 higher than it actually is. In other words, to induce buyers to demand any given quantity, the market price must now be $0.50 lower to make up for the effect of the tax. Thus, the tax shifts the demand curve *downward* from $D_1$ to $D_2$ by the exact size of the tax ($0.50).

**Step Three**  Having determined how the demand curve shifts, we can now see the effect of the tax by comparing the initial equilibrium and the new equilibrium. You can see in Figure 7 that the equilibrium price of ice cream falls from $3.00 to $2.80, and the equilibrium quantity falls from 100 to 90 cones. Once again, the tax on ice cream reduces the size of the ice-cream market. And once again, buyers and sellers share the burden of the tax. Sellers get a lower price for their product; buyers pay a lower market price to sellers than they did previously, but the effective price (including the tax buyers have to pay) rises from $3.00 to $3.30.

**Implications**  If you compare Figures 6 and 7, you will notice a surprising conclusion: *Taxes levied on sellers and taxes levied on buyers are equivalent*. In both cases, the tax places a wedge between the price that buyers pay and the price that sellers receive. The wedge between the buyers' price and the sellers' price is the same, regardless of whether the tax is levied on buyers or sellers. In either case, the wedge shifts the relative position of the supply and demand curves. In the new equilibrium, buyers and sellers share the burden of the tax. The only difference between a tax levied on sellers and a tax levied on buyers is who sends the money to the government.

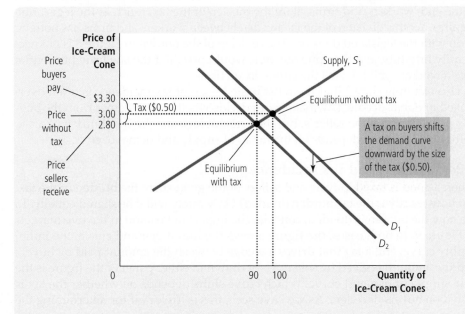

## FIGURE 7

**A Tax on Buyers**
When a tax of $0.50 is levied on buyers, the demand curve shifts down by $0.50 from $D_1$ to $D_2$. The equilibrium quantity falls from 100 to 90 cones. The price that sellers receive falls from $3.00 to $2.80. The price that buyers pay (including the tax) rises from $3.00 to $3.30. Even though the tax is levied on buyers, buyers and sellers share the burden of the tax.

The equivalence of these two taxes is easy to understand if we imagine that the government collects the $0.50 ice-cream tax in a bowl on the counter of each ice-cream store. When the government levies the tax on sellers, the seller is required to place $0.50 in the bowl after the sale of each cone. When the government levies the tax on buyers, the buyer is required to place $0.50 in the bowl every time a cone is bought. Whether the $0.50 goes directly from the buyer's pocket into the bowl, or indirectly from the buyer's pocket into the seller's hand and then into the bowl, does not matter. Once the market reaches its new equilibrium, buyers and sellers share the burden, regardless of how the tax is levied.

### CASE STUDY

**CAN CONGRESS DISTRIBUTE THE BURDEN OF A PAYROLL TAX?**

If you have ever received a paycheck, you probably noticed that taxes were deducted from the amount you earned. One of these taxes is called FICA, an acronym for the Federal Insurance Contributions Act. The federal government uses the revenue from the FICA tax to pay for Social Security and Medicare, the income support and healthcare programs for the elderly. FICA is an example of a *payroll tax*, which is a tax on the wages that firms pay their workers. In 2015, the total FICA tax for the typical worker was 15.3 percent of earnings.

Who do you think bears the burden of this payroll tax—firms or workers? When Congress passed this legislation, it tried to mandate a division of the tax burden. According to the law, half of the tax is paid by firms, and half is paid by workers. That is, half of the tax is paid out of firms' revenues, and half is deducted from workers' paychecks. The amount that shows up as a deduction on your pay stub is the worker contribution.

Our analysis of tax incidence, however, shows that lawmakers cannot dictate the distribution of a tax burden so easily. To illustrate, we can analyze a payroll tax as merely a tax on a good, where the good is labor and the price is the wage. The key feature of the payroll tax is that it places a wedge between the wage that firms pay and the wage that workers receive. Figure 8 shows the outcome. When a payroll tax is enacted, the wage received by workers falls, and the wage paid by firms rises. In the end, workers and firms share the burden of the tax, much as the legislation requires. Yet this division of the tax burden between workers and firms has nothing to do with the legislated division: The division of the burden in Figure 8 is not necessarily fifty-fifty, and the same outcome would prevail if the law levied the entire tax on workers or if it levied the entire tax on firms.

This example shows that the most basic lesson of tax incidence is often overlooked in public debate. Lawmakers can decide whether a tax comes from the buyer's pocket or from the seller's, but they cannot legislate the true burden of a tax. Rather, tax incidence depends on the forces of supply and demand. ●

### 6-2c Elasticity and Tax Incidence

When a good is taxed, buyers and sellers of the good share the burden of the tax. But how exactly is the tax burden divided? Only rarely will it be shared equally. To see how the burden is divided, consider the impact of taxation in the two markets in Figure 9. In both cases, the figure shows the initial demand curve, the initial supply curve, and a tax that drives a wedge between the amount paid by buyers and the amount received by sellers. (Not drawn in either panel of the figure is the new supply or demand curve. Which curve shifts depends on whether the tax is levied on buyers or sellers. As we have seen, this is irrelevant for determining the

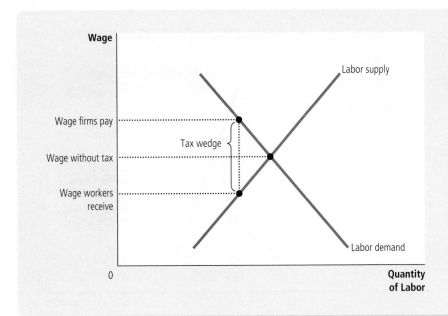

**FIGURE 8**

**A Payroll Tax**
A payroll tax places a wedge between the wage that workers receive and the wage that firms pay. Comparing wages with and without the tax, you can see that workers and firms share the tax burden. This division of the tax burden between workers and firms does not depend on whether the government levies the tax on workers, levies the tax on firms, or divides the tax equally between the two groups.

incidence of the tax.) The difference in the two panels is the relative elasticity of supply and demand.

Panel (a) of Figure 9 shows a tax in a market with very elastic supply and relatively inelastic demand. That is, sellers are very responsive to changes in the price of the good (so the supply curve is relatively flat), whereas buyers are not very responsive (so the demand curve is relatively steep). When a tax is imposed on a market with these elasticities, the price received by sellers does not fall by much, so sellers bear only a small burden. By contrast, the price paid by buyers rises substantially, indicating that buyers bear most of the burden of the tax.

Panel (b) of Figure 9 shows a tax in a market with relatively inelastic supply and very elastic demand. In this case, sellers are not very responsive to changes in the price (so the supply curve is steeper), whereas buyers are very responsive (so the demand curve is flatter). The figure shows that when a tax is imposed, the price paid by buyers does not rise by much, but the price received by sellers falls substantially. Thus, sellers bear most of the burden of the tax.

The two panels of Figure 9 show a general lesson about how the burden of a tax is divided: *A tax burden falls more heavily on the side of the market that is less elastic.* Why is this true? In essence, the elasticity measures the willingness of buyers or sellers to leave the market when conditions become unfavorable. A small elasticity of demand means that buyers do not have good alternatives to consuming this particular good. A small elasticity of supply means that sellers do not have good alternatives to producing this particular good. When the good is taxed, the side of the market with fewer good alternatives is less willing to leave the market and, therefore, bears more of the burden of the tax.

We can apply this logic to the payroll tax discussed in the previous case study. Most labor economists believe that the supply of labor is much less elastic than the demand. This means that workers, rather than firms, bear most of the burden of the payroll tax. In other words, the distribution of the tax burden is far from the fifty-fifty split that lawmakers intended.

## FIGURE 9

**How the Burden of a Tax Is Divided**
In panel (a), the supply curve is elastic, and the demand curve is inelastic. In this case, the price received by sellers falls only slightly, while the price paid by buyers rises substantially. Thus, buyers bear most of the burden of the tax. In panel (b), the supply curve is inelastic, and the demand curve is elastic. In this case, the price received by sellers falls substantially, while the price paid by buyers rises only slightly. Thus, sellers bear most of the burden of the tax.

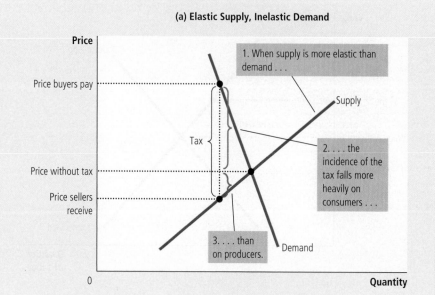

**(a) Elastic Supply, Inelastic Demand**

1. When supply is more elastic than demand . . .

2. . . . the incidence of the tax falls more heavily on consumers . . .

3. . . . than on producers.

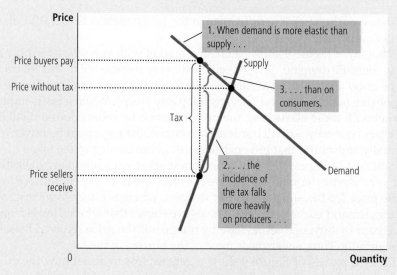

**(b) Inelastic Supply, Elastic Demand**

1. When demand is more elastic than supply . . .

3. . . . than on consumers.

2. . . . the incidence of the tax falls more heavily on producers . . .

**CASE STUDY**

**WHO PAYS THE LUXURY TAX?**

In 1990, Congress adopted a new luxury tax on items such as yachts, private airplanes, furs, jewelry, and expensive cars. The goal of the tax was to raise revenue from those who could most easily afford to pay. Because only the rich could afford to buy such extravagances, taxing luxuries seemed a logical way of taxing the rich.

Yet, when the forces of supply and demand took over, the outcome was quite different from the one Congress intended. Consider, for example, the market for yachts. The demand for yachts is quite elastic. A millionaire can easily not buy a yacht; he can use the money to buy a bigger house, take a European vacation, or leave a larger bequest to his heirs. By contrast, the supply of yachts is relatively inelastic, at least in the short run. Yacht factories are not easily converted to alternative uses, and workers who build yachts are not eager to change careers in response to changing market conditions.

Our analysis makes a clear prediction in this case. With elastic demand and inelastic supply, the burden of a tax falls largely on the suppliers. That is, a tax on yachts places a burden largely on the firms and workers who build yachts because they end up getting a significantly lower price for their product. The workers, however, are not wealthy. Thus, the burden of a luxury tax falls more on the middle class than on the rich.

The mistaken assumptions about the incidence of the luxury tax quickly became apparent after the tax went into effect. Suppliers of luxuries made their congressional representatives well aware of the economic hardship they experienced, and Congress repealed most of the luxury tax in 1993. ●

*"If this boat were any more expensive, we'd be playing golf."*

**QuickQuiz**  *In a supply-and-demand diagram, show how a tax on car buyers of $1,000 per car affects the quantity of cars sold and the price of cars. In another diagram, show how a tax on car sellers of $1,000 per car affects the quantity of cars sold and the price of cars. In both of your diagrams, show the change in the price paid by car buyers and the change in the price received by car sellers.*

# 6-3 Conclusion

The economy is governed by two kinds of laws: the laws of supply and demand and the laws enacted by governments. In this chapter, we have begun to see how these laws interact. Price controls and taxes are common in various markets in the economy, and their effects are frequently debated in the press and among policymakers. Even a little bit of economic knowledge can go a long way toward understanding and evaluating these policies.

In subsequent chapters, we analyze many government policies in greater detail. We examine the effects of taxation more fully and consider a broader range of policies than we considered here. Yet the basic lessons of this chapter will not change: When analyzing government policies, supply and demand are the first and most useful tools of analysis.

## CHAPTER QuickQuiz

1. When the government imposes a binding price floor, it causes
   a. the supply curve to shift to the left.
   b. the demand curve to shift to the right.
   c. a shortage of the good to develop.
   d. a surplus of the good to develop.

2. In a market with a binding price ceiling, an increase in the ceiling will _____ the quantity supplied, _____ the quantity demanded, and reduce the _____.
   a. increase, decrease, surplus
   b. decrease, increase, surplus
   c. increase, decrease, shortage
   d. decrease, increase, shortage

3.  A $1 per unit tax levied on consumers of a good is
    equivalent to
    a.  a $1 per unit tax levied on producers of the good.
    b.  a $1 per unit subsidy paid to producers of the good.
    c.  a price floor that raises the good's price by
        $1 per unit.
    d.  a price ceiling that raises the good's price by
        $1 per unit.

4.  Which of the following would increase quantity
    supplied, decrease quantity demanded, and increase
    the price that consumers pay?
    a.  the imposition of a binding price floor
    b.  the removal of a binding price floor
    c.  the passage of a tax levied on producers
    d.  the repeal of a tax levied on producers

5.  Which of the following would increase quantity
    supplied, increase quantity demanded, and decrease
    the price that consumers pay?
    a.  the imposition of a binding price floor
    b.  the removal of a binding price floor
    c.  the passage of a tax levied on producers
    d.  the repeal of a tax levied on producers

6.  When a good is taxed, the burden of the tax falls
    mainly on consumers if
    a.  the tax is levied on consumers.
    b.  the tax is levied on producers.
    c.  supply is inelastic, and demand is elastic.
    d.  supply is elastic, and demand is inelastic.

## SUMMARY

- A price ceiling is a legal maximum on the price of a
  good or service. An example is rent control. If the price
  ceiling is below the equilibrium price, then the price
  ceiling is binding, and the quantity demanded exceeds
  the quantity supplied. Because of the resulting shortage, sellers must in some way ration the good or service among buyers.

- A price floor is a legal minimum on the price of a
  good or service. An example is the minimum wage.
  If the price floor is above the equilibrium price, then
  the price floor is binding, and the quantity supplied
  exceeds the quantity demanded. Because of the resulting surplus, buyers' demands for the good or service
  must in some way be rationed among sellers.

- When the government levies a tax on a good, the equilibrium quantity of the good falls. That is, a tax on a
  market shrinks the size of the market.

- A tax on a good places a wedge between the price paid
  by buyers and the price received by sellers. When the
  market moves to the new equilibrium, buyers pay
  more for the good and sellers receive less for it. In this
  sense, buyers and sellers share the tax burden. The
  incidence of a tax (that is, the division of the tax burden) does not depend on whether the tax is levied on
  buyers or sellers.

- The incidence of a tax depends on the price elasticities
  of supply and demand. Most of the burden falls on the
  side of the market that is less elastic because that side
  of the market cannot respond as easily to the tax by
  changing the quantity bought or sold.

## KEY CONCEPTS

price ceiling, p. 112               price floor, p. 112                    tax incidence, p. 121

## QUESTIONS FOR REVIEW

1.  Give an example of a price ceiling and an example of
    a price floor.

2.  Which causes a shortage of a good—a price ceiling or
    a price floor? Justify your answer with a graph.

3.  What mechanisms allocate resources when the price
    of a good is not allowed to bring supply and demand
    into equilibrium?

4.  Explain why economists usually oppose controls on
    prices.

5.  Suppose the government removes a tax on buyers of a
    good and levies a tax of the same size on sellers of the
    good. How does this change in tax policy affect the price
    that buyers pay sellers for this good, the amount buy-
    ers are out of pocket (including any tax payments they

make), the amount sellers receive (net of any tax payments they make), and the quantity of the good sold?

6. How does a tax on a good affect the price paid by buyers, the price received by sellers, and the quantity sold?

7. What determines how the burden of a tax is divided between buyers and sellers? Why?

## PROBLEMS AND APPLICATIONS

1. Lovers of classical music persuade Congress to impose a price ceiling of $40 per concert ticket. As a result of this policy, do more or fewer people attend classical music concerts? Explain.

2. The government has decided that the free-market price of cheese is too low.
   a. Suppose the government imposes a binding price floor in the cheese market. Draw a supply-and-demand diagram to show the effect of this policy on the price of cheese and the quantity of cheese sold. Is there a shortage or surplus of cheese?
   b. Producers of cheese complain that the price floor has reduced their total revenue. Is this possible? Explain.
   c. In response to cheese producers' complaints, the government agrees to purchase all the surplus cheese at the price floor. Compared to the basic price floor, who benefits from this new policy? Who loses?

3. A recent study found that the demand-and-supply schedules for Frisbees are as follows:

| Price per Frisbee | Quantity Demanded | Quantity Supplied |
|---|---|---|
| $11 | 1 million Frisbees | 15 million Frisbees |
| 10 | 2 | 12 |
| 9 | 4 | 9 |
| 8 | 6 | 6 |
| 7 | 8 | 3 |
| 6 | 10 | 1 |

   a. What are the equilibrium price and quantity of Frisbees?
   b. Frisbee manufacturers persuade the government that Frisbee production improves scientists' understanding of aerodynamics and thus is important for national security. A concerned Congress votes to impose a price floor $2 above the equilibrium price. What is the new market price? How many Frisbees are sold?
   c. Irate college students march on Washington and demand a reduction in the price of Frisbees. An even more concerned Congress votes to repeal the

price floor and impose a price ceiling $1 below the former price floor. What is the new market price? How many Frisbees are sold?

4. Suppose the federal government requires beer drinkers to pay a $2 tax on each case of beer purchased. (In fact, both the federal and state governments impose beer taxes of some sort.)
   a. Draw a supply-and-demand diagram of the market for beer without the tax. Show the price paid by consumers, the price received by producers, and the quantity of beer sold. What is the difference between the price paid by consumers and the price received by producers?
   b. Now draw a supply-and-demand diagram for the beer market with the tax. Show the price paid by consumers, the price received by producers, and the quantity of beer sold. What is the difference between the price paid by consumers and the price received by producers? Has the quantity of beer sold increased or decreased?

5. A senator wants to raise tax revenue and make workers better off. A staff member proposes raising the payroll tax paid by firms and using part of the extra revenue to reduce the payroll tax paid by workers. Would this accomplish the senator's goal? Explain.

6. If the government places a $500 tax on luxury cars, will the price paid by consumers rise by more than $500, less than $500, or exactly $500? Explain.

7. Congress and the president decide that the United States should reduce air pollution by reducing its use of gasoline. They impose a $0.50 tax on each gallon of gasoline sold.
   a. Should they impose this tax on producers or consumers? Explain carefully using a supply-and-demand diagram.
   b. If the demand for gasoline were more elastic, would this tax be more effective or less effective in reducing the quantity of gasoline consumed? Explain with both words and a diagram.
   c. Are consumers of gasoline helped or hurt by this tax? Why?
   d. Are workers in the oil industry helped or hurt by this tax? Why?

8. A case study in this chapter discusses the federal minimum-wage law.

   a. Suppose the minimum wage is above the equilibrium wage in the market for unskilled labor. Using a supply-and-demand diagram of the market for unskilled labor, show the market wage, the number of workers who are employed, and the number of workers who are unemployed. Also show the total wage payments to unskilled workers.

   b. Now suppose the secretary of labor proposes an increase in the minimum wage. What effect would this increase have on employment? Does the change in employment depend on the elasticity of demand, the elasticity of supply, both elasticities, or neither?

   c. What effect would this increase in the minimum wage have on unemployment? Does the change in unemployment depend on the elasticity of demand, the elasticity of supply, both elasticities, or neither?

   d. If the demand for unskilled labor were inelastic, would the proposed increase in the minimum wage raise or lower total wage payments to unskilled workers? Would your answer change if the demand for unskilled labor were elastic?

9. At Fenway Park, home of the Boston Red Sox, seating is limited to about 38,000. Hence, the number of tickets issued is fixed at that figure. Seeing a golden opportunity to raise revenue, the City of Boston levies a per ticket tax of $5 to be paid by the ticket buyer. Boston sports fans, a famously civic-minded lot, dutifully send in the $5 per ticket. Draw a well-labeled graph showing the impact of the tax. On whom does the tax burden fall—the team's owners, the fans, or both? Why?

10. A market is described by the following supply and demand curves:

$$Q^S = 2P$$
$$Q^D = 300 - P$$

   a. Solve for the equilibrium price and quantity.

   b. If the government imposes a price ceiling of $90, does a shortage or surplus (or neither) develop? What are the price, quantity supplied, quantity demanded, and size of the shortage or surplus?

   c. If the government imposes a price floor of $90, does a shortage or surplus (or neither) develop? What are the price, quantity supplied, quantity demanded, and size of the shortage or surplus?

   d. Instead of a price control, the government levies a tax on producers of $30. As a result, the new supply curve is:

$$Q^S = 2(P - 30).$$

   Does a shortage or surplus (or neither) develop? What are the price, quantity supplied, quantity demanded, and size of the shortage or surplus?

To find additional study resources, visit cengagebrain.com, and search for "Mankiw."

# PART III

# Markets and Welfare

# Consumers, Producers, and the Efficiency of Markets

When consumers go to grocery stores to buy food for Thanksgiving dinner, they may be disappointed see the high price of turkey. At the same time, when farmers bring to market the turkeys they have raised, they probably wish that the price of turkey were even higher. These views are not surprising: Buyers always want to pay less, and sellers always want to be paid more. But is there a "right price" for turkey from the standpoint of society as a whole?

In previous chapters, we saw how, in market economies, the forces of supply and demand determine the prices of goods and services and the quantities sold.

So far, however, we have described the way markets allocate scarce resources without directly addressing the question of whether these market allocations are desirable. In other words, our analysis has been *positive* (what is) rather than *normative* (what should be). We know that the price of turkey adjusts to ensure that the quantity of turkey supplied equals the quantity of turkey demanded. But at this equilibrium, is the quantity of turkey produced and consumed too small, too large, or just right?

**welfare economics**
the study of how the allocation of resources affects economic well-being

In this chapter, we take up the topic of **welfare economics**, the study of how the allocation of resources affects economic well-being. We begin by examining the benefits that buyers and sellers receive from engaging in market transactions. We then examine how society can make these benefits as large as possible. This analysis leads to a profound conclusion: In any market, the equilibrium of supply and demand maximizes the total benefits received by all buyers and sellers combined.

As you may recall from Chapter 1, one of the *Ten Principles of Economics* is that markets are usually a good way to organize economic activity. The study of welfare economics explains this principle more fully. It also answers our question about the right price of turkey: The price that balances the supply and demand for turkey is, in a particular sense, the best one because it maximizes the total welfare of turkey consumers and turkey producers. No consumer or producer of turkeys aims to achieve this goal, but their joint action directed by market prices moves them toward a welfare-maximizing outcome, as if led by an invisible hand.

# 7-1 Consumer Surplus

We begin our study of welfare economics by looking at the benefits buyers receive from participating in a market.

### 7-1a  Willingness to Pay

Imagine that you own a mint-condition recording of Elvis Presley's first album. Because you are not an Elvis Presley fan, you decide to sell it. One way to do so is to hold an auction.

Four Elvis fans show up for your auction: Taylor, Carrie, Rihanna, and Gaga. They would all like to own the album, but each of them has a limit on the amount she is willing to pay for it. Table 1 shows the maximum price that each of the four possible buyers would pay. A buyer's maximum is called her **willingness to pay**, and it measures how much that buyer values the good. Each buyer would be eager to buy the album at a price less than her willingness to pay, and she would refuse to buy the album at a price greater than her willingness to pay. At a price

**willingness to pay**
the maximum amount that a buyer will pay for a good

## TABLE 1

Four Possible Buyers' Willingness to Pay

| Buyer | Willingness to Pay |
|---|---|
| Taylor | $100 |
| Carrie | 80 |
| Rihanna | 70 |
| Gaga | 50 |

equal to her willingness to pay, the buyer would be indifferent about buying the good: If the price is exactly the same as the value she places on the album, she would be equally happy buying it or keeping her money.

To sell your album, you begin the bidding process at a low price, say, $10. Because all four buyers are willing to pay much more, the price rises quickly. The bidding stops when Taylor bids $80 (or slightly more). At this point, Carrie, Rihanna, and Gaga have all dropped out of the bidding because they are unwilling to bid any more than $80. Taylor pays you $80 and gets the album. Note that the album has gone to the buyer who values it most highly.

What benefit does Taylor receive from buying the Elvis Presley album? In a sense, Taylor has found a real bargain: She is willing to pay $100 for the album but pays only $80. We say that Taylor receives *consumer surplus* of $20. **Consumer surplus** is the amount a buyer is willing to pay for a good minus the amount the buyer actually pays for it.

Consumer surplus measures the benefit buyers receive from participating in a market. In this example, Taylor receives a $20 benefit from participating in the auction because she pays only $80 for a good she values at $100. Carrie, Rihanna, and Gaga get no consumer surplus from participating in the auction because they left without the album and without paying anything.

Now consider a somewhat different example. Suppose that you had two identical Elvis Presley albums to sell. Again, you auction them off to the four possible buyers. To keep things simple, we assume that both albums are to be sold for the same price and that no one is interested in buying more than one album. Therefore, the price rises until two buyers are left.

In this case, the bidding stops when Taylor and Carrie bid $70 (or slightly higher). At this price, Taylor and Carrie are each happy to buy an album, and Rihanna and Gaga are not willing to bid any higher. Taylor and Carrie each receive consumer surplus equal to her willingness to pay minus the price. Taylor's consumer surplus is $30, and Carrie's is $10. Taylor's consumer surplus is higher now than in the previous example because she gets the same album but pays less for it. The total consumer surplus in the market is $40.

### 7-1b Using the Demand Curve to Measure Consumer Surplus

Consumer surplus is closely related to the demand curve for a product. To see how they are related, let's continue our example and consider the demand curve for this rare Elvis Presley album.

We begin by using the willingness to pay of the four possible buyers to find the market demand schedule for the album. The table in Figure 1 shows the demand schedule that corresponds to Table 1. If the price is above $100, the quantity demanded in the market is 0 because no buyer is willing to pay that much. If the price is between $80 and $100, the quantity demanded is 1 because only Taylor is willing to pay such a high price. If the price is between $70 and $80, the quantity demanded is 2 because both Taylor and Carrie are willing to pay the price. We can continue this analysis for other prices as well. In this way, the demand schedule is derived from the willingness to pay of the four possible buyers.

The graph in Figure 1 shows the demand curve that corresponds to this demand schedule. Note the relationship between the height of the demand curve and the buyers' willingness to pay. At any quantity, the price given by the demand curve shows the willingness to pay of the *marginal buyer*, the buyer who would leave the market first if the price were any higher. At a quantity of 4 albums, for instance, the demand curve has a height of $50, the price that Gaga

**consumer surplus**
the amount a buyer is willing to pay for a good minus the amount the buyer actually pays for it

## FIGURE 1

**The Demand Schedule and the Demand Curve**

The table shows the demand schedule for the buyers (listed in Table 1) of the mint-condition copy of Elvis Presley's first album. The graph shows the corresponding demand curve. Note that the height of the demand curve reflects the buyers' willingness to pay.

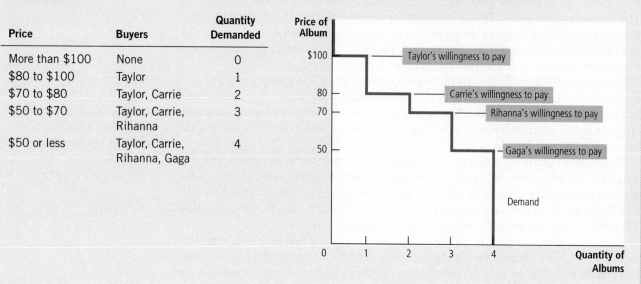

| Price | Buyers | Quantity Demanded |
|---|---|---|
| More than $100 | None | 0 |
| $80 to $100 | Taylor | 1 |
| $70 to $80 | Taylor, Carrie | 2 |
| $50 to $70 | Taylor, Carrie, Rihanna | 3 |
| $50 or less | Taylor, Carrie, Rihanna, Gaga | 4 |

(the marginal buyer) is willing to pay for an album. At a quantity of 3 albums, the demand curve has a height of $70, the price that Rihanna (who is now the marginal buyer) is willing to pay.

Because the demand curve reflects buyers' willingness to pay, we can also use it to measure consumer surplus. Figure 2 uses the demand curve to compute consumer surplus in our two examples. In panel (a), the price is $80 (or slightly above) and the quantity demanded is 1. Note that the area above the price and below the demand curve equals $20. This amount is exactly the consumer surplus we computed earlier when only 1 album is sold.

Panel (b) of Figure 2 shows consumer surplus when the price is $70 (or slightly above). In this case, the area above the price and below the demand curve equals the total area of the two rectangles: Taylor's consumer surplus at this price is $30 and Carrie's is $10. This area equals a total of $40. Once again, this amount is the consumer surplus we computed earlier.

The lesson from this example holds for all demand curves: *The area below the demand curve and above the price measures the consumer surplus in a market.* This is true because the height of the demand curve represents the value buyers place on the good, as measured by their willingness to pay for it. The difference between this willingness to pay and the market price is each buyer's consumer surplus. Thus, the total area below the demand curve and above the price is the sum of the consumer surplus of all buyers in the market for a good or service.

### 7-1c How a Lower Price Raises Consumer Surplus

Because buyers always want to pay less for the goods they buy, a lower price makes buyers of a good better off. But how much does buyers' well-being rise in response to a lower price? We can use the concept of consumer surplus to answer this question precisely.

In panel (a), the price of the good is $80 and the consumer surplus is $20.
In panel (b), the price of the good is $70 and the consumer surplus is $40.

**FIGURE 2**

**Measuring Consumer Surplus with the Demand Curve**

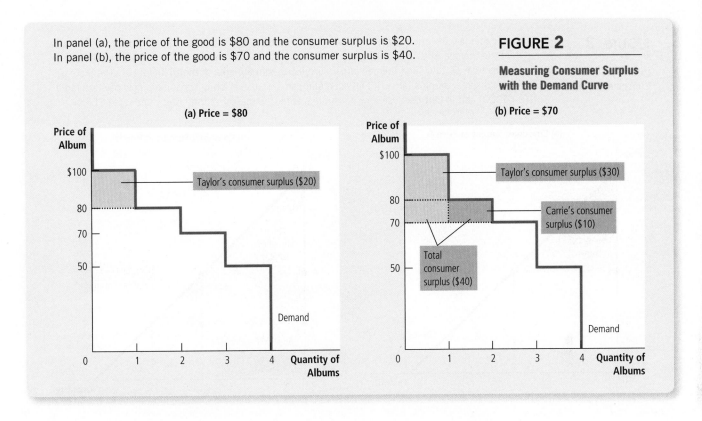

Figure 3 shows a typical demand curve. You may notice that this curve gradually slopes downward instead of taking discrete steps as in the previous two figures. In a market with many buyers, the resulting steps from each buyer dropping out are so small that they form a smooth curve. Although this curve has a different shape, the ideas we have just developed still apply: Consumer surplus is the area above the price and below the demand curve. In panel (a), consumer surplus at a price of $P_1$ is the area of triangle ABC.

Now suppose that the price falls from $P_1$ to $P_2$, as shown in panel (b). The consumer surplus now equals area ADF. The increase in consumer surplus attributable to the lower price is the area BCFD.

This increase in consumer surplus is composed of two parts. First, those buyers who were already buying $Q_1$ of the good at the higher price $P_1$ are better off because now they pay less. The increase in consumer surplus of existing buyers is the reduction in the amount they pay; it equals the area of the rectangle BCED. Second, some new buyers enter the market because they are willing to buy the good at the lower price. As a result, the quantity demanded in the market increases from $Q_1$ to $Q_2$. The consumer surplus these newcomers receive is the area of the triangle CEF.

### 7-1d What Does Consumer Surplus Measure?

Our goal in developing the concept of consumer surplus is to make judgments about the desirability of market outcomes. Now that you have seen what consumer surplus is, let's consider whether it is a good measure of economic well-being.

Imagine that you are a policymaker trying to design a good economic system. Would you care about the amount of consumer surplus? Consumer

**FIGURE 3**

**How Price Affects Consumer Surplus**

In panel (a), the price is $P_1$, the quantity demanded is $Q_1$, and consumer surplus equals the area of the triangle ABC. When the price falls from $P_1$ to $P_2$, as in panel (b), the quantity demanded rises from $Q_1$ to $Q_2$ and the consumer surplus rises to the area of the triangle ADF. The increase in consumer surplus (area BCFD) occurs in part because existing consumers now pay less (area BCED) and in part because new consumers enter the market at the lower price (area CEF).

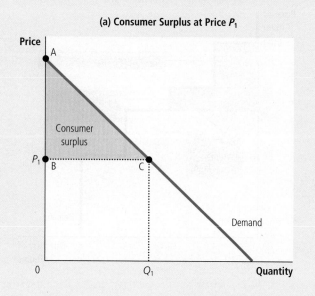

**(a) Consumer Surplus at Price $P_1$**

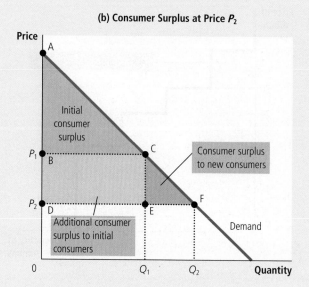

**(b) Consumer Surplus at Price $P_2$**

surplus, the amount that buyers are willing to pay for a good minus the amount they actually pay for it, measures the benefit that buyers receive from a good *as the buyers themselves perceive it*. Thus, consumer surplus is a good measure of economic well-being if policymakers want to satisfy the preferences of buyers.

In some circumstances, policymakers might choose to disregard consumer surplus because they do not respect the preferences that drive buyer behavior. For example, drug addicts are willing to pay a high price for heroin. Yet we would not say that addicts get a large benefit from being able to buy heroin at a low price (even though addicts might say they do). From the standpoint of society, willingness to pay in this instance is not a good measure of the buyers' benefit, and consumer surplus is not a good measure of economic well-being, because addicts are not looking after their own best interests.

In most markets, however, consumer surplus does reflect economic well-being. Economists normally assume that buyers are rational when they make decisions. Rational people do the best they can to achieve their objectives, given their opportunities. Economists also normally assume that people's preferences should be respected. In this case, consumers are the best judges of how much benefit they receive from the goods they buy.

**Quick Quiz** *Draw a demand curve for turkey. In your diagram, show a price of turkey and the consumer surplus at that price. Explain in words what this consumer surplus measures.*

# 7-2 Producer Surplus

We now turn to the other side of the market and consider the benefits sellers receive from participating in a market. As you will see, our analysis of sellers' welfare is similar to our analysis of buyers' welfare.

## 7-2a Cost and the Willingness to Sell

Imagine now that you are a homeowner and want to get your house painted. You turn to four sellers of painting services: Vincent, Claude, Pablo, and Andy. Each painter is willing to do the work for you if the price is right. You decide to take bids from the four painters and auction off the job to the painter who will do the work for the lowest price.

Each painter is willing to take the job if the price he would receive exceeds his cost of doing the work. Here the term **cost** should be interpreted as the painters' opportunity cost: It includes the painters' out-of-pocket expenses (for paint, brushes, and so on) as well as the value that the painters place on their own time. Table 2 shows each painter's cost. Because a painter's cost is the lowest price he would accept for his work, cost is a measure of his willingness to sell his services. Each painter would be eager to sell his services at a price greater than his cost and would refuse to sell his services at a price less than his cost. At a price exactly equal to his cost, he would be indifferent about selling his services: He would be equally happy getting the job or using his time and energy for another purpose.

> **cost**
> the value of everything a seller must give up to produce a good

When you take bids from the painters, the price might start high, but it quickly falls as the painters compete for the job. Once Andy has bid $600 (or slightly less), he is the sole remaining bidder. Andy is happy to do the job for this price because his cost is only $500. Vincent, Claude, and Pablo are unwilling to do the job for less than $600. Note that the job goes to the painter who can do the work at the lowest cost.

What benefit does Andy receive from getting the job? Because he is willing to do the work for $500 but gets $600 for doing it, we say that he receives *producer surplus* of $100. **Producer surplus** is the amount a seller is paid minus the cost of production. Producer surplus measures the benefit sellers receive from participating in a market.

> **producer surplus**
> the amount a seller is paid for a good minus the seller's cost of providing it

Now consider a somewhat different example. Suppose that you have two houses that need painting. Again, you auction off the jobs to the four painters. To keep things simple, let's assume that no painter is able to paint both houses and that you will pay the same amount to paint each house. Therefore, the price falls until two painters are left.

In this case, the bidding stops when Andy and Pablo each offer to do the job for a price of $800 (or slightly less). Andy and Pablo are willing to do the work at this price, while Vincent and Claude are not willing to bid a lower price. At a price of

**TABLE 2**

**The Costs of Four Possible Sellers**

| Seller | Cost |
|--------|------|
| Vincent | $900 |
| Claude | 800 |
| Pablo | 600 |
| Andy | 500 |

## FIGURE 4

**The Supply Schedule and the Supply Curve**

The table shows the supply schedule for the sellers (listed in Table 2) of painting services. The graph shows the corresponding supply curve. Note that the height of the supply curve reflects the sellers' costs.

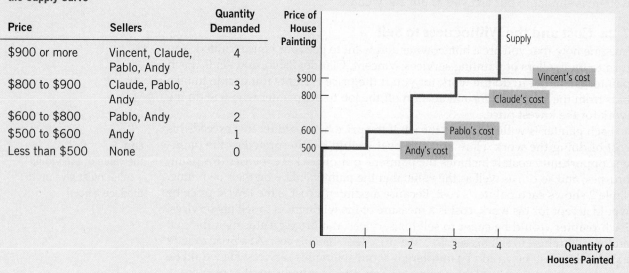

| Price | Sellers | Quantity Demanded |
|---|---|---|
| $900 or more | Vincent, Claude, Pablo, Andy | 4 |
| $800 to $900 | Claude, Pablo, Andy | 3 |
| $600 to $800 | Pablo, Andy | 2 |
| $500 to $600 | Andy | 1 |
| Less than $500 | None | 0 |

$800, Andy receives producer surplus of $300 and Pablo receives producer surplus of $200. The total producer surplus in the market is $500.

### 7-2b Using the Supply Curve to Measure Producer Surplus

Just as consumer surplus is closely related to the demand curve, producer surplus is closely related to the supply curve. To see how, let's continue with our example.

We begin by using the costs of the four painters to find the supply schedule for painting services. The table in Figure 4 shows the supply schedule that corresponds to the costs in Table 2. If the price is below $500, none of the four painters is willing to do the job, so the quantity supplied is zero. If the price is between $500 and $600, only Andy is willing to do the job, so the quantity supplied is 1. If the price is between $600 and $800, Andy and Pablo are willing to do the job, so the quantity supplied is 2, and so on. Thus, the supply schedule is derived from the costs of the four painters.

The graph in Figure 4 shows the supply curve that corresponds to this supply schedule. Note that the height of the supply curve is related to the sellers' costs. At any quantity, the price given by the supply curve shows the cost of the *marginal seller*, the seller who would leave the market first if the price were any lower. At a quantity of 4 houses, for instance, the supply curve has a height of $900, the cost that Vincent (the marginal seller) incurs to provide his painting services. At a quantity of 3 houses, the supply curve has a height of $800, the cost that Claude (who is now the marginal seller) incurs.

Because the supply curve reflects sellers' costs, we can use it to measure producer surplus. Figure 5 uses the supply curve to compute producer surplus in our two examples. In panel (a), we assume that the price is $600 (or slightly less). In this case, the quantity supplied is 1. Note that the area below the price and above

In panel (a), the price of the good is $600 and the producer surplus is $100.
In panel (b), the price of the good is $800 and the producer surplus is $500.

**FIGURE 5**

**Measuring Producer Surplus
with the Supply Curve**

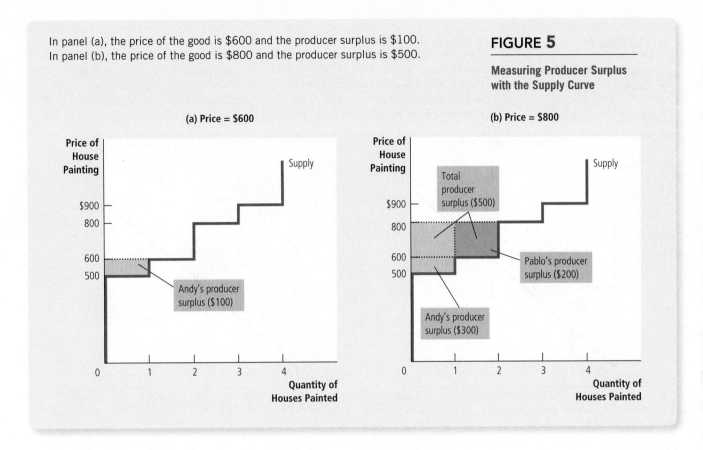

**(a) Price = $600**

**(b) Price = $800**

the supply curve equals $100. This amount is exactly the producer surplus we
computed earlier for Andy.

Panel (b) of Figure 5 shows producer surplus at a price of $800 (or slightly less).
In this case, the area below the price and above the supply curve equals the total
area of the two rectangles. This area equals $500, the producer surplus we com-
puted earlier for Pablo and Andy when two houses needed painting.

The lesson from this example applies to all supply curves: *The area below the
price and above the supply curve measures the producer surplus in a market.* The logic
is straightforward: The height of the supply curve measures sellers' costs, and the
difference between the price and the cost of production is each seller's producer
surplus. Thus, the total area is the sum of the producer surplus of all sellers.

## 7-2c How a Higher Price Raises Producer Surplus

You will not be surprised to hear that sellers always want to receive a higher
price for the goods they sell. But how much does sellers' well-being rise in
response to a higher price? The concept of producer surplus offers a precise
answer to this question.

Figure 6 shows a typical upward-sloping supply curve that would arise in a
market with many sellers. Although this supply curve differs in shape from the
previous figure, we measure producer surplus in the same way: Producer surplus
is the area below the price and above the supply curve. In panel (a), the price is $P_1$
and producer surplus is the area of triangle ABC.

**FIGURE 6**

**How Price Affects Producer Surplus**

In panel (a), the price is $P_1$, the quantity supplied is $Q_1$, and producer surplus equals the area of the triangle ABC. When the price rises from $P_1$ to $P_2$, as in panel (b), the quantity supplied rises from $Q_1$ to $Q_2$ and the producer surplus rises to the area of the triangle ADF. The increase in producer surplus (area BCFD) occurs in part because existing producers now receive more (area BCED) and in part because new producers enter the market at the higher price (area CEF).

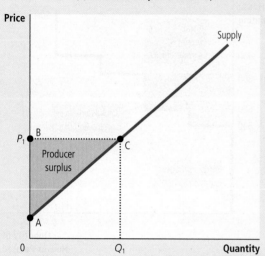

(a) Producer Surplus at Price $P_1$

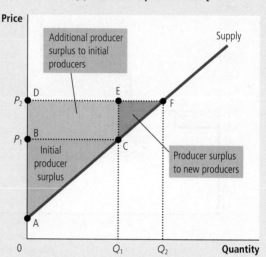

(b) Producer Surplus at Price $P_2$

Panel (b) shows what happens when the price rises from $P_1$ to $P_2$. Producer surplus now equals area ADF. This increase in producer surplus has two parts. First, those sellers who were already selling $Q_1$ of the good at the lower price $P_1$ are better off because they now get more for what they sell. The increase in producer surplus for existing sellers equals the area of the rectangle BCED. Second, some new sellers enter the market because they are willing to produce the good at the higher price, resulting in an increase in the quantity supplied from $Q_1$ to $Q_2$. The producer surplus of these newcomers is the area of the triangle CEF.

As this analysis shows, we use producer surplus to measure the well-being of sellers in much the same way as we use consumer surplus to measure the well-being of buyers. Because these two measures of economic welfare are so similar, it is natural to use them together. Indeed, that is exactly what we do in the next section.

**Quick Quiz**    *Draw a supply curve for turkey. In your diagram, show a price of turkey and the producer surplus at that price. Explain in words what this producer surplus measures.*

# 7-3 Market Efficiency

Consumer surplus and producer surplus are the basic tools that economists use to study the welfare of buyers and sellers in a market. These tools can help us address a fundamental economic question: Is the allocation of resources determined by free markets desirable?

## 7-3a The Benevolent Social Planner

To evaluate market outcomes, we introduce into our analysis a new, hypothetical character called the benevolent social planner. The benevolent social planner is an all-knowing, all-powerful, well-intentioned dictator. The planner wants to maximize the economic well-being of everyone in society. What should this planner do? Should she just leave buyers and sellers at the equilibrium that they reach naturally on their own? Or can she increase economic well-being by altering the market outcome in some way?

To answer this question, the planner must first decide how to measure the economic well-being of a society. One possible measure is the sum of consumer and producer surplus, which we call *total surplus*. Consumer surplus is the benefit that buyers receive from participating in a market, and producer surplus is the benefit that sellers receive. It is therefore natural to use total surplus as a measure of society's economic well-being.

To better understand this measure of economic well-being, recall how we measure consumer and producer surplus. We define consumer surplus as

Consumer surplus = Value to buyers − Amount paid by buyers.

Similarly, we define producer surplus as

Producer surplus = Amount received by sellers − Cost to sellers.

When we add consumer and producer surplus together, we obtain

Total surplus = (Value to buyers − Amount paid by buyers)
+ (Amount received by sellers − Cost to sellers).

The amount paid by buyers equals the amount received by sellers, so the middle two terms in this expression cancel each other. As a result, we can write total surplus as

Total surplus = Value to buyers − Cost to sellers.

Total surplus in a market is the total value to buyers of the goods, as measured by their willingness to pay, minus the total cost to sellers of providing those goods.

If an allocation of resources maximizes total surplus, we say that the allocation exhibits **efficiency**. If an allocation is not efficient, then some of the potential gains from trade among buyers and sellers are not being realized. For example, an allocation is inefficient if a good is not being produced by the sellers with lowest cost. In this case, moving production from a high-cost producer to a low-cost producer will lower the total cost to sellers and raise total surplus. Similarly, an allocation is inefficient if a good is not being consumed by the buyers who value it most highly. In this case, moving consumption of the good from a buyer with a low valuation to a buyer with a high valuation will raise total surplus.

In addition to efficiency, the social planner might also care about **equality**—that is, whether the various buyers and sellers in the market have a similar level of economic well-being. In essence, the gains from trade in a market are like a pie to be shared among the market participants. The question of efficiency concerns whether the pie is as big as possible. The question of equality concerns how

**efficiency**
the property of a resource allocation of maximizing the total surplus received by all members of society

**equality**
the property of distributing economic prosperity uniformly among the members of society

## FIGURE **7**

**Consumer and Producer Surplus in the Market Equilibrium**
Total surplus—the sum of consumer and producer surplus—is the area between the supply and demand curves up to the equilibrium quantity.

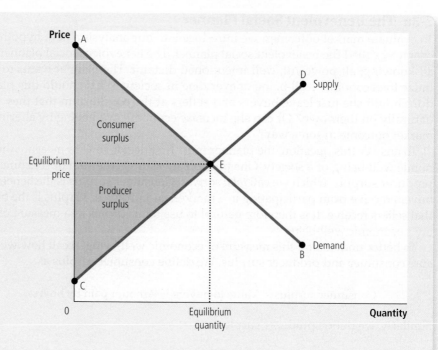

the pie is sliced and how the portions are distributed among members of society. In this chapter, we concentrate on efficiency as the social planner's goal. Keep in mind, however, that real policymakers often care about equality as well.

### 7-3b Evaluating the Market Equilibrium

Figure 7 shows consumer and producer surplus when a market reaches the equilibrium of supply and demand. Recall that consumer surplus equals the area above the price and under the demand curve and producer surplus equals the area below the price and above the supply curve. Thus, the total area between the supply and demand curves up to the point of equilibrium represents the total surplus in this market.

Is this equilibrium allocation of resources efficient? That is, does it maximize total surplus? To answer this question, recall that when a market is in equilibrium, the price determines which buyers and sellers participate in the market. Those buyers who value the good more than the price (represented by the segment AE on the demand curve) choose to buy the good; buyers who value it less than the price (represented by the segment EB) do not. Similarly, those sellers whose costs are less than the price (represented by the segment CE on the supply curve) choose to produce and sell the good; sellers whose costs are greater than the price (represented by the segment ED) do not.

These observations lead to two insights about market outcomes:

1. Free markets allocate the supply of goods to the buyers who value them most highly, as measured by their willingness to pay.
2. Free markets allocate the demand for goods to the sellers who can produce them at the lowest cost.

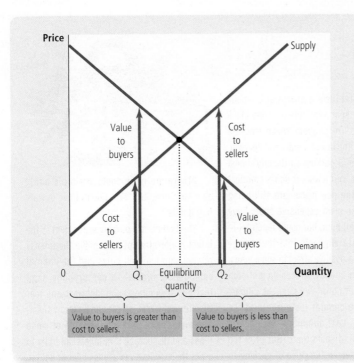

### FIGURE 8

**The Efficiency of the Equilibrium Quantity**
At quantities less than the equilibrium quantity, such as $Q_1$, the value to buyers exceeds the cost to sellers. At quantities greater than the equilibrium quantity, such as $Q_2$, the cost to sellers exceeds the value to buyers. Therefore, the market equilibrium maximizes the sum of producer and consumer surplus.

Thus, given the quantity produced and sold in a market equilibrium, the social planner cannot increase economic well-being by changing the allocation of consumption among buyers or the allocation of production among sellers.

But can the social planner raise total economic well-being by increasing or decreasing the quantity of the good? The answer is no, as stated in this third insight about market outcomes:

3.  Free markets produce the quantity of goods that maximizes the sum of consumer and producer surplus.

Figure 8 illustrates why this is true. To interpret this figure, keep in mind that the demand curve reflects the value to buyers and the supply curve reflects the cost to sellers. At any quantity below the equilibrium level, such as $Q_1$, the value to the marginal buyer exceeds the cost to the marginal seller. As a result, increasing the quantity produced and consumed raises total surplus. This continues to be true until the quantity reaches the equilibrium level. Similarly, at any quantity beyond the equilibrium level, such as $Q_2$, the value to the marginal buyer is less than the cost to the marginal seller. In this case, decreasing the quantity raises total surplus, and this continues to be true until quantity falls to the equilibrium level. To maximize total surplus, the social planner would choose the quantity where the supply and demand curves intersect.

Together, these three insights tell us that the market outcome makes the sum of consumer and producer surplus as large as it can be. In other words, the equilibrium outcome is an efficient allocation of resources. The benevolent social planner can, therefore, leave the market outcome just as she finds it. This policy of leaving well enough alone goes by the French expression *laissez faire*, which literally translates to "leave to do" but is more broadly interpreted as "let people do as they will."

## IN THE NEWS

### The Invisible Hand Can Park Your Car

*In many cities, finding an available parking spot on the street seems about as likely as winning the lottery. But if local governments relied more on the price system, they might be able to achieve a more efficient allocation of this scarce resource.*

#### A Meter So Expensive, It Creates Parking Spots

By Michael Cooper and
Jo Craven McGinty

SAN FRANCISCO—The maddening quest for street parking is not just a tribulation for drivers, but a trial for cities. As much as a third of the traffic in some areas has been attributed to drivers circling as they hunt for spaces. The wearying tradition takes a toll in lost time, polluted air and, when drivers despair, double-parked cars that clog traffic even more.

But San Francisco is trying to shorten the hunt with an ambitious experiment that aims to make sure that there is always at least one empty parking spot available on every block that has meters. The program, which uses new technology and the law of supply and demand, raises the price of parking on the city's most crowded blocks and lowers it on its emptiest blocks. While the new prices are still being phased in—the most expensive spots have risen to $4.50 an hour, but could reach $6— preliminary data suggests that the change may be having a positive effect in some areas.

Change can already be seen on a stretch of Drumm Street downtown near the Embarcadero and the popular restaurants at the Ferry Building. Last summer it was nearly impossible to find spots there. But after the city gradually raised the price of parking to $4.50 an hour from $3.50, high-tech sensors embedded in the street showed that spots were available a little more often—leaving a welcome space the other day for the silver Toyota Corolla driven by Victor Chew, a salesman for a commercial dishwasher company who frequently parks in the area.

"There are more spots available now," said Mr. Chew, 48. "Now I don't have to walk half a mile."

San Francisco's parking experiment is the latest major attempt to improve the uneasy relationship between cities and the internal combustion engine—a century-long saga that has seen cities build highways and tear them down, widen streets and narrow them, and make more parking available at some times and discourage it at others, all to try to make their downtowns accessible but not too congested.

The program here is being closely watched by cities around the country. With the help of a federal grant, San Francisco installed parking sensors and new meters at roughly a quarter of its 26,800 metered spots to track when and where cars are parked. And beginning last

---

Society is lucky that the planner doesn't need to intervene. Although it has been a useful exercise imagining what an all-knowing, all-powerful, well-intentioned dictator would do, let's face it: Such characters are hard to come by. Dictators are rarely benevolent, and even if we found someone so virtuous, she would lack crucial information.

Suppose our social planner tried to choose an efficient allocation of resources on her own, instead of relying on market forces. To do so, she would need to know the value of a particular good to every potential consumer in the market and the cost for every potential producer. And she would need this information not only for this market but for every one of the many thousands of markets in the economy. The task is practically impossible, which explains why centrally planned economies never work very well.

The planner's job becomes easy, however, once she takes on a partner: Adam Smith's invisible hand of the marketplace. The invisible hand takes all the information about buyers and sellers into account and guides everyone in the market to the best outcome as judged by the standard of economic efficiency. It is a truly remarkable feat. That is why economists so often advocate free markets as the best way to organize economic activity.

summer, the city began tweaking its prices every two months—giving it the option of raising them 25 cents an hour, or lowering them by as much as 50 cents—in the hope of leaving each block with at least one available spot. The city also has cut prices at many of the garages and parking lots it manages, to lure cars off the street....

The program is the biggest test yet of the theories of Donald Shoup, a professor of urban planning at the University of California, Los Angeles. His 2005 book, "The High Cost of Free Parking," made him something of a cult figure to city planners—a Facebook group, The Shoupistas, has more than a thousand members. "I think the basic idea is that we will see a lot of benefits if we get the price of curbside parking right, which is the lowest price a city can charge and still have one or two vacant spaces available on every block," he said.

But raising prices is rarely popular. A chapter in Mr. Shoup's book opens with a quote from George Costanza, the "Seinfeld" character: "My father didn't pay for parking, my mother, my brother, nobody. It's like going to a prostitute. Why should I pay when, if I apply myself, maybe I can get it for free?" Some San Francisco neighborhoods recently objected to a proposal to install meters on streets where parking is now free. And raising prices in the most desirable areas raises concerns that it will make them less accessible to the poor.

The new San Francisco electronic parking meter helps equilibrate supply and demand.

That was on the minds of some parkers on Drumm Street, where the midday occupancy rate on one block fell to 86 percent from 98 percent after prices rose. Edward Saldate, 55, a hairstylist who paid nearly $17 for close to four hours of parking there, called it "a big rip-off."

Tom Randlett, 69, an accountant, said that he was pleased to be able to find a spot there for the first time, but acknowledged that the program was "complicated on the social equity level."

Officials note that parking rates are cut as often as they are raised. And Professor Shoup said that the program would benefit many poor people, including the many San Franciscans who do not have cars, because all parking revenues are used for mass transit and any reduction in traffic will speed the buses many people here rely on. And he imagined a day when drivers will no longer attribute good parking spots to luck or karma.

"It will be taken for granted," he said, "the way you take it for granted that when you go to a store you can get fresh bananas or apples." ▪

**Source:** *New York Times,* March 15, 2012.

---

### CASE STUDY

### SHOULD THERE BE A MARKET FOR ORGANS?

Some years ago, the front page of *The Boston Globe* ran the headline "How a Mother's Love Helped Save Two Lives." The newspaper told the story of Susan Stephens, a woman whose son needed a kidney transplant. When the doctor learned that the mother's kidney was not compatible, he proposed a novel solution: If Stephens donated one of her kidneys to a stranger, her son would move to the top of the kidney waiting list. The mother accepted the deal, and soon two patients had the transplants they were waiting for.

The ingenuity of the doctor's proposal and the nobility of the mother's act cannot be doubted. But the story raises some intriguing questions. If the mother could trade a kidney for a kidney, would the hospital allow her to trade a kidney for an expensive, experimental cancer treatment that she could not otherwise afford? Should she be allowed to exchange her kidney for free tuition for her son at the hospital's medical school? Should she be able to sell her kidney and use the cash to trade in her old Chevy for a new Lexus?

As a matter of public policy, our society makes it illegal for people to sell their organs. In essence, in the market for organs, the government has imposed a price

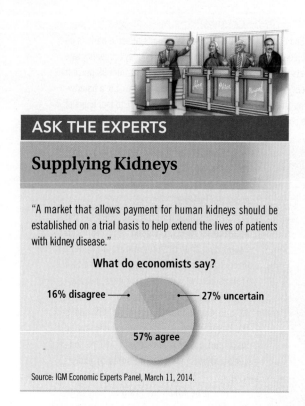

## Supplying Kidneys

"A market that allows payment for human kidneys should be established on a trial basis to help extend the lives of patients with kidney disease."

### What do economists say?

16% disagree ———•       •——— 27% uncertain

57% agree

Source: IGM Economic Experts Panel, March 11, 2014.

ceiling of zero. The result, as with any binding price ceiling, is a shortage of the good. The deal in the Stephens case did not fall under this prohibition because no cash changed hands.

Many economists believe that there would be large benefits to allowing a free market for organs. People are born with two kidneys, but they usually need only one. Meanwhile, some people suffer from illnesses that leave them without any working kidney. Despite the obvious gains from trade, the current situation is dire: The typical patient has to wait several years for a kidney transplant, and every year thousands of people die because a compatible kidney cannot be found. If those needing a kidney were allowed to buy one from those who have two, the price would rise to balance supply and demand. Sellers would be better off with the extra cash in their pockets. Buyers would be better off with the organ they need to save their lives. The shortage of kidneys would disappear.

Such a market would lead to an efficient allocation of resources, but critics of this plan worry about fairness. A market for organs, they argue, would benefit the rich at the expense of the poor because organs would then be allocated to those most willing and able to pay. But you can also question the fairness of the current system. Now, most of us walk around with an extra organ that we don't really need, while some of our fellow citizens are dying to get one. Is that fair? ●

**QuickQuiz**  *Draw the supply and demand curves for turkey. In the equilibrium, show producer and consumer surplus. Explain why producing more turkeys would lower total surplus.*

# 7-4  Conclusion: Market Efficiency and Market Failure

This chapter introduced the basic tools of welfare economics—consumer and producer surplus—and used them to evaluate the efficiency of free markets. We showed that the forces of supply and demand allocate resources efficiently. That is, even though each buyer and seller in a market is concerned only about her own welfare, together they are guided by an invisible hand to an equilibrium that maximizes the total benefits to buyers and sellers.

A word of warning is in order. To conclude that markets are efficient, we made several assumptions about how markets work. When these assumptions do not hold, our conclusion that the market equilibrium is efficient may no longer be true. As we close this chapter, let's briefly consider two of the most important assumptions we made.

First, our analysis assumed that markets are perfectly competitive. In actual economies, however, competition is sometimes far from perfect. In some markets, a single buyer or seller (or a small group of them) may be able to control market prices. This ability to influence prices is called *market power*. Market power can cause markets to be inefficient because it keeps the price and quantity away from the levels determined by the equilibrium of supply and demand.

Second, our analysis assumed that the outcome in a market matters only to the buyers and sellers who participate in that market. Yet sometimes the decisions of buyers and sellers affect people who are not participants in the market at all. Pollution is the classic example. The use of agricultural pesticides, for instance, affects not only the manufacturers who make them and the farmers who use them but also many others who breathe the air or drink the water contaminated by these pesticides. When a market exhibits such side effects, called *externalities*, the welfare implications of market activity depend on more than just the value obtained by the buyers and the cost incurred by the sellers. Because buyers and sellers may ignore these side effects when deciding how much to consume and produce, the equilibrium in a market can be inefficient from the standpoint of society as a whole.

Market power and externalities are examples of a general phenomenon called *market failure*—the inability of some unregulated markets to allocate resources efficiently. When markets fail, public policy can potentially remedy the problem and increase economic efficiency. Microeconomists devote much effort to studying when market failures are likely and how they are best corrected. As you continue your study of economics, you will see that the tools of welfare economics developed here are readily adapted to that endeavor.

Despite the possibility of market failure, the invisible hand of the marketplace is extraordinarily important. In many markets, the assumptions we made in this chapter work well and the conclusion of market efficiency applies directly. Moreover, we can use our analysis of welfare economics and market efficiency to shed light on the effects of various government policies. In the next two chapters, we apply the tools we have just developed to study two important policy issues—the welfare effects of taxation and of international trade.

---

## CHAPTER QuickQuiz

1.  Jen values her time at $60 an hour. She spends
    2 hours giving Colleen a massage.  Colleen was
    willing to pay as much at $300 for the massage, but
    they negotiate a price of $200. In this transaction,
    a. consumer surplus is $20 larger than producer
       surplus.
    b. consumer surplus is $40 larger than producer
       surplus.
    c. producer surplus is $20 larger than consumer
       surplus.
    d. producer surplus is $40 larger than consumer
       surplus.

2.  The demand curve for cookies is downward-sloping.
    When the price of cookies is $2, the quantity
    demanded is 100. If the price rises to $3,
    what happens to consumer surplus?
    a. It falls by less than $100.
    b. It falls by more than $100.
    c. It rises by less than $100.
    d. It rises by more than $100.

3.  John has been working as a tutor for $300 a
    semester. When the university raises the price it pays
    tutors to $400, Jasmine enters the market and begins
    tutoring as well. How much does producer surplus
    rise as a result of this price increase?

    a. by less than $100
    b. between $100 and $200
    c. between $200 and $300
    d. by more than $300

4.  An efficient allocation of resources maximizes
    a. consumer surplus.
    b. producer surplus.
    c. consumer surplus plus producer surplus.
    d. consumer surplus minus producer surplus.

5.  When a market is in equilibrium, the buyers are those
    with the _____ willingness to pay and the sellers
    are those with the _____ costs.
    a. highest, highest
    b. highest, lowest
    c. lowest, highest
    d. lowest, lowest

6.  Producing a quantity larger than the equilibrium
    of supply and demand is inefficient because the
    marginal buyer's willingness to pay is
    a. negative.
    b. zero.
    c. positive but less than the marginal seller's cost.
    d. positive and greater than the marginal seller's cost.

## SUMMARY

- Consumer surplus equals buyers' willingness to pay for a good minus the amount they actually pay, and it measures the benefit buyers get from participating in a market. Consumer surplus can be computed by finding the area below the demand curve and above the price.
- Producer surplus equals the amount sellers receive for their goods minus their costs of production, and it measures the benefit sellers get from participating in a market. Producer surplus can be computed by finding the area below the price and above the supply curve.

- An allocation of resources that maximizes total surplus (the sum of consumer and producer surplus) is said to be efficient. Policymakers are often concerned with the efficiency, as well as the equality, of economic outcomes.
- The equilibrium of supply and demand maximizes total surplus. That is, the invisible hand of the marketplace leads buyers and sellers to allocate resources efficiently.
- Markets do not allocate resources efficiently in the presence of market failures such as market power or externalities.

## KEY CONCEPTS

welfare economics, p. 134
willingness to pay, p. 134
consumer surplus, p. 135

cost, p. 139
producer surplus, p. 139
efficiency, p. 143

equality, p. 143

## QUESTIONS FOR REVIEW

1. Explain how buyers' willingness to pay, consumer surplus, and the demand curve are related.

2. Explain how sellers' costs, producer surplus, and the supply curve are related.

3. In a supply-and-demand diagram, show producer and consumer surplus at the market equilibrium.

4. What is efficiency? Is it the only goal of economic policymakers?

5. Name two types of market failure. Explain why each may cause market outcomes to be inefficient.

## PROBLEMS AND APPLICATIONS

1. Melissa buys an iPhone for $240 and gets consumer surplus of $160.
   a. What is her willingness to pay?
   b. If she had bought the iPhone on sale for $180, what would her consumer surplus have been?
   c. If the price of an iPhone were $500, what would her consumer surplus have been?

2. An early freeze in California sours the lemon crop. Explain what happens to consumer surplus in the market for lemons. Explain what happens to consumer surplus in the market for lemonade. Illustrate your answers with diagrams.

3. Suppose the demand for French bread rises. Explain what happens to producer surplus in the market for French bread. Explain what happens to producer surplus in the market for flour. Illustrate your answers with diagrams.

4. It is a hot day, and Bert is thirsty. Here is the value he places on each bottle of water:

| | |
|---|---|
| Value of first bottle | $7 |
| Value of second bottle | $5 |
| Value of third bottle | $3 |
| Value of fourth bottle | $1 |

a. From this information, derive Bert's demand schedule. Graph his demand curve for bottled water.

b. If the price of a bottle of water is $4, how many bottles does Bert buy? How much consumer surplus does Bert get from his purchases? Show Bert's consumer surplus in your graph.

c. If the price falls to $2, how does quantity demanded change? How does Bert's consumer surplus change? Show these changes in your graph.

5. Ernie owns a water pump. Because pumping large amounts of water is harder than pumping small amounts, the cost of producing a bottle of water rises as he pumps more. Here is the cost he incurs to produce each bottle of water:

| | |
|---|---|
| Cost of first bottle | $1 |
| Cost of second bottle | $3 |
| Cost of third bottle | $5 |
| Cost of fourth bottle | $7 |

a. From this information, derive Ernie's supply schedule. Graph his supply curve for bottled water.

b. If the price of a bottle of water is $4, how many bottles does Ernie produce and sell? How much producer surplus does Ernie get from these sales? Show Ernie's producer surplus in your graph.

c. If the price rises to $6, how does quantity supplied change? How does Ernie's producer surplus change? Show these changes in your graph.

6. Consider a market in which Bert from problem 4 is the buyer and Ernie from problem 5 is the seller.

a. Use Ernie's supply schedule and Bert's demand schedule to find the quantity supplied and quantity demanded at prices of $2, $4, and $6. Which of these prices brings supply and demand into equilibrium?

b. What are consumer surplus, producer surplus, and total surplus in this equilibrium?

c. If Ernie produced and Bert consumed one fewer bottle of water, what would happen to total surplus?

d. If Ernie produced and Bert consumed one additional bottle of water, what would happen to total surplus?

7. The cost of producing flat-screen TVs has fallen over the past decade. Let's consider some implications of this fact.

a. Draw a supply-and-demand diagram to show the effect of falling production costs on the price and quantity of flat-screen TVs sold.

b. In your diagram, show what happens to consumer surplus and producer surplus.

c. Suppose the supply of flat-screen TVs is very elastic. Who benefits most from falling production costs—consumers or producers of these TVs?

8. There are four consumers willing to pay the following amounts for haircuts:

Gloria: $35    Jay: $10    Claire: $40    Phil: $25

There are four haircutting businesses with the following costs:

Firm A: $15    Firm B: $30    Firm C: $20    Firm D: $10

Each firm has the capacity to produce only one haircut. To achieve efficiency, how many haircuts should be given? Which businesses should cut hair and which consumers should have their hair cut? How large is the maximum possible total surplus?

9. One of the largest changes in the economy over the past several decades is that technological advances have reduced the cost of making computers.

a. Draw a supply-and-demand diagram to show what happened to price, quantity, consumer surplus, and producer surplus in the market for computers.

b. Forty years ago, students used typewriters to prepare papers for their classes; today they use computers. Does that make computers and typewriters complements or substitutes? Use a supply-and-demand diagram to show what happened to price, quantity, consumer surplus, and producer surplus in the market for typewriters. Should typewriter producers have been happy or sad about the technological advance in computers?

c. Are computers and software complements or substitutes? Draw a supply-and-demand diagram to show what happened to price, quantity, consumer surplus, and producer surplus in the market for software. Should software producers have been happy or sad about the technological advance in computers?

d. Does this analysis help explain why software producer Bill Gates is one of the world's richest people?

10. A friend of yours is considering two cell phone service providers. Provider A charges $120 per month for the service regardless of the number of phone calls made. Provider B does not have a fixed service fee but instead charges $1 per minute for calls. Your friend's

monthly demand for minutes of calling is given by the equation $Q^D = 150 - 50P$, where $P$ is the price of a minute.

a. With each provider, what is the cost to your friend of an extra minute on the phone?

b. In light of your answer to (a), how many minutes with each provider would your friend talk on the phone?

c. How much would she end up paying each provider every month?

d. How much consumer surplus would she obtain with each provider? (*Hint*: Graph the demand curve and recall the formula for the area of a triangle.)

e. Which provider would you recommend that your friend choose? Why?

11. Consider how health insurance affects the quantity of healthcare services performed. Suppose that the typical medical procedure has a cost of $100, yet a person with health insurance pays only $20 out of pocket. Her insurance company pays the remaining $80. (The insurance company recoups the $80 through premiums, but the premium a person pays does not depend on how many procedures that person chooses to undertake.)

a. Draw the demand curve in the market for medical care. (In your diagram, the horizontal axis should represent the number of medical procedures.) Show the quantity of procedures demanded if each procedure has a price of $100.

b. On your diagram, show the quantity of procedures demanded if consumers pay only $20 per procedure. If the cost of each procedure to society is truly $100, and if individuals have health insurance as described above, will the number of procedures performed maximize total surplus? Explain.

c. Economists often blame the health insurance system for excessive use of medical care. Given your analysis, why might the use of care be viewed as "excessive"?

d. What sort of policies might prevent this excessive use?

To find additional study resources, visit cengagebrain.com, and search for "Mankiw."

# Application: The Costs of Taxation

Taxes are often a source of heated political debate. In 1776, the anger of the American colonists over British taxes sparked the American Revolution. More than two centuries later, the American political parties still debate the proper size and shape of the tax system. Yet no one would deny that some level of taxation is necessary. As Oliver Wendell Holmes, Jr., once said, "Taxes are what we pay for civilized society."

Because taxation has such a major impact on the modern economy, we return to the topic several times throughout this book as we expand the set of tools we have

at our disposal. We began our study of taxes in Chapter 6. There we saw how a tax on a good affects its price and quantity sold and how the forces of supply and demand divide the burden of a tax between buyers and sellers. In this chapter, we extend this analysis and look at how taxes affect welfare, the economic well-being of participants in a market. In other words, we see how high the price of civilized society can be.

The effects of taxes on welfare might at first seem obvious. The government enacts taxes to raise revenue, and this revenue must come out of someone's pocket. As we saw in Chapter 6, both buyers and sellers are worse off when a good is taxed: A tax raises the price buyers pay and lowers the price sellers receive. Yet to fully understand how taxes affect economic well-being, we must compare the reduced welfare of buyers and sellers to the amount of revenue the government raises. The tools of consumer and producer surplus allow us to make this comparison. Our analysis will show that the cost of taxes to buyers and sellers typically exceeds the revenue raised by the government.

## 8-1  The Deadweight Loss of Taxation

We begin by recalling one of the surprising lessons from Chapter 6: The impact of a tax on a market outcome is the same whether the tax is levied on buyers or sellers of a good. When a tax is levied on buyers, the demand curve shifts downward by the size of the tax; when it is levied on sellers, the supply curve shifts upward by that amount. In either case, when the tax is enacted, the price paid by buyers rises, and the price received by sellers falls. In the end, the elasticities of supply and demand determine how the tax burden is distributed between producers and consumers. This distribution is the same regardless of how the tax is levied.

Figure 1 shows these effects. To simplify our discussion, this figure does not show a shift in either the supply or demand curve, although one curve must shift. Which curve shifts depends on whether the tax is levied on sellers (the supply

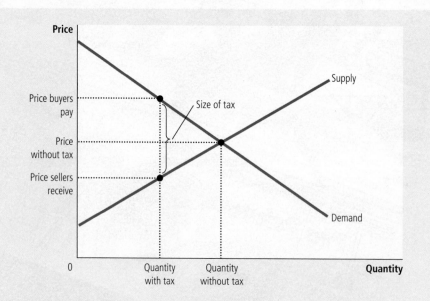

### FIGURE 1

**The Effects of a Tax**
A tax on a good places a wedge between the price that buyers pay and the price that sellers receive. The quantity of the good sold falls.

curve shifts) or buyers (the demand curve shifts). In this chapter, we keep the analysis general and simplify the graphs by not showing the shift. For our purposes here, the key result is that the tax places a wedge between the price buyers pay and the price sellers receive. Because of this tax wedge, the quantity sold falls below the level that would be sold without a tax. In other words, a tax on a good causes the size of the market for the good to shrink. These results should be familiar from Chapter 6.

## 8-1a How a Tax Affects Market Participants

Let's use the tools of welfare economics to measure the gains and losses from a tax on a good. To do this, we must take into account how the tax affects buyers, sellers, and the government. The benefit received by buyers in a market is measured by consumer surplus—the amount buyers are willing to pay for the good minus the amount they actually pay for it. The benefit received by sellers in a market is measured by producer surplus—the amount sellers receive for the good minus their costs. These are precisely the measures of economic welfare we used in Chapter 7.

What about the third interested party, the government? If $T$ is the size of the tax and $Q$ is the quantity of the good sold, then the government gets total tax revenue of $T \times Q$. It can use this tax revenue to provide services, such as roads, police, and public education, or to help the needy. Therefore, to analyze how taxes affect economic well-being, we use the government's tax revenue to measure the public benefit from the tax. Keep in mind, however, that this benefit actually accrues not to the government but to those on whom the revenue is spent.

Figure 2 shows that the government's tax revenue is represented by the rectangle between the supply and demand curves. The height of this rectangle is the size of the tax, $T$, and the width of the rectangle is the quantity of the good sold, $Q$. Because a rectangle's area is its height multiplied by its width, this rectangle's area is $T \times Q$, which equals the tax revenue.

*"You know, the idea of taxation with representation doesn't appeal to me very much, either."*

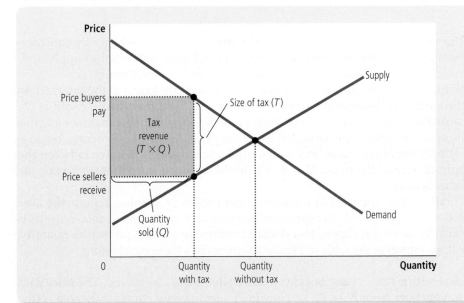

## FIGURE 2

**Tax Revenue**
The tax revenue that the government collects equals $T \times Q$, the size of the tax $T$ times the quantity sold $Q$. Thus, tax revenue equals the area of the rectangle between the supply and demand curves.

## FIGURE 3

**How a Tax Affects Welfare**

A tax on a good reduces consumer surplus (by the area B + C) and producer surplus (by the area D + E). Because the fall in producer and consumer surplus exceeds tax revenue (area B + D), the tax is said to impose a deadweight loss (area C + E).

|  | Without Tax | With Tax | Change |
| --- | --- | --- | --- |
| Consumer Surplus | A + B + C | A | − (B + C) |
| Producer Surplus | D + E + F | F | − (D + E) |
| Tax Revenue | None | B + D | + (B + D) |
| Total Surplus | A + B + C + D + E + F | A + B + D + F | − (C + E) |

The area C + E shows the fall in total surplus and is the deadweight loss of the tax.

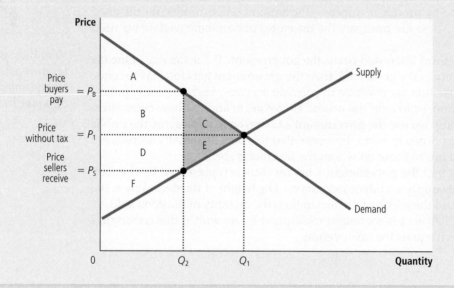

**Welfare without a Tax**   To see how a tax affects welfare, we begin by considering welfare before the government imposes a tax. Figure 3 shows the supply-and-demand diagram with the key areas marked by the letters A through F.

Without a tax, the equilibrium price and quantity are found at the intersection of the supply and demand curves. The price is $P_1$, and the quantity sold is $Q_1$. Because the demand curve reflects buyers' willingness to pay, consumer surplus is the area between the demand curve and the price, A + B + C. Similarly, because the supply curve reflects sellers' costs, producer surplus is the area between the supply curve and the price, D + E + F. In this case, because there is no tax, tax revenue is zero.

Total surplus, the sum of consumer and producer surplus, equals the area A + B + C + D + E + F. In other words, as we saw in Chapter 7, total surplus is the area between the supply and demand curves up to the equilibrium quantity. The first column of the table in Figure 3 summarizes these conclusions.

**Welfare with a Tax**   Now consider welfare after the tax is enacted. The price paid by buyers rises from $P_1$ to $P_B$, so consumer surplus now equals only area A (the area below the demand curve and above the buyers' price). The price received by sellers falls from $P_1$ to $P_S$, so producer surplus now equals only area F (the area above the supply curve and below the sellers' price). The quantity sold falls from $Q_1$ to $Q_2$, and the government collects tax revenue equal to the area B + D.

To compute total surplus with the tax, we add consumer surplus, producer surplus, and tax revenue. Thus, we find that total surplus is area A + B + D + F. The second column of the table summarizes these results.

**Changes in Welfare**   We can now see the effects of the tax by comparing welfare before and after the tax is enacted. The third column of the table in Figure 3 shows the changes. Consumer surplus falls by the area B + C, and producer surplus falls by the area D + E. Tax revenue rises by the area B + D. Not surprisingly, the tax makes buyers and sellers worse off and the government better off.

The change in total welfare includes the change in consumer surplus (which is negative), the change in producer surplus (which is also negative), and the change in tax revenue (which is positive). When we add these three pieces together, we find that total surplus in the market falls by the area C + E. *Thus, the losses to buyers and sellers from a tax exceed the revenue raised by the government.* The fall in total surplus that results when a tax (or some other policy) distorts a market outcome is called a **deadweight loss**. The area C + E measures the size of the deadweight loss.

To understand why taxes cause deadweight losses, recall one of the *Ten Principles of Economics* in Chapter 1: People respond to incentives. In Chapter 7, we saw that free markets normally allocate scarce resources efficiently. That is, in the absence of any tax, the equilibrium of supply and demand maximizes the total surplus of buyers and sellers in a market. When the government imposes a tax, it raises the price buyers pay and lowers the price sellers receive, giving buyers an incentive to consume less and sellers an incentive to produce less. As buyers and sellers respond to these incentives, the size of the market shrinks below its optimum (as shown in the figure by the movement from $Q_1$ to $Q_2$). Thus, because taxes distort incentives, they cause markets to allocate resources inefficiently.

**deadweight loss**
the fall in total surplus that results from a market distortion, such as a tax

## 8-1b  Deadweight Losses and the Gains from Trade

To better understand why taxes cause deadweight losses, consider an example. Imagine that Mike cleans Mei's house each week for $100. The opportunity cost of Mike's time is $80, and the value of a clean house to Mei is $120. Thus, Mike and Mei each receive a $20 benefit from their deal. The total surplus of $40 measures the gains from trade in this particular transaction.

Now suppose that the government levies a $50 tax on the providers of cleaning services. There is now no price that Mei can pay Mike that will leave both of them better off. The most Mei would be willing to pay is $120, but then Mike would be left with only $70 after paying the tax, which is less than his $80 opportunity cost. Conversely, for Mike to receive his opportunity cost of $80, Mei would need to pay $130, which is above the $120 value she places on a clean house. As a result, Mei and Mike cancel their arrangement. Mike loses the income, and Mei lives in a dirtier house.

The tax has made Mike and Mei worse off by a total of $40 because they have each lost $20 of surplus. But note that the government collects no revenue from Mike and Mei because they decide to cancel their arrangement. The $40 is pure deadweight loss: It is a loss to buyers and sellers in a market that is not offset by an increase in government revenue. From this example, we can see the ultimate source of deadweight losses: *Taxes cause deadweight losses because they prevent buyers and sellers from realizing some of the gains from trade.*

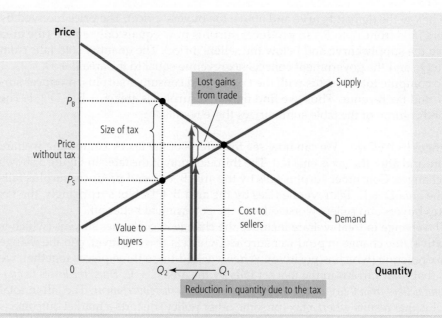

**FIGURE 4**

**The Source of a Deadweight Loss**
When the government imposes a tax on a good, the quantity sold falls from $Q_1$ to $Q_2$. At every quantity between $Q_1$ and $Q_2$, the potential gains from trade among buyers and sellers are not realized. These lost gains from trade create the deadweight loss.

The area of the triangle between the supply and demand curves created by the tax wedge (area C + E in Figure 3) measures these losses. This conclusion can be seen more easily in Figure 4 by recalling that the demand curve reflects the value of the good to consumers and that the supply curve reflects the costs of producers. When the tax raises the price buyers pay to $P_B$ and lowers the price sellers receive to $P_S$, the marginal buyers and sellers leave the market, so the quantity sold falls from $Q_1$ to $Q_2$. Yet as the figure shows, the value of the good to these buyers still exceeds the cost to these sellers. At every quantity between $Q_1$ and $Q_2$, the situation is the same as in our example with Mike and Mei. The gains from trade—the difference between buyers' value and sellers' cost—are less than the tax. As a result, these trades are not made once the tax is imposed. The deadweight loss is the surplus that is lost because the tax discourages these mutually advantageous trades.

**QuickQuiz** *Draw the supply and demand curves for cookies. If the government imposes a tax on cookies, show what happens to the price paid by buyers, the price received by sellers, and the quantity of cookies sold. In your diagram, show the deadweight loss from the tax. Explain the meaning of the deadweight loss.*

# 8-2 The Determinants of the Deadweight Loss

What determines whether the deadweight loss from a tax is large or small? The answer is the price elasticities of supply and demand, which measure how much the quantity supplied and quantity demanded respond to changes in the price.

Let's consider first how the elasticity of supply affects the size of the deadweight loss. In the top two panels of Figure 5, the demand curve and the size of the tax are the same. The only difference in these figures is the elasticity of the supply curve. In panel (a), the supply curve is relatively inelastic: Quantity supplied responds only slightly to changes in the price. In panel (b), the supply curve is relatively elastic: Quantity supplied responds substantially to changes in the

In panels (a) and (b), the demand curve and the size of the tax are the same, but the price elasticity of supply is different. Notice that the more elastic the supply curve, the larger the deadweight loss of the tax. In panels (c) and (d), the supply curve and the size of the tax are the same, but the price elasticity of demand is different. Notice that the more elastic the demand curve, the larger the deadweight loss of the tax.

# FIGURE 5

**Tax Distortions and Elasticities**

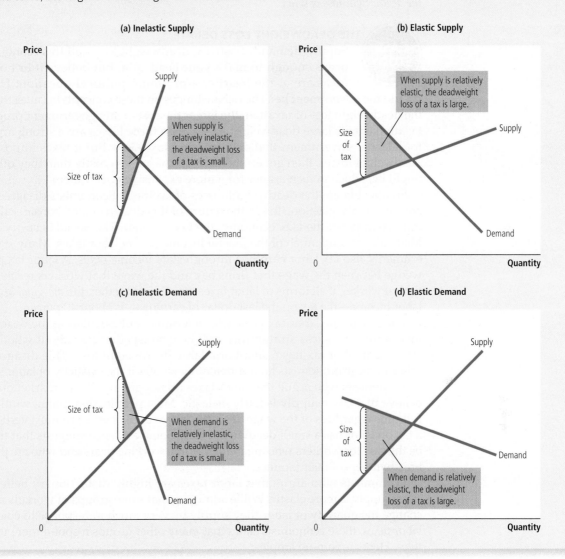

price. Notice that the deadweight loss, the area of the triangle between the supply and demand curves, is larger when the supply curve is more elastic.

Similarly, the bottom two panels of Figure 5 show how the elasticity of demand affects the size of the deadweight loss. Here the supply curve and the size of the tax are held constant. In panel (c), the demand curve is relatively inelastic, and the deadweight loss is small. In panel (d), the demand curve is more elastic, and the deadweight loss from the tax is larger.

The lesson from this figure is apparent. A tax has a deadweight loss because it induces buyers and sellers to change their behavior. The tax raises the price paid by buyers, so they consume less. At the same time, the tax lowers the price received by sellers, so they produce less. Because of these changes in behavior, the equilibrium quantity in the market shrinks below the optimal quantity. The more responsive buyers and sellers are to changes in the price, the more the equilibrium quantity shrinks. Hence, *the greater the elasticities of supply and demand, the greater the deadweight loss of a tax.*

**CASE STUDY**

### THE DEADWEIGHT LOSS DEBATE

Supply, demand, elasticity, deadweight loss—all this economic theory is enough to make your head spin. But believe it or not, these ideas are at the heart of a profound political question: How big should the government be? The debate hinges on these concepts because the larger the deadweight loss of taxation, the larger the cost of any government program. If taxation entails large deadweight losses, then these losses are a strong argument for a leaner government that does less and taxes less. But if taxes impose small deadweight losses, then government programs are less costly than they otherwise might be, which in turn argues for a more expansive government.

So how big are the deadweight losses of taxation? Economists disagree on the answer to this question. To see the nature of this disagreement, consider the most important tax in the U.S. economy: the tax on labor. The Social Security tax, the Medicare tax, and much of the federal income tax are labor taxes. Many state governments also tax labor earnings through state income taxes. A labor tax places a wedge between the wage that firms pay and the wage that workers receive. For a typical worker, if all forms of labor taxes are added together, the *marginal tax rate* on labor income—the tax on the last dollar of earnings—is about 40 percent.

The size of the labor tax is easy to determine, but calculating the deadweight loss of this tax is less straightforward. Economists disagree about whether this 40 percent labor tax has a small or a large deadweight loss. This disagreement arises because economists hold different views about the elasticity of labor supply.

Economists who argue that labor taxes do not greatly distort market outcomes believe that labor supply is fairly inelastic. Most people, they claim, would work full-time regardless of the wage. If so, the labor supply curve is almost vertical, and a tax on labor has a small deadweight loss. Some evidence suggests that this may be the case for workers who are in their prime working years and who are the main breadwinners of their families.

Economists who argue that labor taxes are highly distortionary believe that labor supply is more elastic. While admitting that some groups of workers may not change the quantity of labor they supply by very much in response to changes in labor taxes, these economists claim that many other groups respond more to incentives. Here are some examples:

- Some workers can adjust the number of hours they work—for instance, by working overtime. The higher the wage, the more hours they choose to work.
- Many families have second earners—often married women with children—with some discretion over whether to do unpaid work at home or paid work in the marketplace. When deciding whether to take a job, these second earners compare the benefits of being at home (including savings on the cost of child care) with the wages they could earn.
- Many of the elderly can choose when to retire, and their decisions are partly based on the wage. Once they are retired, the wage determines their incentive to work part-time.

- Some people consider engaging in illegal economic activity, such as the drug trade, or working at jobs that pay "under the table" to evade taxes. Economists call this the *underground economy*. In deciding whether to work in the underground economy or at a legitimate job, these potential criminals compare what they can earn by breaking the law with the wage they can earn legally.

*"What's your position on the elasticity of labor supply?"*

In each of these cases, the quantity of labor supplied responds to the wage (the price of labor). Thus, these workers' decisions are distorted when their labor earnings are taxed. Labor taxes encourage workers to work fewer hours, second earners to stay at home, the elderly to retire early, and the unscrupulous to enter the underground economy.

The debate over the distortionary effects of labor taxation persists to this day. Indeed, whenever you see two political candidates debating whether the government should provide more services or reduce the tax burden, keep in mind that part of the disagreement may rest on different views about the elasticity of labor supply and the deadweight loss of taxation. ●

 *The demand for beer is more elastic than the demand for milk. Would a tax on beer or a tax on milk have a larger deadweight loss? Why?*

## 8-3 Deadweight Loss and Tax Revenue as Taxes Vary

Taxes rarely stay the same for long periods of time. Policymakers in local, state, and federal governments are always considering raising one tax or lowering another. Here we consider what happens to the deadweight loss and tax revenue when the size of a tax changes.

Figure 6 shows the effects of a small, medium, and large tax, holding constant the market's supply and demand curves. The deadweight loss—the reduction in total surplus that results when the tax reduces the size of a market below the optimum—equals the area of the triangle between the supply and demand curves. For the small tax in panel (a), the area of the deadweight loss triangle is quite small. But as the size of the tax rises in panels (b) and (c), the deadweight loss grows larger and larger.

Indeed, the deadweight loss of a tax rises even more rapidly than the size of the tax. This occurs because the deadweight loss is the area of a triangle, and the area of a triangle depends on the *square* of its size. If we double the size of a tax, for instance, the base and height of the triangle double, so the deadweight loss rises by a factor of 4. If we triple the size of a tax, the base and height triple, so the deadweight loss rises by a factor of 9.

The government's tax revenue is the size of the tax times the amount of the good sold. As the first three panels of Figure 6 show, tax revenue equals the area of the rectangle between the supply and demand curves. For the small tax in panel (a), tax revenue is small. As the size of the tax increases from panel (a) to panel (b), tax revenue grows. But as the size of the tax increases further from panel (b) to panel (c), tax revenue falls because the higher tax drastically reduces the size of the market. For a very large tax, no revenue would be raised because people would stop buying and selling the good altogether.

The last two panels of Figure 6 summarize these results. In panel (d), we see that as the size of a tax increases, its deadweight loss quickly gets larger. By contrast, panel (e) shows that tax revenue first rises with the size of the tax, but as the tax increases further, the market shrinks so much that tax revenue starts to fall.

# FIGURE **6**

**How Deadweight Loss and Tax Revenue Vary with the Size of a Tax**

The deadweight loss is the reduction in total surplus due to the tax. Tax revenue is the amount of the tax multiplied by the amount of the good sold. In panel (a), a small tax has a small deadweight loss and raises a small amount of revenue. In panel (b), a somewhat larger tax has a larger deadweight loss and raises a larger amount of revenue. In panel (c), a very large tax has a very large deadweight loss, but because it has reduced the size of the market so much, the tax raises only a small amount of revenue. Panels (d) and (e) summarize these conclusions. Panel (d) shows that as the size of a tax grows larger, the deadweight loss grows larger. Panel (e) shows that tax revenue first rises and then falls. This relationship is called the Laffer curve.

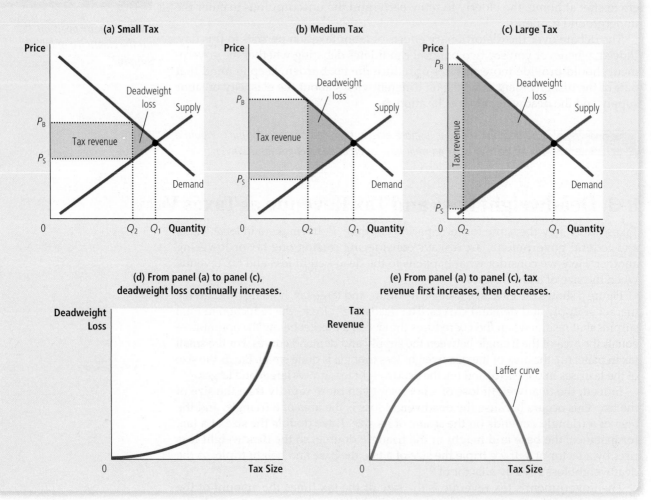

### THE LAFFER CURVE AND SUPPLY-SIDE ECONOMICS

**CASE STUDY**

One day in 1974, economist Arthur Laffer sat in a Washington restaurant with some prominent journalists and politicians. He took out a napkin and drew a figure on it to show how tax rates affect tax revenue. It looked much like panel (e) of our Figure 6. Laffer then suggested that the United States was on the downward-sloping side of this curve. Tax rates were so high, he argued, that reducing them might actually increase tax revenue.

Most economists were skeptical of Laffer's suggestion. They accepted the idea that a cut in tax rates could increase tax revenue as a matter of economic theory, but they doubted whether it would do so in practice. There was scant evidence for Laffer's view that U.S. tax rates had in fact reached such extreme levels.

Nonetheless, the *Laffer curve* (as it became known) captured the imagination of Ronald Reagan. David Stockman, budget director in the first Reagan administration, offers the following story:

> [Reagan] had once been on the Laffer curve himself. "I came into the Big Money making pictures during World War II," he would always say. At that time the wartime income surtax hit 90 percent. "You could only make four pictures and then you were in the top bracket," he would continue. "So we all quit working after four pictures and went off to the country." High tax rates caused less work. Low tax rates caused more. His experience proved it.

When Reagan ran for president in 1980, he made cutting taxes part of his platform. Reagan argued that taxes were so high that they were discouraging hard work and thereby depressing incomes. He argued that lower taxes would give people more incentive to work, which in turn would raise economic well-being. He suggested that incomes could rise by so much that tax revenue might increase, despite the lower tax rates. Because the cut in tax rates was intended to encourage people to increase the quantity of labor they supplied, the views of Laffer and Reagan became known as *supply-side economics*.

Economists continue to debate Laffer's argument. Many believe that subsequent history refuted Laffer's conjecture that lower tax rates would raise tax revenue. Yet because history is open to alternative interpretations, other economists view the events of the 1980s as more favorable to the supply siders. To evaluate Laffer's hypothesis definitively, we would need to rerun history without the Reagan tax cuts and see if tax revenues would have been higher or lower. Unfortunately, that experiment is impossible.

Some economists take an intermediate position on this issue. They believe that while an overall cut in tax rates normally reduces revenue, some taxpayers may occasionally find themselves on the wrong side of the Laffer curve. Other things being equal, a tax cut is more likely to raise tax revenue if the cut applies to those taxpayers facing the highest tax rates. In addition, Laffer's argument may be more compelling for countries with much higher tax rates than the United States. In Sweden in the early 1980s, for instance, the typical worker faced a marginal tax rate of about 80 percent. Such a high tax rate provides a substantial disincentive to work. Studies have suggested that Sweden would have indeed raised more tax revenue if it had lowered its tax rates.

Economists disagree about these issues in part because there is no consensus about the size of the relevant elasticities. The more elastic supply and demand are in any market, the more taxes distort behavior, and the more likely it is that a tax cut will increase tax revenue. There is no debate, however, about the general lesson: How much revenue the government gains or loses from a tax change cannot be computed just by looking at tax rates. It also depends on how the tax change affects people's behavior. ●

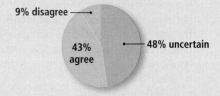

## ASK THE EXPERTS

### The Laffer Curve

"A cut in federal income tax rates in the United States right now would lead to higher national income within five years than without the tax cut."

**What do economists say?**

9% disagree
48% uncertain
43% agree

"A cut in federal income tax rates in the United States right now would raise taxable income enough so that the annual total tax revenue would be higher within five years than without the tax cut."

**What do economists say?**

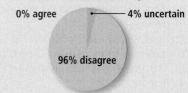

0% agree
4% uncertain
96% disagree

Source: IGM Economic Experts Panel, June 26, 2012.

**QuickQuiz** *If the government doubles the tax on gasoline, can you be sure that revenue from the gasoline tax will rise? Can you be sure that the deadweight loss from the gasoline tax will rise? Explain.*

# 8-4 Conclusion

In this chapter, we have used the tools developed in the previous chapter to further our understanding of taxes. One of the *Ten Principles of Economics* discussed in Chapter 1 is that markets are usually a good way to organize economic activity. In Chapter 7, we used the concepts of producer and consumer surplus to make this principle more precise. Here we have seen that when the government imposes taxes on buyers or sellers of a good, society loses some of the benefits of market efficiency. Taxes are costly to market participants not only because taxes transfer resources from those participants to the government but also because they alter incentives and distort market outcomes.

The analysis presented here and in Chapter 6 should give you a good basis for understanding the economic impact of taxes, but this is not the end of the story. Microeconomists study how best to design a tax system, including how to strike the right balance between equality and efficiency. Macroeconomists study how taxes influence the overall economy and how policymakers can use the tax system to stabilize economic activity and to achieve more rapid economic growth. So as you continue your study of economics, don't be surprised when the subject of taxation comes up yet again.

## CHAPTER QuickQuiz

1.  A tax on a good has a deadweight loss if
    a.  the reduction in consumer and producer surplus is greater than the tax revenue.
    b.  the tax revenue is greater than the reduction in consumer and producer surplus.
    c.  the reduction in consumer surplus is greater than the reduction in producer surplus.
    d.  the reduction in producer surplus is greater than the reduction in consumer surplus.

2.  Sofia pays Sam $50 to mow her lawn every week. When the government levies a mowing tax of $10 on Sam, he raises his price to $60. Sofia continues to hire him at the higher price. What is the change in producer surplus, change in consumer surplus, and deadweight loss?
    a.  $0, $0, $10
    b.  $0, −$10, $0
    c.  +$10, −$10, $10
    d.  +$10, −$10, $0

3.  Eggs have a supply curve that is linear and upward-sloping and a demand curve that is linear and downward-sloping. If a 2 cent per egg tax is increased to 3 cents, the deadweight loss of the tax
    a.  increases by less than 50 percent and may even decline.
    b.  increases by exactly 50 percent.
    c.  increases by more than 50 percent.
    d.  The answer depends on whether supply or demand is more elastic.

4.  Peanut butter has an upward-sloping supply curve and a downward-sloping demand curve. If a 10 cent per pound tax is increased to 15 cents, the government's tax revenue
    a.  increases by less than 50 percent and may even decline.
    b.  increases by exactly 50 percent.
    c.  increases by more than 50 percent.
    d.  The answer depends on whether supply or demand is more elastic.

5.  The Laffer curve illustrates that, in some circumstances, the government can reduce a tax on a good and increase the
    a.  deadweight loss.
    b.  government's tax revenue.
    c.  equilibrium quantity.
    d.  price paid by consumers.

6.  If a policymaker wants to raise revenue by taxing goods while minimizing the deadweight losses, he should look for goods with _____ elasticities of demand and _____ elasticities of supply.
    a.  small, small
    b.  small, large
    c.  large, small
    d.  large, large

## SUMMARY

- A tax on a good reduces the welfare of buyers and sellers of the good, and the reduction in consumer and producer surplus usually exceeds the revenue raised by the government. The fall in total surplus—the sum of consumer surplus, producer surplus, and tax revenue—is called the deadweight loss of the tax.
- Taxes have deadweight losses because they cause buyers to consume less and sellers to produce less, and these changes in behavior shrink the size of the market below the level that maximizes total surplus. Because the elasticities of supply and demand measure how much market participants respond to market conditions, larger elasticities imply larger deadweight losses.
- As a tax grows larger, it distorts incentives more, and its deadweight loss grows larger. Because a tax reduces the size of the market, however, tax revenue does not continually increase. It first rises with the size of a tax, but if the tax gets large enough, tax revenue starts to fall.

## KEY CONCEPT

deadweight loss, p. 157

## QUESTIONS FOR REVIEW

1. What happens to consumer and producer surplus when the sale of a good is taxed? How does the change in consumer and producer surplus compare to the tax revenue? Explain.

2. Draw a supply-and-demand diagram with a tax on the sale of a good. Show the deadweight loss. Show the tax revenue.

3. How do the elasticities of supply and demand affect the deadweight loss of a tax? Why do they have this effect?

4. Why do experts disagree about whether labor taxes have small or large deadweight losses?

5. What happens to the deadweight loss and tax revenue when a tax is increased?

## PROBLEMS AND APPLICATIONS

1. The market for pizza is characterized by a downward-sloping demand curve and an upward-sloping supply curve.
   a. Draw the competitive market equilibrium. Label the price, quantity, consumer surplus, and producer surplus. Is there any deadweight loss? Explain.
   b. Suppose that the government forces each pizzeria to pay a $1 tax on each pizza sold. Illustrate the effect of this tax on the pizza market, being sure to label the consumer surplus, producer surplus, government revenue, and deadweight loss. How does each area compare to the pre-tax case?
   c. If the tax were removed, pizza eaters and sellers would be better off, but the government would lose tax revenue. Suppose that consumers and producers voluntarily transferred some of their gains to the government. Could all parties (including the government) be better off than they were with a tax? Explain using the labeled areas in your graph.

2. Evaluate the following two statements. Do you agree? Why or why not?
   a. "A tax that has no deadweight loss cannot raise any revenue for the government."
   b. "A tax that raises no revenue for the government cannot have any deadweight loss."

3. Consider the market for rubber bands.
   a. If this market has very elastic supply and very inelastic demand, how would the burden of a tax on rubber bands be shared between consumers and producers? Use the tools of consumer surplus and producer surplus in your answer.
   b. If this market has very inelastic supply and very elastic demand, how would the burden of a tax on rubber bands be shared between consumers and producers? Contrast your answer with your answer to part (a).

4. Suppose that the government imposes a tax on heating oil.
   a. Would the deadweight loss from this tax likely be greater in the first year after it is imposed or in the fifth year? Explain.
   b. Would the revenue collected from this tax likely be greater in the first year after it is imposed or in the fifth year? Explain.

5. After economics class one day, your friend suggests that taxing food would be a good way to raise revenue because the demand for food is quite inelastic. In what sense is taxing food a "good" way to raise revenue? In what sense is it not a "good" way to raise revenue?

6. Daniel Patrick Moynihan, the late senator from New York, once introduced a bill that would levy a 10,000 percent tax on certain hollow-tipped bullets.
   a. Do you expect that this tax would raise much revenue? Why or why not?
   b. Even if the tax would raise no revenue, why might Senator Moynihan have proposed it?

7. The government places a tax on the purchase of socks.
   a. Illustrate the effect of this tax on equilibrium price and quantity in the sock market. Identify the following areas both before and after the imposition of the tax: total spending by consumers, total revenue for producers, and government tax revenue.
   b. Does the price received by producers rise or fall? Can you tell whether total receipts for producers rise or fall? Explain.
   c. Does the price paid by consumers rise or fall? Can you tell whether total spending by consumers rises or falls? Explain carefully. (*Hint*: Think about elasticity.) If total consumer spending falls, does consumer surplus rise? Explain.

8. This chapter analyzed the welfare effects of a tax on a good. Now consider the opposite policy. Suppose that the government *subsidizes* a good: For each unit of the good sold, the government pays $2 to the buyer. How does the subsidy affect consumer surplus, producer surplus, tax revenue, and total surplus? Does a subsidy lead to a deadweight loss? Explain.

9. Hotel rooms in Smalltown go for $100, and 1,000 rooms are rented on a typical day.
   a. To raise revenue, the mayor decides to charge hotels a tax of $10 per rented room. After the tax is imposed, the going rate for hotel rooms rises to $108, and the number of rooms rented falls to 900. Calculate the amount of revenue this tax raises for Smalltown and the deadweight loss of the tax. (*Hint*: The area of a triangle is ½ × base × height.)

   b. The mayor now doubles the tax to $20. The price rises to $116, and the number of rooms rented falls to 800. Calculate tax revenue and deadweight loss with this larger tax. Are they double, more than double, or less than double? Explain.

10. Suppose that a market is described by the following supply and demand equations:

$$Q^S = 2P$$
$$Q^D = 300 - P$$

   a. Solve for the equilibrium price and the equilibrium quantity.
   b. Suppose that a tax of $T$ is placed on buyers, so the new demand equation is

$$Q^D = 300 - (P + T)$$

   Solve for the new equilibrium. What happens to the price received by sellers, the price paid by buyers, and the quantity sold?
   c. Tax revenue is $T \times Q$. Use your answer from part (b) to solve for tax revenue as a function of $T$. Graph this relationship for $T$ between 0 and 300.
   d. The deadweight loss of a tax is the area of the triangle between the supply and demand curves. Recalling that the area of a triangle is ½ × base × height, solve for deadweight loss as a function of $T$. Graph this relationship for $T$ between 0 and 300. (*Hint*: Looking sideways, the base of the deadweight loss triangle is $T$, and the height is the difference between the quantity sold with the tax and the quantity sold without the tax.)
   e. The government now levies a tax of $200 per unit on this good. Is this a good policy? Why or why not? Can you propose a better policy?

To find additional study resources, visit cengagebrain.com, and search for "Mankiw."

# Application: International Trade

If you check the labels on the clothes you are wearing, you will probably find that some were made in another country. A century ago, the textile and clothing industry was a major part of the U.S. economy, but that is no longer the case. Faced with foreign competitors that can produce quality goods at low cost, many U.S. firms found it increasingly difficult to produce and sell textiles and clothing at a profit. As a result, they laid off their workers and shut down their factories. Today, most of the textiles and clothing that Americans consume are imported.

The story of the textile industry raises important questions for economic policy: How does international trade affect economic well-being? Who gains and who loses from free trade among countries, and how do the gains compare to the losses?

Chapter 3 introduced the study of international trade by applying the principle of comparative advantage. According to this principle, all countries can benefit from trading with one another because trade allows each country to specialize in doing what it does best. But the analysis in Chapter 3 was incomplete. It did not explain how the international marketplace achieves these gains from trade or how the gains are distributed among the various economic participants.

We now return to the study of international trade to tackle these questions. Over the past several chapters, we have developed many tools for analyzing how markets work: supply, demand, equilibrium, consumer surplus, producer surplus, and so on. With these tools, we can learn more about how international trade affects economic well-being.

# 9-1  The Determinants of Trade

Consider the market for textiles. The textile market is well suited to studying the gains and losses from international trade: Textiles are made in many countries around the world, and there is much world trade in textiles. Moreover, the textile market is one in which policymakers often consider (and sometimes implement) trade restrictions to protect domestic producers from foreign competitors. Here we examine the textile market in the imaginary country of Isoland.

## 9-1a  The Equilibrium without Trade

As our story begins, the Isolandian textile market is isolated from the rest of the world. By government decree, no one in Isoland is allowed to import or export textiles, and the penalty for violating the decree is so large that no one dares try.

Because there is no international trade, the market for textiles in Isoland consists solely of Isolandian buyers and sellers. As Figure 1 shows, the domestic price adjusts to balance the quantity supplied by domestic sellers and the quantity demanded by domestic buyers. The figure shows the consumer and producer surplus in the equilibrium without trade. The sum of consumer and producer surplus measures the total benefits that buyers and sellers receive from participating in the textile market.

**FIGURE 1**

**The Equilibrium without International Trade**

When an economy cannot trade in world markets, the price adjusts to balance domestic supply and demand. This figure shows consumer and producer surplus in an equilibrium without international trade for the textile market in the imaginary country of Isoland.

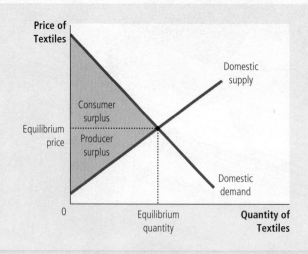

Now suppose that, in a political upset, Isoland elects a new president. The president campaigned on a platform of "change" and promised the voters bold new ideas. Her first act is to assemble a team of economists to evaluate Isolandian trade policy. She asks them to report on three questions:

- If the government allows Isolandians to import and export textiles, what will happen to the price of textiles and the quantity of textiles sold in the domestic textile market?
- Who will gain from free trade in textiles and who will lose, and will the gains exceed the losses?
- Should a tariff (a tax on textile imports) be part of the new trade policy?

After reviewing supply and demand in their favorite textbook (this one, of course), the Isolandian economics team begins its analysis.

## 9-1b The World Price and Comparative Advantage

The first issue our economists take up is whether Isoland is likely to become a textile importer or a textile exporter. In other words, if free trade is allowed, will Isolandians end up buying or selling textiles in world markets?

To answer this question, the economists compare the current Isolandian price of textiles to the price of textiles in other countries. We call the price prevailing in world markets the **world price**. If the world price of textiles is higher than the domestic price, then Isoland will export textiles once trade is permitted. Isolandian textile producers will be eager to receive the higher prices available abroad and will start selling their textiles to buyers in other countries. Conversely, if the world price of textiles is lower than the domestic price, then Isoland will import textiles. Because foreign sellers offer a better price, Isolandian textile consumers will quickly start buying textiles from other countries.

**world price**
the price of a good that prevails in the world market for that good

In essence, comparing the world price with the domestic price before trade reveals whether Isoland has a comparative advantage in producing textiles. The domestic price reflects the opportunity cost of textiles: It tells us how much an Isolandian must give up to obtain one unit of textiles. If the domestic price is low, the cost of producing textiles in Isoland is low, suggesting that Isoland has a comparative advantage in producing textiles relative to the rest of the world. If the domestic price is high, then the cost of producing textiles in Isoland is high, suggesting that foreign countries have a comparative advantage in producing textiles.

As we saw in Chapter 3, trade among nations is ultimately based on comparative advantage. That is, trade is beneficial because it allows each nation to specialize in doing what it does best. By comparing the world price with the domestic price before trade, we can determine whether Isoland is better or worse than the rest of the world at producing textiles.

**QuickQuiz** *The country Autarka does not allow international trade. In Autarka, you can buy a wool suit for 3 ounces of gold. Meanwhile, in neighboring countries, you can buy the same suit for 2 ounces of gold. If Autarka were to allow free trade, would it import or export wool suits? Why?*

# 9-2　The Winners and Losers from Trade

To analyze the welfare effects of free trade, the Isolandian economists begin with the assumption that Isoland is a small economy compared to the rest of the world. This small-economy assumption means that Isoland's actions have little effect on world markets. Specifically, any change in Isoland's trade policy will not affect the world price of textiles. The Isolandians are said to be *price takers* in the world economy. That is, they take the world price of textiles as given. Isoland can be an exporting country by selling textiles at this price or an importing country by buying textiles at this price.

The small-economy assumption is not necessary to analyze the gains and losses from international trade. But the Isolandian economists know from experience (and from reading Chapter 2 of this book) that making simplifying assumptions is a key part of building a useful economic model. The assumption that Isoland is a small economy simplifies the analysis, and the basic lessons do not change in the more complicated case of a large economy.

## 9-2a　The Gains and Losses of an Exporting Country

Figure 2 shows the Isolandian textile market when the domestic equilibrium price before trade is below the world price. Once trade is allowed, the domestic price rises to equal the world price. No seller of textiles would accept less than the world price, and no buyer would pay more than the world price.

## FIGURE 2

**International Trade in an Exporting Country**
Once trade is allowed, the domestic price rises to equal the world price. The supply curve shows the quantity of textiles produced domestically, and the demand curve shows the quantity consumed domestically. Exports from Isoland equal the difference between the domestic quantity supplied and the domestic quantity demanded at the world price. Sellers are better off (producer surplus rises from C to B + C + D), and buyers are worse off (consumer surplus falls from A + B to A). Total surplus rises by an amount equal to area D, indicating that trade raises the economic well-being of the country as a whole.

| | Before Trade | After Trade | Change |
|---|---|---|---|
| Consumer Surplus | A + B | A | −B |
| Producer Surplus | C | B + C + D | + (B + D) |
| Total Surplus | A + B + C | A + B + C + D | + D |

The area D shows the increase in total surplus and represents the gains from trade.

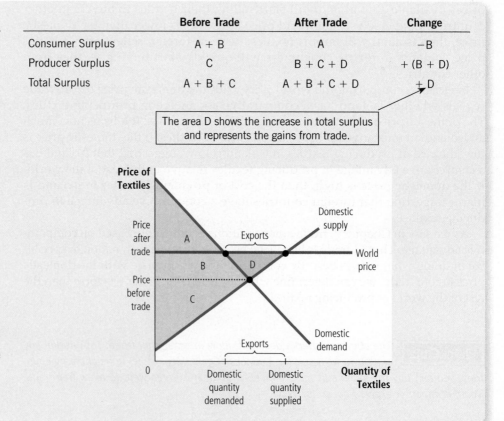

After the domestic price has risen to equal the world price, the domestic quantity supplied differs from the domestic quantity demanded. The supply curve shows the quantity of textiles supplied by Isolandian sellers. The demand curve shows the quantity of textiles demanded by Isolandian buyers. Because the domestic quantity supplied is greater than the domestic quantity demanded, Isoland sells textiles to other countries. Thus, Isoland becomes a textile exporter.

Although domestic quantity supplied and domestic quantity demanded differ, the textile market is still in equilibrium because there is now another participant in the market: the rest of the world. One can view the horizontal line at the world price as representing the rest of the world's demand for textiles. This demand curve is perfectly elastic because Isoland, as a small economy, can sell as many textiles as it wants at the world price.

Consider the gains and losses from opening up trade. Clearly, not everyone benefits. Trade forces the domestic price to rise to the world price. Domestic producers of textiles are better off because they can now sell textiles at a higher price, but domestic consumers of textiles are worse off because they now have to buy textiles at a higher price.

To measure these gains and losses, we look at the changes in consumer and producer surplus. Before trade is allowed, the price of textiles adjusts to balance domestic supply and domestic demand. Consumer surplus, the area between the demand curve and the before-trade price, is area A + B. Producer surplus, the area between the supply curve and the before-trade price, is area C. Total surplus before trade, the sum of consumer and producer surplus, is area A + B + C.

After trade is allowed, the domestic price rises to the world price. Consumer surplus shrinks to area A (the area between the demand curve and the world price). Producer surplus increases to area B + C + D (the area between the supply curve and the world price). Thus, total surplus with trade is area A + B + C + D.

These welfare calculations show who wins and who loses from trade in an exporting country. Sellers benefit because producer surplus increases by the area B + D. Buyers are worse off because consumer surplus decreases by the area B. Because the gains of sellers exceed the losses of buyers by the area D, total surplus in Isoland increases.

This analysis of an exporting country yields two conclusions:

- When a country allows trade and becomes an exporter of a good, domestic producers of the good are better off, and domestic consumers of the good are worse off.
- Trade raises the economic well-being of a nation in the sense that the gains of the winners exceed the losses of the losers.

### 9-2b  The Gains and Losses of an Importing Country

Now suppose that the domestic price before trade is above the world price. Once again, after trade is allowed, the domestic price must equal the world price. As Figure 3 shows, the domestic quantity supplied is less than the domestic quantity demanded. The difference between the domestic quantity demanded and the domestic quantity supplied is bought from other countries, and Isoland becomes a textile importer.

In this case, the horizontal line at the world price represents the supply of the rest of the world. This supply curve is perfectly elastic because Isoland is a small economy and, therefore, can buy as many textiles as it wants at the world price.

# FIGURE 3

**International Trade in an Importing Country**
Once trade is allowed, the domestic price falls to equal the world price. The supply curve shows the amount produced domestically, and the demand curve shows the amount consumed domestically. Imports equal the difference between the domestic quantity demanded and the domestic quantity supplied at the world price. Buyers are better off (consumer surplus rises from A to A + B + D), and sellers are worse off (producer surplus falls from B + C to C). Total surplus rises by an amount equal to area D, indicating that trade raises the economic well-being of the country as a whole.

|  | Before Trade | After Trade | Change |
|---|---|---|---|
| Consumer Surplus | A | A + B + D | + (B + D) |
| Producer Surplus | B + C | C | −B |
| Total Surplus | A + B + C | A + B + C + D | + D |

The area D shows the increase in total surplus and represents the gains from trade.

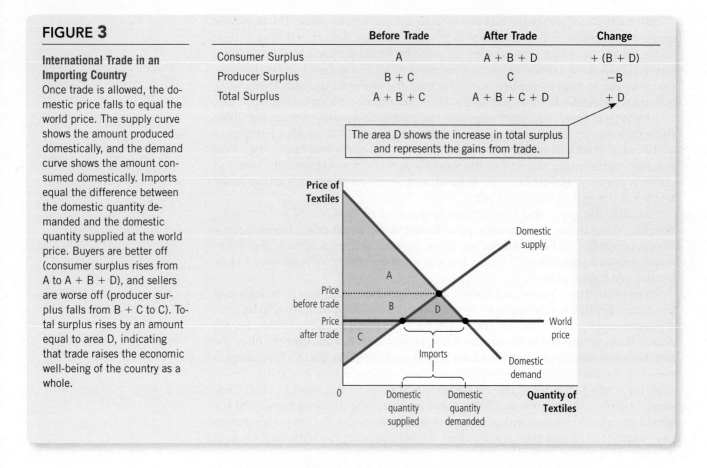

Once again, consider the gains and losses from trade. As in the previous case, not everyone benefits, but here the winners and losers are reversed. When trade forces the domestic price to fall, domestic consumers are better off (they can now buy textiles at a lower price), and domestic producers are worse off (they now have to sell textiles at a lower price). Changes in consumer and producer surplus measure the size of the gains and losses. Before trade, consumer surplus is area A, producer surplus is area B + C, and total surplus is area A + B + C. After trade is allowed, consumer surplus is area A + B + D, producer surplus is area C, and total surplus is area A + B + C + D.

These welfare calculations show who wins and who loses from trade in an importing country. Buyers benefit because consumer surplus increases by the area B + D. Sellers are worse off because producer surplus falls by the area B. The gains of buyers exceed the losses of sellers, and total surplus increases by the area D.

This analysis of an importing country yields two conclusions parallel to those for an exporting country:

- When a country allows trade and becomes an importer of a good, domestic consumers of the good are better off, and domestic producers of the good are worse off.
- Trade raises the economic well-being of a nation in the sense that the gains of the winners exceed the losses of the losers.

Having completed our analysis of trade, we can better understand one of the *Ten Principles of Economics* in Chapter 1: Trade can make everyone better off. If Isoland opens its textile market to international trade, the change creates winners and losers, regardless of whether Isoland ends up exporting or importing textiles. In either case, however, the gains of the winners exceed the losses of the losers, so the winners could compensate the losers and still be better off. In this sense, trade *can* make everyone better off. But *will* trade make everyone better off? Probably not. In practice, compensation for the losers from international trade is rare. Without such compensation, opening an economy to international trade is a policy that expands the size of the economic pie, but it can leave some participants in the economy with a smaller slice.

We can now see why the debate over trade policy is often contentious. Whenever a policy creates winners and losers, the stage is set for a political battle. Nations sometimes fail to enjoy the gains from trade because the losers from free trade are better organized than the winners. The losers may turn their cohesiveness into political clout and lobby for trade restrictions such as tariffs or import quotas.

## 9-2c Effects of a Tariff

The Isolandian economists next consider the effects of a **tariff**—a tax on imported goods. The economists quickly realize that a tariff on textiles will have no effect if Isoland becomes a textile exporter. If no one in Isoland is interested in importing textiles, a tax on textile imports is irrelevant. The tariff matters only if Isoland becomes a textile importer. Concentrating their attention on this case, the economists compare welfare with and without the tariff.

**tariff**
a tax on goods produced abroad and sold domestically

Figure 4 shows the Isolandian market for textiles. Under free trade, the domestic price equals the world price. A tariff raises the price of imported textiles above the world price by the amount of the tariff. Domestic suppliers of textiles, who compete with suppliers of imported textiles, can now sell their textiles for the world price plus the amount of the tariff. Thus, the price of textiles—both imported and domestic—rises by the amount of the tariff and is, therefore, closer to the price that would prevail without trade.

The change in price affects the behavior of domestic buyers and sellers. Because the tariff raises the price of textiles, it reduces the domestic quantity demanded from $Q_1^D$ to $Q_2^D$ and raises the domestic quantity supplied from $Q_1^S$ to $Q_2^S$. *Thus, the tariff reduces the quantity of imports and moves the domestic market closer to its equilibrium without trade.*

Now consider the gains and losses from the tariff. Because the tariff raises the domestic price, domestic sellers are better off, and domestic buyers are worse off. In addition, the government raises revenue. To measure these gains and losses, we look at the changes in consumer surplus, producer surplus, and government revenue. These changes are summarized in the table in Figure 4.

Before the tariff, the domestic price equals the world price. Consumer surplus, the area between the demand curve and the world price, is area A + B + C + D + E + F. Producer surplus, the area between the supply curve and the world price, is area G. Government revenue equals zero. Total surplus, the sum of consumer surplus, producer surplus, and government revenue, is area A + B + C + D + E + F + G.

Once the government imposes a tariff, the domestic price exceeds the world price by the amount of the tariff. Consumer surplus is now area A + B. Producer surplus is area C + G. Government revenue, which is the size of the tariff multiplied by the quantity of after-tariff imports, is the area E. Thus, total surplus with the tariff is area A + B + C + E + G.

## FIGURE 4

### The Effects of a Tariff

A tariff, a tax on imports, reduces the quantity of imports and moves a market closer to the equilibrium that would exist without trade. Total surplus falls by an amount equal to area D + F. These two triangles represent the deadweight loss from the tariff.

|  | Before Tariff | After Tariff | Change |
|---|---|---|---|
| Consumer Surplus | A + B + C + D + E + F | A + B | −(C + D + E + F) |
| Producer Surplus | G | C + G | + C |
| Government Revenue | None | E | + E |
| Total Surplus | A + B + C + D + E + F + G | A + B + C + E + G | −(D + F) |

The area D + F shows the fall in total surplus and represents the deadweight loss of the tariff.

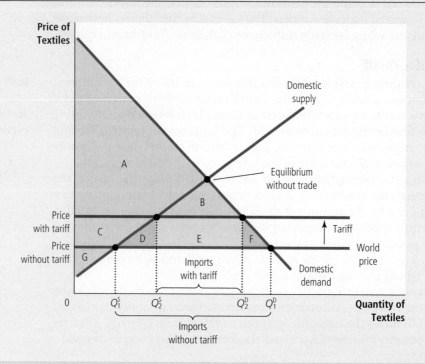

To determine the total welfare effects of the tariff, we add the change in consumer surplus (which is negative), the change in producer surplus (positive), and the change in government revenue (positive). We find that total surplus in the market decreases by the area D + F. This fall in total surplus is called the *deadweight loss* of the tariff.

A tariff causes a deadweight loss because a tariff is a type of tax. Like most taxes, it distorts incentives and pushes the allocation of scarce resources away from the optimum. In this case, we can identify two effects. First, when the tariff raises the domestic price of textiles above the world price, it encourages domestic producers to increase production from $Q_1^S$ to $Q_2^S$. Even though the cost of making these incremental units exceeds the cost of buying them at the world price, the tariff makes it profitable for domestic producers to manufacture them nonetheless. Second, when the tariff raises the price that domestic textile consumers have

## Import Quotas: Another Way to Restrict Trade

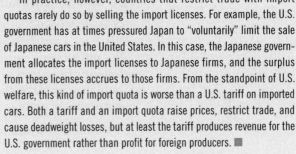

Beyond tariffs, another way that nations sometimes restrict international trade is by putting limits on how much of a good can be imported. In this book, we will not analyze such a policy, other than to point out the conclusion: Import quotas are much like tariffs. Both tariffs and import quotas reduce the quantity of imports, raise the domestic price of the good, decrease the welfare of domestic consumers, increase the welfare of domestic producers, and cause deadweight losses.

There is only one difference between these two types of trade restriction: A tariff raises revenue for the government, whereas an import quota creates surplus for those who obtain the licenses to import. The profit for the holder of an import license is the difference between the domestic price (at which she sells the imported good) and the world price (at which she buys it).

Tariffs and import quotas are even more similar if the government charges a fee for the import licenses. Suppose the government sets the license fee equal to the difference between the domestic price and the world price. In this case, the entire profit of license holders is paid to the government in license fees, and the import quota works exactly like a tariff. Consumer surplus, producer surplus, and government revenue are precisely the same under the two policies.

In practice, however, countries that restrict trade with import quotas rarely do so by selling the import licenses. For example, the U.S. government has at times pressured Japan to "voluntarily" limit the sale of Japanese cars in the United States. In this case, the Japanese government allocates the import licenses to Japanese firms, and the surplus from these licenses accrues to those firms. From the standpoint of U.S. welfare, this kind of import quota is worse than a U.S. tariff on imported cars. Both a tariff and an import quota raise prices, restrict trade, and cause deadweight losses, but at least the tariff produces revenue for the U.S. government rather than profit for foreign producers. ∎

to pay, it encourages them to reduce their consumption of textiles from $Q_1^D$ to $Q_2^D$. Even though domestic consumers value these incremental units at more than the world price, the tariff induces them to cut back their purchases. Area D represents the deadweight loss from the overproduction of textiles, and area F represents the deadweight loss from the underconsumption of textiles. The total deadweight loss of the tariff is the sum of these two triangles.

### 9-2d The Lessons for Trade Policy
The team of Isolandian economists can now write to the new president:

Dear Madam President,

You asked us three questions about opening up trade. After much hard work, we have the answers.

*Question*: If the government allows Isolandians to import and export textiles, what will happen to the price of textiles and the quantity of textiles sold in the domestic textile market?

*Answer*: Once trade is allowed, the Isolandian price of textiles will be driven to equal the price prevailing around the world.

If the world price is now higher than the Isolandian price, our price will rise. The higher price will reduce the amount of textiles Isolandians consume and raise the amount of textiles that Isolandians produce. Isoland will, therefore, become a textile exporter. This occurs because, in this case, Isoland has a comparative advantage in producing textiles.

Conversely, if the world price is now lower than the Isolandian price, our price will fall. The lower price will raise the amount of textiles that Isolandians consume and lower the amount of textiles that Isolandians produce. Isoland will, therefore, become a textile importer. This occurs because, in this case, other countries have a comparative advantage in producing textiles.

*Question*: Who will gain from free trade in textiles and who will lose, and will the gains exceed the losses?

*Answer*: The answer depends on whether the price rises or falls when trade is allowed. If the price rises, producers of textiles gain, and consumers of textiles lose. If the price falls, consumers gain, and producers lose. In both cases, the gains are larger than the losses. Thus, free trade raises the total welfare of Isolandians.

*Question*: Should a tariff be part of the new trade policy?

*Answer*: A tariff has an impact only if Isoland becomes a textile importer. In this case, a tariff moves the economy closer to the no-trade equilibrium and, like most taxes, causes deadweight losses. A tariff improves the welfare of domestic producers and raises revenue for the government, but these gains are more than offset by the losses suffered by consumers. The best policy, from the standpoint of economic efficiency, would be to allow trade without a tariff.

We hope you find these answers helpful as you decide on your new policy.

Your faithful servants,
Isolandian economics team

## 9-2e  Other Benefits of International Trade

The conclusions of the Isolandian economics team are based on the standard analysis of international trade. Their analysis uses the most fundamental tools in the economist's toolbox: supply, demand, and producer and consumer surplus. It shows that there are winners and losers when a nation opens itself up to trade, but the gains of the winners exceed the losses of the losers.

The case for free trade can be made even stronger, however, because there are several other economic benefits of trade beyond those emphasized in the standard analysis. In a nutshell, here are some of these other benefits:

- **Increased variety of goods.** Goods produced in different countries are not exactly the same. German beer, for instance, is not the same as American beer. Free trade gives consumers in all countries greater variety to choose from.
- **Lower costs through economies of scale.** Some goods can be produced at low cost only if they are produced in large quantities—a phenomenon called *economies of scale*. A firm in a small country cannot take full advantage of economies of scale if it can sell only in a small domestic market. Free trade gives firms access to larger world markets and allows them to realize economies of scale more fully.
- **Increased competition.** A company shielded from foreign competitors is more likely to have market power, which in turn gives it the ability to raise prices above competitive levels. This is a type of market failure. Opening up trade fosters competition and gives the invisible hand a better chance to work its magic.

## IN THE NEWS

# Trade as a Tool for Economic Development

*Free international trade can help the world's poorest citizens.*

## Andy Warhol's Guide to Public Policy

By Arthur C. Brooks

I often ask people in my business — public policy — where they get their inspiration. Liberals often point to John F. Kennedy. Conservatives usually cite Ronald Reagan. Personally, I prefer the artist Andy Warhol, who famously declared, "I like boring things." He was referring to art, of course. But the sentiment provides solid public policy guidance as well.

Warhol's work exalted the everyday "boring" items that display the transcendental beauty of life itself. The canonical example is his famous paintings of Campbell Soup cans. Some people sneered, but those willing to look closely could see what he was doing. It is the same idea expressed in an old Zen saying, often attributed to the eighth-century Chinese Buddhist philosopher Layman Pang: "How wondrously supernatural and miraculous! I draw water and I carry wood!"

Warhol's critical insight is usually lost on most of the world. This is not because people are stupid, but because our brains are wired to filter out the mundane and focus on the novel. This turns out to be an important survival adaptation. To discern a predator, you must filter out the constant rustling of leaves and notice the strange snap of a twig.

Warhol believed that defeating this cognitive bias led to greater appreciation of beauty. It also leads to better public policy, especially in relieving poverty. For example, while our attention is naturally drawn to the latest fascinating and expensive innovations in tropical public health, many experts insist it is cheap, boring mosquito bed nets that best protect against malaria. Despite their lifesaving utility, these boring nets tend to be chronically underprovided.

We can look closer to home, too. People love to find ways to get fancy technology into poor schoolchildren's hands, but arguably the best way to help children falling behind in school is simply to devise ways to get them to show up.

But the very best example of the Warhol principle in policy is international trade. If it is progress against poverty that we're pursuing, trade beats the pants off every fancy development program ever devised. The simple mundane beauty of making things and exchanging them freely is the best anti-poverty achievement in history.

For more than two decades, the global poverty rate has been decreasing by roughly 1 percent a year. To put this in perspective, that comes to about 70 million people — equivalent to the whole population of Turkey or Thailand — climbing out of poverty annually. Add it up, and around a billion people have escaped destitution since 1990.

Why? It isn't the United Nations or foreign aid. It is, in the words of the publication YaleGlobal Online, "High growth spillovers originating from large open emerging economies that utilize cross-border supply chains." For readers who don't have tenure, that means free trade in poor countries.

That mug in your hand that says "Made in China" is part of the reason that 680 million Chinese have been pulled out of absolute poverty since the 1980s. No giant collaboration among transnational technocrats or lending initiatives did that. It was because of economic reforms in China, of people making stuff, putting it on boats, and sending it to be sold in America — to you. Critics of free trade often argue that open economies lead to exploitation or environmental degradation. These are serious issues, but protectionism is never the answer. Curbing trade benefits entrenched domestic interests and works against the world's poor.

And what of claims that trade increases global income inequality? They are false. Economists at the World Bank and at LIS (formerly known as the Luxembourg Income Study Center) have shown that, for the world as a whole, income inequality has fallen for most of the past 20 years. This is chiefly because of rising incomes from globalization in the developing world. . . .

Fortunately, President Obama appreciates the benefits of trade and is currently fighting for the latest international trade pact, the Trans-Pacific Partnership (T.P.P.). It would knock down barriers between North American, South American and East Asian nations, benefiting rich and poor people and countries alike. Admirably, the president is standing up to critics in his own party (as well as some in the opposition) who oppose the deal. With luck, T.P.P. will make its way through the House and Senate this spring or summer, and receive the president's signature.

Trade doesn't solve every problem, of course. The world needs democracy, security and many other expressions of American values and leadership as well. But in a policy world crowded with outlandish, wasteful boondoggles, free trade is just the kind of beautifully boring Warholian strategy we need. Americans dedicated to helping others ought to support it without compromise or apology. ∎

**Source:** *New York Times*, April 12, 2015.

- **Enhanced flow of ideas.** The transfer of technological advances around the world is often thought to be linked to the trading of the goods that embody those advances. The best way for a poor agricultural nation to learn about the computer revolution, for instance, is to buy some computers from abroad rather than trying to make them domestically.

Thus, free international trade increases variety for consumers, allows firms to take advantage of economies of scale, makes markets more competitive, and facilitates the spread of technology. If the Isolandian economists also took these effects into account, their advice to the president would be even more forceful.

**QuickQuiz**  *Draw a supply-and-demand diagram for wool suits in the country of Autarka. When trade is allowed, the price of a suit falls from 3 to 2 ounces of gold. In your diagram, show the change in consumer surplus, the change in producer surplus, and the change in total surplus. How would a tariff on suit imports alter these effects?*

# 9-3  The Arguments for Restricting Trade

The letter from the economics team starts to persuade the new president of Isoland to consider allowing trade in textiles. She notes that the domestic price is now high compared to the world price. Free trade would, therefore, cause the price of textiles to fall and hurt domestic textile producers. Before implementing the new policy, she asks Isolandian textile companies to comment on the economists' advice.

Not surprisingly, the textile companies oppose free trade in textiles. They believe that the government should protect the domestic textile industry from foreign competition. Let's consider some of the arguments they might give to support their position and how the economics team would respond.

### 9-3a  The Jobs Argument

Opponents of free trade often argue that trade with other countries destroys domestic jobs. In our example, free trade in textiles would cause the price of

*"You like protectionism as a 'working man.' How about as a consumer?"*

# Should the Winners from Free Trade Compensate the Losers?

*Politicians and pundits often say that the government should help workers made worse off by international trade by, for example, paying for their retraining. In this opinion piece, an economist makes the opposite case.*

## What to Expect When You're Free Trading

**By Steven E. Landsburg**

All economists know that when American jobs are outsourced, Americans as a group are net winners. What we lose through lower wages is more than offset by what we gain through lower prices. In other words, the winners can more than afford to compensate the losers. Does that mean they ought to? Does it create a moral mandate for taxpayer-subsidized retraining programs?...

Um, no. Even if you've just lost your job, there's something fundamentally churlish about blaming the very phenomenon that's elevated you above the subsistence level since the day you were born. If the world owes you compensation for enduring the downside of trade, what do you owe the world for enjoying the upside?

I doubt there's a human being on earth who hasn't benefited from the opportunity to trade freely with his neighbors. Imagine what your life would be like if you had to grow your own food, make your own clothes and rely on your grandmother's home remedies for health care. Access to a trained physician might reduce the demand for grandma's home remedies, but—especially at her age—she's still got plenty of reason to be thankful for having a doctor.

Some people suggest, however, that it makes sense to isolate the moral effects of a single new trading opportunity or free trade agreement. Surely we have fellow citizens who are hurt by those agreements, at least in the limited sense that they'd be better off in a world where trade flourishes, except in this one instance. What do we owe those fellow citizens?

One way to think about that is to ask what your moral instincts tell you in analogous situations. Suppose, after years of buying shampoo at your local pharmacy, you discover you can order the same shampoo for less money on the Web. Do you have an obligation to compensate your pharmacist? If you move to a cheaper apartment, should you compensate your landlord? When you eat at McDonald's, should you compensate the owners of the diner next door? Public policy should not be designed to advance moral instincts that we all reject every day of our lives.

In what morally relevant way, then, might displaced workers differ from displaced pharmacists or displaced landlords? You might argue that pharmacists and landlords have always faced cutthroat competition and

therefore knew what they were getting into, while decades of tariffs and quotas have led manufacturing workers to expect a modicum of protection. That expectation led them to develop certain skills, and now it's unfair to pull the rug out from under them.

Once again, that argument does not mesh with our everyday instincts. For many decades, schoolyard bullying has been a profitable occupation. All across America, bullies have built up skills so they can take advantage of that opportunity. If we toughen the rules to make bullying unprofitable, must we compensate the bullies?

Bullying and protectionism have a lot in common. They both use force (either directly or through the power of the law) to enrich someone else at your involuntary expense. If you're forced to pay $20 an hour to an American for goods you could have bought from a Mexican for $5 an hour, you're being extorted. When a free trade agreement allows you to buy from the Mexican after all, rejoice in your liberation. ∎

*Mr. Landsburg is a professor of economics at the University of Rochester.*

**Source:** *New York Times*, January 16, 2008.

textiles to fall, reducing the quantity of textiles produced in Isoland and thus reducing employment in the Isolandian textile industry. Some Isolandian textile workers would lose their jobs.

Yet free trade creates jobs at the same time that it destroys them. When Isolandians buy textiles from other countries, those countries obtain the resources to buy other goods from Isoland. Isolandian workers would move from the textile industry to those industries in which Isoland has a comparative advantage. The transition may impose hardship on some workers in the short run, but it allows Isolandians as a whole to enjoy a higher standard of living.

Opponents of trade are often skeptical that trade creates jobs. They might respond that *everything* can be produced more cheaply abroad. Under free trade, they might argue, Isolandians could not be profitably employed in any industry. As Chapter 3 explains, however, the gains from trade are based on comparative advantage, not absolute advantage. Even if one country is better than another country at producing everything, each country can still gain from trading with the other. Workers in each country will eventually find jobs in an industry in which that country has a comparative advantage.

### 9-3b  The National-Security Argument

When an industry is threatened with competition from other countries, opponents of free trade often argue that the industry is vital to national security. For example, if Isoland were considering free trade in steel, domestic steel companies might point out that steel is used to make guns and tanks. Free trade would allow Isoland to become dependent on foreign countries to supply steel. If a war later broke out and the foreign supply was interrupted, Isoland might be unable to produce enough steel and weapons to defend itself.

Economists acknowledge that protecting key industries may be appropriate when there are legitimate concerns over national security. Yet they fear that this argument may be used too quickly by producers eager to gain at consumers' expense.

One should be wary of the national-security argument when it is made by representatives of industry rather than the defense establishment. Companies have an incentive to exaggerate their role in national defense to obtain protection from foreign competition. A nation's generals may see things very differently. Indeed, when the military is a consumer of an industry's output, it would benefit from imports. Cheaper steel in Isoland, for example, would allow the Isolandian military to accumulate a stockpile of weapons at lower cost.

### 9-3c  The Infant-Industry Argument

New industries sometimes argue for temporary trade restrictions to help them get started. After a period of protection, the argument goes, these industries will mature and be able to compete with foreign firms. Similarly, older industries sometimes argue that they need temporary protection to help them adjust to new conditions.

Economists are often skeptical about such claims, largely because the infant-industry argument is difficult to implement in practice. To apply protection successfully, the government would need to decide which industries will eventually be profitable and decide whether the benefits of establishing these industries exceed the costs of this protection to consumers. Yet "picking winners" is extraordinarily difficult. It is made even more difficult by the political process, which often awards protection to those industries that are politically powerful. And once a powerful industry is protected from foreign competition, the "temporary" policy is sometimes hard to remove.

In addition, many economists are skeptical about the infant-industry argument in principle. Suppose, for instance, that an industry is young and unable to compete profitably against foreign rivals, but there is reason to believe that the industry can be profitable in the long run. In this case, firm owners should be willing to incur temporary losses to obtain the eventual profits. Protection is not necessary for an infant industry to grow. History shows that start-up firms often incur temporary losses and succeed in the long run, even without protection from competition.

### 9-3d The Unfair-Competition Argument

A common argument is that free trade is desirable only if all countries play by the same rules. If firms in different countries are subject to different laws and regulations, then it is unfair (the argument goes) to expect the firms to compete in the international marketplace. For instance, suppose that the government of Neighborland subsidizes its textile industry by giving textile companies large tax breaks. The Isolandian textile industry might argue that it should be protected from this foreign competition because Neighborland is not competing fairly.

Would it, in fact, hurt Isoland to buy textiles from another country at a subsidized price? Certainly, Isolandian textile producers would suffer, but Isolandian textile consumers would benefit from the low price. The case for free trade is the same as before: The gains of the consumers from buying at the low price would exceed the losses of the producers. Neighborland's subsidy to its textile industry may be a bad policy, but it is the taxpayers of Neighborland who bear the burden. Isoland can benefit from the opportunity to buy textiles at a subsidized price. Rather than objecting to the foreign subsidies, perhaps Isoland should send Neighborland a thank-you note.

### 9-3e The Protection-as-a-Bargaining-Chip Argument

Another argument for trade restrictions concerns the strategy of bargaining. Many policymakers claim to support free trade but, at the same time, argue that trade restrictions can be useful when we bargain with our trading partners. They claim that the threat of a trade restriction can help remove a trade restriction already imposed by a foreign government. For example, Isoland might threaten to impose a tariff on textiles unless Neighborland removes its tariff on wheat. If Neighborland responds to this threat by removing its tariff, the result can be freer trade.

The problem with this bargaining strategy is that the threat may not work. If it doesn't work, the country faces a choice between two bad options. It can carry out its threat and implement the trade restriction, which would reduce its own economic welfare. Or it can back down from its threat, which would cause it to lose prestige in international affairs. Faced with this choice, the country would probably wish that it had never made the threat in the first place.

**CASE STUDY**

**TRADE AGREEMENTS AND THE WORLD TRADE ORGANIZATION**

A country can take one of two approaches to achieving free trade. It can take a *unilateral* approach and remove its trade restrictions on its own. This is the approach that Great Britain took in the 19th century and that Chile and South Korea have taken in recent years. Alternatively, a country can take a *multilateral* approach and reduce its trade restrictions while other countries do the same. In other words, it can bargain with its trading partners in an attempt to reduce trade restrictions around the world.

One important example of the multilateral approach is the North American Free Trade Agreement (NAFTA), which in 1993 lowered trade barriers among the United States, Mexico, and Canada. Another is the General Agreement on Tariffs and Trade (GATT), which is a continuing series of negotiations among many of the world's countries with the goal of promoting free trade. The United States helped

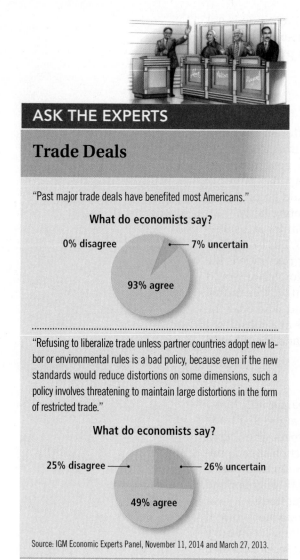

to found GATT after World War II in response to the high tariffs imposed during the Great Depression of the 1930s. Many economists believe that the high tariffs contributed to the worldwide economic hardship of that period. GATT has successfully reduced the average tariff among member countries from about 40 percent after World War II to about 5 percent today.

The rules established under GATT are now enforced by an international institution called the World Trade Organization (WTO). The WTO was established in 1995 and has its headquarters in Geneva, Switzerland. As of 2015, 162 countries have joined the organization, accounting for more than 97 percent of world trade. The functions of the WTO are to administer trade agreements, provide a forum for negotiations, and handle disputes among member countries.

What are the pros and cons of the multilateral approach to free trade? One advantage is that the multilateral approach has the potential to result in freer trade than a unilateral approach because it can reduce trade restrictions abroad as well as at home. If international negotiations fail, however, the result could be more restricted trade than under a unilateral approach.

In addition, the multilateral approach may have a political advantage. In most markets, producers are fewer and better organized than consumers—and thus wield greater political influence. Reducing the Isolandian tariff on textiles, for example, may be politically difficult if considered by itself. The textile companies would oppose free trade, and the buyers of textiles who would benefit are so numerous that organizing their support would be difficult. Yet suppose that Neighborland promises to reduce its tariff on wheat at the same time that Isoland reduces its tariff on textiles. In this case, the Isolandian wheat farmers, who are also politically powerful, would back the agreement. Thus, the multilateral approach to free trade can sometimes win political support when a unilateral approach cannot. ●

**QuickQuiz** *The textile industry of Autarka advocates a ban on the import of wool suits. Describe five arguments its lobbyists might make. Give a response to each of these arguments.*

# 9-4 Conclusion

Economists and the public often disagree about free trade. In 2015, NBC News and *The Wall Street Journal* asked the American public, "In general, do you think that free trade between the United States and foreign countries has helped the United States, has hurt the United States, or has not made much of a difference either way?" Only 29 percent of those polled said free international trade helped, whereas 34 percent thought it hurt. (The rest thought it made no difference or were unsure.) By contrast, economists overwhelmingly support free international trade. They view free trade as a way of allocating production efficiently and raising living standards both at home and abroad.

Economists view the United States as an ongoing experiment that confirms the virtues of free trade. Throughout its history, the United States has allowed unrestricted trade among the states, and the country as a whole has benefited from the specialization that trade allows. Florida grows oranges, Alaska pumps oil, California makes wine, and so on. Americans would not enjoy the high standard of living they do today if people could consume only those goods and services produced in their own states. The world could similarly benefit from free trade among countries.

To better understand economists' view of trade, let's continue our parable. Suppose that the president of Isoland, after reading the latest poll results, ignores the advice of her economics team and decides not to allow free trade in textiles. The country remains in the equilibrium without international trade.

Then, one day, some Isolandian inventor discovers a new way to make textiles at very low cost. The process is quite mysterious, however, and the inventor insists on keeping it a secret. What is odd is that the inventor doesn't need traditional inputs such as cotton or wool. The only material input he needs is wheat. And even more oddly, to manufacture textiles from wheat, he hardly needs any labor input at all.

The inventor is hailed as a genius. Because everyone buys clothing, the lower cost of textiles allows all Isolandians to enjoy a higher standard of living. Workers who had previously produced textiles experience some hardship when their factories close, but they eventually find work in other industries. Some become farmers and grow the wheat that the inventor turns into textiles. Others enter new industries that emerge as a result of higher Isolandian living standards. Everyone understands that the displacement of workers in outmoded industries is an inevitable part of technological progress and economic growth.

After several years, a newspaper reporter decides to investigate this mysterious new textiles process. She sneaks into the inventor's factory and learns that the inventor is a fraud. The inventor has not been making textiles at all. Instead, he has been smuggling wheat abroad in exchange for textiles from other countries. The only thing that the inventor had discovered was the gains from international trade.

When the truth is revealed, the government shuts down the inventor's operation. The price of textiles rises, and workers return to jobs in textile factories. Living standards in Isoland fall back to their former levels. The inventor is jailed and held up to public ridicule. After all, he was no inventor. He was just an economist.

## CHAPTER QuickQuiz

1. If a nation that does not allow international trade in steel has a domestic price of steel lower than the world price, then
   a. the nation has a comparative advantage in producing steel and would become a steel exporter if it opened up trade.
   b. the nation has a comparative advantage in producing steel and would become a steel importer if it opened up trade.
   c. the nation does not have a comparative advantage in producing steel and would become a steel exporter if it opened up trade.
   d. the nation does not have a comparative advantage in producing steel and would become a steel importer if it opened up trade.

2. When the nation of Ectenia opens itself to world trade in coffee beans, the domestic price of coffee beans falls. Which of the following describes the situation?
   a. Domestic production of coffee rises, and Ectenia becomes a coffee importer.
   b. Domestic production of coffee rises, and Ectenia becomes a coffee exporter.
   c. Domestic production of coffee falls, and Ectenia becomes a coffee importer.
   d. Domestic production of coffee falls, and Ectenia becomes a coffee exporter.

3. When a nation opens itself to trade in a good and becomes an importer,
   a. producer surplus decreases, but consumer surplus and total surplus both increase.
   b. producer surplus decreases, consumer surplus increases, and so the impact on total surplus is ambiguous.
   c. producer surplus and total surplus increase, but consumer surplus decreases.
   d. producer surplus, consumer surplus, and total surplus all increase.

4. If a nation that imports a good imposes a tariff, it will increase
   a. the domestic quantity demanded.
   b. the domestic quantity supplied.
   c. the quantity imported from abroad.
   d. all of the above.

5. Which of the following trade policies would benefit producers, hurt consumers, and increase the amount of trade?
   a. the increase of a tariff in an importing country
   b. the reduction of a tariff in an importing country
   c. starting to allow trade when the world price is greater than the domestic price
   d. starting to allow trade when the world price is less than the domestic price

6. The main difference between imposing a tariff and handing out licenses under an import quota is that a tariff increases
   a. consumer surplus.
   b. producer surplus.
   c. international trade.
   d. government revenue.

## SUMMARY

- The effects of free trade can be determined by comparing the domestic price before trade with the world price. A low domestic price indicates that the country has a comparative advantage in producing the good and that the country will become an exporter. A high domestic price indicates that the rest of the world has a comparative advantage in producing the good and that the country will become an importer.
- When a country allows trade and becomes an exporter of a good, producers of the good are better off, and consumers of the good are worse off. When a country allows trade and becomes an importer of a good, consumers are better off, and producers are worse off. In both cases, the gains from trade exceed the losses.

- A tariff—a tax on imports—moves a market closer to the equilibrium that would exist without trade and, therefore, reduces the gains from trade. Although domestic producers are better off and the government raises revenue, the losses to consumers exceed these gains.
- There are various arguments for restricting trade: protecting jobs, defending national security, helping infant industries, preventing unfair competition, and responding to foreign trade restrictions. Although some of these arguments have merit in some cases, most economists believe that free trade is usually the better policy.

## KEY CONCEPTS

world price, p. 169                      tariff, p. 173

## QUESTIONS FOR REVIEW

1. What does the domestic price that prevails without international trade tell us about a nation's comparative advantage?

2. When does a country become an exporter of a good? An importer?

3. Draw the supply-and-demand diagram for an importing country. Identify consumer surplus and producer surplus before trade is allowed. Identify consumer surplus and producer surplus with free trade. What is the change in total surplus?

4. Describe what a tariff is and its economic effects.

5. List five arguments often given to support trade restrictions. How do economists respond to these arguments?

6. What is the difference between the unilateral and multilateral approaches to achieving free trade? Give an example of each.

## PROBLEMS AND APPLICATIONS

1. The world price of wine is below the price that would prevail in Canada in the absence of trade.
   a. Assuming that Canadian imports of wine are a small part of total world wine production, draw a graph for the Canadian market for wine under free trade. Identify consumer surplus, producer surplus, and total surplus in an appropriate table.
   b. Now suppose that an unusual shift of the Gulf Stream leads to an unseasonably cold summer in Europe, destroying much of the grape harvest there. What effect does this shock have on the world price of wine? Using your graph and table from part (a), show the effect on consumer surplus, producer surplus, and total surplus in Canada. Who are the winners and losers? Is Canada as a whole better or worse off?

2. Suppose that Congress imposes a tariff on imported automobiles to protect the U.S. auto industry from foreign competition. Assuming that the United States is a price taker in the world auto market, show the following on a diagram: the change in the quantity of imports, the loss to U.S. consumers, the gain to U.S. manufacturers, government revenue, and the deadweight loss associated with the tariff. The loss to consumers can be decomposed into three pieces: a gain to domestic producers, revenue for the government, and a deadweight loss. Use your diagram to identify these three pieces.

3. When China's clothing industry expands, the increase in world supply lowers the world price of clothing.
   a. Draw an appropriate diagram to analyze how this change in price affects consumer surplus, producer surplus, and total surplus in a nation that imports clothing, such as the United States.
   b. Now draw an appropriate diagram to show how this change in price affects consumer surplus, producer surplus, and total surplus in a nation that exports clothing, such as the Dominican Republic.
   c. Compare your answers to parts (a) and (b). What are the similarities and what are the differences? Which country should be concerned about the expansion of the Chinese textile industry? Which country should be applauding it? Explain.

4. Consider the arguments for restricting trade.
   a. Imagine that you are a lobbyist for timber, an established industry suffering from low-priced foreign competition, and you are trying to get Congress to pass trade restrictions. Which two or three of the five arguments discussed in the chapter do you think would be most persuasive to the average member of Congress? Explain your reasoning.
   b. Now assume you are an astute student of economics (not a hard assumption, we hope). Although all the arguments for restricting trade have their shortcomings, name the two or three arguments that seem to make the most economic sense to you. For each, describe the economic rationale for and against these arguments for trade restrictions.

5. The nation of Textilia does not allow imports of clothing. In its equilibrium without trade, a T-shirt costs $20, and the equilibrium quantity is 3 million T-shirts. One day, after reading Adam Smith's *The Wealth of Nations* while on vacation, the president decides to open the Textilian market to international trade. The market price of a T-shirt falls to the world price of $16. The number of T-shirts consumed in Textilia rises to 4 million, while the number of T-shirts produced declines to 1 million.
   a. Illustrate the situation just described in a graph. Your graph should show all the numbers.
   b. Calculate the change in consumer surplus, producer surplus, and total surplus that results from opening up trade. (*Hint*: Recall that the area of a triangle is ½ × base × height.)

6. China is a major producer of grains, such as wheat, corn, and rice. Some years ago, the Chinese government, concerned that grain exports were driving up food prices for domestic consumers, imposed a tax on grain exports.
   a. Draw the graph that describes the market for grain in an exporting country. Use this graph as the starting point to answer the following questions.
   b. How does an export tax affect domestic grain prices?

c. How does it affect the welfare of domestic consumers, the welfare of domestic producers, and government revenue?

d. What happens to total welfare in China, as measured by the sum of consumer surplus, producer surplus, and tax revenue?

7. Consider a country that imports a good from abroad. For each of following statements, state whether it is true or false. Explain your answer.

a. "The greater the elasticity of demand, the greater the gains from trade."

b. "If demand is perfectly inelastic, there are no gains from trade."

c. "If demand is perfectly inelastic, consumers do not benefit from trade."

8. Having rejected a tariff on textiles (a tax on imports), the president of Isoland is now considering the same-sized tax on textile consumption (including both imported and domestically produced textiles).

a. Using Figure 4, identify the quantity consumed and the quantity produced in Isoland under a textile consumption tax.

b. Construct a table similar to that in Figure 4 for the textile consumption tax.

c. Which raises more revenue for the government—the consumption tax or the tariff? Which has a smaller deadweight loss? Explain.

9. Assume the United States is an importer of televisions and there are no trade restrictions. U.S. consumers buy 1 million televisions per year, of which 400,000 are produced domestically and 600,000 are imported.

a. Suppose that a technological advance among Japanese television manufacturers causes the world price of televisions to fall by $100. Draw a graph to show how this change affects the welfare of U.S. consumers and U.S. producers and how it affects total surplus in the United States.

b. After the fall in price, consumers buy 1.2 million televisions, of which 200,000 are produced domestically and 1 million are imported. Calculate the change in consumer surplus, producer surplus, and total surplus from the price reduction.

c. If the government responded by putting a $100 tariff on imported televisions, what would this do? Calculate the revenue that would be raised and the deadweight loss. Would it be a good policy from the standpoint of U.S. welfare? Who might support the policy?

d. Suppose that the fall in price is attributable not to technological advance but to a $100 per television subsidy from the Japanese government to Japanese industry. How would this affect your analysis?

10. Consider a small country that exports steel. Suppose that a "pro-trade" government decides to subsidize the export of steel by paying a certain amount for each ton sold abroad. How does this export subsidy affect the domestic price of steel, the quantity of steel produced, the quantity of steel consumed, and the quantity of steel exported? How does it affect consumer surplus, producer surplus, government revenue, and total surplus? Is it a good policy from the standpoint of economic efficiency? (*Hint*: The analysis of an export subsidy is similar to the analysis of a tariff.)

To find additional study resources, visit cengagebrain.com, and search for "Mankiw."

# PART IV
# The Economics of the Public Sector

# Externalities

Firms that make and sell paper also create, as a by-product of the manufacturing process, a chemical called dioxin. Scientists believe that once dioxin enters the environment, it raises the population's risk of cancer, birth defects, and other health problems.

Is the production and release of dioxin a problem for society? In Chapters 4 through 9, we examined how markets allocate scarce resources with the forces of supply and demand, and we saw that the equilibrium of supply and demand is typically an efficient allocation of resources. To use Adam Smith's famous

metaphor, the "invisible hand" of the marketplace leads self-interested buyers and sellers in a market to maximize the total benefit that society derives from that market. This insight is the basis for one of the *Ten Principles of Economics* in Chapter 1: Markets are usually a good way to organize economic activity. Should we conclude, therefore, that the invisible hand prevents firms in the paper market from emitting too much dioxin?

Markets do many things well, but they do not do everything well. In this chapter, we begin our study of another of the *Ten Principles of Economics*: Government action can sometimes improve upon market outcomes. We examine why markets sometimes fail to allocate resources efficiently, how government policies can potentially improve the market's allocation, and what kinds of policies are likely to work best.

The market failures examined in this chapter fall under a general category called *externalities*. An **externality** arises when a person engages in an activity that influences the well-being of a bystander but neither pays nor receives compensation for that effect. If the impact on the bystander is adverse, it is called a *negative externality*. If it is beneficial, it is called a *positive externality*. In the presence of externalities, society's interest in a market outcome extends beyond the well-being of buyers and sellers who participate in the market to include the well-being of bystanders who are affected indirectly. Because buyers and sellers neglect the external effects of their actions when deciding how much to demand or supply, the market equilibrium is not efficient when there are externalities. That is, the equilibrium fails to maximize the total benefit to society as a whole. The release of dioxin into the environment, for instance, is a negative externality. Self-interested paper firms will not consider the full cost of the pollution they create in their production process, and consumers of paper will not consider the full cost of the pollution they contribute to as a result of their purchasing decisions. Therefore, the firms will emit too much pollution unless the government prevents or discourages them from doing so.

Externalities come in many varieties, as do the policy responses that try to deal with the market failure. Here are some examples:

**externality**
the uncompensated impact of one person's actions on the well-being of a bystander

- The exhaust from automobiles is a negative externality because it creates smog that other people have to breathe. Because drivers may ignore this externality when deciding what cars to buy and how much to use them, they tend to pollute too much. The federal government addresses this problem by setting emission standards for cars. It also taxes gasoline to reduce the amount that people drive.
- Restored historic buildings convey a positive externality because people who walk or ride by them can enjoy the beauty and sense of history that these buildings provide. Building owners do not get the full benefit of restoration and, therefore, tend to tear down older buildings too quickly. Many local governments respond to this problem by regulating the destruction of historic buildings and by providing tax breaks to owners who restore them.
- Barking dogs create a negative externality because neighbors are disturbed by the noise. Dog owners do not bear the full cost of the noise and, therefore, tend to take too few precautions to prevent their dogs from barking. Local governments address this problem by making it illegal to "disturb the peace."
- Research into new technologies provides a positive externality because it creates knowledge that other people can use. If individual inventors, firms, and

universities cannot capture the benefits of their inventions, they will devote too few resources to research. The federal government addresses this problem partially through the patent system, which gives inventors exclusive use of their inventions for a limited time.

In each of these cases, some decision maker fails to take into account the external effects of his behavior. The government responds by trying to influence this behavior to protect the interests of bystanders.

# 10-1 Externalities and Market Inefficiency

In this section, we use the tools of welfare economics developed in Chapter 7 to examine how externalities affect economic well-being. The analysis shows precisely why externalities cause markets to allocate resources inefficiently. Later in the chapter, we examine various ways private individuals and public policymakers can remedy this type of market failure.

### 10-1a Welfare Economics: A Recap

We begin by recalling the key lessons of welfare economics from Chapter 7. To make our analysis concrete, we consider a specific market—the market for aluminum. Figure 1 shows the supply and demand curves in the market for aluminum.

Recall from Chapter 7 that the supply and demand curves contain important information about costs and benefits. The demand curve for aluminum reflects the value of aluminum to consumers, as measured by the prices they are willing to pay. At any given quantity, the height of the demand curve shows the willingness to pay of the marginal buyer. In other words, it shows the value to the consumer of the last unit of aluminum bought. Similarly, the supply curve reflects the costs of producing aluminum. At any given quantity, the height of the supply curve shows the cost to the marginal seller. In other words, it shows the cost to the producer of the last unit of aluminum sold.

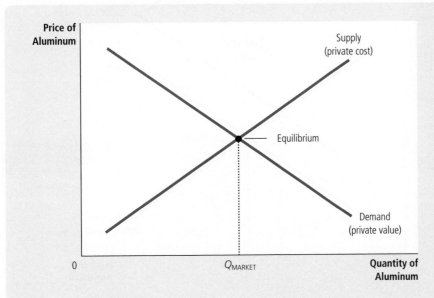

## FIGURE 1

**The Market for Aluminum**
The demand curve reflects the value to buyers, and the supply curve reflects the costs of sellers. The equilibrium quantity, $Q_{MARKET}$, maximizes the total value to buyers minus the total costs of sellers. In the absence of externalities, therefore, the market equilibrium is efficient.

In the absence of government intervention, the price adjusts to balance the supply and demand for aluminum. The quantity produced and consumed in the market equilibrium, shown as $Q_{MARKET}$ in Figure 1, is efficient in the sense that it maximizes the sum of producer and consumer surplus. That is, the market allocates resources in a way that maximizes the total value to the consumers who buy and use aluminum minus the total costs to the producers who make and sell aluminum.

## 10-1b Negative Externalities

Now let's suppose that aluminum factories emit pollution: For each unit of aluminum produced, a certain amount of smoke enters the atmosphere. Because this smoke creates a health risk for those who breathe the air, it is a negative externality. How does this externality affect the efficiency of the market outcome?

Because of the externality, the cost to *society* of producing aluminum is larger than the cost to the aluminum producers. For each unit of aluminum produced, the *social cost* includes the private costs of the aluminum producers plus the costs to those bystanders affected adversely by the pollution. Figure 2 shows the social cost of producing aluminum. The social-cost curve is above the supply curve because it takes into account the external costs imposed on society by aluminum production. The difference between these two curves reflects the cost of the pollution emitted.

What quantity of aluminum should be produced? To answer this question, we once again consider what a benevolent social planner would do. The planner wants to maximize the total surplus derived from the market—the value to consumers of aluminum minus the cost of producing aluminum. The planner understands, however, that the cost of producing aluminum includes the external costs of the pollution.

*"All I can say is that if being a leading manufacturer means being a leading polluter, so be it."*

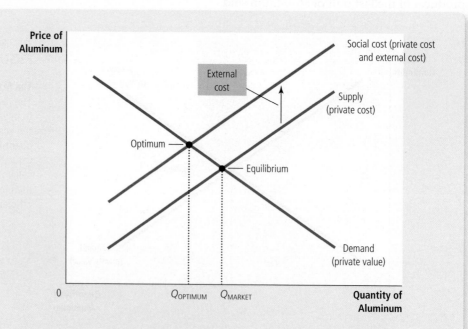

## FIGURE 2

**Pollution and the Social Optimum**
In the presence of a negative externality, such as pollution, the social cost of the good exceeds the private cost. The optimal quantity, $Q_{OPTIMUM}$, is therefore smaller than the equilibrium quantity, $Q_{MARKET}$.

The planner would choose the level of aluminum production at which the demand curve crosses the social-cost curve. This intersection determines the optimal amount of aluminum from the standpoint of society as a whole. Below this level of production, the value of the aluminum to consumers (as measured by the height of the demand curve) exceeds the social cost of producing it (as measured by the height of the social-cost curve). Above this level of production, the social cost of producing additional aluminum exceeds the value to consumers.

Note that the equilibrium quantity of aluminum, $Q_{MARKET}$, is larger than the socially optimal quantity, $Q_{OPTIMUM}$. This inefficiency occurs because the market equilibrium reflects only the private costs of production. In the market equilibrium, the marginal consumer values aluminum at less than the social cost of producing it. That is, at $Q_{MARKET}$, the demand curve lies below the social-cost curve. Thus, reducing aluminum production and consumption below the market equilibrium level raises total economic well-being.

How can the social planner achieve the optimal outcome? One way would be to tax aluminum producers for each ton of aluminum sold. The tax would shift the supply curve for aluminum upward by the size of the tax. If the tax accurately reflected the external cost of pollutants released into the atmosphere, the new supply curve would coincide with the social-cost curve. In the new market equilibrium, aluminum producers would produce the socially optimal quantity of aluminum.

The use of such a tax is called **internalizing the externality** because it gives buyers and sellers in the market an incentive to take into account the external effects of their actions. Aluminum producers would, in essence, take the costs of pollution into account when deciding how much aluminum to supply because the tax would make them pay for these external costs. And, because the market price would reflect the tax on producers, consumers of aluminum would have an incentive to buy a smaller quantity. The policy is based on one of the *Ten Principles of Economics*: People respond to incentives. Later in this chapter, we consider in more detail how policymakers can deal with externalities.

**internalizing the externality**
altering incentives so that people take into account the external effects of their actions

## 10-1c Positive Externalities

Although some activities impose costs on third parties, others yield benefits. Consider education, for example. To a large extent, the benefit of education is private: The consumer of education becomes a more productive worker and thus reaps much of the benefit in the form of higher wages. Beyond these private benefits, however, education also yields positive externalities. One externality is that a more educated population leads to more informed voters, which means better government for everyone. Another externality is that a more educated population tends to result in lower crime rates. A third externality is that a more educated population may encourage the development and dissemination of technological advances, leading to higher productivity and wages for everyone. Because of these three positive externalities, a person may prefer to have neighbors who are well educated.

The analysis of positive externalities is similar to the analysis of negative externalities. As Figure 3 shows, the demand curve does not reflect the value to society of the good. Because the social value is greater than the private value, the social-value curve lies above the demand curve. The optimal quantity is found where the social-value curve and the supply curve intersect. Hence, the socially optimal quantity is greater than the quantity that the private market would naturally reach on its own.

## FIGURE 3

**Education and the Social Optimum**
In the presence of a positive externality, the social value of the good exceeds the private value. The optimal quantity, $Q_{OPTIMUM}$, is therefore larger than the equilibrium quantity, $Q_{MARKET}$.

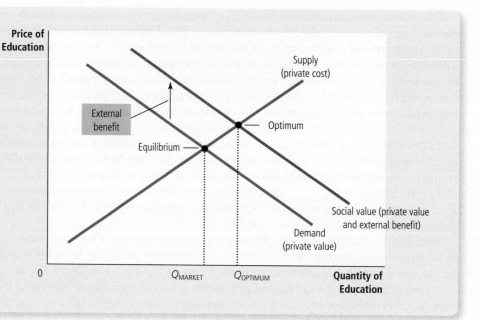

Once again, the government can correct the market failure by inducing market participants to internalize the externality. The appropriate response in the case of positive externalities is exactly the opposite to the case of negative externalities. To move the market equilibrium closer to the social optimum, a positive externality requires a subsidy. In fact, that is exactly the policy the government follows: Education is heavily subsidized through public schools and government scholarships.

To summarize: *Negative externalities lead markets to produce a larger quantity than is socially desirable. Positive externalities lead markets to produce a smaller quantity than is socially desirable. To remedy the problem, the government can internalize the externality by taxing goods that have negative externalities and subsidizing goods that have positive externalities.*

### CASE STUDY

### TECHNOLOGY SPILLOVERS, INDUSTRIAL POLICY, AND PATENT PROTECTION

A potentially important type of positive externality is called a *technology spillover*—the impact of one firm's research and production efforts on other firms' access to technological advance. For example, consider the market for industrial robots. Robots are at the frontier of a rapidly changing technology. Whenever a firm builds a robot, there is some chance that the firm will discover a new and better design. This new design may benefit not only this firm but also society as a whole because the design will enter society's pool of technological knowledge. That is, the new design may have positive externalities for other producers in the economy.

In this case, the government can internalize the externality by subsidizing the production of robots. If the government paid firms a subsidy for each robot produced, the supply curve would shift down by the amount of the subsidy, and this shift would increase the equilibrium quantity of robots. To ensure that the market equilibrium equals the social optimum, the subsidy should equal the value of the technology spillover.

How large are technology spillovers, and what do they imply for public policy? This is an important question because technological progress is the key to raising living standards over time. Yet it is also a difficult question about which economists often disagree.

Some economists believe that technology spillovers are pervasive and that the government should encourage those industries that yield the largest spillovers. For instance, these economists argue that if making computer chips yields greater spillovers than making potato chips, the government should encourage the production of computer chips relative to the production of potato chips. The U.S. tax code does this in a limited way by offering special tax breaks for expenditures on research and development. Some nations go further by subsidizing specific industries that supposedly yield large technology spillovers. Government intervention that aims to promote technology-enhancing industries is sometimes called *industrial policy*.

Other economists are skeptical about industrial policy. Even if technology spillovers are common, pursuing an industrial policy requires the government to gauge the size of the spillovers from different markets. This measurement problem is difficult at best. Without accurate measurements, the political system may end up subsidizing industries with the most political clout rather than those that yield the largest positive externalities.

Another way to deal with technology spillovers is patent protection. The patent laws protect the rights of inventors by giving them exclusive use of their inventions for a period of time. When a firm makes a technological breakthrough, it can patent the idea and capture much of the economic benefit for itself. The patent internalizes the externality by giving the firm a *property right* over its invention. If other firms want to use the new technology, they have to obtain permission from the inventing firm and pay it a royalty. Thus, the patent system gives firms a greater incentive to engage in research and other activities that advance technology. ●

 *Give an example of a negative externality and a positive externality. Explain why market outcomes are inefficient in the presence of these externalities.*

# 10-2 Public Policies toward Externalities

We have discussed why externalities lead markets to allocate resources inefficiently but have mentioned only briefly how this inefficiency can be remedied. In practice, both public policymakers and private individuals respond to externalities in various ways. All of the remedies share the goal of moving the allocation of resources closer to the social optimum.

This section considers governmental solutions. As a general matter, the government can respond to externalities in one of two ways. *Command-and-control policies* regulate behavior directly. *Market-based policies* provide incentives so that private decision makers will choose to solve the problem on their own.

## 10-2a Command-and-Control Policies: Regulation

The government can remedy an externality by either requiring or forbidding certain behaviors. For example, it is a crime to dump poisonous chemicals into the water supply. In this case, the external costs to society far exceed the benefits to the polluter. The government therefore institutes a command-and-control policy that prohibits this act altogether.

## Vaccines

"Declining to be vaccinated against contagious diseases such as measles imposes costs on other people, which is a negative externality."

### What do economists say?

0% disagree          0% uncertain

100% agree

"Considering the costs of restricting free choice, and the share of people in the US who choose not to vaccinate their children for measles, the social benefit of mandating measles vaccines for all Americans (except those with compelling medical reasons) would exceed the social cost."

### What do economists say?

6% disagree ——→   ·— 5% uncertain

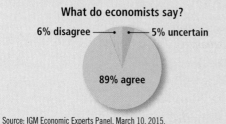

89% agree

Source: IGM Economic Experts Panel, March 10, 2015.

**corrective tax**
a tax designed to induce private decision makers to take into account the social costs that arise from a negative externality

In most cases of pollution, however, the situation is not this simple. Despite the stated goals of some environmentalists, it would be impossible to prohibit all polluting activity. For example, virtually all forms of transportation—even the horse—produce some undesirable polluting by-products. But it would not be sensible for the government to ban all transportation. As a result, instead of trying to eradicate pollution entirely, society has to weigh the costs and benefits to decide the kinds and quantities of pollution it will allow. In the United States, the Environmental Protection Agency (EPA) is the government agency tasked with developing and enforcing regulations aimed at protecting the environment.

Environmental regulations can take many forms. Sometimes the EPA dictates a maximum level of pollution that a factory may emit. Other times the EPA requires that firms adopt a particular technology to reduce emissions. In all cases, to design good rules, the government regulators need to know the details about specific industries and about the alternative technologies that those industries could adopt. This information is often difficult for government regulators to obtain.

### 10-2b  Market-Based Policy 1: Corrective Taxes and Subsidies

Instead of regulating behavior in response to an externality, the government can use market-based policies to align private incentives with social efficiency. For instance, as we saw earlier, the government can internalize the externality by taxing activities that have negative externalities and subsidizing activities that have positive externalities. Taxes enacted to deal with the effects of negative externalities are called **corrective taxes**. They are also called *Pigovian taxes* after economist Arthur Pigou (1877–1959), an early advocate of their use. An ideal corrective tax would equal the external cost from an activity with negative externalities, and an ideal corrective subsidy would equal the external benefit from an activity with positive externalities.

Economists usually prefer corrective taxes to regulations as a way to deal with pollution because they can reduce pollution at a lower cost to society. To see why, let us consider an example.

Suppose that two factories—a paper mill and a steel mill—are each dumping 500 tons of glop into a river every year. The EPA decides that it wants to reduce the amount of pollution. It considers two solutions:

- Regulation: The EPA could tell each factory to reduce its pollution to 300 tons of glop per year.
- Corrective tax: The EPA could levy a tax on each factory of $50,000 for each ton of glop it emits.

The regulation would dictate a level of pollution, whereas the tax would give factory owners an economic incentive to reduce pollution. Which solution do you think is better?

Most economists prefer the tax. To explain this preference, they would first point out that a tax is just as effective as regulation in reducing the overall level of pollution. The EPA can achieve whatever level of pollution it wants by setting the tax at the appropriate level. The higher the tax, the larger the reduction in pollution. If the tax is high enough, the factories will close down altogether, reducing pollution to zero.

Although regulation and corrective taxes are both capable of reducing pollution, the tax accomplishes this goal more efficiently. The regulation requires each factory to reduce pollution by the same amount. An equal reduction, however, is not necessarily the least expensive way to clean up the water. It is possible that the paper mill can reduce pollution at lower cost than the steel mill. If so, the paper mill would respond to the tax by reducing pollution substantially to avoid the tax, whereas the steel mill would respond by reducing pollution less and paying the tax.

In essence, the corrective tax places a price on the right to pollute. Just as markets allocate goods to those buyers who value them most highly, a corrective tax allocates pollution to those factories that face the highest cost of reducing it. Thus, the EPA can achieve any level of pollution at the lowest total cost by using a tax.

Economists also argue that corrective taxes are better for the environment. Under the command-and-control policy of regulation, the factories have no reason to reduce emission further once they have reached the target of 300 tons of glop. By contrast, the tax gives the factories an incentive to develop cleaner technologies because a cleaner technology would reduce the amount of tax the factory has to pay.

Corrective taxes are unlike most other taxes. As we discussed in Chapter 8, most taxes distort incentives and move the allocation of resources away from the social optimum. The reduction in economic well-being—that is, in consumer and producer surplus—exceeds the amount of revenue the government raises, resulting in a deadweight loss. By contrast, when externalities are present, society also cares about the well-being of the affected bystanders. Corrective taxes alter incentives that market participants face to account for the presence of externalities and thereby move the allocation of resources closer to the social optimum. Thus, while corrective taxes raise revenue for the government, they also enhance economic efficiency.

*Arthur Pigou*

### WHY IS GASOLINE TAXED SO HEAVILY?

In many nations, gasoline is among the most heavily taxed goods. The gas tax can be viewed as a corrective tax aimed at addressing three negative externalities associated with driving:

- *Congestion:* If you have ever been stuck in bumper-to-bumper traffic, you have probably wished that there were fewer cars on the road. A gasoline tax keeps congestion down by encouraging people to take public transportation, carpool more often, and live closer to work.
- *Accidents:* Whenever people buy large cars or sport utility vehicles, they may make themselves safer but they certainly put their neighbors at risk. According to the National Highway Traffic Safety Administration, a person driving a typical car is five times as likely to die if hit by a sport utility vehicle than if hit by another car. The gas tax is an indirect way of making

people pay when their large, gas-guzzling vehicles impose risk on others. It would induce them to take this risk into account when choosing what vehicle to purchase.

- *Pollution:* Cars cause smog. Moreover, the burning of fossil fuels such as gasoline is widely believed to be the primary cause of global warming. Experts disagree about how dangerous this threat is, but there is no doubt that the gas tax reduces the threat by discouraging the use of gasoline.

So the gas tax, rather than causing deadweight losses like most taxes, actually makes the economy work better. It means less traffic congestion, safer roads, and a cleaner environment.

How high should the tax on gasoline be? Most European countries impose gasoline taxes that are much higher than those in the United States. Many observers have suggested that the United States should also tax gasoline more heavily. A 2007 study published in the *Journal of Economic Literature* summarized the research on the size of the various externalities associated with driving. It concluded that the optimal corrective tax on gasoline was $2.28 per gallon in 2005 dollars; after adjusting for inflation, that amount is equivalent to about $2.78 per gallon in 2015 dollars. By contrast, the actual tax in the United States in 2015 was only about 50 cents per gallon.

The tax revenue from a gasoline tax could be used to lower taxes that distort incentives and cause deadweight losses, such as income taxes. In addition, some of the burdensome government regulations that require automakers to produce more fuel-efficient cars would prove unnecessary. This idea, however, has never been politically popular. ●

## What Should We Do about Climate Change?

*Many policy analysts believe that taxing carbon is the best approach to dealing with global climate change.*

### The Most Sensible Tax of All

By Yoram Bauman and Shi-Ling Hsu

On Sunday, the best climate policy in the world got even better: British Columbia's carbon tax—a tax on the carbon content of all fossil fuels burned in the province—increased from $25 to $30 per metric ton of carbon dioxide, making it more expensive to pollute.

This was good news not only for the environment but for nearly everyone who pays taxes in British Columbia, because the carbon tax is used to reduce taxes for individuals and businesses. Thanks to this tax swap, British Columbia has lowered its corporate income tax rate to 10 percent from 12 percent, a rate that is among the lowest in the Group of 8 wealthy nations. Personal income taxes for people earning less than $119,000 per year are now the lowest in Canada, and there are targeted rebates for low-income and rural households.

The only bad news is that this is the last increase scheduled in British Columbia. In our view, the reason is simple: the province is waiting for the rest of North America to catch up so that its tax system will not become unbalanced or put energy-intensive industries at a competitive disadvantage.

The United States should jump at the chance to adopt a similar revenue-neutral tax swap. It's an opportunity to reduce existing taxes, clean up the environment and increase personal freedom and energy security.

Let's start with the economics. Substituting a carbon tax for some of our current taxes—on payroll, on investment, on businesses and on workers—is a no-brainer. Why tax good things when you can tax bad things, like emissions? The idea has support from economists across the political spectrum, from Arthur B. Laffer and N. Gregory Mankiw on the right to Peter Orszag and Joseph E. Stiglitz on the left. That's because economists know that a carbon tax swap can reduce the economic drag created by our current tax system and increase long-run growth by nudging the economy away from consumption and borrowing and toward saving and investment.

Of course, carbon taxes also lower carbon emissions. Economic theory suggests that putting a price on pollution reduces emissions more affordably and more effectively than any other measure. This conclusion is supported by empirical evidence from previous market-based policies, like those in the 1990 amendments to the Clean Air Act that targeted sulfur dioxide emissions. British Columbia's carbon tax is only four years old, but preliminary data show that greenhouse gas emissions are down 4.5 percent even as population and gross domestic product have been growing. Sales of motor gasoline have fallen by 2 percent since 2007, compared with a 5 percent increase for Canada as a whole.

What would a British Columbia-style carbon tax look like in the United States? According to our calculations, a British Columbia-style $30 carbon tax would generate about $145 billion a year in the United States. That could be used to reduce individual and corporate income taxes by 10 percent, and afterward there would still be $35 billion left over. If recent budget deals are any guide, Congress might choose to set aside half of that remainder to reduce estate taxes (to please Republicans) and the other half to offset the impacts of higher fuel and electricity prices resulting from the carbon tax on low-income households through refundable tax credits or a targeted reduction in payroll taxes (to please Democrats).

Revenue from a carbon tax would most likely decline over time as Americans reduce their carbon emissions, but for many years to come it could pay for big reductions in existing taxes. It would also promote energy conservation and steer investment into clean technology and other productive economic activities.

Lastly, the carbon tax would actually give Americans more control over how much they pay in taxes. Households and businesses could reduce their carbon tax payments simply by reducing their use of fossil fuels. Americans would trim their carbon footprints—and their tax burdens—by investing in energy efficiency at home and at work, switching to less-polluting vehicles and pursuing countless other innovations. All of this would be driven not by government mandates but by Adam Smith's invisible hand.

A carbon tax makes sense whether you are a Republican or a Democrat, a climate change skeptic or a believer, a conservative or a conservationist (or both). We can move past the partisan fireworks over global warming by turning British Columbia's carbon tax into a made-in-America solution. ■

*Mr. Bauman, an environmental economist, is a fellow at Sightline Institute in Seattle. Mr. Hsu, a law professor at Florida State University, is the author of "The Case for a Carbon Tax."*

**Source:** *New York Times*, July 5, 2012.

## ASK THE EXPERTS

## Carbon Taxes

"The Brookings Institution recently described a U.S. carbon tax of $20 per ton, increasing at 4 percent per year, which would raise an estimated $150 billion per year in federal revenues over the next decade. Given the negative externalities created by carbon dioxide emissions, a federal carbon tax at this rate would involve fewer harmful net distortions to the U.S. economy than a tax increase that generated the same revenue by raising marginal tax rates on labor income across the board."

**What do economists say?**

0% disagree ———•——— 2% uncertain

98% agree

"A tax on the carbon content of fuels would be a less expensive way to reduce carbon-dioxide emissions than would a collection of policies such as 'corporate average fuel economy' requirements for automobiles."

**What do economists say?**

2% disagree ———•——— 3% uncertain

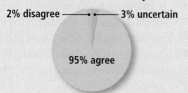

95% agree

Source: IGM Economic Experts Panel, December 4, 2012 and December 20, 2011.

## 10-2c Market-Based Policy 2: Tradable Pollution Permits

Returning to our example of the paper mill and the steel mill, let us suppose that, despite the advice of its economists, the EPA adopts the regulation and requires each factory to reduce its pollution to 300 tons of glop per year. Then one day, after the regulation is in place and both mills have complied, the two firms go to the EPA with a proposal. The steel mill wants to increase its emission of glop from 300 to 400 tons. The paper mill has agreed to reduce its emission from 300 to 200 tons if the steel mill pays it $5 million. The total emission of glop would remain at 600 tons. Should the EPA allow the two factories to make this deal?

From the standpoint of economic efficiency, allowing the deal is good policy. The deal must make the owners of the two factories better off because they are voluntarily agreeing to it. Moreover, the deal does not have any external effects because the total amount of pollution stays the same. Thus, social welfare is enhanced by allowing the paper mill to sell its pollution rights to the steel mill.

The same logic applies to any voluntary transfer of the right to pollute from one firm to another. If the EPA allows firms to make these deals, it will, in essence, create a new scarce resource: pollution permits. A market to trade these permits will eventually develop, and that market will be governed by the forces of supply and demand. The invisible hand will ensure that this new market allocates the right to pollute efficiently. That is, the permits will end up in the hands of those firms that value them most highly, as judged by their willingness to pay. A firm's willingness to pay for the right to pollute, in turn, will depend on its cost of reducing pollution: The more costly it is for a firm to cut back on pollution, the more it will be willing to pay for a permit.

An advantage of allowing a market for pollution permits is that the initial allocation of pollution permits among firms does not matter from the standpoint of economic efficiency. Those firms that can reduce pollution at a low cost will sell whatever permits they get, while firms that can reduce pollution only at a high cost will buy whatever permits they need. As long as there is a free market for the pollution rights, the final allocation will be efficient regardless of the initial allocation.

Reducing pollution using pollution permits may seem very different from using corrective taxes, but the two policies have much in common. In both cases, firms pay for their pollution. With corrective taxes, polluting firms must pay a tax to the government. With pollution permits, polluting firms must pay to buy the permits. (Even firms that already own permits must pay to pollute: The opportunity cost of polluting is what they could have received by selling their permits on the open market.) Both corrective taxes and pollution permits internalize the externality of pollution by making it costly for firms to pollute.

The similarity of the two policies can be seen by considering the market for pollution. Both panels in Figure 4 show the demand curve for the right to pollute.

In panel (a), the EPA sets a price on pollution by levying a corrective tax, and the demand curve determines the quantity of pollution. In panel (b), the EPA limits the quantity of pollution by limiting the number of pollution permits, and the demand curve determines the price of pollution. The price and quantity of pollution are the same in the two cases.

**FIGURE 4**

**The Equivalence of Corrective Taxes and Pollution Permits**

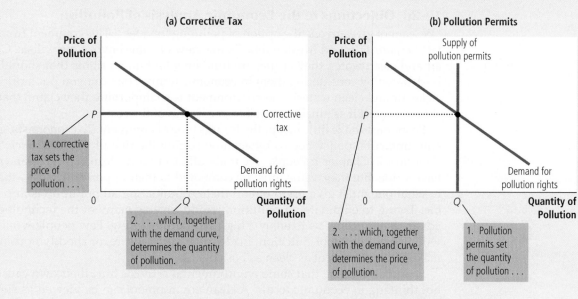

**(a) Corrective Tax**

Price of Pollution

*P* — Corrective tax

1. A corrective tax sets the price of pollution . . .

Demand for pollution rights

0     *Q*     **Quantity of Pollution**

2. . . . which, together with the demand curve, determines the quantity of pollution.

**(b) Pollution Permits**

Price of Pollution

Supply of pollution permits

*P*

2. . . . which, together with the demand curve, determines the price of pollution.

Demand for pollution rights

0     *Q*     **Quantity of Pollution**

1. Pollution permits set the quantity of pollution . . .

This curve shows that the lower the price of polluting, the more firms will choose to pollute. In panel (a), the EPA uses a corrective tax to set a price for pollution. In this case, the supply curve for pollution rights is perfectly elastic (because firms can pollute as much as they want by paying the tax), and the position of the demand curve determines the quantity of pollution. In panel (b), the EPA sets a quantity of pollution by issuing pollution permits. In this case, the supply curve for pollution rights is perfectly inelastic (because the quantity of pollution is fixed by the number of permits), and the position of the demand curve determines the price of pollution. Hence, the EPA can achieve any point on a given demand curve either by setting a price with a corrective tax or by setting a quantity with pollution permits.

In some circumstances, however, selling pollution permits may be better than levying a corrective tax. Suppose the EPA wants no more than 600 tons of glop dumped into the river. But because the EPA does not know the demand curve for pollution, it is not sure what size tax would achieve that goal. In this case, it can simply auction off 600 pollution permits. The auction price would yield the appropriate size of the corrective tax.

The idea of the government auctioning off the right to pollute may at first sound like a creature of some economist's imagination. And in fact, that is how the idea began. But increasingly, the EPA has used this system as a way to control pollution. A notable success story has been the case of sulfur dioxide ($SO_2$), a leading cause of acid rain. In 1990, amendments to the Clean Air Act required power plants to reduce $SO_2$ emissions substantially. At the same time, the amendments set up a system that allowed plants to trade their $SO_2$ allowances. Initially, both industry representatives and environmentalists were skeptical of the proposal, but over time the system reduced pollution with minimal disruption. Pollution permits, like corrective taxes, are now widely viewed as a cost-effective way to keep the environment clean.

### 10-2d  Objections to the Economic Analysis of Pollution

"We cannot give anyone the option of polluting for a fee." This comment from the late Senator Edmund Muskie reflects the view of some environmentalists. Clean air and clean water, they argue, are fundamental human rights that should not be debased by considering them in economic terms. How can you put a price on clean air and clean water? The environment is so important, they claim, that we should protect it as much as possible, regardless of the cost.

Economists have little sympathy for this type of argument. To economists, good environmental policy begins by acknowledging the first of the *Ten Principles of Economics* in Chapter 1: People face trade-offs. Certainly, clean air and clean water have value. But their value must be compared to their opportunity cost—that is, to what one must give up to obtain them. Eliminating all pollution is impossible. Trying to eliminate all pollution would reverse many of the technological advances that allow us to enjoy a high standard of living. Few people would be willing to accept poor nutrition, inadequate medical care, or shoddy housing to make the environment as clean as possible.

Economists argue that some environmental activists hurt their own cause by not thinking in economic terms. A clean environment can be viewed as simply another good. Like all normal goods, it has a positive income elasticity: Rich countries can afford a cleaner environment than poor ones and, therefore, usually have more rigorous environmental protection. In addition, like most other goods, clean air and clean water obey the law of demand: The lower the price of environmental protection, the more the public will want. The economic approach of using pollution permits and corrective taxes reduces the cost of environmental protection and should, therefore, increase the public's demand for a clean environment.

**QuickQuiz**   *A glue factory and a steel mill emit smoke containing a chemical that is harmful if inhaled in large amounts. Describe three ways the town government might respond to this externality. What are the pros and cons of each solution?*

# 10-3  Private Solutions to Externalities

Although externalities tend to cause markets to be inefficient, government action is not always needed to solve the problem. In some circumstances, people can develop private solutions.

### 10-3a  The Types of Private Solutions

Sometimes the problem of externalities is solved with moral codes and social sanctions. Consider, for instance, why most people do not litter. Although there are laws against littering, these laws are not rigorously enforced. Most people choose not to litter just because it is the wrong thing to do. The Golden Rule taught to most children says, "Do unto others as you would have them do unto you." This moral injunction tells us to take account of how our actions affect other people. In economic terms, it tells us to internalize externalities.

Another private solution to externalities involves charities. For example, the Sierra Club, whose goal is to protect the environment, is a nonprofit organization funded with private donations. As another example, colleges and universities receive gifts from alumni, corporations, and foundations in part because education has positive externalities for society. The government encourages this private solution to externalities through the tax system by allowing an income tax deduction for charitable donations.

The private market can often solve the problem of externalities by relying on the self-interest of the relevant parties. Sometimes the solution takes the form of integrating different types of businesses. For example, consider an apple grower and a beekeeper who are located next to each other. Each business confers a positive externality on the other: By pollinating the flowers on the trees, the bees help the orchard produce apples, while the bees use the nectar they get from the apple trees to produce honey. Nonetheless, when the apple grower is deciding how many trees to plant and the beekeeper is deciding how many bees to keep, they neglect the positive externality. As a result, the apple grower plants too few trees and the beekeeper keeps too few bees. These externalities could be internalized if the beekeeper bought the apple orchard or if the apple grower bought the beehives: Both activities would then take place within the same firm, and this single firm could choose the optimal number of trees and bees. Internalizing externalities is one reason that some firms are involved in multiple types of businesses.

Another way for the private market to deal with external effects is for the interested parties to enter into a contract. In the foregoing example, a contract between the apple grower and the beekeeper can solve the problem of too few trees and too few bees. The contract can specify the number of trees, the number of bees, and perhaps a payment from one party to the other. By setting the right number of trees and bees, the contract can solve the inefficiency that normally arises from these externalities and make both parties better off.

## 10-3b The Coase Theorem

How effective is the private market in dealing with externalities? A famous result, called the **Coase theorem** after economist Ronald Coase, suggests that it can be very effective in some circumstances. According to the Coase theorem, if private parties can bargain over the allocation of resources at no cost, then the private market will always solve the problem of externalities and allocate resources efficiently.

To see how the Coase theorem works, consider an example. Suppose that Dick owns a dog named Spot. Spot barks and disturbs Jane, Dick's neighbor. Dick gets a benefit from owning the dog, but the dog confers a negative externality on Jane. Should Dick be forced to send Spot to the pound, or should Jane have to suffer sleepless nights because of Spot's barking?

Consider first what outcome is socially efficient. A social planner, considering the two alternatives, would compare the benefit that Dick gets from the dog to the cost that Jane bears from the barking. If the benefit exceeds the cost, it is efficient for Dick to keep the dog and for Jane to live with the barking. Yet if the cost exceeds the benefit, then Dick should get rid of the dog.

According to the Coase theorem, the private market will reach the efficient outcome on its own. How? Jane can simply offer to pay Dick to get rid of the dog. Dick will accept the deal if the amount of money Jane offers is greater than the benefit of keeping the dog.

By bargaining over the price, Dick and Jane can always reach the efficient outcome. For instance, suppose that Dick gets a $500 benefit from the dog and Jane

**Coase theorem**
the proposition that if private parties can bargain without cost over the allocation of resources, they can solve the problem of externalities on their own

bears an $800 cost from the barking. In this case, Jane can offer Dick $600 to get rid of the dog, and Dick will gladly accept. Both parties are better off than they were before, and the efficient outcome is reached.

It is possible, of course, that Jane would not be willing to offer any price that Dick would accept. For instance, suppose that Dick gets a $1,000 benefit from the dog and Jane bears an $800 cost from the barking. In this case, Dick would turn down any offer below $1,000, while Jane would not offer any amount above $800. Therefore, Dick ends up keeping the dog. Given these costs and benefits, however, this outcome is efficient.

So far, we have assumed that Dick has the legal right to keep a barking dog. In other words, we have assumed that Dick can keep Spot unless Jane pays him enough to induce him to give up the dog voluntarily. But how different would the outcome be if Jane had the legal right to peace and quiet?

According to the Coase theorem, the initial distribution of rights does not matter for the market's ability to reach the efficient outcome. For instance, suppose that Jane can legally compel Dick to get rid of the dog. Having this right works to Jane's advantage, but it probably will not change the outcome. In this case, Dick can offer to pay Jane to allow him to keep the dog. If the benefit of the dog to Dick exceeds the cost of the barking to Jane, then Dick and Jane will strike a bargain in which Dick keeps the dog.

Although Dick and Jane can reach the efficient outcome regardless of how rights are initially distributed, the distribution of rights is not irrelevant: It determines the distribution of economic well-being. Whether Dick has the right to a barking dog or Jane the right to peace and quiet determines who pays whom in the final bargain. But in either case, the two parties can bargain with each other and solve the externality problem. Dick will end up keeping the dog only if his benefit exceeds Jane's cost.

To sum up: *The Coase theorem says that private economic actors can potentially solve the problem of externalities among themselves. Whatever the initial distribution of rights, the interested parties can reach a bargain in which everyone is better off and the outcome is efficient.*

### 10-3c  Why Private Solutions Do Not Always Work

Despite the appealing logic of the Coase theorem, private individuals on their own often fail to resolve the problems caused by externalities. The Coase theorem applies only when the interested parties have no trouble reaching and enforcing an agreement. In the real world, however, bargaining does not always work, even when a mutually beneficial agreement is possible.

**transaction costs**
the costs that parties incur during the process of agreeing to and following through on a bargain

Sometimes the interested parties fail to solve an externality problem because of **transaction costs**, the costs that parties incur in the process of agreeing to and following through on a bargain. In our example, imagine that Dick and Jane speak different languages so that, to reach an agreement, they need to hire a translator. If the benefit of solving the barking problem is less than the cost of the translator, Dick and Jane might choose to leave the problem unsolved. In more realistic examples, the transaction costs are the expenses not of translators but of lawyers required to draft and enforce contracts.

At other times, bargaining simply breaks down. The recurrence of wars and labor strikes shows that reaching agreement can be difficult and that failing to reach agreement can be costly. The problem is often that each party tries to hold out for a better deal. For example, suppose that Dick gets a $500 benefit from having the dog and Jane bears an $800 cost from the barking. Although it is efficient for Jane to pay

## IN THE NEWS

## The Coase Theorem in Action

*Whenever people come in close contact, externalities abound.*

### Don't Want Me to Recline My Airline Seat? You Can Pay Me

**By Josh Barro**

I fly a lot. When I fly, I recline. I don't feel guilty about it. And I'm going to keep doing it, unless you pay me to stop.

I bring this up because of a dispute you may have heard about: On Sunday, a United Airlines flight from Newark to Denver made an unscheduled stop in Chicago to discharge two passengers who had a dispute over seat reclining. According to The Associated Press, a man in a middle seat installed the Knee Defender, a $21.95 device that keeps a seat upright, on the seatback in front of him.

A flight attendant asked him to remove the device. He refused. The woman seated in front of him turned around and threw water at him. The pilot landed the plane and booted both passengers off the flight.

Obviously, it's improper to throw water at another passenger on a flight, even if he deserves it. But I've seen a distressing amount of sympathy for Mr. Knee Defender, who wasn't just instigating a fight but usurping his fellow passenger's property rights. When you buy an airline ticket, one of the things you're buying is the right to use your seat's reclining function. If this passenger so badly wanted the passenger in front of him not to recline, he should have paid her to give up that right.

I wrote an article to that effect in 2011, noting that airline seats are an excellent case study for the Coase Theorem. This is an economic theory holding that it doesn't matter very much who is initially given a property right; so long as you clearly define it and transaction costs are low, people will trade the right so that it ends up in the hands of whoever values it most. That is, I own the right to recline, and if my reclining bothers you, you can pay me to stop. We could (but don't) have an alternative system in which the passenger sitting behind me owns the reclining rights. In that circumstance, if I really care about being allowed to recline, I could pay him to let me.

Donald Marron, a former director of the Congressional Budget Office, agrees with this analysis, but with a caveat. Recline negotiations do involve some transaction costs — passengers don't like bargaining over reclining positions

with their neighbors, perhaps because that sometimes ends with water being thrown in someone's face.

Mr. Marron says we ought to allocate the initial property right to the person likely to care most about reclining, in order to reduce the number of transactions that are necessary. He further argues that it's probably the person sitting behind, as evidenced by the fact people routinely pay for extra-legroom seats.

Mr. Marron is wrong about this last point. I understand people don't like negotiating with strangers, but in hundreds of flights I have taken, I have rarely had anyone complain to me about my seat recline, and nobody has ever offered me money, or anything else of value, in exchange for sitting upright.

If sitting behind my reclined seat was such misery, if recliners like me are "monsters," as Mark Hemingway of *The Weekly Standard* puts it, why is nobody willing to pay me to stop? People talk a big game on social media about the terribleness of reclining, but then people like to complain about all sorts of things; if they really cared that much, someone would have opened his wallet and paid me by now. ■

THE IMAGE BANK/GETTY IMAGES

**Source:** *New York Times*, April 27, 2014.

Dick to find another home for the dog, there are many prices that could lead to this outcome. Dick might demand $750, and Jane might offer only $550. As they haggle over the price, the inefficient outcome with the barking dog persists.

Reaching an efficient bargain is especially difficult when the number of interested parties is large, because coordinating everyone is costly. For example, consider a factory that pollutes the water of a nearby lake. The pollution confers a negative externality on the local fishermen. According to the Coase theorem, if the pollution is inefficient, then the factory and the fishermen could reach a bargain in which the fishermen pay the factory not to pollute. If there are many fishermen, however, trying to coordinate them all to bargain with the factory may be almost impossible.

When private bargaining does not work, the government can sometimes play a role. The government is an institution designed for collective action. In this example, the government can act on behalf of the fishermen, even when it is impractical for the fishermen to act for themselves.

**QuickQuiz**   *Give an example of a private solution to an externality. • What is the Coase theorem? • Why are private economic participants sometimes unable to solve the problems caused by an externality?*

# 10-4 Conclusion

The invisible hand is powerful but not omnipotent. A market's equilibrium maximizes the sum of producer and consumer surplus. When the buyers and sellers in the market are the only interested parties, this outcome is efficient from the standpoint of society as a whole. But when there are external effects, such as pollution, evaluating a market outcome requires taking into account the well-being of third parties as well. In this case, the invisible hand of the marketplace may fail to allocate resources efficiently.

In some cases, people can solve the problem of externalities on their own. The Coase theorem suggests that the interested parties can bargain among themselves and agree on an efficient solution. Sometimes, however, an efficient outcome cannot be reached, perhaps because the large number of interested parties makes bargaining difficult.

When people cannot solve the problem of externalities privately, the government often steps in. Yet even with government intervention, society should not abandon market forces entirely. Rather, the government can address the problem by requiring decision makers to bear the full costs of their actions. Pollution permits and corrective taxes on emissions, for instance, are designed to internalize the externality of pollution. These are increasingly the policies of choice for those interested in protecting the environment. Market forces, properly redirected, are often the best remedy for market failure.

## CHAPTER QuickQuiz

1. Which of the following is an example of a positive externality?
   a. Dev mows Hillary's lawn and is paid $100 for performing the service.
   b. While mowing the lawn, Dev's lawnmower spews out smoke that Hillary's neighbor Kristen has to breathe.
   c. Hillary's newly cut lawn makes her neighborhood more attractive.
   d. Hillary's neighbors pay her if she promises to get her lawn cut on a regular basis.

2. If the production of a good yields a negative externality, then the social-cost curve lies _____ the supply curve, and the socially optimal quantity is _____ than the equilibrium quantity.
   a. above, greater
   b. above, less
   c. below, greater
   d. below, less

3. When the government levies a tax on a good equal to the external cost associated with the good's production, it _____ the price paid by consumers and makes the market outcome _____ efficient.
   a. increases, more
   b. increases, less
   c. decreases, more
   d. decreases, less

4. Which of the following statements about corrective taxes is generally NOT true?
   a. Economists prefer them to command-and-control regulation.
   b. They raise government revenue.
   c. They cause deadweight losses.
   d. They reduce the quantity sold in a market.

5. The government auctions off 500 units of pollution rights. They sell for $50 per unit, raising total revenue of $25,000. This policy is equivalent to a corrective tax of _____ per unit of pollution.
   a. $10
   b. $50
   c. $450
   d. $500

6. The Coase theorem does NOT apply if
   a. there is a significant externality between two parties.
   b. the court system vigorously enforces all contracts.
   c. transaction costs make negotiating difficult.
   d. both parties understand the externality fully.

## SUMMARY

- When a transaction between a buyer and seller directly affects a third party, the effect is called an externality. If an activity yields negative externalities, such as pollution, the socially optimal quantity in a market is less than the equilibrium quantity. If an activity yields positive externalities, such as technology spillovers, the socially optimal quantity is greater than the equilibrium quantity.

- Governments pursue various policies to remedy the inefficiencies caused by externalities. Sometimes the government prevents socially inefficient activity by regulating behavior. Other times it internalizes an externality using corrective taxes. Another public policy is to issue permits. For example, the government could protect the environment by issuing a limited number of pollution permits. The result of this policy is similar to imposing corrective taxes on polluters.

- Those affected by externalities can sometimes solve the problem privately. For instance, when one business imposes an externality on another business, the two businesses can internalize the externality by merging. Alternatively, the interested parties can solve the problem by negotiating a contract. According to the Coase theorem, if people can bargain without cost, then they can always reach an agreement in which resources are allocated efficiently. In many cases, however, reaching a bargain among the many interested parties is difficult, so the Coase theorem does not apply.

## KEY CONCEPTS

externality, p. 190
internalizing the externality, p. 193

corrective tax, p. 196
Coase theorem, p. 203

transaction costs, p. 204

## QUESTIONS FOR REVIEW

1. Give an example of a negative externality and an example of a positive externality.

2. Draw a supply-and-demand diagram to explain the effect of a negative externality that occurs as a result of a firm's production process.

3. In what way does the patent system help society solve an externality problem?

4. What are corrective taxes? Why do economists prefer them to regulations as a way to protect the environment from pollution?

5. List some of the ways that the problems caused by externalities can be solved without government intervention.

6. Imagine that you are a nonsmoker sharing a room with a smoker. According to the Coase theorem, what determines whether your roommate smokes in the room? Is this outcome efficient? How do you and your roommate reach this solution?

## PROBLEMS AND APPLICATIONS

1. Consider two ways to protect your car from theft. The Club (a steering wheel lock) makes it difficult for a car thief to take your car. Lojack (a tracking system) makes it easier for the police to catch the car thief who has stolen it. Which of these methods conveys a negative externality on other car owners? Which conveys a positive externality? Do you think there are any policy implications of your analysis?

2. Consider the market for fire extinguishers.
   a. Why might fire extinguishers exhibit positive externalities?
   b. Draw a graph of the market for fire extinguishers, labeling the demand curve, the social-value curve, the supply curve, and the social-cost curve.
   c. Indicate the market equilibrium level of output and the efficient level of output. Give an intuitive explanation for why these quantities differ.
   d. If the external benefit is $10 per extinguisher, describe a government policy that would yield the efficient outcome.

3. Greater consumption of alcohol leads to more motor vehicle accidents and, thus, imposes costs on people who do not drink and drive.
   a. Illustrate the market for alcohol, labeling the demand curve, the social-value curve, the supply curve, the social-cost curve, the market equilibrium level of output, and the efficient level of output.
   b. On your graph, shade the area corresponding to the deadweight loss of the market equilibrium. (*Hint*: The deadweight loss occurs because some units of alcohol are consumed for which the social cost exceeds the social value.) Explain.

4. Many observers believe that the levels of pollution in our society are too high.
   a. If society wishes to reduce overall pollution by a certain amount, why is it efficient to have different amounts of reduction at different firms?
   b. Command-and-control approaches often rely on uniform reductions among firms. Why are these approaches generally unable to target the firms that should undertake bigger reductions?
   c. Economists argue that appropriate corrective taxes or tradable pollution rights will result in efficient pollution reduction. How do these approaches target the firms that should undertake bigger reductions?

5. The many identical residents of Whoville love drinking Zlurp. Each resident has the following willingness to pay for the tasty refreshment:

   | | |
   |---|---|
   | First bottle | $5 |
   | Second bottle | 4 |
   | Third bottle | 3 |
   | Fourth bottle | 2 |
   | Fifth bottle | 1 |
   | Further bottles | 0 |

   a. The cost of producing Zlurp is $1.50, and the competitive suppliers sell it at this price. (The supply curve is horizontal.) How many bottles will each Whovillian consume? What is each person's consumer surplus?
   b. Producing Zlurp creates pollution. Each bottle has an external cost of $1. Taking this additional cost into account, what is total surplus per person in the allocation you described in part (a)?
   c. Cindy Lou Who, one of the residents of Whoville, decides on her own to reduce her consumption of Zlurp by one bottle. What happens to Cindy's welfare (her consumer surplus minus the cost of pollution she experiences)? How does Cindy's decision affect total surplus in Whoville?
   d. Mayor Grinch imposes a $1 tax on Zlurp. What is consumption per person now? Calculate consumer surplus, the external cost, government revenue, and total surplus per person.
   e. Based on your calculations, would you support the mayor's policy? Why or why not?

6. Bruno loves playing rock 'n' roll music at high volume. Placido loves opera and hates rock 'n' roll. Unfortunately, they are next-door neighbors in an apartment building with paper-thin walls.
   a. What is the externality here?
   b. What command-and-control policy might the landlord impose? Could such a policy lead to an inefficient outcome?
   c. Suppose the landlord lets the tenants do whatever they want. According to the Coase theorem,

how might Bruno and Placido reach an efficient outcome on their own? What might prevent them from reaching an efficient outcome?

7. Figure 4 shows that for any given demand curve for the right to pollute, the government can achieve the same outcome either by setting a price with a corrective tax or by setting a quantity with pollution permits. Suppose there is a sharp improvement in the technology for controlling pollution.
   a. Using graphs similar to those in Figure 4, illustrate the effect of this development on the demand for pollution rights.
   b. What is the effect on the price and quantity of pollution under each regulatory system? Explain.

8. Suppose that the government decides to issue tradable permits for a certain form of pollution.
   a. Does it matter for economic efficiency whether the government distributes or auctions the permits? Why or why not?
   b. If the government chooses to distribute the permits, does the allocation of permits among firms matter for efficiency? Explain.

9. There are three industrial firms in Happy Valley.

| Firm | Initial Pollution Level | Cost of Reducing Pollution by 1 Unit |
|------|-------------------------|--------------------------------------|
| A | 30 units | $20 |
| B | 40 units | $30 |
| C | 20 units | $10 |

The government wants to reduce pollution to 60 units, so it gives each firm 20 tradable pollution permits.
   a. Who sells permits and how many do they sell? Who buys permits and how many do they buy? Briefly explain why the sellers and buyers are each willing to do so. What is the total cost of pollution reduction in this situation?
   b. How much higher would the costs of pollution reduction be if the permits could not be traded?

To find additional study resources, visit cengagebrain.com, and search for "Mankiw."

# Public Goods and Common Resources

An old song lyric maintains that "the best things in life are free." A moment's thought reveals a long list of goods that the songwriter could have had in mind. Nature provides some of them, such as rivers, mountains, beaches, lakes, and oceans. The government provides others, such as playgrounds, parks, and parades. In each case, people often do not pay a fee when they choose to enjoy the benefit of the good.

Goods without prices provide a special challenge for economic analysis. Most goods in our economy are allocated through markets, in which buyers pay for what they receive and sellers are paid for what they provide. For these goods,

prices are the signals that guide the decisions of buyers and sellers, and these decisions lead to an efficient allocation of resources. When goods are available free of charge, however, the market forces that normally allocate resources in our economy are absent.

In this chapter, we examine the problems that arise for the allocation of resources when there are goods without market prices. Our analysis will shed light on one of the *Ten Principles of Economics* in Chapter 1: Governments can sometimes improve market outcomes. When a good does not have a price attached to it, private markets cannot ensure that the good is produced and consumed in the proper amounts. In such cases, government policy can potentially remedy the market failure and increase economic well-being.

## 11-1  The Different Kinds of Goods

How well do markets work in providing the goods that people want? The answer to this question depends on the good being considered. As we discussed in Chapter 7, a market can provide the efficient number of ice-cream cones: The price of ice-cream cones adjusts to balance supply and demand, and this equilibrium maximizes the sum of producer and consumer surplus. Yet as we discussed in Chapter 10, the market cannot be counted on to prevent aluminum manufacturers from polluting the air we breathe: Buyers and sellers in a market typically do not take into account the external effects of their decisions. Thus, markets work well if the good is ice cream, but they don't if the good is clean air.

When thinking about the various goods in the economy, it is useful to group them according to two characteristics:

**excludability**
the property of a good whereby a person can be prevented from using it

- Is the good **excludable**? That is, can people be prevented from using the good?
- Is the good **rival in consumption**? That is, does one person's use of the good reduce another person's ability to use it?

Using these two characteristics, Figure 1 divides goods into four categories:

**rivalry in consumption**
the property of a good whereby one person's use diminishes other people's use

1. **Private goods** are both excludable and rival in consumption. Consider an ice-cream cone, for example. An ice-cream cone is excludable because it is possible to prevent someone from eating one—you just don't give it to her. An ice-cream cone is rival in consumption because if one person eats an ice-cream cone, another person cannot eat the same cone. Most goods in the economy are private goods like ice-cream cones: You don't get one unless you pay for it, and once you have it, you are the only person who benefits. When we analyzed supply and demand in Chapters 4, 5, and 6 and the efficiency of markets in Chapters 7, 8, and 9, we implicitly assumed that goods were both excludable and rival in consumption.

**private goods**
goods that are both excludable and rival in consumption

**public goods**
goods that are neither excludable nor rival in consumption

2. **Public goods** are neither excludable nor rival in consumption. That is, people cannot be prevented from using a public good, and one person's use of a public good does not reduce another person's ability to use it. For example, a tornado siren in a small town is a public good. Once the siren sounds, it is impossible to prevent any single person from hearing it (so it is not excludable). Moreover, when one person gets the benefit of the warning, she does not reduce the benefit to anyone else (so it is not rival in consumption).

## FIGURE 1

**Rival in consumption?**

| | Yes | No |
|---|---|---|
| **Yes** | **Private Goods**<br>• Ice-cream cones<br>• Clothing<br>• Congested toll roads | **Club Goods**<br>• Fire protection<br>• Cable TV<br>• Uncongested toll roads |
| **No** | **Common Resources**<br>• Fish in the ocean<br>• The environment<br>• Congested nontoll roads | **Public Goods**<br>• Tornado siren<br>• National defense<br>• Uncongested nontoll roads |

**Excludable?**

**Four Types of Goods**
Goods can be grouped into four categories according to two characteristics: (1) A good is *excludable* if people can be prevented from using it. (2) A good is *rival in consumption* if one person's use of the good diminishes other people's use of it. This diagram gives examples of goods in each category.

3. **Common resources** are rival in consumption but not excludable. For example, fish in the ocean are rival in consumption: When one person catches fish, there are fewer fish for the next person to catch. But these fish are not an excludable good because it is difficult to stop fishermen from taking fish out of a vast ocean.

4. **Club goods** are excludable but not rival in consumption. For instance, consider fire protection in a small town. It is easy to exclude someone from using this good: The fire department can just let her house burn down. But fire protection is not rival in consumption: Once a town has paid for the fire department, the additional cost of protecting one more house is small. (We discuss club goods again in Chapter 14, where we see that they are one type of a *natural monopoly*.)

**common resources**
goods that are rival in consumption but not excludable

**club goods**
goods that are excludable but not rival in consumption

Although Figure 1 offers a clean separation of goods into four categories, the boundaries between the categories are sometimes fuzzy. Whether goods are excludable or rival in consumption is often a matter of degree. Fish in an ocean may not be excludable because monitoring fishing is so difficult, but a large enough coast guard could make fish at least partly excludable. Similarly, although fish are generally rival in consumption, this would be less true if the population of fishermen were small relative to the population of fish. (Think of North American fishing waters before the arrival of European settlers.) For purposes of our analysis, however, it will be helpful to group goods into these four categories.

In this chapter, we examine goods that are not excludable: public goods and common resources. Because people cannot be prevented from using these goods, they are available to everyone free of charge. The study of public goods and common resources is closely related to the study of externalities. For both of these types of goods, externalities arise because something of value has no price attached to it. If one person were to provide a public good, such as a tornado siren, other people would be better off. They would receive a benefit without paying for it—a positive externality. Similarly, when one person uses a common resource such as the fish in the ocean, other people are worse off because there are fewer fish to catch. They suffer a loss but are not compensated for it—a negative externality. Because of these external effects, private decisions about consumption and production can lead to an inefficient allocation of resources, and government intervention can potentially raise economic well-being.

**QuickQuiz** *Define* public goods *and* common resources *and give an example of each.*

# 11-2 Public Goods

To understand how public goods differ from other goods and why they present problems for society, let's consider an example: a fireworks display. This good is not excludable because it is impossible to prevent someone from seeing fireworks, and it is not rival in consumption because one person's enjoyment of fireworks does not reduce anyone else's enjoyment of them.

## 11-2a The Free-Rider Problem

The citizens of Smalltown, U.S.A., like seeing fireworks on the Fourth of July. Each of the town's 500 residents places a $10 value on the experience for a total benefit of $5,000. The cost of putting on a fireworks display is $1,000. Because the $5,000 benefit exceeds the $1,000 cost, it is efficient for Smalltown to have a fireworks display on the Fourth of July.

Would the private market produce the efficient outcome? Probably not. Imagine that Ella, a Smalltown entrepreneur, decided to put on a fireworks display. Ella would surely have trouble selling tickets to the event because her potential customers would quickly figure out that they could see the fireworks even without a ticket. Because fireworks are not excludable, people have an incentive to be free riders. A **free rider** is a person who receives the benefit of a good but does not pay for it. Because people would have an incentive to be free riders rather than ticket buyers, the market would fail to provide the efficient outcome.

One way to view this market failure is that it arises because of an externality. If Ella puts on the fireworks display, she confers an external benefit on those who see the display without paying for it. When deciding whether to put on the display, however, Ella does not take the external benefits into account. Even though the fireworks display is socially desirable, it is not profitable. As a result, Ella makes the privately rational but socially inefficient decision not to put on the display.

Although the private market fails to supply the fireworks display demanded by Smalltown residents, the solution to Smalltown's problem is obvious: The local government can sponsor a Fourth of July celebration. The town council can raise everyone's taxes by $2 and use the revenue to hire Ella to produce the fireworks. Everyone in Smalltown is better off by $8—the $10 at which residents value the fireworks minus the $2 tax bill. Ella can help Smalltown reach the efficient outcome as a public employee even though she could not do so as a private entrepreneur.

The story of Smalltown is simplified but realistic. In fact, many local governments in the United States pay for fireworks on the Fourth of July. Moreover, the story shows a general lesson about public goods: Because public goods are not excludable, the free-rider problem prevents the private market from supplying them. The government, however, can remedy the problem. If the government decides that the total benefits of a public good exceed its costs, it can provide the public good, pay for it with tax revenue, and potentially make everyone better off.

## 11-2b Some Important Public Goods

There are many examples of public goods. Here we consider three of the most important.

**National Defense** The defense of a country from foreign aggressors is a classic example of a public good. Once the country is defended, it is impossible to prevent any single person from enjoying the benefit of this defense. And when one

**free rider**
a person who receives the benefit of a good but avoids paying for it

person enjoys the benefit of national defense, she does not reduce the benefit to anyone else. Thus, national defense is neither excludable nor rival in consumption.

National defense is also one of the most expensive public goods. In 2014, the U.S. federal government spent a total of $748 billion on national defense, more than $2,346 per person. People disagree about whether this amount is too small or too large, but almost no one doubts that some government spending for national defense is necessary. Even economists who advocate small government agree that national defense is a public good the government should provide.

*"I like the concept if we can do it with no new taxes."*

**Basic Research**   Knowledge is created through research. In evaluating the appropriate public policy toward knowledge creation, it is important to distinguish general knowledge from specific technological knowledge. Specific technological knowledge, such as the invention of a longer-lasting battery, a smaller microchip, or a better digital music player, can be patented. The patent gives the inventor the exclusive right to the knowledge she has created for a period of time. Anyone else who wants to use the patented information must pay the inventor for the right to do so. In other words, the patent makes the knowledge created by the inventor excludable.

By contrast, general knowledge is a public good. For example, a mathematician cannot patent a theorem. Once a theorem is proven, the knowledge is not excludable: The theorem enters society's general pool of knowledge that anyone can use without charge. The theorem is also not rival in consumption: One person's use of the theorem does not prevent any other person from using the theorem.

Profit-seeking firms spend a lot on research trying to develop new products that they can patent and sell, but they do not spend much on basic research. Their incentive, instead, is to free ride on the general knowledge created by others. As a result, in the absence of any public policy, society would devote too few resources to creating new knowledge.

The government tries to provide the public good of general knowledge in various ways. Government agencies, such as the National Institutes of Health and the National Science Foundation, subsidize basic research in medicine, mathematics, physics, chemistry, biology, and even economics. Some people justify government funding of the space program on the grounds that it adds to society's pool of knowledge. Determining the appropriate level of government support for these endeavors is difficult because the benefits are hard to measure. Moreover, the members of Congress who appropriate funds for research usually have little expertise in science and, therefore, are not in the best position to judge what lines of research will produce the largest benefits. So, while basic research is surely a public good, we should not be surprised if the public sector fails to pay for the right amount and the right kinds.

**Fighting Poverty**   Many government programs are aimed at helping the poor. The welfare system (officially called TANF, Temporary Assistance for Needy Families) provides a small income for some poor families. Food stamps (officially called SNAP, Supplemental Nutrition Assistance Program) subsidize the purchase of food for those with low incomes. And various government housing programs make shelter more affordable. These antipoverty programs are financed by taxes paid by families that are financially more successful.

Economists disagree among themselves about what role the government should play in fighting poverty. Here we note one important argument: Advocates of antipoverty programs claim that fighting poverty is a public good. Even if everyone prefers living in a society without poverty, fighting poverty is not a "good" that private actions will adequately provide.

To see why, suppose someone tried to organize a group of wealthy individuals to try to eliminate poverty. They would be providing a public good. This good would not be rival in consumption: One person's enjoyment of living in a society without poverty would not reduce anyone else's enjoyment of it. The good would not be excludable: Once poverty is eliminated, no one can be prevented from taking pleasure in this fact. As a result, there would be a tendency for people to free ride on the generosity of others, enjoying the benefits of poverty elimination without contributing to the cause.

Because of the free-rider problem, eliminating poverty through private charity will probably not work. Yet government action can solve this problem. Taxing the wealthy to raise the living standards of the poor can potentially make everyone better off. The poor are better off because they now enjoy a higher standard of living, and those paying the taxes are better off because they enjoy living in a society with less poverty.

**CASE STUDY**

**ARE LIGHTHOUSES PUBLIC GOODS?**

Some goods can switch between being public goods and being private goods depending on the circumstances. For example, a fireworks display is a public good if performed in a town with many residents. Yet if performed at a private amusement park, such as Walt Disney World, a fireworks display is more like a private good because visitors to the park pay for admission.

Another example is a lighthouse. Economists have long used lighthouses as an example of a public good. Lighthouses mark specific locations along the coast so that passing ships can avoid treacherous waters. The benefit that the lighthouse provides to the ship captain is neither excludable nor rival in consumption, so each captain has an incentive to free ride by using the lighthouse to navigate without paying for the service. Because of this free-rider problem, private markets usually fail to provide the lighthouses that ship captains need. As a result, most lighthouses today are operated by the government.

In some cases, however, lighthouses have been closer to private goods. On the coast of England in the 19th century, for example, some lighthouses were privately owned and operated. Instead of trying to charge ship captains for the service, however, the owner of the lighthouse charged the owner of the nearby port. If the port owner did not pay, the lighthouse owner turned off the light, and ships avoided that port.

In deciding whether something is a public good, one must determine who the beneficiaries are and whether these beneficiaries can be excluded from using the good. A free-rider problem arises when the number of beneficiaries is large and exclusion of any one of them is impossible. If a lighthouse benefits many ship captains, it is a public good. If it primarily benefits a single port owner, it is more like a private good. ●

*KEVIN BRINE/SHUTTERSTOCK.COM*

*What kind of good is this?*

## 11-2c The Difficult Job of Cost–Benefit Analysis

So far we have seen that the government provides public goods because the private market on its own will not produce an efficient quantity. Yet deciding that the government must play a role is only the first step. The government must then determine what kinds of public goods to provide and in what quantities.

Suppose that the government is considering a public project, such as building a new highway. To judge whether to build the highway, it must compare the total benefits for all those who would use it to the costs of building and maintaining it. To make this decision, the government might hire a team of economists and engineers to conduct a study, called a **cost–benefit analysis**, to estimate the total costs and benefits of the project to society as a whole.

Cost–benefit analysts have a tough job. Because the highway will be available to everyone free of charge, there is no price with which to judge the value of the highway. Simply asking people how much they would value the highway is not reliable: Quantifying benefits is difficult using the results from a questionnaire, and respondents have little incentive to tell the truth. Those who would use the highway have an incentive to exaggerate the benefit they receive to get the highway built. Those who would be harmed by the highway have an incentive to exaggerate the costs to them to prevent the highway from being built.

The efficient provision of public goods is, therefore, intrinsically more difficult than the efficient provision of private goods. When buyers of a private good enter a market, they reveal the value they place on it through the prices they are willing to pay. At the same time, sellers reveal their costs with the prices they are willing to accept. The equilibrium is an efficient allocation of resources because it reflects all this information. By contrast, cost–benefit analysts do not have any price signals to observe when evaluating whether the government should provide a public good and how much to provide. Their findings on the costs and benefits of public projects are rough approximations at best.

**cost–benefit analysis**
a study that compares the costs and benefits to society of providing a public good

### HOW MUCH IS A LIFE WORTH?

**CASE STUDY**

Imagine that you have been elected to serve as a member of your local town council. The town engineer comes to you with a proposal: The town can spend $10,000 to install and operate a traffic light at a town intersection that now has only a stop sign. The benefit of the traffic light is increased safety. The engineer estimates, based on data from similar intersections, that the traffic light would reduce the risk of a fatal traffic accident over the lifetime of the traffic light from 1.6 to 1.1 percent. Should you spend the money for the new light?

To answer this question, you turn to cost–benefit analysis. But you quickly run into an obstacle: The costs and benefits must be measured in the same units if you are to compare them meaningfully. The cost is measured in dollars, but the benefit—the possibility of saving a person's life—is not directly monetary. To make your decision, you have to put a dollar value on a human life.

At first, you may be tempted to conclude that a human life is priceless. After all, there is probably no amount of money that you could be paid to voluntarily give up your life or that of a loved one. This suggests that a human life has an infinite dollar value.

For the purposes of cost–benefit analysis, however, this answer leads to nonsensical results. If we truly placed an infinite value on human life, we should place traffic lights on every street corner, and we should all drive large cars loaded with the latest safety features. Yet traffic lights are not at every corner, and people sometimes choose to pay less for smaller cars without safety options such as side-impact air bags or antilock brakes. In both our public and private decisions, we are at times willing to risk our lives to save some money.

Once we have accepted the idea that a person's life has an implicit dollar value, how can we determine what that value is? One approach, sometimes used by courts to award damages in wrongful-death suits, is to look at the total amount of money a person would have earned if she had lived. Economists are often critical of this approach because it ignores other opportunity costs of losing one's life. It thus has the bizarre implication that the life of a retired or disabled person has no value.

A better way to value human life is to look at the risks that people are voluntarily willing to take and how much they must be paid for taking them. For example, mortality risk varies across jobs. Construction workers in high-rise buildings face greater risk of death on the job than office workers do. By comparing wages in risky and less risky occupations, controlling for education, experience, and other determinants of wages, economists can get some sense about what value people put on their own lives. Studies using this approach conclude that the value of a human life is about $10 million.

We can now return to our original example and respond to the town engineer. The traffic light reduces the risk of fatality by 0.5 percentage points. Thus, the expected benefit from installing the traffic light is 0.005 × $10 million, or $50,000. This estimate of the benefit exceeds the cost of $10,000, so you should approve the project. ●

---

**QuickQuiz**   *What is the free-rider problem? Why does the free-rider problem induce the government to provide public goods?* ● *How should the government decide whether to provide a public good?*

# 11-3  Common Resources

Common resources, like public goods, are not excludable: They are available free of charge to anyone who wants to use them. Common resources are, however, rival in consumption: One person's use of the common resource reduces other people's ability to use it. Thus, common resources give rise to a new problem: Once the good is provided, policymakers need to be concerned about how much it is used. This problem is best understood from the classic parable called the **Tragedy of the Commons**.

**Tragedy of the Commons**
a parable that illustrates why common resources are used more than is desirable from the standpoint of society as a whole

## 11-3a  The Tragedy of the Commons

Consider life in a small medieval town. Of the many economic activities that take place in the town, one of the most important is raising sheep. Many of the town's families own flocks of sheep and support themselves by selling the sheep's wool, which is used to make clothing.

As our story begins, the sheep spend much of their time grazing on the land surrounding the town, called the Town Common. No family owns the land. Instead, the town residents own the land collectively, and all the residents are allowed to graze their sheep on it. Collective ownership works well because land is plentiful. As long as everyone can get all the good grazing land they want, the Town Common is not rival in consumption, and allowing residents' sheep to graze for free causes no problems. Everyone in the town is happy.

As the years pass, the population of the town grows, and so does the number of sheep grazing on the Town Common. With a growing number of sheep and a fixed amount of land, the land starts to lose its ability to replenish itself. Eventually, the land is grazed so heavily that it becomes barren. With no grass left on the Town Common, raising sheep is impossible, and the town's once prosperous wool industry disappears. Many families lose their source of livelihood.

What causes the tragedy? Why do the shepherds allow the sheep population to grow so large that it destroys the Town Common? The reason is that social and private incentives differ. Avoiding the destruction of the grazing land depends on the collective action of the shepherds. If the shepherds acted together, they could reduce the sheep population to a size that the Town Common can support. Yet no single family has an incentive to reduce the size of its own flock because each flock represents only a small part of the problem.

In essence, the Tragedy of the Commons arises because of an externality. When one family's flock grazes on the common land, it reduces the quality of the land available for other families. Because people neglect this negative externality when deciding how many sheep to own, the result is an excessive number of sheep.

If the tragedy had been foreseen, the town could have solved the problem in various ways. It could have regulated the number of sheep in each family's flock, internalized the externality by taxing sheep, or auctioned off a limited number of sheep-grazing permits. That is, the medieval town could have dealt with the problem of overgrazing in the way that modern society deals with the problem of pollution.

In the case of land, however, there is a simpler solution. The town can divide the land among town families. Each family can enclose its parcel of land with a fence and then protect it from excessive grazing. In this way, the land becomes a private good rather than a common resource. This outcome in fact occurred during the enclosure movement in England during the 17th century.

The Tragedy of the Commons is a story with a general lesson: When one person uses a common resource, she diminishes other people's enjoyment of it. Because of this negative externality, common resources tend to be used excessively. The government can solve the problem by using regulation or taxes to reduce consumption of the common resource. Alternatively, the government can sometimes turn the common resource into a private good.

This lesson has been known for thousands of years. The ancient Greek philosopher Aristotle pointed out the problem with common resources: "What is common to many is taken least care of, for all men have greater regard for what is their own than for what they possess in common with others."

## 11-3b Some Important Common Resources

There are many examples of common resources. In almost all cases, the same problem arises as in the Tragedy of the Commons: Private decision makers use the common resource too much. As a result, governments often regulate behavior or impose fees to mitigate the problem of overuse.

**Clean Air and Water** As we discussed in Chapter 10, markets do not adequately protect the environment. Pollution is a negative externality that can be remedied with regulations or with corrective taxes on polluting activities. One can view this market failure as an example of a common-resource problem. Clean air and clean water are common resources like open grazing land, and excessive pollution is like excessive grazing. Environmental degradation is a modern Tragedy of the Commons.

**Congested Roads** Roads can be either public goods or common resources. If a road is not congested, then one person's use does not affect anyone else. In this case, use is not rival in

**ASK THE EXPERTS**

## Congestion Pricing

"In general, using more congestion charges in crowded transportation networks — such as higher tolls during peak travel times in cities, and peak fees for airplane takeoff and landing slots — and using the proceeds to lower other taxes would make citizens on average better off."

**What do economists say?**

0% disagree — 2% uncertain

98% agree

Source: IGM Economic Experts Panel, January 11, 2012.

## IN THE NEWS

# The Case for Toll Roads

*Many economists think drivers should be charged more for using roads. Here is why.*

### Why You'll Love Paying for Roads That Used to Be Free

By Eric A. Morris

To end the scourge of traffic congestion, Julius Caesar banned most carts from the streets of Rome during daylight hours. It didn't work—traffic jams just shifted to dusk. Two thousand years later, we have put a man on the moon and developed garments infinitely more practical than the toga, but we seem little nearer to solving the congestion problem.

If you live in a city, particularly a large one, you probably need little convincing that traffic congestion is frustrating and wasteful. According to the Texas Transportation Institute, the average American urban traveler lost 38 hours, nearly one full work week, to congestion in 2005. And congestion is getting worse, not better; urban travelers in 1982 were delayed only 14 hours that year.

Americans want action, but unfortunately there aren't too many great ideas about what that action might be. As Anthony Downs's excellent book *Still Stuck in Traffic: Coping With Peak-Hour Traffic Congestion* chronicles, most of the proposed solutions are too difficult to implement, won't work, or both.

Fortunately, there is one remedy which is both doable and largely guaranteed to succeed. In the space of a year or two we could have you zipping along the 405 or the LIE at the height of rush hour at a comfortable 55 miles per hour.

There's just one small problem with this silver bullet for congestion: many people seem to prefer the werewolf. Despite its merits, this policy, which is known as "congestion pricing," "value pricing," or "variable tolling," is not an easy political sell.

For decades, economists and other transportation thinkers have advocated imposing tolls that vary with congestion levels on roadways. Simply put, the more congestion, the higher the toll, until the congestion goes away.

To many people, this sounds like a scheme by mustache-twirling bureaucrats and their academic apologists to fleece drivers out of their hard-earned cash. Why should drivers have to pay to use roads their tax dollars have already paid for? Won't the remaining free roads be swamped as drivers are forced off the tolled roads? Won't the working-class and poor be the victims here, as the tolled routes turn into "Lexus lanes"?

And besides, adopting this policy would mean listening to economists, and who wants to do that?

There's a real problem with this logic, which is that, on its own terms, it makes perfect sense (except for the listening to economists part). Opponents of tolls are certainly not stupid, and their arguments deserve serious consideration. But in the end, their concerns are largely overblown, and the benefits of tolling swamp the potential costs.

Unfortunately, it can be hard to convey this because the theory behind tolling is somewhat complex and counterintuitive. This is too bad, because variable tolling is an excellent public policy. Here's why: the basic economic theory is that when you give out something valuable—in this case, road space—for less than its true value, shortages result.

Ultimately, there's no free lunch; instead of paying with money, you pay with the effort

consumption, and the road is a public good. Yet if a road is congested, then use of that road yields a negative externality. When one person drives on the road, it becomes more crowded, and other people must drive more slowly. In this case, the road is a common resource.

One way for the government to address the problem of road congestion is to charge drivers a toll. A toll is, in essence, a corrective tax on the externality of congestion. Sometimes, as in the case of local roads, tolls are not a practical solution because the cost of collecting them is too high. But several major cities, including London and Stockholm, have found increasing tolls to be a very effective way to reduce congestion.

Sometimes congestion is a problem only at certain times of day. If a bridge is heavily traveled only during rush hour, for instance, the congestion externality is largest during this time. The efficient way to deal with these externalities is

and time needed to acquire the good. Think of Soviet shoppers spending their lives in endless queues to purchase artificially low-priced but exceedingly scarce goods. Then think of Americans who can fulfill nearly any consumerist fantasy quickly but at a monetary cost. Free but congested roads have left us shivering on the streets of Moscow.

To consider it another way, delay is an externality imposed by drivers on their peers. By driving onto a busy road and contributing to congestion, drivers slow the speeds of others—but they never have to pay for it, at least not directly. In the end, of course, everybody pays, because as we impose congestion on others, others impose it on us. This degenerates into a game that nobody can win.

Markets work best when externalities are internalized: i.e., you pay for the hassle you inflict on others…. Using tolls to help internalize the congestion externality would somewhat reduce the number of trips made on the most congested roads at the peak usage periods; some trips would be moved to less congested times and routes, and others would be foregone entirely. This way we would cut down on the congestion costs we impose on each other.

Granted, tolls cannot fully cope with accidents and other incidents, which are major causes of delay. But pricing can largely eliminate chronic, recurring congestion. No matter how high the demand for a road, there is a level of toll that will keep it flowing freely.

To make tolling truly effective, the price must be right. Too high a price drives away too many cars and the road does not function at its capacity. Too low a price and congestion isn't licked.

The best solution is to vary the tolls in real time based on an analysis of current traffic conditions. Pilot toll projects on roads (like the I-394 in Minnesota and the I-15 in Southern California) use sensors embedded in the pavement to monitor the number and speeds of vehicles on the facility.

A simple computer program then determines the number of cars that should be allowed in. The computer then calculates the level of toll that will attract that number of cars—and no more. Prices are then updated every few minutes on electronic message signs. Hi-tech transponders and antenna arrays make waiting at toll booths a thing of the past.

The bottom line is that speeds are kept high (over 45 m.p.h.) so that throughput is higher than when vehicles are allowed to crowd all at once onto roadways at rush hour, slowing traffic to a crawl.

To maximize efficiency, economists would like to price all travel, starting with the freeways. But given that elected officials have no burning desire to lose their jobs, a more realistic option, for now, is to toll just some freeway lanes that are either new capacity or underused carpool lanes. The other lanes would be left free—and congested. Drivers will then have a choice: wait or pay. Granted, neither is ideal. But right now drivers have no choice at all.

What's the bottom line here? The state of Washington recently opened congestion-priced lanes on its State Route 167. The peak toll in the first month of operation (reached on the evening of Wednesday, May 21) was $5.75. I know, I know, you would never pay such an exorbitant amount when America has taught you that free roads are your birthright. But that money bought Washington drivers a 27-minute time savings. Is a half hour of your time worth $6?

I think I already know the answer, and it is "it depends." Most people's value of time varies widely depending on their activities on any given day. Late for picking the kids up from daycare? Paying $6 to save a half hour is an incredible bargain. Have to clean the house? The longer your trip home takes, the better. Tolling will introduce a new level of flexibility and freedom into your life, giving you the power to tailor your travel costs to fit your schedule. ∎

**Source:** Freakonomics blog, January 6, 2009.

to charge higher tolls during rush hour. This toll would provide an incentive for drivers to alter their schedules, reducing traffic when congestion is greatest.

Another policy that responds to the problem of road congestion (discussed in the previous chapter) is the tax on gasoline. A higher gasoline tax increases the price of gasoline, reduces the amount that people drive, and reduces road congestion. The gasoline tax is an imperfect solution to congestion, however, because it affects other decisions besides the amount of driving on congested roads. In particular, the tax also discourages driving on uncongested roads, even though there is no congestion externality for these roads.

**Fish, Whales, and Other Wildlife**  Many species of animals are common resources. Fish and whales, for instance, have commercial value, and anyone can go to the ocean and catch whatever is available. Each person has little incentive to maintain the species for the next year. Just as excessive grazing can destroy the Town Common, excessive fishing and whaling can destroy commercially valuable marine populations.

Oceans remain one of the least regulated common resources. Two problems prevent an easy solution. First, many countries have access to the oceans, so any solution would require international cooperation among countries that hold different values. Second, because the oceans are so vast, enforcing any agreement is difficult. As a result, fishing rights have been a frequent source of international tension among normally friendly countries.

Within the United States, various laws aim to manage the use of fish and other wildlife. For example, the government charges for fishing and hunting licenses, and it restricts the lengths of the fishing and hunting seasons. Fishermen are often required to throw back small fish, and hunters can kill only a limited number of animals. All these laws reduce the use of a common resource and help maintain animal populations.

**CASE STUDY**

### WHY THE COW IS NOT EXTINCT

Throughout history, many species of animals have been threatened with extinction. When Europeans first arrived in North America, more than 60 million buffalo roamed the continent. Unfortunately, however, hunting the buffalo was so popular during the 19th century that by 1900 the animal's population had fallen to about 400 before the government stepped in to protect the species. In some African countries today, elephants face a similar challenge, as poachers kill them for the ivory in their tusks.

Yet not all animals with commercial value face this threat. The cow, for example, is a valuable source of food, but no one worries that the cow will soon be extinct. Indeed, the great demand for beef seems to ensure that the species will continue to thrive.

Why does the commercial value of ivory threaten the elephant, while the commercial value of beef protects the cow? The reason is that elephants are a common resource, whereas cows are a private good. Elephants roam freely without any owners. Each poacher has a strong incentive to kill as many elephants as she can find. Because poachers are numerous, each poacher has only a slight incentive to preserve the elephant population. By contrast, cattle live on ranches that are privately owned. Each rancher makes a great effort to maintain the cattle population on her ranch because she reaps the benefit.

Governments have tried to solve the elephant's problem in two ways. Some countries, such as Kenya, Tanzania, and Uganda, have made it illegal to kill elephants and sell their ivory. Yet these laws have been hard to enforce, and the battle between the authorities and the poachers has become increasingly violent. Meanwhile, elephant populations have continued to dwindle. By contrast, other countries, such as Botswana, Malawi, Namibia, and Zimbabwe, have made elephants a private good by allowing people to kill elephants, but only those on their own property. Landowners now have an incentive to preserve the species on their own land, and as a result, elephant populations have started to rise. With private ownership and the profit motive now on its side, the African elephant might someday be as safe from extinction as the cow. ●

*"Will the market protect me?"*

 *Why do governments try to limit the use of common resources?*

# 11-4 Conclusion: The Importance of Property Rights

In this and the previous chapter, we have seen there are some "goods" that the market does not provide adequately. Markets do not ensure that the air we breathe is clean or that our country is defended from foreign aggressors. Instead, societies rely on the government to protect the environment and to provide for the national defense.

The problems we considered in these chapters arise in many different markets, but they share a common theme. In all cases, the market fails to allocate resources efficiently because *property rights* are not well established. That is, some item of value does not have an owner with the legal authority to control it. For example, although no one doubts that the "good" of clean air or national defense is valuable, no one has the right to attach a price to it and profit from its use. A factory pollutes too much because no one charges the factory for the pollution it emits. The market does not provide for national defense because no one can charge those who are defended for the benefit they receive.

When the absence of property rights causes a market failure, the government can potentially solve the problem. Sometimes, as in the sale of pollution permits, the solution is for the government to help define property rights and thereby unleash market forces. Other times, as in restricted hunting seasons, the solution is for the government to regulate private behavior. Still other times, as in the provision of national defense, the solution is for the government to use tax revenue to supply a good that the market fails to supply. In each of these cases, if the policy is well planned and well run, it can make the allocation of resources more efficient and thus raise economic well-being.

---

## CHAPTER QuickQuiz

1.  Which categories of goods are excludable?
    a. private goods and club goods
    b. private goods and common resources
    c. public goods and club goods
    d. public goods and common resources

2.  Which categories of goods are rival in consumption?
    a. private goods and club goods
    b. private goods and common resources
    c. public goods and club goods
    d. public goods and common resources

3.  Which of the following is an example of a public good?
    a. residential housing
    b. national defense
    c. restaurant meals
    d. fish in the ocean

4.  Which of the following is an example of a common resource?
    a. residential housing
    b. national defense
    c. restaurant meals
    d. fish in the ocean

5.  Public goods are
    a. efficiently provided by market forces.
    b. underprovided in the absence of government.
    c. overused in the absence of government.
    d. a type of natural monopoly.

6.  Common resources are
    a. efficiently provided by market forces.
    b. underprovided in the absence of government.
    c. overused in the absence of government.
    d. a type of natural monopoly.

## SUMMARY

- Goods differ in whether they are excludable and whether they are rival in consumption. A good is excludable if it is possible to prevent someone from using it. A good is rival in consumption if one person's use of the good reduces others' ability to use the same unit of the good. Markets work best for private goods, which are both excludable and rival in consumption. Markets do not work as well for other types of goods.
- Public goods are neither rival in consumption nor excludable. Examples of public goods include fireworks displays, national defense, and the discovery of fundamental knowledge. Because people are not charged for their use of the public good, they have an incentive to free ride, making private provision of the good untenable. Therefore, governments provide public goods, basing their decision about the quantity of each good on cost–benefit analysis.
- Common resources are rival in consumption but not excludable. Examples include common grazing land, clean air, and congested roads. Because people are not charged for their use of common resources, they tend to use them excessively. Therefore, governments use various methods, such as regulations and corrective taxes, to limit the use of common resources.

## KEY CONCEPTS

excludability, p. 212
rivalry in consumption, p. 212
private goods, p. 212

public goods, p. 212
common resources, p. 213
club goods, p. 213

free rider, p. 214
cost–benefit analysis, p. 217
Tragedy of the Commons, p. 218

## QUESTIONS FOR REVIEW

1. Explain what is meant by a good being "excludable." Explain what is meant by a good being "rival in consumption." Is a slice of pizza excludable? Is it rival in consumption?

2. Define and give an example of a public good. Can the private market provide this good on its own? Explain.

3. What is cost–benefit analysis of public goods? Why is it important? Why is it hard?

4. Define and give an example of a common resource. Without government intervention, will people use this good too much or too little? Why?

## PROBLEMS AND APPLICATIONS

1. Think about the goods and services provided by your local government.
   a. Using the classification in Figure 1, explain which category each of the following goods falls into:
      - police protection
      - snow plowing
      - education
      - rural roads
      - city streets
   b. Why do you think the government provides items that are not public goods?

2. Both public goods and common resources involve externalities.
   a. Are the externalities associated with public goods generally positive or negative? Use examples in your answer. Is the free-market quantity of public goods generally greater or less than the efficient quantity?
   b. Are the externalities associated with common resources generally positive or negative? Use examples in your answer. Is the free-market use of common resources generally greater or less than the efficient use?

3. Fredo loves watching *Downton Abbey* on his local public TV station, but he never sends any money to support the station during its fund-raising drives.
   a. What name do economists have for people like Fredo?
   b. How can the government solve the problem caused by people like Fredo?
   c. Can you think of ways the private market can solve this problem? How does the existence of cable TV alter the situation?

4. Wireless, high-speed Internet is provided for free in the airport of the city of Communityville.
   a. At first, only a few people use the service. What type of a good is this and why?
   b. Eventually, as more people find out about the service and start using it, the speed of the connection begins to fall. Now what type of a good is the wireless Internet service?
   c. What problem might result and why? What is one possible way to correct this problem?

5. Four roommates are planning to spend the weekend in their dorm room watching old movies, and they are debating how many to watch. Here is their willingness to pay for each film:

|             | Steven | Peter | James | Christopher |
|-------------|--------|-------|-------|-------------|
| First film  | $7     | $5    | $3    | $2          |
| Second film | 6      | 4     | 2     | 1           |
| Third film  | 5      | 3     | 1     | 0           |
| Fourth film | 4      | 2     | 0     | 0           |
| Fifth film  | 3      | 1     | 0     | 0           |

   a. Within the dorm room, is the showing of a movie a public good? Why or why not?
   b. If it costs $8 to rent a movie, how many movies should the roommates rent to maximize total surplus?
   c. If they choose the optimal number from part (b) and then split the cost of renting the movies equally, how much surplus does each person obtain from watching the movies?
   d. Is there any way to split the cost to ensure that everyone benefits? What practical problems does this solution raise?
   e. Suppose they agree in advance to choose the efficient number and to split the cost of the movies equally. When Steven is asked his willingness to pay, will he have an incentive to tell the truth? If so, why? If not, what will he be tempted to say?
   f. What does this example teach you about the optimal provision of public goods?

6. Some economists argue that private firms will not undertake the efficient amount of basic scientific research.
   a. Explain why this might be so. In your answer, classify basic research in one of the categories shown in Figure 1.
   b. What sort of policy has the United States adopted in response to this problem?
   c. It is often argued that this policy increases the technological capability of American producers relative to that of foreign firms. Is this argument consistent with your classification of basic research in part (a)? (*Hint*: Can excludability apply to some potential beneficiaries of a public good and not others?)

7. Two towns, each with three members, are deciding whether to put on a fireworks display to celebrate the New Year. Fireworks cost $360. In each town, some people enjoy fireworks more than others.
   a. In the town of Bayport, each of the residents values the public good as follows:

   | Frank  | $50   |
   |--------|-------|
   | Joe    | $100  |
   | Callie | $300  |

   Would fireworks pass a cost–benefit analysis? Explain.
   b. The mayor of Bayport proposes to decide by majority rule and, if the fireworks referendum passes, to split the cost equally among all residents. Who would vote in favor, and who would vote against? Would the vote yield the same answer as the cost–benefit analysis?
   c. In the town of River Heights, each of the residents values the public good as follows:

   | Nancy | $20   |
   |-------|-------|
   | Bess  | $140  |
   | Ned   | $160  |

   Would fireworks pass a cost–benefit analysis? Explain.
   d. The mayor of River Heights also proposes to decide by majority rule and, if the fireworks referendum passes, to split the cost equally among all residents. Who would vote in favor, and who would vote against? Would the vote yield the same answer as the cost–benefit analysis?
   e. What do you think these examples say about the optimal provision of public goods?

8. There is often litter along highways but rarely in people's yards. Provide an economic explanation for this fact.

9. Many transportation systems, such as the Washington, D.C., Metro (subway), charge higher fares during rush hours than during the rest of the day. Why might they do this?

10. High-income people are willing to pay more than lower-income people to avoid the risk of death. For example, they are more likely to pay for safety features on cars. Do you think cost–benefit analysts should take this fact into account when evaluating public projects? Consider, for instance, a rich town and a poor town, both of which are considering the installation of a traffic light. Should the rich town use a higher dollar value for a human life in making this decision? Why or why not?

To find additional study resources, visit cengagebrain.com, and search for "Mankiw."

# PART V
# Firm Behavior and the Organization of Industry

# The Costs of Production

The economy is made up of thousands of firms that produce the goods and services you enjoy every day: General Motors produces automobiles, General Electric produces lightbulbs, and General Mills produces breakfast cereals. Some firms, such as these three, are large; they employ thousands of workers and have thousands of stockholders who share the firms' profits. Other firms, such as the local barbershop or café, are small; they employ only a few workers and are owned by a single person or family.

In previous chapters, we used the supply curve to summarize firms' production decisions. According to the law of supply, firms are willing to produce

and sell a greater quantity of a good when the price of the good is higher. This response leads to a supply curve that slopes upward. For analyzing many questions, the law of supply is all you need to know about firm behavior.

In this chapter and the ones that follow, we examine firm behavior in more detail. This topic will give you a better understanding of the decisions behind the supply curve. In addition, it will introduce you to a part of economics called *industrial organization*—the study of how firms' decisions about prices and quantities depend on the market conditions they face. The town in which you live, for instance, may have several pizzerias but only one cable television company. This raises a key question: How does the number of firms affect the prices in a market and the efficiency of the market outcome? The field of industrial organization addresses exactly this question.

Before turning to these issues, we need to discuss the costs of production. All firms, from Delta Air Lines to your local deli, incur costs while making the goods and services that they sell. As we will see in the coming chapters, a firm's costs are a key determinant of its production and pricing decisions. In this chapter, we define some of the variables that economists use to measure a firm's costs, and we consider the relationships among these variables.

A word of warning: This topic is dry and technical. To be honest, one might even call it boring. But this material provides a crucial foundation for the fascinating topics that follow.

# 12-1 What Are Costs?

We begin our discussion of costs at Caroline's Cookie Factory. Caroline, the owner of the firm, buys flour, sugar, chocolate chips, and other cookie ingredients. She also buys the mixers and ovens and hires workers to run this equipment. She then sells the cookies to consumers. By examining some of the issues that Caroline faces in her business, we can learn some lessons about costs that apply to all firms in an economy.

## 12-1a Total Revenue, Total Cost, and Profit

We begin with the firm's objective. To understand the decisions a firm makes, we must understand what it is trying to do. Although it is conceivable that Caroline started her firm because of an altruistic desire to provide the world with cookies or, perhaps, out of love for the cookie business, it is more likely that she started the business to make money. Economists normally assume that the goal of a firm is to maximize profit, and they find that this assumption works well in most cases.

**total revenue**
the amount a firm receives for the sale of its output

**total cost**
the market value of the inputs a firm uses in production

**profit**
total revenue minus total cost

What is a firm's profit? The amount that the firm receives for the sale of its output (cookies) is called **total revenue**. The amount that the firm pays to buy inputs (flour, sugar, workers, ovens, and so forth) is called **total cost**. Caroline gets to keep any revenue that is not needed to cover costs. **Profit** is a firm's total revenue minus its total cost:

$$\text{Profit} = \text{Total revenue} - \text{Total cost}$$

Caroline's objective is to make her firm's profit as large as possible.

To see how a firm goes about maximizing profit, we must consider fully how to measure its total revenue and its total cost. Total revenue is the easy part: It equals the quantity of output the firm produces multiplied by the price at which it sells its output. If Caroline produces 10,000 cookies and sells them at $2 a cookie, her total revenue is $20,000. The measurement of a firm's total cost, however, is more subtle.

## 12-1b  Costs as Opportunity Costs

When measuring costs at Caroline's Cookie Factory or any other firm, it is important to keep in mind one of the *Ten Principles of Economics* from Chapter 1: The cost of something is what you give up to get it. Recall that the *opportunity cost* of an item refers to all the things that must be forgone to acquire that item. When economists speak of a firm's cost of production, they include all the opportunity costs of making its output of goods and services.

While some of a firm's opportunity costs of production are obvious, others are less so. When Caroline pays $1,000 for flour, that $1,000 is an opportunity cost because Caroline can no longer use that $1,000 to buy something else. Similarly, when Caroline hires workers to make the cookies, the wages she pays are part of the firm's costs. Because these opportunity costs require the firm to pay out some money, they are called **explicit costs**. By contrast, some of a firm's opportunity costs, called **implicit costs**, do not require a cash outlay. Imagine that Caroline is skilled with computers and could earn $100 per hour working as a programmer. For every hour that Caroline works at her cookie factory, she gives up $100 in income, and this forgone income is also part of her costs. The total cost of Caroline's business is the sum of her explicit and implicit costs.

The distinction between explicit and implicit costs highlights an important difference between how economists and accountants analyze a business. Economists are interested in studying how firms make production and pricing decisions. Because these decisions are based on both explicit and implicit costs, economists include both when measuring a firm's costs. By contrast, accountants have the job of keeping track of the money that flows into and out of firms. As a result, they measure the explicit costs but usually ignore the implicit costs.

The difference between the methods of economists and accountants is easy to see in the case of Caroline's Cookie Factory. When Caroline gives up the opportunity to earn money as a computer programmer, her accountant will not count this as a cost of her cookie business. Because no money flows out of the business to pay for this cost, it never shows up on the accountant's financial statements. An economist, however, will count the forgone income as a cost because it will affect the decisions that Caroline makes in her cookie business. For example, if Caroline's wage as a computer programmer rises from $100 to $500 per hour, she might decide that running her cookie business is too costly. She might choose to shut down the factory so she can take a job as a programmer.

**explicit costs**
input costs that require an outlay of money by the firm

**implicit costs**
input costs that do not require an outlay of money by the firm

## 12-1c  The Cost of Capital as an Opportunity Cost

An important implicit cost of almost every business is the opportunity cost of the financial capital that has been invested in the business. Suppose, for instance, that Caroline used $300,000 of her savings to buy the cookie factory from its previous owner. If Caroline had instead left this money in a savings account that pays an interest rate of 5 percent, she would have earned $15,000 per year. To own her cookie factory, therefore, Caroline has given up $15,000 a year in interest income. This forgone $15,000 is one of the implicit opportunity costs of Caroline's business.

As we have already noted, economists and accountants treat costs differently, and this is especially true in their treatment of the cost of capital. An economist views the $15,000 in interest income that Caroline gives up every year as an implicit cost of her business. Caroline's accountant, however, will not show this $15,000 as a cost because no money flows out of the business to pay for it.

To further explore the difference between the methods of economists and accountants, let's change the example slightly. Suppose now that Caroline did not have the entire $300,000 to buy the factory but, instead, used $100,000 of her own savings and borrowed $200,000 from a bank at an interest rate of 5 percent. Caroline's accountant, who only measures explicit costs, will now count the $10,000 interest paid on the bank loan every year as a cost because this amount of money now flows out of the firm. By contrast, according to an economist, the opportunity cost of owning the business is still $15,000. The opportunity cost equals the interest on the bank loan (an explicit cost of $10,000) plus the forgone interest on savings (an implicit cost of $5,000).

### 12-1d Economic Profit versus Accounting Profit

Now let's return to the firm's objective: profit. Because economists and accountants measure costs differently, they also measure profit differently. An economist measures a firm's **economic profit** as the firm's total revenue minus all the opportunity costs (explicit and implicit) of producing the goods and services sold. An accountant measures the firm's **accounting profit** as the firm's total revenue minus only the firm's explicit costs.

Figure 1 summarizes this difference. Notice that because the accountant ignores the implicit costs, accounting profit is usually larger than economic profit. For a business to be profitable from an economist's standpoint, total revenue must exceed all the opportunity costs, both explicit and implicit.

Economic profit is an important concept because it motivates the firms that supply goods and services. As we will see, a firm making positive economic profit will stay in business. It is covering all its opportunity costs and has some revenue left to reward the firm owners. When a firm is making economic losses (that is, when economic profits are negative), the business owners are failing to earn enough revenue to cover all the costs of production. Unless conditions change,

**economic profit**
total revenue minus total cost, including both explicit and implicit costs

**accounting profit**
total revenue minus total explicit cost

---

## FIGURE 1

**Economists versus Accountants**
Economists include all opportunity costs when analyzing a firm, whereas accountants measure only explicit costs. Therefore, economic profit is smaller than accounting profit.

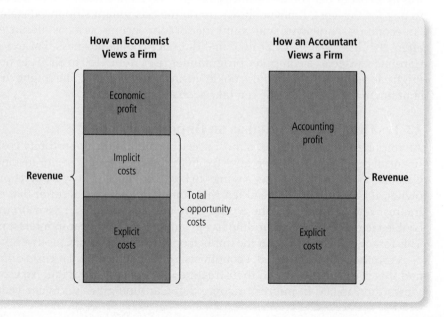

the firm owners will eventually close down the business and exit the industry. To understand business decisions, we need to keep an eye on economic profit.

QuickQuiz *Farmer McDonald gives banjo lessons for $20 an hour. One day, he spends 10 hours planting $100 worth of seeds on his farm. What opportunity cost has he incurred? What cost would his accountant measure? If these seeds yield $200 worth of crops, does McDonald earn an accounting profit? Does he earn an economic profit?*

# 12-2 Production and Costs

Firms incur costs when they buy inputs to produce the goods and services that they plan to sell. In this section, we examine the link between a firm's production process and its total cost. Once again, we consider Caroline's Cookie Factory.

In the analysis that follows, we make an important simplifying assumption: We assume that the size of Caroline's factory is fixed and that Caroline can vary the quantity of cookies produced only by changing the number of workers she employs. This assumption is realistic in the short run but not in the long run. That is, Caroline cannot build a larger factory overnight, but she could do so over the next year or two. This analysis, therefore, describes the production decisions that Caroline faces in the short run. We examine the relationship between costs and time horizon more fully later in the chapter.

### 12-2a The Production Function

Table 1 shows how the quantity of cookies produced per hour at Caroline's factory depends on the number of workers. As you can see in columns (1) and (2), if there are no workers in the factory, Caroline produces no cookies.

| (1)<br>Number of Workers | (2)<br>Output (quantity of cookies produced per hour) | (3)<br>Marginal Product of Labor | (4)<br>Cost of Factory | (5)<br>Cost of Workers | (6)<br>Total Cost of Inputs (cost of factory + cost of workers) |
|---|---|---|---|---|---|
| 0 | 0 | | $30 | $0 | $30 |
| | | 50 | | | |
| 1 | 50 | | 30 | 10 | 40 |
| | | 40 | | | |
| 2 | 90 | | 30 | 20 | 50 |
| | | 30 | | | |
| 3 | 120 | | 30 | 30 | 60 |
| | | 20 | | | |
| 4 | 140 | | 30 | 40 | 70 |
| | | 10 | | | |
| 5 | 150 | | 30 | 50 | 80 |
| | | 5 | | | |
| 6 | 155 | | 30 | 60 | 90 |

**TABLE 1**

A Production Function and Total Cost: Caroline's Cookie Factory

When there is 1 worker, she produces 50 cookies. When there are 2 workers, she produces 90 cookies and so on. Panel (a) of Figure 2 presents a graph of these two columns of numbers. The number of workers is on the horizontal axis, and the number of cookies produced is on the vertical axis. This relationship between the quantity of inputs (workers) and quantity of output (cookies) is called the **production function**.

One of the *Ten Principles of Economics* introduced in Chapter 1 is that rational people think at the margin. As we will see in future chapters, this idea is the key to understanding the decisions a firm makes about how many workers to hire and how much output to produce. To take a step toward understanding these decisions, column (3) in the table gives the marginal product of a worker. The **marginal product** of any input in the production process is the increase in the quantity of output obtained from one additional unit of that input. When the number of workers goes from 1 to 2, cookie production increases from 50 to 90, so the marginal product of the second worker is 40 cookies. And when the number of

**production function**
the relationship between the quantity of inputs used to make a good and the quantity of output of that good

**marginal product**
the increase in output that arises from an additional unit of input

## FIGURE 2

**Caroline's Production Function and Total-Cost Curve**

The production function in panel (a) shows the relationship between the number of workers hired and the quantity of output produced. Here the number of workers hired (on the horizontal axis) is from column (1) in Table 1, and the quantity of output produced (on the vertical axis) is from column (2). The production function gets flatter as the number of workers increases, reflecting diminishing marginal product. The total-cost curve in panel (b) shows the relationship between the quantity of output produced and total cost of production. Here the quantity of output produced (on the horizontal axis) is from column (2) in Table 1, and the total cost (on the vertical axis) is from column (6). The total-cost curve gets steeper as the quantity of output increases because of diminishing marginal product.

**(a) Production function**

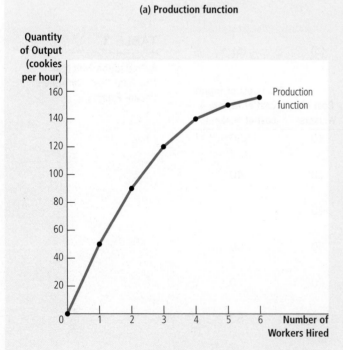

**(b) Total-cost curve**

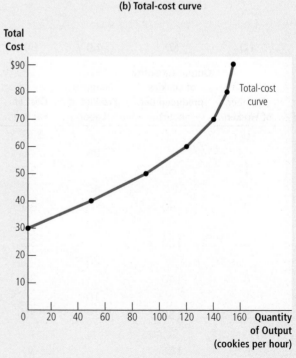

workers goes from 2 to 3, cookie production increases from 90 to 120, so the marginal product of the third worker is 30 cookies. In the table, the marginal product is shown halfway between two rows because it represents the change in output as the number of workers increases from one level to another.

Notice that as the number of workers increases, the marginal product declines. The second worker has a marginal product of 40 cookies, the third worker has a marginal product of 30 cookies, and the fourth worker has a marginal product of 20 cookies. This property is called **diminishing marginal product**. At first, when only a few workers are hired, they have easy access to Caroline's kitchen equipment. As the number of workers increases, additional workers have to share equipment and work in more crowded conditions. Eventually, the kitchen becomes so overcrowded that workers often get in each other's way. Hence, as more workers are hired, each additional worker contributes fewer additional cookies to total production.

Diminishing marginal product is also apparent in Figure 2. The production function's slope ("rise over run") tells us the change in Caroline's output of cookies ("rise") for each additional input of labor ("run"). That is, the slope of the production function measures the marginal product. As the number of workers increases, the marginal product declines, and the production function becomes flatter.

**diminishing marginal product**
the property whereby the marginal product of an input declines as the quantity of the input increases

### 12-2b From the Production Function to the Total-Cost Curve

Columns (4), (5), and (6) in Table 1 show Caroline's cost of producing cookies. In this example, the cost of Caroline's factory is $30 per hour, and the cost of a worker is $10 per hour. If she hires 1 worker, her total cost is $40 per hour. If she hires 2 workers, her total cost is $50 per hour, and so on. With this information, the table now shows how the number of workers Caroline hires is related to the quantity of cookies she produces and to her total cost of production.

Our goal in the next several chapters is to study firms' production and pricing decisions. For this purpose, the most important relationship in Table 1 is between quantity produced [in column (2)] and total cost [in column (6)]. Panel (b) of Figure 2 graphs these two columns of data with quantity produced on the horizontal axis and total cost on the vertical axis. This graph is called the *total-cost curve*.

Now compare the total-cost curve in panel (b) with the production function in panel (a). These two curves are opposite sides of the same coin. The total-cost curve gets steeper as the amount produced rises, whereas the production function gets flatter as production rises. These changes in slope occur for the same reason. High production of cookies means that Caroline's kitchen is crowded with many workers. Because the kitchen is crowded, each additional worker adds less to production, reflecting diminishing marginal product. Therefore, the production function is relatively flat. But now turn this logic around: When the kitchen is crowded, producing an additional cookie requires a lot of additional labor and is thus very costly. Therefore, when the quantity produced is large, the total-cost curve is relatively steep.

| Quick**Quiz** | *If Farmer Jones plants no seeds on her farm, she gets no harvest. If she plants 1 bag of seeds, she gets 3 bushels of wheat. If she plants 2 bags, she gets 5 bushels. If she plants 3 bags, she gets 6 bushels. A bag of seeds costs $100, and seeds are her only cost. Use these data to graph the farmer's production function and total-cost curve. Explain their shapes.* |

## 12-3　The Various Measures of Cost

Our analysis of Caroline's Cookie Factory demonstrated how a firm's total cost reflects its production function. From data on a firm's total cost, we can derive several related measures of cost, which will turn out to be useful when we analyze production and pricing decisions in future chapters. To see how these related measures are derived, we consider the example in Table 2. This table presents cost data on Caroline's neighbor—Conrad's Coffee Shop.

Column (1) in the table shows the number of cups of coffee that Conrad might produce, ranging from 0 to 10 cups per hour. Column (2) shows Conrad's total cost of producing coffee. Figure 3 plots Conrad's total-cost curve. The quantity of coffee [from column (1)] is on the horizontal axis, and total cost [from column (2)] is on the vertical axis. Conrad's total-cost curve has a shape similar to Caroline's. In particular, it becomes steeper as the quantity produced rises, which (as we have discussed) reflects diminishing marginal product.

**TABLE 2**

The Various Measures of Cost: Conrad's Coffee Shop

| (1) Output (cups of coffee per hour) | (2) Total Cost | (3) Fixed Cost | (4) Variable Cost | (5) Average Fixed Cost | (6) Average Variable Cost | (7) Average Total Cost | (8) Marginal Cost |
|---|---|---|---|---|---|---|---|
| 0 | $3.00 | $3.00 | $0.00 | — | — | — | |
| | | | | | | | $0.30 |
| 1 | 3.30 | 3.00 | 0.30 | $3.00 | $0.30 | $3.30 | |
| | | | | | | | 0.50 |
| 2 | 3.80 | 3.00 | 0.80 | 1.50 | 0.40 | 1.90 | |
| | | | | | | | 0.70 |
| 3 | 4.50 | 3.00 | 1.50 | 1.00 | 0.50 | 1.50 | |
| | | | | | | | 0.90 |
| 4 | 5.40 | 3.00 | 2.40 | 0.75 | 0.60 | 1.35 | |
| | | | | | | | 1.10 |
| 5 | 6.50 | 3.00 | 3.50 | 0.60 | 0.70 | 1.30 | |
| | | | | | | | 1.30 |
| 6 | 7.80 | 3.00 | 4.80 | 0.50 | 0.80 | 1.30 | |
| | | | | | | | 1.50 |
| 7 | 9.30 | 3.00 | 6.30 | 0.43 | 0.90 | 1.33 | |
| | | | | | | | 1.70 |
| 8 | 11.00 | 3.00 | 8.00 | 0.38 | 1.00 | 1.38 | |
| | | | | | | | 1.90 |
| 9 | 12.90 | 3.00 | 9.90 | 0.33 | 1.10 | 1.43 | |
| | | | | | | | 2.10 |
| 10 | 15.00 | 3.00 | 12.00 | 0.30 | 1.20 | 1.50 | |

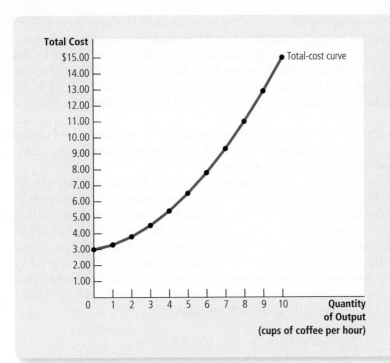

**Total Cost**

Total-cost curve

Quantity
of Output
(cups of coffee per hour)

**FIGURE 3**

**Conrad's Total-Cost Curve**
Here the quantity of output produced (on the horizontal axis) is from column (1) in Table 2, and the total cost (on the vertical axis) is from column (2). As in Figure 2, the total-cost curve gets steeper as the quantity of output increases because of diminishing marginal product.

## 12-3a Fixed and Variable Costs

Conrad's total cost can be divided into two types. Some costs, called **fixed costs**, do not vary with the quantity of output produced. They are incurred even if the firm produces nothing at all. Conrad's fixed costs include any rent he pays because this cost is the same regardless of how much coffee he produces. Similarly, if Conrad needs to hire a full-time bookkeeper to pay bills, regardless of the quantity of coffee produced, the bookkeeper's salary is a fixed cost. The third column in Table 2 shows Conrad's fixed cost, which in this example is $3.00.

Some of the firm's costs, called **variable costs**, change as the firm alters the quantity of output produced. Conrad's variable costs include the cost of coffee beans, milk, sugar, and paper cups: The more cups of coffee Conrad makes, the more of these items he needs to buy. Similarly, if Conrad has to hire more workers to make more cups of coffee, the salaries of these workers are variable costs. Column (4) in the table shows Conrad's variable cost. The variable cost is 0 if he produces nothing, $0.30 if he produces 1 cup of coffee, $0.80 if he produces 2 cups, and so on.

A firm's total cost is the sum of fixed and variable costs. In Table 2, total cost in column (2) equals fixed cost in column (3) plus variable cost in column (4).

**fixed costs**
costs that do not vary with the quantity of output produced

**variable costs**
costs that vary with the quantity of output produced

## 12-3b Average and Marginal Cost

As the owner of his firm, Conrad has to decide how much to produce. One issue he will want to consider when making this decision is how the level of production affects his firm's costs. Conrad might ask his production supervisor the following two questions about the cost of producing coffee:

- How much does it cost to make the typical cup of coffee?
- How much does it cost to increase production of coffee by 1 cup?

These two questions might seem to have the same answer, but they do not. Both answers are important for understanding how firms make production decisions.

To find the cost of the typical unit produced, we divide the firm's costs by the quantity of output it produces. For example, if the firm produces 2 cups of coffee per hour, its total cost is $3.80, and the cost of the typical cup is $3.80/2, or $1.90. Total cost divided by the quantity of output is called **average total cost**. Because total cost is the sum of fixed and variable costs, average total cost can be expressed as the sum of average fixed cost and average variable cost. **Average fixed cost** is the fixed cost divided by the quantity of output, and **average variable cost** is the variable cost divided by the quantity of output.

Average total cost tells us the cost of the typical unit, but it does not tell us how much total cost will change as the firm alters its level of production. Column (8) in Table 2 shows the amount that total cost rises when the firm increases production by 1 unit of output. This number is called **marginal cost**. For example, if Conrad increases production from 2 to 3 cups, total cost rises from $3.80 to $4.50, so the marginal cost of the third cup of coffee is $4.50 minus $3.80, or $0.70. In the table, the marginal cost appears halfway between any two rows because it represents the change in total cost as quantity of output increases from one level to another.

It may be helpful to express these definitions mathematically:

$$\text{Average total cost} = \text{Total cost}/\text{Quantity}$$

$$ATC = TC/Q,$$

and

$$\text{Marginal cost} = \text{Change in total cost}/\text{Change in quantity}$$

$$MC = \Delta TC/\Delta Q$$

Here $\Delta$, the Greek letter delta, represents the change in a variable. These equations show how average total cost and marginal cost are derived from total cost. *Average total cost tells us the cost of a typical unit of output if total cost is divided evenly over all the units produced. Marginal cost tells us the increase in total cost that arises from producing an additional unit of output.* As we will see more fully in the next chapter, business managers like Conrad need to keep in mind the concepts of average total cost and marginal cost when deciding how much of their product to supply to the market.

### 12-3c  Cost Curves and Their Shapes

Just as we found graphs of supply and demand useful when analyzing the behavior of markets in previous chapters, we will find graphs of average and marginal cost useful when analyzing the behavior of firms. Figure 4 graphs Conrad's costs using the data from Table 2. The horizontal axis measures the quantity the firm produces, and the vertical axis measures marginal and average costs. The graph shows four curves: average total cost (*ATC*), average fixed cost (*AFC*), average variable cost (*AVC*), and marginal cost (*MC*).

The cost curves shown here for Conrad's Coffee Shop have some features that are common to the cost curves of many firms in the economy. Let's examine three features in particular: the shape of the marginal-cost curve, the shape of the average-total-cost curve, and the relationship between marginal cost and average total cost.

**average total cost**
total cost divided by the quantity of output

**average fixed cost**
fixed cost divided by the quantity of output

**average variable cost**
variable cost divided by the quantity of output

**marginal cost**
the increase in total cost that arises from an extra unit of production

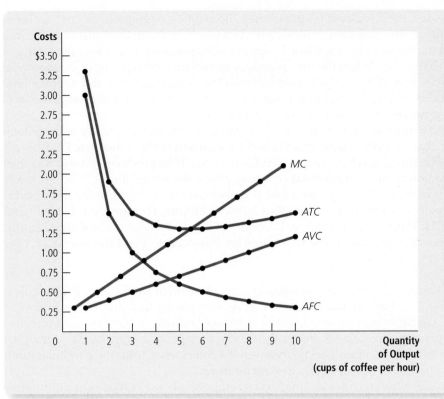

## FIGURE 4

**Conrad's Average-Cost and Marginal-Cost Curves**

This figure shows the average total cost (*ATC*), average fixed cost (*AFC*), average variable cost (*AVC*), and marginal cost (*MC*) for Conrad's Coffee Shop. All of these curves are obtained by graphing the data in Table 2. These cost curves show three common features: (1) Marginal cost rises with the quantity of output. (2) The average-total-cost curve is U-shaped. (3) The marginal-cost curve crosses the average-total-cost curve at the minimum of average total cost.

**Rising Marginal Cost**  Conrad's marginal cost rises as the quantity of output produced increases. This upward slope reflects the property of diminishing marginal product. When Conrad produces a small quantity of coffee, he has few workers, and much of his equipment is not used. Because he can easily put these idle resources to use, the marginal product of an extra worker is large, and the marginal cost of an extra cup of coffee is small. By contrast, when Conrad produces a large quantity of coffee, his shop is crowded with workers, and most of his equipment is fully utilized. Conrad can produce more coffee by adding workers, but these new workers have to work in crowded conditions and may have to wait to use the equipment. Therefore, when the quantity of coffee produced is already high, the marginal product of an extra worker is low, and the marginal cost of an extra cup of coffee is large.

**U-Shaped Average Total Cost**  Conrad's average-total-cost curve is U-shaped, as shown in Figure 4. To understand why, remember that average total cost is the sum of average fixed cost and average variable cost. Average fixed cost always declines as output rises because the fixed cost is getting spread over a larger number of units. Average variable cost usually rises as output increases because of diminishing marginal product.

Average total cost reflects the shapes of both average fixed cost and average variable cost. At very low levels of output, such as 1 or 2 cups per hour, average total cost is very high. Even though average variable cost is low, average fixed cost is high because the fixed cost is spread over only a few units. As output increases, the fixed cost is spread over more units. Average fixed cost declines, rapidly at first and then more slowly. As a result, average total cost also declines until the firm's output reaches 5 cups of coffee per hour, when average total cost is $1.30 per cup. When the firm produces more than 6 cups per hour, however, the increase in average variable cost becomes the dominant force, and average total cost starts rising. The tug of war between average fixed cost and average variable cost generates the U-shape in average total cost.

The bottom of the U-shape occurs at the quantity that minimizes average total cost. This quantity is sometimes called the **efficient scale** of the firm. For Conrad, the efficient scale is 5 or 6 cups of coffee per hour. If he produces more or less than this amount, his average total cost rises above the minimum of $1.30. At lower levels of output, average total cost is higher than $1.30 because the fixed cost is spread over so few units. At higher levels of output, average total cost is higher than $1.30 because the marginal product of inputs has diminished significantly. At the efficient scale, these two forces are balanced to yield the lowest average total cost.

**efficient scale**
the quantity of output that minimizes average total cost

**The Relationship between Marginal Cost and Average Total Cost**    If you look at Figure 4 (or back at Table 2), you will see something that may be surprising at first. *Whenever marginal cost is less than average total cost, average total cost is falling. Whenever marginal cost is greater than average total cost, average total cost is rising.* This feature of Conrad's cost curves is not a coincidence from the particular numbers used in the example: It is true for all firms.

To see why, consider an analogy. Average total cost is like your cumulative grade point average. Marginal cost is like the grade you get in the next course you take. If your grade in your next course is less than your grade point average, your grade point average will fall. If your grade in your next course is higher than your grade point average, your grade point average will rise. The mathematics of average and marginal costs is exactly the same as the mathematics of average and marginal grades.

This relationship between average total cost and marginal cost has an important corollary: *The marginal-cost curve crosses the average-total-cost curve at its minimum.* Why? At low levels of output, marginal cost is below average total cost, so average total cost is falling. But after the two curves cross, marginal cost rises above average total cost. As a result, average total cost must start to rise at this level of output. Hence, this point of intersection is the minimum of average total cost. As we will see in the next chapter, minimum average total cost plays a key role in the analysis of competitive firms.

### 12-3d  Typical Cost Curves

In the examples we have studied so far, the firms have exhibited diminishing marginal product and, therefore, rising marginal cost at all levels of output. This simplifying assumption was useful because it allowed us to focus on the key features of cost curves that are useful in analyzing firm behavior. Yet actual firms are usually more complicated than this. In many firms, marginal product does not start to fall immediately after the first worker is hired. Depending on the production process, the second or third worker might have a higher marginal product than the first because a team of workers can divide tasks and work more productively than a single worker. Firms exhibiting this pattern would experience increasing marginal product for a while before diminishing marginal product set in.

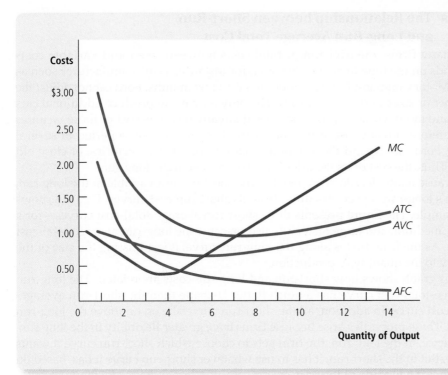

**FIGURE 5**

**Cost Curves for a Typical Firm**
Many firms experience increasing marginal product before diminishing marginal product. As a result, they have cost curves shaped like those in this figure. Notice that marginal cost and average variable cost fall for a while before starting to rise.

Figure 5 shows the cost curves for such a firm, including average total cost (*ATC*), average fixed cost (*AFC*), average variable cost (*AVC*), and marginal cost (*MC*). At low levels of output, the firm experiences increasing marginal product, and the marginal-cost curve falls. Eventually, the firm starts to experience diminishing marginal product, and the marginal-cost curve starts to rise. This combination of increasing then diminishing marginal product also makes the average-variable-cost curve U-shaped.

Despite these differences from our previous example, the cost curves in Figure 5 share the three properties that are most important to remember:

- Marginal cost eventually rises with the quantity of output.
- The average-total-cost curve is U-shaped.
- The marginal-cost curve crosses the average-total-cost curve at the minimum of average total cost.

**QuickQuiz** *Suppose Honda's total cost of producing 4 cars is $225,000 and its total cost of producing 5 cars is $250,000. What is the average total cost of producing 5 cars? What is the marginal cost of the fifth car? • Draw the marginal-cost curve and the average-total-cost curve for a typical firm, and explain why these curves cross where they do.*

## 12-4 Costs in the Short Run and in the Long Run

We noted earlier in this chapter that a firm's costs might depend on the time horizon under consideration. Let's examine more precisely why this might be the case.

### 12-4a  The Relationship between Short-Run and Long-Run Average Total Cost

For many firms, the division of total costs between fixed and variable costs depends on the time horizon. Consider, for instance, a car manufacturer such as Ford Motor Company. Over a period of only a few months, Ford cannot adjust the number or sizes of its car factories. The only way it can produce additional cars is to hire more workers at the factories it already has. The cost of these factories is, therefore, a fixed cost in the short run. By contrast, over a period of several years, Ford can expand the size of its factories, build new factories, or close old ones. Thus, the cost of its factories is a variable cost in the long run.

Because many decisions are fixed in the short run but variable in the long run, a firm's long-run cost curves differ from its short-run cost curves. Figure 6 shows an example. The figure presents three short-run average-total-cost curves—for a small, medium, and large factory. It also presents the long-run average-total-cost curve. As the firm moves along the long-run curve, it is adjusting the size of the factory to the quantity of production.

This graph shows how short-run and long-run costs are related. The long-run average-total-cost curve has a much flatter U-shape than the short-run average-total-cost curve. In addition, all the short-run curves lie on or above the long-run curve. These properties arise because firms have greater flexibility in the long run. In essence, in the long run, the firm gets to choose which short-run curve it wants to use. But in the short run, it has to use whatever short-run curve it has, based on decisions it has made in the past.

The figure shows an example of how a change in production alters costs over different time horizons. When Ford wants to increase production from 1,000 to 1,200 cars per day, it has no choice in the short run but to hire more workers at its existing medium-sized factory. Because of diminishing marginal product, average total cost rises from $10,000 to $12,000 per car. In the long run, however, Ford can expand both the size of the factory and its workforce, and average total cost returns to $10,000.

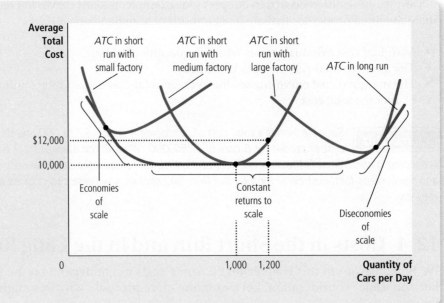

**FIGURE 6**

**Average Total Cost in the Short and Long Runs**
Because fixed costs are variable in the long run, the average-total-cost curve in the short run differs from the average-total-cost curve in the long run.

How long does it take a firm to get to the long run? The answer depends on the firm. It can take a year or more for a major manufacturing firm, such as a car company, to build a larger factory. By contrast, a person running a coffee shop can buy another coffee maker within a few days. There is, therefore, no single answer to the question of how long it takes a firm to adjust its production facilities.

### 12-4b Economies and Diseconomies of Scale

The shape of the long-run average-total-cost curve conveys important information about the production processes that a firm has available for manufacturing a good. In particular, it tells us how costs vary with the scale—that is, the size—of a firm's operations. When long-run average total cost declines as output increases, there are said to be **economies of scale**. When long-run average total cost rises as output increases, there are said to be **diseconomies of scale**. When long-run average total cost does not vary with the level of output, there are said to be **constant returns to scale**. As we can see in Figure 6, Ford has economies of scale at low levels of output, constant returns to scale at intermediate levels of output, and diseconomies of scale at high levels of output.

What might cause economies or diseconomies of scale? Economies of scale often arise because higher production levels allow *specialization* among workers, which permits each worker to become better at a specific task. For instance, if Ford hires a large number of workers and produces a large number of cars, it can reduce costs using modern assembly-line production. Diseconomies of scale can arise because of *coordination problems* that are inherent in any large organization. The more cars Ford produces, the more stretched the management team becomes, and the less effective the managers become at keeping costs down.

**economies of scale**
the property whereby long-run average total cost falls as the quantity of output increases

**diseconomies of scale**
the property whereby long-run average total cost rises as the quantity of output increases

**constant returns to scale**
the property whereby long-run average total cost stays the same as the quantity of output changes

---

**FYI**

## Lessons from a Pin Factory

"Jack of all trades, master of none." This well-known adage sheds light on the nature of cost curves. A person who tries to do everything usually ends up doing nothing very well. If a firm wants its workers to be as productive as they can be, it is often best to give each worker a limited task that she can master. But this organization of work is possible only if a firm employs many workers and produces a large quantity of output.

In his celebrated book *An Inquiry into the Nature and Causes of the Wealth of Nations*, Adam Smith described a visit he made to a pin factory. Smith was impressed by the specialization among the workers and the resulting economies of scale. He wrote,

*One man draws out the wire, another straightens it, a third cuts it, a fourth points it, a fifth grinds it at the top for receiving the head; to make the head requires two or three distinct operations; to put it on is a peculiar business; to whiten it is another; it is even a trade by itself to put them into paper.*

Smith reported that because of this specialization, the pin factory produced thousands of pins per worker every day. He conjectured that if the workers had chosen to work separately, rather than as a team of specialists, "they certainly could not each of them make twenty, perhaps not one pin a day." In other words, because of specialization, a large pin factory could achieve higher output per worker and lower average cost per pin than a small pin factory.

The specialization that Smith observed in the pin factory is prevalent in the modern economy. If you want to build a house, for instance, you could try to do all the work yourself. But most people turn to a builder, who in turn hires carpenters, plumbers, electricians, painters, and many other types of workers. These workers focus their training and experience in particular jobs, and as a result, they become better at their jobs than if they were generalists. Indeed, the use of specialization to achieve economies of scale is one reason modern societies are as prosperous as they are. ∎

This analysis shows why long-run average-total-cost curves are often U-shaped. At low levels of production, the firm benefits from increased size because it can take advantage of greater specialization. Coordination problems, meanwhile, are not yet acute. By contrast, at high levels of production, the benefits of specialization have already been realized, and coordination problems become more severe as the firm grows larger. Thus, long-run average total cost is falling at low levels of production because of increasing specialization and rising at high levels of production because of growing coordination problems.

**Quick Quiz** *If Boeing produces 9 jets per month, its long-run total cost is $9.0 million per month. If it produces 10 jets per month, its long-run total cost is $9.5 million per month. Does Boeing exhibit economies or diseconomies of scale?*

## 12-5 Conclusion

The purpose of this chapter has been to develop some tools to study how firms make production and pricing decisions. You should now understand what economists mean by the term *costs* and how costs vary with the quantity of output a firm produces. To refresh your memory, Table 3 summarizes some of the definitions we have encountered.

By themselves, a firm's cost curves do not tell us what decisions the firm will make. But they are a key component of that decision, as we will see in the next chapter.

**TABLE 3**

**The Many Types of Cost: A Summary**

| Term | Definition | Mathematical Description |
|------|-----------|--------------------------|
| Explicit costs | Costs that require an outlay of money by the firm | |
| Implicit costs | Costs that do not require an outlay of money by the firm | |
| Fixed costs | Costs that do not vary with the quantity of output produced | $FC$ |
| Variable costs | Costs that vary with the quantity of output produced | $VC$ |
| Total cost | The market value of all the inputs that a firm uses in production | $TC = FC + VC$ |
| Average fixed cost | Fixed cost divided by the quantity of output | $AFC = FC / Q$ |
| Average variable cost | Variable cost divided by the quantity of output | $AVC = VC / Q$ |
| Average total cost | Total cost divided by the quantity of output | $ATC = TC / Q$ |
| Marginal cost | The increase in total cost that arises from an extra unit of production | $MC = \Delta TC / \Delta Q$ |

## CHAPTER QuickQuiz

1. Xavier opens up a lemonade stand for two hours. He spends $10 for ingredients and sells $60 worth of lemonade. In the same two hours, he could have mowed his neighbor's lawn for $40. Xavier has an accounting profit of _____ and an economic profit of ____.
   a. $50, $10
   b. $90, $50
   c. $10, $50
   d. $50, $90

2. Diminishing marginal product explains why, as a firm's output increases,
   a. the production function and total-cost curve both get steeper.
   b. the production function and total-cost curve both get flatter.
   c. the production function gets steeper, while the total-cost curve gets flatter.
   d. the production function gets flatter, while the total-cost curve gets steeper.

3. A firm is producing 1,000 units at a total cost of $5,000. If it were to increase production to 1,001 units, its total cost would rise to $5,008. What does this information tell you about the firm?
   a. Marginal cost is $5, and average variable cost is $8.
   b. Marginal cost is $8, and average variable cost is $5.
   c. Marginal cost is $5, and average total cost is $8.
   d. Marginal cost is $8, and average total cost is $5.

4. A firm is producing 20 units with an average total cost of $25 and a marginal cost of $15. If it were to increase production to 21 units, which of the following must occur?
   a. Marginal cost would decrease.
   b. Marginal cost would increase.
   c. Average total cost would decrease.
   d. Average total cost would increase.

5. The government imposes a $1,000 per year license fee on all pizza restaurants. As a result, which cost curves shift?
   a. average total cost and marginal cost
   b. average total cost and average fixed cost
   c. average variable cost and marginal cost
   d. average variable cost and average fixed cost

6. If a higher level of production allows workers to specialize in particular tasks, a firm will likely exhibit _____ of scale and _____ average total cost.
   a. economies, falling
   b. economies, rising
   c. diseconomies, falling
   d. diseconomies, rising

## SUMMARY

- The goal of firms is to maximize profit, which equals total revenue minus total cost.
- When analyzing a firm's behavior, it is important to include all the opportunity costs of production. Some of the opportunity costs, such as the wages a firm pays its workers, are explicit. Other opportunity costs, such as the wages the firm owner gives up by working at the firm rather than taking another job, are implicit. Economic profit takes both explicit and implicit costs into account, whereas accounting profit considers only explicit costs.
- A firm's costs reflect its production process. A typical firm's production function gets flatter as the quantity of an input increases, displaying the property of diminishing marginal product. As a result, a firm's total-cost curve gets steeper as the quantity produced rises.
- A firm's total costs can be divided into fixed costs and variable costs. Fixed costs are costs that do not change when the firm alters the quantity of output produced.

- Variable costs are costs that change when the firm alters the quantity of output produced.
- From a firm's total cost, two related measures of cost are derived. Average total cost is total cost divided by the quantity of output. Marginal cost is the amount by which total cost rises if output increases by 1 unit.
- When analyzing firm behavior, it is often useful to graph average total cost and marginal cost. For a typical firm, marginal cost rises with the quantity of output. Average total cost first falls as output increases and then rises as output increases further. The marginal-cost curve always crosses the average-total-cost curve at the minimum of average total cost.
- A firm's costs often depend on the time horizon considered. In particular, many costs are fixed in the short run but variable in the long run. As a result, when the firm changes its level of production, average total cost may rise more in the short run than in the long run.

## KEY CONCEPTS

total revenue, p. 230
total cost, p. 230
profit, p. 230
explicit costs, p. 231
implicit costs, p. 231
economic profit, p. 232
accounting profit, p. 232

production function, p. 234
marginal product, p. 234
diminishing marginal product, p. 235
fixed costs, p. 237
variable costs, p. 237
average total cost, p. 238
average fixed cost, p. 238

average variable cost, p. 238
marginal cost, p. 238
efficient scale, p. 240
economies of scale, p. 243
diseconomies of scale, p. 243
constant returns to scale, p. 243

## QUESTIONS FOR REVIEW

1. What is the relationship between a firm's total revenue, profit, and total cost?

2. Give an example of an opportunity cost that an accountant would not count as a cost. Why would the accountant ignore this cost?

3. What is marginal product, and what does it mean if it is diminishing?

4. Draw a production function that exhibits diminishing marginal product of labor. Draw the associated total-cost curve. (In both cases, be sure to label the axes.) Explain the shapes of the two curves you have drawn.

5. Define *total cost*, *average total cost*, and *marginal cost*. How are they related?

6. Draw the marginal-cost and average-total-cost curves for a typical firm. Explain why the curves have the shapes that they do and why they intersect where they do.

7. How and why does a firm's average-total-cost curve differ in the short run compared with the long run?

8. Define *economies of scale* and explain why they might arise. Define *diseconomies of scale* and explain why they might arise.

## PROBLEMS AND APPLICATIONS

1. This chapter discusses many types of costs: opportunity cost, total cost, fixed cost, variable cost, average total cost, and marginal cost. Fill in the type of cost that best completes each sentence:
   a. What you give up in taking some action is called the _____.
   b. _____ is falling when marginal cost is below it and rising when marginal cost is above it.
   c. A cost that does not depend on the quantity produced is a(n) _____.
   d. In the ice-cream industry in the short run, _____ includes the cost of cream and sugar but not the cost of the factory.
   e. Profits equal total revenue minus _____.
   f. The cost of producing an extra unit of output is the _____.

2. Your aunt is thinking about opening a hardware store. She estimates that it would cost $500,000 per year to rent the location and buy the stock. In addition, she would have to quit her $50,000 per year job as an accountant.

   a. Define *opportunity cost*.
   b. What is your aunt's opportunity cost of running the hardware store for a year? If your aunt thinks she can sell $510,000 worth of merchandise in a year, should she open the store? Explain.

3. A commercial fisherman notices the following relationship between hours spent fishing and the quantity of fish caught:

   | Hours | Quantity of Fish (in pounds) |
   |---|---|
   | 0 hours | 0 lb. |
   | 1 | 10 |
   | 2 | 18 |
   | 3 | 24 |
   | 4 | 28 |
   | 5 | 30 |

   a. What is the marginal product of each hour spent fishing?

b. Use these data to graph the fisherman's production function. Explain its shape.

c. The fisherman has a fixed cost of $10 (his pole). The opportunity cost of his time is $5 per hour. Graph the fisherman's total-cost curve. Explain its shape.

4. Nimbus, Inc., makes brooms and then sells them door-to-door. Here is the relationship between the number of workers and Nimbus's output during a given day:

| Workers | Output | Marginal Product | Total Cost | Average Total Cost | Marginal Cost |
|---------|--------|------------------|------------|--------------------|---------------|
| 0 | 0 | | — | — | |
| 1 | 20 | — | — | — | — |
| 2 | 50 | — | — | — | — |
| 3 | 90 | — | — | — | — |
| 4 | 120 | — | — | — | — |
| 5 | 140 | — | — | — | — |
| 6 | 150 | — | — | — | — |
| 7 | 155 | — | — | — | — |

a. Fill in the column of marginal products. What pattern do you see? How might you explain it?

b. A worker costs $100 a day, and the firm has fixed costs of $200. Use this information to fill in the column for total cost.

c. Fill in the column for average total cost. (Recall that $ATC = TC/Q$.) What pattern do you see?

d. Now fill in the column for marginal cost. (Recall that $MC = \Delta TC/\Delta Q$.) What pattern do you see?

e. Compare the column for marginal product with the column for marginal cost. Explain the relationship.

f. Compare the column for average total cost with the column for marginal cost. Explain the relationship.

5. You are the chief financial officer for a firm that sells digital music players. Your firm has the following average-total-cost schedule:

| Quantity | Average Total Cost |
|----------|--------------------|
| 600 players | $300 |
| 601 | 301 |

Your current level of production is 600 devices, all of which have been sold. Someone calls, desperate to buy one of your music players. The caller offers you $550 for it. Should you accept the offer? Why or why not?

6. Consider the following cost information for a pizzeria:

| Quantity | Total Cost | Variable Cost |
|----------|------------|---------------|
| 0 dozen pizzas | $300 | $ 0 |
| 1 | 350 | 50 |
| 2 | 390 | 90 |
| 3 | 420 | 120 |
| 4 | 450 | 150 |
| 5 | 490 | 190 |
| 6 | 540 | 240 |

a. What is the pizzeria's fixed cost?

b. Construct a table in which you calculate the marginal cost per dozen pizzas using the information on total cost. Also, calculate the marginal cost per dozen pizzas using the information on variable cost. What is the relationship between these sets of numbers? Explain.

7. Your cousin Vinnie owns a painting company with fixed costs of $200 and the following schedule for variable costs:

| Quantity of Houses Painted per Month | 1 | 2 | 3 | 4 | 5 | 6 | 7 |
|---|---|---|---|---|---|---|---|
| Variable Costs | $10 | $20 | $40 | $80 | $160 | $320 | $640 |

Calculate average fixed cost, average variable cost, and average total cost for each quantity. What is the efficient scale of the painting company?

8. The city government is considering two tax proposals:
- A lump-sum tax of $300 on each producer of hamburgers.
- A tax of $1 per burger, paid by producers of hamburgers.

a. Which of the following curves—average fixed cost, average variable cost, average total cost, and marginal cost—would shift as a result of the lump-sum tax? Why? Show this in a graph. Label the graph as precisely as possible.

b. Which of these same four curves would shift as a result of the per-burger tax? Why? Show this in a new graph. Label the graph as precisely as possible.

9. Jane's Juice Bar has the following cost schedules:

| Quantity | Variable Cost | Total Cost |
| --- | --- | --- |
| 0 vats of juice | $ 0 | $ 30 |
| 1 | 10 | 40 |
| 2 | 25 | 55 |
| 3 | 45 | 75 |
| 4 | 70 | 100 |
| 5 | 100 | 130 |
| 6 | 135 | 165 |

a. Calculate average variable cost, average total cost, and marginal cost for each quantity.
b. Graph all three curves. What is the relationship between the marginal-cost curve and the average-total-cost curve? Between the marginal-cost curve and the average-variable-cost curve? Explain.

10. Consider the following table of long-run total costs for three different firms:

| Quantity | 1 | 2 | 3 | 4 | 5 | 6 | 7 |
| --- | --- | --- | --- | --- | --- | --- | --- |
| Firm A | $60 | $70 | $80 | $90 | $100 | $110 | $120 |
| Firm B | 11 | 24 | 39 | 56 | 75 | 96 | 119 |
| Firm C | 21 | 34 | 49 | 66 | 85 | 106 | 129 |

Does each of these firms experience economies of scale or diseconomies of scale?

To find additional study resources, visit cengagebrain.com, and search for "Mankiw."

# Firms in Competitive Markets

I f your local gas station raised its price for gasoline by 20 percent, it would see a large drop in the amount of gasoline it sold. Its customers would quickly switch to buying their gasoline at other gas stations. By contrast, if your local water company raised the price of water by 20 percent, it would see only a small decrease in the amount of water it sold. People might water their lawns less often and buy more water-efficient showerheads, but they would be hard-pressed to reduce water consumption greatly or to find another supplier. The difference between the gasoline market and the water market is that many firms supply gasoline to the local market, but only one firm supplies water. As you might expect, this difference in market structure shapes the pricing and production decisions of the firms that operate in these markets.

In this chapter, we examine the behavior of competitive firms, such as your local gas station. You may recall that a market is competitive if each buyer and seller is small compared to the size of the market and, therefore, has little ability to influence market prices. By contrast, if a firm can influence the market price of the good it sells, it is said to have *market power*. Later in the book, we examine the behavior of firms with market power, such as your local water company.

Our analysis of competitive firms in this chapter sheds light on the decisions that lie behind the supply curve in a competitive market. Not surprisingly, we find that a market supply curve is tightly linked to firms' costs of production. Less obvious, however, is the question of which among a firm's many types of cost—fixed, variable, average, and marginal—are most relevant for its supply decisions. We see that all these measures of cost play important and interrelated roles.

# 13-1 What Is a Competitive Market?

Our goal in this chapter is to examine how firms make production decisions in competitive markets. As a background for this analysis, we begin by reviewing what a competitive market is.

## 13-1a The Meaning of Competition

**competitive market**
a market with many buyers and sellers trading identical products so that each buyer and seller is a price taker

A **competitive market**, sometimes called a *perfectly competitive market*, has two characteristics:

- There are many buyers and many sellers in the market.
- The goods offered by the various sellers are largely the same.

As a result of these conditions, the actions of any single buyer or seller in the market have a negligible impact on the market price. Each buyer and seller takes the market price as given.

As an example, consider the market for milk. No single consumer of milk can influence the price of milk because each buys a small amount relative to the size of the market. Similarly, each dairy farmer has limited control over the price because many other sellers are offering milk that is essentially identical. Because each seller can sell all he wants at the going price, he has little reason to charge less, and if he charges more, buyers will go elsewhere. Buyers and sellers in competitive markets must accept the price the market determines and, therefore, are said to be *price takers*.

In addition to the previous two conditions for competition, a third condition is sometimes thought to characterize perfectly competitive markets:

- Firms can freely enter or exit the market.

If, for instance, anyone can start a dairy farm, and if any existing dairy farmer can leave the dairy business, then the dairy industry satisfies this condition. Much of the analysis of competitive firms does not require the assumption of free entry and exit because this condition is not necessary for firms to be price takers. Yet, as we see later in this chapter, when there is free entry and exit in a competitive market, it is a powerful force shaping the long-run equilibrium.

## 13-1b The Revenue of a Competitive Firm

A firm in a competitive market, like most other firms in the economy, tries to maximize profit (total revenue minus total cost). To see how it does this, we first consider the revenue of a competitive firm. To keep matters concrete, let's consider a specific firm: the Vaca Family Dairy Farm.

The Vaca Farm produces a quantity of milk, $Q$, and sells each unit at the market price, $P$. The farm's total revenue is $P \times Q$. For example, if a gallon of milk sells for $6 and the farm sells 1,000 gallons, its total revenue is $6,000.

Because the Vaca Farm is small compared to the world market for milk, it takes the price as given by market conditions. This means, in particular, that the price of milk does not depend on the number of gallons that the Vaca Farm produces and sells. If the Vacas double the amount of milk they produce to 2,000 gallons, the price of milk remains the same, and their total revenue doubles to $12,000. As a result, total revenue is proportional to the amount of output.

Table 1 shows the revenue for the Vaca Family Dairy Farm. Columns (1) and (2) show the amount of output the farm produces and the price at which it sells its output. Column (3) is the farm's total revenue. The table assumes that the price of milk is $6 a gallon, so total revenue is $6 times the number of gallons.

Just as the concepts of average and marginal were useful in the preceding chapter when analyzing costs, they are also useful when analyzing revenue. To see what these concepts tell us, consider these two questions:

- How much revenue does the farm receive for the typical gallon of milk?
- How much additional revenue does the farm receive if it increases production of milk by 1 gallon?

Columns (4) and (5) in Table 1 answer these questions.

| (1) Quantity (Q) | (2) Price (P) | (3) Total Revenue (TR = P × Q) | (4) Average Revenue (AR = TR / Q) | (5) Marginal Revenue (MR = ΔTR / ΔQ) |
|---|---|---|---|---|
| 1 gallon | $6 | $6 | $6 | |
| | | | | $6 |
| 2 | 6 | 12 | 6 | |
| | | | | 6 |
| 3 | 6 | 18 | 6 | |
| | | | | 6 |
| 4 | 6 | 24 | 6 | |
| | | | | 6 |
| 5 | 6 | 30 | 6 | |
| | | | | 6 |
| 6 | 6 | 36 | 6 | |
| | | | | 6 |
| 7 | 6 | 42 | 6 | |
| | | | | 6 |
| 8 | 6 | 48 | 6 | |

**TABLE 1**

Total, Average, and Marginal Revenue for a Competitive Firm

**average revenue**
total revenue divided by the quantity sold

Column (4) in the table shows **average revenue**, which is total revenue [from column (3)] divided by the amount of output [from column (1)]. Average revenue tells us how much revenue a firm receives for the typical unit sold. In Table 1, you can see that average revenue equals $6, the price of a gallon of milk. This illustrates a general lesson that applies not only to competitive firms but to other firms as well. Average revenue is total revenue ($P \times Q$) divided by the quantity ($Q$). *Therefore, for all types of firms, average revenue equals the price of the good.*

**marginal revenue**
the change in total revenue from an additional unit sold

Column (5) shows **marginal revenue**, which is the change in total revenue from the sale of each additional unit of output. In Table 1, marginal revenue equals $6, the price of a gallon of milk. This result illustrates a lesson that applies only to competitive firms. Total revenue is $P \times Q$, and $P$ is fixed for a competitive firm. Therefore, when $Q$ rises by 1 unit, total revenue rises by $P$ dollars. *For competitive firms, marginal revenue equals the price of the good.*

 *When a competitive firm doubles the amount it sells, what happens to the price of its output and its total revenue?*

# 13-2 Profit Maximization and the Competitive Firm's Supply Curve

The goal of a firm is to maximize profit, which equals total revenue minus total cost. We have just discussed the competitive firm's revenue, and in the preceding chapter, we discussed the firm's costs. We are now ready to examine how a competitive firm maximizes profit and how that decision determines its supply curve.

### 13-2a  A Simple Example of Profit Maximization

Let's begin our analysis of the firm's supply decision with the example in Table 2. Column (1) in the table shows the number of gallons of milk the Vaca Family Dairy Farm produces. Column (2) shows the farm's total revenue, which is $6 times the number of gallons. Column (3) shows the farm's total cost. Total cost includes fixed costs, which are $3 in this example, and variable costs, which depend on the quantity produced.

Column (4) shows the farm's profit, which is computed by subtracting total cost from total revenue. If the farm produces nothing, it has a loss of $3 (its fixed cost). If it produces 1 gallon, it has a profit of $1. If it produces 2 gallons, it has a profit of $4 and so on. Because the Vaca family's goal is to maximize profit, it chooses to produce the quantity of milk that makes profit as large as possible. In this example, profit is maximized when the farm produces either 4 or 5 gallons of milk, for a profit of $7.

There is another way to look at Vaca Farm's decision: The Vacas can find the profit-maximizing quantity by comparing the marginal revenue and marginal cost from each unit produced. Columns (5) and (6) in Table 2 compute marginal revenue and marginal cost from the changes in total revenue and total cost, and column (7) shows the change in profit for each additional gallon produced. The first gallon of milk the farm produces has a marginal revenue of $6 and a marginal cost of $2; hence, producing that gallon increases profit by $4 (from −$3 to $1). The second gallon produced has a marginal revenue of $6 and a marginal cost of $3, so that gallon increases profit by $3 (from $1 to $4). As long as marginal

| (1) | (2) | (3) | (4) | (5) | (6) | (7) |
|---|---|---|---|---|---|---|
| Quantity (Q) | Total Revenue (TR) | Total Cost (TC) | Profit (TR − TC) | Marginal Revenue (MR = ΔTR / ΔQ) | Marginal Cost (MC = ΔTR / ΔQ) | Change in Profit (MR − MC) |
| 0 gallons | $ 0 | $ 3 | −$3 | | | |
| | | | | $6 | $2 | $4 |
| 1 | 6 | 5 | 1 | | | |
| | | | | 6 | 3 | 3 |
| 2 | 12 | 8 | 4 | | | |
| | | | | 6 | 4 | 2 |
| 3 | 18 | 12 | 6 | | | |
| | | | | 6 | 5 | 1 |
| 4 | 24 | 17 | 7 | | | |
| | | | | 6 | 6 | 0 |
| 5 | 30 | 23 | 7 | | | |
| | | | | 6 | 7 | −1 |
| 6 | 36 | 30 | 6 | | | |
| | | | | 6 | 8 | −2 |
| 7 | 42 | 38 | 4 | | | |
| | | | | 6 | 9 | −3 |
| 8 | 48 | 47 | 1 | | | |

**TABLE 2**

Profit Maximization:
A Numerical Example

revenue exceeds marginal cost, increasing the quantity produced raises profit. Once the Vaca Farm has reached 5 gallons of milk, however, the situation changes. The sixth gallon would have a marginal revenue of $6 and a marginal cost of $7, so producing it would reduce profit by $1 (from $7 to $6). As a result, the Vacas would not produce beyond 5 gallons.

One of the *Ten Principles of Economics* in Chapter 1 is that rational people think at the margin. We now see how the Vaca Family Dairy Farm can apply this principle. If marginal revenue is greater than marginal cost—as it is at 1, 2, and 3 gallons—the Vacas should increase the production of milk because it will put more money in their pockets (marginal revenue) than it takes out (marginal cost). If marginal revenue is less than marginal cost—as it is at 6, 7, and 8 gallons—the Vacas should decrease production. If the Vacas think at the margin and make incremental adjustments to the level of production, they end up producing the profit-maximizing quantity.

## 13-2b The Marginal-Cost Curve and the Firm's Supply Decision

To extend this analysis of profit maximization, consider the cost curves in Figure 1. These cost curves have the three features that, as we discussed in the previous chapter, are thought to describe most firms: The marginal-cost curve (*MC*) is upward-sloping. The average-total-cost curve (*ATC*) is U-shaped. And the marginal-cost curve crosses the average-total-cost curve at the minimum of average total cost. The figure also shows a horizontal line at the market price (*P*). The price line is horizontal because a competitive firm is a price taker: The price

**FIGURE 1**

**Profit Maximization for a Competitive Firm**

This figure shows the marginal-cost curve (*MC*), the average-total-cost curve (*ATC*), and the average-variable-cost curve (*AVC*). It also shows the market price (*P*), which for a competitive firm equals both marginal revenue (*MR*) and average revenue (*AR*). At the quantity $Q_1$, marginal revenue $MR_1$ exceeds marginal cost $MC_1$, so raising production increases profit. At the quantity $Q_2$, marginal cost $MC_2$ is above marginal revenue $MR_2$, so reducing production increases profit. The profit-maximizing quantity $Q_{MAX}$ is found where the horizontal line representing the price intersects the marginal-cost curve.

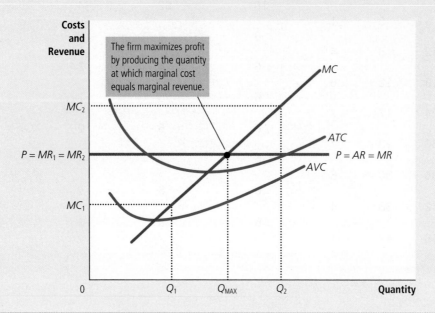

of the firm's output is the same regardless of the quantity that the firm decides to produce. Keep in mind that, for a competitive firm, the price equals both the firm's average revenue (*AR*) and its marginal revenue (*MR*).

We can use Figure 1 to find the quantity of output that maximizes profit. Imagine that the firm is producing at $Q_1$. At this level of output, the marginal-revenue curve is above the marginal-cost curve, showing that marginal revenue is greater than marginal cost. This means that if the firm were to raise production by 1 unit, the additional revenue ($MR_1$) would exceed the additional cost ($MC_1$). Profit, which equals total revenue minus total cost, would increase. Hence, if marginal revenue is greater than marginal cost, as it is at $Q_1$, the firm can increase profit by increasing production.

A similar argument applies when output is at $Q_2$. In this case, the marginal-cost curve is above the marginal-revenue curve, showing that marginal cost is greater than marginal revenue. If the firm were to reduce production by 1 unit, the costs saved ($MC_2$) would exceed the revenue lost ($MR_2$). Therefore, if marginal revenue is less than marginal cost, as it is at $Q_2$, the firm can increase profit by reducing production.

Where do these marginal adjustments to production end? Regardless of whether the firm begins with production at a low level (such as $Q_1$) or at a high level (such as $Q_2$), the firm will eventually adjust production until the quantity produced reaches $Q_{MAX}$. This analysis yields three general rules for profit maximization:

- If marginal revenue is greater than marginal cost, the firm should increase its output.
- If marginal cost is greater than marginal revenue, the firm should decrease its output.
- At the profit-maximizing level of output, marginal revenue and marginal cost are exactly equal.

These rules are the key to rational decision making by any profit-maximizing firm. They apply not only to competitive firms but, as we will see in the next chapter, to other types of firms as well.

We can now see how the competitive firm decides what quantity of its good to supply to the market. Because a competitive firm is a price taker, its marginal revenue equals the market price. For any given price, the competitive firm's profit-maximizing quantity of output is found by looking at the intersection of the price with the marginal-cost curve. In Figure 1, that quantity of output is $Q_{MAX}$.

Suppose that the price prevailing in this market rises, perhaps because of an increase in market demand. Figure 2 shows how a competitive firm responds to the price increase. When the price is $P_1$, the firm produces quantity $Q_1$, the quantity that equates marginal cost to the price. When the price rises to $P_2$, the firm finds that marginal revenue is now higher than marginal cost at the previous level of output, so the firm increases production. The new profit-maximizing quantity is $Q_2$, at which marginal cost equals the new, higher price. *In essence, because the firm's marginal-cost curve determines the quantity of the good the firm is willing to supply at any price, the marginal-cost curve is also the competitive firm's supply curve.* There are, however, some caveats to this conclusion, which we examine next.

### 13-2c The Firm's Short-Run Decision to Shut Down

So far, we have been analyzing the question of how much a competitive firm will produce. In certain circumstances, however, the firm will decide to shut down and not produce anything at all.

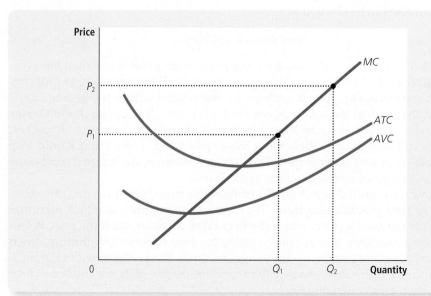

### FIGURE 2

**Marginal Cost as the Competitive Firm's Supply Curve**

An increase in the price from $P_1$ to $P_2$ leads to an increase in the firm's profit-maximizing quantity from $Q_1$ to $Q_2$. Because the marginal-cost curve shows the quantity supplied by the firm at any given price, it is the firm's supply curve.

Here we need to distinguish between a temporary shutdown of a firm and the permanent exit of a firm from the market. A *shutdown* refers to a short-run decision not to produce anything during a specific period of time because of current market conditions. *Exit* refers to a long-run decision to leave the market. The short-run and long-run decisions differ because most firms cannot avoid their fixed costs in the short run but can do so in the long run. That is, a firm that shuts down temporarily still has to pay its fixed costs, whereas a firm that exits the market does not have to pay any costs at all, fixed or variable.

For example, consider the production decision that a farmer faces. The cost of the land is one of the farmer's fixed costs. If the farmer decides not to produce any crops one season, the land lies fallow, and he cannot recover this cost. When making the short-run decision of whether to shut down for a season, the fixed cost of land is said to be a *sunk cost*. By contrast, if the farmer decides to leave farming altogether, he can sell the land. When making the long-run decision of whether to exit the market, the cost of land is not sunk. (We return to the issue of sunk costs shortly.)

Now let's consider what determines a firm's shutdown decision. If the firm shuts down, it loses all revenue from the sale of its product. At the same time, it saves the variable costs of making its product (but must still pay the fixed costs). Thus, *the firm shuts down if the revenue that it would earn from producing is less than its variable costs of production.*

A bit of mathematics can make this shutdown rule more useful. If $TR$ stands for total revenue and $VC$ stands for variable cost, then the firm's decision can be written as

$$\text{Shut down if } TR < VC.$$

The firm shuts down if total revenue is less than variable cost. By dividing both sides of this inequality by the quantity $Q$, we can write it as

$$\text{Shut down if } TR/Q < VC/Q.$$

The left side of the inequality, $TR/Q$, is total revenue $P \times Q$ divided by quantity $Q$, which is average revenue, most simply expressed as the good's price, $P$. The right side of the inequality, $VC/Q$, is average variable cost, $AVC$. Therefore, the firm's shutdown rule can be restated as

$$\text{Shut down if } P < AVC.$$

That is, a firm chooses to shut down if the price of the good is less than the average variable cost of production. This rule is intuitive: When choosing to produce, the firm compares the price it receives for the typical unit to the average variable cost that it must incur to produce the typical unit. If the price doesn't cover the average variable cost, the firm is better off stopping production altogether. The firm still loses money (because it has to pay fixed costs), but it would lose even more money by staying open. The firm can reopen in the future if conditions change so that price exceeds average variable cost.

We now have a full description of a competitive firm's profit-maximizing strategy. If the firm produces anything, it produces the quantity at which marginal cost equals the good's price, which the firm takes as given. Yet if the price is less than average variable cost at that quantity, the firm is better off shutting down temporarily and not producing anything. These results are illustrated in Figure 3. *The competitive firm's short-run supply curve is the portion of its marginal-cost curve that lies above average variable cost.*

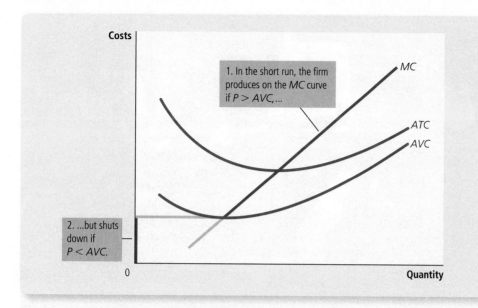

**Costs**

1. In the short run, the firm produces on the *MC* curve if *P* > *AVC*, ...

*MC*

*ATC*

*AVC*

2. ...but shuts down if *P* < *AVC*.

0

**Quantity**

**FIGURE 3**

**The Competitive Firm's Short-Run Supply Curve**
In the short run, the competitive firm's supply curve is its marginal-cost curve (*MC*) above average variable cost (*AVC*). If the price falls below average variable cost, the firm is better off shutting down temporarily.

## 13-2d Spilt Milk and Other Sunk Costs

Sometime in your life you may have been told, "Don't cry over spilt milk," or "Let bygones be bygones." These adages hold a deep truth about rational decision making. Economists say that a cost is a **sunk cost** when it has already been committed and cannot be recovered. Because nothing can be done about sunk costs, you should ignore them when making decisions about various aspects of life, including business strategy.

Our analysis of the firm's shutdown decision is one example of the irrelevance of sunk costs. We assume that the firm cannot recover its fixed costs by temporarily stopping production. That is, regardless of the quantity of output supplied (even if it is zero), the firm still has to pay its fixed costs. As a result, the fixed costs are sunk in the short run, and the firm should ignore them when deciding how much to produce. The firm's short-run supply curve is the part of the marginal-cost curve that lies above average variable cost, and the size of the fixed cost does not matter for this supply decision.

The irrelevance of sunk costs is also important when making personal decisions. Imagine, for instance, that you place a $15 value on seeing a newly released movie. You buy a ticket for $10, but before entering the theater, you lose the ticket. Should you buy another ticket? Or should you now go home and refuse to pay a total of $20 to see the movie? The answer is that you should buy another ticket. The benefit of seeing the movie ($15) still exceeds the opportunity cost (the $10 for the second ticket). The $10 you paid for the lost ticket is a sunk cost. As with spilt milk, there is no point in crying about it.

**sunk cost**
a cost that has already been committed and cannot be recovered

### CASE STUDY

**NEAR-EMPTY RESTAURANTS AND OFF-SEASON MINIATURE GOLF**
Have you ever walked into a restaurant for lunch and found it almost empty? Why, you might have asked, does the restaurant even bother to stay open? It might seem that the revenue from so few customers could not possibly cover the cost of running the restaurant.

In making the decision of whether to open for lunch, a restaurant owner must keep in mind the distinction between fixed and variable costs. Many of

*Staying open can be profitable, even with many tables empty.*

a restaurant's costs—the rent, kitchen equipment, tables, plates, silverware, and so on—are fixed. Shutting down during lunch would not reduce these costs. In other words, these costs are sunk in the short run. When the owner is deciding whether to serve lunch, only the variable costs—the price of the additional food and the wages of the extra staff—are relevant. The owner shuts down the restaurant at lunchtime only if the revenue from the few lunchtime customers would fail to cover the restaurant's variable costs.

An operator of a miniature-golf course in a summer resort community faces a similar decision. Because revenue varies substantially from season to season, the firm must decide when to open and when to close. Once again, the fixed costs—the costs of buying the land and building the course—are irrelevant in making this short-run decision. The miniature-golf course should be open for business only during those times of year when its revenue exceeds its variable costs. ●

### 13-2e  The Firm's Long-Run Decision to Exit or Enter a Market

A firm's long-run decision to exit a market is similar to its shutdown decision. If the firm exits, it will again lose all revenue from the sale of its product, but now it will save not only its variable costs of production but also its fixed costs. Thus, *the firm exits the market if the revenue it would get from producing is less than its total cost.*

We can again make this rule more useful by writing it mathematically. If $TR$ stands for total revenue and $TC$ stands for total cost, then the firm's exit rule can be written as

$$\text{Exit if } TR < TC.$$

The firm exits if total revenue is less than total cost. By dividing both sides of this inequality by quantity $Q$, we can write it as

$$\text{Exit if } TR/Q < TC/Q.$$

We can simplify this further by noting that $TR/Q$ is average revenue, which equals the price $P$, and that $TC/Q$ is average total cost, $ATC$. Therefore, the firm's exit rule is

$$\text{Exit if } P < ATC.$$

That is, a firm chooses to exit if the price of its good is less than the average total cost of production.

A parallel analysis applies to an entrepreneur who is considering starting a firm. He will enter the market if starting the firm would be profitable, which occurs if the price of the good exceeds the average total cost of production. The entry rule is

$$\text{Enter if } P > ATC.$$

The rule for entry is exactly the opposite of the rule for exit.

We can now describe a competitive firm's long-run profit-maximizing strategy. If the firm produces anything, it chooses the quantity at which marginal cost equals the price of the good. Yet if the price is less than the average total cost at that quantity, the firm chooses to exit (or not enter) the market. These results are illustrated in Figure 4. *The competitive firm's long-run supply curve is the portion of its marginal-cost curve that lies above average total cost.*

### 13-2f Measuring Profit in Our Graph for the Competitive Firm

As we study exit and entry, it is useful to analyze the firm's profit in more detail. Recall that profit equals total revenue ($TR$) minus total cost ($TC$):

$$\text{Profit} = TR - TC.$$

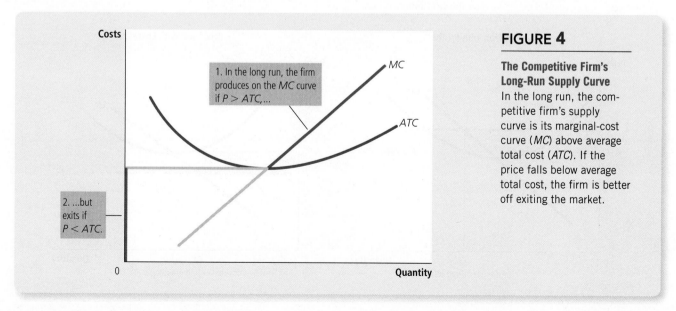

**FIGURE 4**

**The Competitive Firm's Long-Run Supply Curve** In the long run, the competitive firm's supply curve is its marginal-cost curve (*MC*) above average total cost (*ATC*). If the price falls below average total cost, the firm is better off exiting the market.

We can rewrite this definition by multiplying and dividing the right side by $Q$:

$$\text{Profit} = (TR/Q - TC/Q) \times Q.$$

Note that $TR/Q$ is average revenue, which is the price, $P$, and $TC/Q$ is average total cost, $ATC$. Therefore,

$$\text{Profit} = (P - ATC) \times Q.$$

This way of expressing the firm's profit allows us to measure profit in our graphs.

Panel (a) of Figure 5 shows a firm earning positive profit. As we have already discussed, the firm maximizes profit by producing the quantity at which price equals marginal cost. Now look at the shaded rectangle. The height of the rectangle is $P - ATC$, the difference between price and average total cost. The width of the rectangle is $Q$, the quantity produced. Therefore, the area of the rectangle is $(P - ATC) \times Q$, which is the firm's profit.

Similarly, panel (b) of this figure shows a firm with losses (negative profit). In this case, maximizing profit means minimizing losses, a task accomplished once again by producing the quantity at which price equals marginal cost. Now consider the shaded rectangle. The height of the rectangle is $ATC - P$, and the width is $Q$. The area is $(ATC - P) \times Q$, which is the firm's loss. Because a firm in this situation is not making enough revenue on each unit to cover its average total cost, it would choose to exit the market in the long run.

**Quick Quiz**  *How does a competitive firm determine its profit-maximizing level of output? Explain.* • *When does a profit-maximizing competitive firm decide to shut down? When does it decide to exit a market?*

---

### FIGURE 5

**Profit as the Area between Price and Average Total Cost**

The area of the shaded box between price and average total cost represents the firm's profit. The height of this box is price minus average total cost ($P - ATC$), and the width of the box is the quantity of output ($Q$). In panel (a), price is above average total cost, so the firm has positive profit. In panel (b), price is less than average total cost, so the firm incurs a loss.

**(a) A Firm with Profits**

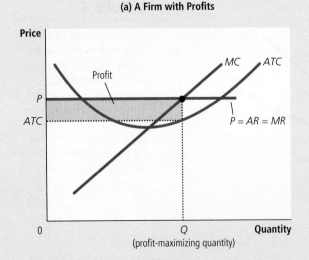

**(b) A Firm with Losses**

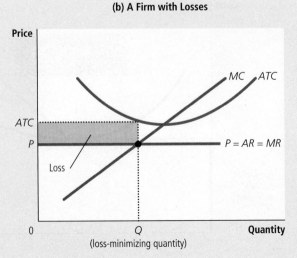

# 13-3 The Supply Curve in a Competitive Market

Now that we have examined the supply decision of a single firm, we can discuss the supply curve for a market. There are two cases to consider. First, we examine a market with a fixed number of firms. Second, we examine a market in which the number of firms can change as old firms exit the market and new firms enter. Both cases are important, for each applies to a specific time horizon. Over short periods of time, it is often difficult for firms to enter and exit, so the assumption of a fixed number of firms is appropriate. But over long periods of time, the number of firms can adjust to changing market conditions.

## 13-3a The Short Run: Market Supply with a Fixed Number of Firms

Consider a market with 1,000 identical firms. For any given price, each firm supplies a quantity of output so that its marginal cost equals the price, as shown in panel (a) of Figure 6. That is, as long as price is above average variable cost, each firm's marginal-cost curve is its supply curve. The quantity of output supplied to the market equals the sum of the quantities supplied by each of the 1,000 individual firms. Thus, to derive the market supply curve, we add the quantity supplied by each firm in the market. As panel (b) of Figure 6 shows, because the firms are identical, the quantity supplied to the market is 1,000 times the quantity supplied by each firm.

## 13-3b The Long Run: Market Supply with Entry and Exit

Now consider what happens if firms are able to enter and exit the market. Let's suppose that everyone has access to the same technology for producing the good

---

In the short run, the number of firms in the market is fixed. As a result, the market supply curve, shown in panel (b), reflects the individual firms' marginal-cost curves, shown in panel (a). Here, in a market of 1,000 firms, the quantity of output supplied to the market is 1,000 times the quantity supplied by each firm.

**FIGURE 6**

**Short-Run Market Supply**

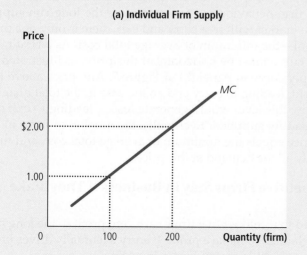

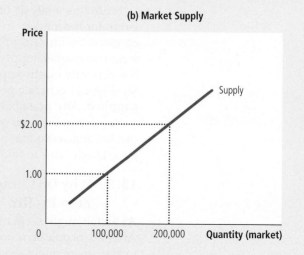

and access to the same markets to buy the inputs for production. Therefore, all current and potential firms have the same cost curves.

Decisions about entry and exit in a market of this type depend on the incentives facing the owners of existing firms and the entrepreneurs who could start new firms. If firms already in the market are profitable, then new firms will have an incentive to enter the market. This entry will expand the number of firms, increase the quantity of the good supplied, and drive down prices and profits. Conversely, if firms in the market are making losses, then some existing firms will exit the market. Their exit will reduce the number of firms, decrease the quantity of the good supplied, and drive up prices and profits. *At the end of this process of entry and exit, firms that remain in the market must be making zero economic profit.*

Recall that we can write a firm's profit as

$$\text{Profit} = (P - ATC) \times Q.$$

This equation shows that an operating firm has zero profit if and only if the price of the good equals the average total cost of producing that good. If price is above average total cost, profit is positive, which encourages new firms to enter. If price is less than average total cost, profit is negative, which encourages some firms to exit. *The process of entry and exit ends only when price and average total cost are driven to equality.*

This analysis has a surprising implication. We noted earlier in the chapter that competitive firms maximize profits by choosing a quantity at which price equals marginal cost. We just noted that free entry and exit force price to equal average total cost. But if price is to equal both marginal cost and average total cost, these two measures of cost must equal each other. Marginal cost and average total cost are equal, however, only when the firm is operating at the minimum of average total cost. Recall from the preceding chapter that the level of production with lowest average total cost is called the firm's *efficient scale*. Therefore, *in the long-run equilibrium of a competitive market with free entry and exit, firms must be operating at their efficient scale.*

Panel (a) of Figure 7 shows a firm in such a long-run equilibrium. In this figure, price *P* equals marginal cost *MC*, so the firm is maximizing profit. Price also equals average total cost *ATC*, so profit is zero. New firms have no incentive to enter the market, and existing firms have no incentive to leave the market.

From this analysis of firm behavior, we can determine the long-run supply curve for the market. In a market with free entry and exit, there is only one price consistent with zero profit—the minimum of average total cost. As a result, the long-run market supply curve must be horizontal at this price, as illustrated by the perfectly elastic supply curve in panel (b) of Figure 7. Any price above this level would generate profit, leading to entry and an increase in the total quantity supplied. Any price below this level would generate losses, leading to exit and a decrease in the total quantity supplied. Eventually, the number of firms in the market adjusts so that price equals the minimum of average total cost, and there are enough firms to satisfy all the demand at this price.

### 13-3c Why Do Competitive Firms Stay in Business If They Make Zero Profit?

At first, it might seem odd that competitive firms earn zero profit in the long run. After all, people start businesses to make a profit. If entry eventually drives profit to zero, there might seem to be little reason to stay in business.

## FIGURE 7

**Long-Run Market Supply**

In the long run, firms will enter or exit the market until profit is driven to zero. As a result, price equals the minimum of average total cost, as shown in panel (a). The number of firms adjusts to ensure that all demand is satisfied at this price. The long-run market supply curve is horizontal at this price, as shown in panel (b).

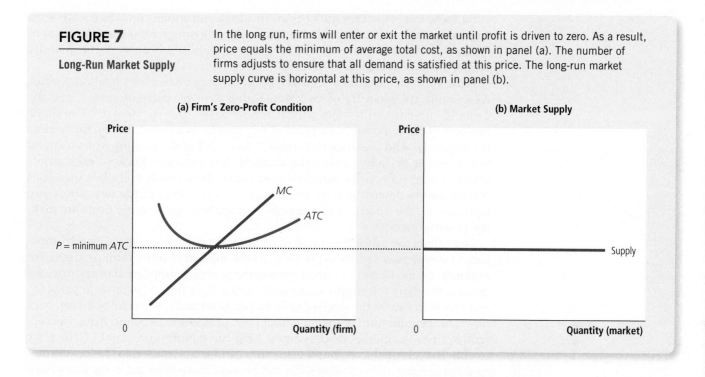

To understand the zero-profit condition more fully, recall that profit equals total revenue minus total cost and that total cost includes all the opportunity costs of the firm. In particular, total cost includes the time and money that the firm owners devote to the business. In the zero-profit equilibrium, the firm's revenue must compensate the owners for these opportunity costs.

Consider an example. Suppose that, to start his farm, a farmer had to invest $1 million, which otherwise he could have deposited in a bank and earned $50,000 a year in interest. In addition, he had to give up another job that would have paid him $30,000 a year. Then the farmer's opportunity cost of farming includes both the interest he could have earned and the forgone wages—a total of $80,000. Even if his profit is driven to zero, his revenue from farming compensates him for these opportunity costs.

Keep in mind that accountants and economists measure costs differently. As we discussed in the previous chapter, accountants keep track of explicit costs but not implicit costs. That is, they measure costs that require an outflow of money from the firm, but they do not include the opportunity costs of production that do not involve an outflow of money. As a result, in the zero-profit equilibrium, economic profit is zero, but accounting profit is positive. Our farmer's accountant, for instance, would conclude that the farmer earned an accounting profit of $80,000, which is enough to keep the farmer in business.

*"We're a nonprofit organization—we don't intend to be, but we are!"*

### 13-3d A Shift in Demand in the Short Run and Long Run

Now that we have a more complete understanding of how firms make supply decisions, we can better explain how markets respond to changes in demand. Because firms can enter and exit in the long run but not in the short run, the response of a market to a change in demand depends on the time horizon. To see this, let's trace the effects of a shift in demand over time.

Suppose the market for milk begins in a long-run equilibrium. Firms are earning zero profit, so price equals the minimum of average total cost. Panel (a) of Figure 8 shows this situation. The long-run equilibrium is point A, the quantity sold in the market is $Q_1$, and the price is $P_1$.

Now suppose scientists discover that milk has miraculous health benefits. As a result, the quantity of milk demanded at every price increases, and the demand curve for milk shifts outward from $D_1$ to $D_2$, as in panel (b). The short-run equilibrium moves from point A to point B; as a result, the quantity rises from $Q_1$ to $Q_2$, and the price rises from $P_1$ to $P_2$. All of the existing firms respond to the higher price by raising the amount they produce. Because each firm's supply curve reflects its marginal-cost curve, how much each firm increases production is determined by the marginal-cost curve. In the new short-run equilibrium, the price of milk exceeds average total cost, so the firms are making positive profit.

Over time, the profit generated in this market encourages new firms to enter. Some farmers may switch to producing milk instead of other farm products, for example. As the number of firms grows, the quantity supplied at every price increases, the short-run supply curve shifts to the right from $S_1$ to $S_2$, as in panel (c), and this shift causes the price of milk to fall. Eventually, the price is driven back down to the minimum of average total cost, profits are zero, and firms stop entering. Thus, the market reaches a new long-run equilibrium, point C. The price of milk has returned to $P_1$, but the quantity produced has risen to $Q_3$. Each firm is again producing at its efficient scale, but because more firms are in the dairy business, the quantity of milk produced and sold is higher.

### 13-3e  Why the Long-Run Supply Curve Might Slope Upward

So far, we have seen that entry and exit can cause the long-run market supply curve to be perfectly elastic. The essence of our analysis is that there are a large number of potential entrants, each of which faces the same costs. As a result, the long-run market supply curve is horizontal at the minimum of average total cost. When the demand for the good increases, the long-run result is an increase in the number of firms and in the total quantity supplied, without any change in the price.

There are, however, two reasons that the long-run market supply curve might slope upward. The first is that some resources used in production may be available only in limited quantities. For example, consider the market for farm products. Anyone can choose to buy land and start a farm, but the quantity of land is limited. As more people become farmers, the price of farmland is bid up, which raises the costs of all farmers in the market. Thus, an increase in demand for farm products cannot induce an increase in quantity supplied without also inducing a rise in farmers' costs, which in turn means a rise in price. The result is a long-run market supply curve that is upward-sloping, even with free entry into farming.

A second reason for an upward-sloping supply curve is that firms may have different costs. For example, consider the market for painters. Anyone can enter the market for painting services, but not everyone has the same costs. Costs vary in part because some people work faster than others and in part because some people have better alternative uses of their time than others. For any given price, those with lower costs are more likely to enter than those with higher costs. To increase the quantity of painting services supplied, additional entrants must be encouraged to enter the market. Because these new entrants have higher costs,

# FIGURE 8

**An Increase in Demand in the Short Run and Long Run**

The market starts in a long-run equilibrium, shown as point A in panel (a). In this equilibrium, each firm makes zero profit, and the price equals the minimum average total cost. Panel (b) shows what happens in the short run when demand rises from $D_1$ to $D_2$. The equilibrium goes from point A to point B, price rises from $P_1$ to $P_2$, and the quantity sold in the market rises from $Q_1$ to $Q_2$. Because price now exceeds average total cost, each firm now makes a profit, which over time encourages new firms to enter the market. This entry shifts the short-run supply curve to the right from $S_1$ to $S_2$, as shown in panel (c). In the new long-run equilibrium, point C, price has returned to $P_1$ but the quantity sold has increased to $Q_3$. Profits are again zero, and price is back to the minimum of average total cost, but the market has more firms to satisfy the greater demand.

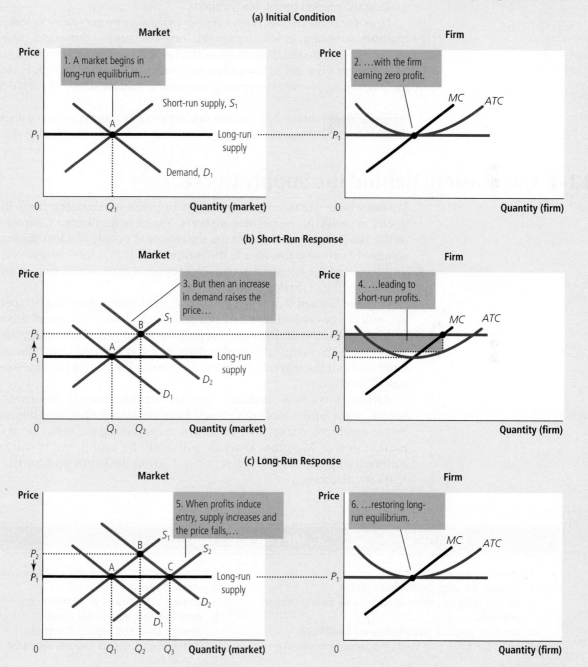

the price must rise to make entry profitable for them. Thus, the long-run market supply curve for painting services slopes upward even with free entry into the market.

Notice that if firms have different costs, some firms earn profit even in the long run. In this case, the price in the market reflects the average total cost of the *marginal firm*—the firm that would exit the market if the price were any lower. This firm earns zero profit, but firms with lower costs earn positive profit. Entry does not eliminate this profit because would-be entrants have higher costs than firms already in the market. Higher-cost firms will enter only if the price rises, making the market profitable for them.

Thus, for these two reasons, a higher price may be necessary to induce a larger quantity supplied, in which case the long-run supply curve is upward-sloping rather than horizontal. Nonetheless, the basic lesson about entry and exit remains true. *Because firms can enter and exit more easily in the long run than in the short run, the long-run supply curve is typically more elastic than the short-run supply curve.*

Quick**Quiz** *In the long run with free entry and exit, is the price in a market equal to marginal cost, average total cost, both, or neither? Explain with a diagram.*

# 13-4 Conclusion: Behind the Supply Curve

We have been discussing the behavior of profit-maximizing firms that supply goods in perfectly competitive markets. You may recall from Chapter 1 that one of the *Ten Principles of Economics* is that rational people think at the margin. This chapter has applied this idea to the competitive firm. Marginal analysis has given us a theory of the supply curve in a competitive market and, as a result, a deeper understanding of market outcomes.

We have learned that when you buy a good from a firm in a competitive market, you can be assured that the price you pay is close to the cost of producing that good. In particular, if firms are competitive and profit-maximizing, the price of a good equals the marginal cost of making that good. In addition, if firms can freely enter and exit the market, the price also equals the lowest possible average total cost of production.

Although we have assumed throughout this chapter that firms are price takers, many of the tools developed here are also useful for studying firms in less competitive markets. We now turn to examining the behavior of firms with market power. Marginal analysis will again be useful, but it will have quite different implications for a firm's production decisions and for the nature of market outcomes.

---

## CHAPTER Quick**Quiz**

1. A perfectly competitive firm
   a. chooses its price to maximize profits.
   b. sets its price to undercut other firms selling similar products.
   c. takes its price as given by market conditions.
   d. picks the price that yields the largest market share.

2. A competitive firm maximizes profit by choosing the quantity at which
   a. average total cost is at its minimum.
   b. marginal cost equals the price.
   c. average total cost equals the price.
   d. marginal cost equals average total cost.

3. A competitive firm's short-run supply curve is its _____ cost curve above its _____ cost curve.
   a. average total, marginal
   b. average variable, marginal
   c. marginal, average total
   d. marginal, average variable

4. If a profit-maximizing, competitive firm is producing a quantity at which marginal cost is between average variable cost and average total cost, it will
   a. keep producing in the short run but exit the market in the long run.
   b. shut down in the short run but return to production in the long run.
   c. shut down in the short run and exit the market in the long run.
   d. keep producing both in the short run and in the long run.

5. In the long-run equilibrium of a competitive market with identical firms, what are the relationships among price $P$, marginal cost $MC$, and average total cost $ATC$?
   a. $P > MC$ and $P > ATC$.
   b. $P > MC$ and $P = ATC$.
   c. $P = MC$ and $P > ATC$.
   d. $P = MC$ and $P = ATC$.

6. Pretzel stands in New York City are a perfectly competitive industry in long-run equilibrium. One day, the city starts imposing a $100 per month tax on each stand. How does this policy affect the number of pretzels consumed in the short run and the long run?
   a. down in the short run, no change in the long run
   b. up in the short run, no change in the long run
   c. no change in the short run, down in the long run
   d. no change in the short run, up in the long run

## SUMMARY

- Because a competitive firm is a price taker, its revenue is proportional to the amount of output it produces. The price of the good equals both the firm's average revenue and its marginal revenue.
- To maximize profit, a firm chooses a quantity of output such that marginal revenue equals marginal cost. Because marginal revenue for a competitive firm equals the market price, the firm chooses quantity so that price equals marginal cost. Thus, the firm's marginal-cost curve is its supply curve.
- In the short run when a firm cannot recover its fixed costs, the firm will choose to shut down temporarily if the price of the good is less than average variable cost. In the long run when the firm can recover both fixed

and variable costs, it will choose to exit if the price is less than average total cost.
- In a market with free entry and exit, profit is driven to zero in the long run. In this long-run equilibrium, all firms produce at the efficient scale, price equals the minimum of average total cost, and the number of firms adjusts to satisfy the quantity demanded at this price.
- Changes in demand have different effects over different time horizons. In the short run, an increase in demand raises prices and leads to profits, and a decrease in demand lowers prices and leads to losses. But if firms can freely enter and exit the market, then in the long run, the number of firms adjusts to drive the market back to the zero-profit equilibrium.

## KEY CONCEPTS

competitive market, p. 250
average revenue, p. 252

marginal revenue, p. 252

sunk cost, p. 257

## QUESTIONS FOR REVIEW

1. What are the main characteristics of a competitive market?

2. Explain the difference between a firm's revenue and its profit. Which do firms maximize?

3. Draw the cost curves for a typical firm. Explain how a competitive firm chooses the level of output that

maximizes profit. At that level of output, show on your graph the firm's total revenue and total cost.

4. Under what conditions will a firm shut down temporarily? Explain.

5. Under what conditions will a firm exit a market? Explain.

6. Does a competitive firm's price equal its marginal cost in the short run, in the long run, or both? Explain.

7. Does a competitive firm's price equal the minimum of its average total cost in the short run, in the long run, or both? Explain.

8. Are market supply curves typically more elastic in the short run or in the long run? Explain.

## PROBLEMS AND APPLICATIONS

1. Many small boats are made of fiberglass and a resin derived from crude oil. Suppose that the price of oil rises.
   a. Using diagrams, show what happens to the cost curves of an individual boat-making firm and to the market supply curve.
   b. What happens to the profits of boat makers in the short run? What happens to the number of boat makers in the long run?

2. Bob's lawn-mowing service is a profit-maximizing, competitive firm. Bob mows lawns for $27 each. His total cost each day is $280, of which $30 is a fixed cost. He mows 10 lawns a day. What can you say about Bob's short-run decision regarding shutdown and his long-run decision regarding exit?

3. Consider total cost and total revenue given in the following table:

| Quantity | 0 | 1 | 2 | 3 | 4 | 5 | 6 | 7 |
|---|---|---|---|---|---|---|---|---|
| Total cost | $8 | 9 | 10 | 11 | 13 | 19 | 27 | 37 |
| Total revenue | $0 | 8 | 16 | 24 | 32 | 40 | 48 | 56 |

   a. Calculate profit for each quantity. How much should the firm produce to maximize profit?
   b. Calculate marginal revenue and marginal cost for each quantity. Graph them. (*Hint*: Put the points between whole numbers. For example, the marginal cost between 2 and 3 should be graphed at 2½.) At what quantity do these curves cross? How does this relate to your answer to part (a)?
   c. Can you tell whether this firm is in a competitive industry? If so, can you tell whether the industry is in a long-run equilibrium?

4. Ball Bearings, Inc., faces costs of production as follows:

| Quantity | Total Fixed Cost | Total Variable Cost |
|---|---|---|
| 0 | $100 | $0 |
| 1 | 100 | 50 |
| 2 | 100 | 70 |
| 3 | 100 | 90 |
| 4 | 100 | 140 |
| 5 | 100 | 200 |
| 6 | 100 | 360 |

   a. Calculate the company's average fixed cost, average variable cost, average total cost, and marginal cost at each level of production.
   b. The price of a case of ball bearings is $50. Seeing that he can't make a profit, the chief executive officer (CEO) decides to shut down operations. What is the firm's profit/loss? Was this a wise decision? Explain.
   c. Vaguely remembering his introductory economics course, the chief financial officer tells the CEO it is better to produce 1 case of ball bearings, because marginal revenue equals marginal cost at that quantity. What is the firm's profit/loss at that level of production? Was this the best decision? Explain.

5. Suppose the book-printing industry is competitive and begins in a long-run equilibrium.
   a. Draw a diagram showing the average total cost, marginal cost, marginal revenue, and supply curve of the typical firm in the industry.
   b. Hi-Tech Printing Company invents a new process that sharply reduces the cost of printing books. What happens to Hi-Tech's profits and to the price of books in the short run when Hi-Tech's patent prevents other firms from using the new technology?
   c. What happens in the long run when the patent expires and other firms are free to use the technology?

6. A firm in a competitive market receives $500 in total revenue and has marginal revenue of $10. What is the average revenue, and how many units were sold?

7. A profit-maximizing firm in a competitive market is currently producing 100 units of output. It has average revenue of $10, average total cost of $8, and fixed cost of $200.
   a. What is its profit?
   b. What is its marginal cost?
   c. What is its average variable cost?
   d. Is the efficient scale of the firm more than, less than, or exactly 100 units?

8. The market for fertilizer is perfectly competitive. Firms in the market are producing output but are currently incurring economic losses.
   a. How does the price of fertilizer compare to the average total cost, the average variable cost, and the marginal cost of producing fertilizer?
   b. Draw two graphs, side by side, illustrating the present situation for the typical firm and for the market.
   c. Assuming there is no change in either demand or the firms' cost curves, explain what will happen in the long run to the price of fertilizer, marginal cost, average total cost, the quantity supplied by each firm, and the total quantity supplied to the market.

9. The market for apple pies in the city of Ectenia is competitive and has the following demand schedule:

   | Price | Quantity Demanded |
   | --- | --- |
   | $1 | 1,200 pies |
   | 2 | 1,100 |
   | 3 | 1,000 |
   | 4 | 900 |
   | 5 | 800 |
   | 6 | 700 |
   | 7 | 600 |
   | 8 | 500 |
   | 9 | 400 |
   | 10 | 300 |
   | 11 | 200 |
   | 12 | 100 |
   | 13 | 0 |

   Each producer in the market has fixed costs of $9 and the following marginal cost:

   | Quantity | Marginal Cost |
   | --- | --- |
   | 1 pie | $2 |
   | 2 | 4 |
   | 3 | 6 |
   | 4 | 8 |
   | 5 | 10 |
   | 6 | 12 |

   a. Compute each producer's total cost and average total cost for 1 to 6 pies.
   b. The price of a pie is now $11. How many pies are sold? How many pies does each producer make? How many producers are there? How much profit does each producer earn?

   c. Is the situation described in part (b) a long-run equilibrium? Why or why not?
   d. Suppose that in the long run there is free entry and exit. How much profit does each producer earn in the long-run equilibrium? What is the market price? How many pies does each producer make? How many pies are sold in the market? How many pie producers are operating?

10. An industry currently has 100 firms, each of which has fixed cost of $16 and average variable cost as follows:

    | Quantity | Average Variable Cost |
    | --- | --- |
    | 1 | $1 |
    | 2 | 2 |
    | 3 | 3 |
    | 4 | 4 |
    | 5 | 5 |
    | 6 | 6 |

    a. Compute a firm's marginal cost and average total cost for each quantity from 1 to 6.
    b. The equilibrium price is currently $10. How much does each firm produce? What is the total quantity supplied in the market?
    c. In the long run, firms can enter and exit the market, and all entrants have the same costs as above. As this market makes the transition to its long-run equilibrium, will the price rise or fall? Will the quantity demanded rise or fall? Will the quantity supplied by each firm rise or fall? Explain your answers.
    d. Graph the long-run supply curve for this market, with specific numbers on the axes as relevant.

11. Suppose that each firm in a competitive industry has the following costs:

    Total cost: $TC = 50 + \frac{1}{2}q^2$
    Marginal cost: $MC = q$

    where $q$ is an individual firm's quantity produced. The market demand curve for this product is

    Demand: $Q^D = 120 - P$

    where $P$ is the price and $Q$ is the total quantity of the good. Currently, there are 9 firms in the market.
    a. What is each firm's fixed cost? What is its variable cost? Give the equation for average total cost.
    b. Graph average-total-cost curve and the marginal-cost curve for $q$ from 5 to 15. At what quantity is average-total-cost curve at its

minimum? What is marginal cost and average total cost at that quantity?

c. Give the equation for each firm's supply curve.

d. Give the equation for the market supply curve for the short run in which the number of firms is fixed.

e. What is the equilibrium price and quantity for this market in the short run?

f. In this equilibrium, how much does each firm produce? Calculate each firm's profit or loss. Is there incentive for firms to enter or exit?

g. In the long run with free entry and exit, what is the equilibrium price and quantity in this market?

h. In this long-run equilibrium, how much does each firm produce? How many firms are in the market?

To find additional study resources, visit cengagebrain.com, and search for "Mankiw."

# Monopoly

I f you own a personal computer, it probably uses some version of Windows, the operating system sold by the Microsoft Corporation. When Microsoft first designed Windows many years ago, it applied for and received a copyright from the government. The copyright gives Microsoft the exclusive right to make and sell copies of the Windows operating system. If a person wants to buy a copy of Windows, she has little choice but to give Microsoft the approximately $100 that the firm has decided to charge for its product. Microsoft is said to have a *monopoly* in the market for Windows.

Microsoft's business decisions are not well described by the model of firm behavior we developed in the previous chapter. In that chapter,

we analyzed competitive markets, in which many firms offer essentially identical products, so each firm has little influence over the price it receives. By contrast, a monopoly such as Microsoft has no close competitors and, therefore, has the power to influence the market price of its product. Whereas a competitive firm is a *price taker*, a monopoly firm is a *price maker*.

In this chapter, we examine the implications of this market power. We will see that market power alters the relationship between a firm's costs and the price at which it sells its product. A competitive firm takes the price of its output as given by the market and then chooses the quantity it will supply so that price equals marginal cost. By contrast, a monopoly charges a price that exceeds marginal cost. Sure enough, we observe this practice in the case of Microsoft's Windows. The marginal cost of Windows—the extra cost that Microsoft incurs by downloading one more copy of the program onto a CD—is only a few dollars. The market price of Windows is many times its marginal cost.

It is not surprising that monopolies charge high prices for their products. Customers of monopolies might seem to have little choice but to pay whatever the monopoly charges. But if so, why does a copy of Windows not cost $1,000? Or $10,000? The reason is that if Microsoft were to set the price that high, fewer people would buy the product. People would buy fewer computers, switch to other operating systems, or make illegal copies. A monopoly firm can control the price of the good it sells, but because a high price reduces the quantity that its customers buy, the monopoly's profits are not unlimited.

As we examine the production and pricing decisions of monopolies, we also consider the implications of monopoly for society as a whole. Monopoly firms, like competitive firms, aim to maximize profit. But this goal has very different ramifications for competitive and monopoly firms. In competitive markets, self-interested consumers and producers reach an equilibrium that promotes general economic well-being, as if guided by an invisible hand. By contrast, because monopoly firms are unchecked by competition, the outcome in a market with a monopoly is often not in the best interest of society.

One of the *Ten Principles of Economics* in Chapter 1 is that governments can sometimes improve market outcomes. The analysis in this chapter sheds more light on this principle. As we examine the problems that monopolies raise for society, we discuss the various ways in which government policymakers might respond to these problems. The U.S. government, for example, keeps a close eye on Microsoft's business decisions. In 1994, it blocked Microsoft from buying Intuit, a leading seller of personal finance software, on the grounds that combining the two firms would concentrate too much market power. Similarly, in 1998, the U.S. Department of Justice objected when Microsoft started integrating its Internet browser into its Windows operating system, claiming that this addition would extend the firm's market power into new areas. In recent years, regulators in the United States and abroad have shifted their focus to firms with growing market power, such as Google and Samsung, but continue to monitor Microsoft's compliance with the antitrust laws.

# 14-1 Why Monopolies Arise

**monopoly**
a firm that is the sole seller of a product without any close substitutes

A firm is a **monopoly** if it is the sole seller of its product and if its product does not have any close substitutes. The fundamental cause of monopoly is *barriers to entry*: A monopoly remains the only seller in its market because other firms cannot enter the market and compete with it. Barriers to entry, in turn, have three main sources:

- *Monopoly resources:* A key resource required for production is owned by a single firm.
- *Government regulation:* The government gives a single firm the exclusive right to produce some good or service.
- *The production process:* A single firm can produce output at a lower cost than can a larger number of firms.

Let's briefly discuss each of these.

*"Rather than a monopoly, we like to consider ourselves 'the only game in town.'"*

## 14-1a  Monopoly Resources

The simplest way for a monopoly to arise is for a single firm to own a key resource. For example, consider the market for water in a small town. If dozens of town residents have working wells, the model of competitive markets discussed in the preceding chapter describes the behavior of sellers. Competition among suppliers drives the price of a gallon of water to equal the marginal cost of pumping an extra gallon. But if there is only one well in town and it is impossible to get water from anywhere else, then the owner of the well has a monopoly on water. Not surprisingly, the monopolist has much greater market power than any single firm in a competitive market. In the case of a necessity like water, the monopolist can command quite a high price, even if the marginal cost of pumping an extra gallon is low.

A classic example of market power arising from the ownership of a key resource is DeBeers, the South African diamond company. Founded in 1888 by Cecil Rhodes, an English businessman (and benefactor of the Rhodes scholarship), DeBeers has at times controlled up to 80 percent of the production from the world's diamond mines. Because its market share is less than 100 percent, DeBeers is not exactly a monopoly, but the company has nonetheless exerted substantial influence over the market price of diamonds.

Although exclusive ownership of a key resource is a potential cause of monopoly, in practice monopolies rarely arise for this reason. Economies are large, and resources are owned by many people. The natural scope of many markets is worldwide, because goods are often traded internationally. There are, therefore, few examples of firms that own a resource for which there are no close substitutes.

## 14-1b  Government-Created Monopolies

In many cases, monopolies arise because the government has given one person or firm the exclusive right to sell some good or service. Sometimes the monopoly arises from the sheer political clout of the would-be monopolist. Kings, for example, once granted exclusive business licenses to their friends and allies. At other times, the government grants a monopoly because doing so is viewed to be in the public interest.

The patent and copyright laws are two important examples. When a pharmaceutical company discovers a new drug, it can apply to the government for a patent. If the government deems the drug to be truly original, it approves the patent, which gives the company the exclusive right to manufacture and sell the drug for 20 years. Similarly, when a novelist finishes a book, she can copyright it. The copyright is a government guarantee that no one can print and sell the work without the author's permission. The copyright makes the novelist a monopolist in the sale of her novel.

The effects of patent and copyright laws are easy to see. Because these laws give one producer a monopoly, they lead to higher prices than would occur under competition. But by allowing these monopoly producers to charge higher prices and earn higher profits, the laws also encourage some desirable behavior. Drug companies are allowed to be monopolists in the drugs they discover to encourage research. Authors are allowed to be monopolists in the sale of their books to encourage them to write more and better books.

Thus, the laws governing patents and copyrights have both benefits and costs. The benefits of the patent and copyright laws are the increased incentives for creative activity. These benefits are offset, to some extent, by the costs of monopoly pricing, which we examine later in this chapter.

### 14-1c  Natural Monopolies

**natural monopoly**
a type of monopoly that arises because a single firm can supply a good or service to an entire market at a lower cost than could two or more firms

An industry is a **natural monopoly** when a single firm can supply a good or service to an entire market at a lower cost than could two or more firms. A natural monopoly arises when there are economies of scale over the relevant range of output. Figure 1 shows the average total costs of a firm with economies of scale. In this case, a single firm can produce any amount of output at the lowest cost. That is, for any given amount of output, a larger number of firms leads to less output per firm and higher average total cost.

An example of a natural monopoly is the distribution of water. To provide water to residents of a town, a firm must build a network of pipes throughout the town. If two or more firms were to compete in the provision of this service, each firm would have to pay the fixed cost of building a network. Thus, the average total cost of water is lowest if a single firm serves the entire market.

We saw other examples of natural monopolies when we discussed public goods and common resources in Chapter 11. We noted that *club goods* are excludable but not rival in consumption. An example is a bridge used so infrequently that it is never congested. The bridge is excludable because a toll collector can prevent someone from using it. The bridge is not rival in consumption because use of the bridge by one person does not diminish the ability of others to use it. Because there is a large fixed cost of building the bridge and a negligible marginal cost of additional users, the average total cost of a trip across the bridge (the total cost divided by the number of trips) falls as the number of trips rises. Hence, the bridge is a natural monopoly.

## FIGURE 1

**Economies of Scale as a Cause of Monopoly**
When a firm's average-total-cost curve continually declines, the firm has what is called a natural monopoly. In this case, when production is divided among more firms, each firm produces less, and average total cost rises. As a result, a single firm can produce any given amount at the lowest cost.

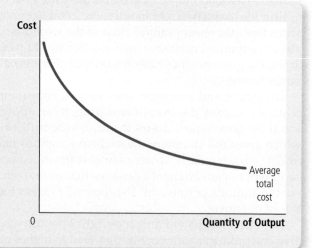

When a firm is a natural monopoly, it is less concerned about new entrants eroding its monopoly power. Normally, a firm has trouble maintaining a monopoly position without ownership of a key resource or protection from the government. The monopolist's profit attracts entrants into the market, and these entrants make the market more competitive. By contrast, entering a market in which another firm has a natural monopoly is unattractive. Would-be entrants know that they cannot achieve the same low costs that the monopolist enjoys because, after entry, each firm would have a smaller piece of the market.

In some cases, the size of the market is one determinant of whether an industry is a natural monopoly. Again, consider a bridge across a river. When the population is small, the bridge may be a natural monopoly. A single bridge can satisfy the entire demand for trips across the river at the lowest cost. Yet as the population grows and the bridge becomes congested, satisfying the entire demand may require two or more bridges across the same river. Thus, as a market expands, a natural monopoly can evolve into a more competitive market.

 *What are the three reasons that a market might have a monopoly? • Give two examples of monopolies and explain the reason for each.*

# 14-2 How Monopolies Make Production and Pricing Decisions

Now that we know how monopolies arise, we can consider how a monopoly firm decides how much of its product to make and what price to charge for it. The analysis of monopoly behavior in this section is the starting point for evaluating whether monopolies are desirable and what policies the government might pursue in monopoly markets.

### 14-2a Monopoly versus Competition

The key difference between a competitive firm and a monopoly is the monopoly's ability to influence the price of its output. A competitive firm is small relative to the market in which it operates and, therefore, has no power to influence the price of its output. It takes the price as given by market conditions. By contrast, because a monopoly is the sole producer in its market, it can alter the price of its good by adjusting the quantity it supplies to the market.

One way to view this difference between a competitive firm and a monopoly is to consider the demand curve that each firm faces. When we analyzed profit maximization by competitive firms in the preceding chapter, we drew the market price as a horizontal line. Because a competitive firm can sell as much or as little as it wants at this price, the competitive firm faces a horizontal demand curve, as in panel (a) of Figure 2. In effect, because the competitive firm sells a product with many perfect substitutes (the products of all the other firms in its market), the demand curve that any one firm faces is perfectly elastic.

By contrast, because a monopoly is the sole producer in its market, its demand curve is the market demand curve. Thus, the monopolist's demand curve slopes downward, as in panel (b) of Figure 2. If the monopolist raises the price of its good, consumers buy less of it. Looked at another way, if the monopolist reduces the quantity of output it produces and sells, the price of its output increases.

The market demand curve provides a constraint on a monopoly's ability to profit from its market power. A monopolist would prefer, if it were possible, to

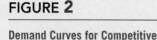

## FIGURE 2

**Demand Curves for Competitive and Monopoly Firms**

Because competitive firms are price takers, they face horizontal demand curves, as in panel (a). Because a monopoly firm is the sole producer in its market, it faces the downward-sloping market demand curve, as in panel (b). As a result, the monopoly has to accept a lower price if it wants to sell more output.

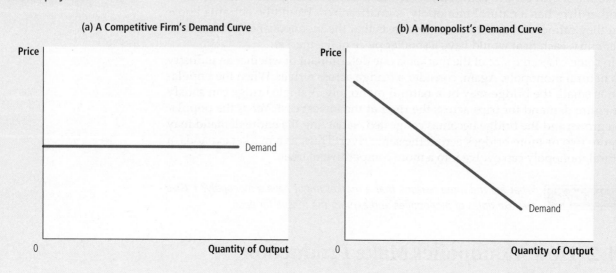

charge a high price and sell a large quantity at that high price. The market demand curve makes that outcome impossible. In particular, the market demand curve describes the combinations of price and quantity that are available to a monopoly firm. By adjusting the quantity produced (or equivalently, the price charged), the monopolist can choose any point on the demand curve, but it cannot choose a point off the demand curve.

What price and quantity of output will the monopolist choose? As with competitive firms, we assume that the monopolist's goal is to maximize profit. Because the firm's profit is total revenue minus total costs, our next task in explaining monopoly behavior is to examine a monopolist's revenue.

### 14-2b A Monopoly's Revenue

Consider a town with a single producer of water. Table 1 shows how the monopoly's revenue might depend on the amount of water produced.

Columns (1) and (2) show the monopolist's demand schedule. If the monopolist produces 1 gallon of water, it can sell that gallon for $10. If it produces 2 gallons, it must lower the price to $9 to sell both gallons. If it produces 3 gallons, it must lower the price to $8. And so on. If you graphed these two columns of numbers, you would get a typical downward-sloping demand curve.

Column (3) of the table presents the monopolist's *total revenue*. It equals the quantity sold [from column (1)] times the price [from column (2)]. Column (4) computes the firm's *average revenue*, the amount of revenue the firm receives per unit sold. We compute average revenue by taking the number for total revenue in column (3) and dividing it by the quantity of output in column (1). As we discussed in the previous chapter, average revenue always equals the price of the good. This is true for monopolists as well as for competitive firms.

TABLE 1

A Monopoly's Total, Average, and Marginal Revenue

| (1) Quantity of Water (Q) | (2) Price (P) | (3) Total Revenue (TR = P × Q) | (4) Average Revenue (AR = TR / Q) | (5) Marginal Revenue (MR = ΔTR / ΔQ) |
|---|---|---|---|---|
| 0 gallons | $11 | $ 0 | — | |
| | | | | $10 |
| 1 | 10 | 10 | $10 | |
| | | | | 8 |
| 2 | 9 | 18 | 9 | |
| | | | | 6 |
| 3 | 8 | 24 | 8 | |
| | | | | 4 |
| 4 | 7 | 28 | 7 | |
| | | | | 2 |
| 5 | 6 | 30 | 6 | |
| | | | | 0 |
| 6 | 5 | 30 | 5 | |
| | | | | −2 |
| 7 | 4 | 28 | 4 | |
| | | | | −4 |
| 8 | 3 | 24 | 3 | |

Column (5) of Table 1 computes the firm's *marginal revenue*, the amount of revenue that the firm receives for each additional unit of output. We compute marginal revenue by taking the change in total revenue when output increases by 1 unit. For example, when the firm is producing 3 gallons of water, it receives total revenue of $24. Raising production to 4 gallons increases total revenue to $28. Thus, marginal revenue from the sale of the fourth gallon is $28 minus $24, or $4.

Table 1 shows a result that is important for understanding monopoly behavior: *A monopolist's marginal revenue is less than the price of its good*. For example, if the firm raises production of water from 3 to 4 gallons, it increases total revenue by only $4, even though it sells each gallon for $7. For a monopoly, marginal revenue is lower than price because a monopoly faces a downward-sloping demand curve. To increase the amount sold, a monopoly firm must lower the price it charges to all customers. Hence, to sell the fourth gallon of water, the monopolist must earn $1 less revenue for each of the first 3 gallons. This $3 loss accounts for the difference between the price of the fourth gallon ($7) and the marginal revenue of that fourth gallon ($4).

Marginal revenue for monopolies is very different from marginal revenue for competitive firms. When a monopoly increases the amount it sells, this action has two effects on total revenue (P × Q):

- *The output effect:* More output is sold, so Q is higher, which tends to increase total revenue.
- *The price effect*: The price falls, so P is lower, which tends to decrease total revenue.

Because a competitive firm can sell all it wants at the market price, there is no price effect. When it increases production by 1 unit, it receives the market price for that unit, and it does not receive any less for the units it was already selling. That is, because the competitive firm is a price taker, its marginal revenue equals the price of its good. By contrast, when a monopoly increases production by 1 unit, it must reduce the price it charges for every unit it sells, and this cut in price reduces revenue on the units it was already selling. As a result, a monopoly's marginal revenue is less than its price.

Figure 3 graphs the demand curve and the marginal-revenue curve for a monopoly firm. (Because the firm's price equals its average revenue, the demand curve is also the average-revenue curve.) These two curves always start at the same point on the vertical axis because the marginal revenue of the first unit sold equals the price of the good. But for the reason we just discussed, the monopolist's marginal revenue on all units after the first is less than the price of the good. Thus, a monopoly's marginal-revenue curve lies below its demand curve.

You can see in Figure 3 (as well as in Table 1) that marginal revenue can even become negative. Marginal revenue is negative when the price effect on revenue is greater than the output effect. In this case, when the firm produces an extra unit of output, the price falls by enough to cause the firm's total revenue to decline, even though the firm is selling more units.

### 14-2c  Profit Maximization

Now that we have considered the revenue of a monopoly firm, we are ready to examine how such a firm maximizes profit. Recall from Chapter 1 that one of the *Ten Principles of Economics* is that rational people think at the margin. This lesson is as true for monopolists as it is for competitive firms. Here we apply the logic of marginal analysis to the monopolist's decision about how much to produce.

Figure 4 graphs the demand curve, the marginal-revenue curve, and the cost curves for a monopoly firm. All these curves should seem familiar: The demand and marginal-revenue curves are like those in Figure 3, and the cost curves are like those we encountered in the last two chapters. These curves contain all the

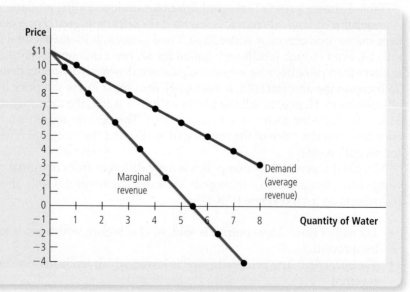

## FIGURE **3**

**Demand and Marginal-Revenue Curves for a Monopoly**
The demand curve shows how the quantity sold affects the price of the good. The marginal-revenue curve shows how the firm's revenue changes when the quantity increases by 1 unit. Because the price on *all* units sold must fall if the monopoly increases production, marginal revenue is less than the price.

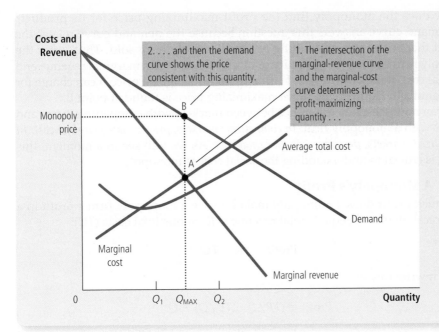

**Costs and Revenue**

2. . . . and then the demand curve shows the price consistent with this quantity.

1. The intersection of the marginal-revenue curve and the marginal-cost curve determines the profit-maximizing quantity . . .

B

Monopoly price

Average total cost

A

Demand

Marginal cost

Marginal revenue

0   $Q_1$   $Q_{MAX}$   $Q_2$   **Quantity**

**FIGURE 4**

**Profit Maximization for a Monopoly**
A monopoly maximizes profit by choosing the quantity at which marginal revenue equals marginal cost (point A). It then uses the demand curve to find the price that will induce consumers to buy that quantity (point B).

information we need to determine the level of output that a profit-maximizing monopolist will choose.

Suppose, first, that the firm is producing at a low level of output, such as $Q_1$. In this case, marginal cost is less than marginal revenue. If the firm increased production by 1 unit, the additional revenue would exceed the additional costs, and profit would rise. Thus, when marginal cost is less than marginal revenue, the firm can increase profit by producing more units.

A similar argument applies at high levels of output, such as $Q_2$. In this case, marginal cost is greater than marginal revenue. If the firm reduced production by 1 unit, the costs saved would exceed the revenue lost. Thus, if marginal cost is greater than marginal revenue, the firm can raise profit by reducing production.

In the end, the firm adjusts its level of production until the quantity reaches $Q_{MAX}$, at which marginal revenue equals marginal cost. Thus, *the monopolist's profit-maximizing quantity of output is determined by the intersection of the marginal-revenue curve and the marginal-cost curve.* In Figure 4, this intersection occurs at point A.

You might recall from the previous chapter that competitive firms also choose the quantity of output at which marginal revenue equals marginal cost. In following this rule for profit maximization, competitive firms and monopolies are alike. But there is also an important difference between these types of firms: The marginal revenue of a competitive firm equals its price, whereas the marginal revenue of a monopoly is less than its price. That is,

For a competitive firm: $P = MR = MC$.

For a monopoly firm:   $P > MR = MC$.

The equality of marginal revenue and marginal cost determines the profit-maximizing quantity for both types of firm. What differs is how the price is related to marginal revenue and marginal cost.

How does the monopoly find the profit-maximizing price for its product? The demand curve answers this question because the demand curve relates the amount that customers are willing to pay to the quantity sold. Thus, after the monopoly firm chooses the quantity of output that equates marginal revenue and marginal cost, it uses the demand curve to find the highest price it can charge for that quantity. In Figure 4, the profit-maximizing price is found at point B.

We can now see a key difference between markets with competitive firms and markets with a monopoly firm: *In competitive markets, price equals marginal cost. In monopolized markets, price exceeds marginal cost.* As we will see in a moment, this finding is crucial to understanding the social cost of monopoly.

### 14-2d A Monopoly's Profit

How much profit does a monopoly make? To see a monopoly firm's profit in a graph, recall that profit equals total revenue (*TR*) minus total costs (*TC*):

$$\text{Profit} = TR - TC.$$

We can rewrite this as

$$\text{Profit} = (TR/Q - TC/Q) \times Q.$$

$TR/Q$ is average revenue, which equals the price, $P$, and $TC/Q$ is average total cost, $ATC$. Therefore,

$$\text{Profit} = (P - ATC) \times Q.$$

This equation for profit (which also holds for competitive firms) allows us to measure the monopolist's profit in our graph.

Consider the shaded box in Figure 5. The height of the box (the segment BC) is price minus average total cost, $P - ATC$, which is the profit on the typical unit sold. The width of the box (the segment DC) is the quantity sold, $Q_{\text{MAX}}$. Therefore, the area of this box is the monopoly firm's total profit.

## Why a Monopoly Does Not Have a Supply Curve

You may have noticed that we have analyzed the price in a monopoly market using the market demand curve and the firm's cost curves. We have not made any mention of the market supply curve. By contrast, when we analyzed prices in competitive markets beginning in Chapter 4, the two most important words were always *supply* and *demand*.

What happened to the supply curve? Although monopoly firms make decisions about what quantity to supply, a monopoly does not have a supply curve. A supply curve tells us the quantity that firms choose to supply at any given price. This concept makes sense when we are analyzing competitive firms, which are price takers. But a monopoly firm is a price maker, not a price taker. It is not meaningful to ask what amount such a firm would produce at any given price because it cannot take the price as given. Instead, when the firm chooses the quantity to supply, that decision (along with the demand curve) determines the price.

Indeed, the monopolist's decision about how much to supply is impossible to separate from the demand curve it faces. The shape of the demand curve determines the shape of the marginal-revenue curve, which in turn determines the monopolist's profit-maximizing quantity. In a competitive market, each firm's supply decisions can be analyzed without knowing the demand curve, but that is not true in a monopoly market. Therefore, we never talk about a monopoly's supply curve. ■

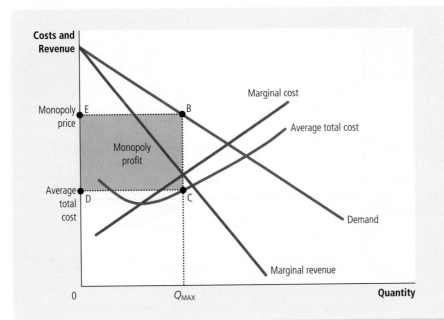

**FIGURE 5**

**The Monopolist's Profit**
The area of the box BCDE equals the profit of the monopoly firm. The height of the box (BC) is price minus average total cost, which equals profit per unit sold. The width of the box (DC) is the number of units sold.

**CASE STUDY**

**MONOPOLY DRUGS VERSUS GENERIC DRUGS**
According to our analysis, prices are determined differently in monopolized markets and competitive markets. A natural place to test this theory is the market for pharmaceutical drugs because this market takes on both market structures. When a firm discovers a new drug, patent laws give the firm a monopoly on the sale of that drug. But eventually, the firm's patent runs out, and any company can make and sell the drug. At that time, the market switches from being monopolistic to being competitive.

What should happen to the price of a drug when the patent runs out? Figure 6 shows the market for a typical drug. In this figure, the marginal cost of producing the drug is constant. (This is approximately true for many drugs.) During the life of the patent, the monopoly firm maximizes profit by producing the quantity at which marginal revenue equals marginal cost and charging a price well above marginal cost. But when the patent runs out, the profit from making the drug should encourage new firms to enter the market. As the market becomes more competitive, the price should fall to equal marginal cost.

Experience is, in fact, consistent with our theory. When the patent on a drug expires, other companies quickly enter and begin selling generic products that are chemically identical to the former monopolist's brand-name product. Just as our analysis predicts, the price of the competitively produced generic drug is well below the price that the monopolist was charging.

The expiration of a patent, however, does not cause the monopolist to lose all of its market power. Some consumers remain loyal to the brand-name drug, perhaps out of fear that the new generic drugs are not actually the same as the drug they have been using for years. As a result, the former monopolist can continue to charge a price above the price charged by its new competitors.

For example, one of the most widely used antidepressants is the drug fluoxetine, which is taken by millions of Americans. Because the patent on this drug expired in 2001, a consumer today has the choice between the original drug, sold under the

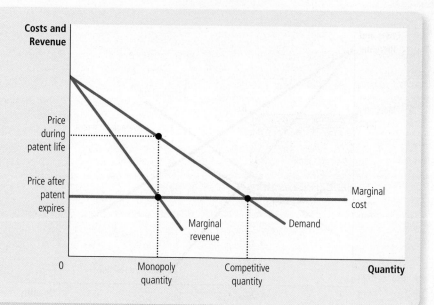

**FIGURE 6**

**The Market for Drugs**
When a patent gives a firm a monopoly over the sale of a drug, the firm charges the monopoly price, which is well above the marginal cost of making the drug. When the patent on a drug runs out, new firms enter the market, making it more competitive. As a result, the price falls from the monopoly price to marginal cost.

brand name Prozac, and a generic version of the same medicine. Prozac sells for about three times the price of generic fluoxetine. This price differential can persist because some consumers are not convinced that the two pills are perfect substitutes. ●

 *Explain how a monopolist chooses the quantity of output to produce and the price to charge.*

# 14-3 The Welfare Cost of Monopolies

Is monopoly a good way to organize a market? We have seen that a monopoly, in contrast to a competitive firm, charges a price above marginal cost. From the standpoint of consumers, this high price makes monopoly undesirable. At the same time, however, the monopoly is earning profit from charging this high price. From the standpoint of the owners of the firm, the high price makes monopoly very desirable. Is it possible that the benefits to the firm's owners exceed the costs imposed on consumers, making monopoly desirable from the standpoint of society as a whole?

We can answer this question using the tools of welfare economics. Recall from Chapter 7 that total surplus measures the economic well-being of buyers and sellers in a market. Total surplus is the sum of consumer surplus and producer surplus. Consumer surplus is consumers' willingness to pay for a good minus the amount they actually pay for it. Producer surplus is the amount producers receive for a good minus their costs of producing it. In this case, there is a single producer—the monopolist.

You can probably guess the result of this analysis. In Chapter 7, we concluded that the equilibrium of supply and demand in a competitive market is not only a natural outcome but also a desirable one. The invisible hand of the market leads to an allocation of resources that makes total surplus as large as it can be. Because a monopoly leads to an allocation of resources different from that in a competitive market, the outcome must, in some way, fail to maximize total economic well-being.

## 14-3a The Deadweight Loss

We begin by considering what the monopoly firm would do if it were run by a benevolent social planner. The social planner cares not only about the profit earned by the firm's owners but also about the benefits received by the firm's consumers. The planner tries to maximize total surplus, which equals producer surplus (profit) plus consumer surplus. Keep in mind that total surplus equals the value of the good to consumers minus the costs of making the good incurred by the monopoly producer.

Figure 7 analyzes how a benevolent social planner would choose the monopoly's level of output. The demand curve reflects the value of the good to consumers, as measured by their willingness to pay for it. The marginal-cost curve reflects the costs of the monopolist. Thus, *the socially efficient quantity is found where the demand curve and the marginal-cost curve intersect.* Below this quantity, the value of an extra unit to consumers exceeds the cost of providing it, so increasing output would raise total surplus. Above this quantity, the cost of producing an extra unit exceeds the value of that unit to consumers, so decreasing output would raise total surplus. At the optimal quantity, the value of an extra unit to consumers exactly equals the marginal cost of production.

If the social planner were running the monopoly, the firm could achieve this efficient outcome by charging the price found at the intersection of the demand and marginal-cost curves. Thus, like a competitive firm and unlike a profit-maximizing monopoly, a social planner would charge a price equal to marginal cost. Because this price would give consumers an accurate signal about the cost of producing the good, consumers would buy the efficient quantity.

We can evaluate the welfare effects of monopoly by comparing the level of output that the monopolist chooses to the level of output that a social planner would

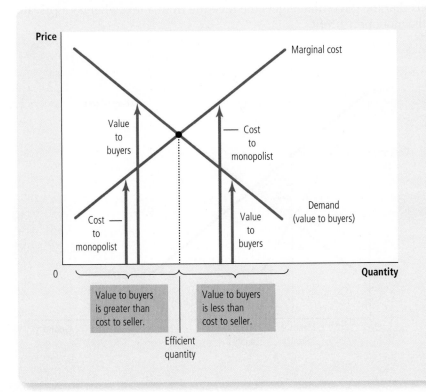

**Price**

Marginal cost

Value to buyers

Cost to monopolist

Cost to monopolist

Value to buyers

Demand (value to buyers)

0

Quantity

Value to buyers is greater than cost to seller.

Value to buyers is less than cost to seller.

Efficient quantity

### FIGURE 7

**The Efficient Level of Output**
A benevolent social planner maximizes total surplus in the market by choosing the level of output where the demand curve and marginal-cost curve intersect. Below this level, the value of the good to the marginal buyer (as reflected in the demand curve) exceeds the marginal cost of making the good. Above this level, the value to the marginal buyer is less than marginal cost.

choose. As we have seen, the monopolist chooses to produce and sell the quantity of output at which the marginal-revenue and marginal-cost curves intersect; the social planner would choose the quantity at which the demand and marginal-cost curves intersect. Figure 8 shows the comparison. *The monopolist produces less than the socially efficient quantity of output.*

We can also view the inefficiency of monopoly in terms of the monopolist's price. Because the market demand curve describes a negative relationship between the price and quantity of the good, a quantity that is inefficiently low is equivalent to a price that is inefficiently high. When a monopolist charges a price above marginal cost, some potential consumers value the good at more than its marginal cost but less than the monopolist's price. These consumers do not buy the good. Because the value these consumers place on the good is greater than the cost of providing it to them, this result is inefficient. Thus, monopoly pricing prevents some mutually beneficial trades from taking place.

The inefficiency of monopoly can be measured with a deadweight loss triangle, as illustrated in Figure 8. Because the demand curve reflects the value to consumers and the marginal-cost curve reflects the costs to the monopoly producer, the area of the deadweight loss triangle between the demand curve and the marginal-cost curve equals the total surplus lost because of monopoly pricing. It represents the reduction in economic well-being that results from the monopoly's use of its market power.

The deadweight loss caused by a monopoly is similar to the deadweight loss caused by a tax. Indeed, a monopolist is like a private tax collector. As we saw in Chapter 8, a tax on a good places a wedge between consumers' willingness to pay (as reflected by the demand curve) and producers' costs (as reflected by the supply curve). Because a monopoly exerts its market power by charging a price above marginal cost, it creates a similar wedge. In both cases, the wedge causes the quantity sold to fall short of the social optimum. The difference between the two cases is that the government gets the revenue from a tax, whereas a private firm gets the monopoly profit.

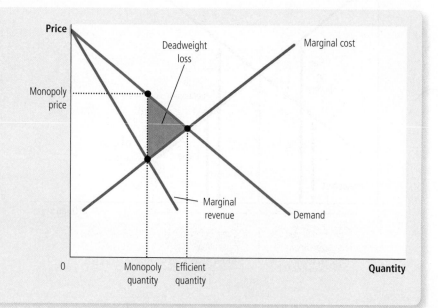

## FIGURE 8

**The Inefficiency of Monopoly**
Because a monopoly charges a price above marginal cost, not all consumers who value the good at more than its cost buy it. Thus, the quantity produced and sold by a monopoly is below the socially efficient level. The deadweight loss is represented by the area of the triangle between the demand curve (which reflects the value of the good to consumers) and the marginal-cost curve (which reflects the costs of the monopoly producer).

### 14-3b The Monopoly's Profit: A Social Cost?

It is tempting to decry monopolies for "profiteering" at the expense of the public. And indeed, a monopoly firm does earn a profit by virtue of its market power. According to the economic analysis of monopoly, however, the firm's profit is not in itself necessarily a problem for society.

Welfare in a monopolized market, as in all markets, includes the welfare of both consumers and producers. Whenever a consumer pays an extra dollar to a producer because of a monopoly price, the consumer is worse off by a dollar and the producer is better off by the same amount. This transfer from the consumers of the good to the owners of the monopoly does not affect the market's total surplus—the sum of consumer and producer surplus. In other words, the monopoly profit itself represents not a reduction in the size of the economic pie but merely a bigger slice for producers and a smaller slice for consumers. Unless consumers are for some reason more deserving than producers—a normative judgment about equity that goes beyond the realm of economic efficiency—the monopoly profit is not a social problem.

The problem in a monopolized market arises because the firm produces and sells a quantity of output below the level that maximizes total surplus. The deadweight loss measures how much the economic pie shrinks as a result. This inefficiency is connected to the monopoly's high price: Consumers buy fewer units when the firm raises its price above marginal cost. But keep in mind that the profit earned on the units that continue to be sold is not the problem. The problem stems from the inefficiently low quantity of output. Put differently, if the high monopoly price did not discourage some consumers from buying the good, it would raise producer surplus by exactly the amount it reduced consumer surplus, leaving total surplus the same as that achieved by a benevolent social planner.

There is, however, a possible exception to this conclusion. Suppose that a monopoly firm has to incur additional costs to maintain its monopoly position. For example, a firm with a government-created monopoly might need to hire lobbyists to convince lawmakers to continue its monopoly. In this case, the monopoly may use up some of its monopoly profits paying for these additional costs. If so, the social loss from monopoly includes both these costs and the deadweight loss resulting from reduced output.

 *How does a monopolist's quantity of output compare to the quantity of output that maximizes total surplus? How does this difference relate to the deadweight loss?*

# 14-4 Price Discrimination

So far, we have been assuming that the monopoly firm charges the same price to all customers. Yet in many cases, firms sell the same good to different customers for different prices, even though the costs of producing for the two customers are the same. This practice is called **price discrimination**.

Before discussing the behavior of a price-discriminating monopolist, we should note that price discrimination is not possible when a good is sold in a competitive market. In a competitive market, many firms are selling the same good at the market price. No firm is willing to charge a lower price to any customer because the firm can sell all it wants at the market price. And if any firm tried to charge a

**price discrimination**
the business practice of selling the same good at different prices to different customers

higher price to a customer, that customer would buy from another firm. For a firm to price discriminate, it must have some market power.

## 14-4a  A Parable about Pricing

To understand why a monopolist would price discriminate, let's consider an example. Imagine that you are the president of Readalot Publishing Company. Readalot's best-selling author has just written a new novel. To keep things simple, let's imagine that you pay the author a flat $2 million for the exclusive rights to publish the book. Let's also assume that the cost of printing the book is zero (as it would be, for example, for an e-book). Readalot's profit, therefore, is the revenue from selling the book minus the $2 million it has paid to the author. Given these assumptions, how would you, as Readalot's president, decide the book's price?

Your first step is to estimate the demand for the book. Readalot's marketing department tells you that the book will attract two types of readers. The book will appeal to the author's 100,000 die-hard fans who are willing to pay as much as $30. In addition, it will appeal to about 400,000 less enthusiastic readers who will pay up to $5.

If Readalot charges a single price to all customers, what price maximizes profit? There are two natural prices to consider: $30 is the highest price Readalot can charge and still get the 100,000 die-hard fans, and $5 is the highest price it can charge and still get the entire market of 500,000 potential readers. Solving Readalot's problem is a matter of simple arithmetic. At a price of $30, Readalot sells 100,000 copies, has revenue of $3 million, and makes profit of $1 million. At a price of $5, it sells 500,000 copies, has revenue of $2.5 million, and makes profit of $500,000. Thus, Readalot maximizes profit by charging $30 and forgoing the opportunity to sell to the 400,000 less enthusiastic readers.

Notice that Readalot's decision causes a deadweight loss. There are 400,000 readers willing to pay $5 for the book, and the marginal cost of providing it to them is zero. Thus, $2 million of total surplus is lost when Readalot charges the higher price. This deadweight loss is the inefficiency that arises whenever a monopolist charges a price above marginal cost.

Now suppose that Readalot's marketing department makes a discovery: These two groups of readers are in separate markets. The die-hard fans live in Australia, and the other readers live in the United States. Moreover, it is hard for readers in one country to buy books in the other.

In response to this discovery, Readalot can change its marketing strategy and increase profits. To the 100,000 Australian readers, it can charge $30 for the book. To the 400,000 American readers, it can charge $5 for the book. In this case, revenue is $3 million in Australia and $2 million in the United States, for a total of $5 million. Profit is then $3 million, which is substantially greater than the $1 million the company could earn charging the same $30 price to all customers. Not surprisingly, Readalot chooses to follow this strategy of price discrimination.

The story of Readalot Publishing is hypothetical, but it describes the business practice of many publishing companies. Consider the price differential between hardcover books and paperbacks. When a publisher has a new novel, it initially releases an expensive hardcover edition and later releases a cheaper paperback edition. The difference in price between these two editions far exceeds the difference in printing costs. The publisher is price discriminating by selling the hardcover to die-hard fans and the paperback to less enthusiastic readers, thereby increasing its profit.

## 14-4b The Moral of the Story

Like any parable, the story of Readalot Publishing is stylized. Yet also like any parable, it teaches some general lessons. In this case, three lessons can be learned about price discrimination.

The first and most obvious lesson is that price discrimination is a rational strategy for a profit-maximizing monopolist. That is, by charging different prices to different customers, a monopolist can increase its profit. In essence, a price-discriminating monopolist charges each customer a price closer to her willingness to pay than is possible with a single price.

The second lesson is that price discrimination requires the ability to separate customers according to their willingness to pay. In our example, customers were separated geographically. But sometimes monopolists choose other differences, such as age or income, to distinguish among customers.

A corollary to this second lesson is that certain market forces can prevent firms from price discriminating. In particular, one such force is *arbitrage*, the process of buying a good in one market at a low price and selling it in another market at a higher price to profit from the price difference. In our example, if Australian bookstores could buy the book in the United States and resell it to Australian readers, the arbitrage would prevent Readalot from price discriminating, because no Australian would buy the book at the higher price.

The third lesson from our parable is the most surprising: Price discrimination can raise economic welfare. Recall that a deadweight loss arises when Readalot charges a single $30 price because the 400,000 less enthusiastic readers do not end up with the book, even though they value it at more than its marginal cost of production. By contrast, when Readalot price discriminates, all readers get the book and the outcome is efficient. Thus, price discrimination can eliminate the inefficiency inherent in monopoly pricing.

Note that in this example the increase in welfare from price discrimination shows up as higher producer surplus rather than higher consumer surplus. Consumers are no better off for having bought the book: The price they pay exactly equals the value they place on the book, so they receive no consumer surplus. The entire increase in total surplus from price discrimination accrues to Readalot Publishing in the form of higher profit.

## 14-4c The Analytics of Price Discrimination

Let's consider a bit more formally how price discrimination affects economic welfare. We begin by assuming that the monopolist can price discriminate perfectly. *Perfect price discrimination* describes a situation in which the monopolist knows exactly each customer's willingness to pay and can charge each customer a different price. In this case, the monopolist charges each customer exactly her willingness to pay, and the monopolist gets the entire surplus in every transaction.

Figure 9 illustrates producer and consumer surplus with and without price discrimination. To keep things simple, this figure is drawn assuming constant per unit costs—that is, marginal cost and average total cost are constant and equal. Without price discrimination, the firm charges a single price above marginal cost, as shown in panel (a). Because some potential customers who value the good at more than marginal cost do not buy it at this high price, the monopoly causes a deadweight loss. Yet when a firm can perfectly price discriminate, as shown in panel (b), each customer who values the good at more than marginal cost buys the good and is charged her willingness to pay. All mutually beneficial trades take

**FIGURE 9**

**Welfare with and without
Price Discrimination**

Panel (a) shows a monopoly that charges the same price to all customers. Total surplus in this market equals the sum of profit (producer surplus) and consumer surplus. Panel (b) shows a monopoly that can perfectly price discriminate. Because consumer surplus equals zero, total surplus now equals the firm's profit. Comparing these two panels, you can see that perfect price discrimination raises profit, raises total surplus, and lowers consumer surplus.

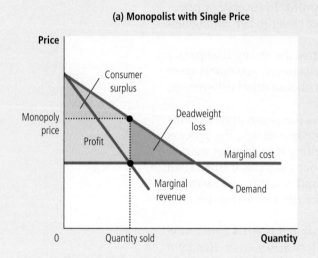

**(a) Monopolist with Single Price**

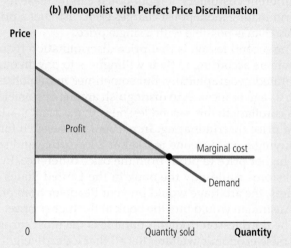

**(b) Monopolist with Perfect Price Discrimination**

place, no deadweight loss occurs, and the entire surplus derived from the market goes to the monopoly producer in the form of profit.

In reality, of course, price discrimination is not perfect. Customers do not walk into stores with signs displaying their willingness to pay. Instead, firms price discriminate by dividing customers into groups: young versus old, weekday versus weekend shoppers, Americans versus Australians, and so on. Unlike those in our parable of Readalot Publishing, customers within each group differ in their willingness to pay for the product, making perfect price discrimination impossible.

How does this imperfect price discrimination affect welfare? The analysis of these pricing schemes is complicated, and it turns out that there is no general answer to this question. Compared with the single-price monopoly outcome, imperfect price discrimination can raise, lower, or leave unchanged the total surplus in a market. The only certain conclusion is that price discrimination raises the monopoly's profit; otherwise, the firm would choose to charge all customers the same price.

### 14-4d  Examples of Price Discrimination

Firms in our economy use various business strategies aimed at charging different prices to different customers. Now that we understand the economics of price discrimination, let's consider some examples.

**Movie Tickets**   Many movie theaters charge a lower price for children and senior citizens than for other patrons. This fact is hard to explain in a competitive market. In a competitive market, price equals marginal cost, and the marginal cost of providing a seat for a child or senior citizen is the same as the marginal cost of providing a seat for anyone else. Yet the differential pricing is easily explained if movie theaters have some local monopoly power and if children and senior citizens have a lower willingness to pay for a ticket. In this case, movie theaters raise their profit by price discriminating.

**Airline Prices** Seats on airplanes are sold at many different prices. Most airlines charge a lower price for a round-trip ticket between two cities if the traveler stays over a Saturday night. At first, this seems odd. Why should it matter to the airline whether a passenger stays over a Saturday night? The reason is that this rule provides a way to separate business travelers and leisure travelers. A passenger on a business trip has a high willingness to pay and, most likely, does not want to stay over a Saturday night. By contrast, a passenger traveling for personal reasons has a lower willingness to pay and is more likely to be willing to stay over a Saturday night. Thus, the airlines can successfully price discriminate by charging a lower price for passengers who stay over a Saturday night.

*"Would it bother you to hear how little I paid for this flight?"*

**Discount Coupons** Many companies offer discount coupons to the public in newspapers, magazines, or online. A buyer simply has to clip the coupon to get $0.50 off her next purchase. Why do companies offer these coupons? Why don't they just cut the price of the product by $0.50?

The answer is that coupons allow companies to price discriminate. Companies know that not all customers are willing to spend time clipping coupons. Moreover, the willingness to clip coupons is related to the customer's willingness to pay for the good. A rich and busy executive is unlikely to spend her time clipping discount coupons out of the newspaper, and she is probably willing to pay a higher price for many goods. A person who is unemployed is more likely to clip coupons and to have a lower willingness to pay. Thus, by charging a lower price only to those customers who clip coupons, firms can successfully price discriminate.

**Financial Aid** Many colleges and universities give financial aid to needy students. One can view this policy as a type of price discrimination. Wealthy students have greater financial resources and, therefore, a higher willingness to pay than needy students. By charging high tuition and selectively offering financial aid, schools in effect charge prices to customers based on the value they place on going to that school. This behavior is similar to that of any price-discriminating monopolist.

**Quantity Discounts** So far in our examples of price discrimination, the monopolist charges different prices to different customers. Sometimes, however, monopolists price discriminate by charging different prices to the same customer for different units that the customer buys. For example, many firms offer lower prices to customers who buy large quantities. A bakery might charge $0.50 for each donut but $5 for a dozen. This is a form of price discrimination because the customer pays a higher price for the first unit she buys than for the twelfth. Quantity discounts are often a successful way of price discriminating because a customer's willingness to pay for an additional unit declines as she buys more units.

 *Give two examples of price discrimination.* • *Explain how perfect price discrimination affects consumer surplus, producer surplus, and total surplus.*

## IN THE NEWS

### Price Discrimination in Higher Education

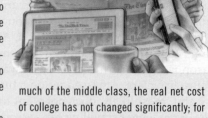

*Colleges and universities are increasingly charging different prices to different students, which makes data on the cost of education harder to interpret.*

#### Misconceptions 101: Why College Costs Aren't Soaring

**By Evan Soltas**

Conventional wisdom suggests that U.S. colleges and universities have become sharply more expensive in recent years.

"When kids do graduate, the most daunting challenge can be the cost of college," President Barack Obama said in his 2012 State of the Union address. "We can't just keep subsidizing skyrocketing tuition; we'll run out of money."

At first, the view that the cost of college is rising appears to have data on its side. Published tuition prices and fees at colleges have risen three times faster than the rate of Consumer Price Index inflation since 1978, according to the Bureau of Labor Statistics....

Real tuition and fees have increased, to be sure, but hardly as significantly as the media often report or the data suggest at face value. The inflation-adjusted net price of college has risen only modestly over the last two decades, according to data from the College Board's Annual Survey of Colleges.

What has happened is a shift toward price discrimination—offering multiple prices for the same product. Universities have offset the increase in sticker price for most families through an expansion of grant-based financial aid and scholarships. That has caused the BLS measure to rise without increasing the net cost.

Wealthier families now pay more than ever to send their children to college. But for

MICHAELJUNG/SHUTTERSTOCK

much of the middle class, the real net cost of college has not changed significantly; for much of the poor, the expansion of aid has increased the accessibility and affordability of a college education....

The nation's most selective institutions are leading the trend toward income-based price discrimination. For example, at Harvard University, the majority of students receive financial aid: In 2012, one year of undergraduate education had a sticker price of $54,496 and came with an average grant of roughly $41,000.

In other words, the cost burden of college has become significantly more progressive since the 1990s. Students from wealthier families not only now pay more for their own educations but also have come to heavily subsidize the costs of the less fortunate. ∎

**Source:** Bloomberg.com, November 27, 2012.

# 14-5 Public Policy toward Monopolies

We have seen that monopolies, in contrast to competitive markets, fail to allocate resources efficiently. Monopolies produce less than the socially desirable quantity of output and charge prices above marginal cost. Policymakers in the government can respond to the problem of monopoly in one of four ways:

- By trying to make monopolized industries more competitive
- By regulating the behavior of the monopolies
- By turning some private monopolies into public enterprises
- By doing nothing at all

## 14-5a Increasing Competition with Antitrust Laws

If Coca-Cola and PepsiCo wanted to merge, the deal would be closely examined by the federal government before it went into effect. The lawyers and economists in the Department of Justice might well decide that a merger between these two large soft-drink companies would make the U.S. soft-drink market substantially less competitive and, as a result, would reduce the economic well-being of the country as a whole. If so, the Department of Justice would challenge the merger in court, and if the judge agreed, the two companies would not be allowed to merge. It is precisely this kind of challenge that prevented software giant Microsoft from buying Intuit in 1994. Similarly, in 2011, the government blocked the phone giant AT&T from buying its competitor T-Mobile.

The government derives this power over private industry from the antitrust laws, a collection of statutes aimed at curbing monopoly power. The first and most important of these laws was the Sherman Antitrust Act, which Congress passed in 1890 to reduce the market power of the large and powerful "trusts" that were viewed as dominating the economy at the time. The Clayton Antitrust Act, passed in 1914, strengthened the government's powers and authorized private lawsuits. As the U.S. Supreme Court once put it, the antitrust laws are "a comprehensive charter of economic liberty aimed at preserving free and unfettered competition as the rule of trade."

The antitrust laws give the government various ways to promote competition. They allow the government to prevent mergers, such as the merger between AT&T and T-Mobile. At times, they allow the government to break up a large company into a group of smaller ones. Finally, the antitrust laws prevent companies from coordinating their activities in ways that make markets less competitive.

Antitrust laws have costs as well as benefits. Sometimes companies merge not to reduce competition but to lower costs through more efficient joint production. These benefits from mergers are sometimes called *synergies*. For example, many U.S. banks have merged in recent years and, by combining operations, have been able to reduce administrative staff. The airline industry has experienced a similar consolidation. If antitrust laws are to raise social welfare, the government must be able to determine which mergers are desirable and which are not. That is, it must be able to measure and compare the social benefit from synergies with the social costs of reduced competition. Critics of the antitrust laws are skeptical that the government can perform the necessary cost–benefit analysis with sufficient accuracy. In the end, the application of antitrust laws is often controversial, even among the experts.

*"But if we do merge with Amalgamated, we'll have enough resources to fight the antitrust violation caused by the merger."*

## 14-5b Regulation

Another way the government deals with the problem of monopoly is by regulating the behavior of monopolists. This solution is common in the case of natural monopolies, such as water and electric companies. These companies are not allowed to charge any price they want. Instead, government agencies regulate their prices.

What price should the government set for a natural monopoly? This question is not as easy as it might at first appear. One might conclude that the price should equal the monopolist's marginal cost. If price equals marginal cost, customers will buy the quantity of the monopolist's output that maximizes total surplus and the allocation of resources will be efficient.

There are, however, two practical problems with marginal-cost pricing as a regulatory system. The first arises from the logic of cost curves. By definition, natural monopolies have

### ASK THE EXPERTS

## Airline Mergers

"If regulators had not approved mergers in the past decade between major networked airlines, travelers would be better off today."

**What do economists say?**

26% disagree

45% uncertain

29% agree

Source: IGM Economic Experts Panel, August 28, 2013.

declining average total cost. As we first discussed in Chapter 12, when average total cost is declining, marginal cost is less than average total cost. This situation is illustrated in Figure 10, which shows a firm with a large fixed cost and then constant marginal cost thereafter. If regulators were to set price equal to marginal cost, that price would be less than the firm's average total cost and the firm would lose money. Instead of charging such a low price, the monopoly firm would just exit the industry.

Regulators can respond to this problem in various ways, none of which is perfect. One way is to subsidize the monopolist. In essence, the government picks up the losses inherent in marginal-cost pricing. Yet to pay for the subsidy, the government needs to raise money through taxation, which involves its own deadweight losses. Alternatively, the regulators can allow the monopolist to charge a price higher than marginal cost. If the regulated price equals average total cost, the monopolist earns exactly zero economic profit. Yet average-cost pricing leads to deadweight losses because the monopolist's price no longer reflects the marginal cost of producing the good. In essence, average-cost pricing is like a tax on the good the monopolist is selling.

The second problem with marginal-cost pricing as a regulatory system (and with average-cost pricing as well) is that it gives the monopolist no incentive to reduce costs. Each firm in a competitive market tries to reduce its costs because lower costs mean higher profits. But if a regulated monopolist knows that regulators will reduce prices whenever costs fall, the monopolist will not benefit from lower costs. In practice, regulators deal with this problem by allowing monopolists to keep some of the benefits from lower costs in the form of higher profit, a practice that requires some departure from marginal-cost pricing.

### 14-5c Public Ownership

The third policy used by the government to deal with monopoly is public ownership. That is, rather than regulating a natural monopoly that is run by a private firm, the government can run the monopoly itself. This solution is common in many European countries, where the government owns and operates utilities

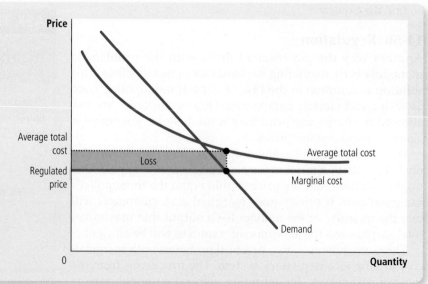

## FIGURE 10

**Marginal-Cost Pricing for a Natural Monopoly**
Because a natural monopoly has declining average total cost, marginal cost is less than average total cost. Therefore, if regulators require a natural monopoly to charge a price equal to marginal cost, price will be below average total cost, and the monopoly will lose money.

such as telephone, water, and electric companies. In the United States, the government runs the Postal Service. The delivery of ordinary first-class mail is often thought to be a natural monopoly.

Economists usually prefer private to public ownership of natural monopolies. The key issue is how the ownership of the firm affects the costs of production. Private owners have an incentive to minimize costs as long as they reap part of the benefit in the form of higher profit. If the firm's managers are doing a bad job of keeping costs down, the firm's owners will fire them. By contrast, if the government bureaucrats who run a monopoly do a bad job, the losers are the customers and taxpayers, whose only recourse is the political system. The bureaucrats may become a special-interest group and attempt to block cost-reducing reforms. Put simply, as a way of ensuring that firms are well run, the voting booth is less reliable than the profit motive.

### 14-5d Doing Nothing

Each of the foregoing policies aimed at reducing the problem of monopoly has drawbacks. As a result, some economists argue that it is often best for the government not to try to remedy the inefficiencies of monopoly pricing. Here is the assessment of economist George Stigler, who won the Nobel Prize for his work in industrial organization:

> A famous theorem in economics states that a competitive enterprise economy will produce the largest possible income from a given stock of resources. No real economy meets the exact conditions of the theorem, and all real economies will fall short of the ideal economy—a difference called "market failure." In my view, however, the degree of "market failure" for the American economy is much smaller than the "political failure" arising from the imperfections of economic policies found in real political systems.

As this quotation makes clear, determining the proper role of the government in the economy requires judgments about politics as well as economics.

 *Describe the ways policymakers can respond to the inefficiencies caused by monopolies. List a potential problem with each of these policy responses.*

## 14-6 Conclusion: The Prevalence of Monopolies

This chapter has discussed the behavior of firms that have control over the prices they charge. We have seen that these firms behave very differently from the competitive firms studied in the previous chapter. Table 2 summarizes some of the key similarities and differences between competitive and monopoly markets.

From the standpoint of public policy, a crucial result is that a monopolist produces less than the socially efficient quantity and charges a price above marginal cost. As a result, a monopoly causes deadweight losses. In some cases, these inefficiencies can be mitigated through price discrimination by the monopolist. But other times, they call for policymakers to take an active role.

How prevalent are the problems of monopoly? There are two answers to this question.

In one sense, monopolies are common. Most firms have some control over the prices they charge. They are not forced to charge the market price for their goods

**TABLE 2**

**Competition versus Monopoly: A Summary Comparison**

|  | Competition | Monopoly |
|---|---|---|
| **Similarities** | | |
| Goal of firms | Maximize profits | Maximize profits |
| Rule for maximizing | $MR = MC$ | $MR = MC$ |
| Can earn economic profits in the short run? | Yes | Yes |
| **Differences** | | |
| Number of firms | Many | One |
| Marginal revenue | $MR = P$ | $MR < P$ |
| Price | $P = MC$ | $P > MC$ |
| Produces welfare-maximizing level of output? | Yes | No |
| Entry in the long run? | Yes | No |
| Can earn economic profits in the long run? | No | Yes |
| Price discrimination possible? | No | Yes |

because their goods are not exactly the same as those offered by other firms. A Ford Taurus is not the same as a Toyota Camry. Ben and Jerry's ice cream is not the same as Breyer's. Each of these goods has a downward-sloping demand curve, which gives each producer some degree of monopoly power.

Yet firms with substantial monopoly power are rare. Few goods are truly unique. Most have substitutes that, even if not exactly the same, are similar. Ben and Jerry can raise the price of their ice cream a little without losing all their sales, but if they raise it a lot, sales will fall substantially as their customers switch to other brands.

In the end, monopoly power is a matter of degree. It is true that many firms have some monopoly power. It is also true that their monopoly power is usually limited. In such a situation, we will not go far wrong assuming that firms operate in competitive markets, even if that is not precisely the case.

## CHAPTER QuickQuiz

1. A firm is a natural monopoly if it exhibits the following as its output increases:
   a. decreasing marginal revenue.
   b. increasing marginal cost.
   c. decreasing average revenue.
   d. decreasing average total cost.

2. For a profit-maximizing monopoly that charges the same price to all consumers, what is the relationship between price $P$, marginal revenue $MR$, and marginal cost $MC$?
   a. $P = MR$ and $MR = MC$.
   b. $P > MR$ and $MR = MC$.
   c. $P = MR$ and $MR > MC$.
   d. $P > MR$ and $MR > MC$.

3.  If a monopoly's fixed costs increase, its price will
    _____ and its profit will _____.
    a.  increase, decrease
    b.  decrease, increase
    c.  increase, stay the same
    d.  stay the same, decrease

4.  Compared to the social optimum, a monopoly firm
    chooses
    a.  a quantity that is too low and a price that is
        too high.
    b.  a quantity that is too high and a price that is
        too low.
    c.  a quantity and a price that are both too high.
    d.  a quantity and a price that are both too low.

5.  The deadweight loss from monopoly arises because
    a.  the monopoly firm makes higher profits than a
        competitive firm would.
    b.  some potential consumers who forgo buying the
        good value it more than its marginal cost.
    c.  consumers who buy the good have to pay more
        than marginal cost, reducing their consumer
        surplus.
    d.  the monopoly firm chooses a quantity that fails to
        equate price and average revenue.

6.  When a monopolist switches from charging a single
    price to practicing perfect price discrimination, it
    reduces
    a.  the quantity produced.
    b.  the firm's profit.
    c.  consumer surplus.
    d.  total surplus.

## SUMMARY

- A monopoly is a firm that is the sole seller in its market. A monopoly arises when a single firm owns a key resource, when the government gives a firm the exclusive right to produce a good, or when a single firm can supply the entire market at a lower cost than many firms could.
- Because a monopoly is the sole producer in its market, it faces a downward-sloping demand curve for its product. When a monopoly increases production by 1 unit, it causes the price of its good to fall, which reduces the amount of revenue earned on all units produced. As a result, a monopoly's marginal revenue is always below the price of its good.
- Like a competitive firm, a monopoly firm maximizes profit by producing the quantity at which marginal revenue equals marginal cost. The monopoly then sets the price at which that quantity is demanded. Unlike a competitive firm, a monopoly firm's price exceeds its marginal revenue, so its price exceeds marginal cost.
- A monopolist's profit-maximizing level of output is below the level that maximizes the sum of consumer and producer surplus. That is, when the monopoly charges a price above marginal cost, some consumers who value the good more than its cost of production do not buy it. As a result, monopoly causes deadweight losses similar to those caused by taxes.
- A monopolist can often increase profits by charging different prices for the same good based on a buyer's willingness to pay. This practice of price discrimination can raise economic welfare by getting the good to some consumers who would otherwise not buy it. In the extreme case of perfect price discrimination, the deadweight loss of monopoly is completely eliminated and the entire surplus in the market goes to the monopoly producer. More generally, when price discrimination is imperfect, it can either raise or lower welfare compared to the outcome with a single monopoly price.
- Policymakers can respond to the inefficiency of monopoly behavior in four ways. They can use the antitrust laws to try to make the industry more competitive. They can regulate the prices that the monopoly charges. They can turn the monopolist into a government-run enterprise. Or, if the market failure is deemed small compared to the inevitable imperfections of policies, they can do nothing at all.

## KEY CONCEPTS

monopoly, p. 272                    natural monopoly, p. 274                    price discrimination, p. 285

## QUESTIONS FOR REVIEW

1. Give an example of a government-created monopoly. Is creating this monopoly necessarily bad public policy? Explain.

2. Define *natural monopoly*. What does the size of a market have to do with whether an industry is a natural monopoly?

3. Why is a monopolist's marginal revenue less than the price of its good? Can marginal revenue ever be negative? Explain.

4. Draw the demand, marginal-revenue, average-total-cost, and marginal-cost curves for a monopolist. Show the profit-maximizing level of output, the profit-maximizing price, and the amount of profit.

5. In your diagram from the previous question, show the level of output that maximizes total surplus. Show the deadweight loss from the monopoly. Explain your answer.

6. Give two examples of price discrimination. In each case, explain why the monopolist chooses to follow this business strategy.

7. What gives the government the power to regulate mergers between firms? Give a good reason and a bad reason (from the perspective of society's welfare) that two firms might want to merge.

8. Describe the two problems that arise when regulators tell a natural monopoly that it must set a price equal to marginal cost.

## PROBLEMS AND APPLICATIONS

1. A publisher faces the following demand schedule for the next novel from one of its popular authors:

   | Price | Quantity Demanded |
   | --- | --- |
   | $100 | 0 novels |
   | 90 | 100,000 |
   | 80 | 200,000 |
   | 70 | 300,000 |
   | 60 | 400,000 |
   | 50 | 500,000 |
   | 40 | 600,000 |
   | 30 | 700,000 |
   | 20 | 800,000 |
   | 10 | 900,000 |
   | 0 | 1,000,000 |

   The author is paid $2 million to write the book, and the marginal cost of publishing the book is a constant $10 per book.
   a. Compute total revenue, total cost, and profit at each quantity. What quantity would a profit-maximizing publisher choose? What price would it charge?
   b. Compute marginal revenue. (Recall that $MR = \Delta TR/\Delta Q$.) How does marginal revenue compare to the price? Explain.

   c. Graph the marginal-revenue, marginal-cost, and demand curves. At what quantity do the marginal-revenue and marginal-cost curves cross? What does this signify?
   d. In your graph, shade in the deadweight loss. Explain in words what this means.
   e. If the author were paid $3 million instead of $2 million to write the book, how would this affect the publisher's decision regarding what price to charge? Explain.
   f. Suppose the publisher was not profit-maximizing but was concerned with maximizing economic efficiency. What price would it charge for the book? How much profit would it make at this price?

2. A small town is served by many competing supermarkets, which have the same constant marginal cost.
   a. Using a diagram of the market for groceries, show the consumer surplus, producer surplus, and total surplus.
   b. Now suppose that the independent supermarkets combine into one chain. Using a new diagram, show the new consumer surplus, producer surplus, and total surplus. Relative to the competitive market, what is the transfer from consumers to producers? What is the deadweight loss?

3. Johnny Rockabilly has just finished recording his latest CD. His record company's marketing department determines that the demand for the CD is as follows:

| Price | Number of CDs |
|-------|---------------|
| $24 | 10,000 |
| 22 | 20,000 |
| 20 | 30,000 |
| 18 | 40,000 |
| 16 | 50,000 |
| 14 | 60,000 |

The company can produce the CD with no fixed cost and a variable cost of $5 per CD.
   a. Find total revenue for quantity equal to 10,000, 20,000, and so on. What is the marginal revenue for each 10,000 increase in the quantity sold?
   b. What quantity of CDs would maximize profit? What would the price be? What would the profit be?
   c. If you were Johnny's agent, what recording fee would you advise Johnny to demand from the record company? Why?

4. A company is considering building a bridge across a river. The bridge would cost $2 million to build and nothing to maintain. The following table shows the company's anticipated demand over the lifetime of the bridge:

| Price per Crossing | Number of Crossings, in Thousands |
|--------------------|-----------------------------------|
| $8 | 0 |
| 7 | 100 |
| 6 | 200 |
| 5 | 300 |
| 4 | 400 |
| 3 | 500 |
| 2 | 600 |
| 1 | 700 |
| 0 | 800 |

   a. If the company were to build the bridge, what would be its profit-maximizing price? Would that be the efficient level of output? Why or why not?
   b. If the company is interested in maximizing profit, should it build the bridge? What would be its profit or loss?
   c. If the government were to build the bridge, what price should it charge?
   d. Should the government build the bridge? Explain.

5. Consider the relationship between monopoly pricing and price elasticity of demand.
   a. Explain why a monopolist will never produce a quantity at which the demand curve is inelastic. (*Hint:* If demand is inelastic and the firm raises its price, what happens to total revenue and total costs?)
   b. Draw a diagram for a monopolist, precisely labeling the portion of the demand curve that is inelastic. (*Hint:* The answer is related to the marginal-revenue curve.)
   c. On your diagram, show the quantity and price that maximize total revenue.

6. You live in a town with 300 adults and 200 children, and you are thinking about putting on a play to entertain your neighbors and make some money. A play has a fixed cost of $2,000, but selling an extra ticket has zero marginal cost. Here are the demand schedules for your two types of customer:

| Price | Adults | Children |
|-------|--------|----------|
| $10 | 0 | 0 |
| 9 | 100 | 0 |
| 8 | 200 | 0 |
| 7 | 300 | 0 |
| 6 | 300 | 0 |
| 5 | 300 | 100 |
| 4 | 300 | 200 |
| 3 | 300 | 200 |
| 2 | 300 | 200 |
| 1 | 300 | 200 |
| 0 | 300 | 200 |

   a. To maximize profit, what price would you charge for an adult ticket? For a child's ticket? How much profit do you make?
   b. The city council passes a law prohibiting you from charging different prices to different customers. What price do you set for a ticket now? How much profit do you make?
   c. Who is worse off because of the law prohibiting price discrimination? Who is better off? (If you can, quantify the changes in welfare.)
   d. If the fixed cost of the play were $2,500 rather than $2,000, how would your answers to parts (a), (b), and (c) change?

7. The residents of the town Ectenia all love economics, and the mayor proposes building an economics museum. The museum has a fixed cost of $2,400,000 and no variable costs. There are 100,000 town residents, and each has the same demand for museum visits: $Q^D = 10 - P$, where $P$ is the price of admission.
   a. Graph the museum's average-total-cost curve and its marginal-cost curve. What kind of market would describe the museum?
   b. The mayor proposes financing the museum with a lump-sum tax of $24 and then opening the museum to the public for free. How many times would each person visit? Calculate the benefit each person would get from the museum, measured as consumer surplus minus the new tax.
   c. The mayor's anti-tax opponent says the museum should finance itself by charging an admission fee. What is the lowest price the museum can charge without incurring losses? (*Hint*: Find the number of visits and museum profits for prices of $2, $3, $4, and $5.)
   d. For the break-even price you found in part (c), calculate each resident's consumer surplus. Compared with the mayor's plan, who is better off with this admission fee, and who is worse off? Explain.
   e. What real-world considerations absent in the problem above might provide reasons to favor an admission fee?

8. Henry Potter owns the only well in town that produces clean drinking water. He faces the following demand, marginal revenue, and marginal cost curves:

$$\text{Demand: } P = 70 - Q$$
$$\text{Marginal Revenue: } MR = 70 - 2Q$$
$$\text{Marginal Cost: } MC = 10 + Q$$

   a. Graph these three curves. Assuming that Mr. Potter maximizes profit, what quantity does he produce? What price does he charge? Show these results on your graph.
   b. Mayor George Bailey, concerned about water consumers, is considering a price ceiling that is 10 percent below the monopoly price derived in part (a). What quantity would be demanded at this new price? Would the profit-maximizing Mr. Potter produce that amount? Explain. (*Hint*: Think about marginal cost.)
   c. George's Uncle Billy says that a price ceiling is a bad idea because price ceilings cause shortages. Is he right in this case? What size shortage would the price ceiling create? Explain.

   d. George's friend Clarence, who is even more concerned about consumers, suggests a price ceiling 50 percent below the monopoly price. What quantity would be demanded at this price? How much would Mr. Potter produce? In this case, is Uncle Billy right? What size shortage would the price ceiling create?

9. Only one firm produces and sells soccer balls in the country of Wiknam, and as the story begins, international trade in soccer balls is prohibited. The following equations describe the monopolist's demand, marginal revenue, total cost, and marginal cost:

$$\text{Demand: } P = 10 - Q$$
$$\text{Marginal Revenue: } MR = 10 - 2Q$$
$$\text{Total Cost: } TC = 3 + Q + 0.5\,Q^2$$
$$\text{Marginal Cost: } MC = 1 + Q,$$

   where $Q$ is quantity and $P$ is the price measured in Wiknamian dollars.
   a. How many soccer balls does the monopolist produce? At what price are they sold? What is the monopolist's profit?
   b. One day, the King of Wiknam decrees that henceforth there will be free trade—either imports or exports—of soccer balls at the world price of $6. The firm is now a price taker in a competitive market. What happens to domestic production of soccer balls? To domestic consumption? Does Wiknam export or import soccer balls?
   c. In our analysis of international trade in Chapter 9, a country becomes an exporter when the price without trade is below the world price and an importer when the price without trade is above the world price. Does that conclusion hold in your answers to parts (a) and (b)? Explain.
   d. Suppose that the world price was not $6 but, instead, happened to be exactly the same as the domestic price without trade as determined in part (a). Would allowing trade have changed anything in the Wiknamian economy? Explain. How does the result here compare with the analysis in Chapter 9?

10. Based on market research, a film production company in Ectenia obtains the following information about the demand and production costs of its new DVD:

$$\text{Demand: } P = 1,000 - 10Q$$
$$\text{Total Revenue: } TR = 1,000Q - 10Q^2$$
$$\text{Marginal Revenue: } MR = 1,000 - 20Q$$
$$\text{Marginal Cost: } MC = 100 + 10Q,$$

where $Q$ indicates the number of copies sold and $P$ is the price in Ectenian dollars.

a. Find the price and quantity that maximize the company's profit.

b. Find the price and quantity that would maximize social welfare.

c. Calculate the deadweight loss from monopoly.

d. Suppose, in addition to the costs above, the director of the film has to be paid. The company is considering four options:

    i.  a flat fee of 2,000 Ectenian dollars.

    ii.  50 percent of the profits.

    iii.  150 Ectenian dollars per unit sold.

    iv.  50 percent of the revenue.

For each option, calculate the profit-maximizing price and quantity. Which, if any, of these compensation schemes would alter the deadweight loss from monopoly? Explain.

11. Larry, Curly, and Moe run the only saloon in town. Larry wants to sell as many drinks as possible without losing money. Curly wants the saloon to bring in as much revenue as possible. Moe wants to make the largest possible profits. Using a single diagram of the saloon's demand curve and its cost curves, show the price and quantity combinations favored by each of the three partners. Explain. (*Hint*: Only one of these partners will want to set marginal revenue equal to marginal cost.)

12. Many schemes for price discrimination involve some cost. For example, discount coupons take up the time and resources of both the buyer and the seller. This question considers the implications of costly price discrimination. To keep things simple, let's assume that our monopolist's production costs are simply proportional to output so that average total cost and marginal cost are constant and equal to each other.

a. Draw the cost, demand, and marginal-revenue curves for the monopolist. Show the price the monopolist would charge without price discrimination.

b. In your diagram, mark the area equal to the monopolist's profit and call it $X$. Mark the area equal to consumer surplus and call it $Y$. Mark the area equal to the deadweight loss and call it $Z$.

c. Now suppose that the monopolist can perfectly price discriminate. What is the monopolist's profit? (Give your answer in terms of $X$, $Y$, and $Z$.)

d. What is the change in the monopolist's profit from price discrimination? What is the change in total surplus from price discrimination? Which change is larger? Explain. (Give your answer in terms of $X$, $Y$, and $Z$.)

e. Now suppose that there is some cost associated with price discrimination. To model this cost, let's assume that the monopolist has to pay a fixed cost $C$ to price discriminate. How would a monopolist make the decision whether to pay this fixed cost? (Give your answer in terms of $X$, $Y$, $Z$, and $C$.)

f. How would a benevolent social planner, who cares about total surplus, decide whether the monopolist should price discriminate? (Give your answer in terms of $X$, $Y$, $Z$, and $C$.)

g. Compare your answers to parts (e) and (f). How does the monopolist's incentive to price discriminate differ from the social planner's? Is it possible that the monopolist will price discriminate even though doing so is not socially desirable?

To find additional study resources, visit cengagebrain.com, and search for "Mankiw."

# PART VI

# The Data of Macroeconomics

PART VI

The Data of

Economics

# Measuring a Nation's Income

When you finish school and start looking for a full-time job, your experience will, to a large extent, be shaped by prevailing economic conditions. In some years, firms throughout the economy are expanding their production of goods and services, employment is rising, and jobs are easy to find. In other years, firms are cutting back production, employment is declining, and finding a good job takes a long time. Not surprisingly, any college graduate would rather enter the labor force in a year of economic expansion than in a year of economic contraction.

Because the health of the overall economy profoundly affects all of us, changes in economic conditions are widely reported by the

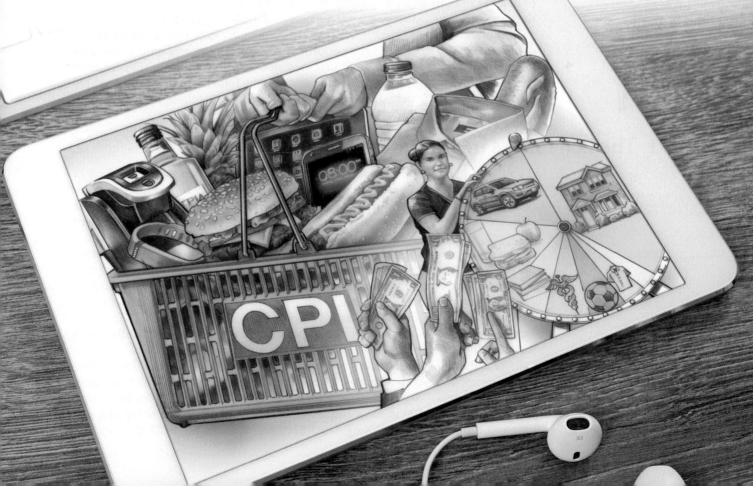

media. Indeed, it is hard to pick up a newspaper, check an online news service, or turn on the TV without seeing some newly reported statistic about the economy. The statistic might measure the total income of everyone in the economy (gross domestic product, or GDP), the rate at which average prices are rising or falling (inflation/deflation), the percentage of the labor force that is out of work (unemployment), total spending at stores (retail sales), or the imbalance of trade between the United States and the rest of the world (the trade deficit). All these statistics are *macroeconomic*. Rather than telling us about a particular household, firm, or market, they tell us something about the entire economy.

As you may recall from Chapter 2, economics is divided into two branches: microeconomics and macroeconomics. **Microeconomics** is the study of how individual households and firms make decisions and how they interact with one another in markets. **Macroeconomics** is the study of the economy as a whole. The goal of macroeconomics is to explain the economic changes that affect many households, firms, and markets simultaneously. Macroeconomists address a broad variety of questions: Why is average income high in some countries and low in others? Why do prices sometimes rise rapidly while at other times they are more stable? Why do production and employment expand in some years and contract in others? What, if anything, can the government do to promote rapid growth in incomes, low inflation, and stable employment? These questions are all macroeconomic in nature because they concern the workings of the entire economy.

Because the economy as a whole is a collection of many households and many firms interacting in many markets, microeconomics and macroeconomics are closely linked. The basic tools of supply and demand, for instance, are as central to macroeconomic analysis as they are to microeconomic analysis. Yet studying the economy in its entirety raises some new and intriguing challenges.

In this and the next chapter, we discuss some of the data that economists and policymakers use to monitor the performance of the overall economy. These data reflect the economic changes that macroeconomists try to explain. This chapter considers *gross domestic product*, which measures the total income of a nation. GDP is the most closely watched economic statistic because it is thought to be the single best measure of a society's economic well-being.

**microeconomics**
the study of how households and firms make decisions and how they interact in markets

**macroeconomics**
the study of economy-wide phenomena, including inflation, unemployment, and economic growth

# 15-1 The Economy's Income and Expenditure

If you were to judge how a person is doing economically, you might first look at her income. A person with a high income can more easily afford life's necessities and luxuries. It is no surprise that people with higher incomes enjoy higher standards of living—better housing, better healthcare, fancier cars, more opulent vacations, and so on.

The same logic applies to a nation's overall economy. When judging whether the economy is doing well or poorly, it is natural to look at the total income that everyone in the economy is earning. That is the task of gross domestic product.

GDP measures two things at once: the total income of everyone in the economy and the total expenditure on the economy's output of goods and services. GDP can perform the trick of measuring both total income and total expenditure because these two things are the same. *For an economy as a whole, income must equal expenditure.*

Why is this true? An economy's income is the same as its expenditure because every transaction has two parties: a buyer and a seller. Every dollar of spending by some buyer is a dollar of income for some seller. Suppose, for instance, that Karen pays Doug $100 to mow her lawn. In this case, Doug is a seller of a service and Karen is a buyer. Doug earns $100 and Karen spends $100. Thus, the transaction contributes equally to the economy's income and to its expenditure. GDP, whether measured as total income or total expenditure, rises by $100.

Another way to see the equality of income and expenditure is with the circular-flow diagram in Figure 1. As you may recall from Chapter 2, this diagram describes all the transactions between households and firms in a simple economy. It simplifies matters by assuming that all goods and services are bought by households and that households spend all of their income. In this economy, when households buy goods and services from firms, these expenditures flow through the markets for goods and services. When the firms use the money they receive from sales to pay workers' wages, landowners' rent, and firm owners' profit, this income flows through the markets for the factors of production. Money continuously flows from households to firms and then back to households.

GDP measures this flow of money. We can compute it for this economy in one of two ways: by adding up the total expenditure by households or by adding up the total income (wages, rent, and profit) paid by firms. Because all expenditure in the economy ends up as someone's income, GDP is the same regardless of how we compute it.

The actual economy is, of course, more complicated than the one illustrated in Figure 1. Households do not spend all of their income; they pay some of it to the government in taxes, and they save some for use in the future. In addition, households do not buy all goods and services produced in the economy; some goods and services are bought by governments, and some are bought by firms that plan to use them in the future to produce their own output. Yet the basic lesson remains the same: Regardless of whether a household, government, or firm buys a good or service, the transaction always has a buyer and a seller. Thus, for the economy as a whole, expenditure and income are the same.

**QuickQuiz**  *What two things does GDP measure? How can it measure two things at once?*

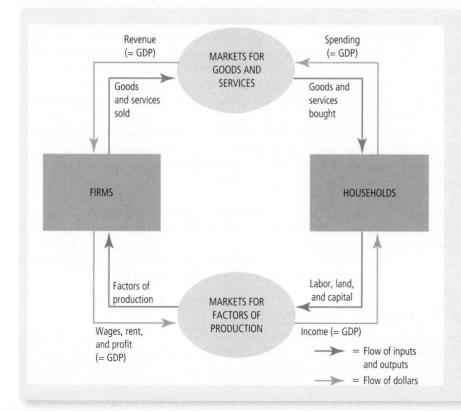

## FIGURE 1

**The Circular-Flow Diagram**
Households buy goods and services from firms, and firms use their revenue from sales to pay wages to workers, rent to landowners, and profit to firm owners. GDP equals the total amount spent by households in the market for goods and services. It also equals the total wages, rent, and profit paid by firms in the markets for the factors of production.

# 15-2 The Measurement of GDP

Having discussed the meaning of gross domestic product in general terms, let's be more precise about how this statistic is measured. Here is a definition of GDP that focuses on GDP as a measure of total expenditure:

**gross domestic product (GDP)**

the market value of all final goods and services produced within a country in a given period of time

- **Gross domestic product (GDP)** is the market value of all final goods and services produced within a country in a given period of time.

This definition might seem simple enough. But in fact, many subtle issues arise when computing an economy's GDP. Let's therefore consider each phrase in this definition with some care.

## 15-2a "GDP Is the Market Value . . ."

You have probably heard the adage "You can't compare apples and oranges." Yet GDP does exactly that. GDP adds together many different kinds of products into a single measure of the value of economic activity. To do this, it uses market prices. Because market prices measure the amount people are willing to pay for different goods, they reflect the value of those goods. If the price of an apple is twice the price of an orange, then an apple contributes twice as much to GDP as does an orange.

## 15-2b ". . . of All . . ."

GDP tries to be comprehensive. It includes all items produced in the economy and sold legally in markets. GDP measures the market value of not just apples and oranges but also pears and grapefruit, books and movies, haircuts and healthcare, and so on.

GDP also includes the market value of the housing services provided by the economy's stock of housing. For rental housing, this value is easy to calculate—the rent equals both the tenant's expenditure and the landlord's income. Yet many people own their homes and, therefore, do not pay rent. The government includes this owner-occupied housing in GDP by estimating its rental value. In effect, GDP is based on the assumption that the owner is renting the house to herself. The imputed rent is included both in the homeowner's expenditure and in her income, so it adds to GDP.

There are some products, however, that GDP excludes because measuring them is difficult. GDP excludes most items produced and sold illicitly, such as illegal drugs. It also excludes most items that are produced and consumed at home and, therefore, never enter the marketplace. Vegetables you buy at the grocery store are part of GDP; vegetables you grow in your garden are not.

These exclusions from GDP can at times lead to paradoxical results. For example, when Karen pays Doug to mow her lawn, that transaction is part of GDP. But suppose Doug and Karen marry. Even though Doug may continue to mow Karen's lawn, the value of the mowing is now left out of GDP because Doug's service is no longer sold in a market. Thus, their marriage reduces GDP.

## 15-2c ". . . Final . . ."

When International Paper makes paper, which Hallmark then uses to make a greeting card, the paper is called an *intermediate good* and the card is called a *final good*. GDP includes only the value of final goods. This is done because the value of intermediate goods is already included in the prices of the final goods. Adding the market value of the paper to the market value of the card would be double counting. That is, it would (incorrectly) count the paper twice.

An important exception to this principle arises when an intermediate good is produced and, rather than being used, is added to a firm's inventory of goods for use or sale at a later date. In this case, the intermediate good is taken to be "final" for the moment, and its value as inventory investment is included as part of GDP. Thus, additions to inventory add to GDP, and when the goods in inventory are later used or sold, the reductions in inventory subtract from GDP.

### 15-2d "...Goods and Services..."

GDP includes both tangible goods (food, clothing, cars) and intangible services (haircuts, housecleaning, doctor visits). When you buy a CD by your favorite band, you are buying a good, and the purchase price is part of GDP. When you pay to hear a concert by the same band, you are buying a service, and the ticket price is also part of GDP.

### 15-2e "...Produced..."

GDP includes goods and services currently produced. It does not include transactions involving items produced in the past. When Ford produces and sells a new car, the value of the car is included in GDP. But when one person sells a used car to another person, the value of the used car is not included in GDP.

### 15-2f "...Within a Country..."

GDP measures the value of production within the geographic confines of a country. When a Canadian citizen works temporarily in the United States, her production is part of U.S. GDP. When an American citizen owns a factory in Haiti, the production at her factory is not part of U.S. GDP. (It is part of Haiti's GDP.) Thus, items are included in a nation's GDP if they are produced domestically, regardless of the nationality of the producer.

### 15-2g "...In a Given Period of Time."

GDP measures the value of production that takes place within a specific interval of time. Usually, that interval is a year or a quarter (3 months). GDP measures the economy's flow of income, as well as its flow of expenditure, during that interval.

When the government reports the GDP for a quarter, it usually presents GDP "at an annual rate." This means that the figure reported for quarterly GDP is the amount of income and expenditure during the quarter multiplied by 4. The government uses this convention so that quarterly and annual figures on GDP can be compared more easily.

In addition, when the government reports quarterly GDP, it presents the data after they have been modified by a statistical procedure called *seasonal adjustment*. The unadjusted data show clearly that the economy produces more goods and services during some times of the year than during others. (As you might guess, December's holiday shopping season is a high point.) When monitoring the condition of the economy, economists and policymakers often want to look beyond these regular seasonal changes. Therefore, government statisticians adjust the quarterly data to take out the seasonal cycle. The GDP data reported in the news are always seasonally adjusted.

Now let's repeat the definition of GDP:

- Gross domestic product (GDP) is the market value of all final goods and services produced within a country in a given period of time.

This definition focuses on GDP as total expenditure in the economy. But don't forget that every dollar spent by a buyer of a good or service becomes a dollar of income to the seller of that good or service. Therefore, in addition to applying this definition, the government adds up total income in the economy. The two ways of calculating GDP give almost exactly the same answer. (Why "almost"? The two measures should be precisely the same, but data sources are not perfect. The difference between the two calculations of GDP is called the *statistical discrepancy*.)

It should be apparent that GDP is a sophisticated measure of the value of economic activity. In advanced courses in macroeconomics, you will learn more about the subtleties that arise in its calculation. But even now you can see that each phrase in this definition is packed with meaning.

Quick**Quiz**　*Which contributes more to GDP—the production of a pound of hamburger or the production of a pound of caviar? Why?*

## FYI

## Other Measures of Income

When the U.S. Department of Commerce computes the nation's GDP, it also computes various other measures of income to get a more complete picture of what's happening in the economy. These other measures differ from GDP by excluding or including certain categories of income. What follows is a brief description of five of these income measures, ordered from largest to smallest.

- *Gross national product* (GNP) is the total income earned by a nation's permanent residents (called *nationals*). It differs from GDP in that it includes income that our citizens earn abroad and excludes income that foreigners earn here. For example, when a Canadian citizen works temporarily in the United States, her production is part of U.S. GDP, but it is not part of U.S. GNP. (It is part of Canada's GNP.) For most countries, including the United States, domestic residents are responsible for most domestic production, so GDP and GNP are quite close.
- *Net national product* (NNP) is the total income of a nation's residents (GNP) minus losses from depreciation. *Depreciation* is the wear and tear on the economy's stock of equipment and structures, such as trucks rusting and old computer models becoming obsolete. In the national income accounts prepared by the Department of Commerce, depreciation is called the "consumption of fixed capital."
- *National income* is the total income earned by a nation's residents in the production of goods and services. It is almost identical to net national product. These two measures differ because of the *statistical discrepancy* that arises from problems in data collection.

- *Personal income* is the income that households and noncorporate businesses receive. Unlike national income, it excludes *retained earnings*, which is income that corporations have earned but have not paid out to their owners. It also subtracts indirect business taxes (such as sales taxes), corporate income taxes, and contributions for social insurance (mostly Social Security taxes). In addition, personal income includes the interest income that households receive from their holdings of government debt and the income that households receive from government transfer programs, such as welfare and Social Security.
- *Disposable personal income* is the income that households and noncorporate businesses have left after satisfying all their obligations to the government. It equals personal income minus personal taxes and certain nontax payments (such as traffic tickets).

Although the various measures of income differ in detail, they almost always tell the same story about economic conditions. When GDP grows rapidly, these other measures of income usually grow rapidly. And when GDP falls, these other measures usually fall as well. For monitoring fluctuations in the overall economy, it does not matter much which measure of income we use. ∎

# 15-3 The Components of GDP

Spending in an economy takes many forms. At any moment, the Smith family may be having lunch at Burger King; Ford may be building a car factory; the U.S. Navy may be procuring a submarine; and British Airways may be buying an airplane from Boeing. GDP includes all of these various forms of spending on domestically produced goods and services.

To understand how the economy is using its scarce resources, economists study the composition of GDP among various types of spending. To do this, GDP (which we denote as $Y$) is divided into four components: consumption ($C$), investment ($I$), government purchases ($G$), and net exports ($NX$):

$$Y = C + I + G + NX.$$

This equation is an *identity*—an equation that must be true because of how the variables in the equation are defined. In this case, because each dollar of expenditure included in GDP is placed into one of the four components of GDP, the total of the four components must be equal to GDP. Let's look at each of these four components more closely.

## 15-3a Consumption

**Consumption** is spending by households on goods and services, with the exception of purchases of new housing. Goods include durable goods, such as automobiles and appliances, and nondurable goods, such as food and clothing. Services include such intangible items as haircuts and medical care. Household spending on education is also included in consumption of services (although one might argue that it would fit better in the next component).

**consumption**
spending by households on goods and services, with the exception of purchases of new housing

## 15-3b Investment

**Investment** is the purchase of goods (called *capital goods*) that will be used in the future to produce more goods and services. Investment is the sum of purchases of business capital, residential capital, and inventories. Business capital includes business structures (such as a factory or office building), equipment (such as a worker's computer), and intellectual property products (such as the software that runs the computer). Residential capital includes the landlord's apartment building and a homeowner's personal residence. By convention, the purchase of a new house is the one type of household spending categorized as investment rather than consumption.

**investment**
spending on business capital, residential capital, and inventories

As mentioned earlier, the treatment of inventory accumulation is noteworthy. When Apple produces a computer and adds it to its inventory instead of selling it, Apple is assumed to have "purchased" the computer for itself. That is, the national income accountants treat the computer as part of Apple's investment spending. (If Apple later sells the computer out of inventory, Apple's inventory investment will then be negative, offsetting the positive expenditure of the buyer.) Inventories are treated this way because one aim of GDP is to measure the value of the economy's production, and goods added to inventory are part of that period's production.

Notice that GDP accounting uses the word *investment* differently from how you might hear the term in everyday conversation. When you hear the word *investment*, you might think of financial investments, such as stocks, bonds, and mutual funds—topics that we study later in this book. By contrast, because GDP measures expenditure on goods and services, here the word *investment* means

## Sex, Drugs, and GDP

*Some nations are debating what to include in their national income accounts.*

### No Sex, Please, We're French

By Zachary Karabell

The government of France has just made what on the face of it appears to be a nonannouncement announcement: It will not include illegal drugs and prostitution in its official calculation of the country's gross domestic product.

What made the announcement odd was that it never has included such activities, nor have most countries. Nor do most governments announce what they do not plan to do. ("The U.S. government has no intention of sending a man to Venus.") Yet the French decision comes in the wake of significant pressure from neighboring countries and from the European Union to integrate these activities into national accounts and economic output. That raises a host of questions: *Should* these activities be included, and if those are, why not others? And what exactly are we measuring—and why?

Few numbers shape our world today more than GDP. It has become the alpha and omega of national success, used by politicians and pundits as the primary gauge of national strength and treated as a numerical proxy for greatness or the lack thereof.

Yet GDP is only a statistic, replete with the limitations of all statistics. Created as an outgrowth of national accounts that were themselves only devised in the 1930s, GDP was never an all-inclusive measure, even as it is treated as such. Multiple areas of economic life were left out, including volunteer work and domestic work.

Now Eurostat, the official statistical agency of the European Union, is leading the drive to include a host of illegal activities in national calculations of GDP, most notably prostitution and illicit drugs. The argument, as a United Nations commission laid out in 2008, is fairly simple: Prostitution and illicit drugs are significant economic activities, and if they're not factored into economic statistics, then we're looking at an incomplete picture—which in turn will make it that much harder to craft smart policy. Additionally, different

---

purchases of goods (such as business capital, residential structures, and inventories) that will be used to produce other goods and services in the future.

### 15-3c Government Purchases

**government purchases**
spending on goods and services by local, state, and federal governments

**Government purchases** include spending on goods and services by local, state, and federal governments. It includes the salaries of government workers as well as expenditures on public works. Recently, the U.S. national income accounts have switched to the longer label *government consumption expenditure and gross investment*, but in this book, we will use the traditional and shorter term *government purchases*.

The meaning of government purchases requires a bit of clarification. When the government pays the salary of an Army general or a schoolteacher, that salary is part of government purchases. But when the government pays a Social Security benefit to a person who is elderly or an unemployment insurance benefit to a worker who was recently laid off, the story is very different: These are called *transfer payments* because they are not made in exchange for a currently produced good or service. Transfer payments alter household income, but they do not reflect the economy's production. (From a macroeconomic standpoint, transfer payments are like negative taxes.) Because GDP is intended to measure income from, and expenditure on, the production of goods and services, transfer payments are not counted as part of government purchases.

### 15-3d Net Exports

**net exports**
spending on domestically produced goods by foreigners (exports) minus spending on foreign goods by domestic residents (imports)

**Net exports** equal the foreign purchases of domestically produced goods (exports) minus the domestic purchases of foreign goods (imports). A domestic firm's sale

countries have different laws: In the Netherlands, for instance, prostitution is legal, as is marijuana. Those commercial transactions (or at least those that are recorded and taxed) are already part of Dutch GDP. Not including them in Italy's or Spain's GDPs can thus make it challenging to compare national numbers.

That is why Spain, Italy, Belgium, and the U.K. have in recent months moved to include illegal drugs and nonlicensed sex trade in their national accounts. The U.K. Office for National Statistics in particular approached its mandate with wonkish seriousness, publishing a 20-page précis of its methodology that explained how it would, say, calculate the dollar amount of prostitution (police records help) or deal with domestically produced drugs versus imported drugs. The result, which will be formally announced in September, will be an additional 10 billion pounds added to Great Britain's GDP.

France, however, has demurred. A nation with a clichéd reputation for a certain savoir faire when it comes to sex and other nocturnal activities has decided (or at least its bureaucrats have) that in spite of an EU directive, it will not calculate the effects of illegal activities that are often nonconsensual or nonvoluntary. That is clearly the case for some prostitution—one French minister stated that "street prostitution" is largely controlled by the Mafia—and the same could be reasonably said of the use of some hard drugs, given their addictive nature.

There is undeniably a strong moralistic component in the French decision. By averring that because they are not voluntary or consensual these exchanges should not be included in GDP, the French government is placing a moral vision of what society *should* be ahead of an economic vision of what society *is*. That in turn makes an already messy statistic far messier, and that serves no one's national interests. . . .

With all of GDP's limitations, adding a new moral dimension would only make the number that much less useful. After all, why stop at not including prostitution because it degrades women? Why not refuse to measure coal production because it degrades the environment? Why not leave out cigarette usage because it causes cancer? The list of possible exclusions on this basis is endless.

If GDP is our current best metric for national output, then at the very least it should attempt to include all measurable output. The usually moralistic United States has actually been including legal prostitution in Nevada and now marijuana sales and consumption in Colorado, California, and Washington without any strong objections based solely on the argument that these are commercial exchanges that constitute this fuzzy entity we call "the economy." . . .

Not measuring drugs and sex won't make them go away, but it will hobble efforts to understand the messy latticework of our economic lives, all in a futile attempt to excise what we do not like. ■

**Source:** *Slate*, June 20, 2014.

to a buyer in another country, such as Boeing's sale of an airplane to British Airways, increases net exports.

The *net* in *net exports* refers to the fact that imports are subtracted from exports. This subtraction is made because other components of GDP include imports of goods and services. For example, suppose that a household buys a $40,000 car from Volvo, the Swedish carmaker. This transaction increases consumption by $40,000 because car purchases are part of consumer spending. It also reduces net exports by $40,000 because the car is an import. In other words, net exports include goods and services produced abroad (with a minus sign) because these goods and services are included in consumption, investment, and government purchases (with a plus sign). Thus, when a domestic household, firm, or government buys a good or service from abroad, the purchase reduces net exports, but because it also raises consumption, investment, or government purchases, it does not affect GDP.

### CASE STUDY

**THE COMPONENTS OF U.S. GDP**

Table 1 shows the composition of U.S. GDP in 2015. In this year, the GDP of the United States was almost $18 trillion. Dividing this number by the 2015 U.S. population of 321 million yields GDP per person (sometimes called GDP per capita). In 2015 the income and expenditure of the average American was $55,882.

Consumption made up 68 percent of GDP, or $38,218 per person. Investment was $9,402 per person. Government purchases were $9,919 per person. Net exports were –$1,657 per person. This number is negative because Americans spent more on foreign goods than foreigners spent on American goods.

**TABLE 1**

**GDP and Its Components**
This table shows total GDP for the U.S. economy in 2015 and the breakdown of GDP among its four components. When reading this table, recall the identity $Y = C + I + G + NX$.

| | Total (in billions of dollars) | Per Person (in dollars) | Percent of Total |
|---|---|---|---|
| Gross domestic product, $Y$ | $17,938 | $55,882 | 100% |
| Consumption, $C$ | 12,268 | 38,218 | 68 |
| Investment, $I$ | 3,018 | 9,402 | 17 |
| Government purchases, $G$ | 3,184 | 9,919 | 18 |
| Net exports, $NX$ | −532 | −1,657 | −3 |

**Source:** U.S. Department of Commerce. Parts may not sum to totals due to rounding.

These data come from the Bureau of Economic Analysis, the part of the U.S. Department of Commerce that produces the national income accounts. You can find more recent data on GDP on its website, http://www.bea.gov. ●

**Quick Quiz**   *List the four components of expenditure. Which is the largest?*

## 15-4   Real versus Nominal GDP

As we have seen, GDP measures the total spending on goods and services in all markets in the economy. If total spending rises from one year to the next, at least one of two things must be true: (1) the economy is producing a larger output of goods and services, or (2) goods and services are being sold at higher prices. When studying changes in the economy over time, economists want to separate these two effects. In particular, they want a measure of the total quantity of goods and services the economy is producing that is not affected by changes in the prices of those goods and services.

To do this, economists use a measure called *real GDP*. Real GDP answers a hypothetical question: What would be the value of the goods and services produced this year if we valued these goods and services at the prices that prevailed in some specific year in the past? By evaluating current production using prices that are fixed at past levels, real GDP shows how the economy's overall production of goods and services changes over time.

To see more precisely how real GDP is constructed, let's consider an example.

### 15-4a   A Numerical Example

Table 2 shows some data for an economy that produces only two goods: hot dogs and hamburgers. The table shows the prices and quantities produced of the two goods in the years 2016, 2017, and 2018.

To compute total spending in this economy, we would multiply the quantities of hot dogs and hamburgers by their prices. In the year 2016, 100 hot dogs are sold at a price of $1 per hot dog, so expenditure on hot dogs equals $100. In the same year, 50 hamburgers are sold for $2 per hamburger, so expenditure on hamburgers also equals $100. Total expenditure in the economy—the sum of expenditure on hot dogs and expenditure on hamburgers—is $200. This amount, the production of goods and services valued at current prices, is called **nominal GDP**.

**nominal GDP**
the production of goods and services valued at current prices

| Prices and Quantities | | | | |
| --- | --- | --- | --- | --- |
| Year | Price of Hot Dogs | Quantity of Hot Dogs | Price of Hamburgers | Quantity of Hamburgers |
| 2016 | $1 | 100 | $2 | 50 |
| 2017 | $2 | 150 | $3 | 100 |
| 2018 | $3 | 200 | $4 | 150 |
| **Calculating Nominal GDP** | | | | |
| 2016 | ($1 per hot dog × 100 hot dogs) + ($2 per hamburger × 50 hamburgers) = $200 | | | |
| 2017 | ($2 per hot dog × 150 hot dogs) + ($3 per hamburger × 100 hamburgers) = $600 | | | |
| 2018 | ($3 per hot dog × 200 hot dogs) + ($4 per hamburger × 150 hamburgers) = $1,200 | | | |
| **Calculating Real GDP (base year 2016)** | | | | |
| 2016 | ($1 per hot dog × 100 hot dogs) + ($2 per hamburger × 50 hamburgers) = $200 | | | |
| 2017 | ($1 per hot dog × 150 hot dogs) + ($2 per hamburger × 100 hamburgers) = $350 | | | |
| 2018 | ($1 per hot dog × 200 hot dogs) + ($2 per hamburger × 150 hamburgers) = $500 | | | |
| **Calculating the GDP Deflator** | | | | |
| 2016 | ($200/$200) × 100 = 100 | | | |
| 2017 | ($600/$350) × 100 = 171 | | | |
| 2018 | ($1,200/$500) × 100 = 240 | | | |

**TABLE 2**

**Real and Nominal GDP**
This table shows how to calculate real GDP, nominal GDP, and the GDP deflator for a hypothetical economy that produces only hot dogs and hamburgers.

The table shows the calculation of nominal GDP for these 3 years. Total spending rises from $200 in 2016 to $600 in 2017 and then to $1,200 in 2018. Part of this rise is attributable to the increase in the quantities of hot dogs and hamburgers, and part is attributable to the increase in the prices of hot dogs and hamburgers.

To obtain a measure of the amount produced that is not affected by changes in prices, we use **real GDP**, which is the production of goods and services valued at constant prices. We calculate real GDP by first designating 1 year as a *base year*. We then use the prices of hot dogs and hamburgers in the base year to compute the value of goods and services in all the years. In other words, the prices in the base year provide the basis for comparing quantities in different years.

**real GDP**
the production of goods and services valued at constant prices

Suppose that we choose 2016 to be the base year in our example. We can then use the prices of hot dogs and hamburgers in 2016 to compute the value of goods and services produced in 2016, 2017, and 2018. Table 2 shows these calculations. To compute real GDP for 2016, we use the prices of hot dogs and hamburgers in 2016 (the base year) and the quantities of hot dogs and hamburgers produced in 2016. (Thus, for the base year, real GDP always equals nominal GDP.) To compute real GDP for 2017, we use the prices of hot dogs and hamburgers in 2016 (the base year) and the quantities of hot dogs and hamburgers produced in 2017. Similarly, to compute real GDP for 2018, we use the prices in 2016 and the quantities in 2018. When we find that real GDP has risen from $200 in 2016 to $350 in 2017 and then to $500 in 2018, we know that the increase is attributable to an increase in the quantities produced because the prices are being held fixed at base-year levels.

To sum up: *Nominal GDP uses current prices to place a value on the economy's produc-tion of goods and services. Real GDP uses constant base-year prices to place a value on the economy's production of goods and services.* Because real GDP is not affected by changes in prices, changes in real GDP reflect only changes in the amounts being produced. Thus, real GDP is a measure of the economy's production of goods and services.

Our goal in computing GDP is to gauge how well the overall economy is per-forming. Because real GDP measures the economy's production of goods and ser-vices, it reflects the economy's ability to satisfy people's needs and desires. Thus, real GDP is a better gauge of economic well-being than is nominal GDP. When economists talk about the economy's GDP, they usually mean real GDP rather than nominal GDP. And when they talk about growth in the economy, they mea-sure that growth as the percentage change in real GDP from one period to another.

### 15-4b  The GDP Deflator

As we have just seen, nominal GDP reflects both the quantities of goods and ser-vices the economy is producing and the prices of those goods and services. By contrast, by holding prices constant at base-year levels, real GDP reflects only the quantities produced. From these two statistics, we can compute a third, called the GDP deflator, which reflects only the prices of goods and services.

The **GDP deflator** is calculated as follows:

**GDP deflator**
a measure of the price level calculated as the ratio of nominal GDP to real GDP times 100

$$\text{GDP deflator} = \frac{\text{Nominal GDP}}{\text{Real GDP}} \times 100.$$

Because nominal GDP and real GDP must be the same in the base year, the GDP deflator for the base year always equals 100. The GDP deflator for subsequent years measures the change in nominal GDP from the base year that cannot be attributable to a change in real GDP.

The GDP deflator measures the current level of prices relative to the level of prices in the base year. To see why this is true, consider a couple of simple exam-ples. First, imagine that the quantities produced in the economy rise over time but prices remain the same. In this case, both nominal and real GDP rise at the same rate, so the GDP deflator is constant. Now suppose, instead, that prices rise over time but the quantities produced stay the same. In this second case, nominal GDP rises but real GDP remains the same, so the GDP deflator rises. Notice that, in both cases, the GDP deflator reflects what's happening to prices, not quantities.

Let's now return to our numerical example in Table 2. The GDP deflator is com-puted at the bottom of the table. For the year 2016, nominal GDP is $200 and real GDP is $200, so the GDP deflator is 100. (The deflator is always 100 in the base year.) For the year 2017, nominal GDP is $600 and real GDP is $350, so the GDP deflator is 171.

Economists use the term *inflation* to describe a situation in which the economy's overall price level is rising. The *inflation rate* is the percentage change in some measure of the price level from one period to the next. Using the GDP deflator, the inflation rate between two consecutive years is computed as follows:

$$\text{Inflation rate in year 2} = \frac{\text{GDP deflator in year 2} - \text{GDP deflator in year 1}}{\text{GDP deflator in year 1}} \times 100.$$

Because the GDP deflator rose in year 2017 from 100 to 171, the inflation rate is $100 \times (171 - 100)/100$, or 71 percent. In 2018, the GDP deflator rose to 240 from 171 the previous year, so the inflation rate is $100 \times (240 - 171)/171$, or 40 percent.

The GDP deflator is one measure that economists use to monitor the average level of prices in the economy and thus the rate of inflation. The GDP deflator gets its name because it can be used to take inflation out of nominal GDP—that is, to "deflate" nominal GDP for the rise that is due to increases in prices. We examine another measure of the economy's price level, called the consumer price index, in the next chapter, where we also describe the differences between the two measures.

**A HALF CENTURY OF REAL GDP**

Now that we know how real GDP is defined and measured, let's look at what this macroeconomic variable tells us about the recent history of the United States. Figure 2 shows quarterly data on real GDP for the U.S. economy since 1965.

The most obvious feature of these data is that real GDP grows over time. The real GDP of the U.S. economy in 2015 was more than four times its 1965 level. Put differently, the output of goods and services produced in the United States has grown on average about 3 percent per year. This continued growth in real GDP enables most Americans to enjoy greater economic prosperity than their parents and grandparents did.

A second feature of the GDP data is that growth is not steady. The upward climb of real GDP is occasionally interrupted by periods during which GDP declines, called *recessions*. Figure 2 marks recessions with shaded vertical bars. (There is no ironclad rule for when the official business cycle dating committee will declare that a recession has occurred, but an old rule of thumb is two consecutive quarters of falling real GDP.) Recessions are associated not only with lower incomes but also with other forms of economic distress: rising unemployment, falling profits, increased bankruptcies, and so on.

Much of macroeconomics is aimed at explaining the long-run growth and short-run fluctuations in real GDP. As we will see in the coming chapters, we need different models for these two purposes. Because the short-run fluctuations represent deviations from the long-run trend, we first examine the behavior of key macroeconomic variables, including real GDP, in the long run. Then in later chapters, we build on this analysis to explain short-run fluctuations. ●

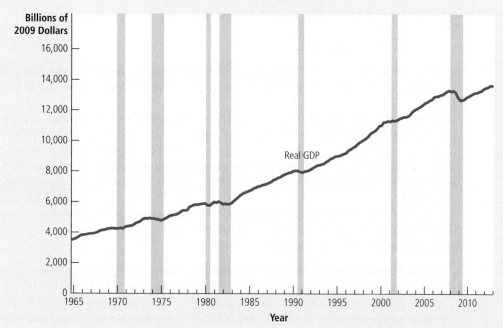

**FIGURE 2**

**Real GDP in the United States**

This figure shows quarterly data on real GDP for the U.S. economy since 1965. Recessions—periods of falling real GDP—are marked with the shaded vertical bars.

**Source:** U.S. Department of Commerce.

## Gauging the High-Tech Economy

*GDP measures the economy's total output. Labor productivity measures output per unit of labor input. If GDP is incorrectly measured, so is productivity.*

### Silicon Valley Doesn't Believe U.S. Productivity Is Down

**By Timothy Aeppel**

MOUNTAIN VIEW, Calif.—Google Inc. chief economist Hal Varian is an evangelist for Silicon Valley's contrarian take on America's productivity slump.

Swiveling to a large screen on the desk behind him, Mr. Varian types in a search for the most commonly asked question on the subject economists elsewhere are

wringing their hands over. Up pops, "What is productivity?"

See, he says, vindicated: "Most people don't know what it even means."

To Mr. Varian and other wealthy brains in the world's most innovative neighborhood, productivity means giving people and companies tools to do things better and faster. By that measure, there is an explosion under way, thanks to the shiny gadgets, apps and digital geegaws spewing out of Silicon Valley.

Official U.S. figures tell a different story. For a decade, economic output per hour worked—the federal government's formula for productivity—has barely budged.... Productivity matters, economists point out, because at a 2% annual growth rate, it takes 35 years to double the standard of living; at 1%,

it takes 70. Low productivity growth slows the economy and holds down wages.

The 68-year-old Mr. Varian, dressed in a purple hoodie and khaki pants, says the U.S. doesn't have a productivity problem, it has a measurement problem, a sound bite shaping up as the gospel according to Silicon Valley.

"There is a lack of appreciation for what's happening in Silicon Valley," he says, "because we don't have a good way to measure it."

One measurement problem is that a lot of what originates here is free or nearly free. Take, for example, a recent walk Mr. Varian

---

**QuickQuiz** *Define* real GDP *and* nominal GDP. *Which is a better measure of economic well-being? Why?*

# 15-5 Is GDP a Good Measure of Economic Well-Being?

Earlier in this chapter, GDP was called the single best measure of the economic well-being of a society. Now that we know what GDP is, we can evaluate this claim.

As we have seen, GDP measures both the economy's total income and the economy's total expenditure on goods and services. Thus, GDP per person tells us the income and expenditure of the average person in the economy. Because most people would prefer to receive higher income and enjoy higher expenditure, GDP per person seems a natural measure of the economic well-being of the average individual.

Yet some people dispute the validity of GDP as a measure of well-being. When Senator Robert Kennedy was running for president in 1968, he gave a moving critique of such economic measures:

> [Gross domestic product] does not allow for the health of our children, the quality of their education, or the joy of their play. It does not include the beauty of our poetry or the strength of our marriages, the intelligence of our public debate or the integrity of our public officials. It measures neither our courage,

arranged with friends. To find each other in the sprawling park nearby, he and his pals used an app that tracked their location, allowing them to meet up quickly. The same tool can track the movement of workers in a warehouse, office or shopping mall.

"Obviously that's a productivity enhancement," Mr. Varian says. "But I doubt that gets measured anywhere."

Consider the efficiency of hailing a taxi with an app on your mobile phone, or finding someone who will meet you at the airport and rent your car while you're away, a new service in San Francisco. Add in online tools that instantly translate conversations or help locate organ donors—the list goes on and on.

Surely, Mr. Varian says, they also make the U.S. more productive....

One problem with the government's productivity measure, Mr. Varian says, is that it is based on gross domestic product, the tally of goods and services produced by the U.S.

economy. GDP was conceived in the 1930s, when economists worried mostly about how much, for example, steel and grain were produced—output easy to measure compared with digital goods and services.

Technological improvements and time-saving apps are trickier. For one thing, it is tough to capture the full impact of quality improvements. For example, if a newer model car breaks down less often than older models but costs the same, the consumers' gain can get lost in the ether....

The U.S. Labor Department has sought to update its GDP measure over the years to include more intangibles, such as adjusting for higher quality. Productivity measures of computer chips, for example, are periodically updated to account for faster speeds. But critics say the process lags behind badly....

Silicon Valley's complaints echo earlier eras. The introduction in the last century of indoor plumbing and household appliances

drastically increased the efficiency of performing domestic chores. But since domestic labor isn't counted in GDP either, the time saved hauling water or washing clothes by hand didn't show up in productivity numbers.

However, these timesaving technologies—among other factors—eventually led to the flood of women into the workforce starting in the 1960s, which, in turn, sent U.S. output soaring.

Mr. Varian is convinced something similar will happen again. At the heart of his argument is the Internet search, cutting short the time to, say, learn how to grow geraniums or find the best Mexican restaurant—a free tool that provides uncounted value at home and at work.... "To be fair," he says, "as we adopt technologies that save time in these nonmarket activities, that frees up time for market-based activities which will show up in GDP." ■

**Source:** *The Wall Street Journal*, July 17, 2015.

nor our wisdom, nor our devotion to our country. It measures everything, in short, except that which makes life worthwhile, and it can tell us everything about America except why we are proud that we are Americans.

Much of what Robert Kennedy said is correct. Why, then, do we care about GDP?

The answer is that a large GDP does in fact help us to lead good lives. GDP does not measure the health of our children, but nations with larger GDP can afford better healthcare for their children. GDP does not measure the quality of their education, but nations with larger GDP can afford better educational systems. GDP does not measure the beauty of our poetry, but nations with larger GDP can afford to teach more of their citizens to read and enjoy poetry. GDP does not take account of our intelligence, integrity, courage, wisdom, or devotion to country, but all of these laudable attributes are easier to foster when people are less concerned about being able to afford the material necessities of life. In short, GDP does not directly measure those things that make life worthwhile, but it does measure our ability to obtain many of the inputs for a worthwhile life.

GDP is not, however, a perfect measure of well-being. Some things that contribute to a good life are left out of GDP. One is leisure. Suppose, for instance, that everyone in the economy suddenly started working every day of the week, rather than enjoying leisure on weekends. More goods and services would be produced, and GDP would rise. But despite the increase in GDP, we should not conclude that everyone would be better off. The loss from reduced leisure would offset the gain from producing and consuming a greater quantity of goods and services.

Because GDP uses market prices to value goods and services, it excludes the value of almost all activity that takes place outside markets. In particular, GDP

## IN THE NEWS

# Measuring Macroeconomic Well-Being

*Can we do better than using gross domestic product?*

### Nations Seek Success Beyond GDP

**By Mark Whitehouse**

Money isn't everything. But in measuring the success of nations, it isn't easy to find a substitute.

Political leaders are increasingly expressing dissatisfaction with gross domestic product—a monetary measure of all the goods and services a country produces—as a gauge of a nation's success in raising living standards.

In November, British Prime Minister David Cameron announced plans to build measures of national well-being that would take into account factors such as peoples' life satisfaction, following a similar effort by French President Nicolas Sarkozy.

Their efforts cut to the core of what economics is supposed to be about: What makes us better off? How can we all have more of it? Anyone hoping for a clear-cut answer, though, is likely to be disappointed.

"There is more to life than GDP, but it will be hard to come up with a single measure to replace it and we are not sure that a single measure is the answer," said Paul Allin, director of the Measuring National Well-Being

Project at the U.K.'s Office of National Statistics. "Maybe we live in a multidimensional world and we have to get used to handling a reasonable number of bits of information."

After a session on creating a national success indicator at the annual meeting of the American Economic Association on Friday, Carol Graham, fellow at the Brookings Institution, summed up the situation thus: "It's like a new science. There's still a lot of work to be done."

For much of the past four decades, economists have puzzled over a paradox that cast doubt on GDP as the world's main indicator of success.

People in richer countries didn't appear to be any happier than people in poor countries. In research beginning in the 1970s, University of Pennsylvania economist Richard Easterlin found no evidence of a link between countries' income—as measured by GDP per person— and peoples' reported levels of happiness.

More recent research suggests GDP isn't quite so bad. Using more data and different statistical techniques, three economists at the University of Pennsylvania's Wharton School—Daniel Sacks, Betsey Stevenson and Justin Wolfers—found that a given percentage increase in GDP per person tends to coincide with a similar increase in reported well-being. The correlation held across different countries and over time.

Still, for measuring the success of policy, GDP is far from ideal. Making everybody work 120 hours a week could radically boost a country's GDP per capita, but it wouldn't make people happier. Removing pollution limits could boost GDP per hour worked, but wouldn't necessarily lead to a world we'd want to live in.

One approach is to enhance GDP with other objective factors such as inequality, leisure and life expectancy. In a paper presented Saturday at the American Economic Association meeting, Stanford economists Peter Klenow and Charles Jones found that doing so can make a big difference.

By their calculation, accounting for longer life expectancy, additional leisure time and lower levels of inequality makes living standards in France and Germany look almost the same as those in the U.S., which otherwise leads the pack by a large margin.

Mr. Klenow points out that the calculation is fraught with difficulties. For one, many countries have poor data on crucial factors such as life expectancy.

omits the value of goods and services produced at home. When a chef prepares a delicious meal and sells it at her restaurant, the value of that meal is part of GDP. But if the chef prepares the same meal for her family, the value she has added to the raw ingredients is left out of GDP. Similarly, child care provided in day-care centers is part of GDP, whereas child care by parents at home is not. Volunteer work also contributes to the well-being of those in society, but GDP does not reflect these contributions.

Another thing that GDP excludes is the quality of the environment. Imagine that the government eliminated all environmental regulations. Firms could then produce goods and services without considering the pollution they create,

For the purpose of comparing well-being across countries, asking people how they feel might be better than monetary measures. Angus Deaton, an economist at Princeton University, notes that placing values on the extremely different goods and services consumed in the U.S. and, say, Tajikistan, can be impossible to do in a comparable way. Just asking people about their situation could be much easier and no less accurate.

Surveys already play a meaningful role in the way many countries assess their performance, from consumer confidence in the U.S. to the Netherlands's Life Situation Index, which accounts for factors such as relationships and community involvement.

As part of its effort to gauge well-being, the U.K. plans to add more subjective questions to its household surveys.

But surveys can also send misleading policy signals. Mr. Wolfers, for example, has found that surveys of women's subjective well-being in the U.S. suggest that they are less happy than they were four decades ago, despite improvements in wages, education and other objective measures. That, he says, doesn't mean the feminist movement should be reversed. Rather, it could be related to rising expectations or greater frankness among the women interviewed.

Peoples' true preferences are often revealed more by what they do than by what they say. Surveys suggest people with children tend to be less happy than those without, yet people keep having children—and nobody would advocate mass sterilization to improve overall well-being.

"What we care about in the world is not just happiness," says Mr. Wolfers. "If you measure just one part of what makes for a full life you're going to end up harming the other parts."

For the time being, that leaves policy makers to choose the measures of success that seem most appropriate for the task at hand. That's not ideal, but it's the best economics has to offer. ■

**Source:** *The Wall Street Journal,* January 10, 2011.

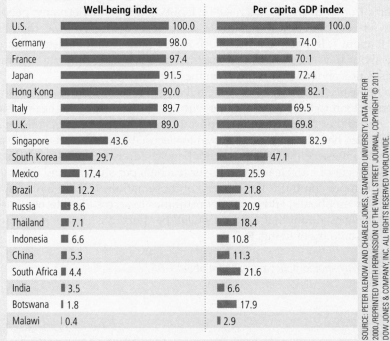

**Happily ever after**

More wealth doesn't always translate into greater quality of life, when factors such as leisure and length of life are included.

| | Well-being index | Per capita GDP index |
|---|---|---|
| U.S. | 100.0 | 100.0 |
| Germany | 98.0 | 74.0 |
| France | 97.4 | 70.1 |
| Japan | 91.5 | 72.4 |
| Hong Kong | 90.0 | 82.1 |
| Italy | 89.7 | 69.5 |
| U.K. | 89.0 | 69.8 |
| Singapore | 43.6 | 82.9 |
| South Korea | 29.7 | 47.1 |
| Mexico | 17.4 | 25.9 |
| Brazil | 12.2 | 21.8 |
| Russia | 8.6 | 20.9 |
| Thailand | 7.1 | 18.4 |
| Indonesia | 6.6 | 10.8 |
| China | 5.3 | 11.3 |
| South Africa | 4.4 | 21.6 |
| India | 3.5 | 6.6 |
| Botswana | 1.8 | 17.9 |
| Malawi | 0.4 | 2.9 |

**Source:** Peter Klenow and Charles Jones, Stanford University. Data are for 2000.

and GDP might rise. Yet well-being would most likely fall. The deterioration in the quality of air and water would more than offset the gains from greater production.

GDP also says nothing about the distribution of income. A society in which 100 people have annual incomes of $50,000 has GDP of $5 million and, not surprisingly, GDP per person of $50,000. So does a society in which 10 people earn $500,000 and 90 suffer with nothing at all. Few people would look at those two situations and call them equivalent. GDP per person tells us what happens to the average person, but behind the average lies a large variety of personal experiences.

In the end, we can conclude that GDP is a good measure of economic well-being for most—but not all—purposes. It is important to keep in mind what GDP includes and what it leaves out.

**CASE STUDY**

**INTERNATIONAL DIFFERENCES IN GDP AND THE QUALITY OF LIFE**
One way to gauge the usefulness of GDP as a measure of economic well-being is to examine international data. Rich and poor countries have vastly different levels of GDP per person. If a large GDP leads to a higher standard of living, then we should observe GDP to be strongly correlated with various measures of the quality of life. And, in fact, we do.

Table 3 shows twelve large nations ranked in order of GDP per person. The table also shows life expectancy at birth, the average years of schooling among adults, and an index of life satisfaction based on asking people to gauge how they feel about their lives on a scale of 0 to 10 (with 10 being the best). These data show a clear pattern. In rich countries, such as the United States and Germany, people can expect to live to about 80, have about 13 years of schooling, and rate their life satisfaction at about 7. In poor countries, such as Bangladesh and Pakistan, people typically die about 10 years earlier, have less than half as much schooling, and rate their life satisfaction about 2 points lower on the 10-point scale.

Data on other aspects of the quality of life tell a similar story. Countries with low GDP per person tend to have more infants with low birth weight, higher rates of infant mortality, higher rates of maternal mortality, and higher rates of child malnutrition. They also have lower rates of access to electricity, paved roads, and clean drinking water. In these countries, fewer school-age children are actually in school, those who are in school must learn with fewer teachers per student, and illiteracy among adults is more common. The citizens of these nations tend to have fewer televisions, fewer telephones, and fewer opportunities to access the Internet. International data leave no doubt that a nation's GDP per person is closely associated with its citizens' standard of living. ●

**QuickQuiz**   *Why should policymakers care about GDP?*

**TABLE 3**

**GDP and the Quality of Life**

The table shows GDP per person and three other measures of the quality of life for twelve major countries.

**Source:** *Human Development Report 2015,* United Nations. Real GDP is for 2014, expressed in 2011 dollars. Average years of schooling is among adults 25 years and older.

| Country | Real GDP per Person | Life Expectancy | Average Years of Schooling | Overall Life Satisfaction (0 to 10 scale) |
|---|---|---|---|---|
| United States | $52,947 | 79 years | 13 years | 7.2 |
| Germany | 43,919 | 81 | 13 | 7.0 |
| Japan | 36,927 | 83 | 12 | 5.9 |
| Russia | 22,352 | 70 | 12 | 6.0 |
| Mexico | 16,056 | 77 | 9 | 6.7 |
| Brazil | 15,175 | 74 | 8 | 7.0 |
| China | 12,547 | 76 | 8 | 5.2 |
| Indonesia | 9,788 | 69 | 8 | 5.6 |
| India | 5,497 | 68 | 5 | 4.4 |
| Nigeria | 5,341 | 53 | 6 | 4.8 |
| Pakistan | 4,866 | 66 | 5 | 5.4 |
| Bangladesh | 3,191 | 72 | 5 | 4.6 |

# 15-6 Conclusion

In this chapter we learned how economists measure the total income of a nation. Measurement is, of course, only a starting point. Much of macroeconomics is aimed at revealing the long-run and short-run determinants of a nation's gross domestic product. Why, for example, is GDP higher in the United States and Japan than in India and Nigeria? What can the governments of the poorest countries do to promote more rapid GDP growth? Why does GDP in the United States rise rapidly in some years and fall in others? What can U.S. policymakers do to reduce the severity of these fluctuations in GDP? These are the questions we will take up shortly.

At this point, it is important to acknowledge the significance of just measuring GDP. We all get some sense of how the economy is doing as we go about our lives. But the economists who study changes in the economy and the policymakers who formulate economic policies need more than this vague sense—they need concrete data on which to base their judgments. Quantifying the behavior of the economy with statistics such as GDP is, therefore, the first step to developing a science of macroeconomics.

## CHAPTER QuickQuiz

1. If the price of a hot dog is $2 and the price of a hamburger is $4, then 30 hot dogs contribute as much to GDP as _____ hamburgers.
   a. 5
   b. 15
   c. 30
   d. 60

2. Angus the sheep farmer sells wool to Barnaby the knitter for $20. Barnaby makes two sweaters, each of which has a market price of $40. Collette buys one of them, while the other remains on the shelf of Barnaby's store to be sold later. What is GDP here?
   a. $40
   b. $60
   c. $80
   d. $100

3. Which of the following does NOT add to U.S. GDP?
   a. Air France buys a plane from Boeing, the U.S. aircraft manufacturer.
   b. General Motors builds a new auto factory in North Carolina.
   c. The city of New York pays a salary to a policeman.
   d. The federal government sends a Social Security check to your grandmother.

4. An American buys a pair of shoes made in Italy. How do the U.S. national income accounts treat the transaction?
   a. Net exports and GDP both rise.
   b. Net exports and GDP both fall.
   c. Net exports fall, while GDP is unchanged.
   d. Net exports are unchanged, while GDP rises.

5. Which is the largest component of GDP?
   a. consumption
   b. investment
   c. government purchases
   d. net exports

6. If all quantities produced rise by 10 percent and all prices fall by 10 percent, which of the following occurs?
   a. Real GDP rises by 10 percent, while nominal GDP falls by 10 percent.
   b. Real GDP rises by 10 percent, while nominal GDP is unchanged.
   c. Real GDP is unchanged, while nominal GDP rises by 10 percent.
   d. Real GDP is unchanged, while nominal GDP falls by 10 percent.

## SUMMARY

- Because every transaction has a buyer and a seller, the total expenditure in the economy must equal the total income in the economy.
- Gross domestic product (GDP) measures an economy's total expenditure on newly produced goods and services and the total income earned from the production of these goods and services. More precisely, GDP is the market value of all final goods and services produced within a country in a given period of time.
- GDP is divided among four components of expenditure: consumption, investment, government purchases, and net exports. Consumption includes spending on goods and services by households, with the exception of purchases of new housing. Investment includes spending on business capital, residential capital, and inventories. Government purchases include spending

on goods and services by local, state, and federal governments. Net exports equal the value of goods and services produced domestically and sold abroad (exports) minus the value of goods and services produced abroad and sold domestically (imports).
- Nominal GDP uses current prices to value the economy's production of goods and services. Real GDP uses constant base-year prices to value the economy's production of goods and services. The GDP deflator—calculated from the ratio of nominal to real GDP—measures the level of prices in the economy.
- GDP is a good measure of economic well-being because people prefer higher to lower incomes. But it is not a perfect measure of well-being. For example, GDP excludes the value of leisure and the value of a clean environment.

## KEY CONCEPTS

microeconomics, p. 304
macroeconomics, p. 304
gross domestic product (GDP), p. 306
consumption, p. 309

investment, p. 309
government purchases, p. 310
net exports, p. 310
nominal GDP, p. 312

real GDP, p. 313
GDP deflator, p. 314

## QUESTIONS FOR REVIEW

1. Explain why an economy's income must equal its expenditure.

2. Which contributes more to GDP—the production of an economy car or the production of a luxury car? Why?

3. A farmer sells wheat to a baker for $2. The baker uses the wheat to make bread, which is sold for $3. What is the total contribution of these transactions to GDP?

4. Many years ago, Peggy paid $500 to put together a record collection. Today, she sold her albums at a garage sale for $100. How does this sale affect current GDP?

5. List the four components of GDP. Give an example of each.

6. Why do economists use real GDP rather than nominal GDP to gauge economic well-being?

7. In the year 2017, the economy produces 100 loaves of bread that sell for $2 each. In the year 2018, the economy produces 200 loaves of bread that sell for $3 each. Calculate nominal GDP, real GDP, and the GDP deflator for each year. (Use 2017 as the base year.) By what percentage does each of these three statistics rise from one year to the next?

8. Why is it desirable for a country to have a large GDP? Give an example of something that would raise GDP and yet be undesirable.

## PROBLEMS AND APPLICATIONS

1. What components of GDP (if any) would each of the following transactions affect? Explain.
   a. Uncle Henry buys a new refrigerator from a domestic manufacturer.
   b. Aunt Jane buys a new house from a local builder.
   c. The Jackson family buys an old Victorian house from the Walker family.
   d. You pay a hairdresser for a haircut.
   e. Ford sells a Mustang from its inventory to the Martinez family.
   f. Ford manufactures a Focus and sells it to Avis, the car rental company.
   g. California hires workers to repave Highway 101.
   h. The federal government sends your grandmother a Social Security check.
   i. Your parents buy a bottle of French wine.
   j. Honda expands its factory in Ohio.

2. Fill in the blanks:

| Year | Real GDP (in 2000 dollars) | Nominal GDP (in current dollars) | GDP Deflator (base year 2000) |
|------|------|------|------|
| 1970 | 3,000 | 1,200 | _____ |
| 1980 | 5,000 | _____ | 60 |
| 1990 | _____ | 6,000 | 100 |
| 2000 | _____ | 8,000 | _____ |
| 2010 | _____ | 15,000 | 200 |
| 2020 | 10,000 | _____ | 300 |
| 2030 | 20,000 | 50,000 | _____ |

3. The government purchases component of GDP does not include spending on transfer payments such as Social Security. Thinking about the definition of GDP, explain why transfer payments are excluded.

4. As the chapter states, GDP does not include the value of used goods that are resold. Why would including such transactions make GDP a less informative measure of economic well-being?

5. Below are some data from the land of milk and honey.

| Year | Price of Milk | Quantity of Milk | Price of Honey | Quantity of Honey |
|------|------|------|------|------|
| 2016 | $1 | 100 quarts | $2 | 50 quarts |
| 2017 | 1 | 200 | 2 | 100 |
| 2018 | 2 | 200 | 4 | 100 |

   a. Compute nominal GDP, real GDP, and the GDP deflator for each year, using 2016 as the base year.
   b. Compute the percentage change in nominal GDP, real GDP, and the GDP deflator in 2017 and 2018 from the preceding year. For each year, identify the variable that does not change. Explain why your answer makes sense.
   c. Did economic well-being increase more in 2017 or 2018? Explain.

6. Consider an economy that produces only chocolate bars. In year 1, the quantity produced is 3 bars and the price is $4. In year 2, the quantity produced is 4 bars and the price is $5. In year 3, the quantity produced is 5 bars and the price is $6. Year 1 is the base year.
   a. What is nominal GDP for each of these three years?
   b. What is real GDP for each of these years?
   c. What is the GDP deflator for each of these years?
   d. What is the percentage growth rate of real GDP from year 2 to year 3?
   e. What is the inflation rate as measured by the GDP deflator from year 2 to year 3?
   f. In this one-good economy, how might you have answered parts (d) and (e) without first answering parts (b) and (c)?

7. Consider the following data on U.S. GDP:

| Year | Nominal GDP (in billions of dollars) | GDP Deflator (base year 2009) |
|------|------|------|
| 2014 | 17,419 | 108.3 |
| 1994 | 7,309 | 73.8 |

   a. What was the growth rate of nominal GDP between 1994 and 2014? (*Hint*: The growth rate of a variable $X$ over an $N$-year period is calculated as $100 \times [(X_{final}/X_{initial})^{1/N} - 1]$.)
   b. What was the growth rate of the GDP deflator between 1994 and 2014?
   c. What was real GDP in 1994 measured in 2009 prices?
   d. What was real GDP in 2014 measured in 2009 prices?
   e. What was the growth rate of real GDP between 1994 and 2014?
   f. Was the growth rate of nominal GDP higher or lower than the growth rate of real GDP? Explain.

8. Revised estimates of U.S. GDP are usually released by the government near the end of each month. Find a newspaper article that reports on the most recent release, or read the news release yourself at http://www.bea.gov, the website of the U.S. Bureau of Economic Analysis. Discuss the recent changes in real and nominal GDP and in the components of GDP.

9. A farmer grows wheat, which she sells to a miller for $100. The miller turns the wheat into flour, which she sells to a baker for $150. The baker turns the wheat

into bread, which she sells to consumers for $180. Consumers eat the bread.

a. What is GDP in this economy? Explain.

b. *Value added* is defined as the value of a producer's output minus the value of the intermediate goods that the producer buys to make the output. Assuming there are no intermediate goods beyond those described above, calculate the value added of each of the three producers.

c. What is total value added of the three producers in this economy? How does it compare to the economy's GDP? Does this example suggest another way of calculating GDP?

10. Goods and services that are not sold in markets, such as food produced and consumed at home, are generally not included in GDP. Can you think of how this might cause the numbers in the second column of Table 3 to be misleading in a comparison of the economic well-being of the United States and India? Explain.

11. The participation of women in the U.S. labor force has risen dramatically since 1970.

a. How do you think this rise affected GDP?

b. Now imagine a measure of well-being that includes time spent working in the home and taking leisure. How would the change in this measure of well-being compare to the change in GDP?

c. Can you think of other aspects of well-being that are associated with the rise in women's labor-force participation? Would it be practical to construct a measure of well-being that includes these aspects?

12. One day, Barry the Barber, Inc., collects $400 for haircuts. Over this day, his equipment depreciates in value by $50. Of the remaining $350, Barry sends $30 to the government in sales taxes, takes home $220 in wages, and retains $100 in his business to add new equipment in the future. From the $220 that Barry takes home, he pays $70 in income taxes. Based on this information, compute Barry's contribution to the following measures of income.

a. gross domestic product

b. net national product

c. national income

d. personal income

e. disposable personal income

To find additional study resources, visit cengagebrain.com, and search for "Mankiw."

# Measuring the Cost of Living

In 1931, as the U.S. economy was suffering through the Great Depression, the New York Yankees paid famed baseball player Babe Ruth a salary of $80,000. At the time, this pay was extraordinary, even among the stars of baseball. According to one story, a reporter asked Ruth whether he thought it was right that he made more than President Herbert Hoover, who had a salary of $75,000. Ruth replied, "I had a better year."

In 2015, the average salary earned by major league baseball players was about $4 million, and Los Angeles Dodgers pitcher Clayton Kershaw was paid $31 million. At first, this fact might lead you to think that baseball has become vastly more lucrative over the past eight decades. But as everyone knows, the prices of goods and services have also risen.

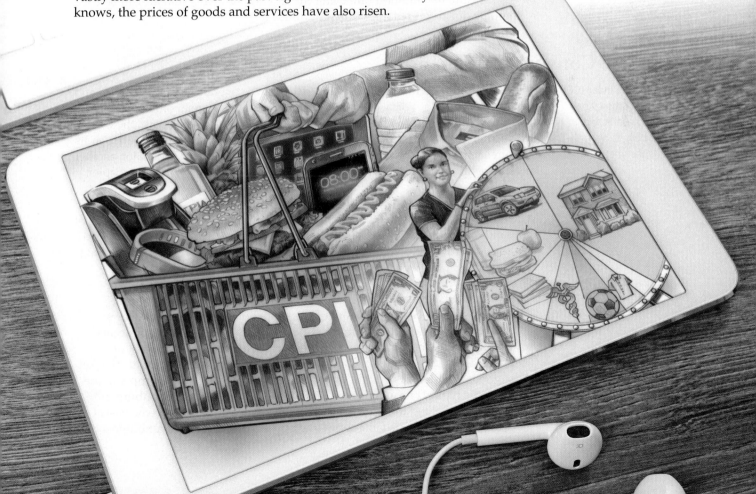

In 1931, a nickel would buy an ice-cream cone and a quarter would buy a ticket at the local movie theater. Because prices were so much lower in Babe Ruth's day than they are today, it is not clear whether Ruth enjoyed a higher or lower standard of living than today's players.

In the preceding chapter, we looked at how economists use gross domestic product (GDP) to measure the quantity of goods and services that the economy is producing. This chapter examines how economists measure the overall cost of living. To compare Babe Ruth's salary of $80,000 to salaries from today, we need to find some way of turning dollar figures into meaningful measures of purchasing power. That is exactly the job of a statistic called the *consumer price index*, or simply the CPI. After seeing how the CPI is constructed, we discuss how we can use such a price index to compare dollar figures from different points in time.

The CPI is used to monitor changes in the cost of living over time. When the CPI rises, the typical family has to spend more money to maintain the same standard of living. Economists use the term *inflation* to describe a situation in which the economy's overall price level is rising. The *inflation rate* is the percentage change in the price level from the previous period. The preceding chapter showed how economists can measure inflation using the GDP deflator. The inflation rate you are likely to hear on the nightly news, however, is calculated from the CPI, which better reflects the goods and services bought by consumers.

As we will see in the coming chapters, inflation is a closely watched aspect of macroeconomic performance and is a key variable guiding macroeconomic policy. This chapter provides the background for that analysis by showing how economists measure the inflation rate using the CPI and how this statistic can be used to compare dollar figures from different times.

# 16-1  The Consumer Price Index

**consumer price index (CPI)**
a measure of the overall cost of the goods and services bought by a typical consumer

The **consumer price index (CPI)** is a measure of the overall cost of the goods and services bought by a typical consumer. Every month, the Bureau of Labor Statistics (BLS), which is part of the Department of Labor, computes and reports the CPI. In this section, we discuss how the CPI is calculated and what problems arise in its measurement. We also consider how this index compares to the GDP deflator, another measure of the overall level of prices, which we examined in the preceding chapter.

### 16-1a  How the CPI Is Calculated

When the BLS calculates the CPI and the inflation rate, it uses data on the prices of thousands of goods and services. To see exactly how these statistics are constructed, let's consider a simple economy in which consumers buy only two goods: hot dogs and hamburgers. Table 1 shows the five steps that the BLS follows.

1. *Fix the basket.* Determine which prices are most important to the typical consumer. If the typical consumer buys more hot dogs than hamburgers, then the price of hot dogs is more important than the price of hamburgers and, therefore, should be given greater weight in measuring the cost of living. The BLS sets these weights by surveying consumers to find the basket of goods and services bought by the typical consumer. In the example in the table, the typical consumer buys a basket of 4 hot dogs and 2 hamburgers.
2. *Find the prices.* Find the prices of each of the goods and services in the basket at each point in time. The table shows the prices of hot dogs and hamburgers for three different years.

**Step 1: Survey Consumers to Determine a Fixed Basket of Goods**

Basket = 4 hot dogs, 2 hamburgers

**Step 2: Find the Price of Each Good in Each Year**

| Year | Price of Hot Dogs | Price of Hamburgers |
|------|------|------|
| 2016 | $1 | $2 |
| 2017 | 2 | 3 |
| 2018 | 3 | 4 |

**Step 3: Compute the Cost of the Basket of Goods in Each Year**

| | |
|---|---|
| 2016 | ($1 per hot dog × 4 hot dogs) + ($2 per hamburger × 2 hamburgers) = $8 per basket |
| 2017 | ($2 per hot dog × 4 hot dogs) + ($3 per hamburger × 2 hamburgers) = $14 per basket |
| 2018 | ($3 per hot dog × 4 hot dogs) + ($4 per hamburger × 2 hamburgers) = $20 per basket |

**Step 4: Choose One Year as a Base Year (2016) and Compute the CPI in Each Year**

| | |
|---|---|
| 2016 | ($8/$8) × 100 = 100 |
| 2017 | ($14/$8) × 100 = 175 |
| 2018 | ($20/$8) × 100 = 250 |

**Step 5: Use the CPI to Compute the Inflation Rate from Previous Year**

| | |
|---|---|
| 2017 | (175 − 100)/100 × 100 = 75% |
| 2018 | (250 − 175)/175 × 100 = 43% |

**TABLE 1**

**Calculating the Consumer Price Index and the Inflation Rate: An Example** This table shows how to calculate the CPI and the inflation rate for a hypothetical economy in which consumers buy only hot dogs and hamburgers.

3. *Compute the basket's cost.* Use the data on prices to calculate the cost of the basket of goods and services at different times. The table shows this calculation for each of the three years. Notice that only the prices in this calculation change. By keeping the basket of goods the same (4 hot dogs and 2 hamburgers), we are isolating the effects of price changes from the effects of any quantity changes that might be occurring at the same time.

4. *Choose a base year and compute the index.* Designate one year as the base year, the benchmark against which other years are to be compared. (The choice of base year is arbitrary. The index is used to measure percentage changes in the cost of living, and these changes are the same regardless of the choice of base year.) Once the base year is chosen, the index is calculated as follows:

$$\text{Consumer price index} = \frac{\text{Price of basket of goods and services in current year}}{\text{Price of basket in base year}} \times 100.$$

That is, the price of the basket of goods and services in each year is divided by the price of the basket in the base year, and this ratio is then multiplied by 100. The resulting number is the CPI.

In the example in Table 1, 2016 is the base year. In this year, the basket of hot dogs and hamburgers costs $8. Therefore, to calculate the CPI, the price of the basket in each year is divided by $8 and multiplied by 100. The CPI is 100 in 2016. (The index is always 100 in the base year.) The CPI is 175 in 2017. This means that the price of the basket in 2017 is 175 percent of its price in the base year. Put differently, a basket of goods that costs $100 in the base year costs

$175 in 2017. Similarly, the CPI is 250 in 2018, indicating that the price level in 2018 is 250 percent of the price level in the base year.

**inflation rate**
the percentage change in the price index from the preceding period

5. *Compute the inflation rate.* Use the CPI to calculate the **inflation rate**, which is the percentage change in the price index from the preceding period. That is, the inflation rate between two consecutive years is computed as follows:

$$\text{Inflation rate in year 2} = \frac{\text{CPI in year 2} - \text{CPI in year 1}}{\text{CPI in year 1}} \times 100.$$

As shown at the bottom of Table 1, the inflation rate in our example is 75 percent in 2017 and 43 percent in 2018.

Although this example simplifies the real world by including only two goods, it shows how the BLS computes the CPI and the inflation rate. The BLS collects and processes data on the prices of thousands of goods and services every month and, by following the five foregoing steps, determines how quickly the cost of living for the typical consumer is rising. When the BLS makes its monthly announcement of the CPI, you can usually hear the number on the evening television news or see it in the next day's newspaper.

In addition to the CPI for the overall economy, the BLS calculates several other price indexes. It reports the index for some narrow categories of goods and services, such as food, clothing, and energy. It also calculates the CPI for all goods

## FYI

# What's in the CPI's Basket?

When constructing the consumer price index, the Bureau of Labor Statistics tries to include all the goods and services that the typical consumer buys. Moreover, it tries to weight these goods and services according to how much consumers buy of each item.

Figure 1 shows the breakdown of consumer spending into the major categories of goods and services. By far the largest category is housing, which makes up 42 percent of the typical consumer's budget. This category includes the cost of shelter (33 percent), fuel and utilities (5 percent), and household furnishings and operation (4 percent). The next largest category, at 16 percent, is transportation, which includes spending on cars, gasoline, buses, subways, and so on. The next category, at 15 percent, is food and beverages; this includes food at home (8 percent), food away from home (6 percent), and alcoholic beverages (1 percent). Next are medical care at 8 percent, education and communication at 7 percent, and recreation at 6 percent. Apparel, which includes clothing, footwear, and jewelry, makes up 3 percent of the typical consumer's budget.

Also included in the figure, at 3 percent of spending, is a category for other goods and services. This is a catchall for consumer purchases (such as cigarettes, haircuts, and funeral expenses) that do not naturally fit into the other categories. ∎

## FIGURE 1

**The Typical Basket of Goods and Services**
This figure shows how the typical consumer divides spending among various categories of goods and services. The Bureau of Labor Statistics calls each percentage the "relative importance" of the category.

**Source:** Bureau of Labor Statistics.

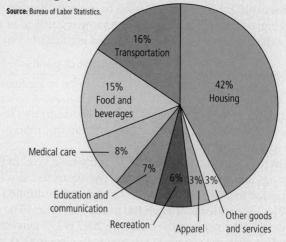

and services excluding food and energy, a statistic called the **core CPI**. Because food and energy prices show substantial short-run volatility, the core CPI better reflects ongoing inflation trends. Finally, the BLS also calculates the **producer price index** (PPI), which measures the cost of a basket of goods and services bought by firms rather than consumers. Because firms eventually pass on their costs to consumers in the form of higher consumer prices, changes in the PPI are often thought to be useful in predicting changes in the CPI.

**core CPI**
a measure of the overall cost of consumer goods and services excluding food and energy

**producer price index**
a measure of the cost of a basket of goods and services bought by firms

## 16-1b Problems in Measuring the Cost of Living

The goal of the consumer price index is to measure changes in the cost of living. In other words, the CPI tries to gauge how much incomes must rise to maintain a constant standard of living. The CPI, however, is not a perfect measure of the cost of living. Three problems with the index are widely acknowledged but difficult to solve.

The first problem is called *substitution bias*. When prices change from one year to the next, they do not all change proportionately: Some prices rise more than others. Consumers respond to these differing price changes by buying less of the goods whose prices have risen by relatively large amounts and by buying more of the goods whose prices have risen less or perhaps even have fallen. That is, consumers substitute toward goods that have become relatively less expensive. If a price index is computed assuming a fixed basket of goods, it ignores the possibility of consumer substitution and, therefore, overstates the increase in the cost of living from one year to the next.

Let's consider a simple example. Imagine that in the base year, apples are cheaper than pears, so consumers buy more apples than pears. When the BLS constructs the basket of goods, it will include more apples than pears. Suppose that next year pears are cheaper than apples. Consumers will naturally respond to the price changes by buying more pears and fewer apples. Yet when computing the CPI, the BLS uses a fixed basket, which in essence assumes that consumers continue buying the now expensive apples in the same quantities as before. For this reason, the index will measure a much larger increase in the cost of living than consumers actually experience.

The second problem with the CPI is the *introduction of new goods*. When a new good is introduced, consumers have more variety from which to choose, and this in turn reduces the cost of maintaining the same level of economic well-being. To see why, consider a hypothetical situation: Suppose you could choose between a $100 gift certificate at a large store that offered a wide array of goods and a $100 gift certificate at a small store with the same prices but a more limited selection. Which would you prefer? Most people would pick the store with greater variety. In essence, the increased set of possible choices makes each dollar more valuable. The same is true with the evolution of the economy over time: As new goods are introduced, consumers have more choices, and each dollar is worth more. But because the CPI is based on a fixed basket of goods and services, it does not reflect the increase in the value of the dollar that arises from the introduction of new goods.

Again, let's consider an example. When the iPod was introduced in 2001, consumers found it more convenient to listen to their favorite music. Devices to play music were available previously, but they were not nearly as portable and versatile. The iPod was a new option that increased consumers' set of opportunities. For any given number of dollars, the introduction of the iPod made people better off; conversely, achieving the same level of economic well-being required a smaller number of dollars. A perfect cost-of-living index would have reflected the introduction of the iPod with a decrease in the cost of living. The CPI, however, did not decrease in response to the introduction of the iPod. Eventually, the BLS revised the basket of goods to include the iPod, and subsequently, the index reflected changes in iPod prices. But the reduction in the cost of living associated with the initial introduction of the iPod never showed up in the index.

The third problem with the CPI is *unmeasured quality change*. If the quality of a good deteriorates from one year to the next while its price remains the same, the value of a dollar falls, because you are getting a lesser good for the same amount of money. Similarly, if the quality rises from one year to the next, the value of a dollar rises. The BLS does its best to account for quality change. When the quality of a good in the basket changes—for example, when a car model has more horsepower or gets better gas mileage from one year to the next—the Bureau adjusts the price of the good to account for the quality change. It is, in essence,

## IN THE NEWS

# Monitoring Inflation in the Internet Age

*The web is providing alternative ways to collect data on the overall level of prices.*

### Do We Need Google to Measure Inflation?

By Annie Lowrey

At some 23,000 retailers and businesses in 90 U.S. cities, hundreds of government workers find and mark down prices on very precise products. And I'm not kidding when I say "very precise."

Say the relevant worker is finding the price for a motel room. She might write a report like this: *Occupancy*—two adults; *Type of accommodation*—deluxe room; *Room classification/location*—ocean view, room 306; *Time of stay*—weekend; *Length of stay*—one night; *Bathroom facilities*—one full bathroom; *Kitchen facilities*—none; *Television*—one, includes free movie channel; *Telephone*—one telephone, free local calls; *Air-conditioned*—yes; *Meals included*—breakfast; *Parking*—free self parking; *Transportation*—Transportation to airport, no charge; *Recreation facilities*—an indoor and an outdoor pool, a private beach, three tennis courts, and an exercise room.

This mind-numbingly tedious process goes on for a dizzying panoply of items:

wine, takeaway meals, bedroom furniture, surgical procedures, pet dogs, college tuition, cigarettes, haircuts, funerals. When all of the prices are marked down, the workers submit forms that are collated, checked, and input into massive spreadsheets. Then the government boils all those numbers down to one. It weights certain prices, taking into account that consumers spend more on rent than cereal, for instance. It considers product improvements and changes in spending habits. Then it comes up with a master number showing how much a customer's spending needed to increase to buy the same goods, month-on-month. That number is the Consumer Price Index, the government's main gauge of inflation.

Each month, the Bureau of Labor Statistics goes through all that hassle because knowing the rate of inflation is such an important measure of economic health—and it's important to the government's own budget. High inflation? Savers panic, watching the spending power of their accounts erode. Deflation? Everyone saves, awaiting cheaper prices in a few months. And wildly changing inflation makes it difficult for businesses and consumers to make economic decisions. Moreover, the government needs to know the rate of inflation to index certain payments, like Social Security benefits or interest payments on TIPS bonds.

But just because the government expends so much energy determining the rate of inflation does not mean it is tallying it in the smartest or most accurate way. The reigning methodology is, well, clunky. It costs Washington around $234 million a year to get all those people to go and bear witness to a $1.57 price increase in a packet of tube socks and then to massage those individual data points down to one number. Moreover, there is a weekslong lag between the checkers tallying up the numbers and the government announcing the changes: The inflation measure comes out only 12 times a year, though prices change, sometimes dramatically, all the time. Plus, the methodology is archaic, given that we live in the Internet age. Prices are easily available online and a lot of shopping happens on the Web rather than in stores.

But there might be a better way. In the last few months, economists have come up with new methods for calculating inflation at Internet speed—nimbler, cheaper, faster, and perhaps even more accurate than Washington's. The first comes from the Massachusetts Institute of Technology. In

trying to compute the price of a basket of goods of constant quality. Despite these efforts, changes in quality remain a problem because quality is hard to measure.

There is still much debate among economists about how severe these measurement problems are and what should be done about them. Several studies written during the 1990s concluded that the CPI overstated inflation by about 1 percentage point per year. In response to this criticism, the BLS adopted several technical changes to improve the CPI, and many economists believe that the bias is now only about half as large as it once was. The issue is important because many government programs use the CPI to adjust for changes in the overall level of prices. Recipients of Social Security, for instance, get annual increases in benefits that are tied to the CPI. Some economists have suggested modifying these programs to correct for the measurement problems by, for instance, reducing the magnitude of the automatic benefit increases.

2007, economists Roberto Rigobon and Alberto Cavallo started tracking prices online and inputting them into a massive database. Then, last month, they unveiled the Billion Prices Project, an inflation measure based on 5 million items sold by 300 online retailers in 70 countries. (For the United States, the BPP collects about 500,000 prices.)

The BPP's inflation measure is markedly different from the government's. The economists just average all the prices culled online, meaning the basket of goods is whatever you can buy on the Web. (Some things, like books, are most often bought online. Some items, like cats, are not.) Plus, the researchers do not weight certain items' prices, even if they tend to make up a bigger proportion of household spending.

Still, thus far, the BPP has tracked the CPI closely. And the online-based measure has additional advantages. It comes out daily, giving a better sense of inflation's direction. It also lets researchers examine minute, day-to-day price changes. For instance, this month Rigobon and Cavallo noted that Black Friday discounts "had a smaller effect on average prices in 2010 than in 2009," contrary to reports of deeper discounting this year. And it has already produced some academic insights. For instance, Cavallo found that retailers change prices less often, but more, percentage-wise, than economists previously thought.

A second inflation measure comes from Web behemoth Google and is a pet project of

the company's chief economist, Hal Varian. As reported by the *Financial Times*, earlier this year, Varian decided to use Google's vast database of Web prices to construct the "Google Price Index," a constantly updated measure of price changes and inflation. (The idea came to him when he was searching for a pepper grinder online.) Google has not yet decided whether it will publish the price index, and has not released its methodology. But Varian said that his preliminary index tracked CPI closely, though it did show periods of

"I wonder how much this costs online."

deflation—the worrisome incidence of prices actually falling—where the CPI did not.

The new indices lead to the big question of whether the government *needs* to update its methods to account for changes in the economy—taking new pricing trends into consideration, rejiggering its formula, updating more frequently. The answer might be yes. (Economists have reformed the CPI before.) But the CPI and its Stone Age method of calculation boasts one huge benefit: It's a stable, tested measure, consistent over time, since its methodology doesn't change much. Moreover, and somewhat remarkably, the Google and Billion Prices Project indices actually seem to confirm the accuracy of the old-fashioned CPI, tracking it closely rather than showing it to be off-base.

Ultimately, there is a good argument for *more* inflation measures, not just better or newer ones. The government already calculates a number of rates of inflation to give a fuller picture of price changes, the value of money, and the economy. Most notably, the BLS publishes a "core inflation" number, a measure of inflation outside volatile food and energy prices. There are dozens of other measures, as well. The new Web-based yardsticks provide even more alternatives and opportunities to examine the accuracy of the CPI—and to make new findings. That means, for now, those detective-like government rubes painstakingly checking prices on clipboards get to stay in work. ∎

**Source:** *Slate*, December 20, 2010.

### 16-1c   The GDP Deflator versus the Consumer Price Index

In the preceding chapter, we examined another measure of the overall level of prices in the economy—the GDP deflator. The GDP deflator is the ratio of nominal GDP to real GDP. Because nominal GDP is current output valued at current prices and real GDP is current output valued at base-year prices, the GDP deflator reflects the current level of prices relative to the level of prices in the base year.

Economists and policymakers monitor both the GDP deflator and the CPI to gauge how quickly prices are rising. Usually, these two statistics tell a similar story. Yet two important differences can cause them to diverge.

The first difference is that the GDP deflator reflects the prices of all goods and services *produced domestically*, whereas the CPI reflects the prices of all goods and services *bought by consumers*. For example, suppose that the price of an airplane produced by Boeing and sold to the Air Force rises. Even though the plane is part of GDP, it is not part of the basket of goods and services bought by a typical consumer. Thus, the price increase shows up in the GDP deflator but not in the CPI.

As another example, suppose that Volvo raises the price of its cars. Because Volvos are made in Sweden, the car is not part of U.S. GDP. But U.S. consumers buy Volvos, so the car is part of the typical consumer's basket of goods. Hence, a price increase in an imported consumption good, such as a Volvo, shows up in the CPI but not in the GDP deflator.

This first difference between the CPI and the GDP deflator is particularly important when the price of oil changes. The United States produces some oil, but much of the oil we use is imported. As a result, oil and oil products such as gasoline and heating oil make up a much larger share of consumer spending than of GDP. When the price of oil rises, the CPI rises by much more than does the GDP deflator.

The second and subtler difference between the GDP deflator and the CPI concerns how various prices are weighted to yield a single number for the overall level of prices. The CPI compares the price of a *fixed* basket of goods and services to the price of the basket in the base year. Only occasionally does the BLS change the basket of goods. By contrast, the GDP deflator compares the price of *currently produced* goods and services to the price of the same goods and services in the base year. Thus, the group of goods and services used to compute the GDP deflator changes automatically over time. This difference is not important when all prices are changing proportionately. But if the prices of different goods and services are changing by varying amounts, the way we weight the various prices matters for the overall inflation rate.

Figure 2 shows the inflation rate as measured by both the GDP deflator and the CPI for each year since 1965. You can see that sometimes the two measures diverge. When they do diverge, it is possible to go behind these numbers and explain the divergence with the two differences we have discussed. For example, in 1979 and 1980, CPI inflation spiked up more than the GDP deflator largely because oil prices more than doubled during these two years. Yet divergence between these two measures is the exception rather than the rule. In the 1970s, both the GDP deflator and the CPI show high rates of inflation. In the late 1980s, 1990s, and the first decade of the 2000s, both measures show low rates of inflation.

THE WALL STREET JOURNAL

| AUDiO - VIDEO |

FROM THE WALL STREET JOURNAL—PERMISSION, CARTOON FEATURES SYNDICATE

*"The price may seem a little high, but you have to remember that's in today's dollars."*

 **QuickQuiz**   *Explain briefly what the CPI measures and how it is constructed.*
• *Identify one reason why the CPI is an imperfect measure of the cost of living.*

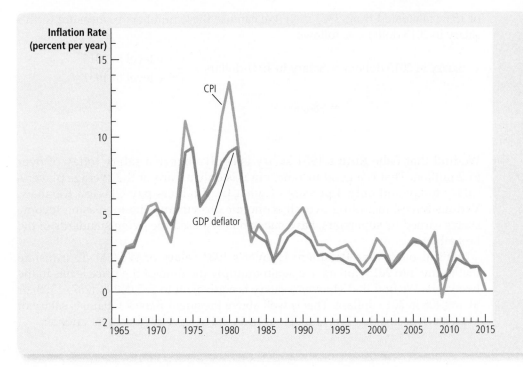

**FIGURE 2**

**Two Measures of Inflation**
This figure shows the inflation rate—the percentage change in the level of prices—as measured by the GDP deflator and the CPI using annual data since 1965. Notice that the two measures of inflation generally move together.

**Source:** U.S. Department of Labor; U.S. Department of Commerce.

## 16-2 Correcting Economic Variables for the Effects of Inflation

The purpose of measuring the overall level of prices in the economy is to allow us to compare dollar figures from different times. Now that we know how price indexes are calculated, let's see how we might use such an index to compare a dollar figure from the past to a dollar figure in the present.

### 16-2a Dollar Figures from Different Times

We first return to the issue of Babe Ruth's salary. Was his salary of $80,000 in 1931 high or low compared to the salaries of today's players?

To answer this question, we need to know the level of prices in 1931 and the level of prices today. Part of the increase in baseball salaries compensates players for higher prices today. To compare Ruth's salary to those of today's players, we need to inflate Ruth's salary to turn 1931 dollars into today's dollars.

The formula for turning dollar figures from year $T$ into today's dollars is the following:

$$\text{Amount in today's dollars} = \text{Amount in year } T \text{ dollars} \times \frac{\text{Price level today}}{\text{Price level in year } T}.$$

A price index such as the CPI measures the price level and thus determines the size of the inflation correction.

Let's apply this formula to Ruth's salary. Government statistics show a CPI of 15.2 for 1931 and 237 for 2015. Thus, the overall level of prices has risen by a factor of 15.6 (calculated from 237/15.2). We can use these numbers to measure Ruth's salary in 2015 dollars, as follows:

$$\text{Salary in 2015 dollars} = \text{Salary in 1931 dollars} \times \frac{\text{Price level in 2015}}{\text{Price level in 1931}}$$

$$= \$80,000 \times \frac{237}{15.2}$$

$$= \$1,247,368.$$

We find that Babe Ruth's 1931 salary is equivalent to a salary today of over $1.2 million. That is a good income, but it is only a third of the average player's salary today and only 4 percent of what the Dodgers pay Clayton Kershaw. Various forces, including overall economic growth and the increasing income shares earned by superstars, have substantially raised the living standards of the best athletes.

Let's also examine President Hoover's 1931 salary of $75,000. To translate that figure into 2015 dollars, we again multiply the ratio of the price levels in the two years. We find that Hoover's salary is equivalent to $75,000 × (237/15.2), or $1,169,408 in 2015 dollars. This is well above President Barack Obama's salary of $400,000. It seems that President Hoover did have a pretty good year after all.

---

## Mr. Index Goes to Hollywood

What is the most popular movie of all time? The answer might surprise you.

Movie popularity is usually gauged by box office receipts. By that measure, *Star Wars: The Force Awakens* is the number-one movie of all time with domestic receipts of $923 million, followed by *Avatar* ($761 million) and *Titanic* ($659 million). But this ranking ignores an obvious but important fact: Prices, including those of movie tickets, have been rising over time. Inflation gives an advantage to newer films.

When we correct box office receipts for the effects of inflation, the story is very different. The number-one movie is now *Gone with the Wind* ($1,758 million), followed by the original *Star Wars* ($1,550 million) and *The Sound of Music* ($1,239 million). *Star Wars: The Force Awakens* falls to number 11.

*Gone with the Wind* was released in 1939, before everyone had televisions in their homes. In the 1930s, about 90 million Americans went to the cinema each week, compared to about 25 million today. But the movies from that era don't show up in conventional popularity rankings because ticket prices were only a quarter. And indeed, in the ranking based on nominal box office receipts, *Gone with the Wind* does not make the top 100 films. Scarlett and Rhett fare a lot better once we correct for the effects of inflation. ■

"May the force of inflation be with you."

LUCAS FILMS/BAD ROBOT/WALT DISNEY PRODUCTIONS / ALBUM/NEWSCOM

**REGIONAL DIFFERENCES IN THE COST OF LIVING**

CASE STUDY

When you graduate from college, you may well have several job offers from which to choose. Not surprisingly, some jobs pay more than others. If the jobs are located in different places, however, be careful when comparing them. The cost of living varies not only over time but also over geography. What seems like a larger paycheck might not turn out to be so once you take into account regional differences in the prices of goods and services.

The Bureau of Economic Analysis has used the data collected for the CPI to compare prices around the United States. The resulting statistic is called *regional price parities*. Just as the CPI measures variation in the cost of living from year to year, regional price parities measure variation in the cost of living from state to state.

Figure 3 shows the regional price parities for 2013. For example, living in the state of New York costs 115.3 percent of what it costs to live in the typical place in the United States (that is, New York is 15.3 percent more expensive than average).

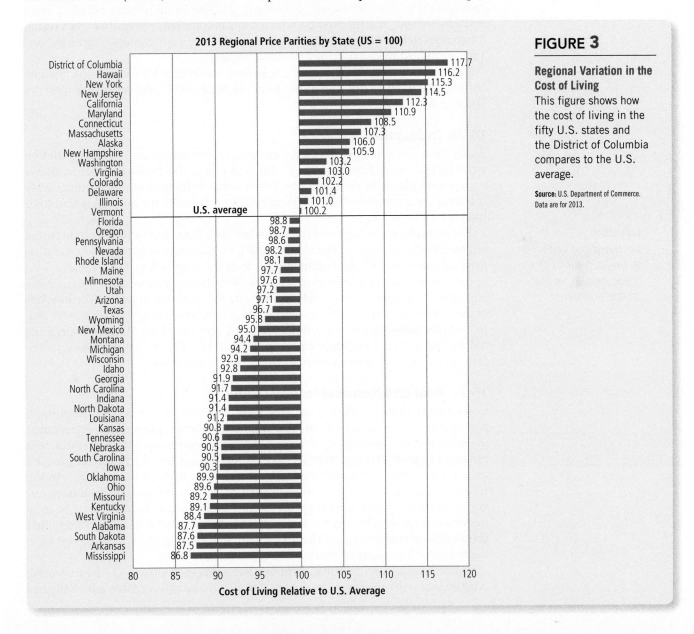

**FIGURE 3**

**Regional Variation in the Cost of Living**
This figure shows how the cost of living in the fifty U.S. states and the District of Columbia compares to the U.S. average.

**Source:** U.S. Department of Commerce. Data are for 2013.

Living in Mississippi costs 86.8 percent of what it costs to live in the typical place (that is, Mississippi is 13.2 percent less expensive than average).

What accounts for these differences? It turns out that the prices of goods, such as food and clothing, explain only a small part of these regional differences. Most goods are tradable: They can be easily transported from one state to another. As a consequence of regional trade, large price disparities are unlikely to persist for long.

Services explain a larger part of these regional differences. A haircut, for example, can cost more in one state than another. If barbers were willing to move to where the price of a haircut is high, or if customers were willing to fly across the country in search of cheap haircuts, then the prices of haircuts across regions might well converge. But because transporting haircuts is so costly, large price disparities can persist.

Housing services are particularly important for understanding regional differences in the cost of living. Such services represent a large share of a typical consumer's budget. Moreover, once built, a house or apartment building can't easily be moved, and the land on which it sits is completely immobile. As a result, differences in housing costs can be persistently large. For example, rents in New York are almost twice what they are in Mississippi.

Keep these facts in mind when it comes time to compare job offers. Look not only at the dollar salaries but also at the local prices of goods and services, especially housing. ●

## 16-2b Indexation

As we have just seen, price indexes are used to correct for the effects of inflation when comparing dollar figures from different times. This type of correction shows up in many places in the economy. When some dollar amount is automatically corrected for changes in the price level by law or contract, the amount is said to be **indexed** for inflation.

**indexation**
the automatic correction by law or contract of a dollar amount for the effects of inflation

For example, many long-term contracts between firms and unions include partial or complete indexation of the wage to the CPI. Such a provision, called a *cost-of-living allowance* (or COLA), automatically raises the wage when the CPI rises.

Indexation is also a feature of many laws. Social Security benefits, for instance, are adjusted every year to compensate the elderly for increases in prices. The brackets of the federal income tax—the income levels at which the tax rates change—are also indexed for inflation. There are, however, many ways in which the tax system is not indexed for inflation, even when perhaps it should be. We discuss these issues more fully when we discuss the costs of inflation later in this book.

## 16-2c Real and Nominal Interest Rates

Correcting economic variables for the effects of inflation is particularly important, and somewhat tricky, when we look at data on interest rates. The very concept of an interest rate necessarily involves comparing amounts of money at different points in time. When you deposit your savings in a bank account, you give the bank some money now, and the bank returns your deposit with interest in the future. Similarly, when you borrow from a bank, you get some money now, but you will have to repay the loan with interest in the future. In both cases, to fully understand the deal between you and the bank, it is crucial to acknowledge that future dollars could have a different value than today's dollars. That is, you have to correct for the effects of inflation.

Let's consider an example. Suppose Sally Saver deposits $1,000 in a bank account that pays an annual interest rate of 10 percent. A year later, after Sally has accumulated $100 in interest, she withdraws her $1,100. Is Sally $100 richer than she was when she made the deposit a year earlier?

The answer depends on what we mean by "richer." Sally does have $100 more than she had before. In other words, the number of dollars in her possession has risen by 10 percent. But Sally does not care about the amount of money itself: She cares about what she can buy with it. If prices have risen while her money was in the bank, each dollar now buys less than it did a year ago. In this case, her purchasing power—the amount of goods and services she can buy—has not risen by 10 percent.

To keep things simple, let's suppose that Sally is a movie fan and buys only DVDs. When Sally made her deposit, a DVD cost $10. Her deposit of $1,000 was equivalent to 100 DVDs. A year later, after getting her 10 percent interest, she has $1,100. How many DVDs can she buy now? It depends on what has happened to the price of a DVD. Here are some examples:

- Zero inflation: If the price of a DVD remains at $10, the amount she can buy has risen from 100 to 110 DVDs. The 10 percent increase in the number of dollars means a 10 percent increase in her purchasing power.
- Six percent inflation: If the price of a DVD rises from $10 to $10.60, then the number of DVDs she can buy has risen from 100 to approximately 104. Her purchasing power has increased by about 4 percent.
- Ten percent inflation: If the price of a DVD rises from $10 to $11, she can still buy only 100 DVDs. Even though Sally's dollar wealth has risen, her purchasing power is the same as it was a year earlier.
- Twelve percent inflation: If the price of a DVD increases from $10 to $11.20, the number of DVDs she can buy has fallen from 100 to approximately 98. Even with her greater number of dollars, her purchasing power has decreased by about 2 percent.

And if Sally were living in an economy with deflation—falling prices—another possibility could arise:

- Two percent deflation: If the price of a DVD falls from $10 to $9.80, then the number of DVDs she can buy rises from 100 to approximately 112. Her purchasing power increases by about 12 percent.

These examples show that the higher the rate of inflation, the smaller the increase in Sally's purchasing power. If the rate of inflation exceeds the rate of interest, her purchasing power actually falls. And if there is deflation (that is, a negative rate of inflation), her purchasing power rises by more than the rate of interest.

To understand how much a person earns in a savings account, we need to consider both the interest rate and the change in prices. The interest rate that measures the change in dollar amounts is called the **nominal interest rate**, and the interest rate corrected for inflation is called the **real interest rate**. The nominal interest rate, the real interest rate, and inflation are related approximately as follows:

**nominal interest rate**
the interest rate as usually reported without a correction for the effects of inflation

$$\text{Real interest rate} = \text{Nominal interest rate} - \text{Inflation rate.}$$

The real interest rate is the difference between the nominal interest rate and the rate of inflation. The nominal interest rate tells you how fast the number of dollars in your bank account rises over time, while the real interest rate tells you how fast the purchasing power of your bank account rises over time.

**real interest rate**
the interest rate corrected for the effects of inflation

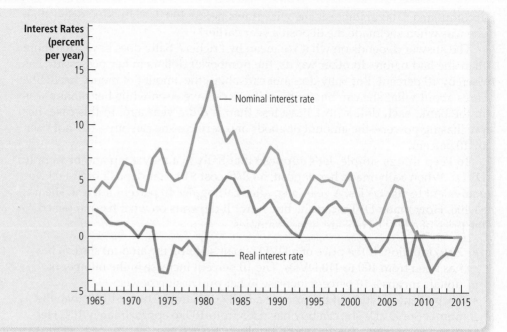

## FIGURE 4

**Real and Nominal Interest Rates**

This figure shows nominal and real interest rates using annual data since 1965. The nominal interest rate is the rate on a three-month Treasury bill. The real interest rate is the nominal interest rate minus the inflation rate as measured by the CPI. Notice that nominal and real interest rates often do not move together.

**Source:** U.S. Department of Labor; U.S. Department of Treasury.

**CASE STUDY**

### INTEREST RATES IN THE U.S. ECONOMY

Figure 4 shows real and nominal interest rates in the U.S. economy since 1965. The nominal interest rate in this figure is the rate on three-month Treasury bills (although data on other interest rates would be similar). The real interest rate is computed by subtracting the rate of inflation from this nominal interest rate. Here the inflation rate is measured as the percentage change in the CPI.

One feature of this figure is that the nominal interest rate almost always exceeds the real interest rate. This reflects the fact that the U.S. economy has experienced rising consumer prices in almost every year during this period. By contrast, if you look at data for the U.S. economy during the late 19th century or for the Japanese economy in some recent years, you will find periods of deflation. During deflation, the real interest rate exceeds the nominal interest rate.

The figure also shows that because inflation is variable, real and nominal interest rates do not always move together. For example, in the late 1970s, nominal interest rates were high. But because inflation was very high, real interest rates were low. Indeed, during much of the 1970s, real interest rates were negative, for inflation eroded people's savings more quickly than nominal interest payments increased them. By contrast, in the late 1990s, nominal interest rates were lower than they had been two decades earlier. But because inflation was much lower, real interest rates were higher. In the coming chapters, we will examine the economic forces that determine both real and nominal interest rates. ●

**QuickQuiz**  *Henry Ford paid his workers $5 a day in 1914. If the CPI was 10 in 1914 and 237 in 2015, how much is the Ford paycheck worth in 2015 dollars?*

# 16-3 Conclusion

"A nickel ain't worth a dime anymore," the late, great baseball player Yogi Berra once observed. Indeed, throughout recent history, the real values behind the nickel, the dime, and the dollar have not been stable. Persistent increases in the overall level of prices have been the norm. Such inflation reduces the purchasing power of each unit of money over time. When comparing dollar figures from different times, it is important to keep in mind that a dollar today is not the same as a dollar 20 years ago or, most likely, 20 years from now.

This chapter has discussed how economists measure the overall level of prices in the economy and how they use price indexes to correct economic variables for the effects of inflation. Price indexes allow us to compare dollar figures from different points in time and, therefore, get a better sense of how the economy is changing.

The discussion of price indexes in this chapter, together with the preceding chapter's discussion of GDP, is only the first step in the study of macroeconomics. We have not yet examined what determines a nation's GDP or the causes and effects of inflation. To do that, we need to go beyond issues of measurement. Indeed, that is our next task. Having explained how economists measure macroeconomic quantities and prices in the last chapter, we are now ready to develop the models that explain movements in these variables.

Here is our strategy in the upcoming chapters. First, we look at the long-run determinants of real GDP and related variables, such as saving, investment, real interest rates, and unemployment. Second, we look at the long-run determinants of the price level and related variables, such as the money supply, inflation, and nominal interest rates. Last of all, having seen how these variables are determined in the long run, we examine the more complex question of what causes short-run fluctuations in real GDP and the price level. In all of these chapters, the measurement issues we have just discussed will provide the foundation for the analysis.

---

## CHAPTER Quick**Quiz**

1. The CPI measures approximately the same economic phenomenon as
   a. nominal GDP.
   b. real GDP.
   c. the GDP deflator.
   d. the unemployment rate.

2. The largest component in the basket of goods and services used to compute the CPI is
   a. food and beverages.
   b. housing.
   c. medical care.
   d. apparel.

3. If a Pennsylvania gun manufacturer raises the price of rifles it sells to the U.S. Army, its price hikes will increase
   a. both the CPI and the GDP deflator.
   b. neither the CPI nor the GDP deflator.
   c. the CPI but not the GDP deflator.
   d. the GDP deflator but not the CPI.

4. Because consumers can sometimes substitute cheaper goods for those that have risen in price,
   a. the CPI overstates inflation.
   b. the CPI understates inflation.
   c. the GDP deflator overstates inflation.
   d. the GDP deflator understates inflation.

5. If the CPI is 200 in year 1980 and 300 today, then $600 in 1980 has the same purchasing power as _____ today.
   a. $400
   b. $500
   c. $700
   d. $900

6. You deposit $2,000 in a savings account, and a year later you have $2,100. Meanwhile, the CPI rises from 200 to 204. In this case, the nominal interest rate is _____ percent, and the real interest rate is _____ percent.
   a. 1, 5
   b. 3, 5
   c. 5, 1
   d. 5, 3

## SUMMARY

- The consumer price index (CPI) shows the cost of a basket of goods and services relative to the cost of the same basket in the base year. The index is used to measure the overall level of prices in the economy. The percentage change in the CPI measures the inflation rate.

- The CPI is an imperfect measure of the cost of living for three reasons. First, it does not take into account consumers' ability to substitute toward goods that become relatively cheaper over time. Second, it does not take into account increases in the purchasing power of the dollar due to the introduction of new goods. Third, it is distorted by unmeasured changes in the quality of goods and services. Because of these measurement problems, the CPI overstates true inflation.

- Like the CPI, the GDP deflator measures the overall level of prices in the economy. The two price indexes usually move together, but there are important differences. The GDP deflator differs from the CPI because it includes goods and services produced rather than goods and services consumed. As a result, imported goods affect the CPI but not the GDP deflator. In addition, while the CPI uses a fixed basket of goods, the GDP deflator automatically changes the group of goods and services over time as the composition of GDP changes.

- Dollar figures from different times do not represent a valid comparison of purchasing power. To compare a dollar figure from the past to a dollar figure today, the older figure should be inflated using a price index.

- Various laws and private contracts use price indexes to correct for the effects of inflation. The tax laws, however, are only partially indexed for inflation.

- A correction for inflation is especially important when looking at data on interest rates. The nominal interest rate is the interest rate usually reported; it is the rate at which the number of dollars in a savings account increases over time. By contrast, the real interest rate takes into account changes in the value of the dollar over time. The real interest rate equals the nominal interest rate minus the rate of inflation.

## KEY CONCEPTS

consumer price index (CPI), p. 326
inflation rate, p. 328
core CPI, p. 329

producer price index, p. 329
indexation, p. 336

nominal interest rate, p. 337
real interest rate, p. 337

## QUESTIONS FOR REVIEW

1. Which do you think has a greater effect on the CPI: a 10 percent increase in the price of chicken or a 10 percent increase in the price of caviar? Why?

2. Describe the three problems that make the CPI an imperfect measure of the cost of living.

3. If the price of imported French wine rises, is the CPI or the GDP deflator affected more? Why?

4. Over a long period of time, the price of a candy bar rose from $0.20 to $1.20. Over the same period, the CPI rose from 150 to 300. Adjusted for overall inflation, how much did the price of the candy bar change?

5. Explain the meaning of *nominal interest rate* and *real interest rate*. How are they related?

## PROBLEMS AND APPLICATIONS

1. Suppose that the year you were born someone bought $100 of goods and services for your baby shower. How much would you guess it would cost today to buy a similar amount of goods and services? Now find data on the CPI and compute the answer based on it. (You can find the BLS's inflation calculator here: http://www.bls.gov/data/inflation_calculator.htm).

2. The residents of Vegopia spend all of their income on cauliflower, broccoli, and carrots. In 2016, they spend a total of $200 for 100 heads of cauliflower, $75 for 50 bunches of broccoli, and $50 for 500 carrots. In 2017, they spend a total of $225 for 75 heads of cauliflower, $120 for 80 bunches of broccoli, and $100 for 500 carrots.
   a. Calculate the price of one unit of each vegetable in each year.
   b. Using 2016 as the base year, calculate the CPI for each year.
   c. What is the inflation rate in 2017?

3. Suppose that people consume only three goods, as shown in this table:

   |              | Tennis Balls | Golf Balls | Bottles of Gatorade |
   | ------------ | ------------ | ---------- | ------------------- |
   | 2017 price    | $2           | $4         | $1                  |
   | 2017 quantity | 100          | 100        | 200                 |
   | 2018 price    | $2           | $6         | $2                  |
   | 2018 quantity | 100          | 100        | 200                 |

   a. What is the percentage change in the price of each of the three goods?
   b. Using a method similar to the CPI, compute the percentage change in the overall price level.
   c. If you were to learn that a bottle of Gatorade increased in size from 2017 to 2018, should that information affect your calculation of the inflation rate? If so, how?
   d. If you were to learn that Gatorade introduced new flavors in 2018, should that information affect your calculation of the inflation rate? If so, how?

4. Go to the website of the Bureau of Labor Statistics (http://www.bls.gov) and find data on the CPI. By how much has the index including all items risen over the past year? For which categories of spending have prices risen the most? The least? Have any categories experienced price declines? Can you explain any of these facts?

5. A small nation of ten people idolizes the TV show *The Voice*. All they produce and consume are karaoke machines and CDs, in the following amounts:

   |      | Karaoke Machines | | CDs | |
   |      | Quantity | Price | Quantity | Price |
   | ---- | -------- | ----- | -------- | ----- |
   | 2017 | 10       | $40   | 30       | $10   |
   | 2018 | 12       | 60    | 50       | 12    |

   a. Using a method similar to the CPI, compute the percentage change in the overall price level. Use 2017 as the base year and fix the basket at 1 karaoke machine and 3 CDs.
   b. Using a method similar to the GDP deflator, compute the percentage change in the overall price level. Also use 2017 as the base year.
   c. Is the inflation rate in 2018 the same using the two methods? Explain why or why not.

6. Which of the problems in the construction of the CPI might be illustrated by each of the following situations? Explain.
   a. the invention of cell phones
   b. the introduction of air bags in cars
   c. increased personal computer purchases in response to a decline in their price
   d. more scoops of raisins in each package of Raisin Bran
   e. greater use of fuel-efficient cars after gasoline prices increase

7. A dozen eggs cost $0.88 in January 1980 and $2.11 in January 2015. The average wage for production workers was $7.58 per hour in January 1980 and $19.64 in January 2015.
   a. By what percentage did the price of eggs rise?
   b. By what percentage did the wage rise?
   c. In each year, how many minutes did a worker have to work to earn enough to buy a dozen eggs?
   d. Did workers' purchasing power in terms of eggs rise or fall?

8. The chapter explains that Social Security benefits are increased each year in proportion to the increase in the CPI, even though most economists believe that the CPI overstates actual inflation.
   a. If the elderly consume the same market basket as other people, does Social Security provide the elderly with an improvement in their standard of living each year? Explain.
   b. In fact, the elderly consume more healthcare compared to younger people, and healthcare costs have risen faster than overall inflation. What would you do to determine whether the elderly are actually better off from year to year?

9. Suppose that a borrower and a lender agree on the nominal interest rate to be paid on a loan. Then inflation turns out to be higher than they both expected.
   a. Is the real interest rate on this loan higher or lower than expected?
   b. Does the lender gain or lose from this unexpectedly high inflation? Does the borrower gain or lose?
   c. Inflation during the 1970s was much higher than most people had expected when the decade began. How did this affect homeowners who obtained fixed-rate mortgages during the 1960s? How did it affect the banks that lent the money?

To find additional study resources, visit cengagebrain.com, and search for "Mankiw."

# PART VII

# The Real Economy in the Long Run

# Production and Growth

**W**hen you travel around the world, you see tremendous variation in the standard of living. The average income in a rich country, such as the United States, Japan, or Germany, is about ten times the average income in a poor country, such as India, Nigeria, or Nicaragua. These large differences in income are reflected in large differences in the quality of life. People in richer countries have better nutrition, safer housing, better healthcare, and longer life expectancy as well as more automobiles, more telephones, and more computers.

Even within a country, there are large changes in the standard of living over time. In the United States over the past century, average income as measured by real gross domestic product (GDP) per person has grown by about 2 percent per year. Although 2 percent might

seem small, this rate of growth implies that average income doubles every 35 years. Because of this growth, most Americans enjoy much greater economic prosperity than did their parents, grandparents, and great-grandparents.

Growth rates vary substantially from country to country. From 2000 to 2014, GDP per person in China grew at a rate of 11 percent per year, accumulating to a 357 percent increase in average income. A country experiencing such rapid growth can, in one generation, go from being among the poorest in the world to being among the richest. By contrast, in the same time span, income per person in Zimbabwe fell by a total of 13 percent, leaving the typical citizen mired in poverty.

What explains these diverse experiences? How can rich countries maintain their high standard of living? What policies can poor countries pursue to promote more rapid growth and join the developed world? These are among the most important questions in macroeconomics. As the Nobel-Prize-winning economist Robert Lucas put it, "The consequences for human welfare in questions like these are simply staggering: Once one starts to think about them, it is hard to think about anything else."

In the previous two chapters, we discussed how economists measure macroeconomic quantities and prices. We can now begin to study the forces that determine these variables. As we have seen, an economy's GDP measures both the total income earned in the economy and the total expenditure on the economy's output of goods and services. The level of real GDP is a good gauge of economic prosperity, and the growth of real GDP is a good gauge of economic progress. In this chapter we focus on the long-run determinants of the level and growth of real GDP. Later, we study the short-run fluctuations of real GDP around its long-run trend.

We proceed here in three steps. First, we examine international data on real GDP per person. These data will give you some sense of how much the level and growth of living standards vary around the world. Second, we examine the role of *productivity*—the amount of goods and services produced for each hour of a worker's time. In particular, we see that a nation's standard of living is determined by the productivity of its workers, and we consider the factors that determine a nation's productivity. Third, we consider the link between productivity and the economic policies that a nation pursues.

# 17-1 Economic Growth around the World

As a starting point for our study of long-run growth, let's look at the experiences of some of the world's economies. Table 1 shows data on real GDP per person for thirteen countries. For each country, the data span over a century of history. The first and second columns of the table present the countries and time periods. (The time periods differ somewhat from country to country because of differences in data availability.) The third and fourth columns show estimates of real GDP per person more than a century ago and for a recent year.

The data on real GDP per person show that living standards vary widely from country to country. Income per person in the United States, for instance, is now about four times that in China and about ten times that in India. The poorest countries have average levels of income not seen in the developed world for many decades. The typical resident of Pakistan in 2014 had about the same real income as the typical resident of the United Kingdom in 1870. The typical Bangladeshi in 2014 had considerably less real income than a typical American in 1870.

TABLE 1

The Variety of Growth Experiences

| Country | Period | Real GDP per Person | | Growth Rate (per year) |
| | | At Beginning of Period[a] | At End of Period[a] | |
|---|---|---|---|---|
| Brazil | 1900–2014 | $ 828 | $15,590 | 2.61% |
| Japan | 1890–2014 | 1,600 | 37,920 | 2.59 |
| China | 1900–2014 | 762 | 13,170 | 2.53 |
| Mexico | 1900–2014 | 1,233 | 16,640 | 2.31 |
| Germany | 1870–2014 | 2,324 | 46,850 | 2.11 |
| Indonesia | 1900–2014 | 948 | 10,190 | 2.10 |
| Canada | 1870–2014 | 2,527 | 43,360 | 1.99 |
| India | 1900–2014 | 718 | 5,630 | 1.82 |
| United States | 1870–2014 | 4,264 | 55,860 | 1.80 |
| Pakistan | 1900–2014 | 785 | 5,090 | 1.65 |
| Argentina | 1900–2014 | 2,440 | 12,510 | 1.44 |
| Bangladesh | 1900–2014 | 663 | 3,330 | 1.43 |
| United Kingdom | 1870–2014 | 5,117 | 39,040 | 1.42 |

[a]Real GDP is measured in 2014 dollars.

**Source:** Robert J. Barro and Xavier Sala-i-Martin, *Economic Growth* (New York: McGraw-Hill, 1995), Tables 10.2 and 10.3; *World Bank* online data; and author's calculations. To account for international price differences, data are PPP-adjusted when available.

The last column of the table shows each country's growth rate. The growth rate measures how rapidly real income per person grew in the typical year. In the United States, for example, where real income per person was $4,264 in 1870 and $55,860 in 2014, the growth rate was 1.80 percent per year. This means that if real income per person, beginning at $4,264, were to increase by 1.80 percent for each of 144 years, it would end up at $55,860. Of course, income did not rise exactly 1.80 percent every year: Some years it rose by more, other years it rose by less, and in still other years it fell. The growth rate of 1.80 percent per year ignores short-run fluctuations around the long-run trend and represents an average rate of growth for real income per person over many years.

The countries in Table 1 are ordered by their growth rate from the most to the least rapid. Here you can see the large variety in growth experiences. High on the list are Brazil and China, which went from being among the poorest nations in the world to being among middle-income nations. Also high on the list is Japan, which went from being a middle-income nation to being among the richest nations.

Near the bottom of the list you can find Pakistan and Bangladesh, which were among the poorest nations at the end of the nineteenth century and remain so today. At the bottom of the list is the United Kingdom. In 1870, the United Kingdom was the richest country in the world, with average income about 20 percent higher than that of the United States and more than twice Canada's. Today, average income in the United Kingdom is 30 percent below that of the United States and 10 percent below Canada's.

These data show that the world's richest countries have no guarantee they will stay the richest and that the world's poorest countries are not doomed to remain forever in poverty. But what explains these changes over time? Why do some countries zoom ahead while others lag behind? These are precisely the questions that we take up next.

**Quick Quiz** *What has been the approximate long-run growth rate of real GDP per person in the United States? Name a country that has had faster growth and a country that has had slower growth.*

# 17-2 Productivity: Its Role and Determinants

Explaining why living standards vary so much around the world is, in one sense, very easy. The answer can be summarized in a single word—*productivity*. But in another sense, the international variation in living standards is deeply puzzling. To explain why incomes are so much higher in some countries than in others, we must look at the many factors that determine a nation's productivity.

### 17-2a Why Productivity Is So Important

Let's begin our study of productivity and economic growth by developing a simple model based loosely on Daniel Defoe's famous novel *Robinson Crusoe* about a sailor stranded on a desert island. Because Crusoe lives alone, he

---

**FYI**

## Are You Richer Than the Richest American?

*A*merican Heritage magazine once published a list of the richest Americans of all time. The number 1 spot went to John D. Rockefeller, the oil entrepreneur who lived from 1839 to 1937. According to the magazine's calculations, his wealth would today be the equivalent of about $200 billion, almost three times that of Bill Gates, the software entrepreneur who is today's richest American.

Despite his great wealth, Rockefeller did not enjoy many of the conveniences that we now take for granted. He couldn't watch television, play video games, surf the Internet, or send e-mail. During the heat of summer, he couldn't cool his home with air-conditioning. For much of his life, he couldn't travel by car or plane, and he couldn't use a telephone to call friends or family. If he became ill, he couldn't take advantage of many medicines, such as antibiotics, that doctors today routinely use to prolong and enhance life.

John D. Rockefeller

Now consider: How much money would someone have to pay you to give up for the rest of your life all the modern conveniences that Rockefeller lived without? Would you do it for $200 billion? Perhaps not. And if you wouldn't, is it fair to say that you are better off than John D. Rockefeller, allegedly the richest American ever?

The preceding chapter discussed how standard price indexes, which are used to compare sums of money from different points in time, fail to fully reflect the introduction of new goods in the economy. As a result, the rate of inflation is overestimated. The flip side of this observation is that the rate of real economic growth is underestimated. Pondering Rockefeller's life shows how significant this problem might be. Because of tremendous technological advances, the average American today is arguably "richer" than the richest American a century ago, even if that fact is lost in standard economic statistics. ■

BETTMANN/GETTY IMAGES

catches his own fish, grows his own vegetables, and makes his own clothes. We can think of Crusoe's activities—his production and consumption of fish, vegetables, and clothing—as a simple economy. By examining Crusoe's economy, we can learn some lessons that also apply to more complex and realistic economies.

What determines Crusoe's standard of living? In a word, **productivity**, the quantity of goods and services produced from each unit of labor input. If Crusoe is good at catching fish, growing vegetables, and making clothes, he lives well. If he is bad at doing these things, he lives poorly. Because Crusoe gets to consume only what he produces, his living standard is tied to his productivity.

In the case of Crusoe's economy, it is easy to see that productivity is the key determinant of living standards and that growth in productivity is the key determinant of growth in living standards. The more fish Crusoe can catch per hour, the more he eats at dinner. If Crusoe finds a better place to catch fish, his productivity rises. This increase in productivity makes Crusoe better off: He can eat the extra fish, or he can spend less time fishing and devote more time to making other goods he enjoys.

Productivity's key role in determining living standards is as true for nations as it is for stranded sailors. Recall that an economy's GDP measures two things at once: the total income earned by everyone in the economy and the total expenditure on the economy's output of goods and services. GDP can measure these two things simultaneously because, for the economy as a whole, they must be equal. Put simply, an economy's income is the economy's output.

Like Crusoe, a nation can enjoy a high standard of living only if it can produce a large quantity of goods and services. Americans live better than Nigerians because American workers are more productive than Nigerian workers. The Japanese have enjoyed more rapid growth in living standards than Argentineans because Japanese workers have experienced more rapid growth in productivity. Indeed, one of the *Ten Principles of Economics* in Chapter 1 is that a country's standard of living depends on its ability to produce goods and services.

Hence, to understand the large differences in living standards we observe across countries or over time, we must focus on the production of goods and services. But seeing the link between living standards and productivity is only the first step. It leads naturally to the next question: Why are some economies so much better at producing goods and services than others?

### 17-2b How Productivity Is Determined

Although productivity is uniquely important in determining Robinson Crusoe's standard of living, many factors determine Crusoe's productivity. Crusoe will be better at catching fish, for instance, if he has more fishing poles, if he has been trained in the best fishing techniques, if his island has a plentiful fish supply, or if he invents a better fishing lure. Each of these determinants of Crusoe's productivity—which we can call *physical capital, human capital, natural resources,* and *technological knowledge*—has a counterpart in more complex and realistic economies. Let's consider each factor in turn.

**Physical Capital per Worker**   Workers are more productive if they have tools with which to work. The stock of equipment and structures used to produce goods and services is called **physical capital**, or just *capital*. For example,

**productivity**
the quantity of goods and services produced from each unit of labor input

**physical capital**
the stock of equipment and structures that are used to produce goods and services

## A Picture Is Worth a Thousand Statistics

George Bernard Shaw once said, "It is the mark of a truly intelligent person to be moved by statistics." Most of us, however, have trouble being moved by data on GDP—until we see with our own eyes what these statistics represent.

The three photos on these pages show a typical family from each of three countries—the United Kingdom, Mexico, and Mali. Each family was photographed outside their home, together with all their material possessions.

These nations have very different standards of living, as judged by these photos, GDP, or other statistics.

- The United Kingdom is an advanced economy. In 2014, its income per person was $39,040. A baby born in the United Kingdom can expect a relatively healthy childhood: Only 4 out of 1,000 children die before reaching age 5. Almost the entire population has access to modern sanitation facilities, such as a bathroom and sewer system, to safely remove human waste. Educational attainment is high: Among individuals of college age, 60 percent are enrolled in higher education.

- Mexico is a middle-income country. In 2014, its income per person was $16,640. About 13 out of 1,000 children die before age 5. About 85 percent have access to modern sanitation. Among those of college age, 30 percent are enrolled.

- Mali is a poor country. In 2014, its income per person was only $1,510. Life is often cut short: 115 out of 1,000 children die before age 5. Only 25 percent of the population has access to modern sanitation. And educational attainment in Mali is low: Among those of college age, only 7 percent are enrolled.

Economists who study economic growth try to understand what causes such large differences in the standard of living. ■

A Typical Family in the United Kingdom

DAVID REED - FROM MATERIAL WORLD

A Typical Family in Mexico

A Typical Family in Mali

when woodworkers make furniture, they use saws, lathes, and drill presses. More tools allow the woodworkers to produce their output more quickly and more accurately: A worker with only basic hand tools can make less furniture each week than a worker with sophisticated and specialized woodworking equipment.

As you may recall, the inputs used to produce goods and services—labor, capital, and so on—are called the *factors of production*. An important feature of capital is that it is a *produced* factor of production. That is, capital is an input into the production process that in the past was an output from the production process. The woodworker uses a lathe to make the leg of a table. Earlier, the lathe itself was the output of a firm that manufactures lathes. The lathe manufacturer in turn used other equipment to make its product. Thus, capital is a factor of production used to produce all kinds of goods and services, including more capital.

**Human Capital per Worker**  A second determinant of productivity is human capital. **Human capital** is the economist's term for the knowledge and skills that workers acquire through education, training, and experience. Human capital includes the skills accumulated in early childhood programs, grade school, high school, college, and on-the-job training for adults in the labor force.

**human capital**
the knowledge and skills that workers acquire through education, training, and experience

Education, training, and experience are less tangible than lathes, bulldozers, and buildings, but human capital is similar to physical capital in many ways. Like physical capital, human capital raises a nation's ability to produce goods and services. Also like physical capital, human capital is a produced factor of production. Producing human capital requires inputs in the form of teachers, libraries, and student time. Indeed, students can be viewed as "workers" who have the important job of producing the human capital that will be used in future production.

**natural resources**
the inputs into the production of goods and services that are provided by nature, such as land, rivers, and mineral deposits

**Natural Resources per Worker**  A third determinant of productivity is **natural resources**. Natural resources are inputs into production that are provided by nature, such as land, rivers, and mineral deposits. Natural resources take two forms: renewable and nonrenewable. A forest is an example of a renewable resource. When one tree is cut down, a seedling can be planted in its place to be harvested in the future. Oil is an example of a nonrenewable resource. Because oil is produced by nature over many millions of years, there is only a limited supply. Once the supply of oil is depleted, it is impossible to create more.

Differences in natural resources are responsible for some of the differences in standards of living around the world. The historical success of the United States was driven in part by the large supply of land well suited for agriculture. Today, some countries in the Middle East, such as Kuwait and Saudi Arabia, are rich simply because they happen to be on top of some of the largest pools of oil in the world.

Although natural resources can be important, they are not necessary for an economy to be highly productive in producing goods and services. Japan, for instance, is one of the richest countries in the world, despite having few natural resources. International trade makes Japan's success possible. Japan imports many of the natural resources it needs, such as oil, and exports its manufactured goods to economies rich in natural resources.

**Technological Knowledge**   A fourth determinant of productivity is **technological knowledge**—the understanding of the best ways to produce goods and services. A hundred years ago, most Americans worked on farms because farm technology required a high input of labor to feed the entire population. Today, thanks to advances in farming technology, a small fraction of the population can produce enough food to feed the entire country. This technological change made labor available to produce other goods and services.

Technological knowledge takes many forms. Some technology is common knowledge—after one person uses it, everyone becomes aware of it. For example, once Henry Ford successfully introduced assembly-line production, other carmakers quickly followed suit. Other technology is proprietary—it is known only by the company that discovers it. Only the Coca-Cola Company, for instance, knows the secret recipe for making its famous soft drink. Still other technology is proprietary for a short time. When a pharmaceutical company discovers a new drug, the patent system gives that company a temporary right to be its exclusive manufacturer. When the patent expires, however, other companies are allowed to make the drug. All these forms of technological knowledge are important for the economy's production of goods and services.

It is worthwhile to distinguish between technological knowledge and human capital. Although they are closely related, there is an important difference.

**technological knowledge** society's understanding of the best ways to produce goods and services

---

## The Production Function

Economists often use a *production function* to describe the relationship between the quantity of inputs used in production and the quantity of output from production. For example, suppose $Y$ denotes the quantity of output, $L$ the quantity of labor, $K$ the quantity of physical capital, $H$ the quantity of human capital, and $N$ the quantity of natural resources. Then we might write

$$Y = AF(L, K, H, N),$$

where $F(\ )$ is a function that shows how the inputs are combined to produce output. $A$ is a variable that reflects the available production technology. As technology improves, $A$ rises, so the economy produces more output from any given combination of inputs.

Many production functions have a property called *constant returns to scale*. If a production function has constant returns to scale, then doubling all inputs causes the amount of output to double as well. Mathematically, we write that a production function has constant returns to scale if, for any positive number $x$,

$$xY = AF(xL, xK, xH, xN).$$

A doubling of all inputs would be represented in this equation by $x = 2$. The right side shows the inputs doubling, and the left side shows output doubling.

Production functions with constant returns to scale have an interesting and useful implication. To see this implication, set $x = 1/L$ so that the preceding equation becomes

$$Y/L = AF(1, K/L, H/L, N/L).$$

Notice that $Y/L$ is output per worker, which is a measure of productivity. This equation says that labor productivity depends on physical capital per worker ($K/L$), human capital per worker ($H/L$), and natural resources per worker ($N/L$). Productivity also depends on the state of technology, as reflected by the variable $A$. Thus, this equation provides a mathematical summary of the four determinants of productivity we have just discussed. ■

Technological knowledge refers to society's understanding about how the world works. Human capital refers to the resources expended transmitting this understanding to the labor force. To use a relevant metaphor, technological knowledge is the quality of society's textbooks, whereas human capital is the amount of time that the population has devoted to reading them. Workers' productivity depends on both.

**CASE STUDY**

### ARE NATURAL RESOURCES A LIMIT TO GROWTH?

Today, the world's population is over 7 billion, more than four times what it was a century ago. At the same time, many people are enjoying a much higher standard of living than did their great-grandparents. A perennial debate concerns whether this growth in population and living standards can continue in the future.

Many commentators have argued that natural resources will eventually limit how much the world's economies can grow. At first, this argument might seem hard to ignore. If the world has only a fixed supply of nonrenewable natural resources, how can population, production, and living standards continue to grow over time? Eventually, won't supplies of oil and minerals start to run out? When these shortages start to occur, won't they stop economic growth and, perhaps, even force living standards to fall?

Despite the apparent appeal of such arguments, most economists are less concerned about such limits to growth than one might guess. They argue that technological progress often yields ways to avoid these limits. If we compare the economy today to the economy of the past, we see various ways in which the use of natural resources has improved. Modern cars have better gas mileage. New houses have better insulation and require less energy to heat and cool. More efficient oil rigs waste less oil in the process of extraction. Recycling allows some nonrenewable resources to be reused. The development of alternative fuels, such as ethanol instead of gasoline, allows us to substitute renewable for nonrenewable resources.

Seventy years ago, some conservationists were concerned about the excessive use of tin and copper. At the time, these were crucial commodities: Tin was used to make many food containers, and copper was used to make telephone wire. Some people advocated mandatory recycling and rationing of tin and copper so that supplies would be available for future generations. Today, however, plastic has replaced tin as a material for making many food containers, and phone calls often travel over fiber-optic cables, which are made from sand. Technological progress has made once crucial natural resources less necessary.

But are all these efforts enough to permit continued economic growth? One way to answer this question is to look at the prices of natural resources. In a market economy, scarcity is reflected in market prices. If the world were running out of natural resources, then the prices of those resources would be rising over time. But in fact, the opposite is more often true. Natural resource prices exhibit substantial short-run fluctuations, but over long spans of time, the prices of most natural resources (adjusted for overall inflation) are stable or falling. It appears that our ability to conserve these resources is growing more rapidly than their supplies are dwindling. Market prices give no reason to believe that natural resources are a limit to economic growth. ●

**QuickQuiz**   *List and describe four determinants of a country's productivity.*

# 17-3 Economic Growth and Public Policy

So far, we have determined that a society's standard of living depends on its ability to produce goods and services and that its productivity in turn depends on physical capital per worker, human capital per worker, natural resources per worker, and technological knowledge. Let's now turn to the question faced by policymakers around the world: What can government policy do to raise productivity and living standards?

## 17-3a Saving and Investment

Because capital is a produced factor of production, a society can change the amount of capital it has. If today the economy produces a large quantity of new capital goods, then tomorrow it will have a larger stock of capital and be able to produce more goods and services. Thus, one way to raise future productivity is to invest more current resources in the production of capital.

One of the *Ten Principles of Economics* presented in Chapter 1 is that people face trade-offs. This principle is especially important when considering the accumulation of capital. Because resources are scarce, devoting more resources to producing capital requires devoting fewer resources to producing goods and services for current consumption. That is, for society to invest more in capital, it must consume less and save more of its current income. The growth that arises from capital accumulation is not a free lunch: It requires that society sacrifice consumption of goods and services in the present to enjoy higher consumption in the future.

The next chapter examines in more detail how an economy's financial markets coordinate saving and investment. It also examines how government policies influence the amount of saving and investment that take place. At this point, it is important to note that encouraging saving and investment is one way that a government can encourage growth and, in the long run, raise an economy's standard of living.

## 17-3b Diminishing Returns and the Catch-Up Effect

Suppose that a government pursues policies that raise the nation's saving rate—the percentage of GDP devoted to saving rather than consumption. What happens? With the nation saving more, fewer resources are needed to make consumption goods and more resources are available to make capital goods. As a result, the capital stock increases, leading to rising productivity and more rapid growth in GDP. But how long does this higher rate of growth last? Assuming that the saving rate remains at its new, higher level, does the growth rate of GDP stay high indefinitely or only for a period of time?

The traditional view of the production process is that capital is subject to **diminishing returns**: As the stock of capital rises, the extra output produced from an additional unit of capital falls. In other words, when workers already have a large quantity of capital to use in producing goods and services, giving them an additional unit of capital increases their productivity only slightly. This is illustrated in Figure 1, which shows how the amount of capital per worker determines the amount of output per worker, holding constant all the other determinants of output (such as natural resources and technological knowledge).

Because of diminishing returns, an increase in the saving rate leads to higher growth only for a while. As the higher saving rate allows more capital to be accumulated, the benefits from additional capital become smaller over time, and

**diminishing returns**
the property whereby the benefit from an extra unit of an input declines as the quantity of the input increases

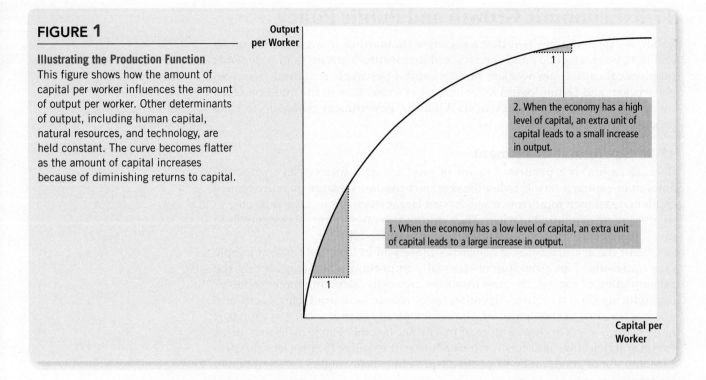

## FIGURE 1

**Illustrating the Production Function**
This figure shows how the amount of capital per worker influences the amount of output per worker. Other determinants of output, including human capital, natural resources, and technology, are held constant. The curve becomes flatter as the amount of capital increases because of diminishing returns to capital.

Output per Worker

2. When the economy has a high level of capital, an extra unit of capital leads to a small increase in output.

1. When the economy has a low level of capital, an extra unit of capital leads to a large increase in output.

Capital per Worker

so growth slows down. *In the long run, the higher saving rate leads to a higher level of productivity and income but not to higher growth in these variables.* Reaching this long run, however, can take quite a while. According to studies of international data on economic growth, increasing the saving rate can lead to substantially higher growth for a period of several decades.

The property of diminishing returns to capital has another important implication: Other things being equal, it is easier for a country to grow fast if it starts out relatively poor. This effect of initial conditions on subsequent growth is sometimes called the **catch-up effect**. In poor countries, workers lack even the most rudimentary tools and, as a result, have low productivity. Thus, small amounts of capital investment can substantially raise these workers' productivity. By contrast, workers in rich countries have large amounts of capital with which to work, and this partly explains their high productivity. Yet with the amount of capital per worker already so high, additional capital investment has a relatively small effect on productivity. Studies of international data on economic growth confirm this catch-up effect: Controlling for other variables, such as the percentage of GDP devoted to investment, poor countries tend to grow at faster rates than rich countries.

This catch-up effect can help explain some otherwise puzzling facts. Here's an example: From 1960 to 1990, the United States and South Korea devoted a similar share of GDP to investment. Yet over this time, the United States experienced only mediocre growth of about 2 percent, while South Korea experienced spectacular growth of more than 6 percent. The explanation is the catch-up effect. In 1960, South Korea had GDP per person less than one-tenth the U.S. level, in part because previous investment had been so low. With a small initial capital stock, the benefits to capital accumulation were much greater in South Korea, and this gave South Korea a higher subsequent growth rate.

**catch-up effect**
the property whereby countries that start off poor tend to grow more rapidly than countries that start off rich

This catch-up effect shows up in other aspects of life. When a school gives an end-of-year award to the "Most Improved" student, that student is usually one who began the year with relatively poor performance. Students who began the year not studying find improvement easier than students who always worked hard. Note that it is good to be "Most Improved," given the starting point, but it is even better to be "Best Student." Similarly, economic growth over the last several decades has been much more rapid in South Korea than in the United States, but GDP per person is still higher in the United States.

## 17-3c Investment from Abroad

So far, we have discussed how policies aimed at increasing a country's saving rate can increase investment and, thereby, long-term economic growth. Yet saving by domestic residents is not the only way for a country to invest in new capital. The other way is investment by foreigners.

Investment from abroad takes several forms. Ford Motor Company might build a car factory in Mexico. A capital investment that is owned and operated by a foreign entity is called *foreign direct investment*. Alternatively, an American might buy stock in a Mexican corporation (that is, buy a share in the ownership of the corporation), and the corporation can use the proceeds from the stock sale to build a new factory. An investment that is financed with foreign money but operated by domestic residents is called *foreign portfolio investment*. In both cases, Americans provide the resources necessary to increase the stock of capital in Mexico. That is, American saving is being used to finance Mexican investment.

When foreigners invest in a country, they do so because they expect to earn a return on their investment. Ford's car factory increases the Mexican capital stock and, therefore, increases Mexican productivity and Mexican GDP. Yet Ford takes some of this additional income back to the United States in the form of profit. Similarly, when an American investor buys Mexican stock, the investor has a right to a portion of the profit that the Mexican corporation earns.

Investment from abroad, therefore, does not have the same effect on all measures of economic prosperity. Recall that gross domestic product (GDP) is the income earned within a country by both residents and nonresidents, whereas gross national product (GNP) is the income earned by residents of a country both at home and abroad. When Ford opens its car factory in Mexico, some of the income the factory generates accrues to people who do not live in Mexico. As a result, foreign investment in Mexico raises the income of Mexicans (measured by GNP) by less than it raises the production in Mexico (measured by GDP).

Nonetheless, investment from abroad is one way for a country to grow. Even though some of the benefits from this investment flow back to the foreign owners, this investment does increase the economy's stock of capital, leading to higher productivity and higher wages. Moreover, investment from abroad is one way for poor countries to learn the state-of-the-art technologies developed and used in richer countries. For these reasons, many economists who advise governments in less developed economies advocate policies that encourage investment from abroad. Often, this means removing restrictions that governments have imposed on foreign ownership of domestic capital.

An organization that tries to encourage the flow of capital to poor countries is the World Bank. This international organization obtains funds from the world's advanced countries, such as the United States, and uses these resources to make loans to less developed countries so that they can invest in roads, sewer systems, schools, and other types of capital. It also offers the countries advice about how the funds might best be used. The World Bank and its sister organization, the International Monetary Fund, were set up after World War II. One lesson from the war was that economic distress often leads to political turmoil, international tensions, and military conflict. Thus, every country has an interest in promoting economic prosperity around the world. The World Bank and the International Monetary Fund were established to achieve that common goal.

### 17-3d Education

Education—investment in human capital—is at least as important as investment in physical capital for a country's long-run economic success. In the United States, each year of schooling has historically raised a person's wage by an average of about 10 percent. In less developed countries, where human capital is especially scarce, the gap between the wages of educated and uneducated workers is even larger. Thus, one way government policy can enhance the standard of living is to provide good schools and to encourage the population to take advantage of them.

Investment in human capital, like investment in physical capital, has an opportunity cost. When students are in school, they forgo the wages they could have earned as members of the labor force. In less developed countries, children often drop out of school at an early age, even though the benefit of additional schooling is very high, simply because their labor is needed to help support the family.

Some economists have argued that human capital is particularly important for economic growth because human capital conveys positive externalities. An *externality* is the effect of one person's actions on the well-being of a bystander. An educated person, for instance, might generate new ideas about how best to produce goods and services. If these ideas enter society's pool of knowledge so that everyone can use them, then the ideas are an external benefit of education. In this case, the return from schooling for society is even greater than the return for the individual. This argument would justify the large subsidies to human-capital investment that we observe in the form of public education.

One problem facing some poor countries is the *brain drain*—the emigration of many of the most highly educated workers to rich countries, where these workers can enjoy a higher standard of living. If human capital does have positive externalities, then this brain drain makes those people left behind even poorer. This problem offers policymakers a dilemma. On the one hand, the United States and other rich countries have the best systems of higher education, and it would seem natural for poor countries to send their best students abroad to earn higher degrees. On the other hand, those students who have spent time abroad may choose not to return home, and this brain drain will reduce the poor nation's stock of human capital even further.

### 17-3e Health and Nutrition

The term *human capital* usually refers to education, but it can also be used to describe another type of investment in people: expenditures that lead to a healthier population. Other things being equal, healthier workers are more productive. The right investments in the health of the population provide one way for a nation to increase productivity and raise living standards.

According to the late economic historian Robert Fogel, improved health from better nutrition has been a significant factor in long-run economic growth. Fogel estimated that in Great Britain in 1780, about one in five people were so malnourished that they were incapable of manual labor. Among those who could work, insufficient caloric intake substantially reduced the work effort they could put forth. As nutrition improved, so did workers' productivity.

Fogel studied these historical trends in part by looking at the height of the population. Short stature can be an indicator of malnutrition, especially during gestation and the early years of life. Fogel found that as nations develop economically, people eat more and the population gets taller. From 1775 to 1975, the average caloric intake in Great Britain rose by 26 percent and the height of the average man rose by 3.6 inches. Similarly, during the spectacular economic growth in South Korea from 1962 to 1995, caloric consumption rose by 44 percent and average male height rose by 2 inches. Of course, a person's height is determined by a combination of genetics and environment. But because the genetic makeup of a population is slow to change, such increases in average height are most likely due to changes in the environment—nutrition being the obvious explanation.

Moreover, studies have found that height is an indicator of productivity. Looking at data on a large number of workers at a point in time, researchers have found that taller workers tend to earn more. Because wages reflect a worker's productivity, this finding suggests that taller workers tend to be more productive. The effect of height on wages is especially pronounced in poorer countries, where malnutrition is a bigger risk.

Fogel won the Nobel Prize in Economics in 1993 for his work in economic history, which includes not only his studies of nutrition but also his studies of American slavery and the role of railroads in the development of the American economy. In the lecture he gave when he was awarded the prize, he surveyed the evidence on health and economic growth. He concluded that "improved gross nutrition accounts for roughly 30 percent of the growth of per capita income in Britain between 1790 and 1980."

Today, malnutrition is fortunately rare in developed nations such as Great Britain and the United States. (Obesity is a more widespread problem.) But for people in developing nations, poor health and inadequate nutrition remain obstacles to higher productivity and improved living standards. The United Nations estimates that almost a third of the population in sub-Saharan Africa is undernourished.

The causal link between health and wealth runs in both directions. Poor countries are poor in part because their populations are not healthy, and their populations are not healthy in part because they are poor and cannot afford adequate healthcare and nutrition. It is a vicious circle. But this fact opens the possibility of a virtuous circle: Policies that lead to more rapid economic growth would naturally improve health outcomes, which in turn would further promote economic growth.

## 17-3f Property Rights and Political Stability

Another way policymakers can foster economic growth is by protecting property rights and promoting political stability. This issue goes to the very heart of how market economies work.

Production in market economies arises from the interactions of millions of individuals and firms. When you buy a car, for instance, you are buying the output of a car dealer, a car manufacturer, a steel company, an iron ore mining company, and so on. This division of production among many firms allows the economy's factors of production to be used as effectively as possible. To achieve this outcome, the economy has to coordinate transactions among these firms, as well as between firms and consumers. Market economies achieve this coordination through market prices. That is, market prices are the instrument with which the invisible hand of the marketplace brings supply and demand into balance in each of the many thousands of markets that make up the economy.

An important prerequisite for the price system to work is an economy-wide respect for *property rights*. Property rights refer to the ability of people to exercise authority over the resources they own. A mining company will not make the effort to mine iron ore if it expects the ore to be stolen. The company mines the ore only if it is confident that it will benefit from the ore's subsequent sale. For this reason, courts serve an important role in a market economy: They enforce property rights. Through the criminal justice system, the courts discourage theft. In addition, through the civil justice system, the courts ensure that buyers and sellers live up to their contracts.

Those of us in developed countries tend to take property rights for granted, but those living in less developed countries understand that a lack of property rights can be a major problem. In many countries, the system of justice does not work well. Contracts are hard to enforce, and fraud often goes unpunished. In more extreme cases, the government not only fails to enforce property rights but actually infringes upon them. To do business in some countries, firms are expected to bribe government officials. Such corruption impedes the coordinating power of markets. It also discourages domestic saving and investment from abroad.

One threat to property rights is political instability. When revolutions and coups are common, there is doubt about whether property rights will be respected in the future. If a revolutionary government might confiscate the capital of some businesses, as was often true after communist revolutions, domestic residents have less incentive to save, invest, and start new businesses. At the same time, foreigners have less incentive to invest in the country. Even the threat of revolution can act to depress a nation's standard of living.

Thus, economic prosperity depends in part on political prosperity. A country with an efficient court system, honest government officials, and a stable constitution will enjoy a higher economic standard of living than a country with a poor court system, corrupt officials, and frequent revolutions and coups.

## 17-3g  Free Trade

Some of the world's poorest countries have tried to achieve more rapid economic growth by pursuing *inward-oriented policies*. These policies attempt to increase productivity and living standards within the country by avoiding interaction with the rest of the world. Domestic firms often advance the infant-industry argument, claiming they need protection from foreign competition to thrive and grow. Together with a general distrust of foreigners, this argument has at times led policymakers in less developed countries to impose tariffs and other trade restrictions.

Most economists today believe that poor countries are better off pursuing *outward-oriented policies* that integrate these countries into the world economy. International trade in goods and services can improve the economic well-being of a country's citizens. Trade is, in some ways, a type of technology. When a country exports wheat and imports textiles, the country benefits as if it had invented a technology for turning wheat into textiles. A country that eliminates trade restrictions will, therefore, experience the same kind of economic growth that would occur after a major technological advance.

The adverse impact of inward orientation becomes clear when one considers the small size of many less developed economies. The total GDP of Argentina, for instance, is about that of Houston, Texas. Imagine what would happen if the Houston city council were to prohibit city residents from trading with people living outside the city limits. Without being able to take advantage of the gains from trade, Houston would need to produce all the goods it consumes. It would also have to produce all its own capital goods, rather than importing state-of-the-art equipment from other cities. Living standards in Houston would fall immediately, and the problem would likely only get worse over time. This is precisely what happened when Argentina pursued inward-oriented policies throughout much of the 20th century. In contrast, countries that pursued outward-oriented policies, such as South Korea, Singapore, and Taiwan, enjoyed high rates of economic growth.

The amount that a nation trades with others is determined not only by government policy but also by geography. Countries with natural seaports find trade easier than countries without this resource. It is not a coincidence that many of the world's major cities, such as New York, San Francisco, and Hong Kong, are located next to oceans. Similarly, because landlocked countries find international trade more difficult, they tend to have lower levels of income than countries with easy access to the world's waterways. For example, countries with more than 80 percent of their population living within 100 kilometers of a coast have an average GDP per person about four times as large as countries with less than 20 percent of their population living near a coast. The critical importance of access to the sea helps explain why the African continent, which contains many landlocked countries, is so poor.

## 17-3h Research and Development

The primary reason that living standards are higher today than they were a century ago is that technological knowledge has advanced. The telephone, the transistor, the computer, and the internal combustion engine are among the thousands of innovations that have improved the ability to produce goods and services.

Most technological advances come from private research by firms and individual inventors, but there is also a public interest in promoting these efforts. To a large extent, knowledge is a *public good*: That is, once one person discovers an idea, the idea enters society's pool of knowledge and other people can freely use it. Just as government has a role in providing a public good such as national defense, it also has a role in encouraging the research and development of new technologies.

The U.S. government has long played a role in the creation and dissemination of technological knowledge. A century ago, the government sponsored research about farming methods and advised farmers how best to use their land. More recently, the U.S. government, through the Air Force and NASA, has supported aerospace research; as a result, the United States is a leading maker of rockets and planes. The government continues to encourage advances in knowledge with research grants from the National Science Foundation and the National Institutes of Health and with tax breaks for firms engaging in research and development.

Yet another way in which government policy encourages research is through the patent system. When a person or firm creates an innovative product, such as a new drug, the inventor can apply for a patent. If the product is deemed truly original,

**ASK THE EXPERTS**

## Innovation and Growth

"Future innovations worldwide will not be transformational enough to promote sustained per-capita economic growth rates in the United States and western Europe over the next century as high as those over the past 150 years."

**What do economists say?**

34% disagree

59% uncertain

7% agree

**Source:** IGM Economic Experts Panel, February 11, 2014.

## IN THE NEWS

# Curmudgeon versus Optimist

*When economists look ahead to future technological progress, their crystal ball is often foggy.*

### Has All the Important Stuff Already Been Invented?

**By Timothy Aeppel**

Robert Gordon, a curmudgeonly 73-year-old economist, believes our best days are over. After a century of life-changing innovations that spurred growth, he says, human progress is slowing to a crawl.

Joel Mokyr, a cheerful 67-year-old economist, imagines a coming age of new inventions, including gene therapies to prolong our life span and miracle seeds that can feed the world without fertilizers.

These big-name colleagues at Northwestern University represent opposite poles in the debate over the future of the 21st century economy: rapid innovation driven by robotic manufacturing, 3-D printing and cloud computing, versus years of job losses, stagnant wages and rising income inequality.

The divergent views are more than academic. For many Americans, the recession left behind the scars of lost jobs, lower wages and depressed home prices. The question is whether tough times are here for good. The answer depends on who you ask.

"I think the rate of innovation is just getting faster and faster," Mr. Mokyr said over noodles and spicy chicken at a Thai restaurant near the campus where he and Mr. Gordon have taught for four decades.

"What's the evidence of that?" snapped Mr. Gordon. "There isn't any."

The men get along fine when talk is limited to, say, faculty gossip. About the future, though, they bicker constantly. When Mr. Mokyr described life-prolonging medical advances, Mr. Gordon cut in: "Extending life without curing Alzheimer's means people who can walk but can't think."

Mr. Gordon landed at Northwestern from the University of Chicago in the fall of 1973, a year before Mr. Mokyr arrived there from Yale after finishing his Ph.D. Their tit-for-tat repartee makes them popular speakers—for economists, at least....

The professors headlined a Bank of Korea event in Seoul earlier this month. "We always go mano-a-mano," Mr. Mokyr said. "But we often end up talking about different things. Bob's a macroeconomist, I'm an economic historian."

Mr. Mokyr has long studied how new tools have led to economic breakthroughs. For example, how the development of telescopes allowed for rapid advances in astronomy. History makes him certain his colleague is wrong.

Mr. Gordon's ideas, in fact, fly in the face of modern economic orthodoxy. Since Nobel economist Robert Solow first argued in the 1950s that growth was driven by new technology, most economists have embraced the idea. Progress may be uneven, according to this view, but there is no reason to expect the world to run out of ideas.

"Bob says the low-hanging fruit has been picked, because we won't invent indoor plumbing again," Mr. Mokyr said. In speeches, Mr. Gordon often displays images of a flush toilet and iPhone and asks: Which would you give up?

Mr. Mokyr said many economists before Mr. Gordon have proclaimed the end of progress, but these pessimists have always been proven wrong. It was a popular theme during the Depression, he said, but modern economists now recognize the 1930s as a period of rapid technological progress with such advances as the development of jet engines and radar.

Today, Mr. Mokyr said, fast computing is a new tool that will open the way to new inventions in the future.

The darkness of Mr. Mokyr's family history contrasts with his optimism for the future. His parents were Dutch Jews who survived the Holocaust. His father, a civil servant, died of cancer when Mr. Mokyr was a year old. He was raised by his mother in a small apartment in the port city of Haifa in Israel. "My mother was not an optimist," he said. "She had lived a very tough life."

Mr. Gordon, the more famous of the two men, has the credentials to buck conventional

Curmudgeon

wisdom. His parents and a brother were Ph.D. economists. His father, an expert on business cycles, taught at the University of California, Berkeley, for decades....

If anything, his family should have made him an optimist. Mr. Gordon's father grew up grindingly poor, at one point supporting three younger brothers after his own father died; his eventual success mirrored the larger transformation of the U.S. into the world's richest country.

"His generation saw the move from crowded tenements in the 1920s to suburbia in the 1950s—with everyone having a yard and a car," Mr. Gordon said, a leap showing how much progress has since slowed.

Mr. Gordon sees a hobbled U.S. economy ahead. Americans are getting older, leaving too few workers to support the aging population. The problem is even worse in other Western economies.

An aging citizenry is among a list of troubles, including the declining share of working-age men with jobs; stagnant rates of Americans earning college degrees; jobs lost abroad and high government debt. The biggest obstacle, he said, is growing income inequality.

To compensate, Mr. Gordon said, economies need technological advances. The problem is that the biggest breakthroughs—like electrification or the discovery of antibiotics—are behind us. Electricity changed how people lived and worked, and it spawned hundreds of new industries. The technology that allowed people to communicate instantly or travel quickly over long distances were 19th- and 20th-century innovations.

More recent inventions—including the Internet—won't pack the same punch, he said: "The rapid progress made over the past 250 years could well turn out to be a unique episode in human history."

Cellphones, he said, are just a refinement of the telephone. "Look at what an ideal kitchen looked like in 1955—it's not that different than today," Mr. Gordon said. "It's nothing like moving from clothes lines to clothes dryers."...

Mr. Gordon said his ideas began taking shape between semesters at graduate school. He worked during the summer of 1965 for a team of economists analyzing the dazzling productivity growth that began around 1920 and ran through World War II and the postwar boom.

Except for an upturn in the 1990s, growth has been tepid ever since.

"Everyone has looked for a big overarching factor to explain this," he said. "But it occurred to me, it could be as simple as that we'd run out of the great inventions."

Mr. Gordon said his ideas evolved from there. In 2000, he published a paper saying that computer technology, hailed as the driver of the "new economy," was far less impressive than earlier big inventions. He generated more controversy with a 2012 academic paper titled "Is U.S. Economic Growth Over?"

The paper included a dire prediction: The economy will grow less than half as fast as the remarkable 2% average it notched

Optimist

between 1870 and 2007. "Americans got used to their standard of living doubling from that of their parents. No more," he told investment managers in Germany this year.

If he is right, the standard of living for the average American—measured in per capita income—will in the future take 78 years to double, compared with the 35 years it took between 1972 and 2007....

Much of Mr. Gordon's work focuses on an economy's output. Mr. Mokyr, meanwhile, is more interested in how new inventions improve the quality of life in ways that don't show up in traditional measures: new medicines that treat chronic pain or allow older people to stay active years longer. A hip replacement, he said, let him keep riding his bike to and from work.

"For Bob, it's all about the measure of input and output—especially output," said Mr. Mokyr. That is why the aging population is such a big problem for Mr. Gordon, since retired people stop producing.

Mr. Gordon countered that many of the innovations Mr. Mokyr anticipates—such as new technology to clean air and water pollution—will solve problems created by past economic growth. Those shouldn't be counted the same way as breakthroughs that add to output, he said.

"Maybe the problem is that we didn't measure growth in the past correctly," Mr. Mokyr retorted, "because we didn't account for the costs."

The two men agree on one point. "One of the main missions I have in life is to point out to my students how lucky they are to be born in the 20th century," Mr. Mokyr said. "Compared to what life was like 100 or 200 years ago, we're incredibly fortunate." ■

**Source:** *The Wall Street Journal*, June 16, 2014.

the government awards the patent, which gives the inventor the exclusive right to make the product for a specified number of years. In essence, the patent gives the inventor a property right over her invention, turning her new idea from a public good into a private good. By allowing inventors to profit from their inventions—even if only temporarily—the patent system enhances the incentive for individuals and firms to engage in research.

### 17-3i Population Growth

Economists and other social scientists have long debated how population affects a society. The most direct effect is on the size of the labor force: A large population means more workers to produce goods and services. The tremendous size of the Chinese population is one reason China is such an important player in the world economy.

At the same time, however, a large population means more people to consume those goods and services. So while a large population means a larger total output of goods and services, it need not mean a higher standard of living for the typical citizen. Indeed, both large and small nations are found at all levels of economic development.

Beyond these obvious effects of population size, population growth interacts with the other factors of production in ways that are more subtle and open to debate.

**Stretching Natural Resources**   Thomas Robert Malthus (1766–1834), an English minister and early economic thinker, is famous for his book called *An Essay on the Principle of Population as It Affects the Future Improvement of Society.* In it, he offered what may be history's most chilling forecast. Malthus argued that an ever-increasing population would continually strain society's ability to provide for itself. As a result, mankind was doomed to forever live in poverty.

Malthus's logic was simple. He began by noting that "food is necessary to the existence of man" and that "the passion between the sexes is necessary and will remain nearly in its present state." He concluded that "the power of population is infinitely greater than the power in the earth to produce subsistence for man." According to Malthus, the only check on population growth was "misery and vice." Attempts by charities or governments to alleviate poverty were counterproductive, he argued, because they merely allowed the poor to have more children, placing even greater strains on society's productive capabilities.

Malthus may have correctly described the world at the time when he lived, but fortunately, his dire forecast was far off the mark. The world population has increased about sixfold over the past two centuries, but living standards around the world are on average much higher. As a result of economic growth, chronic hunger and malnutrition are less common now than they were in Malthus's day. Modern famines occur from time to time but are more often the result of an unequal income distribution or political instability than inadequate food production.

Where did Malthus go wrong? As we discussed in a case study earlier in this chapter, growth in human ingenuity has offset the effects of a larger population. Pesticides, fertilizers, mechanized farm equipment, new crop varieties, and other technological advances that Malthus never imagined have allowed each farmer to feed ever greater numbers of people. Even with more mouths to feed, fewer farmers are necessary because each farmer is much more productive.

**Diluting the Capital Stock**   Whereas Malthus worried about the effects of population on the use of natural resources, some modern theories of economic

*Thomas Robert Malthus*

2002 ARPL / TOPHAM / THE IMAGEWORKS

growth emphasize its effects on capital accumulation. According to these theories, high population growth reduces GDP per worker because rapid growth in the number of workers forces the capital stock to be spread more thinly. In other words, when population growth is rapid, each worker is equipped with less capital. A smaller quantity of capital per worker leads to lower productivity and lower GDP per worker.

This problem is most apparent in the case of human capital. Countries with high population growth have large numbers of school-age children. This places a larger burden on the educational system. It is not surprising, therefore, that educational attainment tends to be low in countries with high population growth.

The differences in population growth around the world are large. In developed countries, such as the United States and those in Western Europe, the population has risen only about 1 percent per year in recent decades and is expected to rise even more slowly in the future. By contrast, in many poor African countries, population grows at about 3 percent per year. At this rate, the population doubles every 23 years. This rapid population growth makes it harder to provide workers with the tools and skills they need to achieve high levels of productivity.

Rapid population growth is not the main reason that less developed countries are poor, but some analysts believe that reducing the rate of population growth would help these countries raise their standards of living. In some countries, this goal is accomplished directly with laws that regulate the number of children families may have. For example, from 1980 to 2015, China allowed only one child per family; couples who violated this rule were subject to substantial fines. In countries with greater freedom, the goal of reduced population growth is accomplished less directly by increasing awareness of birth control techniques.

Another way in which a country can influence population growth is to apply one of the *Ten Principles of Economics*: People respond to incentives. Bearing a child, like any decision, has an opportunity cost. When the opportunity cost rises, people will choose to have smaller families. In particular, women with the opportunity to receive a good education and desirable employment tend to want fewer children than those with fewer opportunities outside the home. Hence, policies that foster equal treatment of women may be one way for less developed economies to reduce the rate of population growth and, perhaps, raise their standards of living.

**Promoting Technological Progress** Rapid population growth may depress economic prosperity by reducing the amount of capital each worker has, but it may also have some benefits. Some economists have suggested that world population growth has been an engine of technological progress and economic prosperity. The mechanism is simple: If there are more people, then there are more scientists, inventors, and engineers to contribute to technological advance, which benefits everyone.

Economist Michael Kremer provided some support for this hypothesis in an article titled "Population Growth and Technological Change: One Million B.C. to 1990," which was published in the *Quarterly Journal of Economics* in 1993. Kremer began by noting that over the broad span of human history, world growth rates have increased with world population. For example, world growth was more rapid when the world population was 1 billion (which occurred around the year 1800) than when the population was only 100 million (around 500 B.C.). This fact is consistent with the hypothesis that a larger population induces more technological progress.

Kremer's second piece of evidence comes from comparing regions of the world. The melting of the polar icecaps at the end of the Ice Age around 10,000 B.C. flooded the land bridges and separated the world into several distinct regions that could not communicate with one another for thousands of years. If technological progress is more rapid when there are more people to discover things, then larger regions should have experienced more rapid growth.

According to Kremer, that is exactly what happened. The most successful region of the world in 1500 (when Columbus reestablished contact) comprised the "Old World" civilizations of the large Eurasia-Africa region. Next in technological development were the Aztec and Mayan civilizations in the Americas, followed by the hunter-gatherers of Australia, and then the primitive people of Tasmania, who lacked even fire-making and most stone and bone tools.

## IN THE NEWS

# Using Experiments to Evaluate Aid

*To figure out what policies work in developing nations, economists are increasingly turning to randomized controlled experiments.*

## What It Takes to Lift Families Out of Poverty

**By Michaeleen Doucleff**

Eighteen years ago, Dean Karlan was a fresh, bright-eyed graduate student in economics at the Massachusetts Institute of Technology. He wanted to answer what seemed like a simple question:

"Does global aid work?" Karlan says.

He was reading a bunch of studies on the topic. But none of them actually answered the question. "We were tearing our hair out reading these papers because it was frustrating," he says. "[We] never really felt like the papers were really satisfactory."

One problem was that no one was actually testing global aid programs—methodically—to see if they really changed people's lives permanently. "They haven't been taking the scientific method to problems of poverty," he says.

Take, for instance, a charity that gives a family a cow. The charity might check on the family a year later and say, "Wow! The family is doing so much better with this cow. Cows must be the reason."

But maybe it wasn't the cow that improved the family's life. Maybe it had a bumper crop that year or property values went up in the neighborhood. Researchers really weren't doing those experiments, Karlan says.

So he and a bunch of his colleagues had a radical idea: Test aid with the same method doctors use to test drugs (that is, randomized control trials).

The idea is quite simple. Give some families aid but others nothing. Then follow both groups, and see if the aid actually made a difference in the long run.

Karlan, who's now a professor at Yale University, says many people were skeptical. "I have many conversations with people who say, 'You want to do what? Why would you want to do that?'"

One issue is that some families go home empty-handed, with no aid. So the idea seems unethical. But Karlan disagrees. "The whole point of this is to help more people," he says. "If we find out what works and what doesn't, in five years we can have a much bigger impact."

So Karlan and collaborators around the world, including those at the Abdul Latif Jameel Poverty Action Lab at MIT and the nonprofit Innovations for Poverty Action, decided to try out the idea with one of the toughest problems out there: helping families get out of extreme poverty.

An anti-poverty program in Bangladesh, called BRAC, looked like it was successful. It seemed to help nearly 400,000 families who were living off less than $1.25 each day. So Karlan and his colleagues wanted to test the program and see if it could work in other countries.

The smallest isolated region was Flinders Island, a tiny island between Tasmania and Australia. With the smallest population, Flinders Island had the fewest opportunities for technological advance and, indeed, seemed to regress. Around 3000 B.C., human society on Flinders Island died out completely. A large population, Kremer concluded, is a prerequisite for technological advance.

**Quick Quiz** *Describe three ways a government policymaker can try to raise the growth in living standards in a society. Are there any drawbacks to these policies?*

They teamed up with a network of researchers and nonprofits in six developing countries. They went to thousands of communities and found the poorest families.

Then they divided the families into two groups. They gave half the families nothing. And the other half a whole smorgasbord of aid for one to two years. They gave them:

1. Some livestock for making money, such as goats for milk, bees for honey, or guinea pigs for selling. "Depending on the site, there were different things specifically appropriate for that context," Karlan says.
2. Training about how to raise the livestock
3. Food or cash so they wouldn't eat the livestock
4. A savings account
5. Help with their health—both physical and mental

Karlan and his colleagues reported the results of the massive experiment in the journal *Science* this week.

So what did they find? Well, the strategy worked pretty well in five of the six countries they tried it in. Families who got the aid started making a little more money, and they had more food to eat.

"We see mental health go up. Happiness go up. We even saw things like female power increase," Karlan says.

But here's what sets this study apart from the rest: Families continued to make a bit more money even a year after the aid stopped.

"People were stuck. They give them this big push, and they seem to be on a sustained increased income level," says Justin Sandefur, an economist at the Center for Global Development in Washington, who wasn't involved in the study.

"What I found exciting and unique about this study is that the impact of the aid was durable and sustainable," he added.

The results suggest that the right kind of aid does help people in multiple places. It lifted

PER-ANDERS PETTERSSON/GETTY IMAGES NEWS/ GETTY IMAGES

the families up just a little bit so they could finally start inching out of extreme poverty.

But we shouldn't get too excited yet. These people are still very poor, says Sarah Baird, an economist at George Washington University.

The effect of the aid was actually quite small, she says. Families' incomes and food consumption together went up by only a small amount — about 5 percent, on average, when compared with the control group.

And it's still unknown how long this bump will last. The researchers looked at the change only a year after the aid stopped.

"Moving poverty is hard," Baird says. "The fact that they [Karlan and colleagues] were able to move it, and it was sustainable after a year, I think is important."

The findings are a leap forward, she says, because it shows charities and governments a basic strategy that often works.

And even a little bit of extra money can make a huge difference in these peoples' lives, she says. It can help them send their kids to school. Or even just give them a little more hope. ■

**Source:** ©2015 National Public Radio, Inc. NPR news report titled "What It Takes To Lift Families Out Of Poverty" by Michaeleen Doucleff was originally published on NPR. org on May 15, 2015, and is used with the permission of NPR. Any unauthorized duplication is strictly prohibited.

# 17-4 Conclusion: The Importance of Long-Run Growth

In this chapter, we have discussed what determines the standard of living in a nation and how policymakers can endeavor to raise it through policies that promote economic growth. Most of this chapter is summarized in one of the *Ten Principles of Economics*: A country's standard of living depends on its ability to produce goods and services. Policymakers who want to encourage growth in living standards must aim to increase their nation's productive ability by encouraging rapid accumulation of the factors of production and ensuring that these factors are employed as effectively as possible.

Economists differ in their views on the role of government in promoting economic growth. At the very least, government can lend support to the invisible hand by maintaining property rights and political stability. More controversial is whether government should target and subsidize specific industries that might be especially important for technological progress. There is no doubt that these issues are among the most important in economics. The success of one generation's policymakers in learning and heeding the fundamental lessons about economic growth determines what kind of world the next generation will inherit.

## CHAPTER QuickQuiz

1. Over the past century, real GDP per person in the United States has grown about _____ percent per year, which means it doubles about every _____ years.
   a. 2, 14
   b. 2, 35
   c. 5, 14
   d. 5, 35

2. The world's rich countries, such as the United States and Germany, have income per person that is about _____ times the income per person in the world's poor countries, such as Pakistan and India.
   a. 2
   b. 4
   c. 10
   d. 30

3. Most economists are _____ that natural resources will eventually limit economic growth. As evidence, they note that the prices of most natural resources, adjusted for overall inflation, have tended to _____ over time.
   a. concerned, rise
   b. concerned, fall
   c. not concerned, rise
   d. not concerned, fall

4. Because capital is subject to diminishing returns, higher saving and investment do not lead to higher
   a. income in the long run.
   b. income in the short run.
   c. growth in the long run.
   d. growth in the short run.

5. When the Japanese car maker Toyota expands one of its car factories in the United States, what is the likely impact of this event on the gross domestic product and gross national product of the United States?
   a. GDP rises and GNP falls.
   b. GNP rises and GDP falls.
   c. GDP shows a larger increase than GNP.
   d. GNP shows a larger increase than GDP.

6. Thomas Robert Malthus believed that population growth would
   a. put stress on the economy's ability to produce food, dooming humans to remain in poverty.
   b. spread the capital stock too thinly across the labor force, lowering each worker's productivity.
   c. promote technological progress, because there would be more scientists and inventors.
   d. eventually decline to sustainable levels, as birth control improved and people had smaller families.

## SUMMARY

- Economic prosperity, as measured by GDP per person, varies substantially around the world. The average income in the world's richest countries is more than ten times that in the world's poorest countries. Because growth rates of real GDP also vary substantially, the relative positions of countries can change dramatically over time.

- The standard of living in an economy depends on the economy's ability to produce goods and services. Productivity, in turn, depends on the physical capital, human capital, natural resources, and technological knowledge available to workers.

- Government policies can try to influence the economy's growth rate in many ways: by encouraging saving and investment, encouraging investment from abroad, fostering education, promoting good health, maintaining property rights and political stability, allowing free trade, and promoting the research and development of new technologies.

- The accumulation of capital is subject to diminishing returns: The more capital an economy has, the less additional output the economy gets from an extra unit of capital. As a result, although higher saving leads to higher growth for a period of time, growth eventually slows down as capital, productivity, and income rise. Also because of diminishing returns, the return to capital is especially high in poor countries. Other things being equal, these countries can grow faster because of the catch-up effect.

- Population growth has a variety of effects on economic growth. On the one hand, more rapid population growth may lower productivity by stretching the supply of natural resources and by reducing the amount of capital available for each worker. On the other hand, a larger population may enhance the rate of technological progress because there are more scientists and engineers.

## KEY CONCEPTS

productivity, p. 349
physical capital, p. 349
human capital, p. 352

natural resources, p. 352
technological knowledge, p. 353

diminishing returns, p. 355
catch-up effect, p. 356

## QUESTIONS FOR REVIEW

1. What does the level of a nation's GDP measure? What does the growth rate of GDP measure? Would you rather live in a nation with a high level of GDP and a low growth rate or in a nation with a low level of GDP and a high growth rate?

2. List and describe four determinants of productivity.

3. In what way is a college degree a form of capital?

4. Explain how higher saving leads to a higher standard of living. What might deter a policymaker from trying to raise the rate of saving?

5. Does a higher rate of saving lead to higher growth temporarily or indefinitely?

6. Why would removing a trade restriction, such as a tariff, lead to more rapid economic growth?

7. How does the rate of population growth influence the level of GDP per person?

8. Describe two ways the U.S. government tries to encourage advances in technological knowledge.

## PROBLEMS AND APPLICATIONS

1. Most countries, including the United States, import substantial amounts of goods and services from other countries. Yet the chapter says that a nation can enjoy a high standard of living only if it can produce a large quantity of goods and services itself. Can you reconcile these two facts?

2. Suppose that society decided to reduce consumption and increase investment.
   a. How would this change affect economic growth?
   b. What groups in society would benefit from this change? What groups might be hurt?

3. Societies choose what share of their resources to devote to consumption and what share to devote to investment. Some of these decisions involve private spending; others involve government spending.
   a. Describe some forms of private spending that represent consumption and some forms that represent investment. The national income accounts include tuition as a part of consumer spending. In your opinion, are the resources you devote to your education a form of consumption or a form of investment?
   b. Describe some forms of government spending that represent consumption and some forms that represent investment. In your opinion, should we view government spending on health programs as a form of consumption or investment? Would you distinguish between health programs for the young and health programs for the elderly?

4. What is the opportunity cost of investing in capital? Do you think a country can overinvest in capital? What is the opportunity cost of investing in human capital? Do you think a country can overinvest in human capital? Explain.

5. In the 1990s and the first decade of the 2000s, investors from the Asian economies of Japan and China made significant direct and portfolio investments in the United States. At the time, many Americans were unhappy that this investment was occurring.
   a. In what way was it better for the United States to receive this foreign investment than not to receive it?
   b. In what way would it have been better still for Americans to have made this investment?

6. In many developing nations, young women have lower enrollment rates in secondary school than do young men. Describe several ways in which greater educational opportunities for young women could lead to faster economic growth in these countries.

7. The International Property Right Index scores countries based on the legal and political environment and how well property rights are protected. Go online and find a recent ranking. Choose three countries with high scores and three countries with low scores. Then find estimates of GDP per person in each of these six countries. What pattern do you find? Give two possible interpretations of the pattern.

8. International data show a positive correlation between income per person and the health of the population.
   a. Explain how higher income might cause better health outcomes.
   b. Explain how better health outcomes might cause higher income.
   c. How might the relative importance of your two hypotheses be relevant for public policy?

9. The great 18th-century economist Adam Smith wrote, "Little else is requisite to carry a state to the highest degree of opulence from the lowest barbarism but peace, easy taxes, and a tolerable administration of justice: all the rest being brought about by the natural course of things." Explain how each of the three conditions Smith describes would promote economic growth.

To find additional study resources, visit cengagebrain.com, and search for "Mankiw."

# Saving, Investment, and the Financial System

Imagine that you have just graduated from college (with a degree in economics, of course) and you decide to start your own business—an economic forecasting firm. Before you make any money selling your forecasts, you have to incur substantial costs to set up your business. You have to buy computers with which to make your forecasts, as well as desks, chairs, and filing cabinets to furnish your new office. Each of these items is a type of capital that your firm will use to produce and sell its services.

How do you obtain the funds to invest in these capital goods? Perhaps you are able to pay for them out of your past savings. More likely, however, like most entrepreneurs, you do not have enough money of your own

to finance the start of your business. As a result, you have to get the money you need from other sources.

There are various ways to finance these capital investments. You could borrow the money, perhaps from a bank or from a friend or relative. In this case, you would promise not only to return the money to the lender at a later date but also to pay the lender interest for the use of the money. Alternatively, you could convince someone to provide the money you need for your business in exchange for a share of your future profits, whatever they might happen to be. In either case, your investment in computers and office equipment is being financed by someone else's saving.

**financial system**
the group of institutions in the economy that help to match one person's saving with another person's investment

The **financial system** consists of the institutions that help to match one person's saving with another person's investment. As we discussed in the previous chapter, saving and investment are key ingredients to long-run economic growth: When a country saves a large portion of its GDP, more resources are available for investment in capital, and higher capital raises a country's productivity and living standard. The previous chapter, however, did not explain how the economy coordinates saving and investment. At any time, some people want to save some of their income for the future and others want to borrow to finance investments in new and growing businesses. What brings these two groups of people together? What ensures that the supply of funds from those who want to save balances the demand for funds from those who want to invest?

This chapter examines how the financial system works. First, we discuss the large variety of institutions that make up the financial system in our economy. Second, we examine the relationship between the financial system and some key macroeconomic variables—notably saving and investment. Third, we develop a model of the supply and demand for funds in financial markets. In the model, the interest rate is the price that adjusts to balance supply and demand. The model shows how various government policies affect the interest rate and, thereby, society's allocation of scarce resources.

# 18-1 Financial Institutions in the U.S. Economy

At the broadest level, the financial system moves the economy's scarce resources from savers (people who spend less than they earn) to borrowers (people who spend more than they earn). Savers save for various reasons—to put a child through college in several years or to retire comfortably in several decades. Similarly, borrowers borrow for various reasons—to buy a house in which to live or to start a business with which to make a living. Savers supply their money to the financial system with the expectation that they will get it back with interest at a later date. Borrowers demand money from the financial system with the knowledge that they will be required to pay it back with interest at a later date.

The financial system is made up of various financial institutions that help coordinate the actions of savers and borrowers. As a prelude to analyzing the economic forces that drive the financial system, let's discuss the most important of these institutions. Financial institutions can be grouped into two categories: financial markets and financial intermediaries. We consider each category in turn.

**financial markets**
financial institutions through which savers can directly provide funds to borrowers

## 18-1a Financial Markets

**Financial markets** are the institutions through which a person who wants to save can directly supply funds to a person who wants to borrow. The two most important financial markets in our economy are the bond market and the stock market.

**The Bond Market** When Intel, the giant maker of computer chips, wants to borrow to finance construction of a new factory, it can borrow directly from the public. It does this by selling bonds. A **bond** is a certificate of indebtedness that specifies the obligations of the borrower to the holder of the bond. Put simply, a bond is an IOU. It identifies the time at which the loan will be repaid, called the *date of maturity*, and the rate of interest that will be paid periodically until the loan matures. The buyer of a bond gives his money to Intel in exchange for this promise of interest and eventual repayment of the amount borrowed (called the *principal*). The buyer can hold the bond until maturity, or he can sell the bond at an earlier date to someone else.

**bond**
a certificate of indebtedness

There are millions of different bonds in the U.S. economy. When large corporations, the federal government, or state and local governments need to borrow to finance the purchase of a new factory, a new jet fighter, or a new school, they usually do so by issuing bonds. If you look at *The Wall Street Journal* or the business section of your local newspaper, you will find a listing of the prices and interest rates on some of the most important bond issues. These bonds differ according to three significant characteristics.

The first characteristic is a bond's *term*—the length of time until the bond matures. Some bonds have short terms, such as a few months, while others have terms as long as 30 years. (The British government has even issued a bond that never matures, called a *perpetuity*. This bond pays interest forever, but the principal is never repaid.) The interest rate on a bond depends, in part, on its term. Long-term bonds are riskier than short-term bonds because holders of long-term bonds have to wait longer for repayment of principal. If a holder of a long-term bond needs his money earlier than the distant date of maturity, he has no choice but to sell the bond to someone else, perhaps at a reduced price. To compensate for this risk, long-term bonds usually pay higher interest rates than short-term bonds.

The second important characteristic of a bond is its *credit risk*—the probability that the borrower will fail to pay some of the interest or principal. Such a failure to pay is called a *default*. Borrowers can (and sometimes do) default on their loans by declaring bankruptcy. When bond buyers perceive that the probability of default is high, they demand a higher interest rate as compensation for this risk. Because the U.S. government is considered a safe credit risk, government bonds tend to pay low interest rates. By contrast, financially shaky corporations raise money by issuing *junk bonds*, which pay very high interest rates. Buyers of bonds can judge credit risk by checking with various private agencies that evaluate the credit risk of different bonds. For example, Standard & Poor's rates bonds from AAA (the safest) to D (those already in default).

The third important characteristic of a bond is its *tax treatment*—the way the tax laws treat the interest earned on the bond. The interest on most bonds is taxable income; that is, the bond owner has to pay a portion of the interest he earns in income taxes. By contrast, when state and local governments issue bonds, called *municipal bonds*, the bond owners are not required to pay federal income tax on the interest income. Because of this tax advantage, bonds issued by state and local governments typically pay a lower interest rate than bonds issued by corporations or the federal government.

**The Stock Market** Another way for Intel to raise funds to build a new semiconductor factory is to sell stock in the company. **Stock** represents ownership in a firm and is, therefore, a claim to the profits that the firm makes. For example, if Intel sells a total of 1,000,000 shares of stock, then each share represents ownership of 1/1,000,000 of the business.

**stock**
a claim to partial ownership in a firm

The sale of stock to raise money is called *equity finance*, whereas the sale of bonds is called *debt finance*. Although corporations use both equity and debt finance to raise money for new investments, stocks and bonds are very different. The owner of shares of Intel stock is a part owner of Intel, while the owner of an Intel bond is a creditor of the corporation. If Intel is very profitable, the stockholders enjoy the benefits of these profits, whereas the bondholders get only the interest on their bonds. And if Intel runs into financial difficulty, the bondholders are paid what they are due before stockholders receive anything at all. Compared to bonds, stocks offer the holder both higher risk and potentially higher return.

After a corporation issues stock by selling shares to the public, these shares trade among stockholders on organized stock exchanges. In these transactions, the corporation itself receives no money when its stock changes hands. The most important stock exchanges in the U.S. economy are the New York Stock Exchange and the NASDAQ (National Association of Securities Dealers Automated Quotations). Most of the world's countries have their own stock exchanges on which the shares of local companies trade.

The prices at which shares trade on stock exchanges are determined by the supply of and demand for the stock in these companies. Because stock represents ownership in a corporation, the demand for a stock (and thus its price) reflects people's perception of the corporation's future profitability. When people become optimistic about a company's future, they raise their demand for its stock and thereby bid up the price of a share of stock. Conversely, when people's expectations of a company's prospects decline, the price of a share falls.

Various stock indexes are available to monitor the overall level of stock prices. A *stock index* is computed as an average of a group of stock prices. The most famous stock index is the Dow Jones Industrial Average, which has been computed regularly since 1896. It is now based on the prices of the stocks of thirty major U.S. companies, such as General Electric, Microsoft, Coca-Cola, Boeing, Apple, and Wal-Mart. Another well-known stock index is the Standard & Poor's 500 Index, which is based on the prices of the stocks of 500 major companies. Because stock prices reflect expected profitability, these stock indexes are watched closely as possible indicators of future economic conditions.

## 18-1b  Financial Intermediaries

**financial intermediaries**
financial institutions through which savers can indirectly provide funds to borrowers

**Financial intermediaries** are financial institutions through which savers can indirectly provide funds to borrowers. The term *intermediary* reflects the role of these institutions in standing between savers and borrowers. Here we consider two of the most important financial intermediaries: banks and mutual funds.

**Banks**   If the owner of a small grocery store wants to finance an expansion of his business, he probably takes a strategy quite different from that of Intel. Unlike Intel, a small grocer would find it difficult to raise funds in the bond and stock markets. Most buyers of stocks and bonds prefer to buy those issued by larger, more familiar companies. The small grocer, therefore, most likely finances his business expansion with a loan from a local bank.

Banks are the financial intermediaries with which people are most familiar. A primary job of banks is to take in deposits from people who want to save and use these deposits to make loans to people who want to borrow. Banks pay depositors interest on their deposits and charge borrowers slightly higher interest on their loans. The difference between these rates of interest covers the banks' costs and returns some profit to the owners of the banks.

FYI

## Key Numbers for Stock Watchers

When following the stock of any company, you should keep an eye on three key numbers. These numbers are reported on the financial pages of some newspapers, and you can easily obtain them online as well (such as at Yahoo! Finance):

- **Price.** The single most important piece of information about a stock is the price of a share. News services usually present several prices. The "last" price is the price at which the stock more recently traded. The "previous close" is the price of the last transaction that occurred before the stock exchange closed on its previous day of trading. A news service may also give the "high" and "low" prices over the past day of trading and, sometimes, over the past year as well. It may also report the change from the previous day's closing price.
- **Dividend.** Corporations pay out some of their profits to their stock-holders; this amount is called the *dividend*. (Profits not paid out are called *retained earnings* and are used by the corporation for additional investment.) News services often report the dividend paid over the previous year for each share of stock. They some-times report the *dividend yield*, which is the dividend expressed as a percentage of the stock's price.
- **Price-earnings ratio.** A corporation's earnings, or account-ing profit, is the amount of revenue it receives for the sale of its products minus its costs of production as measured by

its accountants. *Earnings per share* is the company's total earnings divided by the number of shares of stock outstanding. The *price-earnings ratio*, often called the P/E, is the price of a corporation's stock divided by the amount the corporation earned per share over the past year. Historically, the typical price-earnings ratio is about 15. A higher P/E indicates that a corporation's stock is expensive relative to its recent earnings; this might indicate either that people expect earnings to rise in the future or that the stock is overvalued. Conversely, a lower P/E indicates that a corporation's stock is cheap relative to its recent earnings; this might indicate either that people expect earnings to fall or that the stock is undervalued.

Why do news services report all these data? Many people who invest their savings in stock follow these numbers closely when deciding which stocks to buy and sell. By contrast, other stockholders follow a buy-and-hold strategy: They buy the stock of well-run companies, hold it for long periods of time, and do not respond to the daily fluctuations. ■

Besides being financial intermediaries, banks play another important role in the economy: They facilitate purchases of goods and services by allowing people to write checks against their deposits and to access those deposits with debit cards. In other words, banks help create a special asset that people can use as a *medium of exchange*. A medium of exchange is an item that people can easily use to engage in transactions. A bank's role in providing a medium of exchange distinguishes it from many other financial institutions. Stocks and bonds, like bank deposits, are a possible *store of value* for the wealth that people have accumulated in past saving, but access to this wealth is not as easy, cheap, and immediate as just writing a check or swiping a debit card. For now, we ignore this second role of banks, but we will return to it when we discuss the monetary system later in the book.

**Mutual Funds**   A financial intermediary of increasing importance in the U.S. economy is the mutual fund. A **mutual fund** is an institution that sells shares to the public and uses the proceeds to buy a selection, or *portfolio*, of various types of stocks, bonds, or both stocks and bonds. The shareholder of the mutual fund accepts all the risk and return associated with the portfolio. If the value of the portfolio rises, the shareholder benefits; if the value of the portfolio falls, the shareholder suffers the loss.

The primary advantage of mutual funds is that they allow people with small amounts of money to diversify their holdings. Buyers of stocks and bonds are well advised to heed the adage: Don't put all your eggs in one basket. Because the

**mutual fund**
an institution that sells shares to the public and uses the proceeds to buy a portfolio of stocks and bonds

**ARLO AND JANIS** by Jimmy Johnson

value of any single stock or bond is tied to the fortunes of one company, holding a single kind of stock or bond is very risky. By contrast, people who hold a diverse portfolio of stocks and bonds face less risk because they have only a small stake in each company. Mutual funds make this diversification easy. With only a few hundred dollars, a person can buy shares in a mutual fund and, indirectly, become the part owner or creditor of hundreds of major companies. For this service, the company operating the mutual fund charges shareholders a fee, usually between 0.25 and 2.0 percent of assets each year.

A second advantage claimed by mutual fund companies is that mutual funds give ordinary people access to the skills of professional money managers. The managers of most mutual funds pay close attention to the developments and prospects of the companies in which they buy stock. These managers buy the stock of companies they view as having a profitable future and sell the stock of companies with less promising prospects. This professional management, it is argued, should increase the return that mutual fund depositors earn on their savings.

Financial economists, however, are often skeptical of this argument. With thousands of money managers paying close attention to each company's prospects, the price of a company's stock is usually a good reflection of the company's true value. As a result, it is hard to "beat the market" by buying good stocks and selling bad ones. In fact, mutual funds called *index funds*, which buy all the stocks in a given stock index, perform somewhat better on average than mutual funds that take advantage of active trading by professional money managers. The explanation for the superior performance of index funds is that they keep costs low by buying and selling very rarely and by not having to pay the salaries of professional money managers.

### 18-1c Summing Up

The U.S. economy contains a large variety of financial institutions. In addition to the bond market, the stock market, banks, and mutual funds, there are also pension funds, credit unions, insurance companies, and even the local loan shark. These institutions differ in many ways. When analyzing the macroeconomic role of the financial system, however, it is more important to keep in mind that, despite their differences, these financial institutions all serve the same goal: directing the resources of savers into the hands of borrowers.

 *What is a share of stock? What is a bond? Explain their differences and similarities.*

# 18-2 Saving and Investment in the National Income Accounts

Events that occur within the financial system are central to understanding developments in the overall economy. As we have just seen, the institutions that make up this system—the bond market, the stock market, banks, and mutual funds—have the role of coordinating the economy's saving and investment. And as we saw in the previous chapter, saving and investment are important determinants of long-run growth in GDP and living standards. As a result, macroeconomists need to understand how financial markets work and how various events and policies affect them.

As a starting point for analyzing financial markets, we discuss the key macroeconomic variables that measure activity in these markets. Our emphasis here is not on behavior but on accounting. *Accounting* refers to how various numbers are defined and added up. A personal accountant might help an individual add up his income and expenses. A national income accountant does the same thing for the economy as a whole. The national income accounts include, in particular, GDP and the many related statistics.

The rules of national income accounting include several important identities. Recall that an *identity* is an equation that must be true because of the way the variables in the equation are defined. Identities are useful to keep in mind, for they clarify how different variables are related to one another. Here we consider some accounting identities that shed light on the macroeconomic role of financial markets.

## 18-2a Some Important Identities

Recall that gross domestic product (GDP) is both total income in an economy and the total expenditure on the economy's output of goods and services. GDP (denoted as $Y$) is divided into four components of expenditure: consumption ($C$), investment ($I$), government purchases ($G$), and net exports ($NX$). We write

$$Y = C + I + G + NX.$$

This equation is an identity because every dollar of expenditure that shows up on the left side also shows up in one of the four components on the right side. Because of the way each of the variables is defined and measured, this equation must always hold.

In this chapter, we simplify our analysis by assuming that the economy we are examining is closed. A *closed economy* is one that does not interact with other economies. In particular, a closed economy does not engage in international trade in goods and services, nor does it engage in international borrowing and lending. Actual economies are *open economies*—that is, they interact with other economies around the world. Nonetheless, assuming a closed economy is a useful simplification with which we can learn some lessons that apply to all economies. Moreover, this assumption applies perfectly to the world economy (for interplanetary trade is not yet common).

Because a closed economy does not engage in international trade, imports and exports are exactly zero. Therefore, net exports ($NX$) are also zero. We can now simplify the identity as

$$Y = C + I + G.$$

This equation states that GDP is the sum of consumption, investment, and government purchases. Each unit of output sold in a closed economy is consumed, invested, or bought by the government.

To see what this identity can tell us about financial markets, subtract *C* and *G* from both sides of this equation. We then obtain

$$Y - C - G = I.$$

**national saving (saving)**
the total income in the economy that remains after paying for consumption and government purchases

The left side of this equation ($Y - C - G$) is the total income in the economy that remains after paying for consumption and government purchases: This amount is called **national saving**, or just **saving**, and is denoted *S*. Substituting *S* for $Y - C - G$, we can write the last equation as

$$S = I.$$

This equation states that saving equals investment.

To understand the meaning of national saving, it is helpful to manipulate the definition a bit more. Let *T* denote the amount that the government collects from households in taxes minus the amount it pays back to households in the form of transfer payments (such as Social Security and welfare). We can then write national saving in either of two ways:

$$S = Y - C - G$$

or

$$S = (Y - T - C) + (T - G).$$

These equations are the same because the two *T*'s in the second equation cancel each other, but each reveals a different way of thinking about national saving. In particular, the second equation separates national saving into two pieces: private saving ($Y - T - C$) and public saving ($T - G$).

**private saving**
the income that households have left after paying for taxes and consumption

**public saving**
the tax revenue that the government has left after paying for its spending

**budget surplus**
an excess of tax revenue over government spending

**budget deficit**
a shortfall of tax revenue from government spending

Consider each of these two pieces. **Private saving** is the amount of income that households have left after paying their taxes and paying for their consumption. In particular, because households receive income of *Y*, pay taxes of *T*, and spend *C* on consumption, private saving is $Y - T - C$. **Public saving** is the amount of tax revenue that the government has left after paying for its spending. The government receives *T* in tax revenue and spends *G* on goods and services. If *T* exceeds *G*, the government runs a **budget surplus** because it receives more money than it spends. This surplus of $T - G$ represents public saving. If the government spends more than it receives in tax revenue, then *G* is larger than *T*. In this case, the government runs a **budget deficit**, and public saving ($T - G$) is a negative number.

Now consider how these accounting identities are related to financial markets. The equation $S = I$ reveals an important fact: *For the economy as a whole, saving must be equal to investment.* Yet this fact raises some important questions: What mechanisms lie behind this identity? What coordinates those people who are deciding how much to save and those people who are deciding how much to invest? The answer is the financial system. The bond market, the stock market, banks, mutual funds, and other financial markets and intermediaries stand between the two sides of the $S = I$ equation. They take in the nation's saving and direct it to the nation's investment.

### 18-2b The Meaning of Saving and Investment

The terms *saving* and *investment* can sometimes be confusing. Most people use these terms casually and sometimes interchangeably. By contrast, the macroeconomists who put together the national income accounts use these terms carefully and distinctly.

Consider an example. Suppose that Larry earns more than he spends and deposits his unspent income in a bank or uses it to buy some stock or a bond from a corporation. Because Larry's income exceeds his consumption, he adds to the nation's saving. Larry might think of himself as "investing" his money, but a macroeconomist would call Larry's act saving rather than investment.

In the language of macroeconomics, investment refers to the purchase of new capital, such as equipment or buildings. When Moe borrows from the bank to build himself a new house, he adds to the nation's investment. (Remember, the purchase of a new house is the one form of household spending that is investment rather than consumption.) Similarly, when the Curly Corporation sells some stock and uses the proceeds to build a new factory, it also adds to the nation's investment.

Although the accounting identity $S = I$ shows that saving and investment are equal for the economy as a whole, this does not have to be true for every individual household or firm. Larry's saving can be greater than his investment, and he can deposit the excess in a bank. Moe's saving can be less than his investment, and he can borrow the shortfall from a bank. Banks and other financial institutions make these individual differences between saving and investment possible by allowing one person's saving to finance another person's investment.

 *Define* private saving, public saving, national saving, *and* investment. *How are they related?*

# 18-3 The Market for Loanable Funds

Having discussed some of the important financial institutions in our economy and the macroeconomic role of these institutions, we are ready to build a model of financial markets. Our purpose in building this model is to explain how financial markets coordinate the economy's saving and investment. The model also gives us a tool with which we can analyze various government policies that influence saving and investment.

To keep things simple, we assume that the economy has only one financial market, called the **market for loanable funds**. All savers go to this market to deposit their saving, and all borrowers go to this market to take out their loans. Thus, the term *loanable funds* refers to all income that people have chosen to save and lend out, rather than use for their own consumption, and to the amount that investors have chosen to borrow to fund new investment projects. In the market for loanable funds, there is one interest rate, which is both the return to saving and the cost of borrowing.

The assumption of a single financial market, of course, is not realistic. As we have seen, the economy has many types of financial institutions. But as we discussed in Chapter 2, the art in building an economic model is simplifying the world in order to explain it. For our purposes here, we can ignore the diversity of financial institutions and assume that the economy has a single financial market.

**market for loanable funds**
the market in which those who want to save supply funds and those who want to borrow to invest demand funds

### 18-3a Supply and Demand for Loanable Funds

The economy's market for loanable funds, like other markets in the economy, is governed by supply and demand. To understand how the market for loanable funds operates, therefore, we first look at the sources of supply and demand in that market.

The supply of loanable funds comes from people who have some extra income they want to save and lend out. This lending can occur directly, such as when a household buys a bond from a firm, or it can occur indirectly, such as when a household makes a deposit in a bank, which then uses the funds to make loans. In both cases, *saving is the source of the supply of loanable funds*.

The demand for loanable funds comes from households and firms who wish to borrow to make investments. This demand includes families taking out mortgages to buy new homes. It also includes firms borrowing to buy new equipment or build factories. In both cases, *investment is the source of the demand for loanable funds*.

The interest rate is the price of a loan. It represents the amount that borrowers pay for loans and the amount that lenders receive on their saving. Because a high interest rate makes borrowing more expensive, the quantity of loanable funds demanded falls as the interest rate rises. Similarly, because a high interest rate makes saving more attractive, the quantity of loanable funds supplied rises as the interest rate rises. In other words, the demand curve for loanable funds slopes downward, and the supply curve for loanable funds slopes upward.

Figure 1 shows the interest rate that balances the supply and demand for loanable funds. In the equilibrium shown, the interest rate is 5 percent, and the quantity of loanable funds demanded and the quantity of loanable funds supplied both equal $1,200 billion.

The adjustment of the interest rate to the equilibrium level occurs for the usual reasons. If the interest rate were lower than the equilibrium level, the quantity of loanable funds supplied would be less than the quantity of loanable funds demanded. The resulting shortage of loanable funds would encourage lenders to

### FIGURE 1

**The Market for Loanable Funds**
The interest rate in the economy adjusts to balance the supply and demand for loanable funds. The supply of loanable funds comes from national saving, including both private saving and public saving. The demand for loanable funds comes from firms and households that want to borrow for purposes of investment. Here the equilibrium interest rate is 5 percent, and $1,200 billion of loanable funds are supplied and demanded.

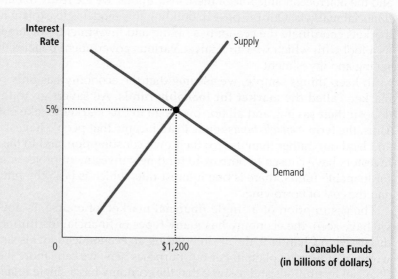

raise the interest rate they charge. A higher interest rate would encourage saving (thereby increasing the quantity of loanable funds supplied) and discourage borrowing for investment (thereby decreasing the quantity of loanable funds demanded). Conversely, if the interest rate were higher than the equilibrium level, the quantity of loanable funds supplied would exceed the quantity of loanable funds demanded. As lenders compete for the scarce borrowers, interest rates would be driven down. In this way, the interest rate approaches the equilibrium level at which the supply and demand for loanable funds exactly balance.

Recall that economists distinguish between the real interest rate and the nominal interest rate. The nominal interest rate is the monetary return to saving and the monetary cost of borrowing. It is the interest rate as usually reported. The real interest rate is the nominal interest rate corrected for inflation; it equals the nominal interest rate minus the inflation rate. Because inflation erodes the value of money over time, the real interest rate more accurately reflects the real return to saving and the real cost of borrowing. Therefore, the supply and demand for loanable funds depend on the real (rather than nominal) interest rate, and the equilibrium in Figure 1 should be interpreted as determining the real interest rate in the economy. For the rest of this chapter, when you see the term *interest rate*, you should remember that we are talking about the real interest rate.

This model of the supply and demand for loanable funds shows that financial markets work much like other markets in the economy. In the market for milk, for instance, the price of milk adjusts so that the quantity of milk supplied balances the quantity of milk demanded. In this way, the invisible hand coordinates the behavior of dairy farmers and the behavior of milk drinkers. Once we realize that saving represents the supply of loanable funds and investment represents the demand, we can see how the invisible hand coordinates saving and investment. When the interest rate adjusts to balance supply and demand in the market for loanable funds, it coordinates the behavior of people who want to save (the suppliers of loanable funds) and the behavior of people who want to invest (the demanders of loanable funds).

We can now use this analysis of the market for loanable funds to examine various government policies that affect the economy's saving and investment. Because this model is just supply and demand in a particular market, we analyze any policy using the three steps discussed in Chapter 4. First, we decide whether the policy shifts the supply curve or the demand curve. Second, we determine the direction of the shift. Third, we use the supply-and-demand diagram to see how the equilibrium changes.

## 18-3b  Policy 1: Saving Incentives

Many economists and policymakers have advocated increases in how much people save. Their argument is simple. One of the *Ten Principles of Economics* in Chapter 1 is that a country's standard of living depends on its ability to produce goods and services. And as we discussed in the preceding chapter, saving is an important long-run determinant of a nation's productivity. If the United States could somehow raise its saving rate, more resources would be available for capital accumulation, GDP would grow more rapidly, and over time, U.S. citizens would enjoy a higher standard of living.

Another of the *Ten Principles of Economics* is that people respond to incentives. Many economists have used this principle to suggest that the low rate of saving is at least partly attributable to tax laws that discourage saving. The U.S. federal government, as well as many state governments, collects revenue by taxing income, including interest and dividend income. To see the effects of this policy, consider a 25-year-old who saves $1,000 and buys a 30-year bond that pays an interest rate of 9 percent. In the absence of taxes, the $1,000 grows to $13,268 when the individual reaches age 55. Yet if that interest is taxed at a rate of, say, 33 percent, the after-tax interest rate is only 6 percent. In this case, the $1,000 grows to only $5,743 over the 30 years. The tax on interest income substantially reduces the future payoff from current saving and, as a result, reduces the incentive for people to save.

In response to this problem, some economists and lawmakers have proposed reforming the tax code to encourage greater saving. For example, one proposal is to expand eligibility for special accounts, such as Individual Retirement Accounts, that allow people to shelter some of their saving from taxation. Let's consider the effect of such a saving incentive on the market for loanable funds, as illustrated in Figure 2. We analyze this policy following our three steps.

First, which curve would this policy affect? Because the tax change would alter the incentive for households to save *at any given interest rate*, it would affect the quantity of loanable funds supplied at each interest rate. Thus, the supply of loanable funds would shift. The demand for loanable funds would remain the same because the tax change would not directly affect the amount that borrowers want to borrow at any given interest rate.

Second, which way would the supply curve shift? Because saving would be taxed less heavily than under current law, households would increase their saving by consuming a smaller fraction of their income. Households would use this additional saving to increase their deposits in banks or to buy more bonds. The supply of loanable funds would increase, and the supply curve would shift to the right from $S_1$ to $S_2$, as shown in Figure 2.

Finally, we can compare the old and new equilibria. In the figure, the increased supply of loanable funds reduces the interest rate from 5 percent to 4 percent. The lower interest rate raises the quantity of loanable funds demanded from $1,200 billion to $1,600 billion. That is, the shift in the supply curve moves the market

## FIGURE 2

**Saving Incentives Increase the Supply of Loanable Funds**
A change in the tax laws to encourage Americans to save more would shift the supply of loanable funds to the right from $S_1$ to $S_2$. As a result, the equilibrium interest rate would fall, and the lower interest rate would stimulate investment. Here the equilibrium interest rate falls from 5 percent to 4 percent, and the equilibrium quantity of loanable funds saved and invested rises from $1,200 billion to $1,600 billion.

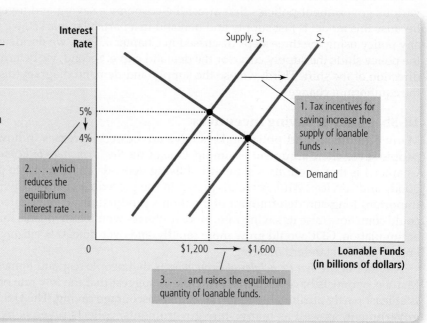

equilibrium along the demand curve. With a lower cost of borrowing, households and firms are motivated to borrow more to finance greater investment. Thus, *if a reform of the tax laws encouraged greater saving, the result would be lower interest rates and greater investment.*

This analysis of the effects of increased saving is widely accepted among economists, but there is less consensus about what kinds of tax changes should be enacted. Many economists endorse tax reform aimed at increasing saving to stimulate investment and growth. Yet others are skeptical that these tax changes would have much effect on national saving. These skeptics also doubt the equity of the proposed reforms. They argue that, in many cases, the benefits of the tax changes would accrue primarily to the wealthy, who are least in need of tax relief.

## 18-3c Policy 2: Investment Incentives

Suppose that Congress passed a tax reform aimed at making investment more attractive. In essence, this is what Congress does when it institutes an *investment tax credit*, which it does from time to time. An investment tax credit gives a tax advantage to any firm building a new factory or buying a new piece of equipment. Let's consider the effect of such a tax reform on the market for loanable funds, as illustrated in Figure 3.

First, would the law affect supply or demand? Because the tax credit would reward firms that borrow and invest in new capital, it would alter investment at any given interest rate and, thereby, change the demand for loanable funds. By contrast, because the tax credit would not affect the amount that households save at any given interest rate, it would not affect the supply of loanable funds.

Second, which way would the demand curve shift? Because firms would have an incentive to increase investment at any interest rate, the quantity of loanable funds demanded would be higher at any given interest rate. Thus, the demand curve for loanable funds would move to the right, as shown by the shift from $D_1$ to $D_2$ in the figure.

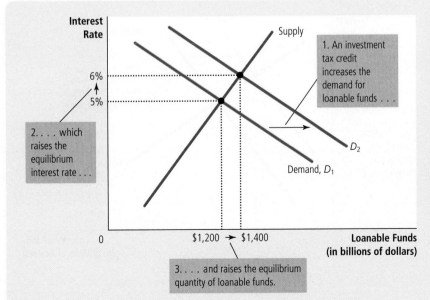

### FIGURE 3

**Investment Incentives Increase the Demand for Loanable Funds**

If the passage of an investment tax credit encouraged firms to invest more, the demand for loanable funds would increase. As a result, the equilibrium interest rate would rise, and the higher interest rate would stimulate saving. Here, when the demand curve shifts from $D_1$ to $D_2$, the equilibrium interest rate rises from 5 percent to 6 percent, and the equilibrium quantity of loanable funds saved and invested rises from $1,200 billion to $1,400 billion.

Third, consider how the equilibrium would change. In Figure 3, the increased demand for loanable funds raises the interest rate from 5 percent to 6 percent, and the higher interest rate in turn increases the quantity of loanable funds supplied from $1,200 billion to $1,400 billion, as households respond by increasing the amount they save. This change in household behavior is represented here as a movement along the supply curve. Thus, *if a reform of the tax laws encouraged greater investment, the result would be higher interest rates and greater saving.*

### 18-3d Policy 3: Government Budget Deficits and Surpluses

A perpetual topic of political debate is the status of the government budget. Recall that a *budget deficit* is an excess of government spending over tax revenue. Governments finance budget deficits by borrowing in the bond market, and the accumulation of past government borrowing is called the *government debt*. A *budget surplus*, an excess of tax revenue over government spending, can be used to repay some of the government debt. If government spending exactly equals tax revenue, the government is said to have a *balanced budget*.

Imagine that the government starts with a balanced budget and then, because of an increase in government spending, starts running a budget deficit. We can analyze the effects of the budget deficit by following our three steps in the market for loanable funds, as illustrated in Figure 4.

First, which curve shifts when the government starts running a budget deficit? Recall that national saving—the source of the supply of loanable funds—is composed of private saving and public saving. A change in the government budget balance represents a change in public saving and, therefore, in the supply of loanable funds. Because the budget deficit does not influence the amount that households and firms want to borrow to finance investment at any given interest rate, it does not alter the demand for loanable funds.

Second, which way does the supply curve shift? When the government runs a budget deficit, public saving is negative, and this reduces national saving. In other words, when the government borrows to finance its budget deficit, it reduces

## FIGURE 4

**The Effect of a Government Budget Deficit**
When the government spends more than it receives in tax revenue, the resulting budget deficit lowers national saving. The supply of loanable funds decreases, and the equilibrium interest rate rises. Thus, when the government borrows to finance its budget deficit, it crowds out households and firms that otherwise would borrow to finance investment. Here, when the supply curve shifts from $S_1$ to $S_2$, the equilibrium interest rate rises from 5 percent to 6 percent, and the equilibrium quantity of loanable funds saved and invested falls from $1,200 billion to $800 billion.

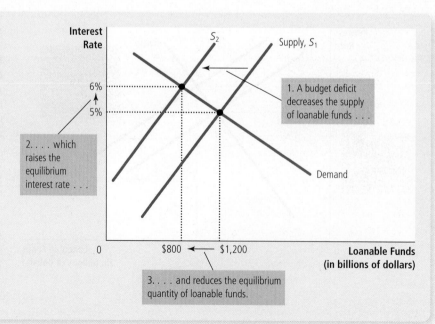

the supply of loanable funds available to finance investment by households and firms. Thus, a budget deficit shifts the supply curve for loanable funds to the left from $S_1$ to $S_2$, as shown in Figure 4.

Third, we can compare the old and new equilibria. In the figure, when the budget deficit reduces the supply of loanable funds, the interest rate rises from 5 percent to 6 percent. This higher interest rate then alters the behavior of the households and firms that participate in the loan market. In particular, many demanders of loanable funds are discouraged by the higher interest rate. Fewer families buy new homes, and fewer firms choose to build new factories. The fall in investment because of government borrowing is called **crowding out** and is represented in Figure 4 by the movement along the demand curve from a quantity of $1,200 billion in loanable funds to a quantity of $800 billion. That is, when the government borrows to finance its budget deficit, it crowds out private borrowers who are trying to finance investment.

Thus, the most basic lesson about budget deficits follows directly from their effects on the supply and demand for loanable funds: *When the government reduces national saving by running a budget deficit, the interest rate rises and investment falls.* Because investment is important for long-run economic growth, government budget deficits reduce the economy's growth rate.

Why, you might ask, does a budget deficit affect the supply of loanable funds, rather than the demand for them? After all, the government finances a budget deficit by selling bonds, thereby borrowing from the private sector. Why does increased borrowing by the government shift the supply curve, whereas increased borrowing by private investors shifts the demand curve? To answer this question, we need to examine more precisely the meaning of "loanable funds." The model as presented here takes this term to mean the *flow of resources available to fund private investment*; thus, a government budget deficit reduces the supply of loanable funds. If, instead, we had defined the term "loanable funds" to mean the *flow of resources available from private saving*, then the government budget deficit would increase demand rather than reduce supply. Changing the interpretation of the term would cause a semantic change in how we described the model, but the bottom line from the analysis would be the same: In either case, a budget deficit increases the interest rate, thereby crowding out private borrowers who are relying on financial markets to fund private investment projects.

So far, we have examined a budget deficit that results from an increase in government spending, but a budget deficit that results from a tax cut has similar effects. A tax cut reduces public saving, $T - G$. Private saving, $Y - T - C$, might increase because of lower $T$, but as long as households respond to the lower taxes by consuming more, $C$ increases, so private saving rises by less than public saving declines. Thus, national saving $(S = Y - C - G)$, the sum of public and private saving, declines. Once again, the budget deficit reduces the supply of loanable funds, drives up the interest rate, and crowds out borrowers trying to finance capital investments.

Now that we understand the impact of budget deficits, we can turn the analysis around and see that government budget surpluses have the opposite effects. When the government collects more in tax revenue than it spends, it saves the difference by retiring some of the outstanding government

**crowding out**
a decrease in investment that results from government borrowing

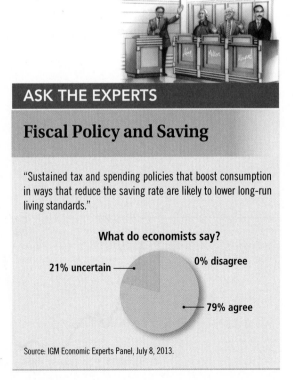

## ASK THE EXPERTS

### Fiscal Policy and Saving

"Sustained tax and spending policies that boost consumption in ways that reduce the saving rate are likely to lower long-run living standards."

**What do economists say?**

21% uncertain

0% disagree

79% agree

Source: IGM Economic Experts Panel, July 8, 2013.

debt. This budget surplus, or public saving, contributes to national saving. Thus, *a budget surplus increases the supply of loanable funds, reduces the interest rate, and stimulates investment.* Higher investment, in turn, means greater capital accumulation and more rapid economic growth.

**CASE STUDY**

### THE HISTORY OF U.S. GOVERNMENT DEBT

How indebted is the U.S. government? The answer to this question varies substantially over time. Figure 5 shows the debt of the U.S. federal government expressed as a percentage of U.S. GDP. It shows that the government debt has fluctuated from zero in 1836 to 107 percent of GDP in 1945.

The behavior of the debt-to-GDP ratio is one gauge of what's happening with the government's finances. Because GDP is a rough measure of the government's tax base, a declining debt-to-GDP ratio indicates that the government indebtedness is shrinking relative to its ability to raise tax revenue. This suggests that the government is, in some sense, living within its means. By contrast, a rising debt-to-GDP ratio means that the government indebtedness is increasing relative to its ability to raise tax revenue. It is often interpreted as meaning that fiscal policy—government spending and taxes—cannot be sustained forever at current levels.

---

**FIGURE 5**

**The U.S. Government Debt**

The debt of the U.S. federal government, expressed here as a percentage of GDP, has varied throughout history. Wartime spending is typically associated with substantial increases in government debt.

**Source:** U.S. Department of Treasury; U.S. Department of Commerce; and T. S. Berry, "Production and Population since 1789," Bostwick Paper No. 6, Richmond, 1988.

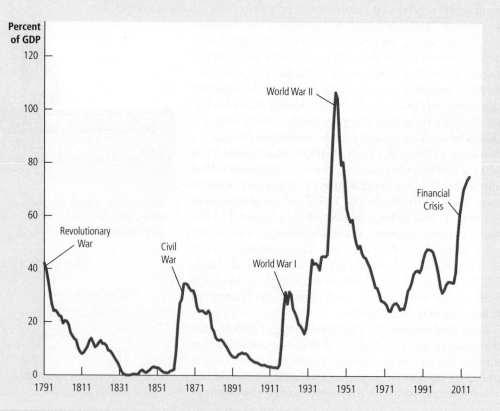

Throughout history, the primary cause of fluctuations in government debt has been war. When wars occur, government spending on national defense rises substantially to pay for soldiers and military equipment. Taxes sometimes rise as well but typically by much less than the increase in spending. The result is a budget deficit and increasing government debt. When the war is over, government spending declines and the debt-to-GDP ratio starts declining as well.

There are two reasons to believe that debt financing of war is an appropriate policy. First, it allows the government to keep tax rates smooth over time. Without debt financing, tax rates would have to rise sharply during wars, and this would cause a substantial decline in economic efficiency. Second, debt financing of wars shifts part of the cost of wars to future generations, who will have to pay off the government debt. This is arguably a fair distribution of the burden, for future generations get some of the benefit when one generation fights a war to defend the nation against foreign aggressors.

One large increase in government debt that cannot be explained by war is the increase that occurred beginning around 1980. When President Ronald Reagan took office in 1981, he was committed to smaller government and lower taxes. Yet he found cutting government spending to be more difficult politically than cutting taxes. The result was the beginning of a period of large budget deficits that continued not only through Reagan's time in office but also for many years thereafter. As a result, government debt rose from 26 percent of GDP in 1980 to 48 percent of GDP in 1993.

Because government budget deficits reduce national saving, investment, and long-run economic growth, the rise in government debt during the 1980s troubled many economists and policymakers. When Bill Clinton moved into the Oval Office in 1993, deficit reduction was his first major goal. Similarly, when the Republicans took control of Congress in 1995, deficit reduction was high on their legislative agenda. Both of these efforts substantially reduced the size of the government budget deficit. In addition, a booming economy in the late 1990s brought in even more tax revenue. Eventually, the federal budget turned from deficit to surplus, and the debt-to-GDP ratio declined significantly for several years.

This fall in the debt-to-GDP ratio, however, stopped during the presidency of George W. Bush, as the budget surplus turned back into a budget deficit. There were three main reasons for this change. First, President Bush signed into law several major tax cuts, which he had promised during the 2000 presidential campaign. Second, in 2001, the economy experienced a *recession* (a reduction in economic activity), which automatically decreased tax revenue and increased government spending. Third, there were increases in government spending on homeland security following the September 11, 2001 attacks and on the subsequent wars in Iraq and Afghanistan.

Truly dramatic increases in the debt-to-GDP ratio started occurring in 2008, as the economy experienced a financial crisis and a deep recession. (The accompanying FYI box addresses this topic briefly, but we will study it more fully in coming chapters.) The recession automatically increased the budget deficit, and several policy measures enacted during the Bush and Obama administrations aimed at combating the recession reduced tax revenue and increased government spending even more. From 2009 to 2012, the federal government's budget deficit averaged about 9 percent of GDP, levels not seen since World War II. The borrowing to finance these deficits led to an increase in the debt-to-GDP ratio from 39 percent in 2008 to 70 percent in 2012. After 2012, as the economy recovered, the budget deficits shrank, and the increases in the debt-to-GDP ratio became smaller. ●

 *If more Americans adopted a "live for today" approach to life, how would this affect saving, investment, and the interest rate?*

## Financial Crises

In 2008 and 2009, the U.S. economy and many other major economies around the world experienced a financial crisis, which in turn led to a deep downturn in economic activity. We will examine these events in detail later in this book. But because this chapter introduces the financial system, let's discuss briefly the key elements of financial crises.

The first element of a financial crisis is a large decline in some asset prices. In 2008 and 2009, that asset was real estate. The price of housing, after experiencing a boom earlier in the decade, fell by about 30 percent over just a few years. Such a large decline in real estate prices had not been seen in the United States since the 1930s.

The second element of a financial crisis is widespread insolvencies at financial institutions. (A company is *insolvent* when its debts exceed the value of its assets.) In 2008 and 2009, many banks and other financial firms had in effect placed bets on real estate prices by holding mortgages backed by that real estate. When house prices fell, large numbers of homeowners stopped repaying their loans. These defaults pushed several major financial institutions toward bankruptcy.

The third element of a financial crisis is a decline in confidence in financial institutions. Although some deposits in banks are insured by government policies, not all are. As insolvencies mounted, every financial institution became a possible candidate for the next bankruptcy. Individuals and firms with uninsured deposits in those institutions pulled out their money. Facing a rash of withdrawals, banks started selling off assets (sometimes at reduced "fire-sale" prices) and cut back on new lending.

The fourth element of a financial crisis is a credit crunch. With many financial institutions facing difficulties, prospective borrowers had trouble getting loans, even if they had profitable investment projects. In essence, the financial system had trouble performing its normal function of directing the resources of savers into the hands of borrowers with the best investment opportunities.

The fifth element of a financial crisis is an economic downturn. With people unable to obtain financing for new investment projects, the overall demand for goods and services declined. As a result, for reasons we discuss more fully later in the book, national income fell and unemployment rose.

The sixth and final element of a financial crisis is a vicious circle. The economic downturn reduced the profitability of many companies and the value of many assets. Thus, we started over again at step one, and the problems in the financial system and the economic downturn reinforced each other.

Financial crises, such as the one of 2008 and 2009, can have severe consequences. Fortunately, they do end. Financial institutions eventually get back on their feet, perhaps with some help from government policy, and they return to their normal function of financial intermediation. ■

# 18-4 Conclusion

"Neither a borrower nor a lender be," Polonius advises his son in Shakespeare's *Hamlet*. If everyone followed this advice, this chapter would have been unnecessary.

Few economists would agree with Polonius. In our economy, people borrow and lend often, and usually for good reason. You may borrow one day to start your own business or to buy a home. And people may lend to you in the hope that the interest you pay will allow them to enjoy a more prosperous retirement. The financial system's job is to coordinate all this borrowing and lending activity.

In many ways, financial markets are like other markets in the economy. The price of loanable funds—the interest rate—is governed by the forces of supply and demand, just as other prices in the economy are. And we can analyze shifts in supply or demand in financial markets as we do in other markets. One of the *Ten Principles of Economics* introduced in Chapter 1 is that markets are usually a good way to organize economic activity. This principle applies to financial markets as well. When financial markets bring the supply and demand for loanable funds into balance, they help allocate the economy's scarce resources to their most efficient uses.

In one way, however, financial markets are special. Financial markets, unlike most other markets, serve the important role of linking the present and the future. Those who supply loanable funds—savers—do so because they want to convert some of their current income into future purchasing power. Those who demand loanable funds—borrowers—do so because they want to invest today in order to have additional capital in the future to produce goods and services. Thus, well-functioning financial markets are important not only for current generations but also for future generations who will inherit many of the resulting benefits.

---

## CHAPTER QuickQuiz

1. Elaine wants to buy and operate an ice-cream truck but doesn't have the financial resources to start the business. She borrows $10,000 from her friend George, to whom she promises an interest rate of 7 percent, and gets another $20,000 from her friend Jerry, to whom she promises a third of her profits. What best describes this situation?
   a. George is a stockholder, and Elaine is a bondholder.
   b. George is a stockholder, and Jerry is a bondholder.
   c. Jerry is a stockholder, and Elaine is a bondholder.
   d. Jerry is a stockholder, and George is a bondholder.

2. If the government collects more in tax revenue than it spends, and households consume more than they get in after-tax income, then
   a. private and public saving are both positive.
   b. private and public saving are both negative.
   c. private saving is positive, but public saving is negative.
   d. private saving is negative, but public saving is positive.

3. A closed economy has income of $1,000, government spending of $200, taxes of $150, and investment of $250. What is private saving?
   a. $100
   b. $200
   c. $300
   d. $400

4. If a popular TV show on personal finance convinces Americans to save more for retirement, the _____ curve for loanable funds would shift, driving the equilibrium interest rate _____.
   a. supply, up
   b. supply, down
   c. demand, up
   d. demand, down

5. If the business community becomes more optimistic about the profitability of capital, the _____ curve for loanable funds would shift, driving the equilibrium interest rate _____.
   a. supply, up
   b. supply, down
   c. demand, up
   d. demand, down

6. From 2008 to 2012, the ratio of government debt to GDP in the United States
   a. increased markedly.
   b. decreased markedly.
   c. was stable at a historically high level.
   d. was stable at a historically low level.

---

## SUMMARY

- The U.S. financial system is made up of many types of financial institutions, such as the bond market, the stock market, banks, and mutual funds. All these institutions act to direct the resources of households that want to save some of their income into the hands of households and firms that want to borrow.

- National income accounting identities reveal some important relationships among macroeconomic variables. In particular, for a closed economy, national saving must equal investment. Financial institutions are the mechanism through which the economy matches one person's saving with another person's investment.

- The interest rate is determined by the supply and demand for loanable funds. The supply of loanable funds comes from households that want to save some of their income and lend it out. The demand for loanable funds comes from households and firms that want to borrow for investment. To analyze how any policy or event affects the interest rate, one must consider how it affects the supply and demand for loanable funds.

- National saving equals private saving plus public saving. A government budget deficit represents negative public saving and, therefore, reduces national saving and the supply of loanable funds available to finance investment. When a government budget deficit crowds out investment, it reduces the growth of productivity and GDP.

## KEY CONCEPTS

financial system, p. 372
financial markets, p. 372
bond, p. 373
stock, p. 373
financial intermediaries, p. 374

mutual fund, p. 375
national saving (saving), p. 378
private saving, p. 378
public saving, p. 378
budget surplus, p. 378

budget deficit, p. 378
market for loanable funds, p. 379
crowding out, p. 385

## QUESTIONS FOR REVIEW

1. What is the role of the financial system? Name and describe two markets that are part of the financial system in the U.S. economy. Name and describe two financial intermediaries.

2. Why is it important for people who own stocks and bonds to diversify their holdings? What type of financial institution makes diversification easier?

3. What is national saving? What is private saving? What is public saving? How are these three variables related?

4. What is investment? How is it related to national saving in a closed economy?

5. Describe a change in the tax code that might increase private saving. If this policy were implemented, how would it affect the market for loanable funds?

6. What is a government budget deficit? How does it affect interest rates, investment, and economic growth?

## PROBLEMS AND APPLICATIONS

1. For each of the following pairs, which bond would you expect to pay a higher interest rate? Explain.
   a. a bond of the U.S. government or a bond of an Eastern European government
   b. a bond that repays the principal in year 2020 or a bond that repays the principal in year 2040
   c. a bond from Coca-Cola or a bond from a software company you run in your garage
   d. a bond issued by the federal government or a bond issued by New York State

2. Many workers hold large amounts of stock issued by the firms at which they work. Why do you suppose companies encourage this behavior? Why might a

person *not* want to hold stock in the company where he works?

3. Explain the difference between saving and investment as defined by a macroeconomist. Which of the following situations represent investment and which represent saving? Explain.
   a. Your family takes out a mortgage and buys a new house.
   b. You use your $200 paycheck to buy stock in AT&T.
   c. Your roommate earns $100 and deposits it in his account at a bank.
   d. You borrow $1,000 from a bank to buy a car to use in your pizza delivery business.

4. Suppose GDP is $8 trillion, taxes are $1.5 trillion, private saving is $0.5 trillion, and public saving is $0.2 trillion. Assuming this economy is closed, calculate consumption, government purchases, national saving, and investment.

5. Economists in Funlandia, a closed economy, have collected the following information about the economy for a particular year:

$Y = 10,000$

$C = 6,000$

$T = 1,500$

$G = 1,700$

The economists also estimate that the investment function is:

$$I = 3,300 - 100r,$$

where $r$ is the country's real interest rate, expressed as a percentage. Calculate private saving, public saving, national saving, investment, and the equilibrium real interest rate.

6. Suppose that Intel is considering building a new chip-making factory.
   a. Assuming that Intel needs to borrow money in the bond market, why would an increase in interest rates affect Intel's decision about whether to build the factory?
   b. If Intel has enough of its own funds to finance the new factory without borrowing, would an increase in interest rates still affect Intel's decision about whether to build the factory? Explain.

7. Three students have each saved $1,000. Each has an investment opportunity in which he or she can invest up to $2,000. Here are the rates of return on the students' investment projects:

   | | |
   |---|---|
   | Harry | 5 percent |
   | Ron | 8 percent |
   | Hermione | 20 percent |

   a. If borrowing and lending are prohibited, so each student uses only personal saving to finance his or her own investment project, how much will each student have a year later when the project pays its return?
   b. Now suppose their school opens up a market for loanable funds in which students can borrow and lend among themselves at an interest rate $r$. What

would determine whether a student would choose to be a borrower or lender in this market?
   c. Among these three students, what would be the quantity of loanable funds supplied and quantity demanded at an interest rate of 7 percent? At 10 percent?
   d. At what interest rate would the loanable funds market among these three students be in equilibrium? At this interest rate, which student(s) would borrow and which student(s) would lend?
   e. At the equilibrium interest rate, how much does each student have a year later after the investment projects pay their return and loans have been repaid? Compare your answers to those you gave in part (a). Who benefits from the existence of the loanable funds market—the borrowers or the lenders? Is anyone worse off?

8. Suppose the government borrows $20 billion more next year than this year.
   a. Use a supply-and-demand diagram to analyze this policy. Does the interest rate rise or fall?
   b. What happens to investment? To private saving? To public saving? To national saving? Compare the size of the changes to the $20 billion of extra government borrowing.
   c. How does the elasticity of supply of loanable funds affect the size of these changes?
   d. How does the elasticity of demand for loanable funds affect the size of these changes?
   e. Suppose households believe that greater government borrowing today implies higher taxes to pay off the government debt in the future. What does this belief do to private saving and the supply of loanable funds today? Does it increase or decrease the effects you discussed in parts (a) and (b)?

9. This chapter explains that investment can be increased both by reducing taxes on private saving and by reducing the government budget deficit.
   a. Why is it difficult to implement both of these policies at the same time?
   b. What would you need to know about private saving to judge which of these two policies would be a more effective way to raise investment?

To find additional study resources, visit cengagebrain.com, and search for "Mankiw."

# The Basic Tools of Finance

Sometime in your life, you will deal with the economy's financial system. You will deposit your savings in a bank account, or you will take out a loan to cover tuition or to buy a house. After you have a job, your employer will start a retirement account for you, and you will decide whether to invest the funds in stocks, bonds, or other financial instruments. If you try to put together your own portfolio, you will have to decide between investing in established companies such as General Electric or newer ones such as Twitter. And in the media, you will hear reports about whether the stock market is up or down, together with the often feeble attempts to explain why the market behaves as it does.

If you reflect for a moment on the many financial decisions you will make during your life, you will see two related elements in almost all of them: time and risk.

As we saw in the preceding two chapters, the financial system coordinates the economy's saving and investment, which in turn are crucial determinants of economic growth. Most fundamentally, the financial system concerns decisions and actions we undertake today that will affect our lives in the future. But the future is unknown. When a person decides to allocate some saving, or a firm decides to undertake an investment, the decision is based on a guess about the likely result. The actual result, however, could end up being very different from what was expected.

**finance**

the field that studies how people make decisions regarding the allocation of resources over time and the handling of risk

This chapter introduces some tools that help us understand the decisions that people make as they participate in financial markets. The field of **finance** develops these tools in great detail, and you may choose to take courses that focus on this topic. But because the financial system is so important to the functioning of the economy, many of the basic insights of finance are central to understanding how the economy works. The tools of finance can also help you think through some of the decisions that you will make in your own life.

This chapter takes up three topics. First, we discuss how to compare sums of money at different points in time. Second, we discuss how to manage risk. Third, we build on our analysis of time and risk to examine what determines the value of an asset, such as a share of stock.

# 19-1 Present Value: Measuring the Time Value of Money

Imagine that someone offers to give you $100 today or $100 in 10 years. Which would you choose? This is an easy question. Getting $100 today is better because you can always deposit the money in a bank, still have it in 10 years, and earn interest on the $100 along the way. The lesson: Money today is more valuable than the same amount of money in the future.

Now consider a harder question: Imagine that someone offers you $100 today or $200 in 10 years. Which would you choose? To answer this question, you need some way to compare sums of money from different points in time. Economists do this with a concept called present value. The **present value** of any future sum of money is the amount today that would be needed, at current interest rates, to produce that future sum.

**present value**

the amount of money today that would be needed, using prevailing interest rates, to produce a given future amount of money

To learn how to use the concept of present value, let's work through a couple of simple examples:

**future value**

the amount of money in the future that an amount of money today will yield, given prevailing interest rates

*Question*: If you put $100 in a bank account today, how much will it be worth in $N$ years? That is, what will be the **future value** of this $100?

*Answer*: Let's use $r$ to denote the interest rate expressed in decimal form (so an interest rate of 5 percent means $r = 0.05$). Suppose that interest is paid annually and that it remains in the bank account to earn more interest—a process called **compounding**. Then the $100 will become

**compounding**

the accumulation of a sum of money in, say, a bank account, where the interest earned remains in the account to earn additional interest in the future

| | |
|---|---|
| $(1 + r) \times \$100$ | after 1 year, |
| $(1 + r) \times (1 + r) \times \$100 = (1 + r)^2 \times \$100$ | after 2 years, |
| $(1 + r) \times (1 + r) \times (1 + r) \times \$100 = (1 + r)^3 \times \$100$ | after 3 years, . . . |
| $(1 + r)^N \times \$100$ | after $N$ years. |

For example, if we are investing at an interest rate of 5 percent for 10 years, then the future value of the $100 will be $(1.05)^{10} \times \$100$, or $163.

*Question*: Now suppose you are going to be paid $200 in $N$ years. What is the *present value* of this future payment? That is, how much would you have to deposit in a bank right now to yield $200 in $N$ years?

*Answer*: To answer this question, just turn the previous answer on its head. In the last question, we computed a future value from a present value by *multiplying* by the factor $(1 + r)^N$. To compute a present value from a future value, we *divide* by the factor $(1 + r)^N$. Thus, the present value of $200 in $N$ years is $200/(1 + r)^N$. If that amount is deposited in a bank today, after $N$ years it will become $(1 + r)^N \times$ [$200/$(1 + r)^N$], which equals $200. For instance, if the interest rate is 5 percent, the present value of $200 to be paid in 10 years is $200/(1.05)^{10}$, or $123. This means that $123 deposited today in a bank account that earned 5 percent would produce $200 after 10 years.

This illustrates the general formula:

- If $r$ is the interest rate, then an amount $X$ to be received in $N$ years has a present value of $X/(1 + r)^N$.

Because the possibility of earning interest reduces the present value below the amount $X$, the process of finding a present value of a future sum of money is called *discounting*. This formula shows precisely how much future sums should be discounted.

Let's now return to our earlier question: Should you choose $100 today or $200 in 10 years? Based on our calculation of present value using an interest rate of 5 percent, you should prefer the $200 in 10 years. The future $200 has a present value of $123, which is greater than $100. You are better off waiting for the future sum.

Notice that the answer to our question depends on the interest rate. If the interest rate were 8 percent, then the $200 in 10 years would have a present value of $200/(1.08)^{10}$, which is only $93. In this case, you should take the $100 today. Why should the interest rate matter for your choice? The answer is that the higher the interest rate, the more you can earn by depositing your money in a bank, so the more attractive getting $100 today becomes.

The concept of present value is useful in many applications, including the decisions that companies face when evaluating investment projects. For instance, imagine that General Motors is thinking about building a new factory. Suppose that the factory will cost $100 million today and will yield the company $200 million in 10 years. Should General Motors undertake the project? You can see that this decision is exactly like the one we have been studying. To make its decision, the company should compare the present value of the $200 million return to the $100 million cost.

The company's decision, therefore, will depend on the interest rate. If the interest rate is 5 percent, then the present value of the $200 million return from the factory is $123 million, and the company will choose to pay the $100 million cost. By contrast, if the interest rate is 8 percent, then the present value of the return is only $93 million, and the company will decide to forgo the project. Thus, the concept of present value helps explain why investment—and thus the quantity of loanable funds demanded—declines when the interest rate rises.

Here is another application of present value: Suppose you win a million-dollar lottery and are given a choice between $20,000 a year for 50 years (totaling $1,000,000) or an immediate payment of $400,000. Which would you choose?

## The Magic of Compounding and the Rule of 70

Suppose you observe that one country has an average growth rate of 1 percent per year, while another has an average growth rate of 3 percent per year. At first, this might not seem like a big deal. What difference can 2 percent make?

The answer is: a big difference. Growth rates that seem small when written in percentage terms are large after they are compounded for many years.

Consider an example. Suppose that two college graduates—Elliot and Darlene—both take their first jobs at the age of 22 earning $30,000 a year. Elliot lives in an economy where all incomes grow at 1 percent per year, while Darlene lives in one where incomes grow at 3 percent per year. Straightforward calculations show what happens. Forty years later, when both are 62 years old, Elliot earns $45,000 a year, while Darlene earns $98,000. Because of that difference of 2 percentage points in the growth rate, Darlene's salary is more than twice Elliot's.

An old rule of thumb, called the *rule of 70*, is helpful in understanding growth rates and the effects of compounding. According to the rule of 70, if some variable grows at a rate of *x* percent per year, then that variable doubles in approximately 70/*x* years. In Elliot's economy, incomes grow at 1 percent per year, so it takes about 70 years for incomes to double. In Darlene's economy, incomes grow at 3 percent per year, so it takes about 70/3, or 23, years for incomes to double.

The rule of 70 applies not only to a growing economy but also to a growing savings account. Here is an example: In 1791, Ben Franklin died and left $5,000 to be invested for a period of 200 years to benefit medical students and scientific research. If this money had earned 7 percent per year (which would, in fact, have been possible), the investment would have doubled in value every 10 years. Over 200 years, it would have doubled 20 times. At the end of 200 years of compounding, the investment would have been worth $2^{20} \times \$5,000$, which is about $5 billion. (In fact, Franklin's $5,000 grew to only $2 million over 200 years because some of the money was spent along the way.)

As these examples show, growth rates and interest rates compounded over many years can lead to some spectacular results. That is probably why Albert Einstein once called compounding "the greatest mathematical discovery of all time." ■

To make the right choice, you need to calculate the present value of the stream of payments. Let's suppose the interest rate is 7 percent. After performing 50 calculations similar to those above (one calculation for each payment) and adding up the results, you would learn that the present value of this million-dollar prize at a 7 percent interest rate is only $276,000. You are better off picking the immediate payment of $400,000. The million dollars may seem like more money, but the future cash flows, once discounted to the present, are worth far less.

 *The interest rate is 7 percent. What is the present value of $150 to be received in 10 years?*

# 19-2  Managing Risk

Life is full of gambles. When you go skiing, you risk breaking your leg in a fall. When you drive to work, you risk a car accident. When you put some of your savings in the stock market, you risk a fall in stock prices. The rational response to this risk is not necessarily to avoid it at any cost but to take it into account in your decision making. Let's consider how a person might do that.

### 19-2a  Risk Aversion

**risk aversion**
a dislike of uncertainty

Most people are **risk averse**. This means more than that people dislike bad things happening to them. It means that they dislike bad things more than they like comparable good things.

For example, suppose a friend offers you the following opportunity. She will toss a coin. If it comes up heads, she will pay you $1,000. But if it comes up tails, you will have to pay her $1,000. Would you accept the bargain? You wouldn't if you were risk averse. For a risk-averse person, the pain of losing the $1,000 would exceed the pleasure from winning $1,000.

Economists have developed models of risk aversion using the concept of *utility*, which is a person's subjective measure of well-being or satisfaction. Every level of wealth provides a certain amount of utility, as shown by the utility function in Figure 1. But the function exhibits the property of diminishing marginal utility: The more wealth a person has, the less utility she gets from an additional dollar. Thus, in the figure, the utility function gets flatter as wealth increases. Because of diminishing marginal utility, the utility lost from losing the $1,000 bet is more than the utility gained from winning it. As a result, people are risk averse.

Risk aversion provides the starting point for explaining various things we observe in the economy. Let's consider three of them: insurance, diversification, and the risk-return trade-off.

### 19-2b The Markets for Insurance

One way to deal with risk is to buy insurance. The general feature of insurance contracts is that a person facing a risk pays a fee to an insurance company, which in return agrees to accept all or part of the risk. There are many types of insurance. Car insurance covers the risk of your being in an auto accident, fire insurance covers the risk that your house will burn down, health insurance covers the risk that you might need expensive medical treatment, and life insurance covers the risk that you will die and leave your family without your income. There is also insurance against the risk of living too long: For a fee paid today, an insurance company will pay you an *annuity*—a regular income every year until you die.

In a sense, every insurance contract is a gamble. It is possible that you will not be in an auto accident, that your house will not burn down, and that you will not need expensive medical treatment. In most years, you will pay the insurance company the premium and get nothing in return except peace of mind. Indeed,

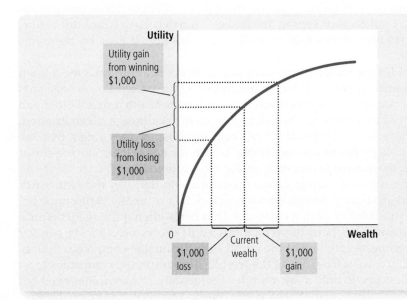

**FIGURE 1**

**The Utility Function**
This utility function shows how utility, a subjective measure of satisfaction, depends on wealth. As wealth rises, the utility function becomes flatter, reflecting the property of diminishing marginal utility. Because of diminishing marginal utility, a $1,000 loss decreases utility by more than a $1,000 gain increases it.

the insurance company is counting on the fact that most people will not make claims on their policies; otherwise, it couldn't pay out large claims to the unlucky few and still stay in business.

From the standpoint of the economy as a whole, the role of insurance is not to eliminate the risks inherent in life but to spread them around more efficiently. Consider fire insurance, for instance. Owning fire insurance does not reduce the risk of losing your home in a fire. But if that unlucky event occurs, the insurance company compensates you. The risk, rather than being borne by you alone, is shared among the thousands of insurance-company shareholders. Because people are risk averse, it is easier for 10,000 people to bear 1/10,000 of the risk than for one person to bear the entire risk herself.

The markets for insurance suffer from two types of problems that impede their ability to spread risk. One problem is *adverse selection*: A high-risk person is more likely to apply for insurance than a low-risk person because a high-risk person would benefit more from insurance protection. A second problem is *moral hazard*: After people buy insurance, they have less incentive to be careful about their risky behavior because the insurance company will cover much of the resulting losses. Insurance companies are aware of these problems, but they cannot fully guard against them. An insurance company cannot perfectly distinguish between high-risk and low-risk customers, and it cannot monitor all of its customers' risky behavior. The price of insurance reflects the actual risks that the insurance company will face after the insurance is bought. The high price of insurance is why some people, especially those who know themselves to be low-risk, decide against buying it and, instead, endure some of life's uncertainty on their own.

### 19-2c  Diversification of Firm-Specific Risk

In 2002, Enron, a large and once widely respected company, went bankrupt amid accusations of fraud and accounting irregularities. Several of the company's top executives were prosecuted and ended up going to prison. The saddest part of the story, however, involved thousands of lower-level employees. Not only did they lose their jobs but many lost their life savings as well. The employees had put about two-thirds of their retirement funds in Enron stock, which became worthless.

If there is one piece of practical advice that finance offers to risk-averse people, it is this: "Don't put all your eggs in one basket." You may have heard this before, but finance has turned this folk wisdom into a science. It goes by the name **diversification**.

**diversification**
the reduction of risk achieved by replacing a single risk with a large number of smaller, unrelated risks

The market for insurance is one example of diversification. Imagine a town with 10,000 homeowners, each facing the risk of a house fire. If someone starts an insurance company and each person in town becomes both a shareholder and a policyholder of the company, they all reduce their risk through diversification. Each person now faces 1/10,000 of the risk of 10,000 possible fires, rather than the entire risk of a single fire in her own home. Unless the entire town catches fire at the same time, the downside that each person faces is much smaller.

When people use their savings to buy financial assets, they can also reduce risk through diversification. A person who buys stock in a company is placing a bet on the future profitability of that company. That bet is often quite risky because companies' fortunes are hard to predict. Microsoft evolved from a start-up by some geeky teenagers into one of the world's most valuable companies in only a few years; Enron went from one of the world's most respected companies to an almost worthless one in only a few months. Fortunately, a shareholder need not

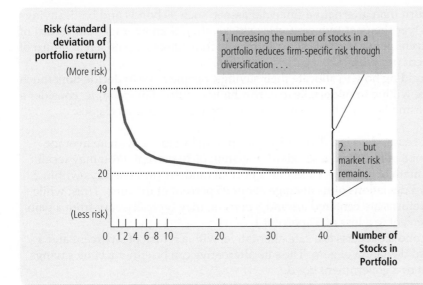

## FIGURE 2

**Diversification Reduces Risk**
This figure shows how the risk of a portfolio, measured here with a statistic called the *standard deviation*, depends on the number of stocks in the portfolio. The investor is assumed to put an equal percentage of her portfolio in each of the stocks. Increasing the number of stocks reduces, but does not eliminate, the amount of risk in a stock portfolio.

**Source:** Adapted from Meir Statman, "How Many Stocks Make a Diversified Portfolio?" *Journal of Financial and Quantitative Analysis* 22 (September 1987): 353–364.

tie her own fortune to that of any single company. Risk can be reduced by placing a large number of small bets, rather than a small number of large ones.

Figure 2 shows how the risk of a portfolio of stocks depends on the number of stocks in the portfolio. Risk is measured here with a statistic called the *standard deviation*, which you may have learned about in a math or statistics class. The standard deviation measures the volatility of a variable—that is, how much the variable is likely to fluctuate. The higher the standard deviation of a portfolio's return, the more volatile its return is likely to be, and the riskier it is that someone holding the portfolio will fail to get the return that she expected.

The figure shows that the risk of a stock portfolio falls substantially as the number of stocks increases. For a portfolio with a single stock, the standard deviation is 49 percent. Going from 1 stock to 10 stocks eliminates about half the risk. Going from 10 to 20 stocks reduces the risk by another 10 percent. As the number of stocks continues to increase, risk continues to fall, although the reductions in risk after 20 or 30 stocks are small.

Notice that it is impossible to eliminate all risk by increasing the number of stocks in the portfolio. Diversification can eliminate **firm-specific risk**—the uncertainty associated with the specific companies. But diversification cannot eliminate **market risk**—the uncertainty associated with the entire economy, which affects all companies traded on the stock market. For example, when the economy goes into a recession, most companies experience falling sales, reduced profit, and low stock returns. Diversification reduces the risk of holding stocks, but it does not eliminate it.

**firm-specific risk**
risk that affects only a single company

**market risk**
risk that affects all companies in the stock market

### 19-2d The Trade-off between Risk and Return

One of the *Ten Principles of Economics* in Chapter 1 is that people face trade-offs. The trade-off that is most relevant for understanding financial decisions is the trade-off between risk and return.

As we have seen, there are risks inherent in holding stocks, even in a diversified portfolio. But risk-averse people are willing to accept this uncertainty because they are compensated for doing so. Historically, stocks have offered much higher rates of return than alternative financial assets, such as bonds and bank savings accounts. Over the past two centuries, stocks offered an average real return of about 8 percent per year, while short-term government bonds paid a real return of only 3 percent per year.

When deciding how to allocate their savings, people have to decide how much risk they are willing to undertake to earn a higher return. For example, consider a person choosing how to allocate her portfolio between two asset classes:

- The first asset class is a diversified group of risky stocks, with an average return of 8 percent and a standard deviation of 20 percent. (You may recall from a math or statistics class that a normal random variable stays within 2 standard deviations of its average about 95 percent of the time. Thus, while actual returns are centered around 8 percent, they typically vary from a gain of 48 percent to a loss of 32 percent.)
- The second asset class is a safe alternative, with a return of 3 percent and a standard deviation of zero. The safe alternative can be either a bank savings account or a government bond.

Figure 3 illustrates the trade-off between risk and return. Each point in this figure represents a particular allocation of a portfolio between risky stocks and the safe asset. The figure shows that the more the individual puts into stocks, the greater both the risk and the return are.

Acknowledging the risk-return trade-off does not, by itself, tell us what a person should do. The choice of a particular combination of risk and return depends on a person's risk aversion, which reflects her own preferences. But it is important for stockholders to recognize that the higher average return that they enjoy comes at the price of higher risk.

**QuickQuiz** *Describe three ways that a risk-averse person might reduce the risk she faces.*

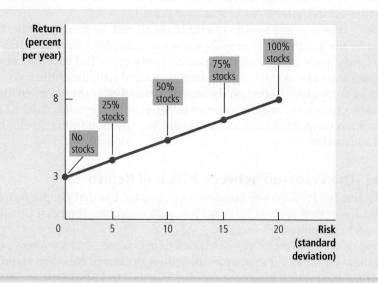

## FIGURE 3

**The Trade-off between Risk and Return**
When people increase the percentage of their savings that they have invested in stocks, they increase the average return they can expect to earn, but they also increase the risks they face.

# 19-3 Asset Valuation

Now that we have developed a basic understanding of the two building blocks of finance—time and risk—let's apply this knowledge. This section considers a simple question: What determines the price of a share of stock? As with most prices, the answer is supply and demand. But that is not the end of the story. To understand stock prices, we need to think more deeply about what determines a person's willingness to pay for a share of stock.

## 19-3a Fundamental Analysis

Let's imagine that you have decided to put 60 percent of your savings into stock, and to achieve diversification, you have decided to buy twenty different stocks. If you open up the newspaper, you will find thousands of stocks listed. How should you pick the twenty for your portfolio?

When you buy stock, you are buying shares in a business. To decide which businesses you want to own, it is natural to consider two things: the value of that share of the business and the price at which the shares are being sold. If the price is less than the value, the stock is said to be *undervalued*. If the price is more than the value, the stock is said to be *overvalued*. If the price and the value are equal, the stock is said to be *fairly valued*. When choosing twenty stocks for your portfolio, you should prefer undervalued stocks. In these cases, you are getting a bargain by paying less than the business is worth.

This is easier said than done. Learning the price is easy: You can just look it up. Determining the value of the business is the hard part. The term **fundamental analysis** refers to the detailed analysis of a company to estimate its value. Many Wall Street firms hire stock analysts to conduct such fundamental analysis and offer advice about which stocks to buy.

The value of a stock to a stockholder is what she gets out of owning it, which includes the present value of the stream of dividend payments and the final sale price. Recall that *dividends* are the cash payments that a company makes to its shareholders. A company's ability to pay dividends, as well as the value of the stock when the stockholder sells her shares, depends on the company's ability to earn profits. Its profitability, in turn, depends on a large number of factors: the demand for its product, how much competition it faces, how much capital it has in place, whether its workers are unionized, how loyal its customers are, what kinds of government regulations and taxes it faces, and so on. The goal of fundamental analysis is to take all these factors into account to determine how much a share of stock in the company is worth.

If you want to rely on fundamental analysis to pick a stock portfolio, there are three ways to do it. One way is to do all the necessary research yourself, such as by reading through companies' annual reports. A second way is to rely on the advice of Wall Street analysts. A third way is to buy shares in a mutual fund, which has a manager who conducts fundamental analysis and makes the decision for you.

**fundamental analysis**
the study of a company's accounting statements and future prospects to determine its value

## 19-3b The Efficient Markets Hypothesis

There is another way to choose twenty stocks for your portfolio: Pick them randomly by, for instance, putting the stock pages on your bulletin board and throwing darts at them. This may sound crazy, but there is reason to believe that it won't lead you too far astray. That reason is called the **efficient markets hypothesis**.

**efficient markets hypothesis**
the theory that asset prices reflect all publicly available information about the value of an asset

To understand this theory, the starting point is to acknowledge that each company listed on a major stock exchange is followed closely by many money managers, such as the individuals who run mutual funds. Every day, these managers monitor news stories and conduct fundamental analysis to try to determine the stock's value. Their job is to buy a stock when its price falls below its fundamental value and to sell it when its price rises above its fundamental value.

The second piece to the efficient markets hypothesis is that the equilibrium of supply and demand sets the market price. This means that, at the market price, the number of shares being offered for sale exactly equals the number of shares that people want to buy. In other words, at the market price, the number of people who think the stock is overvalued exactly balances the number of people who think it's undervalued. As judged by the typical person in the market, all stocks are fairly valued all the time.

**informational efficiency**
the description of asset prices that rationally reflect all available information

According to this theory, the stock market exhibits **informational efficiency**: It reflects all available information about the value of the asset. Stock prices change when information changes. When good news about the company's prospects becomes public, the value and the stock price both rise. When the company's prospects deteriorate, the value and price both fall. But at any moment in time, the market price is the best guess of the company's value based on available information.

**random walk**
the path of a variable whose changes are impossible to predict

One implication of the efficient markets hypothesis is that stock prices should follow a **random walk**. This means that changes in stock prices are impossible to predict from available information. If, based on publicly available information, a person could predict that a stock price would rise by 10 percent tomorrow, then the stock market must be failing to incorporate that information today. According to this theory, the only thing that can move stock prices is news that changes the market's perception of the company's value. But news must be unpredictable—otherwise, it wouldn't really be news. For the same reason, changes in stock prices should be unpredictable.

If the efficient markets hypothesis is correct, then there is little point in spending many hours studying the business page to decide which twenty stocks to add to your portfolio. If prices reflect all available information, no stock is a better buy than any other. The best you can do is to buy a diversified portfolio.

**CASE STUDY**

**RANDOM WALKS AND INDEX FUNDS**

The efficient markets hypothesis is a theory about how financial markets work. The theory may not be completely true: As we discuss in the next section, there is reason to doubt that stockholders are always rational and that stock prices are informationally efficient at every moment. Nonetheless, the efficient markets hypothesis does much better as a description of the world than you might expect.

There is much evidence that stock prices, even if not exactly a random walk, are very close to it. For example, you might be tempted to buy stocks that have recently risen and avoid stocks that have recently fallen (or perhaps just the opposite). But statistical studies have shown that following such trends (or bucking them) fails to outperform the market. The correlation between how well a stock does one year and how well it does the following year is about zero.

Some of the best evidence in favor of the efficient markets hypothesis comes from the performance of index funds. An index fund is a mutual fund that buys all the stocks in a given stock index. The performance of these funds can be compared with that of actively managed mutual funds, where a professional portfolio manager picks stocks based on extensive research and alleged expertise. In essence, an index fund buys all stocks, whereas active funds are supposed to buy only the best stocks.

In practice, active managers usually fail to beat index funds. For example, in the 15-year period ending February 2016, 81 percent of stock mutual funds performed worse than a broadly based index fund holding all stocks traded on U.S. stock exchanges. Over this period, the average annual return on stock funds fell short of the return on the index fund by 0.89 percentage points. Most active portfolio managers failed to beat the market because they trade more frequently, incurring more trading costs, and because they charge greater fees as compensation for their alleged expertise.

What about the 19 percent of managers who did beat the market? Perhaps they are smarter than average, or perhaps they were luckier. If you have 5,000 people flipping coins ten times, on average about 5 will flip ten heads; these 5 might claim an exceptional coin-flipping skill, but they would have trouble replicating the feat. Similarly, studies have shown that mutual fund managers with a history of superior performance usually fail to maintain it in subsequent periods.

The efficient markets hypothesis says that it is impossible to beat the market. The accumulation of many studies of financial markets confirms that beating the market is, at best, extremely difficult. Even if the efficient markets hypothesis is not an exact description of the world, it contains a large element of truth. ●

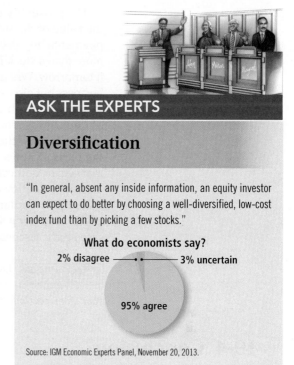

## ASK THE EXPERTS

### Diversification

"In general, absent any inside information, an equity investor can expect to do better by choosing a well-diversified, low-cost index fund than by picking a few stocks."

**What do economists say?**

2% disagree ——— 3% uncertain

95% agree

Source: IGM Economic Experts Panel, November 20, 2013.

### 19-3c Market Irrationality

The efficient markets hypothesis assumes that people buying and selling stock rationally process the information they have about the stock's underlying value. But is the stock market really that rational? Or do stock prices sometimes deviate from reasonable expectations of their true value?

There is a long tradition suggesting that fluctuations in stock prices are partly psychological. In the 1930s, economist John Maynard Keynes suggested that asset markets are driven by the "animal spirits" of investors—irrational waves of optimism and pessimism. In the 1990s, as the stock market soared to new heights, Fed Chairman Alan Greenspan questioned whether the boom reflected "irrational exuberance." Stock prices did subsequently fall, but whether the exuberance of the 1990s was irrational given the information available at the time remains debatable. Whenever the price of an asset rises above what appears to be its fundamental value, the market is said to be experiencing a *speculative bubble*.

The possibility of speculative bubbles in the stock market arises in part because the value of the stock to a stockholder depends not only on the stream of dividend payments but also on the final sale price. Thus, a person might be willing to pay more than a stock is worth today if she expects another person to pay even more for it tomorrow. When evaluating a stock, you have to estimate not only the value of the business but also what other people will think the business is worth in the future.

There is much debate among economists about the frequency and importance of departures from rational pricing. Believers in market irrationality point out (correctly) that the stock market often moves in ways that are hard to explain on the basis of news that might alter a rational valuation. Believers in the efficient markets hypothesis point out (correctly) that it is impossible to know the correct, rational valuation of a company, so one should not quickly jump to the conclusion that any particular valuation is irrational. Moreover, if the market were irrational, a rational person should be able to take advantage of this fact; yet as the previous case study discussed, beating the market is nearly impossible.

> **QuickQuiz**   Fortune *magazine regularly publishes a list of the "most respected" companies. According to the efficient markets hypothesis, if you restrict your stock portfolio to these companies, will you earn a better-than-average return? Explain.*

# 19-4 Conclusion

This chapter has developed some of the basic tools that people should (and often do) use as they make financial decisions. The concept of present value reminds us that a dollar in the future is less valuable than a dollar today, and it gives us a way to compare sums of money at different points in time. The theory of risk management reminds us that the future is uncertain and that risk-averse people can take precautions to guard against this uncertainty. The study of asset valuation tells us that the stock price of any company should reflect its expected future profitability.

Although most of the tools of finance are well established, there is more controversy about the validity of the efficient markets hypothesis and whether stock prices are, in practice, rational estimates of a company's true worth. Rational or not, the large movements in stock prices that we observe have important macroeconomic implications. Stock market fluctuations often go hand in hand with fluctuations in the economy more broadly. We revisit the stock market when we study economic fluctuations later in the book.

## CHAPTER QuickQuiz

1.  If the interest rate is zero, then $100 to be paid in 10 years has a present value that is
    a. less than $100.
    b. exactly $100.
    c. more than $100.
    d. indeterminate.

2.  If the interest rate is 10 percent, then the future value in 2 years of $100 today is
    a. $80.
    b. $83.
    c. $120.
    d. $121.

3.  If the interest rate is 10 percent, then the present value of $100 to be paid in 2 years is
    a. $80
    b. $83.
    c. $120.
    d. $121.

4.  The ability of insurance to spread risk is limited by
    a. risk aversion and moral hazard.
    b. risk aversion and adverse selection.
    c. moral hazard and adverse selection.
    d. risk aversion only.

5. The benefit of diversification when constructing a portfolio is that it can eliminate
   a. speculative bubbles.
   b. risk aversion.
   c. firm-specific risk.
   d. market risk.

6. According to the efficient markets hypothesis,
   a. changes in stock prices are impossible to predict from public information.
   b. excessive diversification can reduce an investor's expected portfolio returns.
   c. the stock market moves based on the changing animal spirits of investors.
   d. actively managed mutual funds should give higher returns than index funds.

## SUMMARY

- Because savings can earn interest, a sum of money today is more valuable than the same sum of money in the future. A person can compare sums from different times using the concept of present value. The present value of any future sum is the amount that would be needed today, given prevailing interest rates, to produce that future sum.
- Because of diminishing marginal utility, most people are risk averse. Risk-averse people can reduce risk by buying insurance, diversifying their holdings, and choosing a portfolio with lower risk and lower return.

- The value of an asset equals the present value of the cash flows the owner will receive. For a share of stock, these cash flows include the stream of dividends and the final sale price. According to the efficient markets hypothesis, financial markets process available information rationally, so a stock price always equals the best estimate of the value of the underlying business. Some economists question the efficient markets hypothesis, however, and believe that irrational psychological factors also influence asset prices.

## KEY CONCEPTS

finance, p. 394
present value, p. 394
future value, p. 394
compounding, p. 394

risk aversion, p. 396
diversification, p. 398
firm-specific risk, p. 399
market risk, p. 399

fundamental analysis, p. 401
efficient markets hypothesis, p. 401
informational efficiency, p. 402
random walk, p. 402

## QUESTIONS FOR REVIEW

1. The interest rate is 7 percent. Use the concept of present value to compare $200 to be received in 10 years and $300 to be received in 20 years.

2. What benefit do people get from the market for insurance? What two problems impede the insurance market from working perfectly?

3. What is diversification? Does a stockholder get a greater benefit from diversification when going from 1 to 10 stocks or when going from 100 to 120 stocks?

4. Comparing stocks and government bonds, which type of asset has more risk? Which pays a higher average return?

5. What factors should a stock analyst think about in determining the value of a share of stock?

6. Describe the efficient markets hypothesis, and give a piece of evidence consistent with this hypothesis.

7. Explain the view of those economists who are skeptical of the efficient markets hypothesis.

## PROBLEMS AND APPLICATIONS

1. According to an old myth, Native Americans sold the island of Manhattan about 400 years ago for $24. If they had invested this amount at an interest rate of 7 percent per year, how much, approximately, would they have today?

2. A company has an investment project that would cost $10 million today and yield a payoff of $15 million in 4 years.
   a. Should the firm undertake the project if the interest rate is 11 percent? 10 percent? 9 percent? 8 percent?
   b. Can you figure out the exact cutoff for the interest rate between profitability and nonprofitability?

3. Bond A pays $8,000 in 20 years. Bond B pays $8,000 in 40 years. (To keep things simple, assume these are zero-coupon bonds, which means the $8,000 is the only payment the bondholder receives.)
   a. If the interest rate is 3.5 percent, what is the value of each bond today? Which bond is worth more? Why? (*Hint*: You can use a calculator, but the rule of 70 should make the calculation easy.)
   b. If the interest rate increases to 7 percent, what is the value of each bond? Which bond has a larger *percentage* change in value?
   c. Based on the example above, complete the two blanks in this sentence: "The value of a bond [rises/falls] when the interest rate increases, and bonds with a longer time to maturity are [more/less] sensitive to changes in the interest rate."

4. Your bank account pays an interest rate of 8 percent. You are considering buying a share of stock in XYZ Corporation for $110. After 1, 2, and 3 years, it will pay a dividend of $5. You expect to sell the stock after 3 years for $120. Is XYZ a good investment? Support your answer with calculations.

5. For each of the following kinds of insurance, give an example of behavior that can be called *moral hazard* and another example of behavior that can be called *adverse selection*.
   a. health insurance
   b. car insurance
   c. life insurance

6. Which kind of stock would you expect to pay the higher average return: stock in an industry that is very sensitive to economic conditions (such as an automaker) or stock in an industry that is relatively insensitive to economic conditions (such as a water company)? Why?

7. A company faces two kinds of risk. A firm-specific risk is that a competitor might enter its market and take some of its customers. A market risk is that the economy might enter a recession, reducing sales. Which of these two risks would more likely cause the company's shareholders to demand a higher return? Why?

8. When company executives buy and sell stock based on private information they obtain as part of their jobs, they are engaged in *insider trading*.
   a. Give an example of inside information that might be useful for buying or selling stock.
   b. Those who trade stocks based on inside information usually earn very high rates of return. Does this fact violate the efficient markets hypothesis?
   c. Insider trading is illegal. Why do you suppose that is?

9. Jamal has a utility function $U = W^{1/2}$, where $W$ is his wealth in millions of dollars and $U$ is the utility he obtains from that wealth. In the final stage of a game show, the host offers Jamal a choice between (A) $4 million for sure, or (B) a gamble that pays $1 million with probability 0.6 and $9 million with probability 0.4.
   a. Graph Jamal's utility function. Is he risk averse? Explain.
   b. Does A or B offer Jamal a higher expected prize? Explain your reasoning with appropriate calculations. (*Hint*: The expected value of a random variable is the weighted average of the possible outcomes, where the probabilities are the weights.)
   c. Does A or B offer Jamal a higher expected utility? Again, show your calculations.
   d. Should Jamal pick A or B? Why?

To find additional study resources, visit cengagebrain.com, and search for "Mankiw."

# Unemployment

Losing a job can be the most distressing economic event in a person's life. Most people rely on their labor earnings to maintain their standard of living, and many people also get a sense of personal accomplishment from working. A job loss means a lower living standard in the present, anxiety about the future, and reduced self-esteem. It is not surprising, therefore, that politicians campaigning for office often speak about how their proposed policies will help create jobs.

In previous chapters, we have seen some of the forces that determine the level and growth of a country's standard of living. A country that saves and invests a high fraction of its income, for instance, enjoys more rapid growth in its capital stock and GDP than a similar country that saves and invests less. An even more obvious determinant of a country's

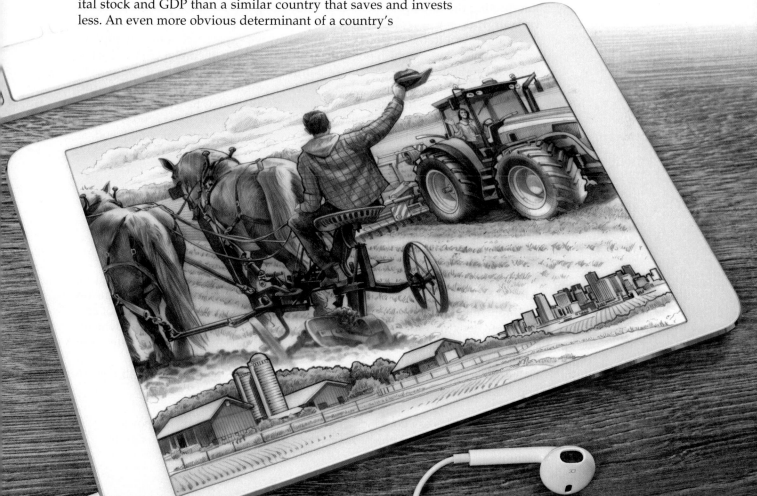

standard of living is the amount of unemployment it typically experiences. People who would like to work but cannot find a job are not contributing to the economy's production of goods and services. Although some degree of unemployment is inevitable in a complex economy with thousands of firms and millions of workers, the amount of unemployment varies substantially over time and across countries. When a country keeps its workers as fully employed as possible, it achieves a higher level of GDP than it would if it left many of its workers idle.

This chapter begins our study of unemployment. The problem of unemployment can be divided into two categories: the long-run problem and the short-run problem. The economy's *natural rate of unemployment* refers to the amount of unemployment that the economy normally experiences. *Cyclical unemployment* refers to the year-to-year fluctuations in unemployment around its natural rate, and it is closely associated with the short-run ups and downs of economic activity. Cyclical unemployment has its own explanation, which we defer until we study short-run economic fluctuations later in this book. In this chapter, we discuss the determinants of an economy's natural rate of unemployment. As we will see, the designation *natural* does not imply that this rate of unemployment is desirable. Nor does it imply that it is constant over time or impervious to economic policy. It just means that this unemployment does not go away on its own even in the long run.

We begin the chapter by looking at some of the relevant facts that describe unemployment. In particular, we examine three questions: How does the government measure the economy's rate of unemployment? What problems arise in interpreting the unemployment data? How long are the unemployed typically without work?

We then turn to the reasons economies always experience some unemployment and the ways in which policymakers can help the unemployed. We discuss four explanations for the economy's natural rate of unemployment: job search, minimum-wage laws, unions, and efficiency wages. As we will see, long-run unemployment does not arise from a single problem that has a single solution. Instead, it reflects a variety of related problems. As a result, there is no easy way for policymakers to reduce the economy's natural rate of unemployment and, at the same time, to alleviate the hardships experienced by the unemployed.

# 20-1 Identifying Unemployment

Let's start by examining more precisely what the term *unemployment* means.

## 20-1a How Is Unemployment Measured?

Measuring unemployment is the job of the Bureau of Labor Statistics (BLS), which is part of the Department of Labor. Every month, the BLS produces data on unemployment and on other aspects of the labor market, including types of employment, length of the average workweek, and the duration of unemployment. These data come from a regular survey of about 60,000 households, called the Current Population Survey.

Based on the answers to survey questions, the BLS places each adult (age 16 and older) in each surveyed household into one of three categories:

- *Employed:* This category includes those who worked as paid employees, worked in their own business, or worked as unpaid workers in a family member's business. Both full-time and part-time workers are counted. This category also includes those who were not working but who had jobs from which they were temporarily absent because of, for example, vacation, illness, or bad weather.

- *Unemployed:* This category includes those who were not employed, were available for work, and had tried to find employment during the previous four weeks. It also includes those waiting to be recalled to a job from which they had been laid off.
- *Not in the labor force:* This category includes those who fit neither of the first two categories, such as full-time students, homemakers, and retirees.

Figure 1 shows the breakdown into these categories for January 2016.

Once the BLS has placed all the individuals covered by the survey in a category, it computes various statistics to summarize the state of the labor market. The BLS defines the **labor force** as the sum of the employed and the unemployed:

$$\text{Labor force} = \text{Number of employed} + \text{Number of unemployed}.$$

The BLS defines the **unemployment rate** as the percentage of the labor force that is unemployed:

$$\text{Unemployment rate} = \frac{\text{Number of unemployed}}{\text{Labor force}} \times 100.$$

The BLS computes unemployment rates for the entire adult population and for specific groups defined by race, gender, and so on.

**labor force**
the total number of workers, including both the employed and the unemployed

**unemployment rate**
the percentage of the labor force that is unemployed

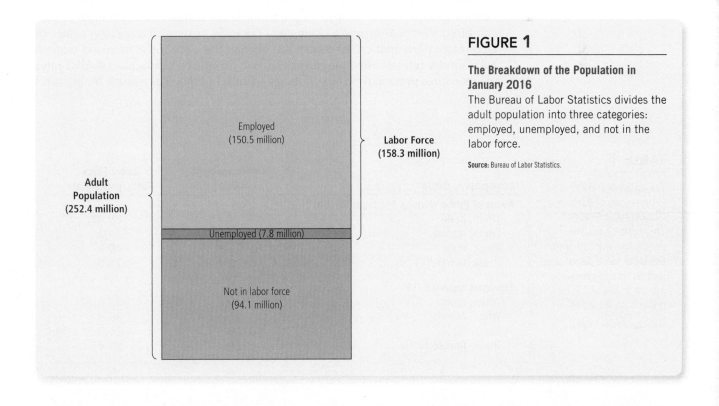

### FIGURE 1

**The Breakdown of the Population in January 2016**
The Bureau of Labor Statistics divides the adult population into three categories: employed, unemployed, and not in the labor force.

**Source:** Bureau of Labor Statistics.

**labor-force participation rate**

the percentage of the adult population that is in the labor force

The BLS uses the same survey to produce data on labor-force participation. The **labor-force participation rate** measures the percentage of the total adult population of the United States that is in the labor force:

$$\text{Labor-force participation rate} = \frac{\text{Labor force}}{\text{Adult population}} \times 100.$$

This statistic tells us the fraction of the population that has chosen to participate in the labor market. The labor-force participation rate, like the unemployment rate, is computed for both the entire adult population and more specific groups.

To see how these data are computed, consider the figures for January 2016. At that time, 150.5 million people were employed, and 7.8 million people were unemployed. The labor force was

$$\text{Labor force} = 150.5 + 7.8 = 158.3 \text{ million.}$$

The unemployment rate was

$$\text{Unemployment rate} = (7.8/158.3) \times 100 = 4.9 \text{ percent.}$$

Because the adult population was 252.4 million, the labor-force participation rate was

$$\text{Labor-force participation rate} = (158.3/252.4) \times 100 = 62.7 \text{ percent.}$$

Hence, in January 2016, almost two-thirds of the U.S. adult population were participating in the labor market, and 4.9 percent of those labor-market participants were without work.

Table 1 shows the statistics on unemployment and labor-force participation for various groups within the U.S. population. Three comparisons are most apparent. First, women of prime working age (25 to 54 years old) have lower rates of labor-force participation than men, but once in the labor force, men and women have similar rates of unemployment. Second, prime-age blacks have similar rates of labor-force participation as prime-age whites, but they have much higher rates

## TABLE 1

**The Labor-Market Experiences of Various Demographic Groups**
This table shows the unemployment rate and the labor-force participation rate of various groups in the U.S. population for 2014.

**Source:** Bureau of Labor Statistics.

| Demographic Group | Unemployment Rate | Labor-Force Participation Rate |
|---|---|---|
| **Adults of Prime Working Age (ages 25–54)** | | |
| White, male | 4.4% | 89.4% |
| White, female | 4.6 | 74.3 |
| Black, male | 10.1 | 80.7 |
| Black, female | 9.1 | 75.8 |
| **Teenagers (ages 16–19)** | | |
| White, male | 19.2 | 35.6 |
| White, female | 15.5 | 36.8 |
| Black, male | 36.5 | 25.9 |
| Black, female | 29.7 | 28.4 |

of unemployment. Third, teenagers have much lower rates of labor-force participation and much higher rates of unemployment than older workers. More generally, these data show that labor-market experiences vary widely among groups
within the economy.

The BLS data on the labor market also allow economists and policymakers to
monitor changes in the economy over time. Figure 2 shows the unemployment rate
in the United States since 1960. The figure shows that the economy always has some
unemployment and that the amount changes from year to year. The normal rate
of unemployment around which the unemployment rate fluctuates is called the
**natural rate of unemployment**, and the deviation of unemployment from its natural rate is called **cyclical unemployment**. The natural rate of unemployment shown
in the figure is a series estimated by economists at the Congressional Budget Office.
For 2015, they estimated a natural rate of 4.9 percent, close to the actual unemployment rate of 5.3 percent. Later in this book, we discuss short-run economic fluctuations, including the year-to-year fluctuations in unemployment around its natural
rate. In the rest of this chapter, however, we ignore the short-run fluctuations and
examine why there is always some unemployment in market economies.

**natural rate of
unemployment**
the normal rate of
unemployment around
which the unemployment
rate fluctuates

**cyclical unemployment**
the deviation of
unemployment from its
natural rate

**CASE STUDY**

**LABOR-FORCE PARTICIPATION OF MEN AND WOMEN IN THE U.S.
ECONOMY**
Women's role in American society has changed dramatically over the
past century. Social commentators have pointed to many causes for
this change. In part, it is attributable to new technologies, such as the
washing machine, clothes dryer, refrigerator, freezer, and dishwasher, which have
reduced the amount of time required to complete routine household tasks. In part, it

This graph uses annual data on the U.S. unemployment rate to show the percentage of
the labor force without a job. The natural rate of unemployment is the normal level of
unemployment around which the unemployment rate fluctuates.

**Source:** U.S. Department of Labor, Congressional Budget Office.

**FIGURE 2**

**Unemployment Rate since
1960**

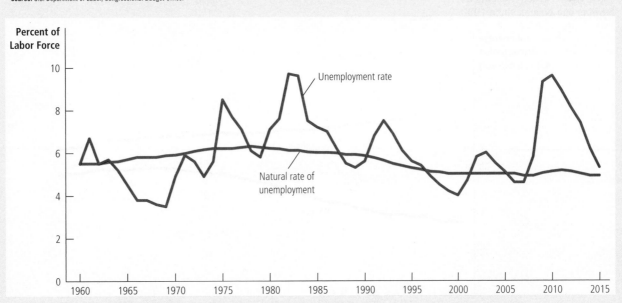

is attributable to improved birth control, which has reduced the number of children born to the typical family. This change in women's role is also partly attributable to changing political and social attitudes, which in turn may have been facilitated by the advances in technology and birth control. Together these developments have had a profound impact on society in general and on the economy in particular.

Nowhere is that impact more obvious than in data on labor-force participation. Figure 3 shows the labor-force participation rates of men and women in the United States since 1950. Just after World War II, men and women had very different roles in society. Only 33 percent of women were working or looking for work, in contrast to 87 percent of men. Since then, this difference in participation rates has gradually diminished, as growing numbers of women have entered the labor force and some men have left it. Data for 2015 show that 57 percent of women were in the labor force, in contrast to 69 percent of men. As measured by labor-force participation, men and women are now playing a more equal role in the economy.

The increase in women's labor-force participation is easy to understand, but the fall in men's may seem puzzling. There are several reasons for this decline. First, young men now stay in school longer than their fathers and grandfathers did. Second, older men now retire earlier and live longer. Third, with more women employed, more fathers now stay at home to raise their children. Full-time students, retirees, and stay-at-home dads are all counted as being out of the labor force. ●

## 20-1b Does the Unemployment Rate Measure What We Want It To?

Measuring the amount of unemployment in the economy might seem a straightforward task, but it is not. While it is easy to distinguish between a person with a full-time job and a person who is not working at all, it is much harder to distinguish between a person who is unemployed and a person who is not in the labor force.

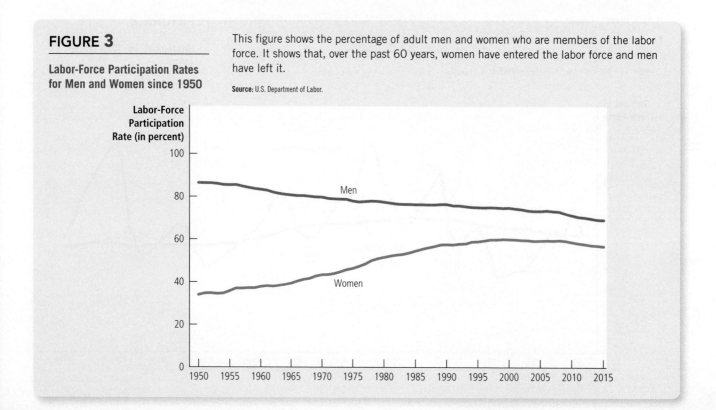

**FIGURE 3**

**Labor-Force Participation Rates for Men and Women since 1950**

This figure shows the percentage of adult men and women who are members of the labor force. It shows that, over the past 60 years, women have entered the labor force and men have left it.

**Source:** U.S. Department of Labor.

Movements into and out of the labor force are, in fact, common. More than one-third of the unemployed are recent entrants into the labor force. These entrants include young workers looking for their first jobs. They also include, in greater numbers, older workers who had previously left the labor force but have now returned to look for work. Moreover, not all unemployment ends with the job seeker finding a job. Almost half of all spells of unemployment end when the unemployed person leaves the labor force.

Because people move into and out of the labor force so often, statistics on unemployment are difficult to interpret. On the one hand, some of those who report being unemployed may not, in fact, be trying hard to find a job. They may be calling themselves unemployed because they want to qualify for a government program that gives financial assistance to the unemployed or because they are working but paid "under the table" to avoid taxes on their earnings. It may be more accurate to view these individuals as out of the labor force or, in some cases, employed. On the other hand, some of those who report being out of the labor force may want to work. These individuals may have tried to find a job and may have given up after an unsuccessful search. Such individuals, called **discouraged workers**, do not show up in unemployment statistics, even though they are truly workers without jobs.

Because of these and other problems, the BLS calculates several other measures of labor underutilization, in addition to the official unemployment rate. These alternative measures are presented in Table 2. In the end, it is best to view the official unemployment rate as a useful but imperfect measure of joblessness.

**discouraged workers**
individuals who would like to work but have given up looking for a job

### TABLE 2

**Measures of Labor Underutilization**
The table shows various measures of joblessness for the U.S. economy. The data are for January 2016.

**Source:** U.S. Department of Labor.

| Measure and Description | Rate |
|---|---|
| U-1   Persons unemployed 15 weeks or longer, as a percent of the civilian labor force (includes only very long-term unemployed) | 2.0% |
| U-2   Job losers and persons who have completed temporary jobs, as a percent of the civilian labor force (excludes job leavers) | 2.3 |
| U-3   Total unemployed, as a percent of the civilian labor force (official unemployment rate) | 4.9 |
| U-4   Total unemployed, plus discouraged workers, as a percent of the civilian labor force plus discouraged workers | 5.3 |
| U-5   Total unemployed plus all marginally attached workers, as a percent of the civilian labor force plus all marginally attached workers | 6.2 |
| U-6   Total unemployed, plus all marginally attached workers, plus total employed part-time for economic reasons, as a percent of the civilian labor force plus all marginally attached workers | 9.9 |

*Note:* The Bureau of Labor Statistics defines terms as follows:

- *Marginally attached workers* are persons who currently are neither working nor looking for work but indicate that they want and are available for a job and have looked for work sometime in the recent past.
- *Discouraged workers* are marginally attached workers who have given a job-market-related reason for not currently looking for a job.
- *Persons employed part-time for economic reasons* are those who want and are available for full-time work but have had to settle for a part-time schedule.

### 20-1c  How Long Are the Unemployed without Work?

In judging how serious the problem of unemployment is, one question to consider is whether unemployment is typically a short-term or long-term condition. If unemployment is short-term, one might conclude that it is not a big problem. Workers may require a few weeks between jobs to find the openings that best suit their tastes and skills. Yet if unemployment is long-term, one might conclude that it is a serious problem. Workers unemployed for many months are more likely to suffer economic and psychological hardship.

Because the duration of unemployment can affect our view about how big a problem unemployment is, economists have devoted much energy to studying data on the duration of unemployment spells. In this work, they have uncovered a result that is important, subtle, and seemingly contradictory: *Most spells of unemployment are short, but most unemployment observed at any given time is long-term.*

To see how this statement can be true, consider an example. Suppose that you visited the government's unemployment office every week for a year to survey the unemployed. Each week you find that there are four unemployed workers. Three of these workers are the same individuals for the whole year, while the fourth person changes every week. Based on this experience, would you say that unemployment is typically short-term or long-term?

Some simple calculations help answer this question. In this example, you meet a total of 55 unemployed people over the course of a year; 52 of them are unemployed for one week, and 3 are unemployed for the full year. This means that 52/55, or 95 percent, of unemployment spells end in one week. Yet whenever you walk into the unemployment office, three of the four people you meet will be unemployed for the entire year. So, even though 95 percent of unemployment spells end in one week, 75 percent of the unemployment observed at any moment is attributable to those individuals who are unemployed for a full year. In this example, as in the world, most spells of unemployment are short, but most unemployment observed at any given time is long-term.

This subtle conclusion implies that economists and policymakers must be careful when interpreting data on unemployment and when designing policies to help the unemployed. Most people who become unemployed will soon find jobs. Yet most of the economy's unemployment problem is attributable to the relatively few workers who are jobless for long periods of time.

### 20-1d  Why Are There Always Some People Unemployed?

We have discussed how the government measures the amount of unemployment, the problems that arise in interpreting unemployment statistics, and the findings of labor economists on the duration of unemployment. You should now have a good idea about what unemployment is.

This discussion, however, has not explained why economies experience unemployment. In most markets in the economy, prices adjust to bring quantity supplied and quantity demanded into balance. In an ideal labor market, wages would adjust to balance the quantity of labor supplied and the quantity of labor demanded. This adjustment of wages would ensure that all workers are always fully employed.

Of course, reality does not resemble this ideal. There are always some workers without jobs, even when the overall economy is doing well. In other words, the unemployment rate never falls to zero; instead, it fluctuates around the natural rate of unemployment. To understand this natural rate, the remaining sections of this chapter examine the reasons actual labor markets depart from the ideal of full employment.

To preview our conclusions, we will find that there are four ways to explain unemployment in the long run. The first explanation is that it takes time for workers to search for the jobs that are best suited for them. The unemployment that results from the process of matching workers and jobs is sometimes called **frictional unemployment**, and it is often thought to explain relatively short spells of unemployment.

The next three explanations for unemployment suggest that the number of jobs available in some labor markets may be insufficient to give a job to everyone who wants one. This occurs when the quantity of labor supplied exceeds the quantity demanded. Unemployment of this sort is sometimes called **structural unemployment**, and it is often thought to explain longer spells of unemployment. As we will see, this kind of unemployment results when wages are set above the level that brings supply and demand into equilibrium. We will examine three possible reasons for an above-equilibrium wage: minimum-wage laws, unions, and efficiency wages.

**frictional unemployment** unemployment that results because it takes time for workers to search for the jobs that best suit their tastes and skills

**structural unemployment** unemployment that results because the number of jobs available in some labor markets is insufficient to provide a job for everyone who wants one

**Quick Quiz** *How is the unemployment rate measured? • How might the unemployment rate overstate the amount of joblessness? How might it understate the amount of joblessness?*

---

## The Jobs Number

When the Bureau of Labor Statistics announces the unemployment rate at the beginning of every month, it also announces the number of jobs the economy has gained or lost. As an indicator of short-run economic trends, the jobs number gets as much attention as the unemployment rate.

Where does the jobs number come from? You might guess that it comes from the same survey of 60,000 households that yields the unemployment rate. And indeed the household survey does produce data on total employment. The jobs number that gets the most attention, however, comes from a separate survey of 160,000 business establishments, which have over 40 million workers on their payrolls. The results from the establishment survey are announced at the same time as the results from the household survey.

Both surveys yield information about total employment, but the results are not always the same. One reason is that the establishment survey has a larger sample, which makes it more reliable. Another reason is that the surveys are not measuring exactly the same thing. For example, a person who has two part-time jobs at different companies would be counted as one employed person in the household survey but as two jobs in the establishment survey. As another example, a person running his own small business would be counted as employed in the household survey but would not show up at all in the establishment survey, because the establishment survey counts only employees on business payrolls.

The establishment survey is closely watched for its data on jobs, but it says nothing about unemployment. To measure the number of unemployed, we need to know how many people without jobs are trying to find them. The household survey is the only source of that information. ■

# 20-2 Job Search

**job search**
the process by which workers find appropriate jobs given their tastes and skills

One reason economies always experience some unemployment is job search. **Job search** is the process of matching workers with appropriate jobs. If all workers and all jobs were the same, so that all workers were equally well suited for all jobs, job search would not be a problem. Laid-off workers would quickly find new jobs that were well suited for them. But in fact, workers differ in their tastes and skills, jobs differ in their attributes, and information about job candidates and job vacancies is disseminated slowly among the many firms and households in the economy.

## 20-2a Why Some Frictional Unemployment Is Inevitable

Frictional unemployment is often the result of changes in the demand for labor among different firms. When consumers decide that they prefer Ford to General Motors cars, Ford increases employment and General Motors lays off workers. The former General Motors workers must now search for new jobs, and Ford must decide which new workers to hire for the various jobs that have opened up. The result of this transition is a period of unemployment.

Similarly, because different regions of the country produce different goods, employment can rise in one region while it falls in another. Consider, for instance, what happens when the world price of oil falls. Oil-producing firms in Texas and North Dakota respond to the lower price by cutting back on production and employment. At the same time, cheaper gasoline stimulates car sales, so auto-producing firms in Michigan and Ohio raise production and employment. The opposite happens when the world price of oil rises. Changes in the composition of demand among industries or regions are called *sectoral shifts*. Because it takes time for workers to search for jobs in the new sectors, sectoral shifts temporarily cause unemployment.

Changing patterns of international trade are also a source of frictional unemployment. In Chapter 3, we learned that nations export goods for which they have a comparative advantage and import goods for which other nations have a comparative advantage. Comparative advantage, however, need not be stable over time. As the world economy evolves, nations may find themselves importing and exporting different goods than they have in the past. Workers will therefore need to move among industries. As they make this transition, they may find themselves unemployed for a period of time.

Frictional unemployment is inevitable simply because the economy is always changing. For example, in the U.S. economy from 2004 to 2014, employment fell by 838,000 in construction and 2.1 million in manufacturing. During the same period, employment rose by 321,000 in mining, 629,000 in computer systems design, 1.9 million in food services, and 2.6 million in healthcare. This churning of the labor force is normal in a well-functioning and dynamic economy. Because workers tend to move toward those industries in which they are most valuable, the long-run result of the process is higher productivity and higher living standards. But along the way, workers in declining industries find themselves out of work and searching for new jobs. The result is some amount of frictional unemployment.

## 20-2b Public Policy and Job Search

Even if some frictional unemployment is inevitable, the precise amount is not. The faster information spreads about job openings and worker availability, the more rapidly the economy can match workers and firms. The Internet, for instance, may help facilitate job search and reduce frictional unemployment. In addition, public policy may play a role. If policy can reduce the time it takes unemployed workers to find new jobs, it can reduce the economy's natural rate of unemployment.

Government programs try to facilitate job search in various ways. One way is through government-run employment agencies, which give out information about job vacancies. Another way is through public training programs, which aim to ease workers' transition from declining to growing industries and to help disadvantaged groups escape poverty. Advocates of these programs believe that they make the economy operate more efficiently by keeping the labor force more fully employed and that they reduce the inequities inherent in a constantly changing market economy.

Critics of these programs question whether the government should get involved with the process of job search. They argue that it is better to let the private market match workers and jobs. In fact, most job search in our economy takes place without intervention by the government. Newspaper ads, online job sites, college career offices, headhunters, and word of mouth all help spread information about job openings and job candidates. Similarly, much worker education is done privately, either through schools or through on-the-job training. These critics contend that the government is no better—and most likely worse—at disseminating the right information to the right workers and deciding what kinds of worker training would be most valuable. They claim that these decisions are best made privately by workers and employers.

## 20-2c Unemployment Insurance

One government program that increases the amount of frictional unemployment, without intending to do so, is **unemployment insurance**. This program is designed to offer workers partial protection against job loss. The unemployed who quit their jobs, were fired for cause, or just entered the labor force are not eligible. Benefits are paid only to the unemployed who were laid off because their previous employers no longer needed their skills. The terms of the program vary over time and across states, but a typical worker covered by unemployment insurance in the United States receives 50 percent of his former wages for 26 weeks.

**unemployment insurance**
a government program that partially protects workers' incomes when they become unemployed

While unemployment insurance reduces the hardship of unemployment, it also increases the amount of unemployment. The explanation is based on one of the *Ten Principles of Economics* in Chapter 1: People respond to incentives. Because unemployment benefits stop when a worker takes a new job, the unemployed devote less effort to job search and are more likely to turn down unattractive job offers. In addition, because unemployment insurance makes unemployment less onerous, workers are less likely to seek guarantees of job security when they negotiate with employers over the terms of employment.

Many studies by labor economists have analyzed the incentive effects of unemployment insurance. One study examined an experiment run by the state of Illinois in 1985. When unemployed workers applied to collect unemployment insurance benefits, the state randomly selected some of them and offered each a $500 bonus if they found new jobs within 11 weeks. This group was then compared to a control group not offered the incentive. The average spell of unemployment for the group offered the bonus was 7 percent shorter than the average spell for the control group. This experiment shows that the design of the unemployment insurance system influences the effort that the unemployed devote to job search.

Several other studies examined search effort by following a group of workers over time. Unemployment insurance benefits, rather than lasting forever, usually run out after 6 months or 1 year. These studies found that when the unemployed become ineligible for benefits, the probability of their finding a new job rises markedly. Thus, receiving unemployment insurance benefits does reduce the search effort of the unemployed.

Even though unemployment insurance reduces search effort and raises unemployment, we should not necessarily conclude that the policy is bad. The program does achieve its primary goal of reducing the income uncertainty that workers face. In addition, when workers turn down unattractive job offers, they have the opportunity to look for jobs that better suit their tastes and skills. Some economists argue that unemployment insurance improves the ability of the economy to match each worker with the most appropriate job.

The study of unemployment insurance shows that the unemployment rate is an imperfect measure of a nation's overall level of economic well-being. Most economists agree that eliminating unemployment insurance would reduce the amount of unemployment in the economy. Yet economists disagree on whether economic well-being would be enhanced or diminished by this change in policy.

**Quick Quiz**  *How would an increase in the world price of oil affect the amount of frictional unemployment? Is this unemployment undesirable? What public policies might affect the amount of unemployment caused by this price change?*

# 20-3 Minimum-Wage Laws

Having seen how frictional unemployment results from the process of matching workers and jobs, let's now examine how structural unemployment results when the number of jobs is insufficient for the number of workers.

To understand structural unemployment, we begin by reviewing how minimum-wage laws can cause unemployment. Minimum wages are not the predominant reason for unemployment in our economy, but they have an important effect on certain groups with particularly high unemployment rates. Moreover, the analysis of minimum wages is a natural place to start because, as we will see, it can be used to understand some of the other reasons for structural unemployment.

Figure 4 reviews the basic economics of a minimum wage. When a minimum-wage law forces the wage to remain above the level that balances supply and demand, it raises the quantity of labor supplied and reduces the quantity of labor demanded compared to the equilibrium level. There is a surplus of labor. Because there are more workers willing to work than there are jobs, some workers are unemployed.

While minimum-wage laws are one reason unemployment exists in the U.S. economy, they do not affect everyone. The vast majority of workers have wages well above the legal minimum, so the law does not prevent most wages from adjusting to balance supply and demand. Minimum-wage laws matter most for the least skilled and least experienced members of the labor force, such as teenagers. Their equilibrium wages tend to be low and, therefore, are more likely to fall below the legal minimum. It is only among these workers that minimum-wage laws explain the existence of unemployment.

Figure 4 is drawn to show the effects of a minimum-wage law, but it also illustrates a more general lesson: *If the wage is kept above the equilibrium level for any reason, the result is unemployment.* Minimum-wage laws are just one reason wages

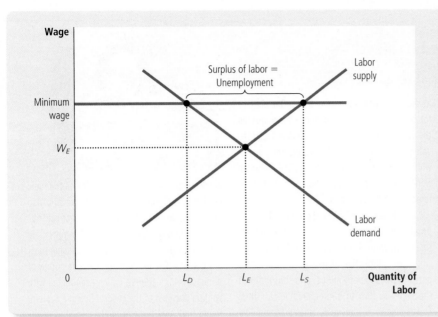

**FIGURE 4**

**Unemployment from a Wage above the Equilibrium Level**
In this labor market, supply and demand are balanced at the wage $W_E$. At this equilibrium wage, the quantity of labor supplied and the quantity of labor demanded both equal $L_E$. By contrast, if the wage is forced to remain above the equilibrium level, perhaps because of a minimum-wage law, the quantity of labor supplied rises to $L_S$ and the quantity of labor demanded falls to $L_D$. The resulting surplus of labor, $L_S - L_D$, represents unemployment.

may be "too high." In the remaining two sections of this chapter, we consider two other reasons wages may be kept above the equilibrium level: unions and efficiency wages. The basic economics of unemployment in these cases is the same as that shown in Figure 4, but these explanations of unemployment can apply to many more of the economy's workers.

At this point, however, we should stop and notice that the structural unemployment that arises from an above-equilibrium wage is, in an important sense, different from the frictional unemployment that arises from the process of job search. The need for job search is not due to the failure of wages to balance labor supply and labor demand. When job search is the explanation for unemployment, workers are *searching* for the jobs that best suit their tastes and skills. By contrast, when the wage is above the equilibrium level, the quantity of labor supplied exceeds the quantity of labor demanded, and workers are unemployed because they are *waiting* for jobs to open up.

**QuickQuiz** *Draw the supply curve and the demand curve for a labor market in which the wage is fixed above the equilibrium level. Show the quantity of labor supplied, the quantity demanded, and the amount of unemployment.*

**CASE STUDY**

**WHO EARNS THE MINIMUM WAGE?**
In 2015, the Department of Labor released a study of which workers reported earnings at or below the minimum wage in 2014, when the minimum wage was $7.25 per hour. (A reported wage below the minimum is possible because some workers are exempt from the statute, because enforcement is imperfect, and because some workers round down when reporting their wages on surveys.) Here is a summary of the findings:

- In 2014, 77 million workers were paid at hourly rates (as opposed to being on salary or self-employed), representing about half of the labor force. Among

## IN THE NEWS

# Should the minimum wage be raised to $15 an hour?

*An economist who studies the minimum wage says there are better ways to help the working poor.*

## Why Market Forces Will Overwhelm a Higher Minimum Wage

**By David Neumark**

The slogans are everywhere: Fight for 15; People Not Profits; One Job Should Be Enough. Worsening income inequality and the persistence of poverty have spurred a movement to raise the minimum wage, at both the national and state levels. Some West Coast cities have already voted to boost their minimum wage to $15, or more than double the federal standard. And Los Angeles is now considering a similarly aggressive move.

The labor market problems that these higher minimum wages are intended to fix are very real. But would a higher wage floor address the underlying problems? A large body of research shows that the answer is almost certainly no, and that there are better solutions, although they are harder for policymakers to embrace.

There are several reasons why workers' wages are currently too low to provide what many view

as an acceptable standard of living. One big factor is that technological changes have increased the value of higher-skilled work and reduced the value of lower-skilled work. Globalization, meanwhile, has brought many lower-skilled American workers into greater competition with their counterparts in other countries.

Simply requiring employers to pay $15 won't provide much ballast against these market forces. In fact, data indicate that minimum wages are ineffective at delivering benefits to poor or low-income families, and that many of the benefits flow to higher-income families. That's because minimum wages target low wages rather than low family incomes. And many minimum-wage workers are not poor or even in low-income families; nearly a quarter are teenagers who will eventually find better-paid jobs. Moreover, most poor families have no workers at all.

As a result, for every $5 in higher wages that a higher minimum imposes on employers, only about $1 goes to poor families, whereas roughly twice as much goes to families with incomes above the median.

Higher minimum wages also reduce employment for the least-skilled workers. Certainly not

every one of the hundreds of studies on the topic confirms this conclusion. But there are also studies claiming that humans have not contributed to climate change, and that supply-side economics did not contribute to massive budget deficits. The most comprehensive survey of minimum wage studies, which I conducted with William Wascher of the Federal Reserve System, found that two-thirds of studies point to negative employment effects, as do over 80% of the more credible studies.

Yet another reason to be wary of raising the minimum wage is that modest job loss overall may mask much steeper job loss among the least skilled. Economists use the phrase "labor-labor substitution" to describe employers responding to a higher minimum wage by replacing their lowest-skilled workers with higher-skilled workers, whom they are more willing to hire at the higher minimum.

Based on my research, I think it is likely that a $15 minimum wage in Los Angeles will lead

hourly paid workers, about 4 percent reported wages at or below the prevailing federal minimum. Thus, the minimum wage directly affects about 2 percent of all workers.

- Minimum-wage workers are more likely to be female. Among hourly paid workers, 5 percent of women had wages at or below the minimum wage, compared with 3 percent of men.
- Minimum-wage workers tend to be young. Among employed teenagers (ages 16 to 19) paid by the hour, about 15 percent earned the minimum wage or less, compared with 3 percent of hourly paid workers age 25 and older.
- Minimum-wage workers tend to be less educated. Among hourly paid workers age 16 and older, about 7 percent of those without a high school diploma earned the minimum wage or less, compared with about 4 percent of those who completed a high school diploma (but did not attend college) and about 2 percent for those who had obtained a college degree.

some teenagers currently focused on their education to take part-time jobs at the new, higher minimum, and displace low-skilled workers from the jobs they now hold. That seems like a bad outcome.

If we really want to help low-skilled workers, we need to recognize that the solutions that actually work are expensive, difficult to achieve or both.

Guaranteeing a minimally acceptable standard of living for those who work entails redistribution of some kind. Minimum wage is one form of redistribution — although we don't always think of it as such — but it's a blunt instrument. Using the tax system is clearly better.

The Earned Income Tax Credit, for instance, targets low-income families very well. Research establishes that it provides generous government subsidies to these families' labor market earnings and that it leads more people to work, which probably explains its bipartisan support.

Some decry the EITC as "corporate welfare," because the labor market entry it encourages pushes down market wages. But that is precisely why it increases employment. If it did not lower wages, employers would not hire additional workers, and those not hired would be more dependent on public programs.

Of course we could still do more. We could make the EITC more generous, including increasing it for those without children who are eligible only for minuscule payments. More radically, we might consider whether all low-income families, irrespective of employment, should receive more general income support in the form of direct cash payments. One might think of these payments as a "public dividend" from the extraordinary productivity of the U.S. economy, which has permitted those at the top to earn dramatically increasing salaries while incomes at the bottom have stagnated.

These alternative policies would have to be financed by higher taxes, but that's a good thing. Redistribution through taxes is paid for by those with the highest incomes. In contrast, higher minimum wages are paid for by those who happen to own businesses in low-wage industries, and the consumers of the products of those industries, who are more likely to be poor.

Progressives who want to help low-income families by pushing for higher minimum wages

would do better to channel their energy toward methods of redistribution that do less to harm the least-skilled, and more to help them.

And assuming that something is going to change in response to stagnating incomes, conservatives may be happier with the consequences of well-designed redistribution policies than the kind of high minimum wage floor Los Angeles is contemplating. For now, redistribution is a dead letter that provokes anguished cries of "socialism." But it doesn't have to be. ■

*David Neumark is Chancellor's Professor of Economics at University of California at Irvine.*

**Source:** *Los Angeles Times,* May 15, 2015.

- Minimum-wage workers are more likely to be working part-time. Among part-time workers (those who usually work less than 35 hours per week), 10 percent were paid the minimum wage or less, compared to 2 percent of full-time workers.
- The industry with the highest proportion of workers with reported hourly wages at or below the minimum wage was leisure and hospitality (18 percent). Over half of all workers paid at or below the minimum wage were employed in this industry, primarily in food services and drinking establishments. For many of these workers, tips supplement the hourly wages received.
- The proportion of hourly paid workers earning the prevailing federal minimum wage or less has changed substantially over time. It trended downward from 13 percent in 1979, when data collection first began on a regular basis, to 2 percent in 2006. It then increased to 4 percent in 2014. This recent increase is in part attributable to a legislated increase in the minimum wage from $5.15 per hour in 2006 to $7.25 per hour in 2014. ●

# 20-4 Unions and Collective Bargaining

**union**
a worker association that bargains with employers over wages, benefits, and working conditions

A **union** is a worker association that bargains with employers over wages, benefits, and working conditions. Only 11 percent of U.S. workers now belong to unions, but unions played a much larger role in the U.S. labor market in the past. In the 1940s and 1950s, when union membership was at its peak, about a third of the U.S. labor force was unionized.

Moreover, for a variety of historical reasons, unions continue to play a large role in many European countries. In Belgium, Norway, and Sweden, for instance, more than half of workers belong to unions. In France and Germany, a majority of workers have wages set by collective bargaining by law, even though only some of these workers are themselves union members. In these cases, wages are not determined by the equilibrium of supply and demand in competitive labor markets.

## 20-4a The Economics of Unions

A union is a type of cartel. Like any cartel, a union is a group of sellers acting together in the hope of exerting their joint market power. Most workers in the U.S. economy discuss their wages, benefits, and working conditions with their employers as individuals. By contrast, workers in a union do so as a group. The process by which unions and firms agree on the terms of employment is called **collective bargaining**.

**collective bargaining**
the process by which unions and firms agree on the terms of employment

**strike**
the organized withdrawal of labor from a firm by a union

When a union bargains with a firm, it asks for higher wages, better benefits, and better working conditions than the firm would offer in the absence of a union. If the union and the firm do not reach agreement, the union can organize a withdrawal of labor from the firm, called a **strike**. Because a strike reduces production, sales, and profit, a firm facing a strike threat is likely to agree to pay higher wages than it otherwise would. Economists who study the effects of unions typically find that union workers earn about 10 to 20 percent more than similar workers who do not belong to unions.

When a union raises the wage above the equilibrium level, it raises the quantity of labor supplied and reduces the quantity of labor demanded, resulting in unemployment. Workers who remain employed at the higher wage are better off, but those who were previously employed and are now unemployed are worse off. Indeed, unions are often thought to cause conflict between different groups of workers—between the *insiders* who benefit from high union wages and the *outsiders* who do not get the union jobs.

The outsiders can respond to their status in one of two ways. Some of them remain unemployed and wait for the chance to become insiders and earn the high union wage. Others take jobs in firms that are not unionized. Thus, when unions raise wages in one part of the economy, the supply of labor increases in other parts of the economy. This increase in labor supply, in turn, reduces wages in industries that are not unionized. In other words, workers in unions reap the benefit of collective bargaining, while workers not in unions bear some of the cost.

The role of unions in the economy depends in part on the laws that govern union organization and collective bargaining. Normally, explicit agreements among members of a cartel are illegal. When firms selling similar products agree to set high prices, the agreement is considered a "conspiracy in restraint of trade," and the government prosecutes the firms in civil and criminal court for violating the antitrust laws. By contrast, unions are exempt from these laws. The policymakers who wrote the antitrust laws believed that workers needed greater market power as they bargained with employers. Indeed, various laws are designed to encourage the formation of unions. In particular, the Wagner Act of 1935 prevents employers from interfering when workers try to organize unions and requires employers to bargain with unions in good faith. The National Labor Relations Board (NLRB) is the government agency that enforces workers' right to unionize.

Legislation affecting the market power of unions is a perennial topic of political debate. State lawmakers sometimes debate *right-to-work laws*, which give workers in a unionized firm the right to choose whether to join the union. In the absence of such laws, unions can insist during collective bargaining that firms make union membership a requirement for employment. At times, lawmakers in Washington have debated a proposed law that would prevent firms from hiring permanent replacements for workers who are on strike. This law would make strikes more costly for firms, thereby increasing the market power of unions. These and similar policy decisions will help determine the future of the union movement.

"*Gentlemen, nothing stands in the way of a final accord except that management wants profit maximization and the union wants more moola.*"

### 20-4b Are Unions Good or Bad for the Economy?

Economists disagree about whether unions are good or bad for the economy as a whole. Let's consider both sides of the debate.

Critics argue that unions are merely a type of cartel. When unions raise wages above the level that would prevail in competitive markets, they reduce the quantity of labor demanded, cause some workers to be unemployed, and reduce the wages in the rest of the economy. The resulting allocation of labor is, critics argue, both inefficient and inequitable. It is inefficient because high union wages reduce employment in unionized firms below the efficient, competitive level. It is inequitable because some workers benefit at the expense of other workers.

Advocates contend that unions are a necessary antidote to the market power of the firms that hire workers. The extreme case of this market power is the "company town," where a single firm does most of the hiring in a geographical region. In a company town, if workers do not accept the wages and working conditions that the firm offers, they have little choice but to move or stop working. In the absence of a union, therefore, the firm could use its market power to pay lower wages and offer worse working conditions than would prevail if it had to compete with other firms for the same workers. In this case, a union may balance the firm's market power and protect the workers from being at the mercy of the firm's owners.

Advocates of unions also claim that unions are important for helping firms respond efficiently to workers' concerns. Whenever a worker takes a job, the worker and the firm must agree on many attributes of the job in addition to the wage: hours of work, overtime, vacations, sick leave, health benefits, promotion schedules, job security, and so on. By representing workers' views on these issues, unions allow firms to provide the right mix of job attributes. Even if unions have the adverse effect of pushing wages above the equilibrium level and causing unemployment, they have the benefit of helping firms keep a happy and productive workforce.

In the end, there is no consensus among economists about whether unions are good or bad for the economy. Like many institutions, their influence is probably beneficial in some circumstances and adverse in others.

 *How does a union in the auto industry affect wages and employment at General Motors and Ford? How does it affect wages and employment in other industries?*

# 20-5 The Theory of Efficiency Wages

A fourth reason economies always experience some unemployment—in addition to job search, minimum-wage laws, and unions—is suggested by the theory of **efficiency wages**. According to this theory, firms operate more efficiently if wages are above the equilibrium level. Therefore, it may be profitable for firms to keep wages high even in the presence of a surplus of labor.

In some ways, the unemployment that arises from efficiency wages is similar to the unemployment that arises from minimum-wage laws and unions. In all three cases, unemployment is the result of wages above the level that balances the quantity of labor supplied and the quantity of labor demanded. Yet there is also an important difference. Minimum-wage laws and unions prevent firms from lowering wages in the presence of a surplus of workers. Efficiency-wage theory states that such a constraint on firms is unnecessary in many cases because firms may be better off keeping wages above the equilibrium level.

Why should firms want to keep wages high? This decision may seem odd at first, for wages are a large part of firms' costs. Normally, we expect profit-maximizing firms to want to keep costs—and therefore wages—as low as possible. The novel insight of efficiency-wage theory is that paying high wages might be profitable because they might raise the efficiency of a firm's workers.

There are several types of efficiency-wage theory. Each type suggests a different explanation for why firms may want to pay high wages. Let's now consider four of these types.

## 20-5a Worker Health

The first and simplest type of efficiency-wage theory emphasizes the link between wages and worker health. Better-paid workers eat a more nutritious diet, and workers who eat a better diet are healthier and more productive. A firm may find it more profitable to pay high wages and have healthy, productive workers than to pay lower wages and have less healthy, less productive workers.

This type of efficiency-wage theory can be relevant for explaining unemployment in less developed countries where inadequate nutrition can be a problem. In these countries, firms may fear that cutting wages would, in fact, adversely influence their workers' health and productivity. In other words, nutrition concerns may explain why firms maintain above-equilibrium wages despite a surplus of labor. Worker health concerns are far less relevant for firms in rich countries such as the United States, where the equilibrium wages for most workers are well above the level needed for an adequate diet.

## 20-5b Worker Turnover

A second type of efficiency-wage theory emphasizes the link between wages and worker turnover. Workers quit jobs for many reasons: to take jobs at other firms, to move to other parts of the country, to leave the labor force, and so on. The frequency with which they quit depends on the entire set of incentives they face, including the benefits of leaving and the benefits of staying. The more a firm pays its workers, the less often its workers will choose to leave. Thus, a firm can reduce turnover among its workers by paying them a high wage.

Why do firms care about turnover? The reason is that it is costly for firms to hire and train new workers. Moreover, even after they are trained, newly hired workers are not as productive as experienced ones. Firms with higher turnover,

therefore, will tend to have higher production costs. Firms may find it profitable to pay wages above the equilibrium level to reduce worker turnover.

## 20-5c Worker Quality

A third type of efficiency-wage theory emphasizes the link between wages and worker quality. All firms want workers who are talented, and they strive to pick the best applicants to fill job openings. But because firms cannot perfectly gauge the quality of applicants, hiring has a degree of randomness to it. When a firm pays a high wage, it attracts a better pool of workers to apply for its jobs and thereby increases the quality of its workforce. If the firm responded to a surplus of labor by reducing the wage, the most competent applicants—who are more likely to have better alternative opportunities than less competent applicants—may choose not to apply. If this influence of the wage on worker quality is strong enough, it may be profitable for the firm to pay a wage above the level that balances supply and demand.

## 20-5d Worker Effort

A fourth and final type of efficiency-wage theory emphasizes the link between wages and worker effort. In many jobs, workers have some discretion over how hard to work. As a result, firms monitor the efforts of their workers, and workers caught shirking their responsibilities are fired. But because monitoring is costly and imperfect, not all shirkers are caught immediately. A firm in such a circumstance is always looking for ways to deter shirking.

One solution is paying wages above the equilibrium level. High wages make workers more eager to keep their jobs and thus motivate them to put forward their best effort. If the wage were at the level that balanced supply and demand, workers would have less reason to work hard because if they were fired, they could quickly find new jobs at the same wage. Therefore, firms may raise wages above the equilibrium level to provide an incentive for workers not to shirk their responsibilities.

**CASE STUDY**

### HENRY FORD AND THE VERY GENEROUS $5-A-DAY WAGE

Henry Ford was an industrial visionary. As founder of the Ford Motor Company, he was responsible for introducing modern techniques of production. Rather than building cars with small teams of skilled craftsmen, Ford built cars on assembly lines in which unskilled workers were taught to perform the same simple tasks over and over again. The output of this assembly process was the Model T Ford, one of the most famous early automobiles.

In 1914, Ford introduced another innovation: the $5 workday. This might not seem like much today, but back then $5 was about twice the going wage. It was also far above the wage that balanced supply and demand. When the new $5-a-day wage was announced, long lines of job seekers formed outside the Ford factories. The number of workers willing to work at this wage far exceeded the number of workers Ford needed.

Ford's high-wage policy had many of the effects predicted by efficiency-wage theory. Turnover fell, absenteeism fell, and productivity rose. Workers were so much more efficient that Ford's production costs were lower despite higher wages. Thus, paying a wage above the equilibrium level was profitable for the firm. An historian of the early Ford Motor Company wrote, "Ford and his associates freely declared on many occasions that the high-wage policy turned out to be good business. By this they meant that it had improved the discipline of the workers, given them a more loyal interest in the institution, and raised their personal efficiency." Henry Ford himself called the $5-a-day wage "one of the finest cost-cutting moves we ever made."

Why did it take a Henry Ford to introduce this efficiency wage? Why were other firms not already taking advantage of this seemingly profitable business strategy? According to some analysts, Ford's decision was closely linked to his use of the assembly line. Workers organized in an assembly line are highly interdependent. If one worker is absent or works slowly, other workers are less able to complete their own tasks. Thus, while assembly lines made production more efficient, they also raised the importance of low worker turnover, high worker effort, and high worker quality. As a result, paying efficiency wages may have been a better strategy for the Ford Motor Company than for other businesses at the time. ●

 *Give four explanations for why firms might find it profitable to pay wages above the level that balances quantity of labor supplied and quantity of labor demanded.*

# 20-6 Conclusion

In this chapter, we discussed the measurement of unemployment and the reasons economies always experience some degree of unemployment. We have seen how job search, minimum-wage laws, unions, and efficiency wages can all help explain why some workers do not have jobs. Which of these four explanations for the natural rate of unemployment are the most important for the U.S. economy and other economies around the world? Unfortunately, there is no easy way to tell. Economists differ in which of these explanations of unemployment they consider most important.

The analysis in this chapter yields an important lesson: Although the economy will always have some unemployment, its natural rate does change over time. Many events and policies can alter the amount of unemployment the economy typically experiences. As the information revolution changes the process of job search, as Congress and state legislatures adjust the minimum wage, as workers form or quit unions, and as firms change their reliance on efficiency wages, the natural rate of unemployment evolves. Unemployment is not a simple problem with a simple solution. But how we choose to organize our society can profoundly influence how prevalent a problem it is.

## CHAPTER QuickQuiz

1. The population of Ectenia is 100 people: 40 work full-time, 20 work half-time but would prefer to work full-time, 10 are looking for a job, 10 would like to work but are so discouraged they have given up looking, 10 are not interested in working because they are full-time students, and 10 are retired. What is the number of unemployed?
   a. 10
   b. 20
   c. 30
   d. 40

2. Using the numbers in the preceding question, what is the size of Ectenia's labor force?
   a. 50
   b. 60
   c. 70
   d. 80

3. The main policy goal of the unemployment insurance system is to reduce the
   a. search effort of the unemployed.
   b. income uncertainty that workers face.
   c. role of unions in wage setting.
   d. amount of frictional unemployment.

4. In a competitive labor market, when the government increases the minimum wage, the result is a(n) _____ in the quantity of labor supplied and a(n) _____ in the quantity of labor demanded.
   a. increase, increase
   b. increase, decrease
   c. decrease, increase
   d. decrease, decrease

5. Unionized workers are paid about _____ percent more than similar nonunion workers.
   a. 2
   b. 5
   c. 15
   d. 40

6. According to the theory of efficiency wages,
   a. firms may find it profitable to pay above-equilibrium wages.
   b. an excess supply of labor puts downward pressure on wages.
   c. sectoral shifts are the main source of frictional unemployment.
   d. right-to-work laws reduce the bargaining power of unions.

## SUMMARY

- The unemployment rate is the percentage of those who would like to work who do not have jobs. The Bureau of Labor Statistics calculates this statistic monthly based on a survey of thousands of households.
- The unemployment rate is an imperfect measure of joblessness. Some people who call themselves unemployed may actually not want to work, and some people who would like to work have left the labor force after an unsuccessful search and therefore are not counted as unemployed.
- In the U.S. economy, most people who become unemployed find work within a short period of time. Nonetheless, most unemployment observed at any given time is attributable to the few people who are unemployed for long periods of time.
- One reason for unemployment is the time it takes workers to search for jobs that best suit their tastes and skills. This frictional unemployment is increased as a result of unemployment insurance, a government policy designed to protect workers' incomes.

- A second reason our economy always has some unemployment is minimum-wage laws. By raising the wage of unskilled and inexperienced workers above the equilibrium level, minimum-wage laws raise the quantity of labor supplied and reduce the quantity demanded. The resulting surplus of labor represents unemployment.
- A third reason for unemployment is the market power of unions. When unions push the wages in unionized industries above the equilibrium level, they create a surplus of labor.
- A fourth reason for unemployment is suggested by the theory of efficiency wages. According to this theory, firms find it profitable to pay wages above the equilibrium level. High wages can improve worker health, lower worker turnover, raise worker quality, and increase worker effort.

## KEY CONCEPTS

labor force, p. 409
unemployment rate, p. 409
labor-force participation rate, p. 410
natural rate of unemployment, p. 411
cyclical unemployment, p. 411

discouraged workers, p. 413
frictional unemployment, p. 415
structural unemployment, p. 415
job search, p. 416
unemployment insurance, p. 417

union, p. 422
collective bargaining, p. 422
strike, p. 422
efficiency wages, p. 424

## QUESTIONS FOR REVIEW

1. What are the three categories into which the Bureau of Labor Statistics divides everyone? How does the BLS compute the labor force, the unemployment rate, and the labor-force participation rate?

2. Is unemployment typically short-term or long-term? Explain.

3. Why is frictional unemployment inevitable? How might the government reduce the amount of frictional unemployment?

4. Are minimum-wage laws a better explanation for structural unemployment among teenagers or among college graduates? Why?

5. How do unions affect the natural rate of unemployment?

6. What claims do advocates of unions make to argue that unions are good for the economy?

7. Explain four ways in which a firm might increase its profits by raising the wages it pays.

## PROBLEMS AND APPLICATIONS

1. In June 2009, at the trough of the Great Recession, the Bureau of Labor Statistics announced that of all adult Americans, 140,196,000 were employed, 14,729,000 were unemployed, and 80,729,000 were not in the labor force. Use this information to calculate:
   a. the adult population
   b. the labor force
   c. the labor-force participation rate
   d. the unemployment rate

2. Explain whether each of the following events increases, decreases, or has no effect on the unemployment rate and the labor-force participation rate.
   a. After a long search, Jon finds a job.
   b. Tyrion, a full-time college student, graduates and is immediately employed.
   c. After an unsuccessful job search, Arya gives up looking and retires.
   d. Daenerys quits her job to become a stay-at-home mom.
   e. Sansa has a birthday, becomes an adult, but has no interest in working.
   f. Jaime has a birthday, becomes an adult, and starts looking for a job.

   g. Cersei dies while enjoying retirement.
   h. Jorah dies working long hours at the office.

3. Go to the website of the Bureau of Labor Statistics (http://www.bls.gov). What is the national unemployment rate right now? Find the unemployment rate for the demographic group that best fits a description of you (for example, based on age, sex, and race). Is it higher or lower than the national average? Why do you think this is so?

4. Between January 2010 and January 2016, U.S. employment increased by 12.1 million workers, but the number of unemployed workers declined by only 7.3 million. How are these numbers consistent with each other? Why might one expect a reduction in the number of people counted as unemployed to be smaller than the increase in the number of people employed?

5. Economists use labor-market data to evaluate how well an economy is using its most valuable resource—its people. Two closely watched statistics are the unemployment rate and the employment–population ratio (calculated as the percentage of the adult population that is employed). Explain what happens to each of these in the following scenarios. In your opinion,

which statistic is the more meaningful gauge of how well the economy is doing?

a. An auto company goes bankrupt and lays off its workers, who immediately start looking for new jobs.

b. After an unsuccessful search, some of the laid-off workers quit looking for new jobs.

c. Numerous students graduate from college but cannot find work.

d. Numerous students graduate from college and immediately begin new jobs.

e. A stock market boom induces newly enriched 60-year-old workers to take early retirement.

f. Advances in healthcare prolong the life of many retirees.

6. Are the following workers more likely to experience short-term or long-term unemployment? Explain.

a. a construction worker who is laid off because of bad weather

b. a manufacturing worker who loses his job at a plant in an isolated area

c. a stagecoach-industry worker who is laid off because of competition from railroads

d. a short-order cook who loses his job when a new restaurant opens across the street

e. an expert welder with little formal education who loses his job when the company installs automatic welding machinery

7. Using a diagram of the labor market, show the effect of an increase in the minimum wage on the wage paid to workers, the number of workers supplied, the number of workers demanded, and the amount of unemployment.

8. Consider an economy with two labor markets—one for manufacturing workers and one for service workers. Suppose initially that neither is unionized.

a. If manufacturing workers formed a union, what impact would you predict on the wages and employment in manufacturing?

b. How would these changes in the manufacturing labor market affect the supply of labor in the market for service workers? What would happen to the equilibrium wage and employment in this labor market?

9. Structural unemployment is sometimes said to result from a mismatch between the job skills that employers want and the job skills that workers have. To explore this idea, consider an economy with two industries: auto manufacturing and aircraft manufacturing.

a. If workers in these two industries require similar amounts of training, and if workers at the beginning of their careers can choose which industry to train for, what would you expect to happen to the wages in these two industries? How long would this process take? Explain.

b. Suppose that one day the economy opens itself to international trade and, as a result, starts importing autos and exporting aircraft. What would happen to the demand for labor in these two industries?

c. Suppose that workers in one industry cannot be quickly retrained for the other. How would these shifts in demand affect equilibrium wages both in the short run and in the long run?

d. If for some reason wages fail to adjust to the new equilibrium levels, what would occur?

10. Suppose that Congress passes a law requiring employers to provide employees some benefit (such as healthcare) that raises the cost of an employee by $4 per hour.

a. What effect does this employer mandate have on the demand for labor? (In answering this and the following questions, be quantitative when you can.)

b. If employees place a value on this benefit exactly equal to its cost, what effect does this employer mandate have on the supply of labor?

c. If the wage can freely adjust to balance supply and demand, how does this law affect the wage and the level of employment? Are employers better or worse off? Are employees better or worse off?

d. Suppose that, before the mandate, the wage in this market was $3 above the minimum wage. In this case, how does the employer mandate affect the wage, the level of employment, and the level of unemployment?

e. Now suppose that workers do not value the mandated benefit at all. How does this alternative assumption change your answers to parts (b) and (c)?

To find additional study resources, visit cengagebrain.com, and search for "Mankiw."

# PART VIII

# Money and Prices in the Long Run

# The Monetary System

When you walk into a restaurant to buy a meal, you get something of value—a full stomach. To pay for this service, you might hand the restaurateur several worn-out pieces of greenish paper decorated with strange symbols, government buildings, and the portraits of famous dead Americans. Or you might hand her a single piece of paper with the name of a bank and your signature. Or you might show her a plastic card and sign a paper slip. Whether you pay by cash, check, or debit card, the restaurateur is happy to work hard to satisfy your gastronomical desires in exchange for these pieces of paper, which, in and of themselves, are worthless.

Anyone who has lived in a modern economy is familiar with this social custom. Even though paper money has no intrinsic value, the restaurateur is confident

that, in the future, some third person will accept it in exchange for something that the restaurateur does value. And that third person is confident that some fourth person will accept the money, with the knowledge that yet a fifth person will accept the money . . . and so on. To the restaurateur and to other people in our society, your cash, check, or debit card receipt represents a claim to goods and services in the future.

The social custom of using money for transactions is extraordinarily useful in a large, complex society. Imagine, for a moment, that there was no item in the economy widely accepted in exchange for goods and services. People would have to rely on *barter*—the exchange of one good or service for another—to obtain the things they need. To get your restaurant meal, for instance, you would have to offer the restaurateur something of immediate value. You could offer to wash some dishes, mow her lawn, or give her your family's secret recipe for meat loaf. An economy that relies on barter will have trouble allocating its scarce resources efficiently. In such an economy, trade is said to require the *double coincidence of wants*—the unlikely occurrence that two people each have a good or service that the other wants.

The existence of money makes trade easier. The restaurateur does not care whether you can produce a valuable good or service for her. She is happy to accept your money, knowing that other people will do the same for her. Such a convention allows trade to be roundabout. The restaurateur accepts your money and uses it to pay her chef; the chef uses her paycheck to send her child to day care; the day care center uses this tuition to pay a teacher; and the teacher hires you to mow her lawn. As money flows from person to person in the economy, it facilitates production and trade, thereby allowing each person to specialize in what she does best and raising everyone's standard of living.

In this chapter, we begin to examine the role of money in the economy. We discuss what money is, the various forms that money takes, how the banking system helps create money, and how the government controls the quantity of money in circulation. Because money is so important in the economy, we devote much effort in the rest of this book to learning how changes in the quantity of money affect various economic variables, including inflation, interest rates, production, and employment. Consistent with our long-run focus in the previous four chapters, in the next chapter we examine the long-run effects of changes in the quantity of money. The short-run effects of monetary changes are a more complex topic, which we take up later in the book. This chapter provides the background for all of this further analysis.

# 21-1 The Meaning of Money

What is money? This might seem like an odd question. When you read that billionaire Mark Zuckerberg has a lot of money, you know what that means: He is so rich that he can buy almost anything he wants. In this sense, the term *money* is used to mean *wealth*.

**money**
the set of assets in an economy that people regularly use to buy goods and services from other people

Economists, however, use the word in a more specific sense: **Money** is the set of assets in the economy that people regularly use to buy goods and services from each other. The cash in your wallet is money because you can use it to buy a meal at a restaurant or a shirt at a store. By contrast, if you happened to own a large share of Facebook, as Mark Zuckerberg does, you would be wealthy, but this asset is not considered a form of money. You could not buy a meal or a shirt with this wealth without first obtaining some cash. According to the economist's definition, money includes only those few types of wealth that are regularly accepted by sellers in exchange for goods and services.

## 21-1a The Functions of Money

Money has three functions in the economy: It is a *medium of exchange*, a *unit of account*, and a *store of value*. These three functions together distinguish money from other assets in the economy, such as stocks, bonds, real estate, art, and even baseball cards. Let's examine each of these functions of money.

A **medium of exchange** is an item that buyers give to sellers when they purchase goods and services. When you go to a store to buy a shirt, the store gives you the shirt and you give the store your money. This transfer of money from buyer to seller allows the transaction to take place. When you walk into a store, you are confident that the store will accept your money for the items it is selling because money is the commonly accepted medium of exchange.

A **unit of account** is the yardstick people use to post prices and record debts. When you go shopping, you might observe that a shirt costs $50 and a hamburger costs $5. Even though it would be accurate to say that the price of a shirt is 10 hamburgers and the price of a hamburger is $1/10$ of a shirt, prices are never quoted in this way. Similarly, if you take out a loan from a bank, the size of your future loan repayments will be measured in dollars, not in a quantity of goods and services. When we want to measure and record economic value, we use money as the unit of account.

A **store of value** is an item that people can use to transfer purchasing power from the present to the future. When a seller accepts money today in exchange for a good or service, that seller can hold the money and become a buyer of another good or service at another time. Money is not the only store of value in the economy: A person can also transfer purchasing power from the present to the future by holding nonmonetary assets such as stocks and bonds. The term *wealth* is used to refer to the total of all stores of value, including both money and nonmonetary assets.

Economists use the term **liquidity** to describe the ease with which an asset can be converted into the economy's medium of exchange. Because money is the economy's medium of exchange, it is the most liquid asset available. Other assets vary widely in their liquidity. Most stocks and bonds can be sold easily with small cost, so they are relatively liquid assets. By contrast, selling a house, a Rembrandt painting, or a 1948 Joe DiMaggio baseball card requires more time and effort, so these assets are less liquid.

When people decide how to allocate their wealth, they have to balance the liquidity of each possible asset against the asset's usefulness as a store of value. Money is the most liquid asset, but it is far from perfect as a store of value. When prices rise, the value of money falls. In other words, when goods and services become more expensive, each dollar in your wallet can buy less. This link between the price level and the value of money is key to understanding how money affects the economy, a topic we start to explore in the next chapter.

## 21-1b The Kinds of Money

When money takes the form of a commodity with intrinsic value, it is called **commodity money**. The term *intrinsic value* means that the item would have value even if it were not used as money. One example of commodity money is gold. Gold has intrinsic value because it is used in industry and in the making of jewelry. Although today we no longer use gold as money, historically gold was a common form of money because it is relatively easy to carry, measure, and verify for impurities. When an economy uses gold as money (or uses paper money that is convertible into gold on demand), it is said to be operating under a *gold standard*.

**medium of exchange**
an item that buyers give to sellers when they want to purchase goods and services

**unit of account**
the yardstick people use to post prices and record debts

**store of value**
an item that people can use to transfer purchasing power from the present to the future

**liquidity**
the ease with which an asset can be converted into the economy's medium of exchange

**commodity money**
money that takes the form of a commodity with intrinsic value

Another example of commodity money is cigarettes. In prisoner-of-war camps during World War II, prisoners traded goods and services with one another using cigarettes as the store of value, unit of account, and medium of exchange. Similarly, as the Soviet Union was breaking up in the late 1980s, cigarettes started replacing the ruble as the preferred currency in Moscow. In both cases, even nonsmokers were happy to accept cigarettes in an exchange, knowing that they could use the cigarettes to buy other goods and services.

**fiat money**

money without intrinsic value that is used as money by government decree

Money without intrinsic value is called **fiat money**. A *fiat* is an order or decree, and fiat money is established as money by government decree. For example, compare the paper dollars in your wallet (printed by the U.S. government) and the paper dollars from a game of Monopoly (printed by the Parker Brothers game company). Why can you use the first to pay your bill at a restaurant but not the second? The answer is that the U.S. government has decreed its dollars to be valid money. Each paper dollar in your wallet reads: "This note is legal tender for all debts, public and private."

Although the government is central to establishing and regulating a system of fiat money (by prosecuting counterfeiters, for example), other factors are also required for the success of such a monetary system. To a large extent, the acceptance of fiat money depends as much on expectations and social convention as on government decree. The Soviet government in the 1980s never abandoned the ruble as the official currency. Yet the people of Moscow preferred to accept cigarettes (or even American dollars) in exchange for goods and services because they were more confident that these alternative monies would be accepted by others in the future.

## IN THE NEWS

# Why Gold?

*For many centuries, when societies have used a form of commodity money, the most common choice has been the gold standard. This outcome may have a sound scientific basis.*

### A Chemist Explains Why Gold Beat Out Lithium, Osmium, Einsteinium...

**By Jacob Goldstein and David Kestenbaum**

The periodic table lists 118 different chemical elements. And yet, for thousands of years, humans have really, really liked one of them in particular: gold. Gold has been used as money for millennia, and its price has been going through the roof.

Why gold? Why not osmium, lithium, or ruthenium?

We went to an expert to find out: Sanat Kumar, a chemical engineer at Columbia University. We asked him to take the periodic table, and start eliminating anything that wouldn't work as money.

The periodic table looks kind of like a bingo card. Each square has a different element in it—one for carbon, another for gold, and so on.

Sanat starts with the far-right column of the table. The elements there have a really appealing characteristic: They're not going to change. They're chemically stable.

But there's also a big drawback: They're gases. You could put all your gaseous money in a jar, but if you opened the jar, you'd be broke. So Sanat crosses out the right-hand column.

Then he swings over to the far left-hand column, and points to one of the elements there: Lithium

"If you expose lithium to air, it will cause a huge fire that can burn through concrete walls," he says.

Money that spontaneously bursts into flames is clearly a bad idea. In fact, you don't want your money undergoing any kind of spontaneous chemical reactions. And it turns out that a lot of the elements in the periodic table are pretty reactive.

Not all of them burst into flames. But sometimes they corrode, start to fall apart.

So Sanat crosses out another 38 elements, because they're too reactive.

Then we ask him about those two weird rows at the bottom of the table. They're always

### 21-1c  Money in the U.S. Economy

As we will see, the quantity of money circulating in the economy, called the *money stock*, has a powerful influence on many economic variables. But before we consider why that is true, we need to ask a preliminary question: What is the quantity of money? In particular, suppose you were given the task of measuring how much money there is in the U.S. economy. What would you include in your measure?

The most obvious asset to include is **currency**—the paper bills and coins in the hands of the public. Currency is clearly the most widely accepted medium of exchange in our economy. There is no doubt that it is part of the money stock.

**currency**
the paper bills and coins in the hands of the public

Yet currency is not the only asset that you can use to buy goods and services. Many stores also accept personal checks. Wealth held in your checking account is almost as convenient for buying things as wealth held in your wallet. To measure the money stock, therefore, you might want to include **demand deposits**—balances in bank accounts that depositors can access on demand simply by writing a check or swiping a debit card at a store.

**demand deposits**
balances in bank accounts that depositors can access on demand by writing a check

Once you start to consider balances in checking accounts as part of the money stock, you are led to consider the large variety of other accounts that people hold at banks and other financial institutions. Bank depositors usually cannot write checks against the balances in their savings accounts, but they can easily transfer funds from savings into checking accounts. In addition, depositors in money market mutual funds can often write checks against their balances. Thus, these other accounts should plausibly be part of the U.S. money stock.

---

broken out separately from the main table, and they have some great names—promethium, einsteinium.

But it turns out they're radioactive—put some einsteinium in your pocket, and a year later, you'll be dead.

So we're down from 118 elements to 30, and we've come up with a list of three key requirements:

1. Not a gas.
2. Doesn't corrode or burst into flames.
3. Doesn't kill you.

Now Sanat adds a new requirement: You want the thing you pick to be rare. This lets him cross off a lot of the boxes near the top of the table, because the elements clustered there tend to be more abundant.

At the same time, you don't want to pick an element that's too rare. So osmium—which apparently comes to earth via meteorites—gets the axe.

In Gold We Trust

FIKMIK/SHUTTERSTOCK

That leaves us with just five elements: rhodium, palladium, silver, platinum and gold. And all of them, as it happens, are considered precious metals.

But even here we can cross things out. Silver has been widely used as money, of course. But it's reactive—it tarnishes. So Sanat says it's not the best choice.

Early civilizations couldn't have used rhodium or palladium, because they weren't discovered until the early 1800s.

That leaves platinum and gold, both of which can be found in rivers and streams.

But if you were in the ancient world and wanted to make platinum coins, you would have needed some sort of magic furnace from the future. The melting point for platinum is over 3,000 degrees Fahrenheit.

Gold happens to melt at a much lower temperature, which made it much easier for pre-industrial people to work with.

So we ask Sanat: If we could run the clock back and start history again, could things go a different way, or would gold emerge again as the element of choice?

"For the earth, with every parameter we have, gold is the sweet spot," he says. "It would come out no other way." ∎

**Source:** *NPR Morning Edition*, February 15, 2011.

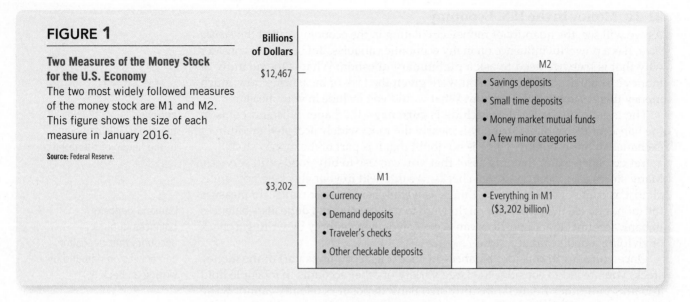

### FIGURE 1

**Two Measures of the Money Stock for the U.S. Economy**
The two most widely followed measures of the money stock are M1 and M2. This figure shows the size of each measure in January 2016.

**Source:** Federal Reserve.

In a complex economy such as ours, it is not easy to draw a line between assets that can be called "money" and assets that cannot. The coins in your pocket clearly are part of the money stock, and the Empire State Building clearly is not, but there are many assets in between these extremes for which the choice is less clear. Because different analysts can reasonably disagree about where to draw the dividing line between monetary and nonmonetary assets, various measures of the money stock are available for the U.S. economy. Figure 1 shows the two most commonly used, designated M1 and M2. M2 includes more assets in its measure of money than does M1.

For our purposes in this book, we need not dwell on the differences between the various measures of money. None of our discussion will hinge on the distinction between M1 and M2. The important point is that the money stock for the U.S. economy includes not only currency but also deposits in banks and other financial institutions that can be readily accessed and used to buy goods and services.

**WHERE IS ALL THE CURRENCY?**

**CASE STUDY**

One puzzle about the money stock of the U.S. economy concerns the amount of currency. In January 2016, there was $1.4 trillion of currency outstanding. To put this number in perspective, we can divide it by 252 million, the number of adults (age 16 and older) in the United States. This calculation implies that the average adult holds over $5,500 of currency. Most people are surprised to learn that our economy has so much currency because they carry far less than this in their wallets.

Who is holding all this currency? No one knows for sure, but there are two plausible explanations.

The first explanation is that much of the currency is held abroad. In foreign countries without a stable monetary system, people often prefer U.S. dollars to domestic assets. Estimates suggest that over half of U.S. dollars circulate outside the United States.

The second explanation is that much of the currency is held by drug dealers, tax evaders, and other criminals. For most people in the U.S. economy, currency is not a particularly good way to hold wealth. Not only can currency be lost or stolen

## Why Credit Cards Aren't Money

It might seem natural to include credit cards as part of the economy's stock of money. After all, people use credit cards to make many of their purchases. Aren't credit cards, therefore, a medium of exchange?

At first this argument may seem persuasive, but credit cards are excluded from all measures of the quantity of money. The reason is that credit cards are not really a method of payment but rather a method of *deferring* payment. When you buy a meal with a credit card, the bank that issued the card pays the restaurant what it is due. At a later date, you will have to repay the bank (perhaps with interest). When the time comes to pay your credit card bill, you will probably do so by writing a check against your checking account. The balance in this checking account is part of the economy's stock of money.

Notice that credit cards are different from debit cards, which automatically withdraw funds from a bank account to pay for items bought. Rather than allowing the user to postpone payment for a purchase, a debit card gives the user immediate access to deposits in a bank account. In this sense, a debit card is more similar to a check than to a credit card. The account balances that lie behind debit cards are included in measures of the quantity of money.

Even though credit cards are not considered a form of money, they are nonetheless important for analyzing the monetary system. People who have credit cards can pay many of their bills together at the end of the month, rather than sporadically as they make purchases. As a result, people who have credit cards probably hold less money on average than people who do not have credit cards. Thus, the introduction and increased popularity of credit cards may reduce the amount of money that people choose to hold. ■

but it also does not earn interest, whereas a bank deposit does. Thus, most people hold only small amounts of currency. By contrast, criminals may avoid putting their wealth in banks because a bank deposit gives police a paper trail that they can use to trace illegal activities. For criminals, currency may be the best store of value available. ●

**QuickQuiz** *List and describe the three functions of money.*

# 21-2 The Federal Reserve System

Whenever an economy uses a system of fiat money, as the U.S. economy does, some agency must be responsible for regulating the system. In the United States, that agency is the **Federal Reserve**, often simply called the **Fed**. If you look at the top of a dollar bill, you will see that it is called a "Federal Reserve Note." The Fed is an example of a **central bank**—an institution designed to oversee the banking system and regulate the quantity of money in the economy. Other major central banks around the world include the Bank of England, the Bank of Japan, and the European Central Bank.

**Federal Reserve (Fed)**
the central bank of the United States

**central bank**
an institution designed to oversee the banking system and regulate the quantity of money in the economy

## 21-2a The Fed's Organization

The Federal Reserve was created in 1913 after a series of bank failures in 1907 convinced Congress that the United States needed a central bank to ensure the health of the nation's banking system. Today, the Fed is run by its board of governors, which has seven members appointed by the president and confirmed by the Senate. The governors have 14-year terms. Just as federal judges are given lifetime appointments to insulate them from politics, Fed governors are given long terms to give them independence from short-term political pressures when they formulate monetary policy.

Among the seven members of the board of governors, the most important is the chair. The chair directs the Fed staff, presides over board meetings, and testifies regularly about Fed policy in front of congressional committees. The president appoints the chair to a 4-year term. As this book was going to press, the chair of the Fed was Janet Yellen, a former economics professor who was appointed to the Fed job by President Barack Obama in 2014.

The Federal Reserve System is made up of the Federal Reserve Board in Washington, D.C., and twelve regional Federal Reserve Banks located in major cities around the country. The presidents of the regional banks are chosen by each bank's board of directors, whose members are typically drawn from the region's banking and business community.

The Fed has two related jobs. The first is to regulate banks and ensure the health of the banking system. This task is largely the responsibility of the regional Federal Reserve Banks. In particular, the Fed monitors each bank's financial condition and facilitates bank transactions by clearing checks. It also acts as a bank's bank. That is, the Fed makes loans to banks when banks themselves want to borrow. When financially troubled banks find themselves short of cash, the Fed acts as a *lender of last resort*—a lender to those who cannot borrow anywhere else—to maintain stability in the overall banking system.

**money supply**
the quantity of money available in the economy

**monetary policy**
the setting of the money supply by policymakers in the central bank

The Fed's second and more important job is to control the quantity of money that is made available in the economy, called the **money supply**. Decisions by policymakers concerning the money supply constitute **monetary policy**. At the Federal Reserve, monetary policy is made by the Federal Open Market Committee (FOMC). The FOMC meets about every six weeks in Washington, D.C., to discuss the condition of the economy and consider changes in monetary policy.

## 21-2b  The Federal Open Market Committee

The Federal Open Market Committee is made up of the seven members of the board of governors and five of the twelve regional bank presidents. All twelve regional presidents attend each FOMC meeting, but only five get to vote. Voting rights rotate among the twelve regional presidents over time. The president of the New York Fed always gets a vote, however, because New York is the traditional financial center of the U.S. economy and because all Fed purchases and sales of government bonds are conducted at the New York Fed's trading desk.

Through the decisions of the FOMC, the Fed has the power to increase or decrease the number of dollars in the economy. In simple metaphorical terms, you can imagine the Fed printing dollar bills and dropping them around the country by helicopter. Similarly, you can imagine the Fed using a giant vacuum cleaner to suck dollar bills out of people's wallets. Although in practice the Fed's methods for changing the money supply are more complex and subtle than this, the helicopter-vacuum metaphor is a good first step to understanding the meaning of monetary policy.

Later in this chapter, we discuss how the Fed actually changes the money supply, but it is worth noting here that the Fed's primary tool is the *open-market operation*—the purchase and sale of U.S. government bonds. (Recall that a U.S.

government bond is a certificate of indebtedness of the federal government.) If the FOMC decides to increase the money supply, the Fed creates dollars and uses them to buy government bonds from the public in the nation's bond markets. After the purchase, these dollars are in the hands of the public. Thus, an open-market purchase of bonds by the Fed increases the money supply. Conversely, if the FOMC decides to decrease the money supply, the Fed sells government bonds from its portfolio to the public in the nation's bond markets. After the sale, the dollars the Fed receives for the bonds are out of the hands of the public. Thus, an open-market sale of bonds by the Fed decreases the money supply.

Central banks are important institutions because changes in the money supply can profoundly affect the economy. One of the *Ten Principles of Economics* introduced in Chapter 1 is that prices rise when the government prints too much money. Another of the *Ten Principles of Economics* is that society faces a short-run trade-off between inflation and unemployment. The power of the Fed rests on these principles. For reasons we discuss more fully in the coming chapters, the Fed's policy decisions are key determinants of the economy's rate of inflation in the long run and the economy's employment and production in the short run. Indeed, the Fed's chair has been called the second most powerful person in the United States.

 *What are the primary responsibilities of the Federal Reserve? If the Fed wants to increase the supply of money, how does it usually do so?*

# 21-3 Banks and the Money Supply

So far, we have introduced the concept of "money" and discussed how the Federal Reserve controls the supply of money by buying and selling government bonds in open-market operations. This explanation of the money supply is correct, but it is not complete. In particular, it omits the key role that banks play in the monetary system.

Recall that the amount of money you hold includes both currency (the bills in your wallet and coins in your pocket) and demand deposits (the balance in your checking account). Because demand deposits are held in banks, the behavior of banks can influence the quantity of demand deposits in the economy and, therefore, the money supply. This section examines how banks affect the money supply and, in doing so, how they complicate the Fed's job of controlling the money supply.

*"I've heard a lot about money, and now I'd like to try some."*

### 21-3a The Simple Case of 100-Percent-Reserve Banking

To see how banks influence the money supply, let's first imagine a world without any banks at all. In this simple world, currency is the only form of money. To be concrete, let's suppose that the total quantity of currency is $100. The supply of money is, therefore, $100.

Now suppose that someone opens a bank, appropriately called First National Bank. First National Bank is only a depository institution—that is, it accepts deposits but does not make loans. The purpose of the bank is to give depositors a safe place to keep their money. Whenever a person deposits some money,

**reserves**
deposits that banks have received but have not loaned out

the bank keeps the money in its vault until the depositor withdraws it, writes a check, or uses a debit card to access her balance. Deposits that banks have received but have not loaned out are called **reserves**. In this imaginary economy, all deposits are held as reserves, so this system is called *100-percent-reserve banking*.

We can express the financial position of First National Bank with a *T-account*, which is a simplified accounting statement that shows changes in a bank's assets and liabilities. Here is the T-account for First National Bank if the economy's entire $100 of money is deposited in the bank:

| **First National Bank** | |
|---|---|
| **Assets** | **Liabilities** |
| Reserves            $100.00 | Deposits            $100.00 |

On the left side of the T-account are the bank's assets of $100 (the reserves it holds in its vaults). On the right side are the bank's liabilities of $100 (the amount it owes to its depositors). Because the assets and liabilities exactly balance, this accounting statement is called a *balance sheet*.

Now consider the money supply in this imaginary economy. Before First National Bank opens, the money supply is the $100 of currency that people are holding. After the bank opens and people deposit their currency, the money supply is the $100 of demand deposits. (There is no longer any currency outstanding, since it is all in the bank vault.) Each deposit in the bank reduces currency and raises demand deposits by exactly the same amount, leaving the money supply unchanged. Thus, *if banks hold all deposits in reserve, banks do not influence the supply of money.*

### 21-3b Money Creation with Fractional-Reserve Banking

Eventually, the bankers at First National Bank may start to reconsider their policy of 100-percent-reserve banking. Leaving all that money idle in their vaults seems unnecessary. Why not lend some of it out and earn a profit by charging interest on the loans? Families buying houses, firms building new factories, and students paying for college would all be happy to pay interest to borrow some of that money for a while. First National Bank has to keep some reserves so that currency is available if depositors want to make withdrawals. But if the flow of new deposits is roughly the same as the flow of withdrawals, First National needs to keep only a fraction of its deposits in reserve. Thus, First National adopts a system called **fractional-reserve banking**.

**fractional-reserve banking**
a banking system in which banks hold only a fraction of deposits as reserves

**reserve ratio**
the fraction of deposits that banks hold as reserves

The fraction of total deposits that a bank holds as reserves is called the **reserve ratio**. This ratio is influenced by both government regulation and bank policy. As we discuss more fully later in the chapter, the Fed sets a minimum amount of reserves that banks must hold, called a *reserve requirement*. In addition, banks may hold reserves above the legal minimum, called *excess reserves*, so they can be more confident that they will not run short of cash. For our purpose here, we take the reserve ratio as given to examine how fractional-reserve banking influences the money supply.

Let's suppose that First National has a reserve ratio of 1/10, or 10 percent. This means that it keeps 10 percent of its deposits in reserve and loans out the rest. Now let's look again at the bank's T-account:

**First National Bank**

| Assets | | Liabilities | |
| --- | --- | --- | --- |
| Reserves | $10.00 | Deposits | $100.00 |
| Loans | 90.00 | | |

First National still has $100 in liabilities because making the loans did not alter the bank's obligation to its depositors. But now the bank has two kinds of assets: It has $10 of reserves in its vault, and it has loans of $90. (These loans are liabilities of the people borrowing from First National, but they are assets of the bank because the borrowers will later repay the loans.) In total, First National's assets still equal its liabilities.

Once again consider the supply of money in the economy. Before First National makes any loans, the money supply is the $100 of deposits. Yet when First National lends out some of these deposits, the money supply increases. The depositors still have demand deposits totaling $100, but now the borrowers hold $90 in currency. The money supply (which equals currency plus demand deposits) equals $190. Thus, *when banks hold only a fraction of deposits in reserve, the banking system creates money.*

At first, this creation of money by fractional-reserve banking may seem too good to be true: It appears that the bank has created money out of thin air. To make this feat seem less miraculous, note that when First National Bank loans out some of its reserves and creates money, it does not create any wealth. Loans from First National give the borrowers some currency and thus the ability to buy goods and services. Yet the borrowers are also taking on debts, so the loans do not make them any richer. In other words, as a bank creates the asset of money, it also creates a corresponding liability for those who borrowed the created money. At the end of this process of money creation, the economy is more liquid in the sense that there is more of the medium of exchange, but the economy is no wealthier than before.

## 21-3c The Money Multiplier

The creation of money does not stop with First National Bank. Suppose the borrower from First National uses the $90 to buy something from someone who then deposits the currency in Second National Bank. Here is the T-account for Second National Bank:

**Second National Bank**

| Assets | | Liabilities | |
| --- | --- | --- | --- |
| Reserves | $ 9.00 | Deposits | $90.00 |
| Loans | 81.00 | | |

After the deposit, this bank has liabilities of $90. If Second National also has a reserve ratio of 10 percent, it keeps assets of $9 in reserve and makes $81 in loans. In this way, Second National Bank creates an additional $81 of money. If this $81 is eventually deposited in Third National Bank, which also has a reserve ratio of

10 percent, this bank keeps $8.10 in reserve and makes $72.90 in loans. Here is the T-account for Third National Bank:

**Third National Bank**

| Assets | | Liabilities | |
|---|---|---|---|
| Reserves | $ 8.10 | Deposits | $81.00 |
| Loans | 72.90 | | |

The process goes on and on. Each time that money is deposited and a bank loan is made, more money is created.

How much money is eventually created in this economy? Let's add it up:

| | |
|---|---|
| Original deposit | = $100.00 |
| First National lending | = $ 90.00 (= .9 × $100.00) |
| Second National lending | = $ 81.00 (= .9 × $90.00) |
| Third National lending | = $ 72.90 (= .9 × $81.00) |
| • | • |
| • | • |
| • | • |
| Total money supply | = $1,000.00 |

It turns out that even though this process of money creation can continue forever, it does not create an infinite amount of money. If you laboriously add the infinite sequence of numbers in the preceding example, you find that the $100 of reserves generates $1,000 of money. The amount of money the banking system generates with each dollar of reserves is called the **money multiplier**. In this imaginary economy, where the $100 of reserves generates $1,000 of money, the money multiplier is 10.

**money multiplier**
the amount of money the banking system generates with each dollar of reserves

What determines the size of the money multiplier? It turns out that the answer is simple: *The money multiplier is the reciprocal of the reserve ratio.* If $R$ is the reserve ratio for all banks in the economy, then each dollar of reserves generates $1/R$ dollars of money. In our example, $R = 1/10$, so the money multiplier is 10.

This reciprocal formula for the money multiplier makes sense. If a bank holds $1,000 in deposits, then a reserve ratio of $1/10$ (10 percent) means that the bank must hold $100 in reserves. The money multiplier just turns this idea around: If the banking system as a whole holds a total of $100 in reserves, it can have only $1,000 in deposits. In other words, if $R$ is the ratio of reserves to deposits at each bank (that is, the reserve ratio), then the ratio of deposits to reserves in the banking system (that is, the money multiplier) must be $1/R$.

This formula shows how the amount of money banks create depends on the reserve ratio. If the reserve ratio were only $1/20$ (5 percent), then the banking system would have 20 times as much in deposits as in reserves, implying a money multiplier of 20. Each dollar of reserves would generate $20 of money. Similarly, if the reserve ratio were $1/4$ (25 percent), deposits would be 4 times reserves, the money multiplier would be 4, and each dollar of reserves would generate $4 of money. Thus, *the higher the reserve ratio, the less of each deposit banks loan out, and the smaller the money multiplier.* In the special case of 100-percent-reserve banking, the reserve ratio is 1, the money multiplier is 1, and banks do not make loans or create money.

## 21-3d Bank Capital, Leverage, and the Financial Crisis of 2008–2009

In the previous sections, we have seen a simplified explanation of how banks work. But the reality of modern banking is a bit more complicated, and these complications played a key role in the financial crisis of 2008 and 2009. Before looking at that crisis, we need to learn a bit more about how banks actually function.

In the bank balance sheets you have seen so far, a bank accepts deposits and either uses those deposits to make loans or holds them as reserves. More realistically, a bank gets financial resources not only from accepting deposits but also, like other companies, from issuing equity and debt. The resources that a bank obtains from issuing equity to its owners are called **bank capital**. A bank uses these financial resources in various ways to generate profit for its owners. It not only makes loans and holds reserves but also buys financial securities, such as stocks and bonds.

**bank capital**
the resources a bank's owners have put into the institution

Here is a more realistic example of a bank's balance sheet:

**More Realistic National Bank**

| Assets | | Liabilities and Owners' Equity | |
|---|---|---|---|
| Reserves | $200 | Deposits | $800 |
| Loans | 700 | Debt | 150 |
| Securities | 100 | Capital (owners' equity) | 50 |

On the right side of this balance sheet are the bank's liabilities and capital (also called *owners' equity*). This bank obtained $50 of resources from its owners. It also took in $800 of deposits and issued $150 of debt. The total of $1,000 was put to use in three ways; these are listed on the left side of the balance sheet, which shows the bank's assets. This bank held $200 in reserves, made $700 in bank loans, and used $100 to buy financial securities, such as government or corporate bonds. The bank decides how to allocate its resources among asset classes based on their risk and return, as well as on any regulations (such as reserve requirements) that restrict the bank's choices.

By the rules of accounting, the reserves, loans, and securities on the left side of the balance sheet must always equal, in total, the deposits, debt, and capital on the right side of the balance sheet. There is no magic in this equality. It occurs because the value of the owners' equity is, by definition, the value of the bank's assets (reserves, loans, and securities) minus the value of its liabilities (deposits and debt). Therefore, the left and right sides of the balance sheet always sum to the same total.

Many businesses in the economy rely on **leverage**, the use of borrowed money to supplement existing funds for investment purposes. Indeed, whenever anyone uses debt to finance an investment project, she is applying leverage. Leverage is particularly important for banks, however, because borrowing and lending are at the heart of what they do. To fully understand banking, therefore, it is crucial to understand how leverage works.

**leverage**
the use of borrowed money to supplement existing funds for purposes of investment

The **leverage ratio** is the ratio of the bank's total assets to bank capital. In this example, the leverage ratio is $1,000/$50, or 20. A leverage ratio of 20 means that for every dollar of capital that the bank owners have contributed, the bank has

**leverage ratio**
the ratio of assets to bank capital

$20 of assets. Of the $20 of assets, $19 are financed with borrowed money—either by taking in deposits or issuing debt.

You may have learned in a science class that a lever can amplify a force: A boulder that you cannot move with your arms alone will move more easily if you use a lever. A similar result occurs with bank leverage. To see how this amplification works, let's continue with this numerical example. Suppose that the bank's assets were to rise in value by 5 percent because, say, some of the securities the bank was holding rose in price. Then the $1,000 of assets would now be worth $1,050. Because the depositors and debt holders are still owed $950, the bank capital rises from $50 to $100. Thus, when the leverage rate is 20, a 5-percent increase in the value of assets increases the owners' equity by 100 percent.

The same principle works on the downside, but with troubling consequences. Suppose that some people who borrowed from the bank default on their loans, reducing the value of the bank's assets by 5 percent, to $950. Because the depositors and debt holders have the legal right to be paid before the bank owners, the value of the owners' equity falls to zero. Thus, when the leverage ratio is 20, a 5-percent fall in the value of the bank's assets leads to a 100-percent fall in bank capital. If the value of assets were to fall by more than 5 percent, the bank's assets would fall below its liabilities. In this case, the bank would be *insolvent*, and it would be unable to pay off its debt holders and depositors in full.

**capital requirement**
a government regulation specifying a minimum amount of bank capital

Bank regulators require banks to hold a certain amount of capital. The goal of such a **capital requirement** is to ensure that banks will be able to pay off their depositors (without having to resort to government-provided deposit insurance funds). The amount of capital required depends on the kind of assets a bank holds. If the bank holds safe assets such as government bonds, regulators require less capital than if the bank holds risky assets such as loans to borrowers whose credit is of dubious quality.

Economic turmoil can result when banks find themselves with too little capital to satisfy capital requirements. An example of this phenomenon occurred in 2008 and 2009, when many banks realized they had incurred sizable losses on some of their assets—specifically, mortgage loans and securities backed by mortgage loans. The shortage of capital induced the banks to reduce lending, a phenomenon called a *credit crunch*, which in turn contributed to a severe downturn in economic activity. (This event is discussed more fully in Chapter 23.) To address this problem, the U.S. Treasury, working together with the Federal Reserve, put many billions of dollars of public funds into the banking system to increase the amount of bank capital. As a result, it temporarily made the U.S. taxpayer a part owner of many banks. The goal of this unusual policy was to recapitalize the banking system so that bank lending could return to a more normal level, which in fact occurred by late 2009.

**QuickQuiz** *Describe how banks create money.*

## 21-4 The Fed's Tools of Monetary Control

As we have already discussed, the Federal Reserve is responsible for controlling the supply of money in the economy. Now that we understand how banking works, we are in a better position to understand how the Fed carries out this job. Because banks create money in a system of fractional-reserve banking, the Fed's control of the money supply is indirect. When the Fed decides to change the money supply, it must consider how its actions will work through the banking system.

The Fed has various tools in its monetary toolbox. We can group the tools into two groups: those that influence the quantity of reserves and those that influence the reserve ratio and thereby the money multiplier.

### 21-4a How the Fed Influences the Quantity of Reserves

The first way the Fed can change the money supply is by changing the quantity of reserves. The Fed alters the quantity of reserves in the economy either by buying or selling bonds in open-market operations or by making loans to banks (or by some combination of the two). Let's consider each of these in turn.

**Open-Market Operations** As we noted earlier, the Fed conducts **open-market operations** when it buys or sells government bonds. To increase the money supply, the Fed instructs its bond traders at the New York Fed to buy bonds from the public in the nation's bond markets. The dollars the Fed pays for the bonds increase the number of dollars in the economy. Some of these new dollars are held as currency, and some are deposited in banks. Each new dollar held as currency increases the money supply by exactly $1. Each new dollar deposited in a bank increases the money supply by more than a dollar because it increases reserves and, thereby, the amount of money that the banking system can create.

To reduce the money supply, the Fed does just the opposite: It sells government bonds to the public in the nation's bond markets. The public pays for these bonds with its holdings of currency and bank deposits, directly reducing the amount of money in circulation. In addition, as people make withdrawals from banks to buy these bonds from the Fed, banks find themselves with a smaller quantity of reserves. In response, banks reduce the amount of lending, and the process of money creation reverses itself.

Open-market operations are easy to conduct. In fact, the Fed's purchases and sales of government bonds in the nation's bond markets are similar to the transactions that any individual might undertake for her own portfolio. (Of course, when two individuals engage in a purchase or sale with each other, money changes hands, but the amount of money in circulation remains the same.) In addition, the Fed can use open-market operations to change the money supply by a small or large amount on any day without major changes in laws or bank regulations. Therefore, open-market operations are the tool of monetary policy that the Fed uses most often.

**Fed Lending to Banks** The Fed can also increase the quantity of reserves in the economy by lending reserves to banks. Banks borrow from the Fed when they feel they do not have enough reserves on hand, either to satisfy bank regulators, meet depositor withdrawals, make new loans, or for some other business reason.

There are various ways banks can borrow from the Fed. Traditionally, banks borrow from the Fed's *discount window* and pay an interest rate on that loan called the **discount rate**. When the Fed makes such a loan to a bank, the banking system has more reserves than it otherwise would, and these additional reserves allow the banking system to create more money.

The Fed can alter the money supply by changing the discount rate. A higher discount rate discourages banks from borrowing reserves from the Fed. Thus, an increase in the discount rate reduces the quantity of reserves in the banking system, which in turn reduces the money supply. Conversely, a lower discount rate encourages banks to borrow from the Fed, increasing the quantity of reserves and the money supply.

**open-market operations**
the purchase and sale of U.S. government bonds by the Fed

**discount rate**
the interest rate on the loans that the Fed makes to banks

At times, the Fed has set up other mechanisms for banks to borrow from it. For example, from 2007 to 2010, under the *Term Auction Facility*, the Fed set a quantity of funds it wanted to lend to banks, and eligible banks then bid to borrow those funds. The loans went to the highest eligible bidders—that is, to the banks that had acceptable collateral and offered to pay the highest interest rate. Unlike at the discount window, where the Fed sets the price of a loan and the banks determine the quantity of borrowing, at the Term Auction Facility the Fed set the quantity of borrowing and competitive bidding among banks determined the price. The more funds the Fed made available, the greater the quantity of reserves and the larger the money supply.

The Fed lends to banks not only to control the money supply but also to help financial institutions when they are in trouble. For example, when the stock market crashed by 22 percent on October 19, 1987, many Wall Street brokerage firms found themselves temporarily in need of funds to finance the high volume of stock trading. The next morning, before the stock market opened, Fed Chair Alan Greenspan announced the Fed's "readiness to serve as a source of liquidity to support the economic and financial system." Many economists believe that Greenspan's reaction to the stock crash was an important reason it had few repercussions.

Similarly, in 2008 and 2009, a fall in housing prices throughout the United States led to a sharp rise in the number of homeowners defaulting on their mortgage loans, and many financial institutions holding those mortgages ran into trouble. In an attempt to prevent these events from having broader economic ramifications, the Fed provided many billions of dollars in loans to financial institutions in distress.

### 21-4b How the Fed Influences the Reserve Ratio

In addition to influencing the quantity of reserves, the Fed changes the money supply by influencing the reserve ratio and thereby the money multiplier. The Fed can influence the reserve ratio either through regulating the quantity of reserves banks must hold or through the interest rate that the Fed pays banks on their reserves. Again, let's consider each of these policy tools in turn.

**reserve requirements**
regulations on the minimum amount of reserves that banks must hold against deposits

**Reserve Requirements**   One way the Fed can influence the reserve ratio is by altering **reserve requirements**, the regulations that set the minimum amount of reserves that banks must hold against their deposits. Reserve requirements influence how much money the banking system can create with each dollar of reserves. An increase in reserve requirements means that banks must hold more reserves and, therefore, can loan out less of each dollar that is deposited. As a result, an increase in reserve requirements raises the reserve ratio, lowers the money multiplier, and decreases the money supply. Conversely, a decrease in reserve requirements lowers the reserve ratio, raises the money multiplier, and increases the money supply.

The Fed changes reserve requirements only rarely because such changes disrupt the business of banking. When the Fed increases reserve requirements, for instance, some banks find themselves short of reserves, even though they have seen no change in deposits. As a result, they have to curtail lending until they build their level of reserves to the new required level. Moreover, in recent years, this particular tool has become less effective because many banks hold excess reserves (that is, more reserves than are required).

**Paying Interest on Reserves**  Traditionally, banks did not earn any interest on the reserves they held. In October 2008, however, the Fed began paying *interest on reserves*. That is, when a bank holds reserves on deposit at the Fed, the Fed now pays the bank interest on those deposits. This change gives the Fed another tool with which to influence the economy. The higher the interest rate on reserves, the more reserves banks will choose to hold. Thus, an increase in the interest rate on reserves will tend to increase the reserve ratio, lower the money multiplier, and lower the money supply.

## 21-4c Problems in Controlling the Money Supply

The Fed's various tools—open-market operations, bank lending, reserve requirements, and interest on reserves—have powerful effects on the money supply. Yet the Fed's control of the money supply is not precise. The Fed must wrestle with two problems, each of which arises because much of the money supply is created by our system of fractional-reserve banking.

The first problem is that the Fed does not control the amount of money that households choose to hold as deposits in banks. The more money households deposit, the more reserves banks have, and the more money the banking system can create. The less money households deposit, the less reserves banks have, and the less money the banking system can create. To see why this is a problem, suppose that one day people lose confidence in the banking system and withdraw some of their deposits to hold more currency. When this happens, the banking system loses reserves and creates less money. The money supply falls, even without any Fed action.

The second problem of monetary control is that the Fed does not control the amount that bankers choose to lend. When money is deposited in a bank, it creates more money only when the bank loans it out. Because banks can choose to hold excess reserves instead, the Fed cannot be sure how much money the banking system will create. For instance, suppose that one day bankers become more cautious about economic conditions and decide to make fewer loans and hold greater reserves. In this case, the banking system creates less money than it otherwise would. Because of the bankers' decision, the money supply falls.

Hence, in a system of fractional-reserve banking, the amount of money in the economy depends in part on the behavior of depositors and bankers. Because the Fed cannot control or perfectly predict this behavior, it cannot perfectly control the money supply. Yet if the Fed is vigilant, these problems need not be large. The Fed collects data on deposits and reserves from banks every week, so it quickly becomes aware of any changes in depositor or banker behavior. It can, therefore, respond to these changes and keep the money supply close to whatever level it chooses.

**CASE STUDY**

**BANK RUNS AND THE MONEY SUPPLY**

Most likely you have never witnessed a bank run in real life, but you may have seen one depicted in movies such as *Mary Poppins* or *It's a Wonderful Life*. A bank run occurs when depositors fear that a bank may be having financial troubles and "run" to the bank to withdraw their deposits. The United States has not seen a major bank run in recent history, but in the United Kingdom, a bank called Northern Rock experienced a run in 2007 and, as a result, was eventually taken over by the government.

Bank runs are a problem for banks under fractional-reserve banking. Because a bank holds only a fraction of its deposits in reserve, it cannot satisfy withdrawal

*A not-so-wonderful bank run*

requests from all depositors. Even if the bank is *solvent* (meaning that its assets exceed its liabilities), it will not have enough cash on hand to allow all depositors immediate access to all of their money. When a run occurs, the bank is forced to close its doors until some bank loans are repaid or until some lender of last resort (such as the Fed) provides it with the currency it needs to satisfy depositors.

Bank runs complicate the control of the money supply. An important example of this problem occurred during the Great Depression in the early 1930s. After a wave of bank runs and bank closings, households and bankers became more cautious. Households withdrew their deposits from banks, preferring to hold their money in the form of currency. This decision reversed the process of money creation, as bankers responded to falling reserves by reducing bank loans. At the same time, bankers increased their reserve ratios so that they would have enough cash on hand to meet their depositors' demands in any future bank runs. The higher reserve ratio reduced the money multiplier, which further reduced the money supply. From 1929 to 1933, the money supply fell by 28 percent, without the Federal Reserve taking any deliberate contractionary action. Many economists point to this massive fall in the money supply to explain the high unemployment and falling prices that prevailed during this period. (In future chapters, we examine the mechanisms by which changes in the money supply affect unemployment and prices.)

## IN THE NEWS

# A Trip to Jekyll Island

*Here's the story of how the Federal Reserve came into being.*

## The Stranger-Than-Fiction Story of How the Fed Was Created

**By Roger Lowenstein**

According to opinion surveys, no institution save the Internal Revenue Service is held in lower regard than the Federal Reserve. It's also a font of conspiracy theories stoked by radical libertarians, who insist the Fed is debauching the currency and will ultimately bankrupt the country.

The Fed's unpopularity would make sense if it had, say, failed to intervene and save the system during the 2008 financial crisis. But, in fact, the Fed did rescue the economy....

Nonetheless, dissatisfaction is alive in Congress, where various bills would strip the Fed's autonomy and subject sensitive monetary decisions to the scrutiny of elected politicians. Some bills would go even further and explore a return to the gold standard.

For central bank watchers, this dynamic — effective policy rewarded with populist scorn — is nothing new. In America, it has always been thus.

At Alexander Hamilton's urging, Congress first chartered a national bank — the ur-Fed — in 1791. However, Thomas Jefferson, who famously mistrusted banks (he thought agriculture more virtuous), and who was fearful of a strong central government, opposed this development. After 20 years, the Jeffersonians won and Congress let the charter expire.

This decision led to disaster: ruinous inflation. So Congress chartered a Second Bank of the United States, which began in 1817, providing the growing country with a better, more uniform currency and improved its public finances. But success couldn't save it. Andrew Jackson despised the Second Bank as a tool of East Coast elites, and it too was abolished.

For most of the 19th century, the U.S., unlike most nations in Europe, did not have a lender of last resort. Frequent panics and

credit shortages were the result. Yet some of the very people who could have benefited most from a central bank, such as farmers who were starved for credit, preferred the status quo. Like Jackson and Jefferson before them, they were fearful that a government bank would tyrannize the people, perhaps in cahoots with Wall Street.

After a financial panic in 1907 virtually shut down the banking system, reformers began to press once more for a central bank. But popular mistrust remained so pronounced that they were afraid to go public.

This is the point — 105 years ago — when the story seems to have been hijacked by a future Hollywood scriptwriter.

On a November evening in 1910, a powerful senator, Rhode Island Republican Nelson W. Aldrich, boarded his private rail car near

Today, bank runs are not a major problem for the U.S. banking system or the Fed. The federal government now guarantees the safety of deposits at most banks, primarily through the Federal Deposit Insurance Corporation (FDIC). Depositors do not make runs on their banks because they are confident that, even if their bank goes bankrupt, the FDIC will make good on the deposits. The policy of government deposit insurance has costs: Bankers whose deposits are guaranteed may have too little incentive to avoid bad risks when making loans. But one benefit of deposit insurance is a more stable banking system. As a result, most people see bank runs only in the movies. ●

## 21-4d The Federal Funds Rate

If you read about U.S. monetary policy in the newspaper, you will find much discussion of the federal funds rate. This raises several questions:

Q: What is the federal funds rate?

A: The **federal funds rate** is the short-term interest rate that banks charge one another for loans. If one bank finds itself short of reserves while another bank has excess reserves, the second bank can lend some reserves to the first. The loans are temporary—typically overnight. The price of the loan is the federal funds rate.

**federal funds rate**
the interest rate at which banks make overnight loans to one another

---

New York. A light snow was falling, muting the hushed, conspiratorial tones of his guests, which is exactly how Aldrich wanted it.

The reform-minded banker Paul Warburg, one of his guests, was toting a hunting rifle, but he had no interest in hunting. The party also included a member of the powerful Morgan bank, as well as an assistant U.S. Treasury secretary, and Frank Vanderlip, head of the country's largest bank, National City.

"On what sort of errand are we going?" Vanderlip inquired.

"It may be a wild-goose chase; it may the biggest thing you and I ever did," Warburg replied.

Masquerading as duck hunters, they disembarked in Brunswick, Ga., and traveled by launch to Jekyll Island, home of an exclusive club surrounded by pine and palmetto groves. Over the course of a week, Aldrich and his bankers mapped out a draft of what was to become the Federal Reserve Act, changing the U.S. economy forever.

Congress was never told that Aldrich's bill had been drafted by Wall Street moguls. His bill did not pass, but it was the basis of a successor bill, the Federal Reserve Act, which Woodrow Wilson signed in 1913. Years

later, when the Jekyll trip was revealed to the public, extremists seized on this stranger-than-fiction episode to bolster their claim that the Fed was a bankers' plot against the American people. For conspiracy theorists, the bankers' conclave on Jekyll became a metaphor for the Fed itself. The obvious irony is that, fearing Americans' irrational suspicion of central banking, Aldrich and his crew

Senator Nelson Aldrich

LIBRARY OF CONGRESS PRINTS AND PHOTOGRAPHS DIVISION WASHINGTON

resorted to a plot that, ultimately, deepened the country's paranoia.

Despite their clandestine tactics, the financiers' motives were actually patriotic. Aldrich had visited Europe and studied its central banks. He wanted expert help to draft an American equivalent. And in between sumptuous meals featuring wild turkey and freshly scalloped oysters, his group of wealthy bankers earnestly wrestled with issues that still provoke us today: How should power over the economy be apportioned between Washington and localities? How should the central bank set interest rates and the money supply?

The Federal Reserve today is not perfect. But it is more transparent than ever, thanks to reforms instituted by the previous chairman, Ben S. Bernanke, and it is no less necessary than was a central bank in 1791. Americans' paranoia is unjustified, just as it has always been. ◼

*Roger Lowenstein is the author of "America's Bank: The Epic Struggle to Create the Federal Reserve."*

**Source:** *Los Angeles Times*, November 2, 2015.

Q: How is the federal funds rate different from the discount rate?

A: The discount rate is the interest rate banks pay to borrow directly from the Federal Reserve through the discount window. Borrowing reserves from another bank in the federal funds market is an alternative to borrowing reserves from the Fed, and a bank short of reserves will typically do whichever is cheaper. In practice, the discount rate and the federal funds rate move closely together.

Q: Does the federal funds rate matter only for banks?

A: Not at all. Although only banks borrow directly in the federal funds market, the economic impact of this market is much broader. Because different parts of the financial system are highly interconnected, interest rates on different kinds of loans are strongly correlated with one another. So when the federal funds rate rises or falls, other interest rates often move in the same direction.

Q: What does the Federal Reserve have to do with the federal funds rate?

A: In recent years, the Federal Reserve has set a target goal for the federal funds rate. When the Federal Open Market Committee meets approximately every 6 weeks, it decides whether to raise or lower that target.

Q: How can the Fed make the federal funds rate hit the target it sets?

A: Although the actual federal funds rate is set by supply and demand in the market for loans among banks, the Fed can use open-market operations to influence that market. For example, when the Fed buys bonds in open-market operations, it injects reserves into the banking system. With more reserves in the system, fewer banks find themselves in need of borrowing reserves to meet reserve requirements. The fall in demand for borrowing reserves decreases the price of such borrowing, which is the federal funds rate. Conversely, when the Fed sells bonds and withdraws reserves from the banking system, more banks find themselves short of reserves, and they bid up the price of borrowing reserves. Thus, open-market purchases lower the federal funds rate, and open-market sales raise the federal funds rate.

Q: But don't these open-market operations affect the money supply?

A: Yes, absolutely. When the Fed announces a change in the federal funds rate, it is committing itself to the open-market operations necessary to make that change happen, and these open-market operations will alter the supply of money. Decisions by the FOMC to change the target for the federal funds rate are also decisions to change the money supply. They are two sides of the same coin. Other things being equal, a decrease in the target for the federal funds rate means an expansion in the money supply, and an increase in the target for the federal funds rate means a contraction in the money supply.

 *If the Fed wanted to use all of its policy tools to decrease the money supply, what would it do?*

# 21-5 Conclusion

Some years ago, a book made the best-seller list with the title *Secrets of the Temple: How the Federal Reserve Runs the Country*. Though no doubt an exaggeration, this title did highlight the important role of the monetary system in our daily lives. Whenever we buy or sell anything, we are relying on the extraordinarily useful social convention called "money." Now that we know what money is and what determines its supply, we can discuss how changes in the quantity of money affect the economy. We begin to address that topic in the next chapter.

## CHAPTER QuickQuiz

1. The money supply includes all of the following EXCEPT
   a. metal coins.
   b. paper currency.
   c. lines of credit accessible with credit cards.
   d. bank balances accessible with debit cards.

2. Chloe takes $100 of currency from her wallet and deposits it into her checking account. If the bank adds the entire $100 to reserves, the money supply _____, but if the bank lends out some of the $100, the money supply _____.
   a. increases, increases even more
   b. increases, increases by less
   c. is unchanged, increases
   d. decreases, decreases by less

3. If the reserve ratio is ¼ and the central bank increases the quantity of reserves in the banking system by $120, the money supply increases by
   a. $90.
   b. $150.
   c. $160.
   d. $480.

4. A bank has capital of $200 and a leverage ratio of 5. If the value of the bank's assets declines by 10 percent, then its capital will be reduced to
   a. $100.
   b. $150.
   c. $180.
   d. $185.

5. Which of the following actions by the Fed would reduce the money supply?
   a. an open-market purchase of government bonds
   b. a reduction in banks' reserve requirements
   c. an increase in the interest rate paid on reserves
   d. a decrease in the discount rate on Fed lending

6. In a system of fractional-reserve banking, even without any action by the central bank, the money supply declines if households choose to hold _____ currency or if banks choose to hold _____ excess reserves.
   a. more, more
   b. more, less
   c. less, more
   d. less, less

## SUMMARY

- The term *money* refers to assets that people regularly use to buy goods and services.
- Money serves three functions. As a medium of exchange, it is the item used to make transactions. As a unit of account, it provides the way to record prices and other economic values. As a store of value, it offers a way to transfer purchasing power from the present to the future.
- Commodity money, such as gold, is money that has intrinsic value: It would be valued even if it were not used as money. Fiat money, such as paper dollars, is money without intrinsic value: It would be worthless if it were not used as money.
- In the U.S. economy, money takes the form of currency and various types of bank deposits, such as checking accounts.
- The Federal Reserve, the central bank of the United States, is responsible for regulating the U.S. monetary system. The Fed chair is appointed by the president and confirmed by Congress every 4 years. The chair is the head of the Federal Open Market Committee, which meets about every 6 weeks to consider changes in monetary policy.
- Bank depositors provide resources to banks by depositing their funds into bank accounts. These deposits are part of a bank's liabilities. Bank owners also provide resources (called bank capital) for the bank. Because of leverage (the use of borrowed funds for investment), a small change in the value of a bank's assets can lead to a large change in the value of the bank's capital. To protect depositors, bank regulators require banks to hold a certain minimum amount of capital.
- The Fed controls the money supply primarily through open-market operations: The purchase of government bonds increases the money supply, and the sale of government bonds decreases the money supply. The Fed also uses other tools to control the money supply. It can expand the money supply by decreasing the discount rate, increasing its lending to banks, lowering reserve requirements, or decreasing the interest rate on reserves. It can contract the money supply by increasing the discount rate, decreasing its lending to banks, raising reserve requirements, or increasing the interest rate on reserves.
- When individuals deposit money in banks and banks loan out some of these deposits, the quantity of money in the economy increases. Because the banking system influences the money supply in this way, the Fed's control of the money supply is imperfect.

- The Federal Reserve has in recent years set monetary policy by choosing a target for the federal funds rate, a short-term interest rate at which banks make loans to one another. As the Fed achieves its target, it adjusts the money supply.

## KEY CONCEPTS

money, p. 434
medium of exchange, p. 435
unit of account, p. 435
store of value, p. 435
liquidity, p. 435
commodity money, p. 435
fiat money, p. 436
currency, p. 437
demand deposits, p. 437

Federal Reserve (Fed), p. 439
central bank, p. 439
money supply, p. 440
monetary policy, p. 440
reserves, p. 442
fractional-reserve banking, p. 442
reserve ratio, p. 442
money multiplier, p. 444
bank capital, p. 445

leverage, p. 445
leverage ratio, p. 445
capital requirement, p. 446
open-market operations, p. 447
discount rate, p. 447
reserve requirements, p. 448
federal funds rate, p. 451

## QUESTIONS FOR REVIEW

1.  What distinguishes money from other assets in the economy?

2.  What is commodity money? What is fiat money? Which kind do we use?

3.  What are demand deposits and why should they be included in the stock of money?

4.  Who is responsible for setting monetary policy in the United States? How is this group chosen?

5.  If the Fed wants to increase the money supply with open-market operations, what does it do?

6.  Why don't banks hold 100-percent reserves? How is the amount of reserves banks hold related to the amount of money the banking system creates?

7.  Bank A has a leverage ratio of 10, while Bank B has a leverage ratio of 20. Similar losses on bank loans at the two banks cause the value of their assets to fall by 7 percent. Which bank shows a larger change in bank capital? Does either bank remain solvent? Explain.

8.  What is the discount rate? What happens to the money supply when the Fed raises the discount rate?

9.  What are reserve requirements? What happens to the money supply when the Fed raises reserve requirements?

10. Why can't the Fed control the money supply perfectly?

## PROBLEMS AND APPLICATIONS

1.  Which of the following are considered money in the U.S. economy? Which are not? Explain your answers by discussing each of the three functions of money.
    a.  a U.S. penny
    b.  a Mexican peso
    c.  a Picasso painting
    d.  a plastic credit card

2.  Explain whether each of the following events increases or decreases the money supply.
    a.  The Fed buys bonds in open-market operations.
    b.  The Fed reduces the reserve requirement.
    c.  The Fed increases the interest rate it pays on reserves.
    d.  Citibank repays a loan it had previously taken from the Fed.
    e.  After a rash of pickpocketing, people decide to hold less currency.
    f.  Fearful of bank runs, bankers decide to hold more excess reserves.
    g.  The FOMC increases its target for the federal funds rate.

3. Your uncle repays a $100 loan from Tenth National Bank (TNB) by writing a $100 check from his TNB checking account. Use T-accounts to show the effect of this transaction on your uncle and on TNB. Has your uncle's wealth changed? Explain.

4. Beleaguered State Bank (BSB) holds $250 million in deposits and maintains a reserve ratio of 10 percent.
   a. Show a T-account for BSB.
   b. Now suppose that BSB's largest depositor withdraws $10 million in cash from her account. If BSB decides to restore its reserve ratio by reducing the amount of loans outstanding, show its new T-account.
   c. Explain what effect BSB's action will have on other banks.
   d. Why might it be difficult for BSB to take the action described in part (b)? Discuss another way for BSB to return to its original reserve ratio.

5. You take $100 you had kept under your mattress and deposit it in your bank account. If this $100 stays in the banking system as reserves and if banks hold reserves equal to 10 percent of deposits, by how much does the total amount of deposits in the banking system increase? By how much does the money supply increase?

6. Happy Bank starts with $200 in bank capital. It then accepts $800 in deposits. It keeps 12.5 percent (1/8th) of deposits in reserve. It uses the rest of its assets to make bank loans.
   a. Show the balance sheet of Happy Bank.
   b. What is Happy Bank's leverage ratio?
   c. Suppose that 10 percent of the borrowers from Happy Bank default and these bank loans become worthless. Show the bank's new balance sheet.
   d. By what percentage do the bank's total assets decline? By what percentage does the bank's capital decline? Which change is larger? Why?

7. The Fed conducts a $10 million open-market purchase of government bonds. If the required reserve ratio is 10 percent, what are the largest and smallest possible increases in the money supply that could result? Explain.

8. Assume that the reserve requirement is 5 percent. All other things being equal, will the money supply expand more if the Fed buys $2,000 worth of bonds or if someone deposits in a bank $2,000 that she had been hiding in her cookie jar? If one creates more, how much more does it create? Support your thinking.

9. Suppose that the reserve requirement for checking deposits is 10 percent and that banks do not hold any excess reserves.
   a. If the Fed sells $1 million of government bonds, what is the effect on the economy's reserves and money supply?
   b. Now suppose the Fed lowers the reserve requirement to 5 percent, but banks choose to hold another 5 percent of deposits as excess reserves. Why might banks do so? What is the overall change in the money multiplier and the money supply as a result of these actions?

10. Assume that the banking system has total reserves of $100 billion. Assume also that required reserves are 10 percent of checking deposits and that banks hold no excess reserves and households hold no currency.
    a. What is the money multiplier? What is the money supply?
    b. If the Fed now raises required reserves to 20 percent of deposits, what are the change in reserves and the change in the money supply?

11. Assume that the reserve requirement is 20 percent. Also assume that banks do not hold excess reserves and there is no cash held by the public. The Fed decides that it wants to expand the money supply by $40 million.
    a. If the Fed is using open-market operations, will it buy or sell bonds?
    b. What quantity of bonds does the Fed need to buy or sell to accomplish the goal? Explain your reasoning.

12. The economy of Elmendyn contains 2,000 $1 bills.
    a. If people hold all money as currency, what is the quantity of money?
    b. If people hold all money as demand deposits and banks maintain 100 percent reserves, what is the quantity of money?
    c. If people hold equal amounts of currency and demand deposits and banks maintain 100 percent reserves, what is the quantity of money?
    d. If people hold all money as demand deposits and banks maintain a reserve ratio of 10 percent, what is the quantity of money?
    e. If people hold equal amounts of currency and demand deposits and banks maintain a reserve ratio of 10 percent, what is the quantity of money?

To find additional study resources, visit cengagebrain.com, and search for "Mankiw."

# Money Growth and Inflation

Today, if you want to buy an ice-cream cone, you need at least a couple of dollars, but that has not always been the case. In the 1930s, my grandmother ran a sweet shop in Trenton, New Jersey, where she sold ice-cream cones in two sizes. A cone with a small scoop of ice cream cost 3 cents. Hungry customers could buy a large scoop for a nickel.

You may not be surprised at the increase in the price of ice cream. In most modern economies, most prices tend to rise over time. This increase in the overall level of prices is called *inflation*. Earlier in the book, we examined how economists

measure the inflation rate as the percentage change in the consumer price index (CPI), the GDP deflator, or some other index of the overall price level. These price indexes show that, in the United States over the past 80 years, prices have risen on average 3.6 percent per year. Accumulated over so many years, a 3.6 percent annual inflation rate leads to a seventeenfold increase in the price level.

Inflation may seem natural and inevitable to a person who grew up in the United States during recent decades, but in fact, it is not inevitable at all. There were long periods in the 19th century during which most prices fell—a phenomenon called *deflation*. The average level of prices in the U.S. economy was 23 percent lower in 1896 than in 1880, and this deflation was a major issue in the presidential election of 1896. Farmers, who had accumulated large debts, suffered when declines in crop prices reduced their incomes and thus their ability to pay off their debts. They advocated government policies to reverse the deflation.

Although inflation has been the norm in more recent history, there has been substantial variation in the rate at which prices rise. From 2005 to 2015, prices rose at an average rate of 1.2 percent per year. By contrast, in the 1970s, prices rose by 7.8 percent per year, which meant the price level more than doubled over the decade. The public often views such high rates of inflation as a major economic problem. In fact, when President Jimmy Carter ran for reelection in 1980, challenger Ronald Reagan pointed to high inflation as one of the failures of Carter's economic policy.

International data show an even broader range of inflation experiences. In 2015, while the inflation rate in the United States was a mere 0.1 percent, it was 1.5 percent in China, 4.9 percent in India, 15 percent in Russia, and 84 percent in Venezuela. And even the high inflation rates in Russia and Venezuela are moderate by some standards. In February 2008, the central bank of Zimbabwe announced the inflation rate in its economy had reached 24,000 percent; some independent estimates put the figure even higher. An extraordinarily high rate of inflation such as this is called *hyperinflation*.

What determines whether an economy experiences inflation and, if so, how much? This chapter answers this question by developing the *quantity theory of money*. Chapter 1 summarized this theory as one of the *Ten Principles of Economics*: Prices rise when the government prints too much money. This insight has a long and venerable tradition among economists. The quantity theory was discussed by the famous 18th-century philosopher and economist David Hume and was advocated more recently by the prominent economist Milton Friedman. This theory can explain moderate inflations, such as those we have experienced in the United States, as well as hyperinflations.

After developing a theory of inflation, we turn to a related question: Why is inflation a problem? At first glance, the answer to this question may seem obvious: Inflation is a problem because people don't like it. In the 1970s, when the United States experienced a relatively high rate of inflation, opinion polls placed inflation as the most important issue facing the nation. President Ford echoed this sentiment in 1974 when he called inflation "public enemy number one." Ford wore a "WIN" button on his lapel—for Whip Inflation Now.

But what, exactly, are the costs that inflation imposes on a society? The answer may surprise you. Identifying the various costs of inflation is not as straightforward as it first appears. As a result, although all economists decry hyperinflation, some economists argue that the costs of moderate inflation are not nearly as large as the public believes.

# 22-1 The Classical Theory of Inflation

We begin our study of inflation by developing the quantity theory of money. This theory is often called "classical" because it was developed by some of the earliest economic thinkers. Most economists today rely on this theory to explain the long-run determinants of the price level and the inflation rate.

## 22-1a The Level of Prices and the Value of Money

Suppose we observe that over some period of time the price of an ice-cream cone rises from a nickel to a dollar. What conclusion should we draw from the fact that people are willing to give up so much more money in exchange for a cone? It is possible that people have come to enjoy ice cream more (perhaps because some chemist has developed a miraculous new flavor). But that is probably not the case. It is more likely that people's enjoyment of ice cream has stayed roughly the same and that, over time, the money used to buy ice cream has become less valuable. Indeed, the first insight about inflation is that it is more about the value of money than about the value of goods.

This insight helps point the way toward a theory of inflation. When the consumer price index and other measures of the price level rise, commentators are often tempted to look at the many individual prices that make up these price indexes: "The CPI rose by 3 percent last month, led by a 20 percent rise in the price of coffee and a 30 percent rise in the price of heating oil." Although this approach does contain some interesting information about what's happening in the economy, it also misses a key point: Inflation is an economy-wide phenomenon that concerns, first and foremost, the value of the economy's medium of exchange.

The economy's overall price level can be viewed in two ways. So far, we have viewed the price level as the price of a basket of goods and services. When the price level rises, people have to pay more for the goods and services they buy. Alternatively, we can view the price level as a measure of the value of money. A rise in the price level means a lower value of money because each dollar in your wallet now buys a smaller quantity of goods and services.

*"So what's it going to be? The same size as last year or the same price as last year?"*

It may help to express these ideas mathematically. Suppose $P$ is the price level as measured by the consumer price index or the GDP deflator. Then $P$ measures the number of dollars needed to buy a basket of goods and services. Now turn this idea around: The quantity of goods and services that can be bought with \$1 equals $1/P$. In other words, if $P$ is the price of goods and services measured in terms of money, $1/P$ is the value of money measured in terms of goods and services.

This mathematics is simplest to understand in an economy that produces only a single good, say, ice-cream cones. In that case, $P$ would be the price of a cone. When the price of a cone ($P$) is \$2, then the value of a dollar ($1/P$) is half a cone. When the price ($P$) rises to \$3, the value of a dollar ($1/P$) falls to a third of a cone. The actual economy produces thousands of goods and services, so we use a price index rather than the price of a single good. But the logic remains the same: When the overall price level rises, the value of money falls.

### 22-1b Money Supply, Money Demand, and Monetary Equilibrium

What determines the value of money? The answer to this question, like many in economics, is supply and demand. Just as the supply and demand for bananas determines the price of bananas, the supply and demand for money determines the value of money. Thus, our next step in developing the quantity theory of money is to consider the determinants of money supply and money demand.

First consider money supply. In the preceding chapter, we discussed how the Federal Reserve, together with the banking system, determines the supply of money. When the Fed sells bonds in open-market operations, it receives dollars in exchange and contracts the money supply. When the Fed buys government bonds, it pays out dollars and expands the money supply. In addition, if any of these dollars are deposited in banks, which hold some as reserves and loan out the rest, the money multiplier swings into action, and these open-market operations can have an even greater effect on the money supply. For our purposes in this chapter, we ignore the complications introduced by the banking system and simply take the quantity of money supplied as a policy variable that the Fed controls.

Now consider money demand. Most fundamentally, the demand for money reflects how much wealth people want to hold in liquid form. Many factors influence the quantity of money demanded. The amount of currency that people hold in their wallets, for instance, depends on how much they rely on credit cards and on whether an automatic teller machine is easy to find. And as we will emphasize in Chapter 24, the quantity of money demanded depends on the interest rate that a person could earn by using the money to buy an interest-bearing bond rather than leaving it in his wallet or low-interest checking account.

Although many variables affect the demand for money, one variable stands out in importance: the average level of prices in the economy. People hold money because it is the medium of exchange. Unlike other assets, such as bonds or stocks, people can use money to buy the goods and services on their shopping lists. How much money they choose to hold for this purpose depends on the prices of those goods and services. The higher prices are, the more money the typical transaction requires, and the more money people will choose to hold in their wallets and checking accounts. That is, a higher price level (a lower value of money) increases the quantity of money demanded.

What ensures that the quantity of money the Fed supplies balances the quantity of money people demand? The answer depends on the time horizon being considered. Later in this book, we examine the short-run answer and learn that interest rates play a key role. The long-run answer, however, is much simpler. *In the long run, money supply and money demand are brought into equilibrium by the overall level of prices.* If the price level is above the equilibrium level, people will want to hold more money than the Fed has created, so the price level must fall to balance supply and demand. If the price level is below the equilibrium level, people will want to hold less money than the Fed has created, and the price level must rise to balance supply and demand. At the equilibrium price level, the quantity of money that people want to hold exactly balances the quantity of money supplied by the Fed.

Figure 1 illustrates these ideas. The horizontal axis of this graph shows the quantity of money. The left vertical axis shows the value of money $1/P$, and the right vertical axis shows the price level $P$. Notice that the price-level axis on the right is inverted: A low price level is shown near the top of this axis, and a high price level is shown near the bottom. This inverted axis illustrates that when the value of money is high (as shown near the top of the left axis), the price level is low (as shown near the top of the right axis).

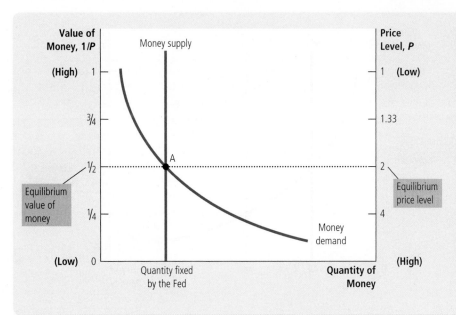

## FIGURE 1

**How the Supply and Demand for Money Determine the Equilibrium Price Level**
The horizontal axis shows the quantity of money. The left vertical axis shows the value of money, and the right vertical axis shows the price level. The supply curve for money is vertical because the quantity of money supplied is fixed by the Fed. The demand curve for money slopes downward because people want to hold a larger quantity of money when each dollar buys less. At the equilibrium, point A, the value of money (on the left axis) and the price level (on the right axis) have adjusted to bring the quantity of money supplied and the quantity of money demanded into balance.

The two curves in this figure are the supply and demand curves for money. The supply curve is vertical because the Fed has fixed the quantity of money available. The demand curve for money slopes downward, indicating that when the value of money is low (and the price level is high), people demand a larger quantity of it to buy goods and services. At the equilibrium, shown in the figure as point A, the quantity of money demanded balances the quantity of money supplied. This equilibrium of money supply and money demand determines the value of money and the price level.

### 22-1c The Effects of a Monetary Injection

Let's now consider the effects of a change in monetary policy. To do so, imagine that the economy is in equilibrium and then, suddenly, the Fed doubles the supply of money by printing some dollar bills and dropping them around the country from helicopters. (Or, less dramatically and more realistically, the Fed could inject money into the economy by buying some government bonds from the public in open-market operations.) What happens after such a monetary injection? How does the new equilibrium compare to the old one?

Figure 2 shows what happens. The monetary injection shifts the supply curve to the right from $MS_1$ to $MS_2$, and the equilibrium moves from point A to point B. As a result, the value of money (shown on the left axis) decreases from $1/2$ to $1/4$, and the equilibrium price level (shown on the right axis) increases from 2 to 4. In other words, when an increase in the money supply makes dollars more plentiful, the result is an increase in the price level that makes each dollar less valuable.

This explanation of how the price level is determined and why it might change over time is called the **quantity theory of money**. According to the quantity theory, the quantity of money available in an economy determines the value of money, and growth in the quantity of money is the primary cause of inflation. As economist Milton Friedman once put it, "Inflation is always and everywhere a monetary phenomenon."

**quantity theory of money**
a theory asserting that the quantity of money available determines the price level and that the growth rate in the quantity of money available determines the inflation rate

## FIGURE 2

**An Increase in the Money Supply**

When the Fed increases the supply of money, the money supply curve shifts from $MS_1$ to $MS_2$. The value of money (on the left axis) and the price level (on the right axis) adjust to bring supply and demand back into balance. The equilibrium moves from point A to point B. Thus, when an increase in the money supply makes dollars more plentiful, the price level increases, making each dollar less valuable.

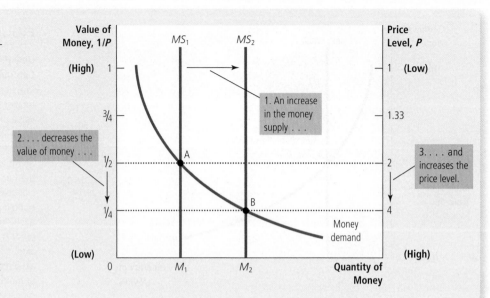

### 22-1d  A Brief Look at the Adjustment Process

So far, we have compared the old equilibrium and the new equilibrium after an injection of money. How does the economy move from the old to the new equilibrium? A complete answer to this question requires an understanding of short-run fluctuations in the economy, which we examine later in this book. Here, we briefly consider the adjustment process that occurs after a change in the money supply.

The immediate effect of a monetary injection is to create an excess supply of money. Before the injection, the economy was in equilibrium (point A in Figure 2). At the prevailing price level, people had exactly as much money as they wanted. But after the helicopters drop the new money and people pick it up off the streets, people have more dollars in their wallets than they want. At the prevailing price level, the quantity of money supplied now exceeds the quantity demanded.

People try to get rid of this excess supply of money in various ways. They might use it to buy goods and services. Or they might use this excess money to make loans to others by buying bonds or by depositing the money in a bank savings account. These loans allow other people to buy goods and services. In either case, the injection of money increases the demand for goods and services.

The economy's ability to supply goods and services, however, has not changed. As we saw in the chapter on production and growth, the economy's output of goods and services is determined by the available labor, physical capital, human capital, natural resources, and technological knowledge. None of these is altered by the injection of money.

Thus, the greater demand for goods and services causes the prices of goods and services to increase. The increase in the price level, in turn, increases the quantity of money demanded because people are using more dollars for every transaction. Eventually, the economy reaches a new equilibrium (point B in Figure 2) at which the quantity of money demanded again equals the quantity of money supplied.

In this way, the overall price level for goods and services adjusts to bring money supply and money demand into balance.

## 22-1e The Classical Dichotomy and Monetary Neutrality

We have seen how changes in the money supply lead to changes in the average level of prices of goods and services. How do monetary changes affect other economic variables, such as production, employment, real wages, and real interest rates? This question has long intrigued economists, including David Hume in the 18th century.

Hume and his contemporaries suggested that economic variables should be divided into two groups. The first group consists of **nominal variables**—variables measured in monetary units. The second group consists of **real variables**— variables measured in physical units. For example, the income of corn farmers is a nominal variable because it is measured in dollars, whereas the quantity of corn they produce is a real variable because it is measured in bushels. Nominal GDP is a nominal variable because it measures the dollar value of the economy's output of goods and services; real GDP is a real variable because it measures the total quantity of goods and services produced and is not influenced by the current prices of those goods and services. The separation of real and nominal variables is now called the **classical dichotomy**. (A *dichotomy* is a division into two groups, and *classical* refers to the earlier economic thinkers.)

Applying the classical dichotomy is tricky when we turn to prices. Most prices are quoted in units of money and, therefore, are nominal variables. When we say that the price of corn is $2 a bushel or that the price of wheat is $1 a bushel, both prices are nominal variables. But what about a *relative* price—the price of one thing compared to another? In our example, we could say that the price of a bushel of corn is 2 bushels of wheat. This relative price is not measured in terms of money. When comparing the prices of any two goods, the dollar signs cancel, and the resulting number is measured in physical units. Thus, while dollar prices are nominal variables, relative prices are real variables.

This lesson has many applications. For instance, the real wage (the dollar wage adjusted for inflation) is a real variable because it measures the rate at which people exchange goods and services for a unit of labor. Similarly, the real interest rate (the nominal interest rate adjusted for inflation) is a real variable because it measures the rate at which people exchange goods and services today for goods and services in the future.

Why separate variables into these groups? The classical dichotomy is useful because different forces influence real and nominal variables. According to classical analysis, nominal variables are influenced by developments in the economy's monetary system, whereas money is largely irrelevant for explaining real variables.

This idea was implicit in our discussion of the real economy in the long run. In previous chapters, we examined how real GDP, saving, investment, real interest rates, and unemployment are determined without mentioning the existence of money. In that analysis, the economy's production of goods and services depends on technology and factor supplies, the real interest rate balances the supply and demand for loanable funds, the real wage balances the supply and demand for labor, and unemployment results when the real wage is kept above the equilibrium level. These conclusions have nothing to do with the quantity of money supplied.

Changes in the supply of money, according to classical analysis, affect nominal variables but not real ones. When the central bank doubles the money supply, the

**nominal variables**
variables measured in monetary units

**real variables**
variables measured in physical units

**classical dichotomy**
the theoretical separation of nominal and real variables

**monetary neutrality**
the proposition that changes in the money supply do not affect real variables

price level doubles, the dollar wage doubles, and all other dollar values double. Real variables, such as production, employment, real wages, and real interest rates, are unchanged. The irrelevance of monetary changes for real variables is called **monetary neutrality**.

An analogy helps explain monetary neutrality. As the unit of account, money is the yardstick we use to measure economic transactions. When a central bank doubles the money supply, all prices double, and the value of the unit of account falls by half. A similar change would occur if the government were to reduce the length of the yard from 36 to 18 inches: With the new, shorter yardstick, all *measured* distances (nominal variables) would double, but the *actual* distances (real variables) would remain the same. The dollar, like the yard, is merely a unit of measurement, so a change in its value should not have real effects.

Is monetary neutrality realistic? Not completely. A change in the length of the yard from 36 to 18 inches would not matter in the long run, but in the short run, it would lead to confusion and mistakes. Similarly, most economists today believe that over short periods of time—within the span of a year or two—monetary changes affect real variables. Hume himself also doubted that monetary neutrality would apply in the short run. (We will study short-run non-neutrality later in the book, and this topic will help explain why the Fed changes the money supply over time.)

Yet classical analysis is right about the economy in the long run. Over the course of a decade, monetary changes have significant effects on nominal variables (such as the price level) but only negligible effects on real variables (such as real GDP). When studying long-run changes in the economy, the neutrality of money offers a good description of how the world works.

## 22-1f Velocity and the Quantity Equation

We can obtain another perspective on the quantity theory of money by considering the following question: How many times per year is the typical dollar bill used to pay for a newly produced good or service? The answer to this question is given by a variable called the **velocity of money**. In physics, the term *velocity* refers to the speed at which an object travels. In economics, the velocity of money refers to the speed at which the typical dollar bill travels around the economy from wallet to wallet.

**velocity of money**
the rate at which money changes hands

To calculate the velocity of money, we divide the nominal value of output (nominal GDP) by the quantity of money. If $P$ is the price level (the GDP deflator), $Y$ the quantity of output (real GDP), and $M$ the quantity of money, then velocity is

$$V = (P \times Y)/M.$$

To see why this makes sense, imagine a simple economy that produces only pizza. Suppose that the economy produces 100 pizzas in a year, that a pizza sells for \$10, and that the quantity of money in the economy is \$50. Then the velocity of money is

$$V = (\$10 \times 100)/\$50$$
$$= 20.$$

In this economy, people spend a total of \$1,000 per year on pizza. For this \$1,000 of spending to take place with only \$50 of money, each dollar bill must change hands on average 20 times per year.

With slight algebraic rearrangement, this equation can be rewritten as

$$M \times V = P \times Y.$$

This equation states that the quantity of money ($M$) times the velocity of money ($V$) equals the price of output ($P$) times the amount of output ($Y$). It is called the **quantity equation** because it relates the quantity of money ($M$) to the nominal value of output ($P \times Y$). The quantity equation shows that an increase in the quantity of money in an economy must be reflected in one of the other three variables: The price level must rise, the quantity of output must rise, or the velocity of money must fall.

In many cases, it turns out that the velocity of money is relatively stable. For example, Figure 3 shows nominal GDP, the quantity of money (as measured by M2), and the velocity of money for the U.S. economy since 1960. During this period, the money supply and nominal GDP both increased more than thirtyfold. By contrast, the velocity of money, although not exactly constant, has not changed

**quantity equation**
the equation $M \times V = P \times Y$, which relates the quantity of money, the velocity of money, and the dollar value of the economy's output of goods and services

---

This figure shows the nominal value of output as measured by nominal GDP, the quantity of money as measured by M2, and the velocity of money as measured by their ratio. For comparability, all three series have been scaled to equal 100 in 1960. Notice that nominal GDP and the quantity of money have grown dramatically over this period, while velocity has been relatively stable.

**Source:** U.S. Department of Commerce; Federal Reserve Board.

**FIGURE 3**

**Nominal GDP, the Quantity of Money, and the Velocity of Money**

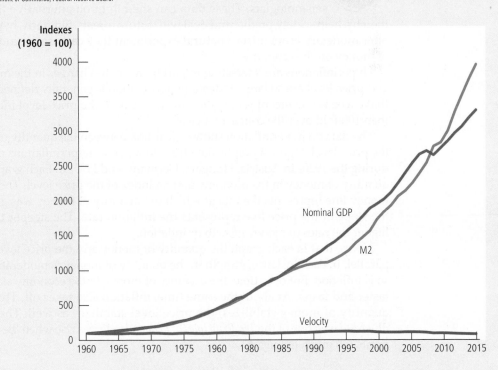

dramatically. Thus, for some purposes, the assumption of constant velocity is a good approximation.

We now have all the elements necessary to explain the equilibrium price level and inflation rate. They are as follows:

1. The velocity of money is relatively stable over time.
2. Because velocity is stable, when the central bank changes the quantity of money ($M$), it causes proportionate changes in the nominal value of output ($P \times Y$).
3. The economy's output of goods and services ($Y$) is primarily determined by factor supplies (labor, physical capital, human capital, and natural resources) and the available production technology. In particular, because money is neutral, money does not affect output.
4. With output ($Y$) determined by factor supplies and technology, when the central bank alters the money supply ($M$) and induces proportional changes in the nominal value of output ($P \times Y$), these changes are reflected in changes in the price level ($P$).
5. Therefore, when the central bank increases the money supply rapidly, the result is a high rate of inflation.

These five steps are the essence of the quantity theory of money.

### CASE STUDY

**MONEY AND PRICES DURING FOUR HYPERINFLATIONS**

Although earthquakes can wreak havoc on a society, they have the beneficial by-product of providing much useful data for seismologists. These data can shed light on alternative theories and, thereby, help society predict and deal with future threats. Similarly, hyperinflations offer monetary economists a natural experiment they can use to study the effects of money on the economy.

Hyperinflations are interesting in part because the changes in the money supply and price level are so large. Indeed, hyperinflation is generally defined as inflation that exceeds 50 percent *per month*. This means that the price level increases more than 100-fold over the course of a year.

The data on hyperinflation show a clear link between the quantity of money and the price level. Figure 4 graphs data from four classic hyperinflations that occurred during the 1920s in Austria, Hungary, Germany, and Poland. Each graph shows the quantity of money in the economy and an index of the price level. The slope of the money line represents the rate at which the quantity of money was growing, and the slope of the price line represents the inflation rate. The steeper the lines, the higher the rates of money growth or inflation.

Notice that in each graph the quantity of money and the price level are almost parallel. In each instance, growth in the quantity of money is moderate at first and so is inflation. But over time, the quantity of money in the economy starts growing faster and faster. At about the same time, inflation also takes off. Then when the quantity of money stabilizes, the price level stabilizes as well. These episodes illustrate well one of the *Ten Principles of Economics*: Prices rise when the government prints too much money. ●

This figure shows the quantity of money and the price level during four hyperinflations. (Note that these variables are graphed on *logarithmic* scales. This means that equal vertical distances on the graph represent equal *percentage* changes in the variable.) In each case, the quantity of money and the price level move closely together. The strong association between these two variables is consistent with the quantity theory of money, which states that growth in the money supply is the primary cause of inflation.

**Source:** Adapted from Thomas J. Sargent, "The End of Four Big Inflations," in Robert Hall, ed., *Inflation* (Chicago: University of Chicago Press, 1983), pp. 41–93.

## FIGURE 4

**Money and Prices during Four Hyperinflations**

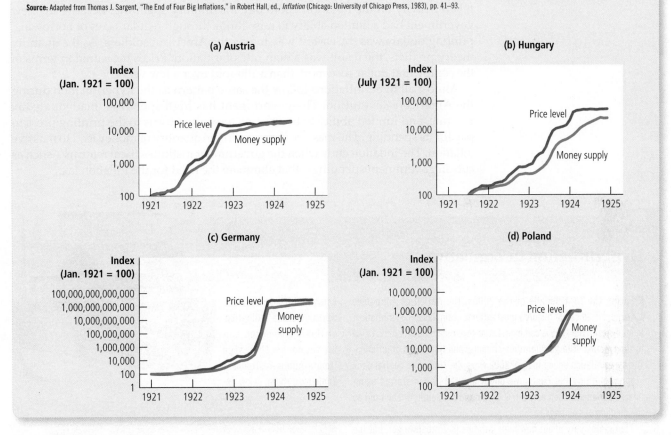

## 22-1g The Inflation Tax

If inflation is so easy to explain, why do countries experience hyperinflation? That is, why do the central banks of these countries choose to print so much money that its value is certain to fall rapidly over time?

The answer is that the governments of these countries are using money creation as a way to pay for their spending. When the government wants to build roads, pay salaries to its soldiers, or give transfer payments to the poor or elderly, it first has to raise the necessary funds. Normally, the government does this by levying taxes, such as income and sales taxes, and by borrowing from the public by selling government bonds. Yet the government can also pay for spending simply by printing the money it needs.

When the government raises revenue by printing money, it is said to levy an **inflation tax**. The inflation tax is not exactly like other taxes, however, because no one receives a bill from the government for this tax. Instead, the inflation tax is

**inflation tax**
the revenue the government raises by creating money

subtler. When the government prints money, the price level rises, and the dollars in your wallet become less valuable. Thus, *the inflation tax is like a tax on everyone who holds money*.

The importance of the inflation tax varies from country to country and over time. In the United States in recent years, the inflation tax has been a trivial source of revenue: It has accounted for less than 3 percent of government revenue. During the 1770s, however, the Continental Congress of the fledgling United States relied heavily on the inflation tax to pay for military spending. Because the new government had a limited ability to raise funds through regular taxes or borrowing, printing dollars was the easiest way to pay the American soldiers. As the quantity theory predicts, the result was a high rate of inflation: Prices measured in terms of the continental dollar rose more than a 100-fold over a few years.

Almost all hyperinflations follow the same pattern as the hyperinflation during the American Revolution. The government has high spending, inadequate tax revenue, and limited ability to borrow. As a result, it turns to the printing press to pay for its spending. The massive increases in the quantity of money lead to massive inflation. The inflation ends when the government institutes fiscal reforms—such as cuts in government spending—that eliminate the need for the inflation tax.

---

**FYI**

## Hyperinflation in Zimbabwe

During the first decade of the 2000s, the nation of Zimbabwe experienced one of history's most extreme examples of hyperinflation. In many ways, the story is common: Large government budget deficits led to the creation of large quantities of money and high rates of inflation. The hyperinflation ended in April 2009 when the Zimbabwe central bank stopped printing the Zimbabwe dollar and the nation started using foreign currencies such as the U.S. dollar and the South African rand as the medium of exchange.

Estimates vary about how high inflation in Zimbabwe got, but the magnitude of the problem is well documented by the denomination of the notes being issued by the central bank. Before the hyperinflation started, the Zimbabwe dollar was worth a bit more than one U.S. dollar, so the denominations of the paper currency were similar to those one would find in the United States. A person might carry, for example, a 10-dollar note in his wallet. In January 2008, however, after years of high inflation, the Reserve Bank of Zimbabwe issued notes worth 10 million Zimbabwe dollars, which was then equivalent to about 4 U.S. dollars. But even that did not prove to be large enough. A year later, the central bank announced it would issue notes worth 10 trillion Zimbabwe dollars, then worth about 3 U.S. dollars.

As prices rose and the central bank printed ever-larger denominations of money, the older, smaller-denomination currency lost value and became almost worthless. One indication of this phenomenon can be found on this sign from a public restroom in Zimbabwe, shown below. ■

ISTOCK/GETTY IMAGES

## 22-1h The Fisher Effect

According to the principle of monetary neutrality, an increase in the rate of money growth raises the rate of inflation but does not affect any real variable. An important application of this principle concerns the effect of money on interest rates. Interest rates are important variables for macroeconomists to understand because they link the economy of the present and the economy of the future through their effects on saving and investment.

To understand the relationship between money, inflation, and interest rates, recall the distinction between the nominal interest rate and the real interest rate. The *nominal interest rate* is the interest rate you hear about at your bank. If you have a savings account, for instance, the nominal interest rate tells you how fast the number of dollars in your account will rise over time. The *real interest rate* corrects the nominal interest rate for the effect of inflation to tell you how fast the purchasing power of your savings account will rise over time. The real interest rate is the nominal interest rate minus the inflation rate:

$$\text{Real interest rate} = \text{Nominal interest rate} - \text{Inflation rate}.$$

For example, if the bank posts a nominal interest rate of 7 percent per year and the inflation rate is 3 percent per year, then the real value of the deposits grows by 4 percent per year.

We can rewrite this equation to show that the nominal interest rate is the sum of the real interest rate and the inflation rate:

$$\text{Nominal interest rate} = \text{Real interest rate} + \text{Inflation rate}.$$

This way of looking at the nominal interest rate is useful because different economic forces determine each of the two terms on the right side of this equation. As we discussed earlier in the book, the supply and demand for loanable funds determine the real interest rate. And according to the quantity theory of money, growth in the money supply determines the inflation rate.

Let's now consider how growth in the money supply affects interest rates. In the long run over which money is neutral, a change in money growth should not affect the real interest rate. The real interest rate is, after all, a real variable. For the real interest rate not to be affected, the nominal interest rate must adjust one-for-one to changes in the inflation rate. Thus, *when the Fed increases the rate of money growth, the long-run result is both a higher inflation rate and a higher nominal interest rate*. This adjustment of the nominal interest rate to the inflation rate is called the **Fisher effect**, after Irving Fisher (1867–1947), the economist who first studied it.

**Fisher effect**
the one-for-one adjustment of the nominal interest rate to the inflation rate

Keep in mind that our analysis of the Fisher effect has maintained a long-run perspective. The Fisher effect need not hold in the short run because inflation may be unanticipated. A nominal interest rate is a payment on a loan, and it is typically set when the loan is first made. If a jump in inflation catches the borrower and lender by surprise, the nominal interest rate they agreed on will fail to reflect the higher inflation. But if inflation remains high, people will eventually come to expect it, and loan agreements will reflect this expectation. To be precise, therefore, the Fisher effect states that the nominal interest rate adjusts to expected inflation. Expected inflation moves with actual inflation in the long run, but that is not necessarily true in the short run.

The Fisher effect is crucial for understanding changes over time in the nominal interest rate. Figure 5 shows the nominal interest rate and the inflation rate in

**FIGURE 5**

**The Nominal Interest Rate and the Inflation Rate**

This figure uses annual data since 1960 to show the nominal interest rate on three-month Treasury bills and the inflation rate as measured by the consumer price index. The close association between these two variables is evidence for the Fisher effect: When the inflation rate rises, so does the nominal interest rate.

**Source:** U.S. Department of Treasury; U.S. Department of Labor.

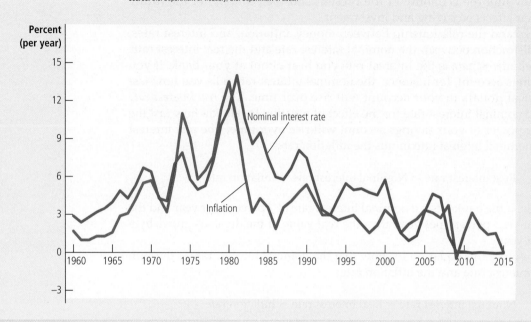

the U.S. economy since 1960. The close association between these two variables is clear. The nominal interest rate rose from the early 1960s through the 1970s because inflation was also rising during this time. Similarly, the nominal interest rate fell from the early 1980s through the 1990s because the Fed got inflation under control. In recent years, both the nominal interest rate and the inflation rate have been low by historical standards.

**QuickQuiz** *The government of a country increases the growth rate of the money supply from 5 percent per year to 50 percent per year. What happens to prices? What happens to nominal interest rates? Why might the government be doing this?*

## 22-2 The Costs of Inflation

In the late 1970s, when the U.S. inflation rate reached about 10 percent per year, inflation dominated debates over economic policy. And even though inflation has been low over the past 20 years, it remains a closely watched macroeconomic variable. One study found that *inflation* is the economic term mentioned most often in U.S. newspapers (ahead of second-place finisher *unemployment* and third-place finisher *productivity*).

Inflation is closely watched and widely discussed because it is thought to be a serious economic problem. But is that true? And if so, why?

### 22-2a A Fall in Purchasing Power? The Inflation Fallacy

If you ask the typical person why inflation is bad, he will tell you that the answer is obvious: Inflation robs him of the purchasing power of his hard-earned dollars. When prices rise, each dollar of income buys fewer goods and services. Thus, it might seem that inflation directly lowers living standards.

Yet further thought reveals a fallacy in this answer. When prices rise, buyers of goods and services pay more for what they buy. At the same time, however, sellers of goods and services get more for what they sell. Because most people earn their incomes by selling their services, such as their labor, inflation in incomes goes hand in hand with inflation in prices. Thus, *inflation does not in itself reduce people's real purchasing power*.

People believe the inflation fallacy because they do not appreciate the principle of monetary neutrality. A worker who receives an annual raise of 10 percent tends to view that raise as a reward for his own talent and effort. When an inflation rate of 6 percent reduces the real value of that raise to only 4 percent, the worker might feel that he has been cheated of what is rightfully his due. In fact, as we discussed in the chapter on production and growth, real incomes are determined by real variables, such as physical capital, human capital, natural resources, and the available production technology. Nominal incomes are determined by those factors and the overall price level. If the Fed were to lower the inflation rate from 6 percent to zero, our worker's annual raise would fall from 10 percent to 4 percent. He might feel less robbed by inflation, but his real income would not rise more quickly.

If nominal incomes tend to keep pace with rising prices, why then is inflation a problem? It turns out that there is no single answer to this question. Instead, economists have identified several costs of inflation. Each of these costs shows some way in which persistent growth in the money supply does, in fact, have some adverse effect on real variables.

### 22-2b Shoeleather Costs

As we have discussed, inflation is like a tax on the holders of money. The tax itself is not a cost to society: It is only a transfer of resources from households to the government. Yet most taxes give people an incentive to alter their behavior to avoid paying the tax, and this distortion of incentives causes deadweight losses for society as a whole. Like other taxes, the inflation tax also causes deadweight losses because people waste scarce resources trying to avoid it.

How can a person avoid paying the inflation tax? Because inflation erodes the real value of the money in your wallet, you can avoid the inflation tax by holding less money. One way to do this is to go to the bank more often. For example, rather than withdrawing $200 every four weeks, you might withdraw $50 once a week. By making more frequent trips to the bank, you can keep more of your wealth in your interest-bearing savings account and less in your wallet, where inflation erodes its value.

The cost of reducing your money holdings is called the **shoeleather cost** of inflation because making more frequent trips to the bank causes your shoes to wear out more quickly. Of course, this term is not to be taken literally: The actual cost of reducing your money holdings is not the wear and tear on your shoes but the time and convenience you must sacrifice to keep less money on hand than you would if there were no inflation.

**shoeleather costs**
the resources wasted when inflation encourages people to reduce their money holdings

The shoeleather costs of inflation may seem trivial. Indeed, they are in the U.S. economy, which has had only moderate inflation in recent years. But this cost is magnified in countries experiencing hyperinflation. Here is a description of one person's experience in Bolivia during its hyperinflation (as reported in the August 13, 1985, issue of *The Wall Street Journal*):

> When Edgar Miranda gets his monthly teacher's pay of 25 million pesos, he hasn't a moment to lose. Every hour, pesos drop in value. So, while his wife rushes to market to lay in a month's supply of rice and noodles, he is off with the rest of the pesos to change them into black-market dollars.
>
> Mr. Miranda is practicing the First Rule of Survival amid the most out-of-control inflation in the world today. Bolivia is a case study of how runaway inflation undermines a society. Price increases are so huge that the figures build up almost beyond comprehension. In one six-month period, for example, prices soared at an annual rate of 38,000 percent. By official count, however, last year's inflation reached 2,000 percent, and this year's is expected to hit 8,000 percent—though other estimates range many times higher. In any event, Bolivia's rate dwarfs Israel's 370 percent and Argentina's 1,100 percent—two other cases of severe inflation.
>
> It is easier to comprehend what happens to the thirty-eight-year-old Mr. Miranda's pay if he doesn't quickly change it into dollars. The day he was paid 25 million pesos, a dollar cost 500,000 pesos. So he received $50. Just days later, with the rate at 900,000 pesos, he would have received $27.

As this story shows, the shoeleather costs of inflation can be substantial. With the high inflation rate, Mr. Miranda does not have the luxury of holding the local money as a store of value. Instead, he is forced to convert his pesos quickly into goods or into U.S. dollars, which offer a more stable store of value. The time and effort that Mr. Miranda expends to reduce his money holdings are a waste of resources. If the monetary authority pursued a low-inflation policy, Mr. Miranda would be happy to hold pesos, and he could put his time and effort to more productive use. In fact, shortly after this article was written, the Bolivian inflation rate was reduced substantially with a more restrictive monetary policy.

### 22-2c  Menu Costs

Most firms do not change the prices of their products every day. Instead, firms often announce prices and leave them unchanged for weeks, months, or even years. One survey found that the typical U.S. firm changes its prices about once a year.

Firms change prices infrequently because there are costs to changing prices. Costs of price adjustment are called **menu costs**, a term derived from a restaurant's cost of printing a new menu. Menu costs include the costs of deciding on new prices, printing new price lists and catalogs, sending these new price lists and catalogs to dealers and customers, advertising the new prices, and even dealing with customer annoyance over price changes.

Inflation increases the menu costs that firms must bear. In the current U.S. economy, with its low inflation rate, annual price adjustment is an appropriate business strategy for many firms. But when high inflation makes firms' costs rise rapidly, annual price adjustment is impractical. During hyperinflations, for example, firms must change their prices daily or even more often just to keep up with all the other prices in the economy.

### 22-2d  Relative-Price Variability and the Misallocation of Resources

Suppose that the Eatabit Eatery prints a new menu with new prices every January and then leaves its prices unchanged for the rest of the year. If there is no inflation, Eatabit's relative prices—the prices of its meals compared to other prices in the

**menu costs**
the costs of changing prices

economy—would be constant over the course of the year. By contrast, if the inflation rate is 12 percent per year, Eatabit's relative prices will automatically fall by 1 percent each month. The restaurant's relative prices will be high in the early months of the year, just after it has printed a new menu, and low in the later months. And the higher the inflation rate, the greater is this automatic variability. Thus, because prices change only once in a while, inflation causes relative prices to vary more than they otherwise would.

Why does this matter? The reason is that market economies rely on relative prices to allocate scarce resources. Consumers decide what to buy by comparing the quality and prices of various goods and services. Through these decisions, they determine how the scarce factors of production are allocated among industries and firms. When inflation distorts relative prices, consumer decisions are distorted and markets are less able to allocate resources to their best use.

### 22-2e Inflation-Induced Tax Distortions

Almost all taxes distort incentives, cause people to alter their behavior, and lead to a less efficient allocation of the economy's resources. Many taxes, however, become even more problematic in the presence of inflation. The reason is that lawmakers often fail to take inflation into account when writing the tax laws. Economists who have studied the tax code conclude that inflation tends to raise the tax burden on income earned from savings.

One example of how inflation discourages saving is the tax treatment of *capital gains*—the profits made by selling an asset for more than its purchase price. Suppose that in 1988 you used some of your savings to buy stock in IBM for $30 and that in 2016 you sold the stock for $130. According to the tax law, you have earned a capital gain of $100, which you must include in your income when computing how much income tax you owe. But because the overall price level doubled from 1988 to 2016, the $30 you invested in 1988 is equivalent (in terms of purchasing power) to $60 in 2016. When you sell your stock for $130, you have a real gain (an increase in purchasing power) of only $70. The tax code, however, does not take account of inflation and assesses you a tax on a gain of $100. Thus, inflation exaggerates the size of capital gains and inadvertently increases the tax burden on this type of income.

Another example is the tax treatment of interest income. The income tax treats the *nominal* interest earned on savings as income, even though part of the nominal interest rate merely compensates for inflation. To see the effects of this policy, consider the numerical example in Table 1. The table compares two economies, both of which tax interest income at a rate of 25 percent. In Economy A, inflation is zero and the nominal and real interest rates are both 4 percent. In this case, the 25 percent tax on interest income reduces the real interest rate from 4 percent to 3 percent. In Economy B, the real interest rate is again 4 percent but the inflation rate is 8 percent. As a result of the Fisher effect, the nominal interest rate is 12 percent. Because the income tax treats this entire 12 percent interest as income, the government takes 25 percent of it, leaving an after-tax nominal interest rate of only 9 percent and an after-tax real interest rate of only 1 percent. In this case, the 25 percent tax on interest income reduces the real interest rate from 4 percent to 1 percent. Because the after-tax real interest rate provides the incentive to save, saving is much less attractive in the economy with inflation (Economy B) than in the economy with stable prices (Economy A).

The taxes on nominal capital gains and on nominal interest income are two examples of how the tax code interacts with inflation. There are many others. Because of these inflation-induced tax changes, higher inflation tends to

## TABLE 1

**How Inflation Raises the Tax Burden on Saving**
In the presence of zero inflation, a 25 percent tax on interest income reduces the real interest rate from 4 percent to 3 percent. In the presence of 8 percent inflation, the same tax reduces the real interest rate from 4 percent to 1 percent.

|  | Economy A (price stability) | Economy B (inflation) |
|---|---|---|
| Real interest rate | 4% | 4% |
| Inflation rate | 0 | 8 |
| Nominal interest rate (real interest rate + inflation rate) | 4 | 12 |
| Reduced interest due to 25 percent tax (0.25 × nominal interest rate) | 1 | 3 |
| After-tax nominal interest rate (0.75 × nominal interest rate) | 3 | 9 |
| After-tax real interest rate (after-tax nominal interest rate − inflation rate) | 3 | 1 |

discourage people from saving. Recall that the economy's saving provides the resources for investment, which in turn is a key ingredient to long-run economic growth. Thus, when inflation raises the tax burden on saving, it tends to depress the economy's long-run growth rate. There is, however, no consensus among economists about the size of this effect.

One solution to this problem, other than eliminating inflation, is to index the tax system. That is, the tax laws could be rewritten to take account of the effects of inflation. In the case of capital gains, for example, the tax code could adjust the purchase price using a price index and assess the tax only on the real gain. In the case of interest income, the government could tax only real interest income by excluding that portion of the interest income that merely compensates for inflation. To some extent, the tax laws have moved in the direction of indexation. For example, the income levels at which income tax rates change are adjusted automatically each year based on changes in the consumer price index. Yet many other aspects of the tax laws—such as the tax treatment of capital gains and interest income—are not indexed.

In an ideal world, the tax laws would be written so that inflation would not alter anyone's real tax liability. In the real world, however, tax laws are far from perfect. More complete indexation would probably be desirable, but it would further complicate a tax code that many people already consider too complex.

### 22-2f Confusion and Inconvenience

Imagine that we took a poll and asked people the following question: "This year the yard is 36 inches. How long do you think it should be next year?" Assuming we could get people to take us seriously, they would tell us that the yard should stay the same length—36 inches. Anything else would just complicate life needlessly.

What does this finding have to do with inflation? Recall that money, as the economy's unit of account, is what we use to quote prices and record debts. In other words, money is the yardstick with which we measure economic transactions. The job of the Federal Reserve is a bit like the job of the Bureau of

Standards—to ensure the reliability of a commonly used unit of measurement. When the Fed increases the money supply and creates inflation, it erodes the real value of the unit of account.

It is difficult to judge the costs of the confusion and inconvenience that arise from inflation. Earlier, we discussed how the tax code incorrectly measures real incomes in the presence of inflation. Similarly, accountants incorrectly measure firms' earnings when prices are rising over time. Because inflation causes dollars at different times to have different real values, computing a firm's profit—the difference between its revenue and costs—is more complicated in an economy with inflation. Therefore, to some extent, inflation makes investors less able to sort successful from unsuccessful firms, which in turn impedes financial markets in their role of allocating the economy's saving to alternative types of investment.

## 22-2g A Special Cost of Unexpected Inflation: Arbitrary Redistributions of Wealth

So far, the costs of inflation we have discussed occur even if inflation is steady and predictable. Inflation has an additional cost, however, when it comes as a surprise. Unexpected inflation redistributes wealth among the population in a way that has nothing to do with either merit or need. These redistributions occur because many loans in the economy are specified in terms of the unit of account—money.

Consider an example. Suppose that Sam Student takes out a $20,000 loan at a 7 percent interest rate from Bigbank to attend college. In 10 years, the loan will come due. After his debt has compounded for 10 years at 7 percent, Sam will owe Bigbank $40,000. The real value of this debt will depend on inflation over the decade. If Sam is lucky, the economy will have a hyperinflation. In this case, wages and prices will rise so high that Sam will be able to pay the $40,000 debt out of pocket change. By contrast, if the economy goes through a major deflation, then wages and prices will fall, and Sam will find the $40,000 debt a greater burden than he anticipated.

This example shows that unexpected changes in prices redistribute wealth among debtors and creditors. A hyperinflation enriches Sam at the expense of Bigbank because it diminishes the real value of the debt; Sam can repay the loan in dollars that are less valuable than he anticipated. Deflation enriches Bigbank at Sam's expense because it increases the real value of the debt; in this case, Sam has to repay the loan in dollars that are more valuable than he anticipated. If inflation were predictable, then Bigbank and Sam could take inflation into account when setting the nominal interest rate. (Recall the Fisher effect.) But if inflation is hard to predict, it imposes risk on Sam and Bigbank that both would prefer to avoid.

This cost of unexpected inflation is important to consider together with another fact: Inflation is especially volatile and uncertain when the average rate of inflation is high. This is seen most simply by examining the experience of different countries. Countries with low average inflation, such as Germany in the late 20th century, tend to have stable inflation. Countries with high average inflation, such as many countries in Latin America, tend to have unstable inflation. There are no known examples of economies with high, stable inflation. This relationship between the level and volatility of inflation points to another cost of inflation. If a country pursues a high-inflation monetary policy, it will have to bear not only the costs of high expected inflation but also the arbitrary redistributions of wealth associated with unexpected inflation.

## 22-2h Inflation Is Bad, but Deflation May Be Worse

In recent U.S. history, inflation has been the norm. But the level of prices has fallen at times, such as during the late 19th century and early 1930s. From 1998 to 2012, Japan experienced a 4-percent decline in its overall price level. So as we conclude our discussion of the costs of inflation, we should briefly consider the costs of deflation as well.

Some economists have suggested that a small and predictable amount of deflation may be desirable. Milton Friedman pointed out that deflation would lower the nominal interest rate (via the Fisher effect) and that a lower nominal interest rate would reduce the cost of holding money. The shoeleather costs of holding money would, he argued, be minimized by a nominal interest rate close to zero, which in turn would require deflation equal to the real interest rate. This prescription for moderate deflation is called the *Friedman rule*.

Yet there are also costs of deflation. Some of these mirror the costs of inflation. For example, just as a rising price level induces menu costs and relative-price variability, so does a falling price level. Moreover, in practice, deflation is rarely as steady and predictable as Friedman recommended. More often, it comes as a surprise, resulting in the redistribution of wealth toward creditors and away from debtors. Because debtors are often poorer, these redistributions in wealth are particularly painful.

Perhaps most important, deflation often arises because of broader macroeconomic difficulties. As we will see in future chapters, falling prices result when some event, such as a monetary contraction, reduces the overall demand for goods and services in the economy. This fall in aggregate demand can lead to falling incomes and rising unemployment. In other words, deflation is often a symptom of deeper economic problems.

**CASE STUDY**

### THE WIZARD OF OZ AND THE FREE-SILVER DEBATE

As a child, you probably saw the movie *The Wizard of Oz*, based on a children's book written in 1900. The movie and book tell the story of a young girl, Dorothy, who finds herself lost in a strange land far from home. You probably did not know, however, that some scholars believe that the story is actually an allegory about U.S. monetary policy in the late 19th century.

From 1880 to 1896, the price level in the U.S. economy fell by 23 percent. Because this event was unanticipated, it led to a major redistribution of wealth. Most farmers in the western part of the country were debtors. Their creditors were the bankers in the east. When the price level fell, it caused the real value of these debts to rise, which enriched the banks at the expense of the farmers.

According to Populist politicians of the time, the solution to the farmers' problem was the free coinage of silver. During this period, the United States was operating with a gold standard. The quantity of gold determined the money supply and, thereby, the price level. The free-silver advocates wanted silver, as well as gold, to be used as money. If adopted, this proposal would have increased the money supply, pushed up the price level, and reduced the real burden of the farmers' debts.

The debate over silver was heated, and it was central to the politics of the 1890s. A common election slogan of the Populists was "We Are Mortgaged. All but Our Votes." One prominent advocate of free silver was William Jennings Bryan, the Democratic nominee for president in 1896. He is remembered in part for a speech at the Democratic Party's nominating convention in which he said, "You shall not press down upon the brow of labor this crown of thorns. You shall not crucify mankind upon a cross of gold." Rarely since then have politicians waxed so poetic about alternative approaches to monetary policy. Nonetheless, Bryan lost the election to Republican William McKinley, and the United States remained on the gold standard.

L. Frank Baum, author of the book *The Wonderful Wizard of Oz*, was a midwestern journalist. When he sat down to write a story for children, he made the characters represent protagonists in the major political battle of his time. Here is how economic historian Hugh Rockoff, writing in the *Journal of Political Economy* in 1990, interprets the story:

| | |
|---|---|
| DOROTHY: | Traditional American values |
| TOTO: | Prohibitionist party, also called the Teetotalers |
| SCARECROW: | Farmers |
| TIN WOODSMAN: | Industrial workers |
| COWARDLY LION: | William Jennings Bryan |
| MUNCHKINS: | Citizens of the East |
| WICKED WITCH OF THE EAST: | Grover Cleveland |
| WICKED WITCH OF THE WEST: | William McKinley |
| WIZARD: | Marcus Alonzo Hanna, chairman of the Republican Party |
| OZ: | Abbreviation for ounce of gold |
| YELLOW BRICK ROAD: | Gold standard |

*An early debate over monetary policy*

At the end of Baum's story, Dorothy does find her way home, but it is not by just following the yellow brick road. After a long and perilous journey, she learns that the wizard is incapable of helping her or her friends. Instead, Dorothy finally discovers the magical power of her *silver* slippers. (When the book was made into a movie in 1939, Dorothy's slippers were changed from silver to ruby. The Hollywood filmmakers were more interested in showing off the new technology of Technicolor than in telling a story about 19th-century monetary policy.)

The Populists lost the debate over the free coinage of silver, but they eventually got the monetary expansion and inflation that they wanted. In 1898, prospectors discovered gold near the Klondike River in the Canadian Yukon. Increased supplies of gold also arrived from the mines of South Africa. As a result, the money supply and the price level started to rise in the United States and in other countries operating on the gold standard. Within 15 years, prices in the United States were back to the levels that had prevailed in the 1880s, and farmers were better able to handle their debts. ●

**Quick Quiz** *List and describe six costs of inflation.*

## 22-3 Conclusion

This chapter discussed the causes and costs of inflation. The primary cause of inflation is growth in the quantity of money. When the central bank creates money in large quantities, the value of money falls quickly. To maintain stable prices, the central bank must maintain strict control over the money supply.

The costs of inflation are more subtle. They include shoeleather costs, menu costs, increased variability of relative prices, unintended changes in tax liabilities, confusion and inconvenience, and arbitrary redistributions of wealth. Are these costs, in total, large or small? All economists agree that they become huge during hyperinflation. But during periods of moderate inflation—when prices rise by less than 10 percent per year—the size of these costs is more open to debate.

This chapter presented many of the most important lessons about inflation, but the analysis is incomplete. When the central bank reduces the rate of money growth, prices rise less rapidly, as the quantity theory suggests. Yet as the economy makes the transition to the lower inflation rate, the change in monetary policy will likely disrupt production and employment. That is, even though monetary policy is neutral in the long run, it has profound effects on real variables in the short run. Later in this book we will examine the reasons for short-run monetary non-neutrality to enhance our understanding of the causes and effects of inflation.

## CHAPTER QuickQuiz

1. The classical principle of monetary neutrality states that changes in the money supply do not influence _____ variables and is thought most applicable in the _____ run.
   a. nominal, short
   b. nominal, long
   c. real, short
   d. real, long

2. If nominal GDP is $400, real GDP is $200, and the money supply is $100, then
   a. the price level is ½, and velocity is 2.
   b. the price level is ½, and velocity is 4.
   c. the price level is 2, and velocity is 2.
   d. the price level is 2, and velocity is 4.

3. According to the quantity theory of money, which variable in the quantity equation is most stable over long periods of time?
   a. money
   b. velocity
   c. price level
   d. output

4. Hyperinflations occur when the government runs a large budget _____, which the central bank finances with a substantial monetary _____.
   a. deficit, contraction
   b. deficit, expansion
   c. surplus, contraction
   d. surplus, expansion

5. According to the quantity theory of money and the Fisher effect, if the central bank increases the rate of money growth,
   a. inflation and the nominal interest rate both increase.
   b. inflation and the real interest rate both increase.
   c. the nominal interest rate and the real interest rate both increase.
   d. inflation, the real interest rate, and the nominal interest rate all increase.

6. If an economy always has inflation of 10 percent per year, which of the following costs of inflation will it NOT suffer?
   a. shoeleather costs from reduced holdings of money
   b. menu costs from more frequent price adjustment
   c. distortions from the taxation of nominal capital gains
   d. arbitrary redistributions between debtors and creditors

## SUMMARY

- The overall level of prices in an economy adjusts to bring money supply and money demand into balance. When the central bank increases the supply of money, it causes the price level to rise. Persistent growth in the quantity of money supplied leads to continuing inflation.

- The principle of monetary neutrality asserts that changes in the quantity of money influence nominal variables but not real variables. Most economists believe that monetary neutrality approximately describes the behavior of the economy in the long run.

- A government can pay for some of its spending simply by printing money. When countries rely heavily on this "inflation tax," the result is hyperinflation.

- One application of the principle of monetary neutrality is the Fisher effect. According to the Fisher effect, when the inflation rate rises, the nominal interest rate rises by the same amount so that the real interest rate remains the same.

- Many people think that inflation makes them poorer because it raises the cost of what they buy. This view is a fallacy, however, because inflation also raises nominal incomes.

- Economists have identified six costs of inflation: shoeleather costs associated with reduced money holdings, menu costs associated with more frequent adjustment of prices, increased variability of relative prices, unintended changes in tax liabilities due to nonindexation of the tax code, confusion and inconvenience resulting from a changing unit of account, and arbitrary redistributions of wealth between debtors and creditors. Many of these costs are large during hyperinflation, but the size of these costs for moderate inflation is less clear.

## KEY CONCEPTS

## QUESTIONS FOR REVIEW

1. Explain how an increase in the price level affects the real value of money.

2. According to the quantity theory of money, what is the effect of an increase in the quantity of money?

3. Explain the difference between nominal and real variables and give two examples of each. According to the principle of monetary neutrality, which variables are affected by changes in the quantity of money?

4. In what sense is inflation like a tax? How does thinking about inflation as a tax help explain hyperinflation?

5. According to the Fisher effect, how does an increase in the inflation rate affect the real interest rate and the nominal interest rate?

6. What are the costs of inflation? Which of these costs do you think are most important for the U.S. economy?

7. If inflation is less than expected, who benefits—debtors or creditors? Explain.

## PROBLEMS AND APPLICATIONS

1. Suppose that this year's money supply is $500 billion, nominal GDP is $10 trillion, and real GDP is $5 trillion.
   a. What is the price level? What is the velocity of money?
   b. Suppose that velocity is constant and the economy's output of goods and services rises by 5 percent each year. What will happen to nominal GDP and the price level next year if the Fed keeps the money supply constant?
   c. What money supply should the Fed set next year if it wants to keep the price level stable?
   d. What money supply should the Fed set next year if it wants inflation of 10 percent?

2. Suppose that changes in bank regulations expand the availability of credit cards so that people need to hold less cash.
   a. How does this event affect the demand for money?
   b. If the Fed does not respond to this event, what will happen to the price level?
   c. If the Fed wants to keep the price level stable, what should it do?

3. It is sometimes suggested that the Federal Reserve should try to achieve zero inflation. If we assume that velocity is constant, does this zero-inflation goal require that the rate of money growth equal zero? If yes, explain why. If no, explain what the rate of money growth should equal.

4. Suppose that a country's inflation rate increases sharply. What happens to the inflation tax on the holders of money? Why is wealth that is held in savings accounts *not* subject to a change in the inflation tax? Can you think of any way holders of savings accounts are hurt by the increase in the inflation rate?

5. Let's consider the effects of inflation in an economy composed of only two people: Bob, a bean farmer, and Rita, a rice farmer. Bob and Rita both always consume equal amounts of rice and beans. In 2016, the price of beans was $1 and the price of rice was $3.
   a. Suppose that in 2017 the price of beans was $2 and the price of rice was $6. What was inflation? Was Bob better off, worse off, or unaffected by the changes in prices? What about Rita?
   b. Now suppose that in 2017 the price of beans was $2 and the price of rice was $4. What was inflation? Was Bob better off, worse off, or unaffected by the changes in prices? What about Rita?
   c. Finally, suppose that in 2017 the price of beans was $2 and the price of rice was $1.50. What was inflation? Was Bob better off, worse off, or unaffected by the changes in prices? What about Rita?

   d. What matters more to Bob and Rita—the overall inflation rate or the relative price of rice and beans?

6. If the tax rate is 40 percent, compute the before-tax real interest rate and the after-tax real interest rate in each of the following cases.
   a. The nominal interest rate is 10 percent, and the inflation rate is 5 percent.
   b. The nominal interest rate is 6 percent, and the inflation rate is 2 percent.
   c. The nominal interest rate is 4 percent, and the inflation rate is 1 percent.

7. Recall that money serves three functions in the economy. What are those functions? How does inflation affect the ability of money to serve each of these functions?

8. Suppose that people expect inflation to equal 3 percent, but in fact, prices rise by 5 percent. Describe how this unexpectedly high inflation rate would help or hurt the following:
   a. the government
   b. a homeowner with a fixed-rate mortgage
   c. a union worker in the second year of a labor contract
   d. a college that has invested some of its endowment in government bonds

9. Explain whether the following statements are true, false, or uncertain.
   a. "Inflation hurts borrowers and helps lenders, because borrowers must pay a higher rate of interest."
   b. "If prices change in a way that leaves the overall price level unchanged, then no one is made better or worse off."
   c. "Inflation does not reduce the purchasing power of most workers."

To find additional study resources, visit cengagebrain.com, and search for "Mankiw."

# PART IX

# Short-Run Economic Fluctuations

# Aggregate Demand and Aggregate Supply

Economic activity fluctuates from year to year. In most years, the production of goods and services rises. Because of increases in the labor force, increases in the capital stock, and advances in technological knowledge, the economy can produce more and more over time. This growth allows everyone to enjoy a higher standard of living. On average, over the past half century, the production of the U.S. economy as measured by real GDP has grown by about 3 percent per year.

In some years, however, instead of expanding, the economy contracts. Firms find themselves unable to sell all the goods and services they have to offer, so

**recession**
a period of declining
real incomes and rising
unemployment

**depression**
a severe recession

they reduce production. Workers are laid off, unemployment becomes widespread, and factories are left idle. With the economy producing fewer goods and services, real GDP and other measures of income decline. Such a period of falling incomes and rising unemployment is called a **recession** if it is relatively mild and a **depression** if it is more severe.

An example of such a downturn occurred in 2008 and 2009. From the fourth quarter of 2007 to the second quarter of 2009, real GDP for the U.S. economy fell by 4.2 percent. The rate of unemployment rose from 4.4 percent in May 2007 to 10.0 percent in October 2009—the highest level in more than a quarter century. Not surprisingly, students graduating during this time found that desirable jobs were hard to come by.

What causes short-run fluctuations in economic activity? What, if anything, can public policy do to prevent periods of falling incomes and rising unemployment? When recessions and depressions occur, how can policymakers reduce their length and severity? These are the questions we take up now.

The variables that we study are largely those we have seen in previous chapters. They include GDP, unemployment, interest rates, and the price level. Also familiar are the policy instruments of government spending, taxes, and the money supply. What differs from our earlier analysis is the time horizon. So far, our goal has been to explain the behavior of these variables in the long run. Our goal now is to explain their short-run deviations from long-run trends. In other words, instead of focusing on the forces that explain economic growth from generation to generation, we are now interested in the forces that explain economic fluctuations from year to year.

There is some debate among economists about how best to analyze short-run fluctuations, but most economists use the *model of aggregate demand and aggregate supply*. Learning how to use this model for analyzing the short-run effects of various events and policies is the primary task ahead. This chapter introduces the model's two pieces: the aggregate-demand curve and the aggregate-supply curve. Before turning to the model, however, let's look at some of the key facts that describe the ups and downs of the economy.

# 23-1 Three Key Facts about Economic Fluctuations

Short-run fluctuations in economic activity have occurred in all countries throughout history. As a starting point for understanding these year-to-year fluctuations, let's discuss some of their most important properties.

## 23-1a Fact 1: Economic Fluctuations Are Irregular and Unpredictable

Fluctuations in the economy are often called *the business cycle*. As this term suggests, economic fluctuations correspond to changes in business conditions. When real GDP grows rapidly, business is good. During such periods of economic expansion, most firms find that customers are plentiful and that profits are growing. When real GDP falls during recessions, businesses have trouble. During such periods of economic contraction, most firms experience declining sales and dwindling profits.

The term *business cycle* is somewhat misleading because it suggests that economic fluctuations follow a regular, predictable pattern. In fact, economic fluctuations are not at all regular, and they are almost impossible to predict with much accuracy. Panel (a) of Figure 1 shows the real GDP of the

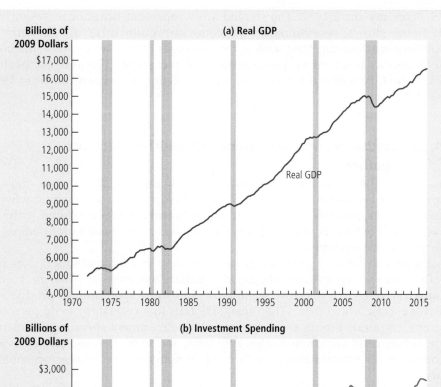

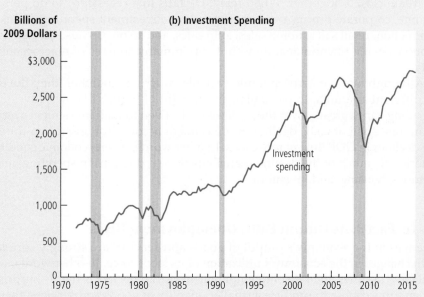

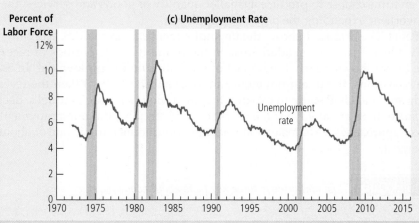

## FIGURE 1

**A Look at Short-Run Economic Fluctuations**
This figure shows real GDP in panel (a), investment spending in panel (b), and unemployment in panel (c) for the U.S. economy. Recessions are shown as the shaded areas. Notice that real GDP and investment spending decline during recessions, while unemployment rises.

**Source:** U.S. Department of Commerce; U.S. Department of Labor.

U.S. economy since 1972. The shaded areas represent times of recession. As the figure shows, recessions do not come at regular intervals. Sometimes recessions are close together, such as the recessions of 1980 and 1982. Sometimes the economy goes many years without a recession. The longest period in U.S. history without a recession was the economic expansion from 1991 to 2001.

### 23-1b   Fact 2: Most Macroeconomic Quantities Fluctuate Together

Real GDP is the variable most commonly used to monitor short-run changes in the economy because it is the most comprehensive measure of economic activity. Real GDP measures the value of all final goods and services produced within a given period of time. It also measures the total income (adjusted for inflation) of everyone in the economy.

It turns out, however, that for monitoring short-run fluctuations, it does not really matter which measure of economic activity one looks at. Most macroeconomic variables that measure some type of income, spending, or production fluctuate closely together. When real GDP falls in a recession, so do personal income, corporate profits, consumer spending, investment spending, industrial production, retail sales, home sales, auto sales, and so on. Because recessions are economy-wide phenomena, they show up in many sources of macroeconomic data.

Although many macroeconomic variables fluctuate together, they fluctuate by different amounts. In particular, as panel (b) of Figure 1 shows, investment spending varies greatly over the business cycle. Even though investment averages about one-sixth of GDP, declines in investment account for about two-thirds of the declines in GDP during recessions. In other words, when economic conditions deteriorate, much of the decline is attributable to reductions in spending on new factories, housing, and inventories.

HOW TO DELEGATE DURING A RECESSION

© ROBERT MANKOFF / THE NEW YORKER COLLECTION/ WWW.CARTOONBANK.COM

*"You're fired. Pass it on."*

### 23-1c   Fact 3: As Output Falls, Unemployment Rises

Changes in the economy's output of goods and services are strongly correlated with changes in the economy's utilization of its labor force. In other words, when real GDP declines, the rate of unemployment rises. This fact is hardly surprising: When firms choose to produce a smaller quantity of goods and services, they lay off workers, expanding the pool of unemployed.

Panel (c) of Figure 1 shows the unemployment rate in the U.S. economy since 1972. Once again, the shaded areas in the figure indicate periods of recession. The figure shows clearly the impact of recessions on unemployment. In each of the recessions, the unemployment rate rises substantially. When the recession ends and real GDP starts to expand, the unemployment rate gradually declines. Because there are always some workers between jobs, the unemployment rate never approaches zero. Instead, it fluctuates around its natural rate of about 5 or 6 percent.

QuickQuiz   *List and discuss three key facts about economic fluctuations.*

# 23-2 Explaining Short-Run Economic Fluctuations

Describing what happens to economies as they fluctuate over time is easy. Explaining what causes these fluctuations is more difficult. Indeed, compared to the topics we have studied in previous chapters, the theory of economic fluctuations remains controversial. In this chapter, we begin to develop the model that most economists use to explain short-run fluctuations in economic activity.

## 23-2a The Assumptions of Classical Economics

In previous chapters, we developed theories to explain what determines most important macroeconomic variables in the long run. Chapter 17 explained the level and growth of productivity and real GDP. Chapters 18 and 19 explained how the financial system works and how the real interest rate adjusts to balance saving and investment. Chapter 20 explained why there is always some unemployment in the economy. Chapters 21 and 22 explained the monetary system and how changes in the money supply affect the price level, the inflation rate, and the nominal interest rate.

All of this previous analysis was based on two related ideas: the classical dichotomy and monetary neutrality. Recall that the classical dichotomy is the separation of variables into real variables (those that measure quantities or relative prices) and nominal variables (those measured in terms of money). According to classical macroeconomic theory, changes in the money supply affect nominal variables but not real variables. As a result of this monetary neutrality, Chapters 17 through 20 were able to examine the determinants of real variables (real GDP, the real interest rate, and unemployment) without introducing nominal variables (the money supply and the price level).

In a sense, money does not matter in a classical world. If the quantity of money in the economy were to double, everything would cost twice as much, and everyone's income would be twice as high. But so what? The change would be *nominal* (by the standard meaning of "nearly insignificant"). The things that people *really* care about—whether they have a job, how many goods and services they can afford, and so on—would be exactly the same.

This classical view is sometimes described by the saying, "Money is a veil." That is, nominal variables may be the first things we see when we observe an economy because economic variables are often expressed in units of money. But what's important are the real variables and the economic forces that determine them. According to classical theory, to understand these real variables, we need to look behind the veil.

## 23-2b The Reality of Short-Run Fluctuations

Do these assumptions of classical macroeconomic theory apply to the world in which we live? The answer to this question is of central importance to understanding how the economy works. *Most economists believe that classical theory describes the world in the long run but not in the short run.*

Consider again the impact of money on the economy. Most economists believe that, beyond a period of several years, changes in the money supply affect prices and other nominal variables but do not affect real GDP, unemployment, and other real variables—just as classical theory says. When studying year-to-year changes in the economy, however, the assumption of monetary neutrality is no longer appropriate. In the short run, real and nominal variables are highly intertwined, and changes in the money supply can temporarily push real GDP away from its long-run trend.

Even the classical economists themselves, such as David Hume, realized that classical economic theory did not hold in the short run. From his vantage point in 18th-century England, Hume observed that when the money supply expanded after gold discoveries, it took some time for prices to rise, and in the meantime, the economy enjoyed higher employment and production.

To understand how the economy works in the short run, we need a new model. This new model can be built using many of the tools we developed in previous chapters, but it must abandon the classical dichotomy and the neutrality of money. We can no longer separate our analysis of real variables such as output and employment from our analysis of nominal variables such as money and the price level. Our new model focuses on how real and nominal variables interact.

### 23-2c The Model of Aggregate Demand and Aggregate Supply

Our model of short-run economic fluctuations focuses on the behavior of two variables. The first variable is the economy's output of goods and services, as measured by real GDP. The second is the average level of prices, as measured by the CPI or the GDP deflator. Notice that output is a real variable, whereas the price level is a nominal variable. By focusing on the relationship between these two variables, we are departing from the classical assumption that real and nominal variables can be studied separately.

We analyze fluctuations in the economy as a whole with the **model of aggregate demand and aggregate supply**, which is illustrated in Figure 2. On the vertical axis is the overall price level in the economy. On the horizontal axis is the overall quantity of goods and services produced in the economy. The **aggregate-demand curve** shows the quantity of goods and services that households, firms,

**model of aggregate demand and aggregate supply**
the model that most economists use to explain short-run fluctuations in economic activity around its long-run trend

**aggregate-demand curve**
a curve that shows the quantity of goods and services that households, firms, the government, and customers abroad want to buy at each price level

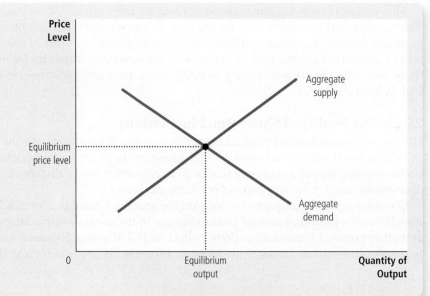

## FIGURE 2

**Aggregate Demand and Aggregate Supply**
Economists use the model of aggregate demand and aggregate supply to analyze economic fluctuations. On the vertical axis is the overall level of prices. On the horizontal axis is the economy's total output of goods and services. Output and the price level adjust to the point at which the aggregate-supply and aggregate-demand curves intersect.

the government, and customers abroad want to buy at each price level. The **aggregate-supply curve** shows the quantity of goods and services that firms produce and sell at each price level. According to this model, the price level and the quantity of output adjust to bring aggregate demand and aggregate supply into balance.

It is tempting to view the model of aggregate demand and aggregate supply as nothing more than a large version of the model of market demand and market supply introduced in Chapter 4. But in fact, this model is quite different. When we consider demand and supply in a specific market—ice cream, for instance—the behavior of buyers and sellers depends on the ability of resources to move from one market to another. When the price of ice cream rises, the quantity demanded falls because buyers will use their incomes to buy products other than ice cream. Similarly, a higher price of ice cream raises the quantity supplied because firms that produce ice cream can increase production by hiring workers away from other parts of the economy. This *microeconomic* substitution from one market to another is impossible for the economy as a whole. After all, the quantity that our model is trying to explain—real GDP—measures the *total* quantity of goods and services produced by *all* firms in *all* markets. To understand why the aggregate-demand curve slopes downward and why the aggregate-supply curve slopes upward, we need a *macroeconomic* theory that explains the total quantity of goods and services demanded and the total quantity of goods and services supplied. Developing such a theory is our next task.

**aggregate-supply curve**
a curve that shows the quantity of goods and services that firms choose to produce and sell at each price level

QuickQuiz *How does the economy's behavior in the short run differ from its behavior in the long run? • Draw the model of aggregate demand and aggregate supply. What variables are on the two axes?*

# 23-3 The Aggregate-Demand Curve

The aggregate-demand curve tells us the quantity of all goods and services demanded in the economy at any given price level. As Figure 3 illustrates, the aggregate-demand curve slopes downward. This means that, other things being equal, a decrease in the economy's overall level of prices (from, say, $P_1$ to $P_2$) raises the quantity of goods and services demanded (from $Y_1$ to $Y_2$). Conversely, an increase in the price level reduces the quantity of goods and services demanded.

### 23-3a Why the Aggregate-Demand Curve Slopes Downward
Why does a change in the price level move the quantity of goods and services demanded in the opposite direction? To answer this question, it is useful to recall that an economy's GDP (which we denote as $Y$) is the sum of its consumption ($C$), investment ($I$), government purchases ($G$), and net exports ($NX$):

$$Y = C + I + G + NX.$$

Each of these four components contributes to the aggregate demand for goods and services. For now, we assume that government spending is fixed by policy. The other three components of spending—consumption, investment, and net exports—depend on economic conditions and, in particular, on the price level. Therefore, to understand the downward slope of the aggregate-demand curve, we must examine how the price level affects the quantity of goods and services demanded for consumption, investment, and net exports.

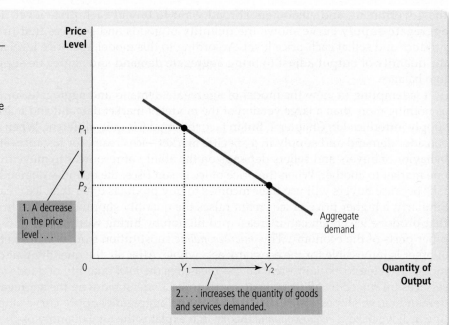

## FIGURE 3

**The Aggregate-Demand Curve**
A fall in the price level from $P_1$ to $P_2$ increases the quantity of goods and services demanded from $Y_1$ to $Y_2$. There are three reasons for this negative relationship. As the price level falls, real wealth rises, interest rates fall, and the exchange rate depreciates. These effects stimulate spending on consumption, investment, and net exports. Increased spending on any or all of these components of output means a larger quantity of goods and services demanded.

**The Price Level and Consumption: The Wealth Effect**   Consider the money that you hold in your wallet and your bank account. The nominal value of this money is fixed: One dollar is always worth one dollar. Yet the *real* value of a dollar is not fixed. If a candy bar costs one dollar, then a dollar is worth one candy bar. If the price of a candy bar falls to 50 cents, then one dollar is worth two candy bars. Thus, when the price level falls, the dollars you are holding rise in value, which increases your real wealth and your ability to buy goods and services.

This logic gives us the first reason the aggregate-demand curve slopes downward. *A decrease in the price level raises the real value of money and makes consumers wealthier, which in turn encourages them to spend more. The increase in consumer spending means a larger quantity of goods and services demanded. Conversely, an increase in the price level reduces the real value of money and makes consumers poorer, which in turn reduces consumer spending and the quantity of goods and services demanded.*

**The Price Level and Investment: The Interest-Rate Effect**   The price level is one determinant of the quantity of money demanded. When the price level is lower, households do not need to hold as much money to buy the goods and services they want. Therefore, when the price level falls, households try to reduce their holdings of money by lending some of it out. For instance, a household might use its excess money to buy interest-bearing bonds. Or it might deposit its excess money in an interest-bearing savings account, and the bank would use these funds to make more loans. In either case, as households try to convert some of their money into interest-bearing assets, they drive down interest rates. (The next chapter analyzes this process in more detail.)

Interest rates, in turn, affect spending on goods and services. Because a lower interest rate makes borrowing less expensive, it encourages firms to borrow more to invest in new plants and equipment, and it encourages households to borrow more to invest in new housing. (A lower interest rate might also stimulate consumer spending, especially spending on large durable purchases such as cars, which are often bought on credit.) Thus, a lower interest rate increases the quantity of goods and services demanded.

This logic gives us the second reason the aggregate-demand curve slopes downward. *A lower price level reduces the interest rate, encourages greater spending on investment goods, and thereby increases the quantity of goods and services demanded. Conversely, a higher price level raises the interest rate, discourages investment spending, and decreases the quantity of goods and services demanded.*

**The Price Level and Net Exports: The Exchange-Rate Effect** As we have just discussed, a lower price level in the United States lowers the U.S. interest rate. In response to the lower interest rate, some U.S. investors will seek higher returns by investing abroad. For instance, as the interest rate on U.S. government bonds falls, a mutual fund might sell U.S. government bonds to buy German government bonds. As the mutual fund tries to convert its dollars into euros to buy the German bonds, it increases the supply of dollars in the market for foreign-currency exchange.

The increased supply of dollars to be turned into euros causes the dollar to depreciate relative to the euro. This leads to a change in the real exchange rate—the relative price of domestic and foreign goods. Because each dollar buys fewer units of foreign currencies, foreign goods become more expensive relative to domestic goods.

The change in relative prices affects spending, both at home and abroad. Because foreign goods are now more expensive, Americans buy less from other countries, causing U.S. imports of goods and services to decrease. At the same time, because U.S. goods are now cheaper, foreigners buy more from the United States, so U.S. exports increase. Net exports equal exports minus imports, so both of these changes cause U.S. net exports to increase. Thus, the fall in the real exchange value of the dollar leads to an increase in the quantity of goods and services demanded.

This logic yields the third reason the aggregate-demand curve slopes downward. *When a fall in the U.S. price level causes U.S. interest rates to fall, the real value of the dollar declines in foreign exchange markets. This depreciation stimulates U.S. net exports and thereby increases the quantity of goods and services demanded. Conversely, when the U.S. price level rises and causes U.S. interest rates to rise, the real value of the dollar increases, and this appreciation reduces U.S. net exports and the quantity of goods and services demanded.*

**Summing Up** There are three distinct but related reasons a fall in the price level increases the quantity of goods and services demanded:

1. Consumers are wealthier, which stimulates the demand for consumption goods.
2. Interest rates fall, which stimulates the demand for investment goods.
3. The currency depreciates, which stimulates the demand for net exports.

The same three effects work in reverse: When the price level rises, decreased wealth depresses consumer spending, higher interest rates depress investment spending, and a currency appreciation depresses net exports.

Here is a thought experiment to hone your intuition about these effects. Imagine that one day you wake up and notice that, for some mysterious reason, the prices of all goods and services have fallen by half, so the dollars you are holding are worth twice as much. In real terms, you now have twice as much money as you had when you went to bed the night before. What would you do with the extra money? You could spend it at your favorite restaurant, increasing consumer spending. You could lend it out (by buying a bond or depositing it in your bank), reducing interest rates and increasing investment spending. Or you could invest it overseas (by buying shares in an international mutual fund), reducing the real exchange value of the dollar and increasing net exports. Whichever of these three responses you choose, the fall in the price level leads to an increase in the quantity of goods and services demanded. This is what the downward slope of the aggregate-demand curve represents.

It is important to keep in mind that the aggregate-demand curve (like all demand curves) is drawn holding "other things equal." In particular, our three explanations of the downward-sloping aggregate-demand curve assume that the money supply is fixed. That is, we have been considering how a change in the price level affects the demand for goods and services, holding the amount of money in the economy constant. As we will see, a change in the quantity of money shifts the aggregate-demand curve. At this point, just keep in mind that the aggregate-demand curve is drawn for a given quantity of the money supply.

### 23-3b  Why the Aggregate-Demand Curve Might Shift

The downward slope of the aggregate-demand curve shows that a fall in the price level raises the overall quantity of goods and services demanded. Many other factors, however, affect the quantity of goods and services demanded at a given price level. When one of these other factors changes, the quantity of goods and services demanded at every price level changes and the aggregate-demand curve shifts.

Let's consider some examples of events that shift aggregate demand. We can categorize them according to the component of spending that is most directly affected.

**Shifts Arising from Changes in Consumption**  Suppose Americans suddenly become more concerned about saving for retirement and, as a result, reduce their current consumption. Because the quantity of goods and services demanded at any price level is lower, the aggregate-demand curve shifts to the left. Conversely, imagine that a stock market boom makes people wealthier and less concerned about saving. The resulting increase in consumer spending means a greater quantity of goods and services demanded at any given price level, so the aggregate-demand curve shifts to the right.

Thus, any event that changes how much people want to consume at a given price level shifts the aggregate-demand curve. One policy variable that has this effect is the level of taxation. When the government cuts taxes, it encourages people to spend more, so the aggregate-demand curve shifts to the right. When the government raises taxes, people cut back on their spending and the aggregate-demand curve shifts to the left.

**Shifts Arising from Changes in Investment**  Any event that changes how much firms want to invest at a given price level also shifts the aggregate-demand curve. For instance, imagine that the computer industry introduces a faster line of computers and many firms decide to invest in new computer systems. Because the quantity of goods and services demanded at any price level is higher, the aggregate-demand curve shifts to the right. Conversely, if firms become pessimistic about future business conditions, they may cut back on investment spending, shifting the aggregate-demand curve to the left.

Tax policy can also influence aggregate demand through investment. For example, an investment tax credit (a tax rebate tied to a firm's investment spending) increases the quantity of investment goods that firms demand at any given interest rate and therefore shifts the aggregate-demand curve to the right. The repeal of an investment tax credit reduces investment and shifts the aggregate-demand curve to the left.

Another policy variable that can influence investment and aggregate demand is the money supply. As we discuss more fully in the next chapter, an increase in the money supply lowers the interest rate in the short run. This decrease in the interest rate makes borrowing less costly, which stimulates investment spending and thereby shifts the aggregate-demand curve to the right. Conversely, a decrease in the money supply raises the interest rate, discourages investment spending, and thereby shifts the aggregate-demand curve to the left. Many economists believe that throughout U.S. history, changes in monetary policy have been an important source of shifts in aggregate demand.

**Shifts Arising from Changes in Government Purchases**   The most direct way that policymakers shift the aggregate-demand curve is through government purchases. For example, suppose Congress decides to reduce purchases of new weapons systems. Because the quantity of goods and services demanded at any price level is lower, the aggregate-demand curve shifts to the left. Conversely, if state governments start building more highways, the result is a greater quantity of goods and services demanded at any price level, so the aggregate-demand curve shifts to the right.

**Shifts Arising from Changes in Net Exports**   Any event that changes net exports for a given price level also shifts aggregate demand. For instance, when Europe experiences a recession, it buys fewer goods from the United States. This reduces U.S. net exports at every price level and shifts the aggregate-demand curve for the U.S. economy to the left. When Europe recovers from its recession, it starts buying U.S. goods again and the aggregate-demand curve shifts to the right.

Net exports can also change because international speculators cause movements in the exchange rate. Suppose, for instance, that these speculators lose confidence in foreign economies and want to move some of their wealth into the U.S. economy. In doing so, they bid up the value of the U.S. dollar in the foreign exchange market. This appreciation of the dollar makes U.S. goods more expensive compared to foreign goods, which depresses net exports and shifts the aggregate-demand curve to the left. Conversely, speculation that causes a depreciation of the dollar stimulates net exports and shifts the aggregate-demand curve to the right.

**Summing Up**   In the next chapter, we analyze the aggregate-demand curve in more detail. There we examine more precisely how the tools of monetary and fiscal policy can shift aggregate demand and whether policymakers should use these tools for that purpose. At this point, however, you should have some idea about why the aggregate-demand curve slopes downward and what kinds of events and policies can shift this curve. Table 1 summarizes what we have learned so far.

**TABLE 1**

The Aggregate-Demand
Curve: Summary

**Why Does the Aggregate-Demand Curve Slope Downward?**
1. *The Wealth Effect:* A lower price level increases real wealth, which stimulates spending on consumption.
2. *The Interest-Rate Effect:* A lower price level reduces the interest rate, which stimulates spending on investment.
3. *The Exchange-Rate Effect:* A lower price level causes the real exchange rate to depreciate, which stimulates spending on net exports.

**Why Might the Aggregate-Demand Curve Shift?**
1. *Shifts Arising from Changes in Consumption:* An event that causes consumers to spend more at a given price level (a tax cut, a stock market boom) shifts the aggregate-demand curve to the right. An event that causes consumers to spend less at a given price level (a tax hike, a stock market decline) shifts the aggregate-demand curve to the left.
2. *Shifts Arising from Changes in Investment:* An event that causes firms to invest more at a given price level (optimism about the future, a fall in interest rates due to an increase in the money supply) shifts the aggregate-demand curve to the right. An event that causes firms to invest less at a given price level (pessimism about the future, a rise in interest rates due to a decrease in the money supply) shifts the aggregate-demand curve to the left.
3. *Shifts Arising from Changes in Government Purchases:* An increase in government purchases of goods and services (greater spending on defense or highway construction) shifts the aggregate-demand curve to the right. A decrease in government purchases on goods and services (a cutback in defense or highway spending) shifts the aggregate-demand curve to the left.
4. *Shifts Arising from Changes in Net Exports:* An event that raises spending on net exports at a given price level (a boom overseas, speculation that causes an exchange-rate depreciation) shifts the aggregate-demand curve to the right. An event that reduces spending on net exports at a given price level (a recession overseas, speculation that causes an exchange-rate appreciation) shifts the aggregate-demand curve to the left.

QuickQuiz    *Explain the three reasons the aggregate-demand curve slopes downward.*
*• Give an example of an event that would shift the aggregate-demand curve. In which direction would this event shift the curve?*

# 23-4 The Aggregate-Supply Curve

The aggregate-supply curve tells us the total quantity of goods and services that firms produce and sell at any given price level. Unlike the aggregate-demand curve, which always slopes downward, the aggregate-supply curve shows a relationship that depends crucially on the time horizon examined. *In the long run, the aggregate-supply curve is vertical, whereas in the short run, the aggregate-supply curve slopes upward.* To understand short-run economic fluctuations, and how the short-run behavior of the economy deviates from its long-run behavior, we need to examine both the long-run aggregate-supply curve and the short-run aggregate-supply curve.

## 23-4a Why the Aggregate-Supply Curve Is Vertical in the Long Run

What determines the quantity of goods and services supplied in the long run? We implicitly answered this question earlier in the book when we analyzed the process of economic growth. *In the long run, an economy's production of goods and services (its real GDP) depends on its supplies of labor, capital, and natural resources and on the available technology used to turn these factors of production into goods and services.*

When we analyzed these forces that govern long-run growth, we did not need to make any reference to the overall level of prices. We examined the price level in a separate chapter, where we saw that it was determined by the quantity of money. We learned that if two economies were identical except that one had twice as much money in circulation, the price level would be twice as high in the economy with more money. But since the amount of money does not affect technology or the supplies of labor, capital, and natural resources, the output of goods and services in the two economies would be the same.

Because the price level does not affect the long-run determinants of real GDP, the long-run aggregate-supply curve is vertical, as in Figure 4. In other words, in the long run, the economy's labor, capital, natural resources, and technology determine the total quantity of goods and services supplied, and this quantity supplied is the same regardless of what the price level happens to be.

The vertical long-run aggregate-supply curve is a graphical representation of the classical dichotomy and monetary neutrality. As we have already discussed, classical macroeconomic theory is based on the assumption that real variables do not depend on nominal variables. The long-run aggregate-supply curve is consistent with this idea because it implies that the quantity of output (a real variable) does not depend on the level of prices (a nominal variable). As noted earlier, most economists believe this principle works well when studying the economy over a period of many years but not when studying year-to-year changes. Thus, *the aggregate-supply curve is vertical only in the long run.*

### 23-4b Why the Long-Run Aggregate-Supply Curve Might Shift

Because classical macroeconomic theory predicts the quantity of goods and services produced by an economy in the long run, it also explains the position of the long-run aggregate-supply curve. The long-run level of production is

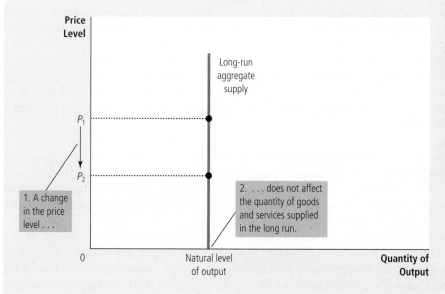

### FIGURE 4

**The Long-Run Aggregate-Supply Curve**
In the long run, the quantity of output supplied depends on the economy's quantities of labor, capital, and natural resources and on the technology for turning these inputs into output. Because the quantity supplied does not depend on the overall price level, the long-run aggregate-supply curve is vertical at the natural level of output.

**natural level of output**
the production of goods and services that an economy achieves in the long run when unemployment is at its normal rate

sometimes called *potential output* or *full-employment output*. To be more precise, we call it the **natural level of output** because it shows what the economy produces when unemployment is at its natural, or normal, rate. The natural level of output is the rate of production toward which the economy gravitates in the long run.

Any change in the economy that alters the natural level of output shifts the long-run aggregate-supply curve. Because output in the classical model depends on labor, capital, natural resources, and technological knowledge, we can categorize shifts in the long-run aggregate-supply curve as arising from these four sources.

**Shifts Arising from Changes in Labor**   Imagine that an economy experiences an increase in immigration. Because there would be a greater number of workers, the quantity of goods and services supplied would increase. As a result, the long-run aggregate-supply curve would shift to the right. Conversely, if many workers left the economy to go abroad, the long-run aggregate-supply curve would shift to the left.

The position of the long-run aggregate-supply curve also depends on the natural rate of unemployment, so any change in the natural rate of unemployment shifts the long-run aggregate-supply curve. For example, if Congress were to raise the minimum wage substantially, the natural rate of unemployment would rise and the economy would produce a smaller quantity of goods and services. As a result, the long-run aggregate-supply curve would shift to the left. Conversely, if a reform of the unemployment insurance system were to encourage unemployed workers to search harder for new jobs, the natural rate of unemployment would fall and the long-run aggregate-supply curve would shift to the right.

**Shifts Arising from Changes in Capital**   An increase in the economy's capital stock increases productivity and, thereby, the quantity of goods and services supplied. As a result, the long-run aggregate-supply curve shifts to the right. Conversely, a decrease in the economy's capital stock decreases productivity and the quantity of goods and services supplied, shifting the long-run aggregate-supply curve to the left.

Notice that the same logic applies regardless of whether we are discussing physical capital such as machines and factories or human capital such as college degrees. An increase in either type of capital will raise the economy's ability to produce goods and services and, thus, shift the long-run aggregate-supply curve to the right.

**Shifts Arising from Changes in Natural Resources**   An economy's production depends on its natural resources, including its land, minerals, and weather. The discovery of a new mineral deposit shifts the long-run aggregate-supply curve to the right. A change in weather patterns that makes farming more difficult shifts the long-run aggregate-supply curve to the left.

In many countries, crucial natural resources are imported. A change in the availability of these resources can also shift the aggregate-supply curve. For example, as we discuss later in this chapter, events occurring in the world oil market have historically been an important source of shifts in aggregate supply for the United States and other oil-importing nations.

**Shifts Arising from Changes in Technological Knowledge** Perhaps the most important reason that the economy today produces more than it did a generation ago is that our technological knowledge has advanced. The invention of the computer, for instance, has allowed us to produce more goods and services from any given amounts of labor, capital, and natural resources. As computer use has spread throughout the economy, it has shifted the long-run aggregate-supply curve to the right.

Although not literally technological, many other events act like changes in technology. For instance, opening up international trade has effects similar to inventing new production processes because it allows a country to specialize in higher-productivity industries; therefore, it also shifts the long-run aggregate-supply curve to the right. Conversely, if the government passes new regulations preventing firms from using some production methods, perhaps to address worker safety or environmental concerns, the result is a leftward shift in the long-run aggregate-supply curve.

**Summing Up** Because the long-run aggregate-supply curve reflects the classical model of the economy we developed in previous chapters, it provides a new way to describe our earlier analysis. Any policy or event that raised real GDP in previous chapters can now be described as increasing the quantity of goods and services supplied and shifting the long-run aggregate-supply curve to the right. Any policy or event that lowered real GDP in previous chapters can now be described as decreasing the quantity of goods and services supplied and shifting the long-run aggregate-supply curve to the left.

## 23-4c Using Aggregate Demand and Aggregate Supply to Depict Long-Run Growth and Inflation

Having introduced the economy's aggregate-demand curve and the long-run aggregate-supply curve, we now have a new way to describe the economy's long-run trends. Figure 5 illustrates the changes that occur in an economy from decade to decade. Notice that both curves are shifting. Although many forces influence the economy in the long run and can in theory cause such shifts, the two most important forces in practice are technology and monetary policy. Technological progress enhances an economy's ability to produce goods and services, and the resulting increases in output are reflected in continual shifts of the long-run aggregate-supply curve to the right. At the same time, because the Fed increases the money supply over time, the aggregate-demand curve also shifts to the right. As the figure illustrates, the result is continuing growth in output (as shown by increasing $Y$) and continuing inflation (as shown by increasing $P$). This is just another way of representing the classical analysis of growth and inflation we conducted in earlier chapters.

The purpose of developing the model of aggregate demand and aggregate supply, however, is not to dress our previous long-run conclusions in new clothing. Instead, it is to provide a framework for short-run analysis, as we will see in a moment. As we develop the short-run model, we keep the analysis simple by omitting the continuing growth and inflation shown by the shifts in Figure 5. But always remember that long-run trends are the background on which short-run fluctuations are superimposed. *The short-run fluctuations in output and the price level that we will be studying should be viewed as deviations from the long-run trends of output growth and inflation.*

## FIGURE 5

**Long-Run Growth and Inflation in the Model of Aggregate Demand and Aggregate Supply**

As the economy becomes better able to produce goods and services over time, primarily because of technological progress, the long-run aggregate-supply curve shifts to the right. At the same time, as the Fed increases the money supply, the aggregate-demand curve also shifts to the right. In this figure, output grows from $Y_{1990}$ to $Y_{2000}$ and then to $Y_{2010}$ and the price level rises from $P_{1990}$ to $P_{2000}$ and then to $P_{2010}$. Thus, the model of aggregate demand and aggregate supply offers a new way to describe the classical analysis of growth and inflation.

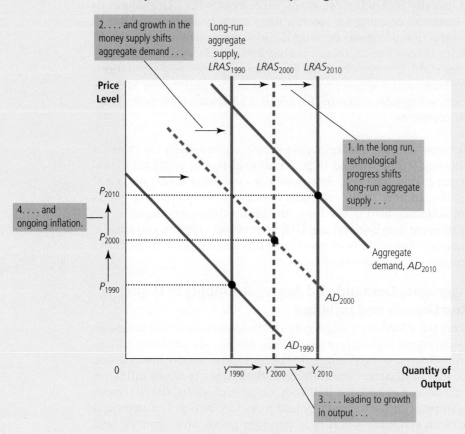

### 23-4d Why the Aggregate-Supply Curve Slopes Upward in the Short Run

The key difference between the economy in the short run and in the long run is the behavior of aggregate supply. The long-run aggregate-supply curve is vertical because, in the long run, the overall level of prices does not affect the economy's ability to produce goods and services. By contrast, in the short run, the price level *does* affect the economy's output. That is, over a period of a year or two, an increase in the overall level of prices in the economy tends to raise the quantity of goods and services supplied, and a decrease in the level of prices tends to reduce the quantity of goods and services supplied. As a result, the short-run aggregate-supply curve slopes upward, as shown in Figure 6.

Why do changes in the price level affect output in the short run? Macro-economists have proposed three theories for the upward slope of the short-run

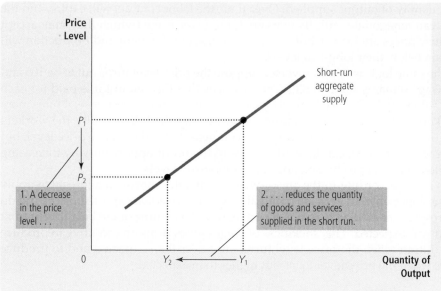

**Price Level**

$P_1$

$P_2$

Short-run aggregate supply

1. A decrease in the price level . . .

2. . . . reduces the quantity of goods and services supplied in the short run.

$Y_2$ ← $Y_1$

0

**Quantity of Output**

**FIGURE 6**

**The Short-Run Aggregate-Supply Curve**
In the short run, a fall in the price level from $P_1$ to $P_2$ reduces the quantity of output supplied from $Y_1$ to $Y_2$. This positive relationship could be due to sticky wages, sticky prices, or misperceptions. Over time, wages, prices, and perceptions adjust, so this positive relationship is only temporary.

aggregate-supply curve. In each theory, a specific market imperfection causes the supply side of the economy to behave differently in the short run than it does in the long run. The following theories differ in their details, but they share a common theme: *The quantity of output supplied deviates from its long-run, or natural, level when the actual price level in the economy deviates from the price level that people expected to prevail.* When the price level rises above the level that people expected, output rises above its natural level, and when the price level falls below the expected level, output falls below its natural level.

**The Sticky-Wage Theory** The first explanation of the upward slope of the short-run aggregate-supply curve is the sticky-wage theory. This theory is the simplest of the three approaches to aggregate supply, and some economists believe it highlights the most important reason why the economy in the short run differs from the economy in the long run. Therefore, it is the theory of short-run aggregate supply that we emphasize in this book.

According to this theory, the short-run aggregate-supply curve slopes upward because nominal wages are slow to adjust to changing economic conditions. In other words, wages are "sticky" in the short run. To some extent, the slow adjustment of nominal wages is attributable to long-term contracts between workers and firms that fix nominal wages, sometimes for as long as 3 years. In addition, this prolonged adjustment may be attributable to slowly changing social norms and notions of fairness that influence wage setting.

An example can help explain how sticky nominal wages can result in a short-run aggregate-supply curve that slopes upward. Imagine that a year ago a firm expected the price level today to be 100, and based on this expectation, it signed a contract with its workers agreeing to pay them, say, $20 an hour. In fact, the price level turns out to be only 95. Because prices have fallen below expectations, the firm gets 5 percent less than expected for each unit of its product that it sells. The cost of labor used to make the output, however, is stuck at $20 per hour. Production is now less profitable, so the firm hires fewer workers and reduces the quantity of output supplied. Over time, the labor contract will expire, and the firm can renegotiate with its workers for a lower wage (which they may accept because prices are lower), but in the meantime, employment and production will remain below their long-run levels.

The same logic works in reverse. Suppose the price level turns out to be 105 and the wage remains stuck at $20. The firm sees that the amount it is paid for each unit sold is up by 5 percent, while its labor costs are not. In response, it hires more workers and increases the quantity of output supplied. Eventually, the workers will demand higher nominal wages to compensate for the higher price level, but for a while, the firm can take advantage of the profit opportunity by increasing employment and production above their long-run levels.

In short, according to the sticky-wage theory, the short-run aggregate-supply curve slopes upward because nominal wages are based on expected prices and do not respond immediately when the actual price level turns out to be different from what was expected. This stickiness of wages gives firms an incentive to produce less output when the price level turns out lower than expected and to produce more when the price level turns out higher than expected.

**The Sticky-Price Theory**    Some economists have advocated another approach to explaining the upward slope of the short-run aggregate-supply curve, called the sticky-price theory. As we just discussed, the sticky-wage theory emphasizes that nominal wages adjust slowly over time. The sticky-price theory emphasizes that the prices of some goods and services also adjust sluggishly in response to changing economic conditions. This slow adjustment of prices occurs in part because there are costs to adjusting prices, called *menu costs*. These menu costs include the cost of printing and distributing catalogs and the time required to change price tags. As a result of these costs, prices as well as wages may be sticky in the short run.

To see how sticky prices explain the aggregate-supply curve's upward slope, suppose that each firm in the economy announces its prices in advance based on the economic conditions it expects to prevail over the coming year. Suppose further that after prices are announced, the economy experiences an unexpected contraction in the money supply, which (as we have learned) will reduce the overall price level in the long run. What happens in the short run? Although some firms reduce their prices quickly in response to the unexpected change in economic conditions, many other firms want to avoid additional menu costs. As a result, they temporarily lag behind in cutting their prices. Because these lagging firms have prices that are too high, their sales decline. Declining sales, in turn, cause these firms to cut back on production and employment. In other words, because not all prices adjust immediately to changing conditions, an unexpected fall in the price level leaves some firms with higher-than-desired prices, and these higher-than-desired prices depress sales and induce firms to reduce the quantity of goods and services they produce.

Similar reasoning applies when the money supply and price level turn out to be above what firms expected when they originally set their prices. While some firms raise their prices quickly in response to the new economic environment, other firms lag behind, keeping their prices at the lower-than-desired levels. These low prices attract customers, which induces these firms to increase employment and production. Thus, during the time these lagging firms are operating with outdated prices, there is a positive association between the overall price level and the quantity of output. This positive association is represented by the upward slope of the short-run aggregate-supply curve.

**The Misperceptions Theory**   A third approach to explaining the upward slope of the short-run aggregate-supply curve is the misperceptions theory. According to this theory, changes in the overall price level can temporarily mislead suppliers about what is happening in the individual markets in which they sell their output. As a result of these short-run misperceptions, suppliers respond to changes in the level of prices, and this response leads to an upward-sloping aggregate-supply curve.

To see how this might work, suppose the overall price level falls below the level that suppliers expected. When suppliers see the prices of their products fall, they may mistakenly believe that their *relative* prices have fallen; that is, they may believe that their prices have fallen compared to other prices in the economy. For example, wheat farmers may notice a fall in the price of wheat before they notice a fall in the prices of the many items they buy as consumers. They may infer from this observation that the reward for producing wheat is temporarily low, and they may respond by reducing the quantity of wheat they supply. Similarly, workers may notice a fall in their nominal wages before they notice that the prices of the goods they buy are also falling. They may infer that the reward for working is temporarily low and respond by reducing the quantity of labor they supply. In both cases, a lower price level causes misperceptions about relative prices, and these misperceptions induce suppliers to respond to the lower price level by decreasing the quantity of goods and services supplied.

Similar misperceptions arise when the price level is above what was expected. Suppliers of goods and services may notice the price of their output rising and infer, mistakenly, that their relative prices are rising. They would conclude that it is a good time to produce. Until their misperceptions are corrected, they respond to the higher price level by increasing the quantity of goods and services supplied. This behavior results in a short-run aggregate-supply curve that slopes upward.

**Summing Up**   There are three alternative explanations for the upward slope of the short-run aggregate-supply curve: (1) sticky wages, (2) sticky prices, and (3) misperceptions about relative prices. Economists debate which of these theories is correct, and it is possible that each contains an element of truth. For our purposes in this book, the similarities of the theories are more important than the differences. All three theories suggest that output deviates in the short run from its natural level when the actual price level deviates from the price level that people had expected to prevail. We can express this mathematically as follows:

$$
\begin{array}{l}
\text{Quantity} \\
\text{of output} \\
\text{supplied}
\end{array}
=
\begin{array}{l}
\text{Natural} \\
\text{level of} \\
\text{output}
\end{array}
+\;
a
\left(
\begin{array}{l}
\text{Actual} \\
\text{price} \\
\text{level}
\end{array}
-
\begin{array}{l}
\text{Expected} \\
\text{price} \\
\text{level}
\end{array}
\right)
$$

where $a$ is a number that determines how much output responds to unexpected changes in the price level.

Notice that each of the three theories of short-run aggregate supply emphasizes a problem that is likely to be temporary. Whether the upward slope of the aggregate-supply curve is attributable to sticky wages, sticky prices, or misperceptions, these conditions will not persist forever. Over time, nominal wages will become unstuck, prices will become unstuck, and misperceptions about relative prices will be corrected. In the long run, it is reasonable to assume that wages and prices are flexible rather than sticky and that people are not confused about relative prices. Thus, while we have several good theories to explain why the short-run aggregate-supply curve slopes upward, they are all consistent with a long-run aggregate-supply curve that is vertical.

### 23-4e Why the Short-Run Aggregate-Supply Curve Might Shift

The short-run aggregate-supply curve tells us the quantity of goods and services supplied in the short run for any given level of prices. This curve is similar to the long-run aggregate-supply curve, but it is upward-sloping rather than vertical because of sticky wages, sticky prices, and misperceptions. Thus, when thinking about what shifts the short-run aggregate-supply curve, we have to consider all those variables that shift the long-run aggregate-supply curve. In addition, we have to consider a new variable—the expected price level—that influences the wages that are stuck, the prices that are stuck, and the perceptions about relative prices that may be flawed.

Let's start with what we know about the long-run aggregate-supply curve. As we discussed earlier, shifts in the long-run aggregate-supply curve normally arise from changes in labor, capital, natural resources, or technological knowledge. These same variables shift the short-run aggregate-supply curve. For example, when an increase in the economy's capital stock increases productivity, the economy is able to produce more output, so both the long-run and short-run aggregate-supply curves shift to the right. When an increase in the minimum wage raises the natural rate of unemployment, the economy has fewer employed workers and thus produces less output, so both the long-run and short-run aggregate-supply curves shift to the left.

The important new variable that affects the position of the short-run aggregate-supply curve is the price level that people expected to prevail. As we have discussed, the quantity of goods and services supplied depends, in the short run, on sticky wages, sticky prices, and misperceptions. Yet wages, prices, and perceptions are set based on the expected price level. So when people change their expectations of the price level, the short-run aggregate-supply curve shifts.

To make this idea more concrete, let's consider a specific theory of aggregate supply—the sticky-wage theory. According to this theory, when workers and firms expect the price level to be high, they are likely to reach a bargain with a higher level of nominal wages. Higher wages raise firms' costs, and for any given actual price level, higher costs reduce the quantity of goods and services supplied. Thus, when the expected price level rises, wages are higher, costs increase, and firms produce a smaller quantity of goods and services at any given actual price level. Thus, the short-run aggregate-supply curve shifts to the left. Conversely, when the expected price level falls, wages are lower, costs decline, firms increase output at any given price level, and the short-run aggregate-supply curve shifts to the right.

A similar logic applies in each theory of aggregate supply. The general lesson is the following: *An increase in the expected price level reduces the quantity of goods and services supplied and shifts the short-run aggregate-supply curve to the left. A decrease in the expected price level raises the quantity of goods and services supplied and shifts the short-run aggregate-supply curve to the right.* As we will see in the next section, the influence of expectations on the position of the short-run aggregate-supply curve plays a key role in explaining how the economy makes the transition from the short run to the long run. In the short run, expectations are fixed and the economy finds itself at the intersection of the aggregate-demand curve and the short-run aggregate-supply curve. In the long run, if people observe that the price level is different from what they expected, their expectations adjust and the short-run aggregate-supply curve shifts. This shift ensures that the economy eventually finds itself at the intersection of the aggregate-demand curve and the long-run aggregate-supply curve.

You should now have some understanding about why the short-run aggregate-supply curve slopes upward and what events and policies can cause this curve to shift. Table 2 summarizes our discussion.

**TABLE 2**

**The Short-Run Aggregate-Supply Curve: Summary**

**Why Does the Short-Run Aggregate-Supply Curve Slope Upward?**

1. *The Sticky-Wage Theory:* An unexpectedly low price level raises the real wage, which causes firms to hire fewer workers and produce a smaller quantity of goods and services.
2. *The Sticky-Price Theory:* An unexpectedly low price level leaves some firms with higher-than-desired prices, which depresses their sales and leads them to cut back production.
3. *The Misperceptions Theory:* An unexpectedly low price level leads some suppliers to think their relative prices have fallen, which induces a fall in production.

**Why Might the Short-Run Aggregate-Supply Curve Shift?**

1. *Shifts Arising from Changes in Labor:* An increase in the quantity of labor available (perhaps due to a fall in the natural rate of unemployment) shifts the aggregate-supply curve to the right. A decrease in the quantity of labor available (perhaps due to a rise in the natural rate of unemployment) shifts the aggregate-supply curve to the left.
2. *Shifts Arising from Changes in Capital:* An increase in physical or human capital shifts the aggregate-supply curve to the right. A decrease in physical or human capital shifts the aggregate-supply curve to the left.
3. *Shifts Arising from Changes in Natural Resources:* An increase in the availability of natural resources shifts the aggregate-supply curve to the right. A decrease in the availability of natural resources shifts the aggregate-supply curve to the left.
4. *Shifts Arising from Changes in Technology:* An advance in technological knowledge shifts the aggregate-supply curve to the right. A decrease in the available technology (perhaps due to government regulation) shifts the aggregate-supply curve to the left.
5. *Shifts Arising from Changes in the Expected Price Level:* A decrease in the expected price level shifts the short-run aggregate-supply curve to the right. An increase in the expected price level shifts the short-run aggregate-supply curve to the left.

**QuickQuiz**   *Explain why the long-run aggregate-supply curve is vertical. • Explain three theories for why the short-run aggregate-supply curve slopes upward. • What variables shift both the long-run and short-run aggregate-supply curves? • What variable shifts the short-run aggregate-supply curve but not the long-run aggregate-supply curve?*

# 23-5 Two Causes of Economic Fluctuations

Now that we have introduced the model of aggregate demand and aggregate supply, we have the basic tools we need to analyze fluctuations in economic activity. In particular, we can use what we have learned about aggregate demand and aggregate supply to examine the two basic causes of short-run fluctuations : shifts in aggregate demand and shifts in aggregate supply.

To keep things simple, we assume the economy begins in long-run equilibrium, as shown in Figure 7. Output and the price level are determined in the long run by the intersection of the aggregate-demand curve and the long-run aggregate-supply curve, shown as point A in the figure. At this point, output is at its natural level. Because the economy is always in a short-run equilibrium, the short-run aggregate-supply curve passes through this point as well, indicating that the expected price level has adjusted to this long-run equilibrium. That is, when an economy is in its long-run equilibrium, the expected price level must equal the actual price level so that the intersection of aggregate demand with short-run

## FIGURE 7

**The Long-Run Equilibrium**
The long-run equilibrium of the economy is found where the aggregate-demand curve crosses the long-run aggregate-supply curve (point A). When the economy reaches this long-run equilibrium, the expected price level will have adjusted to equal the actual price level. As a result, the short-run aggregate-supply curve crosses this point as well.

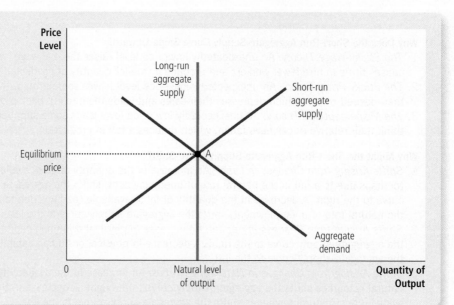

aggregate supply is the same as the intersection of aggregate demand with long-run aggregate supply.

### 23-5a The Effects of a Shift in Aggregate Demand

Suppose that a wave of pessimism suddenly overtakes the economy. The cause might be a scandal in the White House, a crash in the stock market, or the outbreak of war overseas. Because of this event, many people lose confidence in the future and alter their plans. Households cut back on their spending and delay major purchases, and firms put off buying new equipment.

What is the macroeconomic impact of such a wave of pessimism? In answering this question, we can follow the three steps we used in Chapter 4 when analyzing supply and demand in specific markets. First, we determine whether the event affects aggregate demand or aggregate supply. Second, we determine the direction that the curve shifts. Third, we use the diagram of aggregate demand and aggregate supply to compare the initial and the new equilibrium. The new wrinkle is that we need to add a fourth step: We have to keep track of a new short-run equilibrium, a new long-run equilibrium, and the transition between them. Table 3 summarizes the four steps to analyzing economic fluctuations.

## TABLE 3

**Four Steps for Analyzing Macroeconomic Fluctuations**

1. Decide whether the event shifts the aggregate-demand curve or the aggregate-supply curve (or perhaps both).
2. Decide the direction in which the curve shifts.
3. Use the diagram of aggregate demand and aggregate supply to determine the impact on output and the price level in the short run.
4. Use the diagram of aggregate demand and aggregate supply to analyze how the economy moves from its new short-run equilibrium to its new long-run equilibrium.

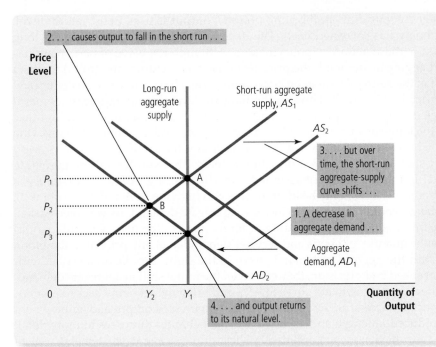

2. . . . causes output to fall in the short run . . .

**FIGURE 8**

**A Contraction in Aggregate Demand**
A fall in aggregate demand is represented with a leftward shift in the aggregate-demand curve from $AD_1$ to $AD_2$. In the short run, the economy moves from point A to point B. Output falls from $Y_1$ to $Y_2$, and the price level falls from $P_1$ to $P_2$. Over time, as the expected price level adjusts, the short-run aggregate-supply curve shifts to the right from $AS_1$ to $AS_2$, and the economy reaches point C, where the new aggregate-demand curve crosses the long-run aggregate-supply curve. In the long run, the price level falls to $P_3$, and output returns to its natural level, $Y_1$.

3. . . . but over time, the short-run aggregate-supply curve shifts . . .

1. A decrease in aggregate demand . . .

4. . . . and output returns to its natural level.

The first two steps are straightforward. First, because the wave of pessimism affects spending plans, it affects the aggregate-demand curve. Second, because households and firms now want to buy a smaller quantity of goods and services for any given price level, the event reduces aggregate demand. As Figure 8 shows, the aggregate-demand curve shifts to the left from $AD_1$ to $AD_2$.

With this figure, we can perform step three: By comparing the initial and the new equilibrium, we can see the effects of the fall in aggregate demand. In the short run, the economy moves along the initial short-run aggregate-supply curve, $AS_1$, going from point A to point B. As the economy moves between these two points, output falls from $Y_1$ to $Y_2$ and the price level falls from $P_1$ to $P_2$. The falling level of output indicates that the economy is in a recession. Although not shown in the figure, firms respond to lower sales and production by reducing employment. Thus, the pessimism that caused the shift in aggregate demand is, to some extent, self-fulfilling: Pessimism about the future leads to falling incomes and rising unemployment.

Now comes step four—the transition from the short-run equilibrium to the new long-run equilibrium. Because of the reduction in aggregate demand, the price level initially falls from $P_1$ to $P_2$. The price level is thus below the level that people were expecting ($P_1$) before the sudden fall in aggregate demand. People can be surprised in the short run, but they will not remain surprised. Over time, their expectations catch up with this new reality, and the expected price level falls as well. The fall in the expected price level alters wages, prices, and perceptions, which in turn influences the position of the short-run aggregate-supply curve. For example, according to the sticky-wage theory, once workers and firms come to expect a lower level of prices, they start to strike bargains for lower nominal wages; the reduction in labor costs encourages firms to hire more workers and expand production at any given level of prices. Thus, the fall in the expected price level shifts the short-run aggregate-supply curve to the right from $AS_1$ to $AS_2$ in Figure 8. This shift allows the economy to approach point C, where the new aggregate-demand curve ($AD_2$) crosses the long-run aggregate-supply curve.

In the new long-run equilibrium, point C, output is back to its natural level. The economy has corrected itself: The decline in output is reversed in the long run, even without action by policymakers. Although the wave of pessimism has reduced aggregate demand, the price level has fallen sufficiently (to $P_3$) to offset the shift in the aggregate-demand curve, and people have come to expect this new lower price level as well. Thus, in the long run, the shift in aggregate demand is reflected fully in the price level and not at all in the level of output. In other words, the long-run effect of a shift in aggregate demand is a nominal change (the price level is lower) but not a real change (output is the same).

What should policymakers do when faced with a sudden fall in aggregate demand? In this analysis, we assumed they did nothing. Another possibility is that, as soon as the economy heads into recession (moving from point A to point B), policymakers could take action to increase aggregate demand. As we noted earlier, an increase in government spending or an increase in the money supply would increase the quantity of goods and services demanded at any price and, therefore, would shift the aggregate-demand curve to the right. If policymakers act with sufficient speed and precision, they can offset the initial shift in aggregate demand, return the aggregate-demand curve to $AD_1$, and bring the economy back to point A. If the policy is successful, the painful period of depressed output and employment can be reduced in length and severity. The next chapter discusses in more detail the ways in which monetary and fiscal policy influence aggregate demand, as well as some of the practical difficulties in using these policy instruments.

To sum up, this story about shifts in aggregate demand has three important lessons:

- In the short run, shifts in aggregate demand cause fluctuations in the economy's output of goods and services.
- In the long run, shifts in aggregate demand affect the overall price level but do not affect output.
- Because policymakers influence aggregate demand, they can potentially mitigate the severity of economic fluctuations.

**FYI**

## Monetary Neutrality Revisited

According to classical economic theory, money is neutral. That is, changes in the quantity of money affect nominal variables such as the price level but not real variables such as output. Earlier in this chapter, we noted that most economists accept this conclusion as a description of how the economy works in the long run but not in the short run. With the model of aggregate demand and aggregate supply, we can illustrate this conclusion and explain it more fully.

Suppose that the Federal Reserve reduces the quantity of money in the economy. What effect does this change have? As we discussed, the money supply is one determinant of aggregate demand. The reduction in the money supply shifts the aggregate-demand curve to the left.

The analysis looks just like Figure 8. Even though the cause of the shift in aggregate demand is different, we would observe the same effects on output and the price level. In the short run, both output and the price level fall. The economy experiences a recession. But over time,

the expected price level falls as well. Firms and workers respond to their new expectations by, for instance, agreeing to lower nominal wages. As they do so, the short-run aggregate-supply curve shifts to the right. Eventually, the economy finds itself back on the long-run aggregate-supply curve.

Figure 8 shows when money matters for real variables and when it does not. In the long run, money is neutral, as represented by the movement of the economy from point A to point C. But in the short run, a change in the money supply has real effects, as represented by the movement of the economy from point A to point B. An old saying summarizes the analysis: "Money is a veil, but when the veil flutters, real output sputters." ∎

**CASE STUDY**

### TWO BIG SHIFTS IN AGGREGATE DEMAND: THE GREAT DEPRESSION AND WORLD WAR II

At the beginning of this chapter, we established three key facts about economic fluctuations by looking at data since 1972. Let's now take a longer look at U.S. economic history. Figure 9 shows data since 1900 on the percentage change in real GDP over the previous 3 years. In an average 3-year period, real GDP grows about 10 percent—a bit more than 3 percent per year. The business cycle, however, causes fluctuations around this average. Two episodes jump out as being particularly significant: the large drop in real GDP in the early 1930s and the large increase in real GDP in the early 1940s. Both of these events are attributable to shifts in aggregate demand.

The economic calamity of the early 1930s is called the *Great Depression*, and it is by far the largest economic downturn in U.S. history. Real GDP fell by 27 percent from 1929 to 1933, and unemployment rose from 3 percent to 25 percent. At the same time, the price level fell by 22 percent over these 4 years. Many other countries experienced similar declines in output and prices during this period.

Economic historians continue to debate the causes of the Great Depression, but most explanations center on a large decline in aggregate demand. What caused aggregate demand to contract? Here is where the disagreement arises.

Many economists place primary blame on the decline in the money supply: From 1929 to 1933, the money supply fell by 28 percent. As you may recall from our discussion of the monetary system, this decline in the money supply was due to problems in the banking system. As households withdrew their money from financially shaky banks and bankers became more cautious and started holding greater reserves, the process of money creation under fractional-reserve banking went into reverse. The Fed, meanwhile, failed to offset this fall in the money multiplier with expansionary open-market operations. As a result, the money supply declined. Many economists blame the Fed's failure to act for the Great Depression's severity.

---

Over the course of U.S. economic history, two fluctuations stand out as especially large. During the early 1930s, the economy went through the Great Depression, when the production of goods and services plummeted. During the early 1940s, the United States entered World War II and the economy experienced rapidly rising production. Both of these events are usually explained by large shifts in aggregate demand.

**Source:** Louis D. Johnston and Samuel H. Williamson, "What Was GDP Then?" http://www.measuringworth.com/usgdp/; Department of Commerce (Bureau of Economic Analysis).

**FIGURE 9**

**U.S. Real GDP Growth since 1900**

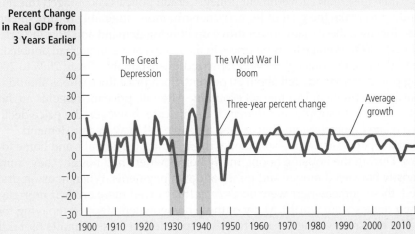

*The outcome of a massive decrease in aggregate demand*

Other economists have suggested alternative reasons for the collapse in aggregate demand. For example, stock prices fell about 90 percent during this period, depressing household wealth and thereby consumer spending. In addition, the banking problems may have prevented some firms from obtaining the financing they wanted for new projects and business expansions, reducing investment spending. It is possible that all these forces may have acted together to contract aggregate demand during the Great Depression.

The second significant episode in Figure 9—the economic boom of the early 1940s—is easier to explain. The cause of this event was World War II. As the United States entered the war overseas, the federal government had to devote more resources to the military. Government purchases of goods and services increased almost fivefold from 1939 to 1944. This huge expansion in aggregate demand almost doubled the economy's production of goods and services and led to a 20 percent increase in the price level (although widespread government price controls limited the rise in prices). Unemployment fell from 17 percent in 1939 to about 1 percent in 1944—the lowest level in U.S. history. ●

### CASE STUDY

**THE GREAT RECESSION OF 2008–2009**

In 2008 and 2009, the U.S. economy experienced a financial crisis and a severe downturn in economic activity. In many ways, it was the worst macroeconomic event in more than half a century.

The story of this downturn begins a few years earlier with a substantial boom in the housing market. The boom was, in part, fueled by low interest rates. In the aftermath of the recession of 2001, the Federal Reserve lowered interest rates to historically low levels. Low interest rates helped the economy recover, but by making it less expensive to get a mortgage and buy a home, they also contributed to a rise in housing prices.

In addition to low interest rates, various developments in the mortgage market made it easier for *subprime borrowers*—those borrowers with a higher risk of default based on their income and credit history—to get loans to buy homes. One development was *securitization*, the process by which a financial institution (specifically, a mortgage originator) makes loans and then (with the help of an investment bank) bundles them together into financial instruments called *mortgage-backed securities*. These mortgage-backed securities were then sold to other institutions (such as banks and insurance companies), which may not have fully appreciated the risks in these securities. Some economists blame inadequate regulation for these high-risk loans. Others blame misguided government policy: Certain policies encouraged this high-risk lending to make the goal of homeownership more attainable for low-income families. Together, these many forces drove up housing demand and housing prices. From 1995 to 2006, average housing prices in the United States more than doubled.

The high price of housing, however, proved unsustainable. From 2006 to 2009, housing prices nationwide fell about 30 percent. Such price fluctuations should not necessarily be a problem in a market economy. After all, price movements are how markets equilibrate supply and demand. In this case, however, the price decline had two related repercussions that caused a sizable fall in aggregate demand.

The first repercussion was a substantial rise in mortgage defaults and home foreclosures. During the housing boom, many homeowners had bought their homes with mostly borrowed money and minimal down payments. When housing prices declined, these homeowners were *underwater* (they owed more on their mortgages than their homes were worth). Many of these homeowners stopped repaying their loans. The banks servicing the mortgages responded to these defaults by taking the houses away in foreclosure procedures and then selling them off. The banks' goal was to recoup whatever they could from the bad loans. As you might have expected from your study of supply and demand, the increase in the number of homes for sale exacerbated the downward spiral of house prices. As house prices fell, spending on the construction of housing also collapsed.

A second repercussion was that the various financial institutions that owned mortgage-backed securities suffered huge losses. In essence, by borrowing large sums to buy high-risk mortgages, these companies had bet that house prices would keep rising; when this bet turned bad, they found themselves at or near the point of bankruptcy. Because of these large losses, many financial institutions did not have funds to loan out and the ability of the financial system to channel resources to those who could best use them was impaired. Even creditworthy customers found themselves unable to borrow to finance investment spending.

As a result of all these events, the economy experienced a large contractionary shift in aggregate demand. Real GDP and employment both fell sharply. The introduction to this chapter has already cited the figures, but they are worth repeating: Real GDP declined by 4.2 percent between the fourth quarter of 2007 and the second quarter of 2009, and the rate of unemployment rose from 4.4 percent in May 2007 to 10.0 percent in October 2009. This experience served as a vivid reminder that deep economic downturns and personal hardship they cause are not a relic of history but a constant risk in the modern economy.

As the crisis unfolded, the U.S. government responded in a variety of ways. Three policy actions—all aimed in part at returning aggregate demand to its previous level—are most noteworthy.

First, the Fed cut its target for the federal funds rate from 5.25 percent in September 2007 to about zero in December 2008. The Federal Reserve also started buying mortgage-backed securities and other private loans in open-market operations. By purchasing these instruments from the banking system, the Fed provided banks with additional funds in the hope that the banks would makes loans more readily available.

Second, in an even more unusual move in October 2008, Congress appropriated $700 billion for the Treasury to use to rescue the financial system. Much of this money was used for equity injections into banks. That is, the Treasury put funds into the banking system, which the banks could use to make loans and otherwise continue their normal operations; in exchange for these funds, the U.S. government became a part owner of these banks, at least temporarily. The goal of this policy was to stem the crisis on Wall Street and make it easier for businesses and individuals to obtain loans.

Finally, when Barack Obama became president in January 2009, his first major initiative was a large increase in government spending. After a relatively brief congressional debate over the form of the legislation, the new president signed a $787 billion stimulus bill on February 17, 2009. This policy move is discussed more fully in the next chapter when we consider the impact of fiscal policy on aggregate demand.

The recovery from this recession officially began in June 2009. But it was, by historical standards, only a meager recovery. From the second quarter of 2009 to the fourth quarter of 2015, real GDP growth averaged only 2.1 percent per year, well below the average rate of growth over the past half century of about 3 percent. Although unemployment fell to 5.0 percent by the end of 2015, much of the decline was attributable to individuals leaving the labor force rather than finding jobs. In December 2015, the employment-to-population ratio was only 1.3 percentage points higher than at its trough during the Great Recession and was more than 3 percentage points lower than before the downturn began.

Which, if any, of the many policy moves were most important for ending the recession? And what other policies might have promoted a more robust recovery? These are surely questions that macroeconomic historians will debate in the years to come. ●

### IN THE NEWS

## What Have We Learned?

*Since the financial crisis and Great Recession of 2008–2009, economists have asked themselves how this episode should change the field of macroeconomics.*

### Olivier Blanchard's Five Lessons for Economists from the Financial Crisis

**By David Wessel**

**W**hat did the worst financial crisis and deepest recession in 75 years teach academic economists and policymakers on whose watch it happened? At a recent London School of Economics forum, convened to honor Bank of England Governor Mervyn King, Olivier Blanchard offered some answers.

Mr. Blanchard, 64 years old, is well positioned to offer such reconsideration. An internationally prominent macroeconomist, he spent 25 years on the MIT faculty before becoming chief economist at the International Monetary Fund in September 2008, just before the collapse of Lehman Brothers.

Here are Mr. Blanchard's five lessons in his own words, lightly edited by The Wall Street Journal's David Wessel:

#### #1: Humility is in order.

The Great Moderation [the economically tranquil period from 1987 to 2007] convinced too many of us that the large-economy crisis—a financial crisis, a banking crisis— was a thing of the past. It wasn't going to happen again, except maybe in emerging markets. History was marching on.

My generation, which was born after World War II, lived with the notion that the world was getting to be a better and better place. We knew how to do things better, not only in economics but in other fields as well. What we have learned is that's not true. History repeats itself. We should have known.

#### #2: The financial system matters— a lot.

It's not the first time that we're confronted with what [former U.S. Defense Secretary Donald] Rumsfeld called "unknown unknowns," things that happened that we hadn't thought about. There is another example in macroeconomics:

The oil shocks of the 1970s during which we were students and we hadn't thought about it. It took a few years, more than a few years, for economists to understand what was going on. After a few years, we concluded that we could think of the oil shock as yet another macroeconomic shock. We did not need to understand the plumbing. We didn't need to understand the details of the oil market. When there's an increase in the price of energy or materials, we can just integrate it into our macro models—the implications of energy prices on inflation and so on.

This is different. What we have learned about the financial system is that the problem is in the plumbing and that we have to understand the plumbing. Before I came to the Fund, I thought of the financial system as a set of arbitrage equations. Basically the Federal Reserve would choose one interest rate, and then the expectations hypothesis would give all the rates everywhere else with premia which might vary, but not very much.

It was really easy. I thought of people on Wall Street as basically doing this for me so I didn't have to think about it.

What we have learned is that that's not the case. In the financial system, a myriad of distortions or small shocks build on each other. When there are enough small shocks, enough distortions, things can go very bad. This has fundamental implications for macroeconomics. We do macro on the assumption that we can look at aggregates in some way and then just have them interact in simple models. I still think that's the way to go, but this shows the limits of that approach. When it comes to the financial system, it's very clear that the details of the plumbing matter.

#### #3 Interconnectedness matters.

This crisis started in the U.S. and across the ocean in a matter of days and weeks. Each crisis, even in small islands, potentially has effects on the rest of the world. The complexity of the cross border claims by creditors and by debtors clearly is something that many of us had not fully realized: the cross border movements triggered by the risk-on/risk-off movements, which countries are safe havens, and when and why? Understanding this has become absolutely essential. What happens in one part of the world cannot be ignored by the rest of the world. The fact that we all spend so

## 23-5b  The Effects of a Shift in Aggregate Supply

Imagine once again an economy in its long-run equilibrium. Now suppose that suddenly some firms experience an increase in their costs of production. For example, bad weather in farm states might destroy some crops, driving up the

much time thinking about Cyprus in the last few days is an example of that.

It's also true on the trade side. We used to think if one country was doing badly, then exports to that country would do badly and therefore the exporting countries would do badly. In our models, the effect was relatively small. One absolutely striking fact of the crisis is the collapse of trade in 2009. Output went down. Trade collapsed. Countries which felt they were not terribly exposed through trade turned out to be enormously exposed.

### #4 We don't know if macro-prudential tools work.

It's very clear that the traditional monetary and fiscal tools are just not good enough to deal with the very specific problems in the financial system. This has led to the development of macro-prudential tools, which may or may not become the third leg of macroeconomic policies.

[Macro-prudential tools allow a central bank to restrain lending in specific sectors without raising interest rates for the whole economy, such as increasing the minimum down payment required to get a mortgage, which reduces the loan-to-value ratio.] In principle, they can address specific issues in the financial sector. If there is a problem somewhere you can target the tool at the problem and not use the policy interest rate, which basically is kind of an atomic bomb without any precision.

The big question here is: How reliable are these tools? How much can they be used? The answer—from some experiments before the crisis with loan-to-value ratios and during the crisis with variations in cyclical bank capital ratios or loan-to-value ratios or capital controls, such as in Brazil—is this: They work but they don't work great. People

and institutions find ways around them. In the process of reducing the problem somewhere you tend to create distortions elsewhere.

### #5 Central bank independence wasn't designed for what central banks are now asked to do.

There is two-way interaction between monetary policy and macro-prudential tools. When [Fed chair] Ben Bernanke does expansionary monetary policy, quantitative easing, and interest rates on many assets

Olivier Blanchard

are close to zero, there's a tendency by many players to take risks to increase their rate of return. Some of this risk actually we want them to take. Some we don't want them to take. That is the interaction of monetary policy on the financial system.

You also have it the other way around. If you use macro-prudential tools to, say, slow down the building in the housing sector you have an effect on aggregate demand, which is going to decrease output.

The question is: How do you organize the use of these tools? It makes sense to have them under the same roof. In practice this means the central bank. But that poses questions not only about coordination between the two functions, but also about central bank independence.

One of the major achievements of the last 20 years is that most central banks have become independent of elected governments. Independence was given because the mandate and the tools were very clear. The mandate was primarily inflation, which can be observed over time. The tool was some short-term interest rate that could be used by the central bank to try to achieve the inflation target. In this case, you can give some independence to the institution in charge of this because the objective is perfectly well defined, and everybody can basically observe how well the central bank does..

If you think now of central banks as having a much larger set of responsibilities and a much larger set of tools, then the issue of central bank independence becomes much more difficult. Do you actually want to give the central bank the independence to choose loan-to-value ratios without any supervision from the political process? Isn't this going to lead to a democratic deficit in a way in which the central bank becomes too powerful? I'm sure there are ways out. Perhaps there could be independence with respect to some dimensions of monetary policy—the traditional ones—and some supervision for the rest or some interaction with a political process. ■

**Source:** Republished with permission of *The Wall Street Journal*, from, "What Have We Learned? *The Wall Street Journal*, April 1, 2013"; permission conveyed through Copyright Clearance Center, Inc. "

cost of producing food products. Or a war in the Middle East might interrupt the shipping of crude oil, driving up the cost of producing oil products.

To analyze the macroeconomic impact of such an increase in production costs, we follow the same four steps as always. First, which curve is affected? Because production costs affect the firms that supply goods and services, changes in

## FIGURE 10

**An Adverse Shift in Aggregate Supply**
When some event increases firms' costs, the short-run aggregate-supply curve shifts to the left from $AS_1$ to $AS_2$. The economy moves from point A to point B. The result is stagflation: Output falls from $Y_1$ to $Y_2$, and the price level rises from $P_1$ to $P_2$.

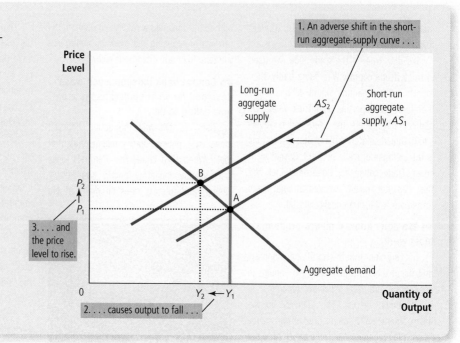

1. An adverse shift in the short-run aggregate-supply curve . . .

3. . . . and the price level to rise.

2. . . . causes output to fall . . .

production costs alter the position of the aggregate-supply curve. Second, in which direction does the curve shift? Because higher production costs make selling goods and services less profitable, firms now supply a smaller quantity of output for any given price level. Thus, as Figure 10 shows, the short-run aggregate-supply curve shifts to the left, from $AS_1$ to $AS_2$. (Depending on the event, the long-run aggregate-supply curve might also shift. To keep things simple, however, we will assume that it does not.)

The figure allows us to perform step three of comparing the initial and the new equilibrium. In the short run, the economy goes from point A to point B, moving along the existing aggregate-demand curve. The output of the economy falls from $Y_1$ to $Y_2$, and the price level rises from $P_1$ to $P_2$. Because the economy is experiencing both *stagnation* (falling output) and *inflation* (rising prices), such an event is sometimes called **stagflation**.

Now consider step four—the transition from the short-run equilibrium to the long-run equilibrium. According to the sticky-wage theory, the key issue is how stagflation affects nominal wages. Firms and workers may at first respond to the higher level of prices by raising their expectations of the price level and setting higher nominal wages. In this case, firms' costs will rise yet again, and the short-run aggregate-supply curve will shift farther to the left, making the problem of stagflation even worse. This phenomenon of higher prices leading to higher wages, in turn leading to even higher prices, is sometimes called a *wage-price spiral*.

At some point, this spiral of ever-rising wages and prices will slow. The low level of output and employment will put downward pressure on workers' wages because workers have less bargaining power when unemployment is high. As nominal wages fall, producing goods and services becomes more profitable and the short-run aggregate-supply curve shifts to the right. As it shifts back toward $AS_1$, the price level falls and the quantity of output approaches its natural level. In

**stagflation**
a period of falling output and rising prices

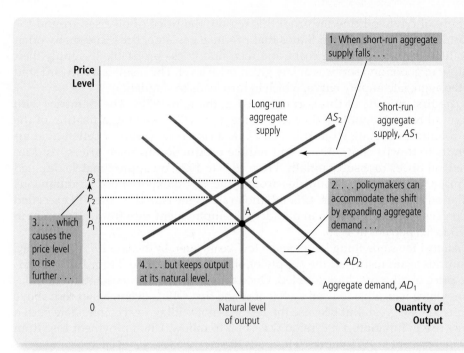

**FIGURE 11**

**Accommodating an Adverse Shift in Aggregate Supply**
Faced with an adverse shift in aggregate supply from $AS_1$ to $AS_2$, policymakers who can influence aggregate demand might try to shift the aggregate-demand curve to the right from $AD_1$ to $AD_2$. The economy would move from point A to point C. This policy would prevent the supply shift from reducing output in the short run, but the price level would permanently rise from $P_1$ to $P_3$.

the long run, the economy returns to point A, where the aggregate-demand curve crosses the long-run aggregate-supply curve.

This transition back to the initial equilibrium assumes, however, that aggregate demand is held constant throughout the process. In the real world, that may not be the case. Policymakers who control monetary and fiscal policy might attempt to offset some of the effects of the shift in the short-run aggregate-supply curve by shifting the aggregate-demand curve. This possibility is shown in Figure 11. In this case, changes in policy shift the aggregate-demand curve to the right, from $AD_1$ to $AD_2$—exactly enough to prevent the shift in aggregate supply from affecting output. The economy moves directly from point A to point C. Output remains at its natural level, and the price level rises from $P_1$ to $P_3$. In this case, policymakers are said to *accommodate* the shift in aggregate supply. An accommodative policy accepts a permanently higher level of prices to maintain a higher level of output and employment.

To sum up, this story about shifts in aggregate supply has two important lessons:

- Shifts in aggregate supply can cause stagflation—a combination of recession (falling output) and inflation (rising prices).
- Policymakers who can influence aggregate demand can potentially mitigate the adverse impact on output but only at the cost of exacerbating the problem of inflation.

**CASE STUDY**

**OIL AND THE ECONOMY**
Some of the largest economic fluctuations in the U.S. economy since 1970 have originated in the oil fields of the Middle East. Crude oil is a key input into the production of many goods and services, and much of the world's oil comes from Saudi Arabia, Kuwait, and other Middle Eastern countries. When some event (usually political in origin) reduces the

supply of crude oil flowing from this region, the price of oil rises around the world. Firms in the United States that produce gasoline, tires, and many other products experience rising costs, and they find it less profitable to supply their output of goods and services at any given price level. The result is a leftward shift in the aggregate-supply curve, which in turn leads to stagflation.

The first episode of this sort occurred in the mid-1970s. The countries with large oil reserves got together as members of OPEC, the Organization of the Petroleum Exporting Countries. OPEC is a *cartel*—a group of sellers that attempts to thwart competition and reduce production to raise prices. And indeed, oil prices rose substantially. From 1973 to 1975, oil approximately doubled in price. Oil-importing countries around the world experienced simultaneous inflation and recession. The U.S. inflation rate as measured by the CPI exceeded 10 percent for the first time in decades. Unemployment rose from 4.9 percent in 1973 to 8.5 percent in 1975.

Almost the same thing happened a few years later. In the late 1970s, the OPEC countries again restricted the supply of oil to raise the price. From 1978 to 1981, the price of oil more than doubled. Once again, the result was stagflation. Inflation, which had subsided somewhat after the first OPEC event, again rose above 10 percent per year. But because the Fed was not willing to accommodate such a large rise in inflation, a recession was soon to follow. Unemployment rose from about 6 percent in 1978 and 1979 to about 10 percent a few years later.

The world market for oil can also be a source of favorable shifts in aggregate supply. In 1986, squabbling broke out among members of OPEC. Member countries reneged on their agreements to restrict oil production. In the world market for crude oil, prices fell by about half. This fall in oil prices reduced costs to U.S. firms, which now found it more profitable to supply goods and services at any given price level. As a result, the aggregate-supply

## The Origins of the Model of Aggregate Demand and Aggregate Supply

John Maynard Keynes

Now that we have a preliminary understanding of the model of aggregate demand and aggregate supply, it is worthwhile to step back from it and consider its history. How did this model of short-run fluctuations develop? The answer is that this model, to a large extent, is a by-product of the Great Depression of the 1930s. Economists and policymakers at the time were puzzled about what had caused this calamity and were uncertain about how to deal with it.

In 1936, economist John Maynard Keynes published a book titled *The General Theory of Employment, Interest, and Money*, which attempted to explain short-run economic fluctuations in general and the Great Depression in particular. Keynes's primary message was that recessions and depressions can occur because of inadequate aggregate demand for goods and services.

Keynes had long been a critic of classical economic theory—the theory we examined earlier in the book—because it could explain only the long-run effects of policies. A few years before offering *The General Theory*, Keynes had written the following about classical economics:

> The long run is a misleading guide to current affairs. In the long run we are all dead. Economists set themselves too easy, too useless a task if in tempestuous seasons they can only tell us when the storm is long past, the ocean will be flat.

Keynes's message was aimed at policymakers as well as economists. As the world's economies suffered with high unemployment, Keynes advocated policies to increase aggregate demand, including government spending on public works.

In the next chapter, we examine in detail how policymakers can use the tools of monetary and fiscal policy to influence aggregate demand. The analysis in the next chapter, as well as in this one, owes much to the legacy of John Maynard Keynes. ∎

curve shifted to the right. The U.S. economy experienced the opposite of stagflation: Output grew rapidly, unemployment fell, and the inflation rate reached its lowest level in many years.

In recent years, the world market for oil has not been as important a source of economic fluctuations for the U.S. economy. Part of the reason is that conservation efforts, changes in technology, and the availability of alternative energy sources have reduced the economy's dependence on oil. The amount of oil used to produce a unit of real GDP has declined by more than 50 percent since the OPEC shocks of the 1970s. As a result, the economic impact of any change in oil prices on the U.S. economy is much smaller today than it was in the past. (Of course, some nations rely on oil exports as a major source of their income, and this makes oil prices crucial for them, but that is another story.) ●

*Changes in Middle East oil production are one source of U.S. economic fluctuations.*

**QuickQuiz**  *Suppose that the election of a popular presidential candidate suddenly increases people's confidence in the future. Use the model of aggregate demand and aggregate supply to analyze the effect on the economy.*

# 23-6 Conclusion

This chapter has achieved two goals. First, we have discussed some of the important facts about short-run fluctuations in economic activity. Second, we have introduced a basic model to explain those fluctuations, called the model of aggregate demand and aggregate supply. We continue our study of this model in the next chapter to understand more fully what causes fluctuations in the economy and how policymakers might respond to these fluctuations.

## CHAPTER QuickQuiz

1. When the economy goes into a recession, real GDP _____ and unemployment _____.
   a. rises, rises
   b. rises, falls
   c. falls, rises
   d. falls, falls

2. A sudden crash in the stock market shifts
   a. the aggregate-demand curve.
   b. the short-run aggregate-supply curve, but not the long-run aggregate-supply curve.
   c. the long-run aggregate-supply curve, but not the short-run aggregate-supply curve.
   d. both the short-run and the long-run aggregate-supply curves.

3. A change in the expected price level shifts
   a. the aggregate-demand curve.
   b. the short-run aggregate-supply curve, but not the long-run aggregate-supply curve.
   c. the long-run aggregate-supply curve, but not the short-run aggregate-supply curve.
   d. both the short-run and the long-run aggregate-supply curves.

4. An increase in the aggregate demand for goods and services has a larger impact on output _____ and a larger impact on the price level _____.
   a. in the short run, in the long run
   b. in the long run, in the short run
   c. in the short run, also in the short run
   d. in the long run, also in the long run

5. Stagflation is caused by
   a. a leftward shift in the aggregate-demand curve.
   b. a rightward shift in the aggregate-demand curve.
   c. a leftward shift in the aggregate-supply curve.
   d. a rightward shift in the aggregate-supply curve.

6. The idea that economic downturns result from an inadequate aggregate demand for goods and services is derived from the work of which economist?
   a. Adam Smith
   b. David Hume
   c. David Ricardo
   d. John Maynard Keynes

## SUMMARY

- All societies experience short-run economic fluctuations around long-run trends. These fluctuations are irregular and largely unpredictable. When recessions occur, real GDP and other measures of income, spending, and production fall, while unemployment rises.

- Classical economic theory is based on the assumption that nominal variables such as the money supply and the price level do not influence real variables such as output and employment. Most economists believe that this assumption is accurate in the long run but not in the short run. Economists analyze short-run economic fluctuations using the model of aggregate demand and aggregate supply. According to this model, the output of goods and services and the overall level of prices adjust to balance aggregate demand and aggregate supply.

- The aggregate-demand curve slopes downward for three reasons. The first is the wealth effect: A lower price level raises the real value of households' money holdings, which stimulates consumer spending. The second is the interest-rate effect: A lower price level reduces the quantity of money households demand; as households try to convert money into interest-bearing assets, interest rates fall, which stimulates investment spending. The third is the exchange-rate effect: As a lower price level reduces interest rates, the dollar depreciates in the market for foreign-currency exchange, which stimulates net exports.

- Any event or policy that raises consumption, investment, government purchases, or net exports at a given price level increases aggregate demand. Any event or policy that reduces consumption, investment, government purchases, or net exports at a given price level decreases aggregate demand.

- The long-run aggregate-supply curve is vertical. In the long run, the quantity of goods and services supplied depends on the economy's labor, capital, natural resources, and technology but not on the overall level of prices.

- Three theories have been proposed to explain the upward slope of the short-run aggregate-supply curve. According to the sticky-wage theory, an unexpected fall in the price level temporarily raises real wages, which induces firms to reduce employment and production. According to the sticky-price theory, an unexpected fall in the price level leaves some firms with prices that are temporarily too high, which reduces their sales and causes them to cut back production. According to the misperceptions theory, an unexpected fall in the price level leads suppliers to mistakenly believe that their relative prices have fallen, which induces them to reduce production. All three theories imply that output deviates from its natural level when the actual price level deviates from the price level that people expected.

- Events that alter the economy's ability to produce output, such as changes in labor, capital, natural resources, or technology, shift the short-run aggregate-supply curve (and may shift the long-run aggregate-supply curve as well). In addition, the position of the short-run aggregate-supply curve depends on the expected price level.

- One possible cause of economic fluctuations is a shift in aggregate demand. When the aggregate-demand curve shifts to the left, for instance, output and prices fall in the short run. Over time, as a change in the expected price level causes wages, prices, and perceptions to adjust, the short-run aggregate-supply curve shifts to the right. This shift returns the economy to its natural level of output at a new, lower price level.

- A second possible cause of economic fluctuations is a shift in aggregate supply. When the short-run aggregate-supply curve shifts to the left, the effect is falling output and rising prices—a combination called stagflation. Over time, as wages, prices, and perceptions adjust, the short-run aggregate-supply curve shifts back to the right, returning the price level and output to their original levels.

## KEY CONCEPTS

recession, p. 484
depression, p. 484

model of aggregate demand and
    aggregate supply, p. 488
aggregate-demand curve, p. 488

aggregate-supply curve, p. 489
natural level of output, p. 496
stagflation, p. 512

## QUESTIONS FOR REVIEW

1. Name two macroeconomic variables that decline when the economy goes into a recession. Name one macroeconomic variable that rises during a recession.

2. Draw a diagram with aggregate demand, short-run aggregate supply, and long-run aggregate supply. Be careful to label the axes correctly.

3. List and explain the three reasons the aggregate-demand curve slopes downward.

4. Explain why the long-run aggregate-supply curve is vertical.

5. List and explain the three theories for why the short-run aggregate-supply curve slopes upward.

6. What might shift the aggregate-demand curve to the left? Use the model of aggregate demand and aggregate supply to trace through the short-run and long-run effects of such a shift on output and the price level.

7. What might shift the aggregate-supply curve to the left? Use the model of aggregate demand and aggregate supply to trace through the short-run and long-run effects of such a shift on output and the price level.

## PROBLEMS AND APPLICATIONS

1. Suppose the economy is in a long-run equilibrium.
   a. Draw a diagram to illustrate the state of the economy. Be sure to show aggregate demand, short-run aggregate supply, and long-run aggregate supply.
   b. Now suppose that a stock market crash causes aggregate demand to fall. Use your diagram to show what happens to output and the price level in the short run. What happens to the unemployment rate?
   c. Use the sticky-wage theory of aggregate supply to explain what will happen to output and the price level in the long run (assuming no change in policy). What role does the expected price level play in this adjustment? Be sure to illustrate your analysis in a graph.

2. Explain whether each of the following events will increase, decrease, or have no effect on long-run aggregate supply.
   a. The United States experiences a wave of immigration.
   b. Congress raises the minimum wage to $15 per hour.
   c. Intel invents a new and more powerful computer chip.
   d. A severe hurricane damages factories along the East Coast.

3. Suppose an economy is in long-run equilibrium.
   a. Use the model of aggregate demand and aggregate supply to illustrate the initial equilibrium (call it point A). Be sure to include both short-run and long-run aggregate supply.
   b. The central bank raises the money supply by 5 percent. Use your diagram to show what happens to output and the price level as the economy moves from the initial to the new short-run equilibrium (call it point B).

   c. Now show the new long-run equilibrium (call it point C). What causes the economy to move from point B to point C?
   d. According to the sticky-wage theory of aggregate supply, how do nominal wages at point A compare to nominal wages at point B? How do nominal wages at point A compare to nominal wages at point C?
   e. According to the sticky-wage theory of aggregate supply, how do real wages at point A compare to real wages at point B? How do real wages at point A compare to real wages at point C?
   f. Judging by the impact of the money supply on nominal and real wages, is this analysis consistent with the proposition that money has real effects in the short run but is neutral in the long run?

4. In 1939, with the U.S. economy not yet fully recovered from the Great Depression, President Roosevelt proclaimed that Thanksgiving would fall a week earlier than usual so that the shopping period before Christmas would be longer. Explain what President Roosevelt might have been trying to achieve, using the model of aggregate demand and aggregate supply.

5. Explain why the following statements are false.
   a. "The aggregate-demand curve slopes downward because it is the horizontal sum of the demand curves for individual goods."
   b. "The long-run aggregate-supply curve is vertical because economic forces do not affect long-run aggregate supply."
   c. "If firms adjusted their prices every day, then the short-run aggregate-supply curve would be horizontal."
   d. "Whenever the economy enters a recession, its long-run aggregate-supply curve shifts to the left."

6.  For each of the three theories for the upward slope of the short-run aggregate-supply curve, carefully explain the following:
    a.  how the economy recovers from a recession and returns to its long-run equilibrium without any policy intervention
    b.  what determines the speed of that recovery

7.  The economy begins in long-run equilibrium. Then one day, the president appoints a new chair of the Federal Reserve. This new chairman is well known for her view that inflation is not a major problem for an economy.
    a.  How would this news affect the price level that people would expect to prevail?
    b.  How would this change in the expected price level affect the nominal wage that workers and firms agree to in their new labor contracts?
    c.  How would this change in the nominal wage affect the profitability of producing goods and services at any given price level?
    d.  How does this change in profitability affect the short-run aggregate-supply curve?
    e.  If aggregate demand is held constant, how does this shift in the aggregate-supply curve affect the price level and the quantity of output produced?
    f.  Do you think this Fed chairman was a good appointment?

8.  Explain whether each of the following events shifts the short-run aggregate-supply curve, the aggregate-demand curve, both, or neither. For each event that does shift a curve, draw a diagram to illustrate the effect on the economy.
    a.  Households decide to save a larger share of their income.
    b.  Florida orange groves suffer a prolonged period of below-freezing temperatures.
    c.  Increased job opportunities overseas cause many people to leave the country.

9.  For each of the following events, explain the short-run and long-run effects on output and the price level, assuming policymakers take no action.
    a.  The stock market declines sharply, reducing consumers' wealth.
    b.  The federal government increases spending on national defense.
    c.  A technological improvement raises productivity.
    d.  A recession overseas causes foreigners to buy fewer U.S. goods.

10. Suppose firms become very optimistic about future business conditions and invest heavily in new capital equipment.
    a.  Draw an aggregate-demand/aggregate-supply diagram to show the short-run effect of this optimism on the economy. Label the new levels of prices and real output. Explain in words why the aggregate quantity of output *supplied* changes.
    b.  Now use the diagram from part (a) to show the new long-run equilibrium of the economy. (For now, assume there is no change in the long-run aggregate-supply curve.) Explain in words why the aggregate quantity of output *demanded* changes between the short run and the long run.
    c.  How might the investment boom affect the long-run aggregate-supply curve? Explain.

To find additional study resources, visit cengagebrain.com, and search for "Mankiw."

# The Influence of Monetary and Fiscal Policy on Aggregate Demand

I magine that you are a member of the Federal Open Market Committee, the group at the Federal Reserve that sets monetary policy. You observe that the president and Congress have agreed to raise taxes. How should the Fed respond to this change in fiscal policy? Should it expand the money supply, contract the money supply, or leave it unchanged?

To answer this question, you need to consider the impact of monetary and fiscal policy on the economy. In the preceding chapter, we used the model of aggregate demand and aggregate supply to explain short-run economic

fluctuations. We saw that shifts in the aggregate-demand curve or the aggregate-supply curve cause fluctuations in the economy's overall output of goods and services and its overall level of prices. As we noted in the previous chapter, both monetary and fiscal policy influence aggregate demand. Thus, a change in one of these policies can lead to short-run fluctuations in output and prices. Policy-makers will want to anticipate this effect and, perhaps, adjust the other policy in response.

In this chapter, we examine in more detail how the government's policy tools influence the position of the aggregate-demand curve. These tools include monetary policy (the supply of money set by the central bank) and fiscal policy (the levels of government spending and taxation set by the president and Congress). We have previously discussed the long-run effects of these policies. In Chapters 17 and 18, we saw how fiscal policy affects saving, investment, and long-run economic growth. In Chapters 21 and 22, we saw how monetary policy influences the price level in the long run. We now look at how these policy tools can shift the aggregate-demand curve and thereby affect macroeconomic variables in the short run.

As we have already learned, many factors influence aggregate demand besides monetary and fiscal policy. In particular, desired spending by households and firms determines the overall demand for goods and services. When desired spending changes, aggregate demand shifts. If policymakers do not respond, such shifts in aggregate demand cause short-run fluctuations in output and employment. As a result, monetary and fiscal policymakers sometimes use the policy levers at their disposal to try to offset these shifts in aggregate demand and stabilize the economy. Here we discuss the theory behind these policy actions and some of the difficulties that arise in using this theory in practice.

# 24-1 How Monetary Policy Influences Aggregate Demand

The aggregate-demand curve shows the total quantity of goods and services demanded in the economy for any price level. The preceding chapter discussed three reasons why the aggregate-demand curve slopes downward:

- *The wealth effect:* A lower price level raises the real value of households' money holdings, which are part of their wealth. Higher real wealth stimulates consumer spending and thus increases the quantity of goods and services demanded.
- *The interest-rate effect:* A lower price level reduces the amount of money people want to hold. As people try to lend out their excess money holdings, the interest rate falls. The lower interest rate stimulates investment spending and thus increases the quantity of goods and services demanded.
- *The exchange-rate effect:* When a lower price level reduces the interest rate, investors move some of their funds overseas in search of higher returns. This movement of funds causes the real value of the domestic currency to fall in the market for foreign-currency exchange. Domestic goods become less expensive relative to foreign goods. This change in the real exchange rate stimulates spending on net exports and thus increases the quantity of goods and services demanded.

These three effects occur simultaneously to increase the quantity of goods and services demanded when the price level falls and to decrease it when the price level rises.

Although all three effects work together to explain the downward slope of the aggregate-demand curve, they are not of equal importance. Because money holdings are a small part of household wealth, the wealth effect is the least important of the three. In addition, because exports and imports represent only a small fraction of U.S. GDP, the exchange-rate effect is not large for the U.S. economy. (This effect is more important for smaller countries, which typically export and import a higher fraction of their GDP.) *For the U.S. economy, the most important reason for the downward slope of the aggregate-demand curve is the interest-rate effect.*

To better understand aggregate demand, we now examine the short-run determination of interest rates in more detail. Here we develop the **theory of liquidity preference**. This theory of interest rates helps explain the downward slope of the aggregate-demand curve, as well as how monetary and fiscal policy can shift this curve. By shedding new light on aggregate demand, the theory of liquidity preference expands our understanding of what causes short-run economic fluctuations and what policymakers can potentially do about them.

**theory of liquidity preference**
Keynes's theory that the interest rate adjusts to bring money supply and money demand into balance

### 24-1a The Theory of Liquidity Preference

In his classic book *The General Theory of Employment, Interest, and Money*, John Maynard Keynes proposed the theory of liquidity preference to explain the factors that determine an economy's interest rate. The theory is, in essence, an application of supply and demand. According to Keynes, the interest rate adjusts to balance the supply of and demand for money.

You may recall that economists distinguish between two interest rates: The *nominal interest rate* is the interest rate as usually reported, and the *real interest rate* is the interest rate corrected for the effects of inflation. When there is no inflation, the two rates are the same. But when borrowers and lenders expect prices to rise over the course of the loan, they agree to a nominal interest rate that exceeds the real interest rate by the expected rate of inflation. The higher nominal interest rate compensates for the fact that they expect the loan to be repaid in less valuable dollars.

Which interest rate are we now trying to explain with the theory of liquidity preference? The answer is both. In the analysis that follows, we hold constant the expected rate of inflation. This assumption is reasonable for studying the economy in the short run, because expected inflation is typically stable over short periods of time. In this case, nominal and real interest rates differ by a constant. When the nominal interest rate rises or falls, the real interest rate that people expect to earn rises or falls by a similar amount. For the rest of this chapter, when we discuss changes in the interest rate, these changes refer to both the real and nominal interest rates.

Let's now develop the theory of liquidity preference by considering the supply and demand for money and how each depends on the interest rate.

**Money Supply** The first piece of the theory of liquidity preference is the supply of money. As we first discussed in Chapter 21, the money supply in the U.S. economy is controlled by the Federal Reserve. The Fed alters the money supply primarily by changing the quantity of reserves in the banking system through the purchase and sale of government bonds in open-market operations. When the Fed buys government bonds, the dollars it pays for the bonds are typically deposited in banks, and these dollars are added to bank reserves. When the Fed sells government bonds, the dollars it receives for the bonds are withdrawn from the banking system, and bank reserves fall. These changes in bank reserves, in turn, lead to changes in banks' ability to make loans and create money. Thus, by buying and selling bonds in open-market operations, the Fed alters the supply of money in the economy.

In addition to open-market operations, the Fed can influence the money supply using a variety of other tools. One option is for the Fed to change how much it lends to banks. For example, a decrease in the discount rate (the interest rate at which banks can borrow reserves from the Fed) encourages more bank borrowing, which increases bank reserves and thereby the money supply. Conversely, an increase in the discount rate discourages bank borrowing, which decreases bank reserves and the money supply. The Fed also alters the money supply by changing reserve requirements (the amount of reserves banks must hold against deposits) and by changing the interest rate it pays banks on the reserves they are holding.

These details of monetary control are important for the implementation of Fed policy, but they are not crucial for the analysis in this chapter. Our goal here is to examine how changes in the money supply affect the aggregate demand for goods and services. For this purpose, we can ignore the details of how Fed policy is implemented and assume that the Fed controls the money supply directly. In other words, the quantity of money supplied in the economy is fixed at whatever level the Fed decides to set it.

Because the quantity of money supplied is fixed by Fed policy, it does not depend on other economic variables. In particular, it does not depend on the interest rate. Once the Fed has made its policy decision, the quantity of money supplied is the same, regardless of the prevailing interest rate. We represent a fixed money supply with a vertical supply curve, as in Figure 1.

## FIGURE 1

**Equilibrium in the Money Market**

According to the theory of liquidity preference, the interest rate adjusts to bring the quantity of money supplied and the quantity of money demanded into balance. If the interest rate is above the equilibrium level (such as at $r_1$), the quantity of money people want to hold ($M_1^d$) is less than the quantity the Fed has created, and this surplus of money puts downward pressure on the interest rate. Conversely, if the interest rate is below the equilibrium level (such as at $r_2$), the quantity of money people want to hold ($M_2^d$) is greater than the quantity the Fed has created, and this shortage of money puts upward pressure on the interest rate. Thus, the forces of supply and demand in the market for money push the interest rate toward the equilibrium interest rate, at which people are content holding the quantity of money the Fed has created.

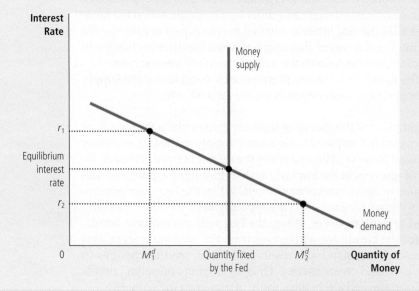

**Money Demand** The second piece of the theory of liquidity preference is the demand for money. As a starting point for understanding money demand, recall that an asset's *liquidity* refers to the ease with which that asset can be converted into the economy's medium of exchange. Because money is the economy's medium of exchange, it is by definition the most liquid asset available. The liquidity of money explains the demand for it: People choose to hold money instead of other assets that offer higher rates of return because money can be used to buy goods and services.

Although many factors determine the quantity of money demanded, the one emphasized by the theory of liquidity preference is the interest rate. The reason is that the interest rate is the opportunity cost of holding money. That is, when you hold wealth as cash in your wallet, instead of as an interest-bearing bond, you lose the interest you could have earned. An increase in the interest rate raises the cost of holding money and, as a result, reduces the quantity of money demanded. A decrease in the interest rate reduces the cost of holding money and raises the quantity demanded. Thus, as shown in Figure 1, the money demand curve slopes downward.

**Equilibrium in the Money Market** According to the theory of liquidity preference, the interest rate adjusts to balance the supply and demand for money. There is one interest rate, called the *equilibrium interest rate*, at which the quantity of money demanded exactly balances the quantity of money supplied. If the interest rate is at any other level, people will try to adjust their portfolios of assets and, as a result, drive the interest rate toward the equilibrium.

For example, suppose that the interest rate is above the equilibrium level, such as $r_1$ in Figure 1. In this case, the quantity of money that people want to hold, $M_1^d$, is less than the quantity of money that the Fed has supplied. Those people who are holding the surplus of money will try to get rid of it by buying interest-bearing bonds or by depositing it in interest-bearing bank accounts. Because bond issuers and banks prefer to pay lower interest rates, they respond to this surplus of money by lowering the interest rates they offer. As the interest rate falls, people become more willing to hold money until, at the equilibrium interest rate, people are happy to hold exactly the amount of money the Fed has supplied.

Conversely, at interest rates below the equilibrium level, such as $r_2$ in Figure 1, the quantity of money that people want to hold, $M_2^d$, is greater than the quantity of money that the Fed has supplied. As a result, people try to increase their holdings of money by reducing their holdings of bonds and other interest-bearing assets. As people cut back on their holdings of bonds, bond issuers find that they have to offer higher interest rates to attract buyers. Thus, the interest rate rises until it reaches the equilibrium level.

## 24-1b The Downward Slope of the Aggregate-Demand Curve

Having seen how the theory of liquidity preference explains the economy's equilibrium interest rate, we now consider the theory's implications for the aggregate demand for goods and services. As a warm-up exercise, let's begin by using the theory to reexamine a topic we already understand—the interest-rate effect and the downward slope of the aggregate-demand curve. In particular, suppose that the overall level of prices in the economy rises. What happens to the interest rate that balances the supply and demand for money, and how does that change affect the quantity of goods and services demanded?

As we discussed in Chapter 22, the price level is one determinant of the quantity of money demanded. At higher prices, more money is exchanged every time a good or service is sold. As a result, people will choose to hold a larger quantity of money. That is, a higher price level increases the quantity of money demanded for any given interest rate. Thus, an increase in the price level from $P_1$ to $P_2$ shifts the money demand curve to the right from $MD_1$ to $MD_2$, as shown in panel (a) of Figure 2.

Notice how this shift in money demand affects the equilibrium in the money market. For a fixed money supply, the interest rate must rise to balance money supply and money demand. Because the higher price level has increased the amount of money people want to hold, it has shifted the money demand curve to the right. Yet the quantity of money supplied is unchanged, so the interest rate must rise from $r_1$ to $r_2$ to discourage the additional demand.

This increase in the interest rate has ramifications not only for the money market but also for the quantity of goods and services demanded, as shown in panel (b). At

## FYI

# Interest Rates in the Long Run and the Short Run

In an earlier chapter, we said that the interest rate adjusts to balance the supply of loanable funds (national saving) and the demand for loanable funds (desired investment). Here we just said that the interest rate adjusts to balance the supply of and demand for money. Can we reconcile these two theories?

To answer this question, we need to focus on three macroeconomic variables: the economy's output of goods and services, the interest rate, and the price level. According to the classical macroeconomic theory we developed earlier in the book, these variables are determined as follows:

1. *Output* is determined by the supplies of capital and labor and the available production technology for turning capital and labor into output. (We call this the natural level of output.)
2. For any given level of output, the *interest rate* adjusts to balance the supply and demand for loanable funds.
3. Given output and the interest rate, the *price level* adjusts to balance the supply and demand for money. Changes in the supply of money lead to proportionate changes in the price level.

These are three of the essential propositions of classical economic theory. Most economists believe that these propositions do a good job of describing how the economy works *in the long run*.

Yet these propositions do not hold in the short run. As we discussed in the preceding chapter, many prices are slow to adjust to changes in the money supply; this fact is reflected in a short-run aggregate-supply curve that is upward-sloping rather than vertical. As a result, *in the short run*, the overall price level cannot, by itself, move to balance the supply of and demand for money. This stickiness of the price level requires the interest rate to move to bring the money market into equilibrium. These changes in the interest rate, in turn, affect the aggregate demand for goods and services. As aggregate demand fluctuates, the economy's output of goods and services moves away from the level determined by factor supplies and technology.

To think about the operation of the economy in the short run (day to day, week to week, month to month, or quarter to quarter), it is best to keep in mind the following logic:

1. The *price level* is stuck at some level (based on previously formed expectations) and, in the short run, is relatively unresponsive to changing economic conditions.
2. For any given (stuck) price level, the *interest rate* adjusts to balance the supply of and demand for money.
3. The interest rate that balances the money market influences the quantity of goods and services demanded and thus the level of *output*.

Notice that this precisely reverses the order of analysis used to study the economy in the long run.

The two different theories of the interest rate are useful for different purposes. When thinking about the long-run determinants of the interest rate, it is best to keep in mind the loanable-funds theory, which highlights the importance of an economy's saving propensities and investment opportunities. By contrast, when thinking about the short-run determinants of the interest rate, it is best to keep in mind the liquidity-preference theory, which highlights the importance of monetary policy. ∎

An increase in the price level from $P_1$ to $P_2$ shifts the money demand curve to the right, as in panel (a). This increase in money demand causes the interest rate to rise from $r_1$ to $r_2$. Because the interest rate is the cost of borrowing, the increase in the interest rate reduces the quantity of goods and services demanded from $Y_1$ to $Y_2$. This negative relationship between the price level and quantity demanded is represented with a downward-sloping aggregate-demand curve, as in panel (b).

**FIGURE 2**

**The Money Market and the Slope of the Aggregate-Demand Curve**

(a) The Money Market

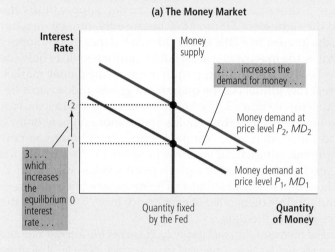

(b) The Aggregate-Demand Curve

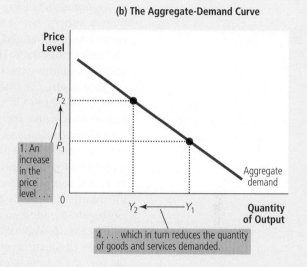

a higher interest rate, the cost of borrowing and the return to saving are greater. Fewer households choose to borrow to buy a new house, and those who do buy smaller houses, so the demand for residential investment falls. Fewer firms choose to borrow to build new factories and buy new equipment, so business investment falls. Thus, when the price level rises from $P_1$ to $P_2$, increasing money demand from $MD_1$ to $MD_2$ and raising the interest rate from $r_1$ to $r_2$, the quantity of goods and services demanded falls from $Y_1$ to $Y_2$.

This analysis of the interest-rate effect can be summarized in three steps: (1) A higher price level raises money demand. (2) Higher money demand leads to a higher interest rate. (3) A higher interest rate reduces the quantity of goods and services demanded. The same logic works for a decline in the price level: A lower price level reduces money demand, which leads to a lower interest rate, and this in turn increases the quantity of goods and services demanded. The result of this analysis is a negative relationship between the price level and the quantity of goods and services demanded, as illustrated by a downward-sloping aggregate-demand curve.

## 24-1c  Changes in the Money Supply

So far, we have used the theory of liquidity preference to explain more fully how the total quantity of goods and services demanded in the economy changes as the price level changes. That is, we have examined movements along a downward-sloping aggregate-demand curve. The theory also sheds light, however, on some of the other events that alter the quantity of goods and services demanded. Whenever the quantity of goods and services demanded changes *for any given price level*, the aggregate-demand curve shifts.

One important variable that shifts the aggregate-demand curve is monetary policy. To see how monetary policy affects the economy in the short run, suppose that the Fed increases the money supply by buying government bonds in open-market operations. (Why the Fed might do this will become clear later, after we understand the effects of such a move.) Let's consider how this monetary injection influences the equilibrium interest rate for a given price level. This will tell us what the injection does to the position of the aggregate-demand curve.

As panel (a) of Figure 3 shows, an increase in the money supply shifts the money supply curve to the right from $MS_1$ to $MS_2$. Because the money demand curve has not changed, the interest rate falls from $r_1$ to $r_2$ to balance money supply and money demand. That is, the interest rate must fall to induce people to hold the additional money the Fed has created, restoring equilibrium in the money market.

Once again, the interest rate influences the quantity of goods and services demanded, as shown in panel (b) of Figure 3. The lower interest rate reduces the cost of borrowing and the return to saving. Households spend more on new homes, stimulating the demand for residential investment. Firms spend more on new factories and new equipment, stimulating business investment. As a result, the quantity of goods and services demanded at a given price level, $\overline{P}$, rises from $Y_1$ to $Y_2$. Of course, there is nothing special about $\overline{P}$: The monetary injection raises the quantity of goods and services demanded at every price level. Thus, the entire aggregate-demand curve shifts to the right.

To sum up: *When the Fed increases the money supply, it lowers the interest rate and increases the quantity of goods and services demanded for any given price level, shifting the aggregate-demand curve to the right. Conversely, when the Fed contracts the money supply, it raises the interest rate and reduces the quantity of goods and services demanded for any given price level, shifting the aggregate-demand curve to the left.*

## FIGURE 3

**A Monetary Injection**

In panel (a), an increase in the money supply from $MS_1$ to $MS_2$ reduces the equilibrium interest rate from $r_1$ to $r_2$. Because the interest rate is the cost of borrowing, the fall in the interest rate raises the quantity of goods and services demanded at a given price level from $Y_1$ to $Y_2$. Thus, in panel (b), the aggregate-demand curve shifts to the right from $AD_1$ to $AD_2$.

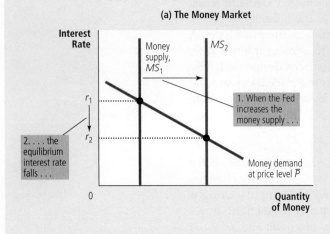

(a) The Money Market

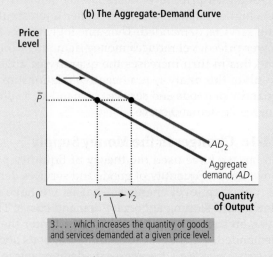

(b) The Aggregate-Demand Curve

### 24-1d  The Role of Interest-Rate Targets in Fed Policy

How does the Federal Reserve affect the economy? Our discussion here and earlier in the book has treated the money supply as the Fed's policy instrument. When the Fed buys government bonds in open-market operations, it increases the money supply and expands aggregate demand. When the Fed sells government bonds in open-market operations, it decreases the money supply and contracts aggregate demand.

Discussions of Fed policy often treat the interest rate, rather than the money supply, as the Fed's policy instrument. Indeed, in recent years, the Federal Reserve has conducted policy by setting a target for the *federal funds rate*—the interest rate that banks charge one another for short-term loans. This target is reevaluated every six weeks at meetings of the Federal Open Market Committee (FOMC). The FOMC has chosen to set a target for the federal funds rate, rather than for the money supply, as it did at times in the past.

There are several related reasons for the Fed's decision to use the federal funds rate as its target. One is that the money supply is hard to measure with sufficient precision. Another is that money demand fluctuates over time. For any given money supply, fluctuations in money demand would lead to fluctuations in interest rates, aggregate demand, and output. By contrast, when the Fed announces a target for the federal funds rate, it essentially accommodates the day-to-day shifts in money demand by adjusting the money supply accordingly.

The Fed's decision to target an interest rate does not fundamentally alter our analysis of monetary policy. The theory of liquidity preference illustrates an important principle: *Monetary policy can be described either in terms of the money supply or in terms of the interest rate.* When the FOMC sets a target for the federal funds rate of, say, 6 percent, the Fed's bond traders are told: "Conduct whatever open-market operations are necessary to ensure that the equilibrium interest rate is 6 percent." In other words, when the Fed sets a target for the interest rate, it commits itself to adjusting the money supply to make the equilibrium in the money market hit that target.

As a result, changes in monetary policy can be viewed either in terms of changing the interest rate target or in terms of changing the money supply. When you read in the newspaper that "the Fed has lowered the federal funds rate from 6 to 5 percent," you should understand that this occurs only because the Fed's bond traders are doing what it takes to make it happen. To lower the federal funds rate, the Fed's bond traders buy government bonds, and this purchase increases the money supply and lowers the equilibrium interest rate (just as in Figure 3). Similarly, when the FOMC raises the target for the federal funds rate, the bond traders sell government bonds, and this sale decreases the money supply and raises the equilibrium interest rate.

The lessons from this analysis are simple: *Changes in monetary policy aimed at expanding aggregate demand can be described either as increasing the money supply or as lowering the interest rate. Changes in monetary policy aimed at contracting aggregate demand can be described either as decreasing the money supply or as raising the interest rate.*

**CASE STUDY**

**WHY THE FED WATCHES THE STOCK MARKET (AND VICE VERSA)**
"The stock market has predicted nine out of the past five recessions." So quipped Paul Samuelson, the famed economist (and textbook author). Samuelson was right that the stock market is highly volatile and can give wrong signals about the economy. But fluctuations in stock prices are often a sign of broader economic developments. The economic boom of the 1990s, for example, appeared not only in rapid GDP growth and falling unemployment but also in rising stock prices, which increased about fourfold during this decade.

Similarly, the deep recession of 2008 and 2009 was reflected in falling stock prices: From November 2007 to March 2009, the stock market lost about half its value.

How should the Fed respond to stock market fluctuations? The Fed has no reason to care about stock prices in themselves, but it does have the job of monitoring and responding to developments in the overall economy, and the stock market is a piece of that puzzle. When the stock market booms, households become wealthier, and this increased wealth stimulates consumer spending. In addition, a rise in stock prices makes it more attractive for firms to sell new shares of stock, and this stimulates investment spending. For both reasons, a booming stock market expands the aggregate demand for goods and services.

As we discuss more fully later in the chapter, one of the Fed's goals is to stabilize aggregate demand, because greater stability in aggregate demand means greater stability in output and the price level. To promote stability, the Fed might respond to a stock market boom by keeping the money supply lower and interest rates higher than it otherwise would. The contractionary effects of higher interest rates would offset the expansionary effects of higher stock prices. In fact, this analysis does describe Fed behavior: Real interest rates were kept high by historical standards during the stock market boom of the late 1990s.

The opposite occurs when the stock market falls. Spending on consumption and investment tends to decline, depressing aggregate demand and pushing the economy toward recession. To stabilize aggregate demand, the Fed would increase the money supply and lower interest rates. And indeed, that is what it typically does. For example, on October 19, 1987, the stock market fell by 22.6 percent—one of the biggest one-day drops in history. The Fed responded to the market crash by increasing the money supply and lowering interest rates. The federal funds rate fell from 7.7 percent at the beginning of October to 6.6 percent at the end of the month. In part because of the Fed's quick action, the economy avoided a recession. Similarly, as we discussed in a case study in the preceding chapter, the Fed also reduced interest rates during the economic downturn and stock market decline of 2008 and 2009, but this time monetary policy was not sufficient to avert a deep recession.

While the Fed keeps an eye on the stock market, stock market participants also keep an eye on the Fed. Because the Fed can influence interest rates and economic activity, it can alter the value of stocks. For example, when the Fed raises interest rates by reducing the money supply, it makes owning stocks less attractive for two reasons. First, a higher interest rate means that bonds, the alternative to stocks, are earning a higher return. Second, the Fed's tightening of monetary policy reduces the demand for goods and services, which reduces profits. As a result, stock prices often fall when the Fed raises interest rates. ●

**QuickQuiz**  *Use the theory of liquidity preference to explain how a decrease in the money supply affects the equilibrium interest rate. How does this change in monetary policy affect the aggregate-demand curve?*

## 24-1e  The Zero Lower Bound

As we have just seen, monetary policy works through interest rates. This conclusion raises a question: What if the Fed's target interest rate has fallen as far as it can? In the recession of 2008 and 2009, the federal funds rate fell to about zero. In this situation, what, if anything, can monetary policy do to stimulate the economy?

Some economists describe this situation as a *liquidity trap*. According to the *theory of liquidity preference*, expansionary monetary policy works by reducing interest rates and stimulating investment spending. But if interest rates have already fallen to around zero, monetary policy may no longer be effective. Nominal interest rates cannot fall much below zero: Rather than making a loan at a negative nominal interest rate, a person would just hold cash. In this environment, expansionary monetary policy raises the supply of money, making the public's asset portfolio more liquid, but because interest rates can't fall any further, the extra liquidity might not have any effect. Aggregate demand, production, and employment may be "trapped" at low levels.

Other economists are skeptical about the relevance of liquidity traps and believe that a central bank continues to have tools to expand the economy, even after its interest rate target hits its lower bound of zero. One possibility is that the central bank could commit itself to keeping interest rates low for an extended period of time. Such a policy is sometimes called *forward guidance*. Even if the central bank's current target for the interest rate cannot fall any further, the promise that interest rates will remain low may help stimulate investment spending.

A second possibility is that the central bank could conduct expansionary open-market operations with a larger variety of financial instruments. Normally, the Fed conducts expansionary open-market operations by buying short-term government bonds. But it could also buy mortgages, corporate debt, and longer-term government bonds and thereby lower the interest rates on these kinds of loans. The Federal Reserve actively pursued this last option in the aftermath of the financial crisis of 2008 and 2009. This type of unconventional monetary policy is sometimes called *quantitative easing* because it increases the quantity of bank reserves.

Some economists have suggested that the possibility of hitting the zero lower bound for interest rates justifies setting the target rate of inflation well above zero. Under zero inflation, the real interest rate, like the nominal interest, can never fall below zero. But if the normal rate of inflation is, say, 4 percent, then the central bank can easily push the real interest rate to negative 4 percent by lowering the nominal interest rate toward zero. Thus, moderate inflation gives monetary policymakers more room to stimulate the economy when needed, reducing the risk of hitting the zero lower bound and having the economy fall into a liquidity trap.

# 24-2 How Fiscal Policy Influences Aggregate Demand

The government can influence the behavior of the economy not only with monetary policy but also with fiscal policy. **Fiscal policy** refers to the government's choices regarding the overall level of government purchases and taxes. Earlier in the book, we examined how fiscal policy influences saving, investment, and growth in the long run. In the short run, however, the primary effect of fiscal policy is on the aggregate demand for goods and services.

**fiscal policy**
the setting of the level of government spending and taxation by government policymakers

## 24-2a Changes in Government Purchases

When policymakers change the money supply or the level of taxes, they shift the aggregate-demand curve indirectly by influencing the spending decisions of firms or households. By contrast, when the government alters its own purchases of goods and services, it shifts the aggregate-demand curve directly.

Suppose, for instance, that the U.S. Department of Defense places a $20 billion order for new fighter planes with Boeing, the large aircraft manufacturer. This order raises the demand for the output produced by Boeing, which induces the company to hire more workers and increase production. Because Boeing is part of the economy, the increase in the demand for Boeing planes means an increase in the total quantity of goods and services demanded at each price level. As a result, the aggregate-demand curve shifts to the right.

By how much does this $20 billion order from the government shift the aggregate-demand curve? At first, one might guess that the aggregate-demand curve shifts to the right by exactly $20 billion. It turns out, however, that this is not the case. There are two macroeconomic effects that cause the size of the shift in aggregate demand to differ from the change in government purchases. The first—the multiplier effect—suggests the shift in aggregate demand could be *larger* than $20 billion. The second—the crowding-out effect—suggests the shift in aggregate demand could be *smaller* than $20 billion. We now discuss these two effects in turn.

### 24-2b  The Multiplier Effect

When the government buys $20 billion of goods from Boeing, that purchase has repercussions. The immediate impact of the higher demand from the government is to raise employment and profits at Boeing. Then, as the workers see higher earnings and the firm owners see higher profits, they respond to this increase in income by raising their own spending on consumer goods. As a result, the government purchase from Boeing raises the demand for the products of many other firms in the economy. Because each dollar spent by the government can raise the aggregate demand for goods and services by more than a dollar, government purchases are said to have a **multiplier effect** on aggregate demand.

This multiplier effect continues even after this first round. When consumer spending rises, the firms that produce these consumer goods hire more people and experience higher profits. Higher earnings and profits stimulate consumer spending once again and so on. Thus, there is positive feedback as higher demand leads to higher income, which in turn leads to even higher demand. Once all these effects are added together, the total impact on the quantity of goods and services demanded can be much larger than the initial impulse from higher government spending.

Figure 4 illustrates the multiplier effect. The increase in government purchases of $20 billion initially shifts the aggregate-demand curve to the right from $AD_1$ to $AD_2$ by exactly $20 billion. But when consumers respond by increasing their spending, the aggregate-demand curve shifts still further to $AD_3$.

This multiplier effect arising from the response of consumer spending can be strengthened by the response of investment to higher levels of demand. For instance, Boeing might respond to the higher demand for planes by deciding to buy more equipment or build another plant. In this case, higher government demand spurs higher demand for investment goods. This positive feedback from demand to investment is sometimes called the *investment accelerator*.

### 24-2c  A Formula for the Spending Multiplier

Some simple algebra permits us to derive a formula for the size of the multiplier effect that arises when an increase in government purchases induces increases in consumer spending. An important number in this formula is the *marginal propensity to consume (MPC)*—the fraction of extra income that a household consumes rather than saves. For example, suppose that the marginal propensity to consume is ¾. This means that for every extra dollar that a household earns, the household

**multiplier effect**
the additional shifts in aggregate demand that result when expansionary fiscal policy increases income and thereby increases consumer spending

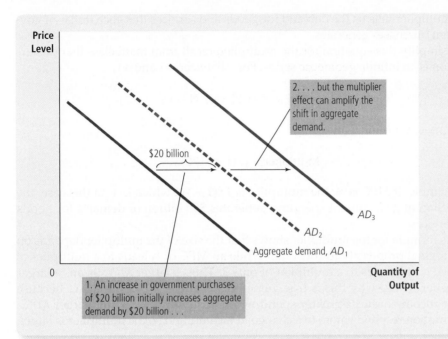

Price
Level

2. . . . but the multiplier effect can amplify the shift in aggregate demand.

$20 billion

$AD_3$

$AD_2$

Aggregate demand, $AD_1$

0

Quantity of
Output

1. An increase in government purchases of $20 billion initially increases aggregate demand by $20 billion . . .

## FIGURE 4

**The Multiplier Effect**
An increase in government purchases of $20 billion can shift the aggregate-demand curve to the right by more than $20 billion. This multiplier effect arises because increases in aggregate income stimulate additional spending by consumers.

spends $0.75 (¾ of the dollar) and saves $0.25. With an $MPC$ of ¾, when the workers and owners of Boeing earn $20 billion from the government contract, they increase their consumer spending by ¾ × $20 billion, or $15 billion.

To gauge the impact on aggregate demand of a change in government purchases, we follow the effects step-by-step. The process begins when the government spends $20 billion, which implies that national income (earnings and profits) also rises by this amount. This increase in income in turn raises consumer spending by $MPC$ × $20 billion, which raises the income for the workers and owners of the firms that produce the consumption goods. This second increase in income again raises consumer spending, this time by $MPC$ × ($MPC$ × $20 billion). These feedback effects go on and on.

To find the total impact on the demand for goods and services, we add up all these effects:

$$\begin{aligned}
\text{Change in government purchases} &= &\$20 \text{ billion} \\
\text{First change in consumption} &= MPC &\times \$20 \text{ billion} \\
\text{Second change in consumption} &= MPC^2 &\times \$20 \text{ billion} \\
\text{Third change in consumption} &= MPC^3 &\times \$20 \text{ billion} \\
&\vdots & \vdots \\
\end{aligned}$$

Total change in demand
$= (1 + MPC + MPC^2 + MPC^3 + \ldots) \times \$20 \text{ billion}.$

Here ". . ." represents an infinite number of similar terms. Thus, we can write the multiplier as follows:

$$\text{Multiplier} = 1 + MPC + MPC^2 + MPC^3 + \ldots.$$

This multiplier tells us the demand for goods and services that each dollar of government purchases generates.

To simplify this equation for the multiplier, recall from math class that this expression is an infinite geometric series. For $x$ between $-1$ and $+1$,

$$1 + x + x^2 + x^3 + \ldots = 1 / (1 - x).$$

In our case, $x = MPC$. Thus,

$$\text{Multiplier} = 1/(1 - MPC).$$

For example, if $MPC$ is ¾, the multiplier is $1/(1 - ¾)$, which is 4. In this case, the $20 billion of government spending generates $80 billion of demand for goods and services.

This formula for the multiplier shows that the size of the multiplier depends on the marginal propensity to consume. While an $MPC$ of ¾ leads to a multiplier of 4, an $MPC$ of ½ leads to a multiplier of only 2. Thus, a larger $MPC$ means a larger multiplier. To see why this is true, remember that the multiplier arises because higher income induces greater spending on consumption. With a larger $MPC$, consumption responds more to a change in income, and so the multiplier is larger.

### 24-2d  Other Applications of the Multiplier Effect

Because of the multiplier effect, a dollar of government purchases can generate more than a dollar of aggregate demand. The logic of the multiplier effect, however, is not restricted to changes in government purchases. Instead, it applies to any event that alters spending on any component of GDP—consumption, investment, government purchases, or net exports.

For example, suppose that a recession overseas reduces the demand for U.S. net exports by $10 billion. This reduced spending on U.S. goods and services depresses U.S. national income, which reduces spending by U.S. consumers. If the marginal propensity to consume is ¾ and the multiplier is 4, then the $10 billion fall in net exports leads to a $40 billion contraction in aggregate demand.

As another example, suppose that a stock market boom increases households' wealth and stimulates their spending on goods and services by $20 billion. This extra consumer spending increases national income, which in turn generates even more consumer spending. If the marginal propensity to consume is ¾ and the multiplier is 4, then the initial impulse of $20 billion in consumer spending translates into an $80 billion increase in aggregate demand.

The multiplier is an important concept in macroeconomics because it shows how the economy can amplify the impact of changes in spending. A small initial change in consumption, investment, government purchases, or net exports can end up having a large effect on aggregate demand and, therefore, the economy's production of goods and services.

### 24-2e  The Crowding-Out Effect

The multiplier effect seems to suggest that when the government buys $20 billion of planes from Boeing, the resulting expansion in aggregate demand is necessarily larger than $20 billion. Yet another effect works in the opposite direction. While an increase in government purchases stimulates the aggregate demand for goods and services, it also causes the interest rate to rise, which reduces investment spending and puts downward pressure on aggregate demand. The reduction in aggregate demand that results when a fiscal expansion raises the interest rate is called the **crowding-out effect**.

To see why crowding out occurs, let's consider what happens in the money market when the government buys planes from Boeing. As we have discussed, this increase in demand raises the incomes of the workers and owners of this firm (and, because of the multiplier effect, of other firms as well). As incomes rise, households plan to buy more goods and services and, as a result, choose to hold more of their wealth in liquid form. That is, the increase in income caused by the fiscal expansion raises the demand for money.

The effect of the increase in money demand is shown in panel (a) of Figure 5. Because the Fed has not changed the money supply, the vertical supply curve remains the same. When the higher level of income shifts the money demand curve to the right from $MD_1$ to $MD_2$, the interest rate must rise from $r_1$ to $r_2$ to keep supply and demand in balance.

The increase in the interest rate, in turn, reduces the quantity of goods and services demanded. In particular, because borrowing is more expensive, the demand for residential and business investment goods declines. In other words, as the increase in government purchases increases the demand for goods and services, it may also crowd out investment. This crowding-out effect partially offsets the impact of government purchases on aggregate demand, as illustrated in panel (b) of Figure 5. The increase in government purchases initially shifts the aggregate-demand curve from $AD_1$ to $AD_2$, but once crowding out takes place, the aggregate-demand curve drops back to $AD_3$.

**crowding-out effect**
the offset in aggregate demand that results when expansionary fiscal policy raises the interest rate and thereby reduces investment spending

---

Panel (a) shows the money market. When the government increases its purchases of goods and services, the resulting increase in income raises the demand for money from $MD_1$ to $MD_2$, and this causes the equilibrium interest rate to rise from $r_1$ to $r_2$. Panel (b) shows the effects on aggregate demand. The initial impact of the increase in government purchases shifts the aggregate-demand curve from $AD_1$ to $AD_2$. Yet because the interest rate is the cost of borrowing, the increase in the interest rate tends to reduce the quantity of goods and services demanded, particularly for investment goods. This crowding out of investment partially offsets the impact of the fiscal expansion on aggregate demand. In the end, the aggregate-demand curve shifts only to $AD_3$.

## FIGURE 5

### The Crowding-Out Effect

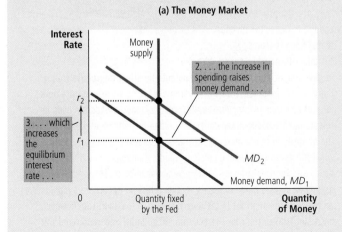

(a) The Money Market

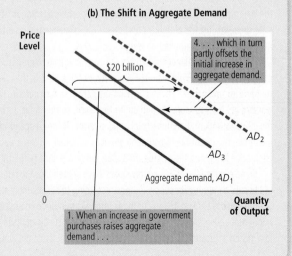

(b) The Shift in Aggregate Demand

To sum up: *When the government increases its purchases by $20 billion, the aggregate demand for goods and services could rise by more or less than $20 billion depending on the sizes of the multiplier and crowding-out effects.* The multiplier effect makes the shift in aggregate demand greater than $20 billion. The crowding-out effect pushes the aggregate-demand curve in the opposite direction and, if large enough, could result in an aggregate-demand shift of less than $20 billion.

### 24-2f  Changes in Taxes

The other important instrument of fiscal policy, besides the level of government purchases, is the level of taxation. When the government cuts personal income taxes, for instance, it increases households' take-home pay. Households will save some of this additional income, but they will also spend some of it on consumer goods. Because it increases consumer spending, the tax cut shifts the aggregate-demand curve to the right. Similarly, a tax increase depresses consumer spending and shifts the aggregate-demand curve to the left.

The size of the shift in aggregate demand resulting from a tax change is also affected by the multiplier and crowding-out effects. When the government cuts taxes and stimulates consumer spending, earnings and profits rise, which further stimulates consumer spending. This is the multiplier effect. At the same time, higher income leads to higher money demand, which tends to raise interest rates. Higher interest rates make borrowing more costly, which reduces investment spending. This is the crowding-out effect. Depending on the sizes of the multiplier and crowding-out effects, the shift in aggregate demand could be larger or smaller than the tax change that causes it.

---

## FYI

### How Fiscal Policy Might Affect Aggregate Supply

So far, our discussion of fiscal policy has stressed how changes in government purchases and changes in taxes influence the quantity of goods and services demanded. Most economists believe that the short-run macroeconomic effects of fiscal policy work primarily through aggregate demand. Yet fiscal policy can potentially influence the quantity of goods and services supplied as well.

For instance, consider the effects of tax changes on aggregate supply. One of the *Ten Principles of Economics* in Chapter 1 is that people respond to incentives. When government policymakers cut tax rates, workers get to keep more of each dollar they earn, so they have a greater incentive to work and produce goods and services. If they respond to this incentive, the quantity of goods and services supplied will be greater at each price level, and the aggregate-supply curve will shift to the right.

Some economists, called *supply siders*, have argued that the influence of tax cuts on aggregate supply is large. According to some supply siders, the influence is so large that a cut in tax rates will stimulate enough additional production and income that tax revenue will actually increase. This is certainly a theoretical possibility, but most economists do not consider it the normal case. While the supply-side effects of taxes are important to consider, they are usually not large enough to cause tax revenue to rise when tax rates fall.

Like changes in taxes, changes in government purchases can also potentially affect aggregate supply. Suppose, for instance, that the government increases expenditure on a form of government-provided capital, such as roads. Roads are used by private businesses to make deliveries to their customers; an increase in the quantity of roads increases these businesses' productivity. Hence, when the government spends more on roads, it increases the quantity of goods and services supplied at any given price level and, thus, shifts the aggregate-supply curve to the right. This effect on aggregate supply is probably more important in the long run than in the short run, however, because it takes time for the government to build new roads and put them into use. ∎

In addition to the multiplier and crowding-out effects, there is another important determinant of the size of the shift in aggregate demand that results from a tax change: households' perceptions about whether the tax change is permanent or temporary. For example, suppose that the government announces a tax cut of $1,000 per household. In deciding how much of this $1,000 to spend, households must ask themselves how long this extra income will last. If they expect the tax cut to be permanent, they will view it as adding substantially to their financial resources and, therefore, increase their spending by a large amount. In this case, the tax cut will have a large impact on aggregate demand. By contrast, if households expect the tax change to be temporary, they will view it as adding only slightly to their financial resources and, therefore, will increase their spending by only a small amount. In this case, the tax cut will have a small impact on aggregate demand.

An extreme example of a temporary tax cut was the one announced in 1992. In that year, President George H. W. Bush faced a lingering recession and an upcoming reelection campaign. He responded to these circumstances by announcing a reduction in the amount of income tax that the federal government was withholding from workers' paychecks. Because legislated income tax rates did not change, however, every dollar of reduced withholding in 1992 meant an extra dollar of taxes due on April 15, 1993, when income tax returns for 1992 were to be filed. Thus, this "tax cut" actually represented only a short-term loan from the government. Not surprisingly, the impact of the policy on consumer spending and aggregate demand was relatively small.

**QuickQuiz**   *Suppose that the government reduces spending on highway construction by $10 billion. Which way does the aggregate-demand curve shift? Explain why the shift might be larger or smaller than $10 billion.*

# 24-3 Using Policy to Stabilize the Economy

We have seen how monetary and fiscal policy can affect the economy's aggregate demand for goods and services. These theoretical insights raise some important policy questions: Should policymakers use these instruments to control aggregate demand and stabilize the economy? If so, when? If not, why not?

### 24-3a The Case for Active Stabilization Policy

Let's return to the question that began this chapter: When the president and Congress raise taxes, how should the Federal Reserve respond? As we have seen, the level of taxation is one determinant of the position of the aggregate-demand curve. When the government raises taxes, aggregate demand will fall, depressing production and employment in the short run. If the Federal Reserve wants to prevent this adverse effect of the fiscal policy, it can expand aggregate demand by increasing the money supply. A monetary expansion would reduce interest rates, stimulate investment spending, and expand aggregate demand. If monetary policy is set appropriately, the combined changes in monetary and fiscal policy could leave the aggregate demand for goods and services unaffected.

This analysis is exactly the sort followed by members of the Federal Open Market Committee. They know that monetary policy is an important determinant of aggregate demand. They also know that there are other important determinants as well, including fiscal policy set by the president and Congress. As a result, the FOMC watches the debates over fiscal policy with a keen eye.

This response of monetary policy to the change in fiscal policy is an example of a more general phenomenon: the use of policy instruments to stabilize aggregate demand and, as a result, production and employment. Economic stabilization has been an explicit goal of U.S. policy since the Employment Act of 1946. This act states that "it is the continuing policy and responsibility of the federal government to . . . promote full employment and production." In essence, the government has chosen to hold itself accountable for short-run macroeconomic performance.

The Employment Act has two implications. The first, more modest, implication is that the government should avoid being a cause of economic fluctuations. Thus, most economists advise against large and sudden changes in monetary and fiscal policy, for such changes are likely to cause fluctuations in aggregate demand. Moreover, when large changes do occur, it is important that monetary and fiscal policymakers be aware of and respond to each others' actions.

The second, more ambitious, implication of the Employment Act is that the government should respond to changes in the private economy to stabilize aggregate demand. The act was passed not long after the publication of Keynes's *The General Theory of Employment, Interest, and Money*, which has been one of the most influential books ever written about economics. In it, Keynes emphasized the key role of aggregate demand in explaining short-run economic fluctuations. Keynes

---

## IN THE NEWS

## How Large Is the Fiscal Policy Multiplier?

*In the global economic downturn of 2008 and 2009, governments around the world turned to fiscal policy to prop up aggregate demand. This episode ignited a debate about the size of the multipliers, which remains a topic of much research.*

### Much Ado about Multipliers

It is the biggest peacetime fiscal expansion in history. Across the globe countries have countered the recession by cutting taxes and by boosting government spending. The G20 group of economies, whose leaders meet this week in Pittsburgh, have introduced stimulus packages worth an average of 2% of GDP this year [2009] and 1.6% of GDP in 2010. Coordinated action on this scale might suggest a consensus about the effects of fiscal stimulus. But economists are in fact deeply divided about how well, or indeed whether, such stimulus works.

The debate hinges on the scale of the "fiscal multiplier." This measure, first formalised

in 1931 by Richard Kahn, a student of John Maynard Keynes, captures how effectively tax cuts or increases in government spending stimulate output. A multiplier of one means that a $1 billion increase in government spending will increase a country's GDP by $1 billion.

The size of the multiplier is bound to vary according to economic conditions. For an economy operating at full capacity, the fiscal multiplier should be zero. Since there are no spare resources, any increase in government demand would just replace spending elsewhere. But in a recession, when workers and factories lie idle, a fiscal boost can increase overall demand. And if the initial stimulus triggers a cascade of expenditure among consumers and businesses, the multiplier can be well above one.

The multiplier is also likely to vary according to the type of fiscal action. Government spending on building a bridge may have a bigger multiplier than a tax cut if consumers save a portion of their tax windfall. A tax cut

targeted at poorer people may have a bigger impact on spending than one for the affluent, since poorer folk tend to spend a higher share of their income.

Crucially, the overall size of the fiscal multiplier also depends on how people react to higher government borrowing. If the government's actions bolster confidence and revive animal spirits, the multiplier could rise as demand goes up and private investment is "crowded in." But if interest rates climb in response to government borrowing then some private investment that would otherwise have occurred could get "crowded out." And if consumers expect higher future taxes in order to finance new government borrowing, they could spend less today. All that would reduce the fiscal multiplier, potentially to below zero.

claimed that the government should actively stimulate aggregate demand when aggregate demand appeared insufficient to maintain production at its full-employment level.

Keynes (and his many followers) argued that aggregate demand fluctuates because of largely irrational waves of pessimism and optimism. He used the term "animal spirits" to refer to these arbitrary changes in attitude. When pessimism reigns, households reduce consumption spending and firms reduce investment spending. The result is reduced aggregate demand, lower production, and higher unemployment. Conversely, when optimism reigns, households and firms increase spending. The result is higher aggregate demand, higher production, and inflationary pressure. Notice that these changes in attitude are, to some extent, self-fulfilling.

In principle, the government can adjust its monetary and fiscal policy in response to these waves of optimism and pessimism and, thereby, stabilize the economy. For example, when people are excessively pessimistic, the Fed can expand the money supply to lower interest rates and expand aggregate demand. When they are excessively optimistic, it can contract the money supply to raise interest rates and dampen aggregate demand. Former Fed Chairman William McChesney Martin described this view of monetary policy very simply: "The Federal Reserve's job is to take away the punch bowl just as the party gets going."

Different assumptions about the impact of higher government borrowing on interest rates and private spending explain wild variations in the estimates of multipliers from today's stimulus spending. Economists in the Obama administration, who assume that the federal funds rate stays constant for a four-year period, expect a multiplier of 1.6 for government purchases and 1.0 for tax cuts from America's fiscal stimulus. An alternative assessment by John Cogan, Tobias Cwik, John Taylor and Volker Wieland uses models in which interest rates and taxes rise more quickly in response to higher public borrowing. Their multipliers are much smaller. They think America's stimulus will boost GDP by only one-sixth as much as the Obama team expects.

When forward-looking models disagree so dramatically, careful analysis of previous fiscal stimuli ought to help settle the debate. Unfortunately, it is extremely tricky to isolate the impact of changes in fiscal policy. One approach is to use microeconomic case studies to examine consumer behaviour in response to specific tax rebates and cuts. These studies, largely based on tax changes in America, find that permanent cuts have a bigger impact on consumer spending than temporary ones and that consumers who find it hard to borrow, such as those close to their credit-card limit, tend to spend more of their tax windfall. But case studies do not measure the overall impact of tax cuts or spending increases on output.

An alternative approach is to try to tease out the statistical impact of changes in government spending or tax cuts on GDP. The difficulty here is to isolate the effects of fiscal-stimulus measures from the rises in social-security spending and falls in tax revenues that naturally accompany recessions. This empirical approach has narrowed the range of estimates in some areas. It has also yielded interesting cross-country comparisons. Multipliers are bigger in closed economies than open ones (because less of the stimulus leaks abroad via imports). They have traditionally been bigger in rich countries than emerging ones (where investors tend to take fright more quickly, pushing interest rates up). But overall economists find as big a range of multipliers from empirical estimates as they do from theoretical models.

To add to the confusion, the post-war experiences from which statistical analyses are drawn differ in vital respects from the current situation. Most of the evidence on multipliers for government spending is based on military outlays, but today's stimulus packages are heavily focused on infrastructure. Interest rates in many rich countries are now close to zero, which may increase the potency of, as well as the need for, fiscal stimulus. Because of the financial crisis relatively more people face borrowing constraints, which would increase the effectiveness of a tax cut. At the same time, highly indebted consumers may now be keen to cut their borrowing, leading to a lower multiplier. And investors today have more reason to be worried about rich countries' fiscal positions than those of emerging markets.

Add all this together and the truth is that economists are flying blind. They can make relative judgments with some confidence. Temporary tax cuts pack less punch than permanent ones, for instance. Fiscal multipliers will probably be lower in heavily indebted economies than in prudent ones. But policymakers looking for precise estimates are deluding themselves. ■

**Source:** *The Economist*, September 24, 2009.

**CASE STUDY**

### KEYNESIANS IN THE WHITE HOUSE

When a reporter in 1961 asked President John F. Kennedy why he advocated a tax cut, Kennedy replied, "To stimulate the economy. Don't you remember your Economics 101?" Kennedy's policy was, in fact, based on the analysis of fiscal policy we have developed in this chapter. His goal was to enact a tax cut, which would raise consumer spending, expand aggregate demand, and increase the economy's production and employment.

In choosing this policy, Kennedy was relying on his team of economic advisers. This team included such prominent economists as James Tobin and Robert Solow, both of whom would later win Nobel Prizes for their contributions to the field. As students in the 1940s, these economists had closely studied John Maynard Keynes's *General Theory*, which was then only a few years old. When the Kennedy advisers proposed cutting taxes, they were putting Keynes's ideas into action.

Although tax changes can have a potent influence on aggregate demand, they have other effects as well. In particular, by changing the incentives that people face, taxes can alter the aggregate supply of goods and services. Part of the Kennedy proposal was an investment tax credit, which gives a tax break to firms that invest in new capital. Higher investment would not only stimulate aggregate demand immediately but also increase the economy's productive capacity over time. Thus, the short-run goal of increasing production through higher aggregate demand was coupled with a long-run goal of increasing production through higher aggregate supply. And indeed, when the tax cut Kennedy proposed was finally enacted in 1964, it helped usher in a period of robust economic growth.

Since the 1964 tax cut, policymakers have from time to time used fiscal policy as a tool for controlling aggregate demand. For example, when President Barack Obama moved into the Oval Office in 2009, he faced an economy in the midst of a recession. One of his first policy initiatives was a stimulus bill, called the American Recovery and Reinvestment Act (ARRA), which included substantial increases in government spending. The In the News box on the preceding two pages discusses some of the debate over this policy initiative. ●

### ASK THE EXPERTS

## Economic Stimulus

"Because of the American Recovery and Reinvestment Act of 2009, the U.S. unemployment rate was lower at the end of 2010 than it would have been without the stimulus bill."

**What do economists say?**

3% disagree — 0% uncertain

97% agree

"Taking into account all of the ARRA's economic consequences—including the economic costs of raising taxes to pay for the spending, its effects on future spending, and any other likely future effects—the benefits of the stimulus will end up exceeding its costs."

**What do economists say?**

6% disagree — 19% uncertain

75% agree

Source: IGM Economic Experts Panel, July 29, 2014.

### 24-3b The Case against Active Stabilization Policy

Some economists argue that the government should avoid active use of monetary and fiscal policy to try to stabilize the economy. They claim that these policy instruments should be set to achieve long-run goals, such as rapid economic growth and low inflation, and that the economy should be left to deal with short-run fluctuations on its own. These economists may admit that monetary and fiscal policy can stabilize the economy in theory, but they doubt whether it can do so in practice.

The primary argument against active monetary and fiscal policy is that these policies affect the economy with a long lag. As we have seen, monetary policy works by changing interest rates, which in turn influence investment spending. But many firms make investment plans far in advance. Thus, most economists believe that it takes at least 6 months for changes in monetary policy to have much effect on output and employment. Moreover, once these effects occur, they can last for several years. Critics of stabilization policy argue that because of this lag, the Fed should not try to fine-tune the economy. They claim that the Fed often reacts too late to changing economic conditions and, as a result, ends up being a cause of rather than a cure for economic fluctuations. These critics advocate a passive monetary policy, such as slow and steady growth in the money supply.

Fiscal policy also works with a lag, but unlike the lag in monetary policy, the lag in fiscal policy is largely attributable to the political process. In the United States, most changes in government spending and taxes must go through congressional committees in both the House and the Senate, be passed by both legislative bodies, and then be signed by the president. Completing this process can take months or, in some cases, years. By the time the change in fiscal policy is passed and ready to implement, the condition of the economy may have changed.

These lags in monetary and fiscal policy are a problem in part because economic forecasting is so imprecise. If forecasters could accurately predict the condition of the economy a year in advance, then monetary and fiscal policymakers could look ahead when making policy decisions. In this case, policymakers could stabilize the economy despite the lags they face. In practice, however, major recessions and depressions arrive without much advance warning. The best that policymakers can do is to respond to economic changes as they occur.

### 24-3c Automatic Stabilizers

**automatic stabilizers**

changes in fiscal policy that stimulate aggregate demand when the economy goes into a recession without policymakers having to take any deliberate action

All economists—both advocates and critics of stabilization policy—agree that the lags in implementation reduce the efficacy of policy as a tool for short-run stabilization. The economy would be more stable, therefore, if policymakers could find a way to avoid some of these lags. In fact, they have. **Automatic stabilizers** are changes in fiscal policy that stimulate aggregate demand when the economy goes into a recession without policymakers having to take any deliberate action.

The most important automatic stabilizer is the tax system. When the economy goes into a recession, the amount of taxes collected by the government falls automatically because almost all taxes are closely tied to economic activity. The personal income tax depends on households' incomes, the payroll tax depends on workers' earnings, and the corporate income tax depends on firms' profits. Because incomes, earnings, and profits all fall in a recession, the government's tax revenue falls as well. This automatic tax cut stimulates aggregate demand and, thereby, reduces the magnitude of economic fluctuations.

Some government spending also acts as an automatic stabilizer. In particular, when the economy goes into a recession and workers are laid off, more people apply for unemployment insurance benefits, welfare benefits, and other forms of income support. This automatic increase in government spending stimulates aggregate demand at exactly the time when aggregate demand is insufficient to maintain full employment. Indeed, when the unemployment insurance system was first enacted in the 1930s, economists who advocated this policy did so in part because of its power as an automatic stabilizer.

The automatic stabilizers in the U.S. economy are not sufficiently strong to prevent recessions completely. Nonetheless, without these automatic stabilizers, output and employment would probably be more volatile than they are. For this reason, many economists oppose a constitutional amendment that would require the federal government always to run a balanced budget, as some politicians have proposed. When the economy goes into a recession, taxes fall, government spending rises, and the government's budget moves toward deficit. If the government faced a strict balanced-budget rule, it would be forced to look for ways to raise taxes or cut spending in a recession. In other words, a strict balanced-budget rule would eliminate the automatic stabilizers inherent in our current system of taxes and government spending.

**Quick Quiz** *Suppose a wave of negative "animal spirits" overruns the economy, and people become pessimistic about the future. What happens to aggregate demand? If the Fed wants to stabilize aggregate demand, how should it alter the money supply? If it does this, what happens to the interest rate? Why might the Fed choose not to respond in this way?*

## 24-4 Conclusion

Before policymakers make any change in policy, they need to consider all the effects of their decisions. Earlier in the book, we examined classical models of the economy, which describe the long-run effects of monetary and fiscal policy. There we saw how fiscal policy influences saving, investment, and long-run growth and how monetary policy influences the price level and the inflation rate.

In this chapter, we examined the short-run effects of monetary and fiscal policy. We saw how these policy instruments can change the aggregate demand for goods and services and alter the economy's production and employment in the short run. When Congress reduces government spending to balance the budget, it needs to consider both the long-run effects on saving and growth and the short-run effects on aggregate demand and employment. When the Fed reduces the growth rate of the money supply, it must take into account the long-run effect on inflation as well as the short-run effect on production. In all parts of government, policymakers must keep in mind both long-run and short-run goals.

---

**CHAPTER QuickQuiz**

1. If the central bank wants to expand aggregate demand, it can _____ the money supply, which would _____ the interest rate.
   a. increase, increase
   b. increase, decrease
   c. decrease, increase
   d. decrease, decrease

2. If the government wants to contract aggregate demand, it can _____ government purchases or _____ taxes.
   a. increase, increase
   b. increase, decrease
   c. decrease, increase
   d. decrease, decrease

3. The Federal Reserve's target rate for the federal funds rate
   a. is an extra policy tool for the central bank, in addition to and independent of the money supply.
   b. commits the Fed to set a particular money supply so that it hits the announced target.
   c. is a goal that is rarely achieved, because the Fed can determine only the money supply.
   d. matters to banks that borrow and lend federal funds but does not influence aggregate demand.

4. With the economy in a recession because of inadequate aggregate demand, the government increases its purchases by $1,200. Suppose the central bank adjusts the money supply to hold the interest rate constant, investment spending is fixed, and the marginal propensity to consume is $2/_3$. How large is the increase in aggregate demand?
   a. $400
   b. $800
   c. $1,800
   d. $3,600

5. If the central bank in the preceding question instead holds the money supply constant and allows the interest rate to adjust, the change in aggregate demand resulting from the increase in government purchases will be
   a. larger.
   b. the same.
   c. smaller but still positive.
   d. negative.

6. Which of the following is an example of an automatic stabilizer? When the economy goes into a recession,
   a. more people become eligible for unemployment insurance benefits.
   b. stock prices decline, particularly for firms in cyclical industries.
   c. Congress begins hearings about a possible stimulus package.
   d. the Federal Reserve changes its target for the federal funds rate.

## SUMMARY

- In developing a theory of short-run economic fluctuations, Keynes proposed the theory of liquidity preference to explain the determinants of the interest rate. According to this theory, the interest rate adjusts to balance the supply and demand for money.
- An increase in the price level raises money demand and increases the interest rate that brings the money market into equilibrium. Because the interest rate represents the cost of borrowing, a higher interest rate reduces investment and, thereby, the quantity of goods and services demanded. The downward-sloping aggregate-demand curve expresses this negative relationship between the price level and the quantity demanded.
- Policymakers can influence aggregate demand with monetary policy. An increase in the money supply reduces the equilibrium interest rate for any given price level. Because a lower interest rate stimulates investment spending, the aggregate-demand curve shifts to the right. Conversely, a decrease in the money supply raises the equilibrium interest rate for any given price level and shifts the aggregate-demand curve to the left.

- Policymakers can also influence aggregate demand with fiscal policy. An increase in government purchases or a cut in taxes shifts the aggregate-demand curve to the right. A decrease in government purchases or an increase in taxes shifts the aggregate-demand curve to the left.
- When the government alters spending or taxes, the resulting shift in aggregate demand can be larger or smaller than the fiscal change. The multiplier effect tends to amplify the effects of fiscal policy on aggregate demand. The crowding-out effect tends to dampen the effects of fiscal policy on aggregate demand.

- Because monetary and fiscal policy can influence aggregate demand, the government sometimes uses these policy instruments in an attempt to stabilize the economy. Economists disagree about how active the government should be in this effort. According to advocates of active stabilization policy, changes in attitudes by households and firms shift aggregate demand; if the government does not respond, the result is undesirable and unnecessary fluctuations in output and employment. According to critics of active stabilization policy, monetary and fiscal policy work with such long lags that attempts at stabilizing the economy often end up being destabilizing.

## KEY CONCEPTS

theory of liquidity preference, p. 521
fiscal policy, p. 529

multiplier effect, p. 530
crowding-out effect, p. 533

automatic stabilizers, p. 540

## QUESTIONS FOR REVIEW

1. What is the theory of liquidity preference? How does it help explain the downward slope of the aggregate-demand curve?

2. Use the theory of liquidity preference to explain how a decrease in the money supply affects the aggregate-demand curve.

3. The government spends $3 billion to buy police cars. Explain why aggregate demand might increase by more or less than $3 billion.

4. Suppose that survey measures of consumer confidence indicate a wave of pessimism is sweeping the country. If policymakers do nothing, what will happen to aggregate demand? What should the Fed do if it wants to stabilize aggregate demand? If the Fed does nothing, what might Congress do to stabilize aggregate demand?

5. Give an example of a government policy that acts as an automatic stabilizer. Explain why the policy has this effect.

## PROBLEMS AND APPLICATIONS

1. Explain how each of the following developments would affect the supply of money, the demand for money, and the interest rate. Illustrate your answers with diagrams.
   a. The Fed's bond traders buy bonds in open-market operations.
   b. An increase in credit-card availability reduces the amount of cash people want to hold.
   c. The Federal Reserve reduces banks' reserve requirements.
   d. Households decide to hold more money to use for holiday shopping.
   e. A wave of optimism boosts business investment and expands aggregate demand.

2. The Federal Reserve expands the money supply by 5 percent.
   a. Use the theory of liquidity preference to illustrate in a graph the impact of this policy on the interest rate.
   b. Use the model of aggregate demand and aggregate supply to illustrate the impact of this change in the interest rate on output and the price level in the short run.
   c. When the economy makes the transition from its short-run equilibrium to its new long-run equilibrium, what will happen to the price level?

d. How will this change in the price level affect the demand for money and the equilibrium interest rate?

e. Is this analysis consistent with the proposition that money has real effects in the short run but is neutral in the long run?

3. Suppose a computer virus disables the nation's automatic teller machines, making withdrawals from bank accounts less convenient. As a result, people want to keep more cash on hand, increasing the demand for money.

   a. Assume the Fed does not change the money supply. According to the theory of liquidity preference, what happens to the interest rate? What happens to aggregate demand?

   b. If instead the Fed wants to stabilize aggregate demand, how should it change the money supply?

   c. If it wants to accomplish this change in the money supply using open-market operations, what should it do?

4. Consider two policies—a tax cut that will last for only one year and a tax cut that is expected to be permanent. Which policy will stimulate greater spending by consumers? Which policy will have the greater impact on aggregate demand? Explain.

5. The economy is in a recession with high unemployment and low output.

   a. Draw a graph of aggregate demand and aggregate supply to illustrate the current situation. Be sure to include the aggregate-demand curve, the short-run aggregate-supply curve, and the long-run aggregate-supply curve.

   b. Identify an open-market operation that would restore the economy to its natural rate.

   c. Draw a graph of the money market to illustrate the effect of this open-market operation. Show the resulting change in the interest rate.

   d. Draw a graph similar to the one in part *a* to show the effect of the open-market operation on output and the price level. Explain in words why the policy has the effect that you have shown in the graph.

6. In the early 1980s, new legislation allowed banks to pay interest on checking deposits, which they could not do previously.

   a. If we define money to include checking deposits, what effect did this legislation have on money demand? Explain.

   b. If the Federal Reserve had maintained a constant money supply in the face of this change, what would have happened to the interest rate? What

would have happened to aggregate demand and aggregate output?

   c. If the Federal Reserve had maintained a constant market interest rate (the interest rate on nonmonetary assets) in the face of this change, what change in the money supply would have been necessary? What would have happened to aggregate demand and aggregate output?

7. Suppose economists observe that an increase in government spending of $10 billion raises the total demand for goods and services by $30 billion.

   a. If these economists ignore the possibility of crowding out, what would they estimate the marginal propensity to consume (*MPC*) to be?

   b. Now suppose the economists allow for crowding out. Would their new estimate of the *MPC* be larger or smaller than their initial one?

8. An economy is operating with output that is $400 billion below its natural level, and fiscal policymakers want to close this recessionary gap. The central bank agrees to adjust the money supply to hold the interest rate constant, so there is no crowding out. The marginal propensity to consume is $4/_5$, and the price level is completely fixed in the short run. In what direction and by how much would government spending need to change to close the recessionary gap? Explain your thinking.

9. Suppose government spending increases. Would the effect on aggregate demand be larger if the Federal Reserve held the money supply constant in response or if the Fed were committed to maintaining a fixed interest rate? Explain.

10. In which of the following circumstances is expansionary fiscal policy more likely to lead to a short-run increase in investment? Explain.

   a. When the investment accelerator is large or when it is small?

   b. When the interest sensitivity of investment is large or when it is small?

11. Consider an economy described by the following equations:

$$Y = C + I + G$$
$$C = 100 + 0.75(Y - T)$$
$$I = 500 - 50\,r$$
$$G = 125$$
$$T = 100$$

where *Y* is GDP, *C* is consumption, *I* is investment, *G* is government purchases, *T* is taxes, and *r* is the interest rate. If the economy were at full employment (that is, at its natural rate), GDP would be 2,000.

a. Explain the meaning of each of these equations.
b. What is the marginal propensity to consume in this economy?
c. Suppose the central bank's policy is to adjust the money supply to maintain the interest rate at 4 percent, so $r = 4$. Solve for GDP. How does it compare to the full-employment level?

d. Assuming no change in monetary policy, what change in government purchases would restore full employment?
e. Assuming no change in fiscal policy, what change in the interest rate would restore full employment?

To find additional study resources, visit cengagebrain.com, and search for "Mankiw."

# Glossary

## A

**absolute advantage** the ability to produce a good using fewer inputs than another producer

**accounting profit** total revenue minus total explicit cost

**aggregate-demand curve** a curve that shows the quantity of goods and services that households, firms, the government, and customers abroad want to buy at each price level

**aggregate-supply curve** a curve that shows the quantity of goods and services that firms choose to produce and sell at each price level

arise from a negative externality

**automatic stabilizers** changes in fiscal policy that stimulate aggregate demand when the economy goes into a recession without policymakers having to take any deliberate action

**average fixed cost** fixed cost divided by the quantity of output

**average revenue** total revenue divided by the quantity sold

**average total cost** total cost divided by the quantity of output

**average variable cost** variable cost divided by the quantity of output

## B

**bank capital** the resources a bank's owners have put into the institution

**bond** a certificate of indebtedness

**budget deficit** a shortfall of tax revenue from government spending

**budget surplus** an excess of tax revenue over government spending

**business cycle** fluctuations in economic activity, such as employment and production

## C

**capital requirement** a government regulation specifying a minimum amount of bank capital

**catch-up effect** the property whereby countries that start off poor tend to grow more rapidly than countries that start off rich

**central bank** an institution designed to oversee the banking system and regulate the quantity of money in the economy

**circular-flow diagram** a visual model of the economy that shows how dollars flow through markets among households and firms

**classical dichotomy** the theoretical separation of nominal and real variables

**club goods** goods that are excludable but not rival in consumption

**Coase theorem** the proposition that if private parties can bargain without cost over the allocation of resources, they can solve the problem of externalities on their own

**collective bargaining** the process by which unions and firms agree on the terms of employment

**commodity money** money that takes the form of a commodity with intrinsic value

**common resources** goods that are rival in consumption but not excludable

**comparative advantage** the ability to produce a good at a lower opportunity cost than another producer

**competitive market** a market in which there are many buyers and many sellers

so that each has a negligible impact on the market price

**complements** two goods for which an increase in the price of one leads to a decrease in the demand for the other

**compounding** the accumulation of a sum of money in, say, a bank account, where the interest earned remains in the account to earn additional interest in the future

**constant returns to scale** the property whereby long-run average total cost stays the same as the quantity of output changes

**consumer price index (CPI)** a measure of the overall cost of the goods and services bought by a typical consumer

**consumer surplus** the amount a buyer is willing to pay for a good minus the amount the buyer actually pays for it

**consumption** spending by households on goods and services, with the exception of purchases of new housing

**core CPI** a measure of the overall cost of consumer goods and services excluding food and energy

**corrective tax** a tax designed to induce private decision makers to take into account the social costs that

**cost** the value of everything a seller must give up to produce a good

**cost–benefit analysis** a study that compares the costs and benefits to society of providing a public good

**cross-price elasticity of demand** a measure of how much the quantity demanded of one good responds to a change in the price of another good, computed as the percentage change in quantity demanded of the first good divided by the percentage change in price of the second good

**crowding out** a decrease in investment that results from government borrowing

**crowding-out effect** the offset in aggregate demand that results when expansionary fiscal policy raises the interest rate and thereby reduces investment spending

**currency** the paper bills and coins in the hands of the public

**cyclical unemployment** the deviation of unemployment from its natural rate

# D

**deadweight loss** the fall in total surplus that results from a market distortion, such as a tax

**demand curve** a graph of the relationship between the price of a good and the quantity demanded

**demand deposits** balances in bank accounts that depositors can access on demand by writing a check

**demand schedule** a table that shows the relationship between the price of a good and the quantity demanded

**depression** a severe recession

**diminishing marginal product** the property whereby the marginal product of an input declines as the quantity of the input increases

**diminishing returns** the property whereby the benefit from an extra unit of an input declines as the quantity of the input increases

**discount rate** the interest rate on the loans that the Fed makes to banks

**discouraged workers** individuals who would like to work but have given up looking for a job

**diseconomies of scale** the property whereby long-run average total cost rises as the quantity of output increases

**diversification** the reduction of risk achieved by replacing a single risk with a large number of smaller, unrelated risks

# E

**economic profit** total revenue minus total cost, including both explicit and implicit costs

**economics** the study of how society manages its scarce resources

**economies of scale** the property whereby long-run average total cost falls as the quantity of output increases

**efficiency** the property of a resource allocation of maximizing the total surplus received by all members of society

**efficiency wages** above-equilibrium wages paid by firms to increase worker productivity

**efficient markets hypothesis** the theory that asset prices reflect all publicly available information about the value of an asset

**efficient scale** the quantity of output that minimizes average total cost

**elasticity** a measure of the responsiveness of quantity demanded or quantity supplied to a change in one of its determinants

**equality** the property of distributing economic prosperity uniformly among the members of society

**equilibrium** a situation in which the market price has reached the level at which quantity supplied equals quantity demanded

**equilibrium price** the price that balances quantity supplied and quantity demanded

**equilibrium quantity** the quantity supplied and the quantity demanded at the equilibrium price

**excludability** the property of a good whereby a person can be prevented from using it

**explicit costs** input costs that require an outlay of money by the firm

**exports** goods produced domestically and sold abroad

**externality** the uncompensated impact of one person's actions on the well-being of a bystander

# F

**federal funds rate** the interest rate at which banks make overnight loans to one another

**Federal Reserve (Fed)** the central bank of the United States

**fiat money** money without intrinsic value that is used as money by government decree

**finance** the field that studies how people make decisions regarding the allocation of resources over time and the handling of risk

**financial intermediaries** financial institutions through which savers can indirectly provide funds to borrowers

**financial markets** financial institutions through which savers can directly provide funds to borrowers

**financial system** the group of institutions in the economy that help to match one person's saving with another person's investment

**firm-specific risk** risk that affects only a single company

**fiscal policy** the setting of the level of government spending and taxation by government policymakers

**Fisher effect** the one-for-one adjustment of the nominal interest rate to the inflation rate

**fixed costs** costs that do not vary with the quantity of output produced

**fractional-reserve banking** a banking system in which banks hold only a fraction of deposits as reserves

**free rider** a person who receives the benefit of a good but avoids paying for it

**frictional unemployment** unemployment that results because it takes time for workers to search for the jobs that best suit their tastes and skills

**fundamental analysis** the study of a company's accounting statements and future prospects to determine its value

**future value** the amount of money in the future that an amount of money today will yield, given prevailing interest rates

# G

**GDP deflator** a measure of the price level calculated as the ratio of nominal GDP to real GDP times 100

**government purchases** spending on goods and services by local, state, and federal governments

**gross domestic product (GDP)** the market value of all final goods and services produced within a country in a given period of time

# H

**human capital** the knowledge and skills that workers acquire through education, training, and experience

# I

**implicit costs** input costs that do not require an outlay of money by the firm

**imports** goods produced abroad and sold domestically

**incentive** something that induces a person to act

**income elasticity of demand** a measure of how much the quantity demanded of a good responds to a change in consumers' income, computed as the percentage change in quantity demanded divided by the percentage change in income

**indexation** the automatic correction by law or contract of a dollar amount for the effects of inflation

**inferior good** a good for which, other things being equal, an increase in income leads to a decrease in demand

**inflation** an increase in the overall level of prices in the economy

**inflation rate** the percentage change in the price index from the preceding period

**inflation tax** the revenue the government raises by creating money

**informational efficiency** the description of asset prices that rationally reflect all available information

**internalizing the externality** altering incentives so that people take into account the external effects of their actions

**investment** spending on business capital, residential capital, and inventories

# J

**job search** the process by which workers find appropriate jobs given their tastes and skills

# L

**labor force** the total number of workers, including both the employed and the unemployed

**labor-force participation rate** the percentage of the adult population that is in the labor force

**law of demand** the claim that, other things being equal, the quantity demanded of a good falls when the price of the good rises

**law of supply** the claim that, other things being equal, the quantity supplied of a good rises when the price of the good rises

**law of supply and demand** the claim that the price of any good adjusts to bring the quantity supplied and the quantity demanded for that good into balance

**leverage** the use of borrowed money to supplement existing funds for purposes of investment

**leverage ratio** the ratio of assets to bank capital

**liquidity** the ease with which an asset can be converted into the economy's medium of exchange

# M

**macroeconomics** the study of economy-wide phenomena, including inflation, unemployment, and economic growth

**marginal change** a small incremental adjustment to a plan of action

**marginal cost** the increase in total cost that arises from an extra unit of production

**marginal product** the increase in output that arises from an additional unit of input

**marginal revenue** the change in total revenue from an additional unit sold

**market** a group of buyers and sellers of a particular good or service

**market economy** an economy that allocates resources through the decentralized decisions of many firms and households as they interact in markets for goods and services

**market failure** a situation in which a market left on its own fails to allocate resources efficiently

**market for loanable funds** the market in which those who want to save supply funds and those who want to borrow to invest demand funds

**market power** the ability of a single economic actor (or small group of actors) to have a substantial influence on market prices

**market risk** risk that affects all companies in the stock market

**medium of exchange** an item that buyers give to sellers when they want to purchase goods and services

**menu costs** the costs of changing prices

**microeconomics** the study of how households and firms make decisions and how they interact in markets

**model of aggregate demand and aggregate supply** the model that most economists use to explain short-run fluctuations in economic activity around its long-run trend

**monetary neutrality** the proposition that changes in the money supply do not affect real variables

**monetary policy** the setting of the money supply by policymakers in the central bank

**money** the set of assets in an economy that people regularly use to buy goods and services from other people

**money multiplier** the amount of money the banking system generates with each dollar of reserves

**money supply** the quantity of money available in the economy

**monopoly** a firm that is the sole seller of a product without any close substitutes

**multiplier effect** the additional shifts in aggregate demand that result when expansionary fiscal policy increases income and thereby increases consumer spending

**mutual fund** an institution that sells shares to the public and uses the proceeds to buy a portfolio of stocks and bonds

# N

**national saving (saving)** the total income in the economy that remains after paying for consumption and government purchases

**natural level of output** the production of goods and services that an economy achieves in the long run when unemployment is at its normal rate

**natural monopoly** a type of monopoly that arises because a single firm can supply a good or service to an entire market at a lower cost than could two or more firms

**natural rate of unemployment** the normal rate of unemployment around which the unemployment rate fluctuates

**natural resources** the inputs into the production of goods and services that are provided by nature, such as land, rivers, and mineral deposits

**net exports** spending on domestically produced goods by foreigners (exports) minus spending on foreign goods by domestic residents (imports)

**nominal GDP** the production of goods and services valued at current prices

**nominal interest rate** the interest rate as usually reported without a correction for the effects of inflation

**nominal variables** variables measured in monetary units

**normal good** a good for which, other things being equal, an increase in income leads to an increase in demand

**normative statements** claims that attempt to prescribe how the world should be

# O

**open-market operations** the purchase and sale of U.S. government bonds by the Fed

**opportunity cost** whatever must be given up to obtain some item

# P

**physical capital** the stock of equipment and structures that are used to produce goods and services

**positive statements** claims that attempt to describe the world as it is

**present value** the amount of money today that would be needed, using prevailing interest rates, to produce a given future amount of money

**price ceiling** a legal maximum on the price at which a good can be sold

**price discrimination** the business practice of selling the same good at different prices to different customers

**price elasticity of demand** a measure of how much the quantity demanded of a good responds to a change in the price of that good, computed as the percentage change in quantity demanded divided by the percentage change in price

**price elasticity of supply** a measure of how much the quantity supplied of a good responds to a change in the price of that good, computed as the percentage change in quantity supplied divided by the percentage change in price

**price floor** a legal minimum on the price at which a good can be sold

**private goods** goods that are both excludable and rival in consumption

**private saving** the income that households have left after paying for taxes and consumption

**producer price index** a measure of the cost of a basket of goods and services bought by firms

**producer surplus** the amount a seller is paid for a good minus the seller's cost of providing it

**production function** the relationship between the quantity of inputs used to make a good and the quantity of output of that good

**production possibilities frontier** a graph that shows the combinations of output that the economy can possibly produce given the available factors of production and the available production technology

**productivity** the quantity of goods and services produced from each unit of labor input

**profit** total revenue minus total cost

**property rights** the ability of an individual to own and exercise control over scarce resources

**public goods** goods that are neither excludable nor rival in consumption

**public saving** the tax revenue that the government has left after paying for its spending

# Q

**quantity demanded** the amount of a good that buyers are willing and able to purchase

**quantity equation** the equation $M \times V = P \times Y$, which relates the quantity of money, the velocity of money, and the dollar value of the economy's output of goods and services

**quantity supplied** the amount of a good that sellers are willing and able to sell

**quantity theory of money** a theory asserting that the quantity of money available determines the price level and that the growth rate in the quantity of money available determines the inflation rate

# R

**random walk** the path of a variable whose changes are impossible to predict

**rational people** people who systematically and purposefully do the best they can to achieve their objectives

**real GDP** the production of goods and services valued at constant prices

**real interest rate** the interest rate corrected for the effects of inflation

**real variables** variables measured in physical units

**recession** a period of declining real incomes and rising unemployment

**reserve ratio** the fraction of deposits that banks hold as reserves

**reserve requirements** regulations on the minimum amount of reserves that banks must hold against deposits

**reserves** deposits that banks have received but have not loaned out

**risk aversion** a dislike of uncertainty

**rivalry in consumption** the property of a good whereby one person's use diminishes other people's use

# S

**scarcity** the limited nature of society's resources

**shoeleather costs** the resources wasted when inflation encourages people to reduce their money holdings

**shortage** a situation in which quantity demanded is greater than quantity supplied

**stagflation** a period of falling output and rising prices

**stock** a claim to partial ownership in a firm

**store of value** an item that people can use to transfer purchasing power from the present to the future

**strike** the organized withdrawal of labor from a firm by a union

**structural unemployment** unemployment that results because the number of jobs available in some labor markets is insufficient to provide a job for everyone who wants one

**substitutes** two goods for which an increase in the price of one leads to an increase in the demand for the other

**sunk cost** a cost that has already been committed and cannot be recovered

**supply curve** a graph of the relationship between the price of a good and the quantity supplied

**supply schedule** a table that shows the relationship between the price of a good and the quantity supplied

**surplus** a situation in which quantity supplied is greater than quantity demanded

# T

**tariff** a tax on goods produced abroad and sold domestically

**tax incidence** the manner in which the burden of a tax is shared among participants in a market

**technological knowledge** society's understanding of the best ways to produce goods and services

**theory of liquidity preference** Keynes's theory that the interest rate adjusts to bring money supply and money demand into balance

**total cost** the market value of the inputs a firm uses in production

**total revenue** the amount paid by buyers and received by sellers of a good, computed as the price of the good times the quantity sold

**Tragedy of the Commons** a parable that illustrates why common resources are used more than is desirable from the standpoint of society as a whole

**transaction costs** the costs that parties incur during the process of agreeing to and following through on a bargain

# U

**unemployment insurance** a government program that partially protects workers' incomes when they become unemployed

**unemployment rate** the percentage of the labor force that is unemployed

**union** a worker association that bargains with employers over wages, benefits, and working conditions

**unit of account** the yardstick people use to post prices and record debts

# V

**variable costs** costs that vary with the quantity of output produced

**velocity of money** the rate at which money changes hands

# W

**welfare economics** the study of how the allocation of resources affects economic well-being

**willingness to pay** the maximum amount that a buyer will pay for a good

**world price** the price of a good that prevails in the world market for that good

# Index

Page numbers in **boldface** refer to pages where key terms are defined.